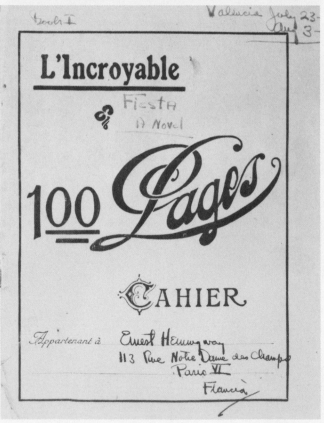

Catalog of the
Ernest Hemingway Collection

at the
John F. Kennedy Library

Volume 2

Incoming Correspondence M—Z
Photographs
Newspaper Clippings
Other Material

G.K. HALL & CO.
70 LINCOLN STREET
BOSTON, MASSACHUSETTS
1982

Frontispiece:

First page of the manuscript of "The Doctor and
the Doctor's Wife", item #368.

Hemingway, soon after his wound from the falling
skylight in his apartment, 1928. Photo by
Helen Breaker. EH731OP

Hemingway in Venice, 1948. EH3734P

Cover of the first notebook of the draft of *The Sun
Also Rises*, item #194.

This publication is printed on
permanent/durable acid-free paper.

ISBN 0-8161-0380-1

Incoming Correspondence

MacAndrews & Co., Ltd.   (Spanish publisher)
TLS J. H. P. Marks
            undated, Madrid
                1p.

MacArthur   (acquaintance)
ANS   [28 Aug 1926, Naples]
           1p., w/envelope

Macaulay Company
        See The American Caravan

MacBride, Burt   (Cosmopolitan)
TLS   6 Apr 1934, N.Y.
                1p.

MacBride, Burt
TLS   28 May 1934, N.Y.
           1p. bearing EH note

MacBride, Burt
ALS   21 Jan [1935], Key West
                2pp.

MacBride, Burt
ALS   Wednseday morning [23 Jan 1935],
           Key West
                2pp.

MacBride, Burt
ALS   25 Jan 1935, en route to Sebruig
                2pp.

MacBride, Burt
TLS   27 May [1935, N.Y.]
           1p., w/newspaper clipping and
           envelope

MacBride, Burt
ANS   20 June [1935, N.Y.]
           1p., w/newspaper clipping and
           envelope

MacCarthy, Adeline D. (well-wisher)
ALS   9 Oct 1918, Rochester
            3pp., w/envelope

Macdonald, Elsie
ALS   24 June 1927, S.S. Veendam, Atlantic
            Ocean
            3pp., w/envelope

Macdonald, Elsie
ALS   27 Oct 1919, Milwaukee
            6pp., w/envelope

Macdonald, Elsie
ALS   20 Jan 1928, N.Y.
            3pp., w/newspaper clipping and
            envelope

Macdonald, Elsie (Red Cross nurse)
ALS   2 Nov 1926, Haverford
            3pp., w/envelope

[Macdonald, Elsie]
ALS Mac
            20 Oct 1929, N.Y.
            4pp.

Macdonald, E[lsie]
ALS   14 Dec 1926, West Philadelphia
            6pp., w/envelope

[Macdonald, Elsie]
Newspaper clippings, a typescript of Thomas
Wolfe's "Two Dark Angels", w/envelope, postmarked
Dec 1929, N.Y.

Macdonald Elsie Murdock
ALS   5 June 1927, Haverford
            3pp., w/envelope

Macdonald, Elsie
ALS   30 Apr 1933, N.Y.
            2pp., w/TL from the Veteran's
            Association of the A.R.C. in Italy
            and envelope

Macdonald, Elsie
ALS   27 Oct 1935, N.Y.
           3pp., w/photographs and envelope

[MacLeish], Ada
ALS   [1927], to EH/Pauline/Jinny
           4pp., w/enclosure

Macdonald, Elsie
ALS   23 May 1937, N.Y.
           5pp.

[MacLeish], Ada
ALS   29 Sept [1952], Conway
           3pp. bearing EH note

MacGregor, Charles (acquaintance, friend)
ALS Mac   [28 July 1934], Ocean Beach, Fire
           Island
           1p., w/envelope bearing Pauline
           note

[MacLeish], Ada
ALS   undated, Saranac Lake, N.Y.
           2pp.

MacHaney, Miriam
Cable   undated, Guethary, to Mr. Barron
           1p.

[MacLeish, Archibald]
TLS Archie
           [1926]
           1p.

[MacLeish], Ada (friend, Archibald's wife)
ALS   [21 Dec 1926], Paris
           1p., w/envelope

MacLeish, Archi[bald] (poet, friend)
ANS   [6 Nov 1926, Paris]
           1p.

[MacLeish, Archibald]
TL   19 June [1927], Ashfield, Mass.,
            to EH/Pauline

            2pp., w/envelope bearing EH note

[MacLeish, Archibald]
ALS "A"

            [20 Feb 1927, Paris]

            3pp., w/envelope

[MacLeish, Archibald]
TLS "A"

            13 Aug [1927], Ashfield
            2pp.

[MacLeish, Archibald]
Cable   5 Mar 1927, La Rochelle
            1p.

[MacLeish, Archibald]
TLS "A"

            18 Sept [1927], Ashfield
            2pp.

[MacLeish, Archibald]
ALS Archie

            Saturday [1928]
            1p., w/envelope

MacLeish, [Archibald]
Cable   [Nov 1927], President Harding
            1p.

[MacLeish, Archibald]
A Post Card S "Archie in automobile"

            [27 May 1928, Budapest]

[MacLeish, Archibald]
ALS "A"

            [14 Feb 1927, Paris]
            1p., w/envelope

[MacLeish, Archibald]
Cable   7 Aug 1928, Conway
            1p.

[MacLeish, Archibald]
ALS "A"

        12 Aug 1928, Conway

        1p., w/envelope

[MacLeish, Archibald]
Cable   26 Dec 1928, Conway

        1p.

[MacLeish, Archibald]
ALS A. Macharchie

        20 Sept 1928, Conway

        1p., w/envelope

[MacLeish, Archibald]
Cable   5 Jan 1929, Greenfield, Mass.

        1p.

[MacLeish, Archibald]
Cable from Ada and Archie

        7 Dec 1928, Conway

        1p.

[MacLeish, Archibald]
Cable   5 Jan 1929, Conway

        1p.

[MacLeish, Archibald]
TLS Archie

        14 Dec [1928], Conway

        1p., w/envelope

MacLeish, Archibald
ALS Archie

        11 Jan [1929, Conway]

        2pp., w/envelope

[MacLeish, Archibald]
Tearsheets from Hound and Horn, pp. 167-169,
"Am Not Prince Hamlet nor was Meant to Be,"
by R. P. Blackmur, w/envelope postmarked
17 Dec 1928, Northampton

MacLeish, Archibald
TLS "A"

        4 Feb [1929], Glencoe, Ill.

        2pp.

[MacLeish, Archibald]
TLS Archie
                11 Mar 1929, Glencoe
                3pp., w/envelope

[MacLeish, Archibald]
TLS A MacL
                [12 Apr 1930, N.Y.]
                1p., w/envelope

MacLeish, Archibald
ALS Archie
                24 June 1929, Conway
                2pp., w/envelope bearing EH note

[MacLeish, Archibald]
Cable from Ada and Archie
                12 May 1931, Conway
                1p.

MacLeish, Archibald
ALS "A"
                1 Sept [1929], Conway
                3pp., w/envelope

[MacLeish, Archibald]
TLS Archie
                2 Feb [1932, N.Y.]
                1p., w/envelope bearing EH note

[MacLeish, Archibald]
Cable from Archie and Ada
                [4 Sept 1929], Conway
                1p. bearing EH notes on verso

[MacLeish, Archibald]
ALS Archie
                [29 Feb 1932, N.Y.]
                1p., w/envelope

[MacLeish, Archibald]
TLS Archie
                [10 Feb 1930, N.Y.]
                2pp. bearing EH note, w/envelope

[MacLeish, Archibald]
TLS Archie
                [Mar 1932], N.Y.
                1p.

[MacLeish, Archibald]
TLS Archie

      [7 Apr 1932, N.Y.]

      1p., w/envelope

MacLeish, Archibald
TLS   26 May 1933, N.Y.

      1p.

[MacLeish, Archibald]
TLS "A"

      [1 June 1932, N.Y.]

      1p., w/envelope

[MacLeish, Archibald]
TLS Archie

      [31 May 1933, N.Y.]

      2pp., w/envelope

[MacLeish, Archibald]
Cable   8 June 1932, N.Y.

      1p.

[MacLeish, Archibald]
TLS "A"

      [c. 7 June 1933]

      1p., w/newspaper clipping and TLcc
from MacLeish to the editor of The
New Republic

[MacLeish, Archibald]
TLS "A"

      [11 June 1932, N.Y.]

      2pp., w/envelope

[MacLeish, Archibald]
Cable   12 June 1933, N.Y.

      1p.

[MacLeish, Archibald]
TLS Archie

      [pre May 1933], Tokyo, to EH/
Pauline

      2pp., w/ANS Ada

[MacLeish, Archibald]
TLS "A"

      [12 June 1933]

      1p.

[MacLeish, Archibald]

TLS Archie

[14 June 1933]

1p., w/correspondence between MacLeish and Bruce Bliven

[MacLeish, Archibald]

Cable   2 May 1934, N.Y.

1p.

[MacLeish, Archibald]

TLS "A"

[20 June 1933], N.Y.

1p., w/correspondence between Max Eastman and MacLeish

[MacLeish, Archibald]

TLS Archie

21 Nov 1934, N.Y.

1p.

[MacLeish, Archibald]

Cable   [31 Oct 1933], N.Y.

1p.

[MacLeish, Archibald]

ALS Archie

[14 Jan 1935, N.Y.

4pp., w/envelope

[MacLeish, Archibald]

TLS "A"

[spring 1934], Conway

2pp.

[MacLeish, Archibald]

ALS Archie

[23 Jan 1935, N.Y.]

3pp., w/envelope

[MacLeish, Archibald]

Cable   20 Apr 1934, Conway

1p.

[MacLeish, Archibald]

ALS "A"

[15 Apr 1935, London]

1p., w/envelope

[MacLeish, Archibald]

TLS Archie

      [5 June 1935, N.Y.]

      2pp., w/Typescript of "Words to be Spoken" and envelope

---

[MacLeish, Archibald]

Cable   27 Jan 1937, N.Y.

      1p.

[MacLeish, Archibald]

ALS Archie

      [August 1935]

      1p.

[MacLeish, Archibald]

Cable   8 Feb 1937, N.Y.

      1p.

[MacLeish, Archibald]

TLS Archie

      [1936]

      2pp.

[MacLeish, Archibald]

ALS Archie

      [8 Feb 1937, N.Y.

      4pp., w/envelope

[MacLeish, Archibald]

TLS Archie

      [10 Aug 1936, Amherst, Mass.]

      3pp., w/enclosure and envelope

[MacLeish, Archibald]

Cable   15 Feb 1937, N.Y.

      1p.

[MacLeish, Archibald]

TLS Archie

      [14 Oct 1936, Conway]

      2pp., w/envelope

[MacLeish, Archibald]

Cable   16 Feb 1937, N.Y.

      1p.

[MacLeish, Archibald]
Cable   [7 Apr 1937], N.Y.
             2pp.

[MacLeish, Archibald]
TLS Archie
             16 June 1937, N.Y.
             2pp., w/envelope

[MacLeish, Archibald]
TLS Archie
             27 May 1937, N.Y.
             2pp.

[MacLeish, Archibald]
TLS Louise Eaton
             .   10 July 1937
                 1p.

[MacLeish, Archibald]
ALS Archie
             28 May 1937
             1p., w/enclosure

[MacLeish, Archibald]
A Receipt S. Louise Eaton
             19 July 1937
             1p.

[MacLeish, Archibald]
Correspondence between Louis P. Birk and
MacLeish
             [4 June 1937]
             5pp.

[MacLeish, Archibald]
TLS Louise Eaton
             [20 July 1937], N.Y.
             1p.

[MacLeish, Archibald]
TLS Archie
             10 June 1937, N.Y.
             1p.

[MacLeish, Archibald]
TLS Archie (LE)   [by Louise Eaton]
             26 July 1937
             1p.

[MacLeish, Archibald]

TLS Archie

8 Aug [1937], Conway

1p.

[MacLeish, Archibald]

Cable   1 Dec [1938], Cambridge

1p.

[MacLeish, Archibald]

TLS Archie

24 July 1938, Conway

1p., w/copy of TL from MacLeish to
Mac [Ralph McA. Ingersoll], 24 July
1938

[MacLeish, Archibald]

TLS Archie

[30 Jan 1939, Farmington, Conn.]

1p., w/envelope

[MacLeish, Archibald]

TLS Archie

6 Aug [1938], Conway

1p., w/envelope

MacLeish, Archiblad

TLS Archie

27 July 1943, Washington

1p., w/envelope

[MacLeish, Archibald]

Cable   [19 Nov 1938, Cambridge]

1p.

[MacLeish, Archibald]

TLS Archie

17 Aug 1943, Washington

1p., w/envelope

[MacLeish, Archibald]

TLS Archie

28 Nov 1938

1p.

MacLeish, Archibald

TLS Archie

1 Dec [1948], N.Y.

2pp., w/envelope bearing EH note

MacLeish, Archibald
TLS Archie

[4 Oct 1952], Conway
2pp. bearing EH note

MacLeish, Archibald
TLS Archie

8 Jan 1957, Conway
1p., w/envelope

[MacLeish, Archibald]
A Poem S Archie

24 June [1953, Conway]
1p., w/envelope

[MacLeish, Archibald]
TLS Archie

[15 Apr 1957], Cambridge
1p., w/envelope postmarked from N.Y.

MacLeish, Archibald
TLS Archie

17 Feb 1954, [Cambridge]
1p., w/envelope

[MacLeish, Archibald]
TLS Felicia Geffen

24 May 1957, N.Y.

1p., w/copy of TL from Robert Frost,
T. S. Eliot and EH, 14 Jan 1957, to
the Attorney-General of the United
States

MacLeish, Archibald
TLS Archie

5 May 1954, Cambridge
1p., w/envelope bearing EH note

MacLeish, Archibald
TLS Archie

3 June [1957], Conway
1p.

[MacLeish, Archibald]
TLS Archie

15 Dec [1956], Cambridge
1p., w/envelope

MacLeish, Archibald
TLS Archie

19 June 1957, Conway
3pp.

MacLeish, Archibald

TLS Archie

21 July 1957, Conway

1p., w/envelope

[MacLeish, Archibald]

Envelope only

undated

MacLeish, Archibald

TLS Archie

[30 Sept 1958], Conway [Cambridge]

2pp., w/envelope bearing EH note

MacLeish, Archibald
See also Birk, Louis P.
Pfeiffer, Gustavus A.
8 May 1933
1 Apr 1932
Pound, Ezra
19 Nov 1926
Ingersoll, Ralph McA.
EH 1932
Houghton Mifflin

MacLeish, Archibald

TL3   11 Nov 1959, N.Y.

1p., w/envelope

MacMillan Co.
See Scribner, Charles, Jr.
7 Apr 1959

[MacLeish, Archibald]

TL3 1yarchieandlove to Pfeiffersand skifers

Saturday

1p.

[MacMullen, Forrest] (friend)

TLS Mac

24 May 1960, Sun Valley

2pp., w/enclosure and envelope

[MacLeish, Archibald]

TL'   undated

1p.

Macomber, Francis (reader)

TLS   20 Aug 1936, N.Y.

1p.

Madden, Cecil (British playwright, aficionado)
TLS   20 Nov 1932, London
              2pp.

Malraux, [Andre]
Cable from Aragon, Malraux, Bloch, Chamson
              8 June 1937, Paris
              1p.

Madill, George J. (Oak Park friend)
ALS   3 Apr 1919, Nantes
              3pp., w/photographs and
              envelope

Malraux, [Andre]
Cable from Malraux, Aragon, Koltsov
              14 June 1937, Paris
              1p.

Mainland, Ken[neth] (Sunny Hemingway's first
                      husband)
ALS   8 Aug 1950, Petoskey
              3pp.

Manfredi, P[ietro] F. (W.W. I friend from Oak
                        Park)
A Post Card S
              15 Mar 1920, Cosenza

Malabu, George (Cuban acquaintance)
ALS   [13 Aug 1960], Oriente, Cuba ,
              to MH
              2pp. bearing MH note and envelope

Manfredi, Pietro F.
AN   9 Feb 1921, [Chicago]
              2pp., w/envelope bearing EH note

Malraux, [Andre] (writer)
Cable from Malraux, Aragon, Chamson, Bloch
              [21 May 1937], Paris
              1p.

Malraux, [Andre]
ALS   [Mar 1937, Paris], to Cher
              camarades
              2pp.

Manley, J. F. (Tanganyika guide)
TLS   23 Feb 1934, Nairobi
           1p.

[Manning, Robert]
TLS Bob M.
                18 Sept 1958, N.Y., to EH/MH
                3pp.

Manley, J. F.
TLS   14 Mar 1934, Nairobi
           1p.

Mansbart, H.
            See Pound, Ezra 10 Dec 1958

Manning, John A.
        See Hayward, Leland
            21 Feb 1955

Manthorp, John C.
        See Time-Life

[Manning, Robert] (Time-Life, friend)
TLS Bob M.
        22 Nov 1954, N.Y.
        2pp., w/enclosure and envelope
        bearing EH note

Marilueha   (reader)
TLS   23 Dec 1960, Lima
           2pp., w/envelope

[Manning, Robert]
TLS Bob
        28 Sept 1957, N.Y., to EH/MH
        2pp.

Marks, John (friend)
A Post Card S
        [1950's]

Marsh, Roy (pilot)

ALS   [11 Apr 1954], Nairobi

           3pp., w/address leaf

Mason, [Frank] (International News Service)

Cable   1 Oct 1922, Paris

           1p.

Marshall, Margaret

           See Beach, Sylvia   7 Sept 1956

Mason, [Frank]

Cable   4 Oct 1922, Paris

           1p.

Martin, W. T.

           See Saturday Evening Post

Mason, [Frank]

Cable   6 Oct [1922], Paris

           1p.

Marton, George (producer)

TLS   25 June 1931, Vienna

           2pp.

[Mason], Frank

Cable   [Nov 1922]

           1p.

Mason, [Frank]

Cable   [1922], N.Y.

           1p.

[Mason, Frank E.]

Western Union Telegraph Card for the Near East
Peace Conference, Lausanne, Nov 1922 for both
Mason and Guglielmo Emmanuel

           2pp.

[Mason], Frank

Cable   24 Nov 1922

   1p.

Mason, [Frank]

Cable   29 Nov 1922

   1p.

[Mason, Frank]

TLS A. Langelier

   25 Nov 1922, Paris

   1p.

[Mason, Frank]

TLS A. Langelier

   4 Dec 1922, Paris

   1p.

Mason, [Frank]

Cable   25 Nov 1922

   1p.

Mason, [Frank]

Cable   14 Dec 1922, [Paris]

   1p.

Mason, [Frank]

Cable   [27 Nov 1922]

   1p. bearing EH notes on verso

Mason, [Frank]

Cable   15 Dec 1922, [Paris]

   1p.

Mason, [Frank]

Cable   28 Nov 1922

   1p.

Mason, [Gran] (husband of Jane, Pan Am
     Airways)

ALS Stoneface Mason

   1 P.M. Sat. [7 Feb 1934], Havana,
   to EH/Pauline

   2pp.

[Mason], Grant

ALS   2 May 1934, Havana

        1p.

[Mason], Jane

ALS   2 Sept [1933, N.Y.], to EH/Pauline

        8pp., w/envelope

[Mason], Jane (friend)

Cable   10 May 1932, Jacksonville

        1p.

[Mason], Jane

ALS   1 Nov 1933, [N.Y.]

        10pp.

[Mason], Jane

Cable   11 May 1932, N.Y.

        1p.

[Mason], Jane

TLS   30 Sept [1934], Tuxedo Park, N.Y.,
        to EH/Pauline

        6pp.

[Mason], Jane

Cable   6 June 1932, Tuxedo Park, N.Y.

        1p.

[Mason], Jane

TLS   17 May apromoxitly [1935], to EH/
        Pauline

        2pp.

Mason, Jane

Cable   4 Aug 1933, N.Y., to EH/Pauline

        1p.

[Mason, Jane]

ALS "J"

        [17 May 1935], to EH/Pauline

        1p.

[Mason], Jane

ALS   [c. June 1935, Miami, to EH/
Pauline

     6pp.

[Mason], Jane

ALS   [30 July 1935], Miami, to EH/
Pauline

    4pp., w/envelope

[Mason], Jane

Cable   10 June 1935, Miami, to EH/Dos Passos

    1p.

Mason, [Jane]

Cable from Masons

      7 Mar 1936, Miami, to EH/Pauline

    1p.

[Mason], Jane

Cable   19 June 1935, Havana

    1p. bearing EH notes

[Mason], Jane

Cable   15 May 1936, Delray Beach, Florida,
to EH/Pauline

    1p.

[Mason], Jane

Cable   29 June 1935, Miami

    1p.

[Mason], Jane

ALS   27 Aug [1936, Havana], to EH/Pauline

    4pp., w/envelope

[Mason], Jane

TLS   2 July [1935], to EH/Pauline

    4pp., w/correspondence between
Jane Mason and Lawrence S. Kubie

[Mason], Jane

Cable   21 July 1938, Washington, to EH/
Pauline

    1p.

[Mason], Jane

TLS   [23 Jan n.y., Havana]

      2pp., w/envelope

Masson, Andre
    See Miro, Joan 18 Sept [1936]

Mason, Jane
    See Hemingway, Pauline
        10 May 1932
        23 Apr 1933
        to others

Masters, Violet (reader)

ALS   undated, Gary, Indiana

      3pp.

Masses & Mainstream
    See Sillen, Samuel

Mathieu, A. Papineau (lawyer)

TLS   11 Oct 1923, Montreal

      1p., w/envelope

[Masson], Andre (artist)

A Post Card S Andre and Paule Vezelay

     [1930]?

Mathieu, Beatrice (writer)

TLS   18 Sept 1934, Paris

      1p.

[Masson], Andre

A Post Card S

    [17 Sept 1937, Saint Pierre Quiberon]

Matisse, Pierre (art gallery owner)

TLS   13 Oct 1934, N.Y.

      1p.

Matisse, Pierre
Cable   14 Nov 1934, N.Y.
               1p. bearing EH notes

[Matthews, Herbert L.]
Transcript of telephone message by "GHA"
               20 Mar 1938
               1p.

Matisse, Pierre
Cable   18 Feb 1935, N.Y.
               1p.

[Matthews, Herbert L.]
TLS "HLM"
               12 Apr [1939] ?
               2pp.

Matisse, Pierre
Cable   9 Jan 1936, N.Y.
               1p.

[Matthews, Herbert L.]
TLS "H.L.M."
               17 Feb [1956], N.Y.
               1p., w/newspaper clipping

Matthews, [Herbert L.] (news correspondent)
Cable   [4 May 1937], Paris
               1p.

Matthews, Herbert L.
TLS Herbert
               27 Aug 1958, N.Y.
               1p., w/envelope

Matthews, [Herbert L.]
Cable   9 Feb 1938, Nice
               1p.

Matthews, Herbert L.
TLS Herbert
               14 Jan 1960, N.Y.
               1p.

Matthews, Herbert L.

TLS Herbert

       21 Mar 1960, N.Y.

       1p., w/photographs and envelope
bearing EH notes

[McAlmon, Robert]   (publisher, Contact Editions)

ALS Bob

       [1924]

       2pp., w/envelope

Matthews, Herbert [L.]

TLS   11 Apr 1960, N.Y., to MH

       2pp. bearing MH note, w/envelope

[McAlmon, Robert]

TLS Bob McA.

       18 May 1926, London

       1p.

Matthews, Hilliard H. (relative of Herbert)

TLS   2 Jan 1941, N.Y.

       2pp., w/photograph and envelope

[McAlmon, Robert]

Pamphlets advertising Contact Editions

   1. Note on "What Happens" a novel by John
      Hermann
   2. Forewarned as regards H D's Prose

Mattox, Roy Lee (Kansas City Star associate)

TLS   23 Dec 1919, Kansas City

       3pp., w/envelope

McCarthy, Frank (filmmaker)

Cable   18 Nov 1954, Richmond, Va.

       1p.

Maugham, William Somerset
      See Time-Life 15 Aug 1952

McClure, John
      See The Double Dealer

McEvoy, J. P. (<u>Reader's Digest</u> editor)

TLS Mac

22 Mar 1955, Pleasantville, N.Y.

1p., w/newspaper clipping and
envelope bearing EH note

McGrath, Thomas J. S., S.J.

TLS   26 Sept 1933, Shreveport

1p.

McFarland, William C. (student)

TLS   13 Dec 1927, Ann Arbor

1p.

McGrath, Thomas J. S., S.J.

TLS Padre Jose del Amor

21 May 1934, Miami

2pp.

McGill, Ralph (editor, <u>The Atlanta
Constitution</u>, reader)

TLS   5 Jan 1951, Atlanta

2pp. bearing EH date notation, w/
typescript of letter from Frances
Morton Minton to McGill, 24 June 1950

McGrath, Thomas J. S., S.J.

TLS   26 May 1954, Shreveport

3pp.

McGill, Ralph

TLS   28 Jan 1954, to EH/MH

2pp., w/envelope

McGrath, Thomas J. S., S.J.

TLS   1 June 1934, Miami

2pp.

McGrath, Thomas, J. S., S.J. (reverand, author,
fisherman)

TL   27 Apr 1933, Shreveport

2pp. bearing EH note

McGrath, Thomas J. S., S.J.

TLS   5 Sept 1934, Miami

4pp., w/TLS Seth Briggs (Field and
Stream) to McGrath, 27 June 1934,
N.Y., and enclosure

McGrath, Thomas J. S., S.J.
TLS Padre Jose del Amor
            29 Oct 1934, Shreveport
            3pp.

McNeil, Oscar B. (sailing acquaintance)
ALS   18 May 1933, Corpus Christie
            4pp.

McGrath, Thomas J. S., S.J.
ALS   28 Feb 1935, Tampa
            4pp., w/newspaper clipping

McNeil, Oscar [B.]
TLS   28 July 1933, Corpus Christie
            3pp., w/17pp. typescript

McKenzie, Vernon
            See *Cosmopolitan*

McPherson, Fanny and Donald
Xmas Greeting S
            1940
            1p.

McLean, Chuck (reader)
TLS   12 Mar 1951, Mont-Boron, Nice
            1p.

Medical Bureau to Aid Spanish Democracy
TLS Walter B. Cannon
            23 Dec 1937, Boston
            1p., w/copies of correspondence
            between Cannon and Ellery
            Sedgwick

McNeary, Walter Nolloth
Cable [26 Jan 1954, Hongkong]
            1p.

Medical Bureau to Aid Spanish Democracy
            See also North American Committee
                        to Aid Spanish Democracy

Medical Center for Federal Prisoners
See Montgomery, Bert

Mendez, Luis (reader)

TLS   12 Oct 1956, Malaga

             4pp., w/envelope bearing EH date

Mees, Hollis R.
             See Hemingway, Pauline
             14 May 1933

Mendez, Raphael
             See Allen, Jay 25 Aug 1937

Meeter, George F. (reader, re: Blaise Centrars

TLS   undated

             1p.

[Menocal], Mayito, [Sr.] (friend)

ALS   4 June 1939, Camaguey, Cuba

             2pp.

Mencken, H. L. (author, editor)

A Statement by the Editor of The American
Mercury, inscribed and signed by Mencken

             16 Apr 1926

             7pp.

[Menocal], Mayito, [Sr.]

ALS   8 Apr 1940, Camaguey

             2pp.

[Mencken, H. L.]

TLS Theodore Rousseau introducing EH to
Mencken

             14 Mar 1928, Paris

             1p., w/envelope

Menocal, Mayito, Sr.

Cable   [3 July 1953], Havana

             1p. bearing EH note

[Menocal], Mayito
Cable   [26 Jan 1954, Havana]
          1p.

[Menocal], Mayito, [Jr.]
ALS   24 Oct 1955, [Camaguey]
          3pp.

[Menocal], Mayito, [Jr.]
ALS   25 Oct 1949, Camaguey, to MH
          4pp.

Mercier, Louis F. V.
          See Holiday

[Menocal], Mayito, [Jr.] (friend)
ALS   28 Apr 1950, Camaguey, to EH/MH
          5pp.

[Merito, Peps, Marquex de Valpariaso y del
Mento] (friend)

Cable   4 Dec 1937, Madrid
          1p.

[Menocal], Mayito, [Jr.]
ALS   16 Dec 1951, to EH/MH
          6pp.

Merner, Garfield David
TLS Garfield
          27 Aug 1936, San Mateo, California
          1p.

[Menocal], Mayito., [Jr.]
ALS M. (little)
          24 Jan 1954, [Camaguey], to EH/MH
          4pp.

Merner, Ward P.
TLS Ward
          21 Sept 1934, Menlo Park, California
          1p.

Meyer, Art
        See Jenkins, Howell
          11 Aug 1918

[Meyer], Wallace

TLS   1 Aug 1952, N.Y.

        3pp.

Meyer, Ben F. (Associated Press)

TLS   22 Aug 1950, Havana

        1p. bearing EH note, w/typescript of
        interview w/EH

[Meyer], Wallace

TLS   8 Aug 1952, N.Y.

        1p.

Meyer, Wallace (editor, Scribner's)

ALS   [July 1928], N.Y.

        6pp.

[Meyer], Wallace

TLS   22 Oct 1953, N.Y.

        2pp.

Meyer, Wallace

TLS   20 July 1950, N.Y., to MH

        1p.

[Meyer], Wallace

TLS   8 Feb 1954, N.Y.

        2pp., w/copy of letter from Earl
        Theisen to Meyer, 26 Jan 1954, Los
        Angeles and envelope bearing EH note

Meyer, Wallace

Cable   [11 Feb 1952], N.Y., to EH/MH

        1p.

[Meyer], Wallace

TLS   17 Feb 1955, N.Y.

        1p., w/book orders and envelope

[Meyer], Wallace
TLS   29 Mar 1955, N.Y.
      1p. bearing EH note, w/photograph

[Meyer], Wallace
TLS   7 Nov 1957, N.Y.
      1p.

[Meyer], Wallace
TLS   20 Dec 1955, N.Y., to MH
      2pp.

Michelson, Herman   (editor, The New Masses)
TLS   3 Mar 1938, N.Y.
      1p. bearing EH note

[Meyer], Wallace
TLS   6 Dec 1956, N.Y.
      2pp. bearing EH notes

Miguelillo   (bullfighter)
Cable   28 Dec 1959
      1p.

[Meyer], Wallace
TLS   14 Mar 1957, N.Y.
      1p., w/envelope bearing EH note

Miguelillo
Cable   [16 Aug 1960], Biarritz
      1p.

[Meyer], Wallace
TLS   29 Mar 1957, N.Y.
      1p. w/envelope bearing EH notes

Miguelillo
Cable   [4 Sept 1960], Malaga 6238-16-4-1555
      1p.

Miguelillo

Cable   [4 Sept 1960], Malaga   6259-13:
           419/48

            1p.

Miller, George J.

TLS   22 June 1943, Nuevitas

            2pp.

Miguel[illo]

Cable   [7 Sept 1960], Malaga

            1p.

Miller, George J.

TLS   29 June 1943, Nuevitas

            2pp. bearing EH notes

Milewski, Szymon (congratulator)

TLS   2 Dec 1954, Warsaw, Poland

            1p. bearing EH note

[Miller, George J.]

Coded message

            [9 July 1943]

            1p. bearing EH notes

[Miller, George J.] (U.S. Naval Liaison Office)

Typed Memo S J. M. Rabassa

            2 June 1943, Nuevitas, Cuba

            1p.

Miller, George J.

TLS   9 July 1943, Nuevitas

            2pp.

Miller, George J.

TLS   15 June 1943, Nuevitas

            2pp. bearing EH notes

[Miller, John W.] (W.W. I Red Cross ambulance
                        driver)

ALS Johnnie

            23 Apr 1919, [Minneapolis]

            6pp., w/envelope

[Miller, John W.]
TLS Giovanni

    16 Nov 1926, [Duluth]·

    4pp.

[Miller, John W.]
ANS Giovanni on Typescript of Miller's "A Flea
to the Dew (or what have you)"

    4 Jan 1935, Chicago

    2pp., w/envelope

[Miller, Madelaine HEMINGWAY Mainland) (sister)
ALS Nunbones

    21 Oct 1918, Oak Park

    7pp., w/envelope

[Miller, Madelaine HEMINGWAY]
ALS Nunbones

    5 Dec 1925, Oak Park

    3pp., w/envelope

[Miller, Madelaine HEMINGWAY]
TL   5 June 1926, Oak Park

    1p., w/envelope

[Miller, Madelaine HEMINGWAY]
ALS Nunbones

    Bath night in the States [pre Feb
1927], to EH and Hadley

    3pp.

[Miller, Madelaine HEMINGWAY]
ALS Nunbones

    26 Feb 1927

    2pp.

[Miller, Madelaine HEMINGWAY]
TLS Sunny

    23 Apr 1927

    2pp.

[Miller, Madelaine HEMINGWAY]
Cable   [7 May 1927], Oak Park

    1p. bearing EH notes

[Miller, Madelaine HEMINGWAY]
ALS Sunny

    12 May [1927, Chicago]

    2pp., w/envelope

[Miller, Madelaine HEMINGWAY]

TLS Sunny

      6 Jan 1928, Oak Park

      2pp., w/envelope

[Miller, Madelaine HEMINGWAY]

ALS Sunny

      30 Oct [1929], Oak Park, to EH/
Pauline

      4pp., w/envelope

[Miller, Madelaine HEMINGWAY]

ALS Sunny

      4 Aug [1928], Petoskey

      4pp., w/envelope

[Miller, Madelaine HEMINGWAY]

TL   27 Jan 1931, Chicago, to EH/Pauline

      2pp.

[Miller, Madelaine HEMINGWAY]

ALS Nunbones

      5 Mar 1928, Oak Park

      6pp., w/envelope

[Miller, Madelaine HEMINGWAY]

TL   8 Feb 1931, Chicago

      2pp.

[Miller, Madelaine HEMINGWAY]

ALS Sunny

      26 Sept [1928, Oak Park]

      6pp., w/envelope

[Miller, Madelaine HEMINGWAY]

TL   28 Dec 1931, Oak Park, to EH/
[Carol] Hemingway]

      2pp.

[Miller, Madelaine HEMINGWAY]

ALS Sunny

      May 18, [1929, Nice]

      5pp., w/envelope

[Miller, Madelaine HEMINGWAY]

TL   6 May 1932, Chicago

      2pp., w/envelope

[Miller, Madelaine HEMINGWAY]

TL   21 July 1933

        2pp.

[Miller, Madelaine HEMINGWAY]

TL   6 June 1935, Oak Park

        3pp., w/envelope

[Miller, Madelaine HEMINGWAY

TL   9 Mar 1934, [Oak Park]

        2pp., w/newspaper clipping and
        envelope

[Miller, Madelaine HEMINGWAY]

TL   11 June1935,

        1p.

[Miller, Madelaine HEMINGWAY]

TL   21 May 1934

        2pp.

[Miller, Madelaine HEMINGWAY]

TL   16 June 1935

        2pp.

[Miller, Madelaine HEMINGWAY]

TL   12 Sept 1934

        2pp.

[Miller, Madelaine HEMINGWAY]

TL   Friday [1936]

        1p., w/sheet music written by
        Sunny Hemingway and publicity

[Miller, Madelaine HEMINGWAY]

TL   3 May 1935, [Oak Park], to EH/
        Pauline

        2pp., w/envelope bearing EH note

[Miller, Madelaine HEMINGWAY]

TL   14 Oct 1936, [Berwyn, Ill.]

        1p., w/envelope

[Miller, Madelaine HEMINGWAY]

TLS Sunny

    15 Mar 1937, [Berwyn, Ill.], to Pauline

    1p., w/envelope

[Miller, Madelaine Hemingway MAINLAND]

ALS Sunny

    [8 Mar 1939, Oak Park], to EH/Pauline

    4pp.,w/envelope and photograph

[Miller, Madelaine HEMINGWAY]

ALS Sunny

    20 Jan 1938, River Forest, to EH/Pauline

    2pp., w/envelope

[Miller, Madelaine Hemingway MAINLAND]

ALS Sunny

    [26 Mar 1939, Oak Park,]

    3pp., w/envelope

[Miller, Madelaine Hemingway MAINLAND]

TLS Sunny

    14 Aug 1938, Oak Park, to EH/Pauline

    1p.

[Miller, Madelaine Hemingway MAINLAND]

ALS Sunny

    11 July 1943, [Memphis]

    1p.

[Miller, Madelaine Hemingway MAINLAND]

ALS Sunny

    22 Dec 1938, [Oak Park]

    4pp., w/envelope

[Miller, Madelaine Hemingway MAINLAND]

TLS Sister Sunny the Nunbones

    18 July 1943, Memphis

    2pp., w/enclosure and envelope

[Miller, Madealine Hemingway] MAINLAND

ALS Sunny

    16 Jan [1939, Oak Park]

    3pp., w/photograph and envelope

[Miller, Madelaine Hemingway MAINLAND]

ALS Nunbones

    29 June 1950

    2pp. bearing EH note

[Miller, Madelaine Hemingway MAINLAND]
ALS Sunny

      [27 July 1950], Petoskey

      7pp. bearing EH note

[Miller, Madelaine Hemingway MAINLAND]
ALS Nunbones

      25 Aug [1952]

      7pp. bearing EH note

[Miller, Madelaine Hemingway MAINLAND]
ALS Nunbones

      23 Oct 1950

      1p. bearing EH note, w/enclosures

[Miller, Madelaine Hemingway MAINLAND]
ALS Nunones

      11 Dec 1952

      1p., w/newspaper clipping and
      photograph

[Miller, Madelaine Hemingway MAINLAND]
ALS Sunny the Nunbones

      [14 Nov 1950]

      2pp., w/newspaper clipping

[Miller, Madelaine Hemingway] MAINLAND
ALS Nunbones

      17 June 1953, Petoskey

      2pp. bearing EH note

[Miller, Madelaine Hemingway MAINLAND]
Xmas Greeting S Sunny, Ken & Uncle Ernie

      [25 Dec] 1951

[Miller, Madelaine Hemingway MAINLAND]
ALS Sunny

      23 June 1953, Petoskey

      4pp., w/envelope bearing EH note

[Miller, Madelaine Hemingway MAINLAND]
ALS Old Nunbones

      [3 June 1952]

      2pp.

[Miller, Madelaine Hemingway] MAINLAND
ALS Nunbones

      [after June 1953], Petoskey

      2pp.

[Miller, Madlaine Hemingway MAINLAND]
Cable   [26 Jan 1954, Petoskey]
                1p.

[Miller, Madelaine Hemingway Mainland]
ALS Sunny
                Sunday even, A Board
                2pp.

[Miller, Madelaine Hemingway MAINLAND]
ALS Nunbones
                13 Sept 1954, [Riverside, Ill.]
                2pp., w/photographs and envelope

[Miller, Madelaine Hemingway Mainland]
ALS Sunny
                undated, on the 'L"
                1p.

[Miller, Madelaine Hemingway MAINLAND]
TLS Nunbones
                1 Apr 1955, Petoskey
                1p., w/envelope

[Miller, Madelaine HEMINGWAY]
TL   undated
                1p.

[MILLER, Madelaine Hemingway]
Birthday Greeting S Nunbones/Sunny
                [14 July 1958, Petoskey]
                W/envelope

[Miller, Madelaine HEMINGWAY]
ALS Sunny the Nunbones
                19 Dec n.y.
                2pp.

[MILLER, Madelaine Hemingway]
ALS Nunbones
                28 Dec [1960, Wolverine, Michigan],
                to EH/MH
                2pp.,w/envelope

Miller, Madelaine Hemingway Mainland
        See also Hemingway, Leicester
                        Summer 1938
                Sanford, Marcelline H.
                        4 Jan 1924

Miller, Webb (newspaperman)
TLS   2 Nov 1936, London
           2pp.

Miller, Webb
TLS Webb
           10 Aug 1937, London
           1p., w/cc signed

Miller, Webb
TLS Webb
           29 Dec 1937, London
           1p.

Milner, Hugh (newspaperman)
ALS   15 May 1954, Madrid
           1p., w/check to EH

Minton, Francis Morton
           See McGill, Ralph 5 Jan 1951

Miro, Joan (painter)
ALS   17 July 1926, Barcelona
           4pp., w/envelope bearing EH note

[Miro, Joan]
Visiting card w/inscription
           21 June 1927, [Paris]
           w/newspaper article and envelope

[Miro], Joan
ALS   22 Nov 1929, Paris
           2pp., w/envelope

[Miro], Joan
ANS   ce Samedi [30 Nov 1929], Paris
           1p., w/envelope

Miro, [Joan]
A Post Card S
           1 Jan 1930, Barcelona
           1p.

Miro, [Joan]

ALS   31 Oct 1933, Paris

          1p., w/enclosure and envelope

Miro, [Joan]

ALS   31 May 1947, N.Y.

          2pp.

[Miro], Joan

ALS   2 Feb 1934, Barcelona

          1p., w/envelope

Miro, [Joan]

ALS   8 Jan 1938, Paris

          1p., w/envelope

[Miro], Joan

A Post Card S Joan & Andre Masson

          18 Sept [1936], Barcelona, to EH/
          Pauline

Miro, Joan

ALS   2 July 1952, Montroig

          1p. bearing EH note, w/envelope

Miro, [Joan]

A Post Card S Miro and Pilar

          23 Dec 1936, Paris, to EH/Pauline

Miro, Joan

Visiting card bearing address

          undated

          1p.

Miro, Joan

ALS   19 May 1937, Paris

          1p., w/envelope

Miro, Joan

          See Mowrer, Hadley R. Hemingway
          25 Aug 1933
          Soby, James T.

Mizener, Arthur (biographer)

TLS   6 Dec 1949, Northfield, Minn.

           1p., w/enclosures

Monck, E. B. (shipmate)

ALS   7 May 1928, Lima

           1p., w/photograph and envelope

Modern Age Books
        See Birk, Louis P.

Mondadori Editore

Cable   1 June 1937, Milan

           1p.

Modern Language Association of America
        See Baker, Carlos   28 Nov 1960
            Stone, George W.

Mondadori Editore

Memorandum of Agreement

           13 Oct 1951

           2pp. bearing EH note

Molano, Joaquin C. (Asociacion Nacional de
        Piscicultra y Pesca)

TLS   25 Jan 1954, Bogota

           1p.

Mondadori Editore

TLS Alberto

           9 May 1952, Milan, to MH

           1p.

Molyneux, Patrice (handwriting analyst)

ALS   29 May 1951, Havana

           2pp.

Mondadori Editore

Cable   [26 Jan 1954, Milan]

           1p.

Mondodori Editore

TLS Arnoldo

        20 Nov 1957, Milan

        1p.

Mondadori Editore
        See also University of
        Oregon Greenburger
        File

Mondadori Editore

TLS Alberto

        2 May 1960, Milan

        1p.,tw/envelope bearing EH note

Monnier, Adrienne (La Maison des Amis des
                        Livres)

ALS   14 Nov 1927, Paris

        1p.

Mondodori Editore

Cable from Alberto Mondadori

        [27 Sept 1960], Milan

        3pp.

Monnier, Jean (ship's doctor)

ALS   5 June [1953], N.Y.

        2pp., w/envelope

Mondodori Editore

Cable from Alberto Mondadori

        [29 Sept 1960], Milan

        2pp.

Monro, Harold
        See The Chapbook

Mondodori, Editore

TLS Ablerto

        10 Jan 1961, Milan

        2pp.

Montes Junco, Josc' (congratulator)

TLS   28 Oct 1954, Havana

        1p. bearing EH note

Montgomery, Bert
TLS   31 Mar 1953, Springfield, Mo.
           1p.

Moorhead, Ethel
           See EH 19 Apr 1925

[Moorhead], Alan
ALS   14 Nov [1948], to MH
           1p.

[Morgan], Pat (friend)
ALS   [Jan 1930], 169 East 74th Street,
           [New York]
           8pp.

[Moorhead, Alan]
TLS "A"
           13 Feb [1949], to MH
           1p.

[Morgan], Pat
ALS   [20 Feb 1930], 27 West 44th
           Street, [New York]
           4pp., w/envelope

[Moorhead], Alan
ALS   22 Sept [1956], London, to MH
           2pp.

Morgan, W. B. (acquaintance in Hendaye)
ALS   7 May 1933, Barcelona
           2pp.

[Moorhead], Alan (historian, friend)
ALS   6 Nov [1956], London, to EH/MH
           4pp.

[Morgan], Pat
ALS   undated, On board S.S. Olympic
           6pp., w/envelope

Morgenstern, George
     See Wilder, Thornton 13 Mar 1935

Moscow Art Theatre
TLS L. Berthensson .
          14 Oct 1923, Paris
          1p.

Morrison, Graham (reader)
ALS   2 Dec 1950, Wheatridge, Colorado
        1p., w/envelope

Mourelet, R. (concierge, Ritz Hotel)
TLS   4 Apr 1950, Paris
        1p. bearing MH notes

Morrison, Theodore (anthologist, professor)
TLS   27 Mar 1939, Cambridge
        1p.

[Mowrer, Edgar A.] (Chicago Daily News, Paul
                Scott Mowrer's brother)
ALS Winifred Mowrer
        26 May [1926], Paris
        1p., w/TLS Edgar to Winnifred, 21 May
        1926, Berlin

Morrow, Elise (columnist)
TLS   9 Jan 1951, Washington
        2pp. bearing EH note

Mowrer, Edgar A.
TLS   28 May 1926, Berlin
        1p. bearing EH note, w/envelope

Morton, Paul (newspaperman)
TLS   1 June 1960, Ontario
        1p., w/enclosure

Mowrer, Edgar A.
ALS   12 June 1926, Berlin
        1p., w/TLS Jean Watson, Curtis
        Brown, 10 June 1926, to Mowrer

Mowrer, Edgar A.

TLS 25 July [1926], Berlin

   1p.

Mowrer, Edgar

   See also Mowrer, Hadley

    25 Aug 1933

Mowrer, Edgar A.

TLS 29 Dec 1926, Berlin

   1p.

[Mowrer, Hadley RICHARDSON]

Certificate of Membership in the Permanent
Blind Relief War Fund for E. Hadley Richardson

   20 Dec 1919, N.Y.

    1p.

Mowrer, Edgar A.

TLS 1 June 1927, Berlin

   1p.

[Mowrer, Hadley RICHARDSON Hemingway] (first
           wife)

ALS Hash

   5 Nov [1920], St. Louis

    4pp., w/envelope

[Mowrer,] Edgar [A.]

TLS Edgar

   8 Oct [1936], Chicago

   2pp., w/envelope

[Mowrer, Hadley RICHARDSON]

ALS Hash

   Monday Morning [8 Nov 1920], St.
   Louis

   6pp., w/envelope

[Mowrer], Edgar [A.]

TLS 14 June n.y., Paris

   2pp.

[Mowrer, Hadley RICHARDSON]

ALS Hash

   11 Nov [1920], St. Louis

   10pp., w/envelope

[Mowrer, Hadley RICHARDSON]
ALS Hash

[20 Nov 1920], St. Louis

6pp., w/envelope

[Mowrer, Hadley RICHARDSON]
Cable   3 Dec 1920, St. Louis

1p.

[Mowrer, Hadley RICHARDSON]
Envelope only postmarked 25 Nov 1920, St. Louis

donor JH

[Mowrer, Hadley RICHARDSON]
ALS Hash

7 Dec [1920, St. Louis]

1p., w/envelope

donor JH

[Mowrer, Hadley RICHARDSON]
ALS Hash/ovitch/ronoff/Me

'sgiving noon [25 Nov (?) 1920]

12 pp.

donor JH

[Mowrer, Hadley RICHARDSON]
ALS Hash

Fri Noon [10 Dec 1920, St. Louis]

8pp., w/envelope

[Mowrer, Hadley RICHARDSON]
ALS Hashlemore

Tuesday morn 30 Nov [1920],
Allentown, Missouri

8 pp., w/envelope

donor JH

[Mowrer, Hadley RICHARDSON]
ALS Hash

Saturday night [11 Dec 1920, St. Louis]

8pp., w/envelope

[Mowrer, Hadley RICHARDSON]
Cable   2 Dec 1920, St. Louis

1p.

[Mowrer, Hadley RICHARDSON]
ALS Hash

Monday night [13 Dec 1920, St. Louis]

7pp.

[Mowrer, Hadley RICHARDSON]

ALS Hash

Tuesday Evening [14 Dec 1920,
St. Louis]

2pp., w/envelope

[Mowrer, Hadley RICHARDSON]

ALS Hash

Thusday 2 P.M. [23 Dec 1920, St.
Louis]

4pp., w/envelope

[Mowrer, Hadley RICHARDSON]

ALS Hash

Wed noon [15 Dec 1920, St. Louis]

2 pp., w/envelope

donor JH

[Mowrer, Hadley RICHARDSON]

ALS Hash

Christmas Eve Noon-before Lunch
[24 Dec 1920, St. Louis]

4pp., w/envelope

[Mowrer, Hadley RICHARDSON]

ALS Hash

Wed 6 P.M. [15 Dec 1920, St.
Louis]

6pp., w/envelope

[Mowrer, Hadley RICHARDSON]

ALS Hash

Monday evening--just dusk. . .
[27 Dec 1920, St. Louis]

10pp., w/envelope

[Mowrer, Hadley RICHARDSON]

ALS Hash/Hashovitch

Monday [20 Dec 1920, St. Louis]

8pp., w/envelope

[Mowrer, Hadley RICHARDSON]

ALS Hash

[31 Dec 1920, St. Louis]

6 pp., w/envelope

donor JH

[Mowrer, Hadley RICHARDSON]

ALS Hash

Tuesday 9 P.M. [21 Dec 1920,
St. Louis]

2pp., w/envelope

[Mowrer, Hadley RICHARDSON]

ALS Hash

New Years Day [1 Jan 1921, St.
Louis]

1 p., w/envelope

donor JH

[Mowrer, Hadley RICHARDSON]

ALS Hash

       Sunday night [2 Jan 1921, St. Louis]

       8 pp., w/envelope

       donor JH

[Mowrer, Hadley RICHARDSON]

ALS Hashovitch

       Saturday Morning [15 Jan 1921, St. Louis]

       11 pp., w/envelope

       donor JH

[Mowrer, Hadley RICHARDSON]

ALS Hash

       Friday Morning [7 Jan 1921, St. Louis]

       11 pp., w/envelope

       donor JH

[Mowrer, Hadley RICHARDSON]

ALS Hashovitch

       Sunday Morning 12 Noon [16 Jan 1921, St. Louis]

       12 pp., w/envelope

       donor JH

[Mowrer, Hadley RICHARDSON]

ALS Hash

       Saturday night [8 Jan 1921, St. Louis]

       11 pp., w/envelope

       donor JH

[Mowrer, Hadley RICHARDSON]

ALS Hash

       [18 Jan 1921, St. Louis]

       14pp., w/envelope

[Mowrer, Hadley RICHARDSON]

ALS his Girl

       Wednesday 3 P.M. [12 Jan 1921, St. Louis]

       2 pp., w/envelope

       donor JH

[Mowrer, Hadley RICHARDSON]

ALS Hashovitch

       Wednesday Night [19 Jan 1921, St. Louis]

       10pp., w/envelope

[Mowrer, Hadley RICHARDSON]

ALS Hash/Hashovitch

       Wednesday noon [12 Jan 1921, St. Louis]

       20 pp., w/envelope

       donor JH

[Mowrer, Hadley RICHARDSON]

ALS Hashovitch

       [20 Jan 1921, St. Louis]

       15 pp., w/envelope

       donor JH

[Mowrer, Hadley RICHARDSON]

Cable   21 Jan 1921, St. Louis

          1p.

[Mowrer, Hadley RICHARDSON]

ALS Hash

          Wednesday night [26 Jan 1921, St. Louis]

          7 pp., w/ envelope

          donor JH

[Mowrer, Hadley RICHARDSON]

ALS Hashovitch

          Friday night [21 Jan 1921, St. Louis]

          8 pp., w/envelope

          donor JH

[Mowrer, Hadley RICHARDSON]

ALS Hashmaninoff

          Thursday Evening [27 Jan 1921, St. Louis]

          8 pp., w/envelope

          donor JH

[Mowrer, Hadley RICHARDSON]

ALS li'l Hasha/Hashovitch

          [22 Jan 1921, St. Louis]

          7 pp., w/envelope

          donor JH

[Mowrer, Hadley RICHARDSON]

ALS Hashovitchissing

          [28 Jan 1921, St. Louis]

          10 pp., w/envelope

          donor JH

[Mowrer, Hadley RICHARDSON]

ALS Hash

          [24 Jan 1921, St. Louis]

          6 pp., w/envelope

          donor JH

[Mowrer,] Hadley [RICHARDSON]

ALS Hashomervitch or Hadley

          Sunday afternoon [30 Jan 1921, St. Louis]

          11 pp., w/envelope

          donor JH

[Mowrer, Hadley RICHARDSON]

ALS Hashovitch

          Monday afternoon [24 Jan 1921, St. Louis]

          7 pp., w/envelope

          donor JH

[Mowrer, Hadley RICHARDSON]

ALS Had

          Monday afternoon [31 Jan 1921, St. Louis]

          4 pp., w/envelope

          donor JH

[Mowrer, Hadley RICHARDSON]
ALS Hashlemore/Hash

      Tuesday night [1 Feb 1921]

      10 pp.

      donor JH

[Mowrer, Hadley RICHARDSON]
ALS Hash

      [8 Feb 1921, St. Louis]

      6 pp., w/envelope

      donor JH

[Mowrer,] Hadley [RICHARDSON]
ALS

      Friday night [4 Feb 1921, St. Louis]

      6 pp., w/envelope

      donor JH

[Mowrer, Hadley RICHARDSON]
ALS Hash

      Tuesday nacht [8 Feb 1921, St. Louis]

      4 pp., w/envelope

      donor JH

[Mowrer, Hadley RICHARDSON]
ALS Hash (Muck) (Mick)

      Saturday afternoon late [5 Feb 1921, St. Louis]

      8pp., w/envelope

[Mowrer], Hadley [RICHARDSON]
AL

      Friday noon [11 Feb 1921, St. Louis]

      4 pp., w/envelope

      donor JH

[Mowrer, Hadley RICHARDSON]
ALS Hash

      Sunday morning or rather 1:20 [6 Feb 1921, St. Louis]

      8pp., w/envelope

[Mowrer,] Hadley [RICHARDSON]
ALS Hash Mic Hadley/Haddum/Hash

      Saturday night [12 Feb 1921, St. Louis]

      6 pp., w/ALS from Oliver E. Bagg, 21 Dec 1920, Chicago, to Hadley, 5 pp., and envelope

      donor JH

[Mowrer, Hadley RICHARDSON]
ALS Hash

      [7 Feb 1921, St. Louis]

      7 pp., w/envelope

      donor JH

[Mowrer,] Hadley [RICHARDSON]
ALS Hadley Mic Hash

      Monday morning [14 Feb 1921, St. Louis]

      8 pp., w/envelope

      donor JH

[Mowrer, Hadley RICHARDSON]

ALS Hash

Tuesday afternoon [15 Feb 1921, St. Louis]

4pp., w/envelope

[Mowrer], Hadley [RICHARDSON]

ALS Hadley Hash

Tuesday Morning [19 Feb 1921]

10pp.

[Mowrer, Hadley RICHARDSON]

ALS Hash

Wednesday afternoon [16 Feb 1921, St. Louis]

2 pp., w/card from Roddy to Amie, and envelope

donor JH

[Mowrer], Hadley [RICHARDSON]

ALS   Thursday noon [24 Feb 1921], St. Louis

10pp., w/envelope

[Mowrer, Hadley RICHARDSON]

ALS Hash

Thursday late afternoon [17 Feb 1921, St. Louis]

5pp., w/envelope

[Mowrer, Hadley RICHARDSON]

ALS Hashovitch/Your lil Hash

Saturday morning [27 Feb 1921], St. Louis

4 pp.

donor JH

[Mowrer, Hadley RICHARDSON]

ALS Hash

Friday night [18 Feb 1921]

4 pp.

donor JH

[Mowrer, Hadley RICHARDSON]

ALS Hash

Sunday morning [27 Feb 1921] St. Louis

8pp., w/envelope

donor JH

[Mowrer, Hadley RICHARDSON]

ALS Hash

Bath night [19 Feb 1921]

6 pp.

donor JH

[Mowrer, Hadley RICHARDSON]

ALS Hash

[March/Apr 1921], St. Louis

4 pp.

donor JH

[Mowrer, Hadley RICHARDSON]

ALS Your own loving Hash

[March/Apr 1921], St. Louis

8 pp.

donor JH

[Mowrer, Hadley RICHARDSON]

ALS Hashovitch

Saturday noon [5 March 1921, St. Louis]

6 pp., w/envelope

donor JH

[Mowrer, Hadley RICHARDSON]

ALS Hash

[1 March 1921] St. Louis

4 pp., w/envelope

donor JH

[Mowrer, Hadley RICHARDSON]

Cable   5 Mar 1921, St. Louis

1p.

[Mowrer, Hadley RICHARDSON]

ALS Hash

[1 March 1921] St. Louis

8 pp., w/envelope

donor JH

[Mowrer, Hadley RICHARDSON]

Cable   6 Mar 1921, St. Louis

1p.

[Mowrer, Hadley RICHARDSON]

ALS Hash

Thursday night, The Breakers
[3 March 1921, St. Louis]

12 pp., w/envelope

donor JH

[Mowrer, Hadley RICHARDSON]

ALS Hasho

Sunday night [6 March 1921, St. Louis]

12 pp., w/envelope

donor JH

[Mowrer, Hadley RICHARDSON]

ALS Hashovitch

[4 March 1921, St. Louis]

5 pp.

donor JH

[Mower, Hadley RICHARDSON]

ALS Hash

Monday morning [7 March 1921, St. Louis]

6 pp.

donor JH

[Mowrer, Hadley RICHARDSON]

Cable   8 Mar 1921, St. Louis

          1p.

[Mowrer, Hadley RICHARDSON]

ALS Hash

          [16 March 1921, St. Louis]

          6 pp., w/envelope

          donor JH

[Mowrer, Hadley RICHARDSON]

ALS Hashovitch

          Tuesday - 4 P.M. [8 March 1921,
          St. Louis]

          6 pp., w/envelope

          donor JH

[Mowrer, Hadley RICHARDSON]

Cable   17 Mar 1921, St. Louis

          1p.

[Mowrer, Hadley RICHARDSON]

ALS Hash

          [9 March 1921, St. Louis]

          1 p., w/envelope

          donor JH

[Mowrer, Hadley RICHARDSON]

ALS Hash

          Tuesday morning [29 March 1921,
          St. Louis]

          8 pp., w/envelope

          donor JH

[Mowrer], Hadley [RICHARDSON]

ALS

          This morning [15 Mar 1921, St. Louis]

          6 pp., w/unrelated enclosures bearing
          EH notation, and envelope

          donor JH

[Mowrer, Hadley RICHARDSON]

ALS Your own Hash

          Wednesday morning [30 March 1921]

          8 pp., w/EH notation

          donor JH

[Mowrer, Hadley RICHARDSON]

Cable   16 Mar 1921, St. Louis

          1p.

[Mowrer, Hadley RICHARDSON]

ALS Hash

          Friday morning [1 April 1921, St.
          Louis]

          10 pp., w/envelope

          donor JH

[Mowrer, Hadley RICHARDSON]

ALS Hash

        Saturday morning [2 April 1921, St. Louis]

        5 pp., w/envelope

        donor JH

[Mowrer, Hadley RICHARDSON]

ALS Hash

        Wensdy Club morning [6 Apr 1921]

        10 pp.

        donor JH

[Mowrer, Hadley RICHARDSON]

ALS Hash

        Sunday morning [3 April 1921, St. Louis]

        7 pp., w/envelope

        donor JH

[Mowrer], Hadley RICHARDSON

ALS

        8 April [1921], St. Louis, to Grace Hall Hemingway

        4 pp., w/envelope

        donor JH

[Mowrer, Hadley RICHARDSON]

ALS Hash

        Monday morning [4 Apr 1921]

        8 pp.

        donor JH

[Mowrer, Hadley RICHARDSON]

ALS Hashlemore/Hash

        Friday night/Saturday mo'nin [8 and 9 Apr 1921]

        15 pp.

        donor JH

[Mowrer, Hadley RICHARDSON]

ALS Hash

        [4 April 1921] St. Louis

        6 pp., w/envelope

        donor JH

[Mowrer, Hadley RICHARDSON]

ALS Hash/H/Hasheovitch

        Sunday 6 PM [10 and 11 April 1921, St. Louis]

        14 pp., w/envelope

        donor JH

[Mowrer, Hadley RICHARDSON]

Envelope only postmarked 5 Apr 1921, St. Louis

        donor JH

[Mowrer, Hadley RICHARDSON]

ALS Hash

        Same afternoon [12 April 1921, St. Louis]

        8 pp., w/envelope

        donor JH

[Mowrer, Hadley RICHARDSON]

ALS Hash

Wednesday 11:30 A.M. [13 Apr 1921, St. Louis]

9pp., w/photograph and envelope

[Mowrer, Hadley RICHARDSON]

ALS 'ash

Wednesday morning [20 April 1921, St. Louis]

8 pp., w/envelope

donor JH

[Mowrer, Hadley RICHARDSON]

ALS Hash

[15 Apr 1921, St. Louis]

6pp., w/envelope

[Mowrer, Hadley RICHARDSON]

ALS Hash

Thursday 4:30 PM [21 April 1921, St. Louis]

4 pp., w/envelope

donor JH

[Mowrer, Hadley RICHARDSON]

ALS Hash

Saturday morning [16 April 1921, St. Louis]

12 pp., w/envelope

donor JH

[Mowrer, Hadley RICHARDSON]

ALS Hashovtich/Hash

[22 April 1921, St. Louis]

6 pp., w/envelope

donor JH

[Mowrer, Hadley RICHARDSON]

ALS Hash

Same afternoon late/late Sunday afternoon [16 and 17 Apr 1921, St. Louis]

4pp., w/envelope

donor JH

[Mowrer, Hadley RICHARDSON]

ALS Hash

Saturday morning [23 April 1921, St. Louis]

8 pp., w/envelope

donor JH

[Mowrer, Hadley RICHARDSON]

ALS Hash

Monday afternoon [18 Apr 1921, St. Louis]

3pp., w/envelope

donor JH

[Mowrer, Hadley RICHARDSON]

ALS Hash

Sunday 12:45 P.M. [24 Apr 1921]

12 pp.

donor JH

[Mowrer, Hadley RICHARDSON]

ALS Hash

Monday morning [25 April 1921, St. Louis]

6 pp., w/envelope

donor JH

[Mowrer, Hadley RICHARDSON]

ALS Hasho

Monday morning [2 May 1921, St. Louis]

6 pp., w/envelope

donor JH

[Mowrer, Hadley RICHARDSON]

ALS Hash

Wednesday morning [27 April 1921, St. Louis]

14 pp., w/envelope

donor JH

[Mowrer, Hadley RICHARDSON]

ALS Hash/Hash

Wednesday night/Thursday morning 4 and 5 May 1921, St. Louis]

16 pp., w/envelope

donor JH

[Mowrer, Hadley RICHARDSON]

ALS Hash

Friday night [29 April 1921] St. Louis

13 pp., w/envelope

donor JH

[Mowrer, Hadley RICHARDSON]

ALS Hash

At night [5 May 1921] St. Louis

6 pp., w/envelope

donor JH

[Mowrer, Hadley RICHARDSON]

ALS Hasho

Saturday 11 AM [30 April 1921] St. Louis

9 pp., w/envelope

donor JH

[Mowrer, Hadley RICHARDSON]

ALS Your own l'il pink-eyed Hash/Hash

Friday 4 P.M./ Saturday morning [6 and 7 May 1921]

12 pp.

donor JH

[Mowrer, Hadley RICHARDSON]

ALS Hash

Sunday 1 P.M. [1 May 1921]

10 pp.

donor JH

[Mowrer, Hadley RICHARDSON]

ALS Hash

Monday 4 P.M. [9 May 1921]

8 pp.

donor JH

[Mowrer, Hadley RICHARDSON]

ALS Hash

Tuesday 4 P.M. [10 May 1921]

8 pp.

donor JH

[Mowrer, Hadley RICHARDSON]

ALS Hash

Tuesday 3 P.M. [17 May 1921]

10 pp.

donor JH

[Mowrer, Hadley RICHARDSON]

ALS Hash

Wednesday After [11 May 1921]

7 pp.

donor JH

[Mowrer, Hadley RICHARDSON]

ALS Hash

Thursday night [19 May 1921]

10 pp.

donor JH

[Mowrer, Hadley RICHARDSON]

ALS Hash

Thursday morning [12 May 1921, St. Louis] bearing EH note

12 pp., w/envelope

donor JH

[Mowrer, Hadley RICHARDSON]

ALS Hashelman

[20 May 1921], St. Louis

12pp., w/envelope

[Mowrer, Hadley RICHARDSON]

ALS Hash

Friday [13 May 1921]

10 pp.

donor JH

[Mowrer, Hadley RICHARDSON]

ALS Hash

Sunday night [22 May 1921,] St. Louis

12 pp., w/envelope

donor JH

[Mowrer, Hadley RICHARDSON]

ALS Hash

Monday noon [16 May 1921]

6 pp.

donor JH

[Mowrer, Hadley RICHARDSON]

ALS Hash

4:30 Monday [23 May 1921,] St. Louis

4 pp., w/envelope

donor JH

[Mowrer, Hadley RICHARDSON]

ALS Hash

Tuesday afternoon [24 May 1921, St. Louis]

15 pp., w/envelope

donor JH

[Mowrer, Hadley RICHARDSON]

ALS Hash

Sunday afternoon [5 June 1921,] St. Louis

12 pp., w/envelope

donor JH

[Mowrer, Hadley RICHARDSON]

ALS Hash

Wednesday noon [25 May 1921]

13 pp.

donor JH

[Mowrer, Hadley RICHARDSON]

ALS Hash

[6 June 1921] St. Louis

8 pp., w/page from Reedy's Mirror, [1916], and envelope

donor JH

[Mowrer, Hadley RICHARDSON]

ALS Hash

Thursday afternoon/Next night [2 and 3 June 1921, St. Louis]

20 pp., w/envelope

donor JH

[Mowrer, Hadley RICHARDSON]

ALS Hash

[7 June 1921] St. Louis

18 pp., w/envelope

donor JH

[Mowrer, Hadley RICHARDSON]

ALS Hashie/Hash

[3 June 1921, St. Louis]

25 pp., w/envelope

donor JH

[Mowrer, Hadley RICHARDSON]

ALS Hash

[8 June 1921,] St. Louis

12 pp., w/envelope

donor JH

[Mowrer, Hadley RICHARDSON]

ALS Hash

[4 June 1921, St. Louis]

5 pp., w/enclosures, 3 pp., and envelope

donor JH

[Mowrer, Hadley RICHARDSON]

ALS Hash

[9 June 1921,] St. Louis

8 pp., w/envelope

donor JH

[Mowrer, Hadley RICHARDSON]
ALS Hash

[10 June 1921] St. Louis
16 pp., w/envelope
donor JH

[Mowrer, Hadley RICHARDSON]
ALS Hash

[15 June 1921], St. Louis
2pp., w/envelope

[Mowrer, Hadley RICHARDSON]
ALS Hash

[11 June 1921] St. Louis
8 pp., w/envelope
donor JH

[Mowrer, Hadley RICHARDSON]
ALS Hash

[16 June 1921] St. Louis
4 pp., w/envelope
donor JH

[Mowrer, Hadley RICHARDSON]
ALS Hash

[11 June 1921], St. Louis
14pp., w/envelope

[Mowrer, Hadley RICHARDSON]
ALS Hash

[16 June 1921] St. Louis
15 pp., w/envelope
donor JH

[Mowrer], Hadley [RICHARDSON]
ALS

12 June [1921], St. Louis, to Grace Hall Hemingway
4 pp.
donor JH

[Mowrer, Hadley RICHARDSON]
ALS Hash

Friday afternoon – Early [17 June 1921, St. Louis]
4 pp., w/envelope
donor JH

[Mowrer, Hadley RICHARDSON]
ALS Hash

[12 June 1921] St. Louis
7 pp., w/envelope
donor JH

[Mowrer, Hadley RICHARDSON]
ALS Hash

Saturday morning [18 June 1921]
6 pp.
donor JH

[Mowrer, Hadley RICHARDSON]

ALS Hash

Sunday Apres midi [19 June 1921, St. Louis]

2pp., w/EH Typescript of "Lines to a Young Lady on Her Having Very Nearly Won a Vogel" and 1 page of EH notes and envelope

[Mowrer, Hadley RICHARDSON]

ALS Hash

Friday morning [24 June 1921, St. Louis]

6 pp., w/envelope

donor JH

[Mowrer, Hadley RICHARDSON]

ALS Hash

Monday noon [20 June 1921, St. Louis]

6 pp., w/envelope

donor JH

[Mowrer, Hadley RICHARDSON]

ALS Hash

Saturday afternoon [25 June 1921] St. Louis

4 pp., w/envelope

donor JH

[Mowrer, Hadley RICHARDSON]

ALS Hash

Tuesday morning [21 June 1921, St. Louis]

10 pp., w/typed list of EH stories bearing EH notations, 1 p., and envelope

donor JH

[Mowrer, Hadley RICHARDSON]

ALS Hash

Sunday – 11 A.M. [26 June 1921] St. Louis

18 pp., w/envelope

donor JH

[Mowrer, Hadley RICHARDSON]

ALS Hash

[22 June 1921, St. Louis]

6 pp., w/envelope

donor JH

[Mowrer, Hadley RICHARDSON]

ALS Hash

Monday 5:30 [27 June 1921, St. Louis]

15 pp., w/envelope

donor JH

[Mowrer, Hadley RICHARDSON]

ALS Hash

Thursday Morning [23 June 1921, St. Louis]

6pp., w/envelope

[Mowrer, Hadley RICHARDSON]

ALS Hash

Wednesday 4 PM [29 June 1921, St. Louis]

18 pp., w/envelope

donor JH

[Mowrer, Hadley RICHARDSON]

ALS Hash

        [30 June 1921, St. Louis]

        9 pp., w/envelope

        donor JH

[Mowrer, Hadley RICHARDSON]

ALS Hash

        Sunday morning [3 July 1921, St. Louis]

        7pp., w/envelope

        donor JH

[Mowrer, Hadley RICHARDSON]

ALS Hash

        Sunday 11:15 A.M. [late June 1921], St. Louis

        10pp.

[Mowrer, Hadley RICHARDSON]

ALS Hash

        4 July [1921, St. Louis]

        11 pp., w/envelope

        donor JH

[Mowrer, Hadley RICHARDSON]

ALS Hash/Hashti

        [July 1921], St. Louis

        15 pp.

        donor JH

[Mowrer, Hadley RICHARDSON]

ALS Hash

        Tuesday morning [5 July 1921, St. Louis]

        12 pp., w/envelope bearing note from Hadley

        donor JH

[Mowrer, Hadley RICHARDSON]

ALS Hash

        1 July [1921, St. Louis]

        6 pp., w/envelope

        donor JH

[Mowrer, Hadley RICHARDSON]

ALS Hash

        [6 July 1921, St. Louis]

        28 pp., w/envelope

        donor JH

[Mowrer, Hadley RICHARDSON]

ALS Hash

        Saturday afternoon [2 July 1921, St. Louis]

        4pp., w/envelope

        donor JH

[Mowrer, Hadley RICHARDSON]

ALS Hash

        Thursday apres-midi [7 July 1921, St. Louis]

        10 pp., w/envelope

        donor JH

[Mowrer, 'Hadley RICHARDSON]

Cable   7 July 1921, St. Louis

        1p. bearing EH cable draft on verso

[Mowrer, Hadley RICHARDSON]

ALS Hash

        Wednesday afternoon late [13 July 1921, St. Louis]

        12 pp., w/envelope

        donor JH

[Mowrer, Hadley RICHARDSON]

Cable   8 July 1921, St. Louis

        1p.

[Mowrer, Hadley RICHARDSON]

ALS Hash

        Thursday [14 July 1921, St. Louis]

        12 pp., w/envelope

        donor JH

[Mowrer], Hadley [RICHARDSON]

ALS

        12 July [1921], St. Louis, to Grace Hall Hemingway

        8 pp.

        donor JH

[Mowrer, Hadley RICHARDSON]

ALS Hash

        [15 July 1921, St. Louis]

        8 pp., w/envelope

        donor JH

[Mowrer, Hadley RICHARDSON]

ALS Hashish

        [12 July 1921,] St. Louis

        1 p., w/envelope

        donor JH

[Mowrer, Hadley RICHARDSON]

ALS Hash

        Saturday 6:15 [16 July 1921]

        13 pp.

        donor JH

[Mowrer, Hadley RICHARDSON]

ALS Hash

        [12 July 1921,] St. Louis

        10 pp., w/envelope

        donor JH

[Mowrer, Hadley RICHARDSON]

ALS Hash

        Sunday morning [17 July 1921,] St. Louis

        9 pp., w/envelope

        donor JH

[Mowrer, Hadley RICHARDSON]

ALS Hash

Monday morning [18 July 1921, St. Louis]

11 pp., w/envelope

donor JH

[Mowrer, Hadley RICHARDSON]

ALS Hash

[23 July 1921] St. Louis

11 pp., w/envelope

donor JH

[Mowrer, Hadley RICHARDSON]

ALS Hash/Hashs

Tuesday A.M. [19 July 1921] St. Louis

10 pp., w/envelope

donor JH

[Mowrer, Hadley RICHARDSON]

ALS Hash

Monday 3 P.M. [25 July 1921] St. Louis

13 pp., w/envelope

donor JH

[Mowrer, Hadley RICHARDSON]

ALS Hash/Hasho

[20 July 1921] St. Louis

7 pp., w/envelope

donor JH

[Mowrer, Hadley RICHARDSON]

ALS Hash

[26 July 1921] St. Louis

6 pp., w/envelope

donor JH

[Mowrer, Hadley RICHARDSON]

ALS Hash

Thursday, 7 P.M., [20 July 1921]

8pp.

[Mowrer, Hadley RICHARDSON]

ALS Hash

Wednesday night [27 July 1921] St. Louis

11 pp., w/envelope

donor JH

[Mowrer, Hadley RICHARDSON]

ALS Harsh

Friday 3 P.M. [21 July 1921, St. Louis]

4pp., w/envelope

[Mowrer, Hadley RICHARDSON]

ALS Hooie

[7 Aug 1921, State Line, Wisconsin]

12pp., w/envelope

[Mowrer, Hadley RICHARDSON]

ALS Hash/Hooie/H

Saturday noon [7 August 1921, State
Line, Wis.]

8 pp., w/envelope

donor JH

[Mowrer, Hadley RICHARDSON]

ALS Hooie

[11 Aug 1921, State Line,
Wisconsin]

3pp., w/envelope

[Mowrer, Hadley RICHARDSON]

ALS Hooie

[8 August 1921], Vilas Cy., Wisconsin

8 pp., w/envelope

donor JH

[Mowrer, Hadley RICHARDSON]

ALS Hooie

Saturday afternoon [13 August 1921,
State Line, Wis]

6 pp., w/envelope

donor JH

[Mowrer, Hadley RICHARDSON]

ALS Hooie

Tuesday morning [9 Aug 1921, State
Line]

7 pp., w/envelope

donor JH

[Mowrer, Hadley RICHARDSON]

ALS Hooie

Sunday early afternoon [14 August
1921, State Line, Wis.]

25 pp.

donor JH

[Mowrer, Hadley RICHARDSON]

ALS Hooie

Wednesday morning [10 August 1921,
Vilas City, Wis.]

16 pp., w/envelope

donor JH

[Mowrer, Hadley RICHARDSON]

ALS Hooie

Wednesday afternoon [17 August 1921,
State Line, Wis.]

16 pp., w/envelope

donor JH

[Mowrer, Hadley RICHARDSON]

ALS Hooie

Thursday night [11 Aug 1921]

11 pp.

donor JH

[Mowrer, Hadley RICHARDSON]

AL

[18 August 1921], State Line, Wis.

2 pp., w/wedding invitation and
envelope

donor JH

[Mowrer, Hadley RICHARDSON]

ALS Hooie

      Thursday morgen [18 August 1921, State Line, Wis.]

      11 pp., w/envelope

      donor JH

[Mowrer, Hadley RICHARDSON]

ALS Hooie

      [23 Aug 1921], State Line

      4pp., w/envelope

[Mowrer, Hadley RICHARDSON]

ALS Hooie

      Friday morning [19 August 1921, State Line, Wis.]

      12 pp., w/envelope

      donor JH

[Mowrer], Hadley [RICHARDSON]

ALS

      29 August 1921, State Line, Wis., to Grace Hall Hemingway

      2 pp.

      donor JH

[Mowrer, Hadley RICHARDSON]

ALS Hooie

      Saturday morning [21 August 1921, State Line, Wis.]

      16 pp., w/envelope

      donor JH

[Mowrer], Hadley [Richardson HEMINGWAY]

ALS

      22 Sept [1921], Walloon Lake, Michigan, to Grace Hall Hemingway

      6 pp., w/envelope

      donor JH

[Mowrer, Hadley RICHARDSON]

ALS Hooie

      Early afternoon, 21 Aug 1921, State Line, Wis.

      6 pp., w/envelope

      donor JH

[Mowrer, Hadley RICHARDSON]

ALS Hash

      Thursday Morning [1921]

      6pp.

[Mowrer, Hadley RICHARDSON]

ALS Hooie/Hooie

      Bent's - Tuesday morning [23 Aug 1921], State Line, Wis. bearing EH note

      19 pp., w/envelope bearing EH notations

      donor JH

[Mowrer, Hadley RICHARDSON]

ALS Hash

      [1921]

      10pp.

[Mowrer, Hadley Richardson HEMINGWAY]

Envelope only postmarked 2 Feb 1922, Paris, to Grace Hall Hemingway

donor JH

[Mowrer], Hadley [Richardson HEMINGWAY]

ALS

Chalet Chamby, Chamby-sur-Montreus, [Jan 1923], Suisse, to Grace Hall Hemingway

2 pp.

donor JH

[Mowrer], Hadley [Richardson HEMINGWAY]

ALS

20 February 1922, Paris, to Grace Hall Hemingway

6 pp., w/envelope

donor JH

[Mowrer], Hadley [Richardson HEMINGWAY]

ALS

Thursday, 27 Sept [1923], Toronto, to Dr. and Mrs. Clarence E. Hemingway

4 pp., w/envelope

donor JH

[Mowrer], Hadley [Richardson HEMINGWAY]

ALS

5 Oct [1922, Paris], to Dr. and Mrs. Clarence E. Hemingway

5 pp., w/envelope

donor JH

[Mowrer], Hadley [Richardson HEMINGWAY]

ALS

Thursday, 18 October [1923], Wellesley Hospital, [Toronto], to Dr. and Mrs. Clarence E. Hemingway

6 pp., w/envelope

donor JH

[Mowrer], Hadley HEMINGWAY

ALS   16 Nov [1922], Paris, to Mr. Ganguisch

1p.

[Mowrer], Hadley [Richardson HEMINGWAY]

ALS

Saturday [8 Dec 1923, Totonto], to Dr. and Mrs. Clarence E. Hemingway

6 pp., w/envelope

donor JH

[Mowrer], Hadley [Richardson HEMINGWAY]

ALS

11 Dec [1922], Lausanne, Switzerland, to Dr. and Mrs. Clarence E. Hemingway

3 pp.

donor JH

[Mowrer], Hadley [Richardson HEMINGWAY]

ALS

2 Jan 1924, [Toronto], to Dr. and Mrs. Clarence E. Hemingway

9 pp., w/envelope

donor JH

[Mowrer], Hadley [Richardson HEMINGWAY]

ALS

20 Feb 1924, Paris, to Dr. and Mrs. Clarence E. Hemingway

2 pp., w/envelope

donor JH

[Mowrer], Hadley [Richardson HEMINGWAY]

ALS

[1927], St. Louis, to Grace Hall Hemingway

2 pp.

donor JH

[Mowrer], Hadley R[ichardson] HEMINGWAY

TCcc   11 May 1924, Paris, to George J. Breaker

1p. bearing EH note

[Mowrer, Hadley HEMINGWAY]

AL   21 May 1927, St. Louis

3pp.

[Mowrer], Hadley [Richardson HEMINGWAY]

TC   20 May [1924, Paris], to George Breaker

1p.

[Mowrer], Hadley [HEMINGWAY]

ALS Hadley or Katherine

13 Aug 1927, [Carmel, California]

3pp., w/newspaper clippings

[Mowrer], Hadley HEMINGWAY

ANS   [September 1926]

1p.

[Mowrer, Hadley HEMINGWAY]

ALS Your original F. Puss

[17 Sept 1927], Carmel

3pp., w/envelope

[Mowrer], Hadley [HEMINGWAY]

New Year's Greeting

[28 Dec 1926, Paris]

W/envelope

[Mowrer, Hadley HEMINGWAY]

ALS Katherine Kat

[17 Nov 1927, Paris]

1p.

[Mowrer, Hadley HEMINGWAY]

Cable   [21 Nov 1927], Paris

              1p.

[Mowrer, Hadley HEMINGWAY]

ALS Katherine/Bumbie

              10 July [1928, Paris]

              4pp., w/enclosure and
              photograph and envelope

[Mowrer], Hadley [HEMINGWAY]

ALS Hadley Katherine/Humsdaddles

              26 Mar [1928], Paris

              8pp., w/envelope

[Mowrer, Hadley HEMINGWAY]

ALS Hadcat on three post cards

              [28 July 1928, Veyrier du Lac]

              W/envelope

[Mowrer, Hadley HEMINGWAY]

AL   [17 Apr 1928, Paris]

              2pp., w/envelope

[Mowrer, Hadley HEMINGWAY]

ALS A mountain and lake cat

              4 Aug [1928], Veyrier du Lac

              2pp., w/envelope

[Mowrer, Hadley HEMINGWAY]

ALS Kat

              14 May 1928, Paris

              5pp.

[Mowrer, Hadley HEMINGWAY]

Cable from Bumbichad

              [10 Aug1928]

              1p.

[Mowrer, Hadley HEMINGWAY]

A Post Cards S Cat

              12 June [1928, Paris]

              4pp.

[Mowrer, Hadley HEMINGWAY]

ALS Hadkat/Bumbie on three post cards

              10 Aug [1928, Veyrier du Lac]

              W/envelope

[Mowrer, Hadley HEMINGWAY]

A Post Card S Kat & Small Pup

        23 Aug [1928, Veyrier du Lac]

[Mowrer, Hadley HEMINGWAY]

ALS H.H.

        [5 Oct 1929], Crecy-en-Brie

        2pp., w/envelope

[Mowrer, Hadley HEMINGWAY]

A Post Card S Bumbie Hemingway

        6 Sept 1928, [Veyrier du Lac]

[Mowrer, Hadley HEMINGWAY]

ALS Haddlekat

        Monday evening [7 Oct 1929, Paris]

        3pp., w/envelope

[Mowrer, Hadley HEMINGWAY]

ALS Kat

        22 Nov 1928, Paris

        4pp., w/envelope bearing EH note

[Mowrer], Hadley HEMINGWAY

ALS   Tuesday evening [8 or 15 Oct 1929, Paris]

        1p., w/TLS Maxwell Aley, 6 Oct 1929

[Mowrer, Hadley HEMINGWAY]

ALS Mamma or Catherine Cat the grateful

        16 Dec [1928], on board the Cunard R.M.S. Berengaria

        8pp., w/envelope postmarked 21 Dec 1928, Cherbourg

[Mowrer] Hadley [HEMINGWAY]

ANS   Friday afternoon, [8 Nov 1929, Paris], to Pauline

        1p.

[Mowrer, Hadley HEMINGWAY]

ALS A Cat.

        [1929]; Geneva

        2pp.

[Mowrer], Hadley [HEMINGWAY]

ANS   [16 Dec 1929, Paris]

        1p. bearing EH notes

[Mowrer, Hadley HEMINGWAY]
ALS Hadlein

4 Jan [1930, Paris]

2pp., w/envelope

[Mowrer, Hadley HEMINGWAY]
ALS Catherine Cat

[15 June 1931], Crecy-en-Brie

4pp., w/envelope

[Mowrer, Hadley HEMINGWAY]
ALS Katherine Cat

26 Jan [1930], Paris

6pp., w/envelope

[Mowrer], Hadley [HEMINGWAY]
Cable   [29 June 1931], Paris

1p.

[Mowrer, Hadley HEMINGWAY]
ALS "H"

11 Feb [1930, Paris]

2pp., w/envelope

[Mowrer], Hadley [HEMINGWAY]
ALS   5 Aug [1931], Paris, to Pauline

4pp., w/envelope

[Mowrer, Hadely Hemingway]
ALS H. Cat

March 10th or so [1930], Paris

6pp.

[Mowrer, Hadley HEMINGWAY]
ALS Cat

16 Dec [1931, Paris], to EH/
Pauline

4pp., w/check made out to EH,
and report cards for John
Hemingway

[Mowrer, Hadley HEMINGWAY]
ALS Kat

[Apr 1931], Paris

6pp., w/envelope

[Mowrer, Hadley HEMINGWAY]
ALS Hadlein Kat

22 Jan [1932, Paris]

4pp., w/copy of letter to IRS,
21 Jan 1932 and envelope

[MOWRER], Hadley

Cable   [21 Aug 1933], Paris

                    1p.

MOWRER, [Hadley]

ALS Katherine Kat

                    [2 May 1935], Chicago

                    4pp., w/envelope

[MOWRER, Hadley]

AN   [25 Aug 1933, Paris]

          2pp. on verso of ALS Joan Miro,
          2 Aug 1933, Montroig, to Hadley,
          w/TLS Edgar [Mowrer], to Hadley
          3 July [1933], Berlin, and
          envelope

MOWRER, [Hadley]

ALS Katherine Kat

                    9 May [1935], Chicago

                    4pp., w/envelope

[MOWRER, Hadley]

ALS Katherine Kat

                    11 Apr 1934, Chicago, to EH/
                    Pauline

                    6pp.

[MOWRER, Hadley]

ALS Haddles or Katherine

                    4 July [1935], Holm Lodge,
                    Wyoming

                    1p., w/ALS Billy Sidley to Jack,
                    3 June 1935, and ALS Thelma
                    Sidley, 12 June 1935, to Hadley,
                    and envelope

[MOWRER, Hadley]

Envelope only postmarked 23 Sept 1934, Chicago

[MOWRER, Hadley]

ALS Le Chat

                    5 Dec [1935], Chicago

                    4pp., w/envelope

[MOWRER, Hadley]

Cable   31 Jan 1935, Miami Beach

                    1p.

[MOWRER, Hadley]

ALS Katherine Kat

                    19 Jan [1937, Chicago]

                    8pp., w/envelope

[MOWRER, Hadley]
ALS Katherine Kat
          21 Nov [1938], Lake Bluff, Ill.
          2pp., w/envelope bearing EH note

MOWRER, Hadley
Cable   29 Dec [1942], Lake Bluff
          1p.

[MOWRER, Hadley]
ALS Katherine Kountry Kat
          6 Dec [1938], Lake Bluff
          2pp., w/envelope

[MOWRER, Hadley]
ALS Katherine
          15 Dec 1943, Lake Bluff
          4pp., w/envelope

MOWRER, [Hadley]
ALS Katherine Ever the Kat
          [21 Sept 1942], Lake Bluff
          3pp.

[MOWRER, Hadley]
ALS Katherine Kat
          14 Jan 1944, Lake Bluff
          2pp.

MOWRER, Hadley
Cable   9 Nov [1942], Lake Forest, Ill.
          1p.

[MOWRER, Hadley]
ALS Katherine Kat
          30 July [1946], Paris
          4pp., w/envelope

MOWRER, [Hadley]
ALS Katherine Puss Cat
          11 Nov [1942], Lake Bluff
          7pp.

MOWRER, [Hadley]
ALS The Cat or Feather Puss
          20 May [1961], Chocorua, NH
          1p., w/newspaper clipping, sel-
          addressed post card and envelope

[Mowrer, Hadley Richardson Hemingway]

ALS Feathercat

        undated

        2pp.

MOWRER, Hadley [Hemingway]

ALS   5 May n.y., Chicago, to Pauline

        4pp.

[Morwer], Hadley [HEMINGWAY]

ALS   14 Dec [1929-1933], to EH/
        Pauline

        2pp., w/ALS Paul and ALS Bumby,
        and photos

[Mowrer], Hadley [RICHARDSON]

ALS Child Hadley

        undated, to Mamma

        3pp.

[Mowrer, Hadley HEMINGWAY]

ALS Hadley Kat

        [pre 1932]

        9pp.

[Mowrer, Hadley] HEMINGWAY

A Letter Draft S

        undated, to Mademoiselle Sylvine

        2pp.

[Mowrer, Hadley Richardson Hemingway]

ALS Kat

        undated, Chicago, to EH/Pauline

        1p. bearing Pauline's notes

[Mowrer, Hadley HEMINGWAY]

Typescript titled "Axioms forumlated on a
wedding anniversary"

        2pp.

[Mowrer, Hadley Hemingway]

ALS Kat, Katherine beginning "Hail Pamplonists"

        undated

        2pp., w/envelope

[Mowrer, Hadley RICHARDSON Hemingway]

TLS A.B. Sturgis

        7 June 1921, St. Louis, to Hadley
        Richardson

        3 pp.

        donor JH

[Mowrer, Hadley HEMINGWAY]

ALS [?]

[20 Nov 1922, Paris], to Mme. Hemingway

1p., w/address-leaf

[Mowrer, Hadley HEMINGWAY]

TLS Manuel [Komroff]

16 Sept 1926, Meaux, to Hadley

1p.

[Mowrer, Hadley HEMINGWAY]

A Post Card S Caroline [?]

[30 June 1924, Cherbourg], to Hadley/Ernest

[Mowrer, Hadley HEMINGWAY]

A Post Card S Howard

31 May [1928, Granada], to Hadley

[Mowrer, Hadley HEMINGWAY]

ALS Ninette [Walter]

15 July 1925, [Paris], to Hadley

2pp., w/envelope

[MOWRER, Hadley]

A Post Card S [?]

Sun. [1939, Sun Valley], to Mrs. Paul Mowrer

[Mowrer, Hadley HEMINGWAY]

ALS Ninette [Walter]

5 Sept 1925, Seninsgrove, Pa., to Hadley

4pp., w/envelope

[MOWRER, Hadley]

A Post Card S [?]

9 Jan 1939, Sun Valley, to Hadley

[Mowrer, Hadley HEMINGWAY]

ALS Ninette Walter

6 Dec 1925, [Paris], to Hadley

2pp., w/envelope

[MOWRER, Hadley]

A Post Card S Elizabeth

2 Sept 1942, Walhalla, Michigan, to Mrs. Paul Scott Mowrer

Mowrer, Hadley Richardson Hemingway
See also EH 15 Dec 1925
June 1926
22 July 1926
Perkins, Maxwell E.
11 June 1932
Hemingway, Pauline
4 Dec 1926
to Hadley
Murphy, Gerald
Manuscripts -- Not EH

Mowrer, Paul Scott

TLS   4 Dec 1929, Paris

1p.

[Mowrer], Paul [Scott] (newscorrespondent,
Hadley's second husband)

ALS   [23 June 1926, Paris], to Hem
and company

2pp., w/envelope bearing EH note

[Mowrer], Paul [Scott]

TLS   27 June 1931, Paris

1p.

[Mowrer], Paul [Scott]

ALS   [4 Oct 1926, Paris]

2pp., w/envelope

[Mowrer], Paul [Scott]

Cable   [22 Mar 1934], Chicago

1p.

[Mowrer], Paul [Scott]

A Post Card S

Sunday [9 Jan 1927, Paris]

[Mowrer, Paul Scott]

T Post Card S Tom Danemann

26 Apr n.y., Florence, to Mr.
Mowrer

Mowrer, Paul Scott

A Post Card S

11 Sept 1927

Mowrer, Paul
See also Mowrer, Hadley R. H.
14 Dec 1929-1933

[Mowrer], Winifred (Paul Scott Mowrer's
                    first wife)

ALS   undated, Pamplona

           2pp.

[Murphy, Gerald] (friend, artist)

A Post Card

                [19 Nov 1925, Cannes]

Munroe, [Robert] (fishing friend)

TLS Bob Munroe

           3 Feb 1938, Coral Gables

           3pp.

[Murphy], Gerald

ALS   3 Mar [1926], Cap d'Antibes, to
           Hadley

           2pp., w/envelope

Munroe, [Robert]

TLS Bob Munroe

           1 June 1939, Coral Gables

           2pp.

[Murphy], Gerald

ALS   22 May 1926, Cap d'Antibes

           2pp., w/envelope

Munroe, [Robert]

TLS Bob Munroe

           27 June 1938, Coral Gables

           1p.

[Murphy, Gerald]

A Post Card S "G"

                15 June [1926, Cannes]

[Murphy], Baoth (son of Gerald and Sara)

ALS   [22 Oct 1929, Antibes]

           1p., w/envelope

[Murphy, Gerald]

ALS dow dow and ALS Agna calliente Sol [Sara
Murphy]

           Tuesday [14 July 1926], Cap
           d'Antibes

           5pp., w/envelope

[Murphy], Gerald

ALS   Saturday [6 Sept 1926], Cap
               d'Antibes

               5pp., w/enclosure and envelope

[Murphy], Gerald

TLS   22 May 1927, Cap d'Antibes

               1p., w/envelope

[Murphy, Gerald]

A Post Card S "G.S."

               [Nov 1926, N.Y.]

[Murphy, Gerald]

TL   18 June 1927, Cap d'Antibes

               2pp., w/envelope bearing EH note

[Murphy], Gerald

Xmas Greeting S Sar and Gerald

               [6 Dec 1926, N.Y.]

               W/envelope

M[urphy], Gerald

A Post Card S

               24 Sept 1927, [Baden-Baden]

               1p., w/newspaper clipping

[Murphy, Gerald]

A Post Card S "G.M."

               13 Feb 1927

[Murphy, Gerald]

TLS daou-daou (French spelling)

               16 Oct 1927, Cap d'Antibes

               1p.

[Murphy], Gerald

A Post Card S

               19 Mar [1927], en route
               [Nurenburg]

               2pp.

[Murphy], Gerald

T Post Card S

               5 Jan 1928, [Paris]

[Murphy], Gerald

ALS 12 Oct 1929, [Paris], to EH/
Pauline

  2pp., w/photograph and envelope

[Murphy], Gerald

Cable from Sara Gerald

  21 Mar 1935, N.Y.

  1p.

[Murphy], Gerald

Cable from Sara Gerald

  [Sept 1932], N.Y.

  1p.

[Murphy, Gerald]

A Post Card S "G"

  8 Jan 1937, [Saranac Lake, N.Y.]

[Murphy, Gerald]

A Post Card S G. and Sara

  4 July 1934, [Antibes], to EH/
Pauline

Murphy, Gerald

TLS 22 Jan 1937, [Saranac Lake], to
Pauline

  2pp., w/envelope

[Murphy, Gerald]

A Post Card S G., Sara, and others

  7 Aug [1934, Antibes]

[Murphy, Gerald]

ANS Dowdow & Sara

  undated, East Hampton, L.I., N.Y.,
to Mr. and Mrs. Hemingway

  1p.

Murphy, [Gerald]

Cable from Murphys

  21 Nov 1934, N.Y.

  1p.

[Murphy], Gerald

A Post Card S "G" and Sara

  21 June n.y., to EH/Pauline

[Murphy], Gerald

ALS   10 a.m. undated

               2pp.

Murphy, Honoria (daughter ofSara and Gerald)

ANS   [1926, Antibes]

               2pp., w/enclosure and envelope

[Murphy], Gerald

ALS   undated, 23, Quai des Grands
               Augustins, [Paris]

               2pp.

[Murphy], Sara

ANS   [Oct 1927]

               1p., originally w/galleys of
               Men Without Women, 1p.

[Murphy], Gerald

ANS on advertisement for Hartmann Trunks

               undated

               1p.

[Murphy], Sara

ALS   Sat eve [12 Oct 1929, Paris], to
               Pauline

               3pp.

[Murphy], Gerald

ANS and ANS Sara

               undated [1926, Paris]

               2pp., w/envelope

[Murphy], Sara (wife of Gerald, friend)

ALS   18 Sept [1934], East Hampton, L.I.,
               to EH/Pauline

               3pp.

Murphy, Gerald and Sara
          See also Hemingway, Pauline
                    12 July 1926
                    to others
               Quintanilla
                    2 May 1938

[Murphy], Sara

A Post Card S Sara, Dos, Katy

          [pre 1935]

Murphy, Sara

ALS   11 Sept [1935], Saranac Lake, to
            EH/Pauline

            7pp.

[Murphy], Sara

ALS   [May 1936], Havana

            2pp.

Murphy, Sara

ALS   18 Sept [1935], Saranac Lake

            5pp., w/envelope

[Murphy], Sara

ALS   Monday noon [May 1936], Havana, to
            Pauline

            2pp.

Murphy, Sara

ALS   18 Sept [1935], Saranac Lake, to
            Pauline

            5pp., w/envelope

[Murphy], Sara

TL   20 May [1936], Saranac Lake

            5pp., w/envelope

Murphy, [Sara]

ALS Biguine

            Oct 18 (Patrick's Birthday) [1935-
1936], Saranac Lake, to Pauline

            3pp., w/EH notes on verso

[Murphy], Sara

ALS   29 July [1936], Paul Smith's, N.Y.,
            to EH/Pauline

            5pp., w/envelope

[Murphy], Sara

Cable   29 Apr 1936, Saranac Lake

            1p.

[Murphy, Sara]

ALS Alice Lee Meyer [?]

            Saturday [6 Feb 1937], Saranac
Lake

            4pp., w/envelope

[Murphy], Sara

TL   22 June [1937], R.M.S. Aquitania,
            to Pauline

            2pp., w/envelope

Museum of Modern Art
            See Barr, Alfred H.

[Murphy, Sara]

Receipt S, w/typed list of items

            20 Sept 1937, Paris

            2pp.

Musgrave, Eric (newspaperman)

ALS   5 Mar 1934, London

            2pp.

Murphy, Sara

ALS   Monday [29 July 1940], East
            Hampton, L.I.

            3pp., w/envelope

[Musselman, Morris M.]   (friend)

T Post Card

            [19 July 1917, Oak Park]

[Murphy], Sara

ALS   24 May 1961, [Palisades, N.Y.]

            2pp., w/envelope

[Musselman, Morris M.]

ALS Mussey and ALS Jack [Pentacost]

            [3 Aug 1917, Chicago]

            3pp., w/envelope

[Murry, Michael E. (student)

TLS   29 Apr 1959, St. Louis Park,
            Minnesota

            4pp.

Musselman, Morris M.

TLS   20 Aug 1917, [Oak Park]

            1p., w/envelope

[Musselman, Morris M.]
TLS Mussey

[1918], Oak Park
2pp.

[Musselman, Morris M.]
TLS Mussey

10 Nov 1920, Chicago
1p.

[Musselman, Morris M.]
A Post Card S Mussey

[25 July 1918, Chicago]

Musselman, Morris M.
TLS Mussey

2 June 1926, Chicago
2pp., w/envelope bearing EH note

[Musselman, Morris M.]
TLS Mussey

[1919], Champaign
2pp.

Musselman, Morris M.
TLS Mussey

18 June 1926, Chicago
1p., w/envelope bearing EH note

[Musselman, Morris M.]
TLS Mussey

30 Jan 1919, Champaign
1p., w/envelope

Musselman, Morris M.
TLS Mussey

10 Aug 1926, Chicago
2pp., w/envelope

[Musselman, Morris M.]
TLS Mussey

24 Apr 1920, Champaign
1p., w/envelope

Musselman, Morris M.
TLS Mussey

8 Nov 1926, Chicago
2pp., w/envelope

[Musselman, Morris M.]
ANS Mussey

[27 Nov 1926]

1p., w/newspaper clippings

[Musselman, Morris M.]
TLS Mussey

22 Dec 1929, Cuyahoga Falls, Ohio

1p.

Musselman, [Morris M.]
A Post Card S Mussey

[7 Jan 1927, Chicago]

[Musselman, Morris M.]
TLS Mussey

[1932], N.Y.

2pp.

[Musselman, Morris M.]
Envelope only postmarked 2 Feb 1927, Chicago

Musselman, [Morris M.]
TLS Mussey

29 Oct 1932, N.Y.

2pp., w/newspaper clipping

[Musselman, Morris M.]
TLS Mussey

4 Mar 1929, Akron, Ohio

1p., w/newspaper clipping and
envelope

[Musselman, Morris M.]
TLS Mussey

[13 May 1934, N.Y.]

1p., w/envelope

Musselman, [Morris M.]
TLS Mussey

1 Oct 1929, Lexington, Kentucky

1p.

Musselman, [Morris M.]
TLS Mussey

20 Feb 1935, N.Y.

1p.

Musselman, [Morris M.]

TLS Mussey

       undated, N.Y.

       1p.

Nathan, J. F.
      See Hogarth, G.

Musselman, Morris McNeil
      See also Manuscripts -- Not EH

Nathan, George Jean
      see The American Mercury

[Nahas, Alexander]

Envelope only bearing EH notes

National 4th Division Association

TLS Iz Goldstein

      17 Nov 1954, Brooklyn, to unknown

      1p., w/newspaper clipping

NANA (North American News Alliance)
      See Wheeler, John
         Zilmer, Bertram G.
         Sargint, H. J. J.

National Institute of Arts and Letters
      See Train, Arthur
         Wescott, Glenway

Nash's--Paul Mall

TLS Ian D. Coster

      13 May 1932, London

      1p. bearing EH note

N.C.W.C. News Service

TLS Frank A. Hall

      4 Oct 1933, Washington, D.C.

      1p.

Neagoé, Peter
      See Fangel, Guy   10 June 1931

Nelson, Paul
ALS   Tuesday, undated [Paris]
           1p.

Neary, Frank
      See Pflaum

Nerber, John (friend)
TLS   23 Nov 1937, Olivet
           2pp.

Negrin, Juan
Cable   [25 Jan 1954, London]
           1p.

New American Library
           See Scribner, Charles, Jr.
                 19 Oct 1960

Nels, P[aul] (Hotel Taube, Schruns)
ALS   23 Apr 1932, Schruns
           2pp., w/envelope

The New Colophon
           See Scribner, Charles, Sr.
                 9 June 1949

[Nelson], Paul (friend)
ALS   30 Dec [1929]
           3pp.

New Directions
           See Laughlin, James

New Masses

TLS J. Rorty

13 May 1926, N.Y.

1p.

New Masses

TLS James Rorty

8 Sept 1926, N.Y.

1p., w/envelope

New Masses

TLS Michael Gold and Bernard Smith

6 Sept n.y., New York

1p.

New Masses
See also Michelson, Herman
North, Joseph

The New Republic

TL   20 May 1927, N.Y.

1p.

The New Republic
See also Bliven, Bruce
Cowley, Malcolm
MacLeish, Archibald
7 June 1933
Wilson, Edmund

The New Review

TLS Samuel Putnam

22 May 1932, Fontenay-aux-Roses

2pp.

Newsweek

Cable   28 Aug 1950, N.Y.

1p.

The New Yorker

TLS K. S. Angell

14 Feb 1927, N.Y.

1p., w/envelope

The New Yorker

TLS Malcolm Johnson

15 July 1931, Garden City, N.Y.

1p. bearing EH note on verso

The <u>New Yorker</u>

TLS "B"

12 Mar 1932, N.Y.

1p.

The <u>New York Times</u>

Cable from Raymond Walters

[15 July 1959], N.Y.

1p. bearing EH cable drafts

The <u>New Yorker</u>

See Ross

<u>New York Times</u>

See also Pfeiffer, Gustavus A.
7 June 1935
Wheeler, John
20 July 1938
Robinson, Layhmond
Sulzberger, C. L.

The <u>New York Herald Tribune</u>

TLS Renee Brasier

4 Nov 1938, Paris

1p. bearing EH notes

<u>New York Times Book Review</u>
See Breit, Harvey

The <u>New York Herald Tribune</u>

TLS Irita Van Doren

17 June 1952, N.Y.

1p.

<u>New York World Telegram and Sun</u>
See Taylor, Alexander

New York Public Library
See Samuels, Lee

Nielsen, Svend Aage (journalist, shipmate)

TL Fragment

14 July 1938, Copenhagen

1p. only

Nizen, Paul
        See Durtain, Luc

Nobel Foundation
Memorandum
        undated, Stockholm
        1p.

Nobby, Frank (Clark Illustrated)
Cable   [25 Jan 1954, London]
        1p.

Non-Sectarian Anti-Nazi League
Cable from Samuel Untermeyer
        5 Dec 1936, N.Y.
        1p.

Nobel Foundation
TLS Anders Osterling
        12 Nov 1954, Stockholm
        1p.

Nordquist, Lawrence (L-T Ranch)
TLS Lawrence and Olive
        11 Dec 1931, Painter, Wyoming
        2pp., w/photograph

Nobel Foundation
TLS Nils K. Stahle
        .   20 Nov 1954, Stockholm
        1p.

Nordquist, Lawrence
TLS   8 Mar 1932, Painter
        1p.

Nobel Foundation
ALS Nils K. Stahle
        6 Dec 1954, Stockholm
        1p.

[Nordquist], Lawrence
ALS Lawrence and Olive
        17 Apr 1932, Billings
        3pp. bearing EH notes

Nordquist, Lawrence

TLS   10 Apr 1935, Painter

      1p., w/enclosure

North, Joseph   (<u>The New Masses</u>)

TLS   5 Sept 1935, N.Y.

      1p.

Nordquist, Lawrence

Advertising Material S

      28 Apr 1936, Painter

      2pp.

North, Joseph

Cable   7 Sept 1935, N.Y.

      1p.

Nordquist, Olive
      See Hemingway, Pauline
          to others

North, Joseph

Cable   9 Sept 1935, N.Y.

      1p.

North American Committee to Aid Spanish
Democracy
      See also Medical Bureau to Aid
          Spanish Democracy

North, Joseph

TLS   10 Sept 1935, N.Y.

      1p.

[North, Henry W. R.   (Ringling Bros. & Barnum
               & Bailey)

TLS Buddy

      23 Apr 1950

      1p.

[North,Joseph]

Cable   14 Sept 1935, N.Y.

      5pp.

North, [Joseph]
Cable   17 Dec 1935, N.Y.
            1p.

North, [Joseph]
Cable   12 Jan 1937, N.Y.
            1p.

North, Joseph
Cable   10 Feb 1936, N.Y.
            1p.

North, [Joseph]
Cable   1 Dec 1938, N.Y.
            1p.

North, Joseph
Cable   17 Mar 1936, N.Y.
            1p.

North, [Joseph]
Cable   13 Dec 1938, N.Y.
            1p.

North, [Joseph]
TLS Joe North
            3 Sept 1936, N.Y.
            1p.

North, [Joseph]
TLS Joe
            16 Dec [1938], N.Y.
            1p.

[North, Joseph]
Cable   12 Jan 1937, N.Y.
            1p.

[North, Joseph]
Cable   8 Feb 1938, N.Y.
            1p.

[North, Joseph]

TLS Joe

2 Feb 1939, N.Y.

2pp.

North, Sterling

TLS   24 Oct 1942 [1952], Morristown

1p., w/envelope bearing EH note

North, Sterling (editor, author)

TLS   23 Nov 1939, Chicago

1p. bearing EH note

North American Committee to Aid Spanish Democracy

Cable from Varian Fay

28 May 1937, N.Y.

1p.

North, Sterling

Cable   1 Oct 1952, Morristown, N.J.

1p.

North American Committee to Aid Spanish Democracy

Cable from Herman F. Reissig

27 June 1937, N.Y.

1p.

North, [Sterling]

Cable   22 Oct 1952, Morristown

1p.

North American Committee to Aid Spanish Democracy

Cable from Sheelagh Kennedy

31 Jan 1938

1p.

North, Sterling

Cable   24 Oct 1952, Morristown

1p.

North American Committee to Aid Spanish Democracy

TLS Robert Cornwall

24 Dec 1938, Jacksonville

1p.

Oak Park: First Congregational Church
            See Barton, William E.
            Hemingway, Anson T.
                18 Mar 1920
            Hemingway, Clarence E.
                13 Oct 1918
                3 Nov 1918
                28 Mar 1920
            Hunter, Marie C.

O'Brien, Edward [G.]
ALS   19 Mar 1927, London
            1p., w/envelope

Ober, Harold (literary agent)
Cable   17 Dec 1938, N.Y.
            1p.

[O'Brien], Edward [G.]
ALS   20 Dec 1936, Oxford
            2pp.

Ober, Harold
            See Fitzgerald, F. Scott
                12 Aug 1926
                Oct 1929

O'Brien, Edward G.
ALS   13 Jan 1937, N.Y.
            2pp.

O'Brien, Edward G. (poet, editor The Best
                        Short Stories)
TLS   3 Sept 1926, London
            1p.

O'Brien, Edward [G.]
ALS   8 Aug 1937, Oxford
            2pp.

O'Brien, [Edward G.]
ALS   [8 Oct 1923, Oxford]
            2pp., w/envelope

O'Brien, Edward [G.]
ALS   22 Apr 1927, London
            2pp.

The Observer
TLS Terence Kilmartin

       2 Sept 1952, London

       1p., w/enclosure

O'Hara, John
ALS   undated, N.Y.

       2pp.

Odlin, Reno
     See Pound, Ezra 20 Jan 1958

O'Hara, John
     See also Reynolds, Quentin
      6 Nov 1935

O'Hara, John (author)
TLS   [May 1935], East Sandwich, Ma.

     1p.

[Ohlsen, Ray]
ALS Cohen

      undated, Chicago

      7pp.

O'Hara, J[ohn]
A Post Card S

     14 Jan [1938], Key West

     1p.

Olgin, M. J. (Pravda)
Cable   23 July 1938, Denver

      1p. bearing EH draft reply on verso

O'Hara, [John]
Cable   11 Jan 1961, Princeton

     1p.

Olgin, M. J.
Cable   25 July 1938, Denver

     1p.

Olgin, M. J.
Cable   24 Oct 1938, N.Y.
        1p.

Ordonez, Antonio (friend, bullfighter)
Cable from Carmen and Antonio Ordonez
        [late Jan 1954], Bogota, Colombia
        1p. bearing EH draft reply

Olgin, M. J.
Cable   27 Feb 1939, N.Y.
        1p.

[Ordonez], Antonio
ALS   [Feb 1959], Bogota
        1p., w/envelope bearing EH notes

Olgin, M. J.
Cable   22 July 1939, N.Y.
        1p.

[Ordonez], Carmen and Antonio
Cable   [9 June 1959], Malaga
        1p.

Oliver & Boyd, Ltd.
        See Scribner, Charles, Jr. 6 Jan 1961

[Ordonez, Antonio]
Cable   [1 Aug 1959], Malaga
        1p.

[Opher], Ivan
ALS   10 Nov 1933, [London]
        3pp.

[Ordonez], Antonio
Cable   [11 Aug 1959], Malaga
        1p.

Ordonez, Antonio

Cable   [27 Aug 1959], Malaga

    1p.

[Ordonez], Antonio

Cable   26 Mar 1960, Jerez de la Frontera

    1p.

[Ordonez], Antonio

Cable   [12 Oct 1959], Lima

    1p.

[Ordonez], Antonio

Cable   26 Mar 1960, Jerez de la Frontera

    1p.

[Ordonez], Antonio

Cable   3 Nov 1959, Madrid

    1p.

Ordonez, Antonio

Cable   [23 Aug 1960], Madrid

    1p.

[Ordonez], Antonio

Cable   28 Jan 1960, Manizales, Colombia

    1p.

Ordonez, Antonio

Newspaper clipping dated 11 Nov 1960

    W/envelope

[Ordonez], Antonio

Cable   29 Jan 1960, Manizales

    1p.

[Ordonez], Antonio

TLS   8 Dec 1960, Madrid

    1p., w/envelope and newspaper
    clippings

[Ordonez], Antonio
Cable   12 Jan 1961, Madrid, to MH
         1p.

Orshevsky
         See Time-Life

[Ordonez], Antonio
Cable   8 May 1961, Puerto Santamaria
         1p. w/envelope bearing EH notes

Osterling, Anders
         See Nobel Foundation

[Ordonez], Antonio
ANS   undated, Paris
         1p.

[Otis, Grace QUINLAN] (friend)
ALS Luke
         27 Dec 1919
         6pp., w/envelope

[Ordonez], Antonio
TLS   undated, Mexico, to EH/MH
         1p.

[Otis, Grace QUINLAN]
ALS "L___"
         20 Jan 1920, Home [Petoskey]
         9pp., w/envelope

[Ordonez], Carmen (friend, wife of Antonio)
Cable   [6 June 1959], Malaga
         1p.

[Otis, Grace QUINLAN]
ALS Luke
         27 and 29 Jan 1920, [Petoskey]
         4pp., w/envelope

[Otis, Grace QUINLAN]

T/ALS Luke

     31 Jan and 2 Feb 1920, Petoskey

     4pp., w/photographs and envelope

[Otis, Grace QUINLAN]

ALS "G"

     4 Aug 1920, Mayfield, Mich.

     4pp.

[Otis, Grace QUINLAN]

ALS Luke

     15 Feb 1920, Detroit

     4pp., w/envelope

[Otis, Grace QUINLAN]

ALS "G"

     Monday [14 Nov 1920, Petoskey]

     4pp., w/envelope

[Otis, Grace QUINLAN]

ALS Luke

     14 Mar 1920, Petoskey

     4pp., w/envelope

[Otis, Grace QUINLAN]

ALS "G"

     10 Aug 1921, Mayfield, Mich.

     4pp., w/envelope

[Otis, Grace QUINLAN]

ALS "G.E."

     23 Mar and 17 Apr 1920, Petoskey

     7pp., w/envelope

[Otis, Grace QUINLAN]

ALS "GC"

     1:30 P.M., undated, to EH, Pudge, and Marge

     2pp., w/envelope

[Otis, Grace QUINLAN]

ALS "G"

     1 June 1920, At the Grind [Petoskey]

     4pp., w/photographs and envelope

OTIS, Grace Quinlan

ALS "G"

     undated, Chicago

     6pp.

Oxford University Press
          See Valentine, O.C.

[Pailthorp, Edwin G.] (friend)
ALS Dutch
          3 June 1920, [Soo, Ontario]
          5pp., w/envelope

Pace, Frank, Jr.
          See Bruce, David

Pailthorp, Edwin [G.]
Xmas Greeting S Dutch
          [15 Dec 1920], Windsor, Ontario
          2pp., w/envelope

Pacific Digest
TLS Chen Pin-ho
          22 Feb 1938, Hong Kong
          1p.

[Pailthorp, Ediwn G.]
TLS Dutch
          22 Jan 1921, Petoskey
          2pp.

Paddock, Robert L.
          See American Friends of
          Spanish Democracy

Pailthorp, E[dwin] G.
TLS Dutch
          26 Apr 1934, Petoskey
          3pp., w/photograph

Paige, D. D. (Ezra Pound scholar)
TLS   15 Oct 1951, Rapallo
          3pp. bearing EH note

Palmer, W. B. (U.S. Army, friend of Buck
                              Lanham)
TLS   25 Aug 1945
          1p. bearing EH notes

Palmer, Paul
    See <u>The American Mercury</u>

Parker, Austin (producer)
Cable   1 Mar 1938, N.Y.
        1p.

Pantheon
    See <u>C</u>urtis Brown 8 Sept 1937

Parker, Austin
Cable   14 Mar 1938, Los Angeles
        1p.

Paramount Pictures
TLS Richard Halliday
    11 Apr 1934, N.Y.
    1p. bearing EH notes

Parker, Austin
    See Dart, Rollin 18 Feb 1938

Paramount Pictures
    See Stitt, Ralph

[Parker], Dorothy
ALS   [31 Oct 1924, Paris]
    1p., w/ALS Lewis [Galantiere], 3 Nov
    [1924, Paris], and his envelope

Parke, Fred C. N. (taxidermist)
TLS   22 Sept 1934, Bangor, Maine
    1p., w/1p. enclosure

[Parker, Dorothy] (author)
Cable   [23 Nov 1928], N.Y.
        1p.

[Parker], Dorothy

TLS   [Sept 1929]

       1p. bearing EH note on verso

Partisan Review

TLS Mary Wickware

       25 Oct 1949, N.Y.

       1p. bearing EH draft reply

[Parker], Dorothy

ALS   undated

       1p.

Patrick, T$_e$d

       See Holiday 17 June 1948
                       4 Jan 1952

    Parker, Dorothy
         See Ross

Pattou, Victor E. (reader)

TLS   17 Aug 1936, Boston

       1p.

Parraga, Carlos N. (motion picture agent)

TLS   21 Dec 1954, Havana

       1p. bearing MH notes

Pattullo, George (fishing friend, reader)

TLS   23 May 1935, N.Y.

       2pp.

Partisan Review

TLS William Phillips

       6 May 1936, N.Y.

       1p.

Pattulo, George

TLS Pat

       8 Dec 1938, [N.Y.]

       1p.

Paul Zsolnay Verlag
See Perkins, Maxwell 9 Mar 1935

Peace Information Center
See Fast, Howard

Paulhan, Jean
See Gallimard 13 Dec 1926

Pearsall, Robert   (congratulator)
TLS   29 Oct 1954, Austin, Texas
1p. bearing EH note

Paz Borrero, Joaquin (Feria de Cali)
TLS J. Paz
29 Oct 1959, Cali, Colombia
2pp.

Pease, Warren
See Jenkins, Howell 11 Aug 1918

Paz Borrero, Joaquin
TLS J. Paz
6 Nov 1959, Cali
2pp.

Pegler, Westbrook (writer)
TLS   [17 Nov 1954], N.Y.
2pp., w/envelope

Peabody, Sam[uel E.] (reader, writer)
TLS   9 Oct 1936, Groton, Mass.
1p.

Peirce, Jonathan (Waldo Peirce's son)
ALS   12 July 1959, Searsport
2pp., w/envelope

[Peirce, Waldo] (artist, friend)
ALS "WP"
        [16 July 1927, Arachon]
        3pp., w/envelope

[Peirce], Waldo
ALS   10 Mar 1928, [N.Y.
        2pp., w/envelope bearing EH note

[Peirce, Waldo]
ALS "WP"
        [21 July 1927], Paris
        1p., w/envelope

[Peirce, Waldo]
ALS Valdo
        9 June 1928, Bangor
        7pp., w/envelope

[Peirce], Waldo
ALS   12 Sept [1927], Paris
        3pp.

[Peirce, Waldo]
TL   12 June 1928, Bangor
        1p., w/envelope

[Peirce, Waldo]
ALS Don Valdo
        28 Dec 1927, Barcelona
        14pp., w/envelope

[Peirce, Waldo]
TL   28 June 1928, Bangor
        2pp.
        oversize

[Peirce, Waldo]
AL Fragment S Valdito
        [Feb 1928]
        2pp.

[Peirce, Waldo]
Portrait of EH and newspaper clipping, w/
envelope postmarked 2 July 1928, Greene Lake,
Maine

[Peirce], Waldo

ALS   11 July 1928, Boston

4pp., w/envelope

[Peirce, Waldo]

ALS "WP"

12 Sept 1928, Bangor

7pp., w/newspaper clipping and photographs and envelope

[Peirce, Waldo]

T/AL   12 July [1928, Bangor]

1p., w/envelope

[Peirce, Waldo]

ALS "W"

18 Sept 1928, Bangor

3pp.

[Peirce], Waldo

TLS   20 July 1928, Bangor

1p.

[Peirce], Waldo

TLS   26 Sept 1928, Bangor

3pp., w/envelope
oversize

[Peirce], Waldo

TLS   26 July 1928, Bangor

1p., w/envelope

[Peirce, Waldo]

ALS "V"

27 Sept [1928]

2pp.

[Peirce, Waldo]

TLS "W"

28 July [1928, Bangor]

1p., w/photograph and newspaper clipping

[Peirce, Waldo]

ALS "V"

9 Oct 1928, Bangor

1p. bearing art work w/ envelope

[Peirce], Waldo

ALS   24 Oct [1928], N.Y.

      3pp., w/envelope

[Peirce], Waldo

ALS   16 Jan [1929], Bangor

      4pp., w/envelope

[Peirce], Waldo

ALS   2 Feb 1929, Bangor

      3pp. bearing art work w/envelope

[Peirce], Waldo

TLS   29 Jan 1929, Bangor

      2pp., w/envelope

[Peirce], Waldo

TLS   [late 1928], Bangor

      7pp.
      oversize

[Peirce], Waldo

ALS   29 Jan [1929, Bangor]

      4pp.

[Peirce], Waldo

ALS   1 Jan 1929, Bangor

      2pp., w/envelope

[Peirce, Waldo]

AL   29 Jan 1929, [Bangor]

      3pp. bearing art work
      oversize

[Peirce], Waldo

ALS   11 Jan [1929], Bangor

      4pp., w/ALS Renee, 11 Jan 1929,
      Bangor, 1p., and envelope

[Peirce, Waldo]

ALS "W"

      8 Feb 1929, Bangor

      2pp.

[Peirce], Waldo
TLS   15/19 Feb [1929], Bangor
        3pp.

[Peirce], Waldo
ALS   25 Sept 1929, Bangor
        1p.

[Peirce, Waldo]
TLS [James R.] Wells
        21 Mar 1929, N.Y., to Peirce
        1p.

[Peirce, Waldo]
AL   2 Nov 1929, Bangor
        2pp., w/photograph and envelope
        bearing EH note

[Peirce], Waldo
ALS   17 June 1929, Bangor
        2pp., w/envelope

[Peirce, Waldo]
TL   1 Dec 1929, Bangor
        3pp.

[Peirce], Waldo
ALS   10 July 1929, Bangor
        7pp., w/envelope

[Peirce], Waldo
TLS   2 Dec 1929, Bangor
        1p.

[Peirce], Waldo
ALS Waldo and Renee
        12 Aug 1929, Bangor
        9pp., w/envelope bearing EH note

[Peirce], Waldo
TLS   27 Jan 1930, Bangor
        2pp., w/photographs and envelope

[Peirce, Waldo]

ANS "W"

        11 Feb [1930, Bangor]

        1p. on verso of an invitation to a vernissage of the Salon d'Automne w/a drawing by Van Dongen

---

[Peirce], Waldo

ALS   17 Apr 1930, Paris

      4pp., w/envelope

[Peirce], Waldo

TLS   21 Feb 1930

      2pp.

[Peirce], Waldo

ALS   [May 1930, Paris]

      3pp.

[Peirce], Waldo

ALS   12 Mar 1930, [Paris]

      1p., w/envelope

[Peirce], Waldo

ALS   15 May 1930

      3pp., w/newspaper clippings and envelope

[Peirce, Waldo]

TLS "W"

        28 Mar 1930, Paris

        2pp.

[Peirce, Waldo]

ALS "W"

        15 May [1930], Paris

        3pp., w/envelope

[Peirce], Waldo

ALS   4 Apr [1930, Paris]

      3pp.

[Perice], Waldo

ALS   22 May 1930, Paris

      4pp., w/envelope

[Perice], Waldo

ALS   29 May [1930, Paris]

    3pp.

[Peirce, Waldo]

ALS "W"

    2 Apr [1932], Bangor

    1p., w/newspaper clippings and envelope

[Peirce], Waldo

ALS   [7 July 1931], not on board <u>S. S. De Grasse</u>, [Bangor]

    2pp., w/photographs and envelope

[Peirce], Waldo

TLS   18 Apr 1932, Bangor

    3pp., w/envelope bearing EH note

[Peirce], Waldo

ALS Waldo, Aly & Uncle Bill

    18 Dec 1931

    3pp.

[Peirce], Waldo

TLS   22 Apr 1932, Bangor

    3pp., w/photograph, newspaper clipping and envelope

[Peirce], Waldo

TLS   11 Mar 1932, Bangor

    1p., w/AL from Mrs. Yorke, 1 Mar 1933, Paris, to Mr. Peirce, and envelope

---

[Peirce], Waldo

TLS   25 May 1932, Bangor

    3pp.

[Peirce], Waldo

TLS   29 Mar 1932, [Bangor]

    1p.

[Peirce, Waldo]

Xmas Greeting

    [25 Dec] 1932, Bangor

    1p., w/art work

[Peirce], Waldo
TLS   25 Apr 1934, N.Y.
         2pp.

[Peirce, Waldo]
TLS "W"
         3 Dec1934, Bangor
         1p., w/draft of letter to Homer
         [Saint-Gaudens]

Peirce, Waldo
ALS "W"
         1 June 1934, Bangor
         1p., w/envelope

[Peirce], Waldo
TLS   6 Dec 1934, Bangor
         2pp.

[Peirce], Waldo
TLS   13 June 1934, Bangwhor [Bangor]
         1p., w/envelope

[Peirce], Waldo
TLS   10 May 1935, N.Y.
         1p., w/envelope

[Peirce], Waldo
ALS   22 Sept 1934, Bangor
         5pp., w/envelope

[Peirce], Waldo
TLS   11 Jan 1937, Tucson
         2pp., w/photographs and envelope

[Peirce], Waldo
Cable   2 Dec 1934, Banjou [Bangor]
         1p.

Peirce, Waldo
TLS Waldo
         25 Jan 1958 [1959], Tucson
         2pp., w/envelope bearing art work

Peirce, W[aldo]

ALS "W"

30 Apr 1959, Tucson, to EH/MH

2pp., w/address-leaf

[Peirce], Waldo

TLS Waldo and Ellen

13 Jan 1960, Tucson

1p., w/newspaper clipping, post card and envelope bearing art work

Peirce, Waldo

AL   23 Mar 1959, Tucson, to EH/MH

4pp.

Peirce, Waldo

ALS   undated, [Paris]

1p., w/envelope

Peirce, W[aldo]

ALS "WP"

14 June 1959, Searsport, Maine

2pp., w/address-leaf

Pellou, Charles D.   (Station Manager, AFRS Madrid)

A Statement S

23 May 1959

1p.

[Peirce, Waldo]

Birthday Greeting S "E.J.K. & W.P."

12 July 1959, Searsport

2pp. bearing art work, w/A Post Card S "F.L.S." [Freddy Stagg], 15 May 1950, Madrid, to Peice, and envelope bearing art work

PEN Club

ALS Benjamin Cremiere

[Nov 1920's], Paris

2pp.

[Peirce, Waldo]

TL   18 Sept 1959, Searsport, to EH/MH

1p., w/"Un Poco de Viento por la Dulzaina" and envelope bearing art work

Penney, Joe

see Farrington,   Aug 1936
Selwyn K.

[Pentacost, Jack] (friend)

ALS Pock

    12 Jan [1920, Ann Arbor]

    3pp., w/envelope

[Percival, Philip H.]

AL   28 Mar 1938, Machakos

    1p., w/2pp. of Percival's diary

[Pentacost, Jack]

ALS Pock

    Thursday [25 Mar 1920, Ann Arbor]

    4pp., w/envelope

[Percival], Philip [H.]

ALS   13 July 1939, N.Y.

    2pp., w/envelope bearing EH note

Pentacost, Jack.

        See also Musselman, Morris M.
                3 Aug 1917

Percival, [Philip] H.

ALS "PHP"

        1 Feb 1952, Machakos

        2pp., w/address-leaf postmarked both
        1952 and 1953 bearing EH note
        "received Feb 7, 1953"

Percival, Philip H. (white hunter, friend)

ALS   10 Nov 1934, Machakos, Kenya

    4pp., w/envelope

Percival, P[hilip] H.

ALS "PHP"

        2 Oct 1952, Machakos

        2pp., w/address-leaf bearing EH note

Percival, P[hilip] H.

ALS   17 May 1936, Machakos

    3pp.

Percival, P[hilip] H.

ALS "PHP"

        1 Nov 1952, [Machakos]

        2pp., w/address-leaf bearing EH note

Percival, P[hilip] H.
ALS "PHP"

      1 Dec 1952, Machakos

      2pp., w/address-leaf bearing EH note

[Percival, Philip H.]
ALS "PHP"

      3 Dec 1953, Kitanga [Machakos]

      2pp.

Percival, P[hilip] H.
ALS "PHP"

      11 June 1953, Machakos

      4pp., w/2 address-leaves

[Percival, Philip H.]
ALS "PHP"

      16 Dec 1953, Machakos

      3pp., w/envelope

Percival, P[hilip] H.
ALS   19 July 1953, Machakos

      2pp., w/address-leaf

[Percival, Philip H.]
ALS "Pop"

      18 and 19 Dec 1953, Machakos

      4pp.

Percival, P[hilip] H.
ALS "PHP"

      30 July 1953, Machakos

      2pp., w/address-leaf

[Percival], Philip [H.]
ALS   1 Mar 1954, Machakos, to EH/MH

      2pp., w/envelope

[Percival], Philip [H.]
ALS   1 Sept 1953, Kitanga [Machakos]

      3pp.

[Percival, Philip H.]
ALS "PHP"

      27 Mar [1954], Machakos

      2pp., w/address-leaf

[Percival, Philip H.]

ALS Pop

    3 May 1954, Kitanga [Machakos]

    2pp., w/address-leaf bearing EH note

Percival, Philip [H.]

ALS   6 Sept 1958, Machakos, to EH/MH

    2pp., w/address-leaf

[Percival], Philip [H.]

ALS   8 July 1955, Machakos, to MH

    2pp., w/address-leaf

[Percival], Philip [H.]

ALS   9 May 1961, Machakos, to EH/MH

    2pp., w/address-leaf

[Percival, Philip H.]

ALS Pop

    22 July 1956, Machakos

    2pp., w/address-leaf

Percival, Vivien (wife of Philip)

ALS   28 June 1953, Machakos

    2pp., w/address-leaf bearing EH note

[Percival, Philip H.]

ALS Pop

    2 Jan 1957, Machakos

    2pp., w/address-leaf

Percival, Vivien

ALS   18 Dec 1953, to EH/MH

    2pp., w/address-leaf

[Percival, Philip H.]

ALS Pop

    8 Feb 1958, Machakos, to EH/MH

    2pp.

Pereda, Prudencio de (writer)

TLS   3 Oct 1935, Ozone Park, N.Y.

    2pp.

Pereda, Prudencio de
TLS   11 Oct 1936, Ozone Park
          1p.

Pereda, Prudencio de
TLS   17 Feb 1938, Ozone Park
          2pp.

Pereda, Prudencio de
TLS   7 Dec 1936
          3pp.

Pereda, Prudencio de
TLS   15 Oct 1938, Richmond Hill, L.I.
          1p.

Pereda, Prudencio de
ALS   20 Dec 1936
          3pp.

[Pereda], Prudencio [de]
TLS   2 Dec 1938, Richmond Hill
          1p.

Pereda, Prudencio de
TLS   5 June 1937, Ozone Park
          1p.

[Pereda], Prudencio [de]
TLS   14 Aug 1943, Camp Campbell, Kentucky
          2pp.

Pereda, Prudencio de
TLS   9 Feb 1937 [1938]
          6pp.

[Perkins, Maxwell E.] (editor, Scribner's)
TLcc   1 Feb 1926, [N.Y.]
          4pp.

Perkins, Maxwell E.
TLS   12 Apr 1926, N.Y.
          2pp.

Perkins, Maxwell E.
TLS   30 June 1926, N.Y.
          1p.

Perkins, Maxwell E.
TLS   18 May 1926, N.Y.
          4pp.

Perkins, Maxwell E.
TLS   20 July 1926, N.Y.
          3pp.

[Perkins, Maxwell E.]
AL Fragment
          29 May 1926, to Scott [Fitzgerald]
          pp. 1-3 only

Perkins, Maxwell E.
TLS   27 July 1926, N.Y.
          1p.

Perkins, Maxwell E.
TLS   14 June 1926, N.Y.
          2pp.

Perkins, Maxwell E.
TLS   23 Aug 1926, N.Y.
          1p.

Perkins, Maxwell E.
TLS   29 June 1926, N.Y.
          2pp.

Perkins, [Maxwell E.]
Cable   [8 Sept 1926], N.Y.
          1p.

Perkins, Maxwell E.
TLS   8 Sept 1926, N.Y.
        4pp.

Perkins, Maxwell [E.]
ALS   11 Nov 1926, [N.Y.]
        1p., w/proof for advertisement of SAR

Perkins, Maxwell E.
TLS   9 Sept 1926, N.Y.
        1p.

Perkins, Maxwell E.
TLS   22 Nov 1926, N.Y.
        4pp.

Perkins, Maxwell E.
TLS   17 Sept 1926, N.Y.
        1p.

Perkins, Maxwell E.
TLS   26 Nov 1926, N.Y.
        4pp.

Perkins, Maxwell E.
TLS   30 Oct 1926, N.Y.
        4pp.

[Perkins, Maxwell E.]
ANS "MEP"
                [26 Nov 1926, N.Y.]
        1p., w/ALS John Biggs, Jr.,
        24 Nov 1926, Wilmington, Del.,
        to Perkins, and envelope

[Perkins, Maxwell E.]
Envelope only postmarked 6 Nov 1926, N.Y.

Perkins, Maxwell E.
TLS   1 Dec 1926, N.Y.
        3pp., w/TLS Benjamin L. Harvey, 22 Nov
        1926, to Scribner's

Perkins, Maxwell E.

TLS   3 Dec 1926, N.Y.

        3pp., w/copy of letter from Dwight
        Deere Wiman, 2 Dec 1926, N.Y., to
        Perkins and envelope w/EH notes

Perkins, Maxwell E.

TLS   14 Jan 1927, N.Y.

        3pp., w/envelope

Perkins, Maxwell [E.]

TLS   10 Dec 1926, N.Y.

        4pp.,w/enclosures and envelope

Perkins, Maxwell E.

TLS   25 Jan 1927, N.Y.

        1p., w/envelope

Perkins, Maxwell E.

TLS   18 Dec 1926, N.Y.

        3pp., w/envelope

Perkins, Maxwell E.

TLS   28 Jan 1927, N.Y.

        1p.

[Perkins, Maxwell E.]

ANS "MEP"

        [Jan 1927], N.Y.

        1p.

Perkins, Maxwell E.

TLS   4 Feb 1927, N.Y.

        3pp.

Perkins, Maxwell [E.]

ALS   [Jan 1927]

        1p.

Perkins, Maxwell E.

TLS   7 Feb 1927, N.Y.

        1p.

Perkins, Maxwell E.

TLS   21 Feb 1927, N.Y.

     3pp., w/enclosure

Perkins, Maxwell [E.]

TLS   13 Apr 1927, N.Y.

     3pp.

Perkins, Maxwell E.

TLS   28 Feb 1927, N.Y.

     2pp., w/envelope

Perkins, Maxwell [E.]

TLS   29 Apr 1927, N.Y.

     4pp.

Perkins, Maxwell E.

TLS   2 Mar 1927, N.Y.

     3pp., w/envelope

Perkins, Maxwell E.

TLS   9 May 1927, N.Y.

     3pp., w/envelope

Perkins, Maxwell [E.]

Cable   9 Mar 1927, N.Y.

     1p.

Perkins, Maxwell E.

TLS   16 May 1927, N.Y.

     2pp.

Perkins, Maxwell E.

TLS   9 Mar 1927, N.Y.

     3pp., w/TLS Ellery Sedgwick, 8 Mar 1927, Boston, to Perkins

---

Perkins, Maxwell [E.]

TLS   27 May 1927, N.Y.'

     2pp., w/envelope

Perkins, Maxwell [E.]
TLS   8 June 1927, N.Y.
            4pp., w/envelope

Perkins, Maxwell E.
TLS   8 Dec 1927, N.Y.
            2pp.

Perkins, Maxwell [E.]
TNS   31 Aug 1927, N.Y.
            1p., w/newspaper clipping

Perkins, Maxwell E.
TLS   18 Jan 1928, N.Y.
            2pp.

Perkins, Maxwell E.]
Cable   29 Oct 1927, N.Y.
            1p.

Perkins, Maxwell E.
TLS   10 Apr 1928, N.Y.
            3pp. bearing EH note

Perkins, Maxwell E.
TLS   18 Nov 1927, N.Y.
            1p.

Perkins, Maxwell E.
TLS   19 Apr 1928, N.Y.
            2pp., w/enclosure

Perkins, Maxwell E.
ALS   30 Nov 1927, N.Y.
            3pp., w/newspaper clipping and
            envelope

Perkins, Maxwell [E.]
TLS   27 Apr 1928, N.Y.
            4pp.

Perkins, Maxwell E.

TLS   24 May 1928, N.Y.

    4pp.

Perkins, Maxwell [E.]

TLS   1 Aug 1928, N.Y.

    1p.

Perkins, Maxwell E.

TLS   25 May 1928, N.Y.

    3pp.

Perkins, Maxwell E.

TLS   8 Aug 1928, N.Y.

    4pp.

Perkins, Maxwell E.

TLS   6 June 1928, N.Y.

    2pp.

Perkins, Maxwell E.

TLS   14 Aug 1928

    2pp.

Perkins, Maxwell E.

TLS   18 June 1928, N.Y.

    4pp., w/enclosure

Perkins, Maxwell [E.]

TLS   30 Aug 1928, N.Y.

    3pp., w/enclosure and envelope

Perkins, Maxwell E.

TLS   26 June 1928, N.Y.

    3pp.

Perkins, Maxwell [E.]

ALS   17 Sept 1928, N.Y.

    6pp.,w/envelope

Perkins, Maxwell [E.]
TLS   21 Sept 1928, N.Y.
    2pp.

Perkins, Maxwell [E.]
Cable   23 Jan 1929, NY
    1p.

Perkins, Maxwell [E.]
TLS   2 Oct 1928, N.Y.
    2pp., w/TM from Whitney Darrow to
    Perkins, 1 Oct 1928, 1p., and
    envelope

Perkins, Maxwell E.
TLS   25 Jan 1929, N.Y.
    2pp.

Perkins, Maxwell E.
TLS   24 Oct 1928, N.Y.
    4pp.

Perkins, Maxwell [E.]
ALS   [9 Feb 1929], Havana Special
    3pp.

Perkins, Maxwell [E.]
ALS   19 Dec 1928, N.Y.
    2pp., w/envelope

Perkins, Maxwell [E.]
Cable   13 Feb 1929, N.Y.
    1p.

Perkins, Maxwell [E.]
ALS   9 Jan 1929
    4pp.

Perkins, Maxwell [E.]
TLS   13 Feb 1929, N.Y.
    2pp.

Perkins, Maxwell [E.]
TLS   19 Feb 1929, N.Y.
         3pp.

Perkins, Maxwell E.
TLS   15 Mar 1929, N.Y.
         3pp., w/envelope

Perkins, Maxwell E.
TLS   27 Feb 1929, N.Y.
         3pp.

Perkins, Maxwell E.
TLS   25 Mar 1929, N.Y.
         1p., w/envelope

Perkins, Maxwell [E.]
TLS   1 Mar 1929, N.Y.
         1p.

Perkins, Maxwell [E.]
Cable   4 Apr 1929, N.Y.
         1p., w/envelope

Perkins, Maxwell [E.]
TLS   8 Mar 1929, N.Y.
         3pp. bearing EH note, w/enclosure

Perkins, Maxwell E.
TLS   1 June 1929, N.Y.
         1p., w/envelope

Perkins, Maxwell E.
TLS   14 Mar 1929, N.Y.
         2pp.

Perkins, Maxwell [E.]
TLS   4 Oct 1929, N.Y.
         3pp.

Perkins, Maxwell [E.]
TLS   8 Oct 1929, N.Y.
         1p.

Perkins, Maxwell [E.]
TLS   8 Apr 1930, N.Y.
         2pp.

Perkins, Maxwell [E.]
TLS   14 Oct 1929, N.Y.
         1p.

[Perkins, Maxwell E.]
TLS Max
         28 May 1930, N.Y.
         2pp.

Perkins, Maxwell [E.]
TLS   15 Oct 1929, N.Y.
         5pp., w/envelope

[Perkins, Maxwell E.]
Cable   5 Jan 1932, N.Y.
         1p.

Perkins, Maxwell [E.]
TLS   3 Feb 1930, N.Y.
         3pp. bearing EH note

[Perkins], Max[well E.]
TLS   14 Jan 1932, N.Y.
         4pp., w/envelope

Perkins, Maxwell [E.]
TLS   4 Mar 1930, N.Y.
         1p. bearing EH note, w/enclosure

[Perkins], Max[well E.]
TLS   19 Feb 1932, N.Y.
         3pp., w/envelope

[Perkins], Max[well E.]

Cable   24 Feb 1932, N.Y.

    1p.

[Perkins], Max[well E.]

Cable   4 Apr 1932, N.Y.

    1p.

[Perkins], Max[well E.]

TLS   24 Feb 1932, N.Y.

    1p.

[Perkins], Max[well E.]

TLS   7 Apr 1932, N.Y.

    3pp.

[Perkins], Max[well E.]

Cable   [Apr 1932], N.Y.

    1p.

[Perkins], Max[well E.]

Cable   8 Apr 1932, N.Y.

    1p.

[Perkins], Max[well E.]

TLS   1 Apr 1932, N.Y.

    3pp.

[Perkins], Max[well E.]

TLS   8 Apr 1932, N.Y.

    3pp.

[Perkins], Max[well E.]

TLS   2 Apr 1932, N.Y.

    3pp.

[Perkins], Max[well E.]

TLS   13 Apr 1932, N.Y.

    2pp.

[Perkins], Max[well E.]

TLS   19 Apr 1932, N.Y.

       2pp., w/envelope

[Perkins], Max[well E.]

TLS   11 June 1932, N.Y.

       2pp., w/copy of letter to Hadley
Hemingway, 31 May 1932, and envelope

[Perkins], Max[well E.]

TLS   28 Apr 1932, N.Y.

       4pp.

[Perkins], Max[well E.]

TLS   23 June 1932, N.Y.

       4pp., w/TMemoS Mr. Chapin, 15 June
1932, N.Y., to Perkins

[Perkins], Max[well E.]

TLS   10 May 1932, N.Y.

       3pp.,w/envelope

[Perkins], Max[well E.]

TLS   7 July 1932, N.Y.

       3pp.

[Perkins], Max[well E.]

Cable   16 May 1932, N.Y.

       1p.

Perkins, Maxwell [E.]

TLS   29 Sept 1932, N.Y., to Pauline

       3pp.

Perkins, Maxwell [E.]

Cable   8 June 1932, N.Y.

       1p.

[Perkins], Max[well E.]

TLS   8 Oct 1932, N.Y.

       3pp.

[Perkins], Max[well E.]
TLS   12 Nov 1932, N.Y.
         4pp.

[Perkins], Max[well E.]
TLS   12 Apr 1933, N.Y.
         4pp.

[Perkins], Max[well E.]
TLS   12 Jan 1933, N.Y.
         3pp.

[Perkins], Max[well E.]
TLS   25 May 1933, N.Y.
         3pp.

[Perkins], Max[well E.]
TLS   3 Apr 1933, N.Y.
         6pp.

Perkins, Maxwell [E.]
TLS   9 June 1933, N.Y., to Pauline
         1p.

[Perkins], Max[well E.]
TLS   3 Apr 1933, N.Y.
         2pp.

[Perkins], Max[well E.]
Cable   12 June 1933, N.Y.
         1p.

[Perkins], Max[well E.]
Cable   10 Apr 1933, N.Y.
         1p.

[Perkins], Max[well E.]
TLS   16 June 1933, N.Y.
         2pp.

[Perkins], Max[well E.]

TLS   19 June 1933, N.Y.

    2pp.

[Perkins], Max[well E.]

TLS   22 Sept 1933, N.Y.

    3pp.

[Perkins], Max[well E.]

Cable   18 July 1933, N.Y.

    1p.

[Perkins], Max[well E.]

TLS   25 Sept 1933, N.Y.

    1p., w/TLS from M.C. Wagner, 13 Sept
1933, Paris, to Scribner's and envelope

[Perkins], Max[well E.]

TLS   2 Aug 1933, N.Y.

    3pp.,w/newspaper clipping and envelope

[Perkins], Max[well E.]

ALS   undated

    3pp., possibly w/envelope postmarked
3 Oct 1933, N.Y.

[Perkins], Max[well E.]

TLS   14 Aug 1933, N.Y.

    2pp., w/envelope

[Perkins], Max[well E.]

TLS   5 Oct 1933, N.Y.

    3pp.

[Perkins], Max[well E.]

Cable   [15 Sept 1933], N.Y.

    1p.

[Perkins], Max[well E.]

Cable   25 Oct 1933, N.Y.

    1p.

[Perkins], Max[well E.]
Cable   4 Nov 1933, N.Y.
        1p.

[Perkins], Max[well E.]
Cable   2 May 1934, N.Y.
        1p.

[Perkins], Max[well E.]
TLS   6 Nov 1933, N.Y.
        3pp.

[Perkins], Max[well E.]
TLS   28 June 1934
        5pp.

[Perkins], Max[well E.]
TLS   10 Nov 1933, N.Y.
        3pp.

[Perkins], Max[well E.]
TLS   1 Oct 1934, N.Y.
        4pp.

[Perkins], Max[well E.]
Cable   18 Nov 1933, N.Y.
        1p.

[Perkins], Max[well E.]
TLS   6 Oct 1934, N.Y.
        3pp.

[Perkins], Max[well E.]
TLS   7 Feb 1934, N.Y.
        4pp., w/envelope

[Perkins], Max[well E.]
TLS   9 Oct 1934, N.Y.
        1p., w/enclosures and envelope

[Perkins], Max[well E.]
TLS   10 Nov 1934, N.Y.
      2pp., w/envelope

[Perkins], Max[well E.]
TLS   8 Feb 1935, N.Y.
      2pp.

[Perkins], Max[well E.
TLS   22 Nov 1934, N.Y.
      1p.

[Perkins], Max[well E.]
ALS   [11 Feb 1935, N.Y.]
      5pp., w/envelope

[Perkins], Max[well E.]
TLS   28 Nov 1934, N.Y.
      4pp., w/envelope bearing EH note

[Perkins], Max[well E.]
Cable   15 Feb 1935, N.Y.
      1p.

[Perkins], Max[well E.]
TLS   18 Dec 1934, N.Y.
      4pp., w/enclosure and envelope

[Perkins], Max[well E.]
TLS   16 Feb 1935, N.Y.
      2pp.

[Perkins], Max[well E.]
Cable   4 Feb 1935, N.Y.
      1p.

Perkins, Maxwell [E.]
Cable   19 Feb 1935, N.Y.
      1p.

[Perkins], Max[well E.]

TLS   19 Feb 1935, N.Y.

        4pp.

[Perkins], Max[well E.]

Cable   20 Feb 1935, N.Y.

        1p.

[Perkins], Max[well E.]

TLS   27 Feb 1935, N.Y.

        2pp.

[Perkins], Max[well E.]

TLS   9 Mar 1935, N.Y.

        2pp., w/TL from Paul Zsolnay Verlag,
26 Feb 1935, Vienna, to Jonathan Cape,
and envelope

[Perkins], Max[well E.]

TLS   2 Apr 1935, N.Y.

        4pp., w/envelope

[Perkins], Max[well E.]

TLS   4 Apr 1935, N.Y.

        3pp.

[Perkins], Max[well E.]

TLS   25 Apr 1935, N.Y.

        4pp., w/enclosure and envelope bearing
EH note

[Perkins], Max[well E.]

TLS   21 May 1935, N.Y.

        4pp.

[Perkins], Max[well E.]

TLS   5 June 1935, N.Y.

        4pp.

[Perkins], Max[well E.]

TLS   14 June 1935, N.Y.

        2pp.

[Perkins], Max[well E.]
Cable   31 July 1935, N.Y.
        1p.

[Perkins], Max[well E.]
TLS   20 Dec 1935, N.Y.
        3pp.

[Perkins], Max[well E.]
TLS   5 Aug 1935, N.Y.
        2pp., w/envelope

[Perkins], Max[well E.]
TLS   6 Apr 1936, N.Y.
        3pp.

[Perkins], Max[well E.]
Cable   19 Aug 1935, N.Y.
        1p.

[Perkins], Max[well E.]
TLS   15 Apr 1936, N.Y.
        3pp. bearing EH note

[Perkins], Max[well E.]
ALS   30 Aug 1935, [N.Y.]
        12pp., w/envelope

[Perkins], Max[well E.]
TLS   9 May 1936, N.Y.
        4pp., w/enclosures and envelope

[Perkins], Max[well E.]
TLS   17 Sept 1935, N.Y.
        1p., w/enclosures

[Perkins], Max[well E.]
TLS   21 July 1936, N.Y.
        4pp., w/envelope

[Perkins], Max[well E.]
TLS   27 Aug 1936, N.Y.
          1p., w/enclosures and envelope

[Perkins, Max[well E.]
TLS   20 Nov 1936, N.Y.
          2pp.

[Perkins], Max[well E.]
TLS   18 Sept 1936, N.Y.
          3pp.

[Perkins], Max[well E.]
TLS   9 Dec 1936, N.Y.
          4pp.

[Perkins], Max[well E.]
TLS   1 Oct 1936, N.Y.
          4pp., w/envelope

[Perkins], Max[well E.]
Cable   16 Dec 1936, N.Y.
          1p.

[Perkins], Max[well E.]
TLS   13 Nov 1936, N.Y.
          2pp.

[Perkins], Max[well E.]
TLS   7 Jan 1937, N.Y.
          2pp., w/envelope

[Perkins], Max[well E.]
TLS   17 Nov 1936, N.Y.
          2pp.

[Perkins], Max[well E.]
TNS   8 Feb 1937
          1p., w/enclosure

[Perkins], Max[well E.]
TLS   18 Feb 1937, N.Y.
          2pp.

[Perkins], Max[well E.]
Cable   [30 Dec 1937], N.Y.
          1p.

[Perkins], Max[well E.]
Cable   20 Feb 1937, N.Y.
          1p.

[Perkins], Max[well E.]
Cable   [3 Jan 1938], N.Y.
          1p.

Perkins, [Maxwell E.]
Cable from Marshall Perkins
          20 May 1937, Baltimore, Maryland
          1p.

[Perkins], Max[well E.]
Cable   1 Feb 1938, N.Y.
          1p.

[Perkins], Max[well E.]
TLS   17 June 1937, N.Y.
          4pp., w/envelope

[Perkins], Max[well E.]
TLS   3 Feb 1938, N.Y.
          4pp., w/envelope

[Perkins], Max[well E.]
TLS   5 Aug 1937, N.Y.
          4pp., w/enclosures

[Perkins], Max[well E.]
TLS   4 Feb 1938, N.Y.
          3pp., w/enclosures

[Perkins], Max[well E.]

TLS   8 Feb 1938, N.Y.

2pp., w/envelope

[Perkins], Max[well E.]

Cable   [7 Apr 1938], N.Y.

1p.

[Perkins], Max[well E.]

Cable   [11 Feb 1938], N.Y.

1p.

[Perkins], Max[well E.]

TLS   7 Apr 1938, N.Y.

3pp.

[Perkins], Max[well E.]

TLS   21 Feb 1938, N.Y.

3pp., w/envelope

[Perkins], Max[well E.]

TLS   13 May 1938, N.Y.

4pp., w/enclosure and envelope

[Perkins], Max[well E.]

TLS   3 Mar 1938, N.Y.

3pp.

[Perkins], Max[well E.]

TLS   1 July 1938,

4pp., w/newspaper clipping

[Perkins], Max[well E.]

TLS   8 Mar 1938, N.Y.

4pp.

[Perkins], Max[well E.]

TLS   18 July 1938, N.Y.

5pp.

[Perkins], Max[well E.]
Cable   21 July 1938, N.Y.
          1p.

[Perkins], Max[well E.]
Cable   [6 Nov 1938], N.Y.
          1p.

[Perkins, Maxwell E.]
Cable from Irma Wyckoff
          21 July 1938, N.Y.
          1p.

[Perkins], Max[well E.]
TLS   20 Dec 1938, N.Y.
          2pp.

[Perkins], Max[well E.]
TLS   25 July 1938, N.Y.
          3pp.

[Perkins], Max[well E.]
Cable   23 Dec 1938, N.Y.
          1p.

[Perkins], Max[well E.]
TLS   29 July 1938, N.Y.
          2pp.

[Perkins], Max[well E.]
TLS   26 Jan 1939, N.Y.
          3pp.

[Perkins], Max[well E.]
TLS   9 Aug 1938, N.Y.
          3pp.

[Perkins], Max[well E.]
TNS   3 Feb 1939, N.Y.
          1p.

[Perkins], Max[well E.]
TLS   21 Mar 1939, N.Y.
         3pp.

[Perkins], Max[well E.]
TLS   1 July 1942, N.Y.
         3pp.

[Perkins], Max[well E.]
TLS   18 Apr 1939, N.Y.
         3pp.

Perkins, Maxwell [E.]
 TLS Max
          14 July 1943, N.Y.
          4pp.

[Perkins], Max[well E.]
TLS   27 Apr 1939, N.Y.
         3pp.

Perkins, Maxwell [E.]
TLS Max
          28 July 1943, N.Y.
          4pp.

[Perkins], Max[well E.]
TNS   2 May 1939, N.Y.
         1p.

[Perkins],Max[well E.]
TLS   16 Aug 1943, N.Y.
          2pp.

[Perkins], Max[well E.]
TLS   9 Jan 1942, N.Y.
         3pp. bearing EH notes

Perkins, Maxwell E.
TLS   7 Feb 1944, N.Y.
         2pp., w/envelope

Perkins, Maxwell E.

TLS Max

28 July 1944

2pp.

Pessino, Pedro Sanchez (doctor)

TLS   24 Aug 1954, Havana

1p., w/TLS Pessino to Edward W.
Scott, 23 Aug 1954, and envelope

[Perkins], Max[well E.]

TLS   5 Sept 1945, N.Y.

2pp., w/envelope

Peterson, E. L. (reader)

TLS   13 June 1926, Windber, Pa.

5pp., w/photograph and envelope

[Perkins], Max[well E.]

TLS   23 Dec 1946, N.Y.

2pp.

Peterson, Harold S. (reader)

TLS   3 Apr 1959, Miami

1p., w/envelope bearing EH note

Perkins, Maxwell E.
    See Brague, Harry   undated
        Darrow, Whitney 16 Aug 1943
        Fitzgerald, F. Scott
            17 Aug 1926
        Reynolds, Paul 12 Aug 1929
        EH   Aug 1933

Petitclerc, Denne

TLS Denne

2 Aug 1956, Miami

2pp.

Perry, Everett R. (city librarian)

Copy of a letter

28 Jan 1933, [Los Angeles]

1p.

Petitclerc, Denne

TLS Denne

8 July 1960, San Francisco

3pp.

Pettus, Charles
          See ARC

[Pfeiffer, Gustavus A.]
TLS Uncle Gus
          18 Oct 1927, N.Y.
          1p.

[Pfeiffer, Gustavus A.]
ALS Uncle Gus
          [1927, Cherbourg], to EH/Pauline
          1p., w/envelope

[Pfeiffer, Gustavus A.]
ALS "G.A."
          20 Nov 1927, N.Y.
          6pp., w/envelope

Pfeiffer, G[ustavus] A. (Pauline's uncle)
ALS "G.A.P."
          17 Sept 1927, Homestead
          8pp.

[Pfeiffer], Gus[tavus A.]
TLS   1 Dec 1927, to Virginia Pfeiffer
          1p.

Pfeiffer, G[ustavus] A.
TLS "G.A.P."
          27 Sept 1927, N.Y.
          1p.

[Pfeiffer, Gustavus A.]
ALS Uncle Gus
          22 Jan 1928, N.Y.
          8pp., w/envelope

Pfeiffer, [Gustavus A.]
Cable   17 Oct 1927
          1p.

[Pfeiffer, Gustavus A.]
A Post Card S Uncle Gus
          7 Apr 1928, [Piggott], to EH/Pauline
          1p.

Pfeiffer, G[ustavus] A.
TLS Uncle Gus
    29 June 1928, N.Y., to EH/Pauline
    2pp., w/envelope

[Pfeiffer], Gus[tavus A.]
ALS   5 Feb 1929, On Board S.S. Majestic
    7pp., w/newspaper clipping and envelope

[Pfeiffer, Gustavus A.]
ALS "G.A.P."
    17 July 1928, N.Y.
    2pp., w/envelope bearing Pauline's notes

[Pfeiffer], Gus[tavus A.]
ALS   28 Feb 1929, N.Y.
    7pp.

Pfeiffer, G[ustavus] A.
TLS "G.A.P."
    16 Oct 1928, N.Y.
    2pp. bearing ALS Pauline, and envelope bearing EH note

Pfeiffer, G[ustavus] A.
Cable   27 Feb 1929, N.Y.
    1p.

[Pfeiffer], Gus[tavus A.]
ALS   [2 Dec 1928], Havana, to Pauline
    1p.

Pfeiffer, [Gustavus A.]
Cable   [1 Oct 1929, St. Louis]
    1p.

[Pfeiffer, Gustavus A.]
ALS "G.A.P."
    2 Dec 1928, Havana
    1p., w/photograph, enclosures, and envelope

[Pfeiffer, Gustavus A.]
A Post Card S "G.A.P."
    21 Nov 1929, Moscow
    1p.

[Pfeiffer, Gustavus A.]

TLS "G.A.P."

  7 Dec 1929, Berlin

  1p., w/envelope

[Pfeiffer], Gus[tavus A.]

TLS 3 June 1930, Paris

  1p., w/cc of letters to A. Matas
  Teixidor, 3 and 4 June 1930

[Pfeiffer, Gustavus A.]

ALS "GAP"

  13 Dec 1929, en route to ?

  3pp. bearing EH notes

Pfeiffer, [Gustavus A.]

Cable 4 June 1930

  1p.

[Pfeiffer], Gus[tavus A.]

ALS 8 Jan 1930, D. Bremen, to EH/Pauline

  2pp.

[Pfeiffer], Gus[tavus A.]

TLS 11 May 1931, N.Y.

  1p.

[Pfeiffer], Gus[tavus A.]

ALS 8 Mar 1930, Washington

  3pp.

[Pfeiffer, Gustavus A.]

TLS G. E. Esperson

  12 June and 7 July 1931, Suresnes,
  France, to Pauline

  2pp.

[Pfeiffer, Gustavus A.]

TLcc 24 Mar 1930

  1p.

Pfeiffer, Gus[tavus] A.

ALS 16 July 1931, N.Y.

  12pp.

[Pfeiffer, Gustavus A.]

TLcc   21 Oct 1931, to Dr. Don Carlos Guffey

    1p.

[Pfeiffer], Gus[tavus A.]

TLS   24 Feb 1932, N.Y.

    1p., w/enclosures

Pfeiffer, G[ustavus] A.

TLScc   21 Oct 1931, to Dr. Don Carlos Guffey

    1p., w/ALS Guffey, 16 Oct 1931, Kansas City, to GAP

[Pfeiffer], Gus[tavus A.]

TLS   1 Apr 1932, N.Y., to EH/Henry Strater/ Archibald MacLeish

    1p.

[Pfeiffer], Gus[tavus A.]

TNS   14 Dec 1931, N.Y.

    1p.

[Pfeiffer], Gus[tavus A.]

TLS   5 Apr 1932, N.Y.

    2pp.

[Pfeiffer], Gus[tavus A.]

TLS   14 Dec 1931, N.Y.

    1p., w/enclosure

[Pfeiffer], Gus[tavus A.]

TLS   14 May 1932, N.Y., to Pauline

    2pp.

[Pfeiffer], Gus[tavus A.]

TLS   5 Feb 1932, N.Y.

    1p., w/enclosures

[Pfeiffer], Gus[tavus A.]

TLS   23 May 1932, N.Y.

    1p., w/enclosure

[Pfeiffer], Gus[tavus A.]

TLS   27 Sept 1932, N.Y.

     1p.

[Pfeiffer, Gustavus A.]

Itinerary for St. Louis Trip

     15 Mar 1933

     1p.

[Pfeiffer, Gustavus A.]

TLS Adele C. Brockhoff

     7 Oct 1932, New York

     1p., w/newspaper clippings

[Pfeiffer], Gus[tavus A.]

ALS   30 Apr [1933], en Route N.Y.

     4pp.

[Pfeiffer], Gus[tavus A.]

Cable   8 Dec [1932], N.Y.

     1p.

Pfeiffer, Gustavus A.

Copy of a letter

     1 May 1933, Nearing N.Y., to Sister Emma and Al

     4pp.

[Pfeiffer], Gus[tavus A.]

TLS   9 Dec 1932

     1p., w/newspaper clipping and copy of telegram to EH, 8 Dec 1932

[Pfeiffer, Gustavus A.]

TLScc   8 May 1933, to Archibald MacLeish

     1p.

[Pfeiffer], Gus[tavus A.]

Cable   10 Dec [1932], N.Y.

     1p.

[Pfeiffer], Gus[tavus A.]

TLS   1 June 1933, N.Y.

     2pp.

[Pfeiffer], Gus[tavus A.]
TLS   20 June 1933, N.Y.
         2pp.

[Pfeiffer], Gus[tavus A.]
TLS   25 Aug 1933, N.Y.
         1p.

[Pfeiffer], Gus[tavus A.]
TNS   20 June 1933
         1p.

Pfeiffer, [Gustavus A.]
Cable   3 Oct 1933
         1p.

[Pfeiffer], Gus[tavus A.]
Cable from All the Family and Uncle Gus
         8 July 1933, Piggott
         1p.

[Pfeiffer], Gus[tavus A.]
TLS   5 Oct 1933, N.Y.
         1p.

Pfeiffer, Gustavus A.
TLS   18 July 1933, N.Y., to EH/Pauline
         1p., w/envelope

[Pfeiffer], Gus[tavus A.]
TLS   5 Oct 1933, N.Y.
         1p., w/enclosure

[Pfeiffer], Gus[tavus A.]
TLS   14 Aug 1933, N.Y.
         1p., w/newspaper clippings

[Pfeiffer], Gus[tavus A.]
TLS   23 Dec 1933, N.Y.
         5pp.

[Pfeiffer], Gus[tavus A.]

TLS   24 Jan 1934, N.Y., to Pauline

1p.

[Pfeiffer], Gus[tavus A.]

TLS   30 Apr 1934, N.Y.

2pp. bearing EH note, w/enclosure

[Pfeiffer, Gustavus A.]

TLcc   24 Jan 1934, N.Y.

3pp., w/enclosure

[Pfeiffer], Gus[tavus A.]

TLS   5 June 1934, N.Y.

4pp., w/copy of a cable from
Pfeiffer to Hemingway, 4 June
1954, and enclosure

[Pfeiffer, Gustavus A.]

TLS "G.A.P."

25 Jan 1934, N.Y.

1p.

Pfeiffer, Gustavus A.

TNS Uncle Gus

22 June 1934, N.Y.

1p.

[Pfeiffer], Gus[tavus A.]

TLS   12 Feb 1934, N.Y.

1p.

[Pfeiffer], Gus[tavus A.]

TLS   26 June 1934, N.Y.

2pp. bearing EH note

Pfeiffer, Gustavus A.

TLS Uncle Gus

12 Apr 1934, N.Y.

1p.

[Pfeiffer], Gus[tavus A.]

TLS   10 Aug 1934, N.Y.

1p.

[Pfeiffer], Gus[tavus A.]
Cable   16 Aug 1934, N.Y.

     1p.

Pfeiffer, Gustavus A.
TLS Uncle Gus

    24 Oct 1934, N.Y.

     1p.

Pfeiffer, Gustavus A.
TLS   16 Aug1934, N.Y.

    1p., w/enclosures, including copy of
cable from GAP to EH, 16 Aug 1934

Peiffer, Gustavus A.
TLS Uncle Gus

    29 Oct 1934, N.Y.

     1p.

Pfeiffer, Gustavus A.
TL   24 Aug 1934, N.Y.

    2pp.

[Pfeiffer], Gus[tavus A.]
Cable   20 Nov 1934

    1p. two copies

Pfeiffer, Gustavus A.
TLS   25 Sept 1934, N.Y.

    2pp., w/enclosure, newspaper clipping,
and envelope

Pfeiffer, Gustavus A.
TLS Uncle Gus

    23 Nov 1934, N.Y., beginning "Thanks
for your two telegrams. . .

    1p.

Pfeiffer, Gustavus A.
TLS Uncle Gus

    19 Oct 1934, N.Y.

    2pp., w/envelope bearing EH note

Pfeiffer, Gustavus A.
TLS Uncle Gus

    23 Nov 1934, N.Y., beginning "Pleased
to receive your telegram. . .

Pfeiffer, Gustavus A.
TLS Uncle Gus
27 Nov 1934, N.Y.
2pp., w/envelope bearing EH note

Pfeiffer, Gustavus A.
TLS Uncle Gus
19 Mar 1935, N.Y.
1p. bearing EH note

Pfeiffer, Gustavus A.
ALS Uncle Gus
24 Dec 1934, N.Y.
2pp.

Pfeiffer, Gustavus A.
TLS Uncle Gus
25 Mar 1935, N.Y.
2pp. bearing EH note

[Pfeiffer, Gustavus A.]
AL   26 Jan 1935, Berlin
4pp.

Pfeiffer, Gustavus A.
TLS Uncle Gus
25 Mar 1935, N.Y.
1p.

[Pfeiffer, Gustavus A.]
TLS Uncle Gus
7 Mar 1935, S.S. Bremen
2pp.

[Pfeiffer, Gustavus A.]
G. A. Pfeiffer's Itinerary Trip West
11 Apr 1935
1p., w/envelope

[Pfeiffer], Gus[tavus A.]
Cable   9 Mar 1935, N.Y.
1p.

Pfeiffer, [Gustavus A.]
Cable   30 Apr 1935, N.Y.
1p.

[Pfeiffer], Gus[tavus A.]
ALS   23 May 1935, Miami
          4pp.

Pfeiffer, Gustavus A.
TLS Uncle Gus
          21 June 1935, N.Y., to Pauline
          1p., w/newspaper clipping

Pfeiffer, Gustavus A.
TLS Uncle Gus
          27 May 1935, N.Y., beginning "Enclosed
          find draft. . ."
          1p.

Pfeiffer, Gustavus A.
TLS Uncle Gus
          12 Aug 1935, N.Y.
          2pp., w/envelope

Pfeiffer, Gustavus A.
TLS Uncle Gus
          27 May 1935, N.Y., beginning "Pair of
          Glasses"
          1p.

Pfeiffer, Gustavus A.
TLS Uncle Gus
          16 Aug 1935, N.Y.
          1p.

Pfeiffer, Gustavus A.
TLS Uncle Gus
          5 June 1935, N.Y.
          1p.

Pfeiffer, Gustavus A.
TLS Uncle Gus
          20 Aug 1935, N.Y.
          1p., w/envelope

Pfeiffer, Gustavus A.
TLS Uncle Gus
          7 June 1935, N.Y.
          1p., w/copy of letter to New York
          Times, 7 June 1935

Pfeiffer, Gustavus A.
TLS Uncle Gus
          30 Aug 1935, N.Y.
          1p.

Pfeiffer, Gustavus A.
TLS Uncle Gus

   7 Oct 1935, N.Y.
   2pp.

Pfeiffer, Gustavus A.
TLS Uncle Gus

   26 June 1936, N.Y.
   2pp.

Pfeiffer, Gustavus A.
TLS Uncle Gus

   7 Oct 1935, N.Y.
   1p.

Pfeiffer, Gustavus A.
TLS Uncle Gus

   16 July 1936, N.Y.

   1p., w/TLS Leonard Kluftinger, 2 July
   1936, to GAP, and newspaper clipping

Pfeiffer, Gustavus A.
TLS Uncle Gus

   10 Oct 1935, N.Y.
   1p., w/enclosure

Pfeiffer, Gustavus A.
TLS Uncle Gus

   28 July 1936, N.Y., to Sister Emma
   and All
   1p.

Pfeiffer, Gustavus A.
TLS Uncle Gus

   15 Oct 1935, N.Y.
   1p.

Pfeiffer, Gustavus A.
TLS Uncle Gus

   28 July 1936, N.Y., to Sister Emma
   and All
   2pp.

[Pfeiffer], Gus[tavus A.]
ALS 1 Mar 1936, D. Bremen
   9pp.

Pfeiffer, Gustavus A.
TLS Uncle Gus

   26 Aug 1936, N.Y.
   1p.

Pfeiffer, Gustavus A.
TLS Uncle Gus
      26 Aug 1936, N.Y.
      2pp.

[Pfeiffer], Gus[tavus A.]
ALS   8 Feb [1937], D. Europa
      4pp., w/envelope

Pfeiffer, Gustavus A.
TLS Uncle Gus
      26 Aug 1936, N.Y., to Sister Emma and All
      1p.

Pfeiffer, Gustavus A.
TLS Uncle Gus
      24 May 1937, N.Y.
      1p., w/enclosure

Pfeiffer, Gustavus A.
TLS Uncle Gus
      28 Aug 1936, N.Y.
      1p., w/enclosure, newspaper clipping, and envelope

[Pfeiffer], Gus[tavus A.]
Cable   21 May 1937
      1p.

Pfeiffer, Gustavus A.
TLS Uncle Gus
      8 Sept 1936, N.Y.
      1p., w/newspaper clipping

[Pfeiffer], Gus[tavus A.]
ALS   31 May 1937
      2pp.

Pfeiffer, Gustavus A.
TMemo   4 Nov 1936, N.Y.
      2pp.

[Pfeiffer], Gus[tavus A.]
TLS   25 Apr 1938
      2pp.

[Pfeiffer], Gus[tavus A.]

Cable   6 June 1938, N.Y.

      1p.

[Pfeiffer], Gus[tavus A.]

Cable from Aunt Annie, Uncle Henry, Aunt Louise, and Uncle Gus

      [25 Dec n.y.], N.Y.

      1p.

Pfeiffer, Gustavus A.

TLS Uncle Gus

      21 June 1938, N.Y.

      1p., w/envelope

Pfeiffer, Gustavus A.

Xmas Greeting

      undated

Pfeiffer, Gustavus A.

TL   2 Mar 1939, N.Y., to Louise, Sister Emma, and All

    6p., w/enclosure

Pfeiffer, Gustavus A.
    See Pauline 22 Oct 1928

[Pfeiffer], Gus[tavus A.]

Cable   13 Apr 1939, N.Y., to EH/Pauline/ Virginia Pfeiffer

      1p.

Pfeiffer, Gustavus A.
    See Samuels, Lee 5 Jan 1955
    Brockhoff, Adele C.

[Pfeiffer, Gustavus A.]

Excerpt from Letter

      3 Dec 1940

      1p.

Pfeiffer, Gustavus A.
    See also #64 and #83

[Pfeiffer], Karl   (Pauline's brother)

TLS   2 May 1933, Piggott

        1p.

Pfeiffer, [Mary A.]

TL From Mother Pfeiffer

        7 Sept [1927], Piggott

        2pp., w/TLS Karl [Pfeiffer], 2 Aug 1927,
Orange, to Father and Mother, newspaper
clipping and envelope

Pfeiffer, Karl

TLS Karl

        18 May 1933, Piggott

        1p.

[Pfeiffer, Mary A.]

TL   1 July 1928, Piggott

        1p.

Pfeiffer, Karl

ALS Karl

        18 Mar 1935, Piggott

        2pp., w/newspaper clipping

[Pfeiffer, Mary A.]   (Pauline's mother)

TLS Bro Gus

        18 Aug 1928, N.Y., to Sister Mary and
ALS Connie to Aunt Mary, 6 Sept 1928,
w/newspaper clipping and envelope
postmarked 18 Sept 1928, St. Louis and
Jonesboro R.P.O.

Pfeiffer, Karl

ALS Karl

        28 Nov 1935, Piggott

        2pp., w/envelope

[Pfeiffer, Mary A.]

TL   2 Nov [1928], Piggott, to EH/Pauline

        1p.

Pfeiffer, Karl
        See Pfeiffer, Mary 7 Sept 1927

Pfeiffer, [Mary A.]

ALS   [12 Dec 1928, Piggott]

        2pp., w/envelope

Pfeiffer, [Mary A.]

TL   4 May 1929, Piggott

     2pp.

[Pfeiffer], Mary [A.]

TL   July [1933], Piggott, to dear
     Children

     3pp., w/photographs

Pfeiffer, [Mary A.]

TL   9 Oct 1929, Piggott

     3pp., w/envelope

[Pfeiffer], Mary [A.]

TL   18 July 1934, Piggott, to dear
     Children

     3pp.

[Pfeiffer, Mary A.]

ALS Mother

     20 Jan 1930, Phoenix, to My dear
     Children

     3pp.

Pfeiffer, Mary [A.]

TL   Sept [1936],

     3pp.

Pfeiffer, [Mary A.]

TL   7 June 1932, Piggott, to Dear Children

     1p., w/envelope

[Pfeiffer], Mary [A.]

TL   18 July 1938, to dear Children

     2pp., w/tear affecting text

[Pfeiffer], Mary [A.]

TL   4 May [1933, Piggott]

     2pp., w/envelope

Pfeiffer, [Mary A.]

TLS   30 Nov 1938, Piggott

     3pp., w/envelope and check signed
     Mary A. Pfeiffer

[Pfeiffer, Mary A.]

A Post Card S Mother

      31 Jan [1930], Phoenix, to Pauline

1p.

[Pfeiffer, Paul M.]

ALS Father

      10 Mar 1929, Piggott, to dear Children

5pp., w/envelope

[Pfeiffer, Mary A.]

TL   31 Oct [1933], Piggott, to Pauline

3pp., w/envelope

[Pfeiffer, Paul M.]

ALS Father

      30 Mar 1929, Piggott, to dear Children

4pp., w/envelope

[Pfeiffer, Mary A.]

ALS Mother

      Tuesday 9 Feb n.y., Miami, to Pauline

3pp.

[Pfeiffer, Paul M.]

ALS Father

      10 July 1929, Piggott, to EH and all

5pp.

Pfeiffer, [Mary A.]

TL   12 Mar n.y., Piggott, to Pauline

3pp.

[Pfeiffer, Paul M.]

TLS Father

      14 Oct 1929, Piggott, to EH and all

1p., w/envelope

[Pfeiffer, Paul M.] (Pauline's father)

ALS Father

      1 July 1928, Piggott, to Pauline and all

4pp., w/envelope

[Pfeiffer, Paul M.]

ANS Father on TL from W. A. Sheaffer Pen Company, 10 Jan 1930, to EH

      1p., w/envelope

[Pfeiffer, Paul M.]

TLS Father

      20 May 1930, Piggott, to Dear
      Children

      2pp.

Pfeiffer, Paul M.

ALS Father

      16 Oct 1933, Piggott, to Ernest and
      all

      2pp.

Pfeiffer, Paul M.

TLS Father

      18 June 1931, Piggott, to Dear
      Children

      2pp.

Pfeiffer, Paul M.

TLS Father

      10 Dec 1934, Piggott, to Dear
      Children

      2pp.

Pfeiffer, Paul M.

TLS Father

      17 July 1933, Piggott, to Dear
      Children

      2pp.

[Pfeiffer, Paul M.]

ALS Father

      24 Feb 1935, Phoenix

      2pp.

Pfeiffer, Paul M.

TLS Father

      19 Sept 1933, Piggott, to dear
      Pauline and all

      3pp., w/envelope

Pfeiffer, Paul M.

TLS Father

      15 Nov 1937, Piggott

      2pp.

Pfeiffer, Paul M.

TLS Father

      30 Sept 1933, Piggott, to dear
      Pauline and all

      2pp.

[Pfeiffer, Paul M.]

ALS Father

      1 Mar 1938, Phoenix, to Dear
      Children

      2pp., w/envelope

Pfeiffer, Paul M.

TLS Father

    20 June 1938, Piggott, to Dear
    Children

    1p.

[Pfeiffer, Paul M.]

ALS Father

    10 F$_e$b n.y., Miami

    2pp.

Pfeiffer, [Paul M.]

Cable from Pfeiffers

        undated, Piggott

        1p.

Pfeiffer, [Paul M.]

Cable from Father, Mother, Karl and Matilda

        undated

        1p.

Pfeiffer, Robert H. (Pauline's cousin)

TLS   21 Oct 1935, Cambridge, Mass.

        1p.

[Pfeiffer, Virginia] (Pauline's sister)

ANS Gin

        [2 Nov 1926, Paris]

        1p., w/address-leaf

[Pfeiffer, Virginia]

ALS Jin

        1p., on verso of TL from Pauline to
        Jinny, 6 Nov [1926], w/envelope
        postmarked 17 Nov 1926, Paris

[Pfeiffer, Virginia]

ALS Gin

        [Dec 1926, Paris]

        1p., w/address-leaf

[Pfeiffer, Virginia]

TL   [Dec 1926, Paris]

        1p.

[Pfeiffer, Virginia]

ANS Gin

        Wednesday [21 Dec 1926, Paris]

        1p., w/address-leaf

[Pfeiffer, Virginia]
ALS Gin

[5 Aug 1929], Hendaye, to EH/
Pauline

3pp.

[Pfeiffer, Virginia]
Cable   10 Feb 1933, Kitzbuhel

1p.

[Pfeiffer, Virginia]
ALS Jinny

3 Feb [1932], Kitzbuhel, to Pauline

4pp.

[Pfeiffer, Virginia]
ALS Jinny

[late Feb 1933], Kitzbuhel

2pp., w/photograph

[Pfeiffer, Virginia]
ALS Jinny

8 Mar [1932], Kitzbuhel, Tirol, to
EH/Pauline

3pp.

[Pfeiffer, Virginia]
ALS Jinny

[25] June [1933], Piggott, to Pauline

4pp., w/envelope

[Pfeiffer, Virginia]
ALS Jinny

[17 May 1932], Piggott, to EH/
Pauline

6pp., w/envelope

[Pfeiffer, Virginia]
ALS Gin

[24 Aug 1929], Interlaken, to EH/
Pauline

2pp., w/envelope

[Pfeiffer, Virginia]
ALS J. A. Wilkin

14 Nov 1932, Watson, Arkansas, to
Virginia Pfeiffer

3pp.,bearing EH pencil notes, w/envelope
bearing EH notes

[Pfeiffer, Virginia]
ALS Jinny

27 Dec [1933], Piggott, to EH/
Pauline

3pp.

[Pfeiffer, Virginia]

TL   Monday [12 Oct 1936, N.Y.], to dear
Homs

2pp., w/envelope

[Pfeiffer, Virginia]

TL   24 Apr n.y., [Paris]

1p.

[Pfeiffer, Virginia]

Cable   7 Jan 1937, N.Y.

1p.

[Pfeiffer, Virginia]

ALS Jinny

6 Feb n.y., [N.Y.], to Dear
Travelers

3pp.

[Pfeiffer, Virginia]

ALS Jinny

[9 Feb 1937, N.Y.]

3pp., w/envelope

[Pfeiffer, Virginia]

ALS Jinny

[Aug n.y.], Cat Cay, to Mr. and Mrs.
B.F.

4pp.

[Pfeiffer, Virginia]

TL   29 Aug [1946], Rome, to MH

1p.

[Pfeiffer, Virginia]

ALS Jinny

undated, [New York], to Rajahs or
Memhibs

3pp.

[Pfeiffer, Virginia]

TLS Gin

12 Feb n.y., Hotel

2pp.

[Pfeiffer, Virginia]

TL   undated, Hotel de Fleurus [Paris],
to EH/Pauline

2pp.

[Pfeiffer, Virginia]

ALS Jinny

      26 Feb n.y., Vienna

      4pp.

[Pfeiffer, Virginia]

TL   20 Aug n.y., Piggott, to Pauline

      2pp.

[Pfeiffer, Virginia]

ALS Jinny

      30 Mar n.y., Hotel Paris Dinard, to
      EH/Pauline

      2pp.

[Pfeiffer], Virginia

ALS   Monday [N.Y.], to Mother and Father
      [Pfeiffer?]

      3pp.

[Pfeiffer, Virginia]

TL   18 Aug n.y., N.Y.

      1p.

Pfeiffer, Virginia
      See Hemingway, Pauline 15 Nov 1926
                                 18 Nov 1926

      Hemingway, Pauline to
      Virginia Pfeiffer

[Pfeiffer, Virginia]

TL Fragment?

      undated, beginning "Got all your fine
      letters. . ."

      1p.

Pflaum   (Spanish Civil War acquaintance)

TLS   undated

      1p., w/enclosures concerning Joseph
      Selligman

[Pfeiffer, Virginia]

ALS Jinny

      Sunday, Cap d'Antibes, to EH/Pauline

      1p.

Phillips, William
      See Partisan Review

Pinder, Albert
       See Lerner, Michael 6 Nov 1935

Pivano Sottsass, Fernanda (Italian translator)
TLS Nanda
       13 Dec 1949, Torino, to EH/MH
       2pp.

Pinker and Morrison (literary representatives)
TLS Frances Pindyck
       3 Dec 1934, N.Y.
       1p. bearing EH note

[Pivano Sottsass, Fernanda]
TLS Nanda
       17 June 1952, Torino
       1p., w/envelope

Pinker and Morrison
TLS Frances Pindyck
       7 Mar 1935, N.Y.
       1p.

[Pivano Sottsass, Fernanda]
Cable [27 Jan 1954, Milan]
       1p.

Pinnell, Charles H. (reader)
TNS   [24 Mar 1946], West Palm Beach, to
       EH/MH
       1p. each, w/TLS to Reader's Digest
       and newspaper clippings

Pivano Sottsass, Fernanda
TLS Nanda
       22 Apr 1959, Milano, to EH/MH
       2pp., w/enclosure

Pitt and Scott Ltd.
       See Continental Express Co.,
       8 Nov 1950

Plan
       See Curtis Brown, 11 July 1938

Planned Parenthood Federation of America
See Huxley, Sir Julian

[Plimpton], George

TLS   10 Dec 1960, N.Y.

      6pp.

Plimpton, George A. (author, editor)

TLS   [1957], Paris

      1p.

[Plimpton], George

TLS   16 Jan 1961, N.Y.

      2pp.,w/envelope bearing EH notes

[Plimpton], George

ALS   3 July 1957, N.Y.

      4pp., w/envelope

[Plimpton], George

TLS   20 Jan 1961, N.Y.

      2pp., w/envelope bearing EH note

[Plimpton], George

ALS   27 Apr 1958

      1p.

[Plimpton], George

TLS   4 Mar 1961, [N.Y.]

      2pp., w/TLScc, 4 Mar 1961, N.Y., to
Charles Scribner's & Sons, and
envelope

Plimpton, George

ALS George

      22 Oct 1959, N.Y.

      2pp.

Plimpton, George

TLS George

      undated, N.Y.

      1p.

Plummer, William L. (W.W. II friend)

TLS   12 Apr 1950, Atlanta, to EH/MH

          1p., w/newspaper clipping

[Pound], Dorothy (Ezra's wife)

ALS   18 Oct [1923], London

          1p., w/envelope

Poetry

TN   15 Jan 1923, Chicago

          1p., w/envelope

[Pound], Dorothy

ALS   22 Dec [1923, Paris]

          2pp., w/envelope

Polik, William   (congratulator)

TLS .Bill Polik

          31 Oct 1954, New York

          1p. bearing EH note

Pound, Dorothy

ALS Dorothy

          Wednesday, [8 Dec 1926], Rapallo

          1p., w/TLS Paul Rosenfeld, 24 Nov
          1928, N.Y., to Ezra Pound, and
          envelope

Poling, Alonzo (father of a member of the
              Abraham Lincoln Brigade)

ALS   13 Apr 1938, Wilburton, Oklahoma

          1p.

Pound, Dorothy

ALS Dorothy

          [1931?], Rapallo

          2pp.

Pollinger, L. E.
          See Curtis Brown
              E. Morrill Cody, 19 Jan 1934

[Pound], Dorothy

ALS   25 Apr 1933, Rapallo

          2pp., w/post card and envelope

Pound, Dorothy
ALS   15 Aug [1936], London
                1p.

[Pound, Ezra] (poet, friend)
A Post Card
                [10 Apr 1922, Siena]

[Pound], Dorothy
ALS   22   [1957], Washington
                2pp., w/envelope

[Pound, Ezra]
Invitation to tea and a showing of paintings
by Tami Koume
                [6 July 1922, Paris]
                1p., w/envelope

Pound, Dorothy
Post card bearing art work and Note S
                undated
                2pp.

[Pound, Ezra]
A Post Card S "E.P."
                [6 July 1922, Paris]

Pound, Dorothy
        See also Ezra Pound

[Pound, Ezra]
TLS "E"
                [1 Nov 1922, Paris]
                1p., w/envelope

Pound, Ezra
AN on Pound's visiting card
                [1922-1923, Paris]

[Pound, Ezra]
A Post Card S "E. & D.P."
                [20 Dec 1922, Paris], to EH/Hadley
                1p.

[Pound, Ezra]
ALS "E"
        [27 Jan 1922], Rapallo
        4pp., w/envelope

[Pound, Ezra]
A Post Card S "E"
        [23 Nov 1923, Roma]
        1p., w/envelope

[Pound, Ezra]
AL   26 Mar 1923, Rimini
        2pp.

[Pound, Ezra]
TLS "E"
        [3 Dec 1923, Paris]
        1p. bearing EH notes on verso,
        w/envelope

[Pound, Ezra]
TLS "E"
        21 Sept 1923, [Paris]
        3pp., w/envelope

[Pound, Ezra]
TLS "E.P."
        17 Dec [1923, Paris]
        1p.

[Pound, Ezra]
ANS "E"
        [25 Sept 1923, Paris]
        1p., w/ALS Bill [William Bird],
        17 Sept 1923, Venice, to Ezra

[Pound, Ezra]
TL   [1924]
        1p.

[Pound, Ezra]
TLS "E.P."
        [24 Oct 1923], Paris
        3pp., w/envelope

[Pound, Ezra]
TL   [10 June 1924, Paris]
        1p., w/envelope

[Pound, Ezra]
ALS "E.P."

31 July [1926], Paris
3pp., w/envelope

Pound, Ezra
TLS   18 Nov 1926, Rapallo
3pp., w/envelope

[Pound, Ezra]
TLS "E.P."

28 Oct 1926, [Rapallo]
1p., w/envelope

Pound, Ezra
TLS "E"

20 Nov [1926], Rapallo
1p., w/TLS "E.P.", 19 Nov 1926,
Rapallo, to [Archibald] MacLeish,
7pp., w/envelope

Pound, Ezra
TLS "E.P."

3 Nov 1926, Rapallo
6pp., w/envelope

Pound, Ezra
TLS "E"

22 Nov [1926], Rapallo
3pp., w/envelope

Pound, Ezra
TLS "E"

5 Nov [1926], Rapallo
1p., w/envelope

Pound, Ezra
TLS "E"

2 Dec [1926], Rapallo
1p., w/newspaper clipping and
envelope

Pound, Ezra
TLS "E"

8 or 9 Nov [1926], Rapallo
5pp., w/2pp. enclosure and envelope

[Pound, Ezra]
TLS "E"

[4 Dec 1926, Rapallo]
1p., w/envelope

Pound, Ezra

TL   21 Dec 1926, Rapallo

3pp.

Pound, Ezra

TLS "E.P."

            29 Jan [1927], Rapallo

            2pp., w/envelope

[Pound, Ezra]

New Year's greeting S "E.P."

            [23 Dec 1926, Rapallo]

            W/envelope

Pound, Ezra

TLS "EP"

            30 Jan [1927], Rapallo

            1p.

Pound, Ezra

TLS "E.P."

            5 Jan [1927], Rapallo

            2pp., w/newspaper clipping and
            envelope

Pound, Ezra

TLS "EP"

            11 Feb 1927, Rapallo

            3pp., w/envelope

Pound, Ezra

TLS "E"

            18 Jan 1927, Rapallo

            1p., w/envelope bearing EH note

Pound, Ezra

TLS "EP"

            15 Feb [1927], Rapallo

            2pp., w/newspaper clipping and
            envelope

[Pound, Ezra]

TLS "E"

            25 Jan [1927, Rapallo]

            2pp., w/envelope

Pound, Ezra

Post Card

            [17 Feb 1927, Rapallo]

[Pound, Ezra]

T Post Card

      11 Mar [1927, Rapallo]

Pound, Ezra

TLS "E"

      26 Dec [1927], Rapallo

    1p., w/newspaper clipping and envelope

Pound, E[zra]

TNS on ALS Maurice Darantiere

      14 Mar 1927, [Rapallo]

      2pp., w/envelope

Pound, Ezra

TLS "E"

      7 Jan 1928, Rapallo

      2pp., w/envelope

Pound, Ezra

TLS "E"

      [21 Mar 1927], Rapallo

      1p., w/envelope

Pound, Ezra

TLS "E"

      [11 Jan 1928], Rapallo

      2pp., w/envelope

[Pound, Ezra]

T Post Card

      1 Aug [1927], Rapallo

Pound, Ezra

TLS "EP"

      11 Mar 1928, Rapallo

      1p., w/envelope

[Pound, Ezra]

T Post Card

      27 Aug 1927, [Rapallo]

      2pp.

Pound, Ezra

TLS "E"

      24 July 1928, Rapallo

      1p., w/envelope

Pound, Ezra
TLS "E"
16 Jan 1929, Rapallo
1p.

[Pound, Ezra]
ALS "E"
[Summer/fall 1933], Rapallo
3pp.

Pound, Ez[ra]
TLS Ez
15 or 14 Jan [1933], Rapallo
2pp., w/envelope

Pound, E[zra]
TL   13 Aug [1933], Rapallo
2pp.

Pound, E[zra]
TLS "E"
26 Apr [1933], Rapallo
3pp., w/envelope bearing EH note

Pound, E[zra]
TLS "E"
29 Sept [1933], Rapallo
1p.

Pound, E[zra]
TLS "E"
28 Apr [1933], Rapallo
3pp.

Pound, Ez[ra]
TLS Ez
17 Nov [1933], Rapallo
2pp., w/enclosure and envelope

[Pound, Ezra]
ALS "E Z PO"
[7 Aug 1933, Siena]
3pp., w/envelope

Pound, Ezra
TLS Ez
13 and 14 Mar 1934, Rapallo
2pp.

Pound, Ez[ra]
TLS Ez

    4 Aug [1934], Rapallo
    2pp., w/envelope

[Pound, Ezra]
TL, w/ANS "D.P." [Dorothy Pound]

    7 July [1955, Washington]
    2pp., w/envelope

Pound, Ez[ra]
TLS Ez

    7 Aug [1934], Rapallo
    2pp., w/envelope

[Pound, Ezra]
TL   7 Aug 1955, [Washington]
    1p., w/envelope

Pound, Ezra
TLS Ez

    12 June 1936, Rapallo
    1p., w/envelope

[Pound, Ezra]
TLS "Ez"

    [3 July 1956, Washington]
    2pp. bearing EH note

Pound, Ezra
T Post Card

    2 Nov [1937], Rapallo

[Pound, Ezra]
TL   9 Aug [1956, Washington]
    2pp., w/envelope

[Pound, Ezra]
TL, w/ANS "D.P" [Dorothy Pound]

    16 June [1955, Washington]
    1p., w/envelope

[Pound, Ezra]
TLS "Ez"

    27 Aug [1956, Washington]
    2pp., w/envelope

[Pound, Ezra]

TLS Ez

8 Nov [1956, Washington]

1p., w/address-leaf

[Pound, Ezra]

TL   20 Sept [1957, Washington]

1p., w/address-leaf

[Pound, Ezra]

TLS Ez

[14 Apr] 1957, [Washington]

1p., w/envelope

[Pound, Ezra]

TLS Reno Odlin

20 Jan 1958, Washington

1p., containing statement by Ezra
Pound, 6 Dec 1957, and envelope

[Pound], Ezra

TLS "EP"

12 June 1957, [Washington]

1p., w/envelope

Pound, Ezra

TNS Ez on statement dated 6 Dec 1957, w/
enclosure and envelope postmarked 22 Jan 1958,
Washington

[Pound, Ezra]

TLS "E"

13 July [1957, Washington]

1p., w/envelope

[Pound], Ez[ra]

TLS   3 Apr 1958, [Washington]

2pp., w/address-leaf

[Pound, Ezra]

TLS Ez

13 Sept 1957, [Washington]

2pp., w/envelope bearing EH note

[Pound, Ezra]

TLS Ez

16 July [1958], Schloss Brunnenburg-
Tirolo

1p. bearing ANS D[orothy Pound],
w/envelope

[Pound], Ez[ra]

T Post Card S

        22 July [1958], Schloss Brunnenburg-Tirolo

        1p. bearing ANS D[orothy Pound], w/envelope bearing EH note

---

[Pound], Ez[ra]

TLS   1 Oct 1959, Rapallo

        2pp., w/envelope postmarked 30 Sept 1959

[Pound], Ez[ra]

TLS   7 Aug [1958], Schloss Brunnenburg-Tirolo

        2pp., w/envelope

[Pound], Ez[ra]

TLS   6 Sept n.y.

        1p., w/photograph

[Pound], Ez[ra]

ALS   [11 Nov 1958], Venice

        1p., w/enclosure and envelope

[Pound, Ezra]

AN bearing ANS D[orothy Pound]

        undated

        2pp.

[Pound], Ez[ra]

TLS   [10 Dec 1958, Merano]

        1p., w/envelope

[Pound, Ezra]

Copies of correspondence concerning the release of Pound from St. Elizabeth's. Originals filed elsewhere in collection

---

[Pound], Ez[ra]

TNS on envelope from TLS Dr. H. Mansbart, 5 Dec 1958, Innsbruck, to EH

        w/envelope postmarked 27 Jan 1959, Tirol

Pound, Ezra

    See Guy Hickok 20 Aug 1928
      Pound, Dorothy 8 Dec 1926
      Sandburg, Carl 4 June 1955

Pounds, Bob (reader)

TLS   16 June 1928, Angolo, Louisiana

          1p., w/envelope

Pravda
     See Olgin, M. J.

[Powell], Dawn (author, friend)

A Post Card S

          [8 May 1936, Saratoga Springs]

Preteceille, M. E. Ogier (Spanish Civil War
                            Comrade, Editorial
                            Espana)

TLS   13 Mar 1935, Madrid

          2pp.

[Powell], Dawn

TLS   [22 Feb 1944, N.Y.]

          2pp., w/envelope

Preteceille, [M. E.] Ogier

TLS   13 Mar 1937, Paris

          1p.

[Powell], Dawn

TLS   19 Nov 1952, N.Y.

          2pp. bearing EH note

Preteceille, [M. E.] Ogier

TLS   28 Apr 1937, Paris, to Luis Rubio
          Hidalgo

          1p.

[Powell, Dawn]

Name, address, and telephone number

          undated

          1p.

Preteceille, M. E. Ogier
     See also Jonathan Cape 30 Dec 1929
              Quintanilla, Luis
                            13 Mar 1937

Preteceille, [M. E.] Ogier

TLS   undated, Madrid, to Carlos J.
          Contreras

          1p., w/envelope

Putnam, Samuel
          See The New Review

Prentiss, Mark O.   (Mark Twain School Memorial
                    Committee)

TLS   12 Jan 1937, N.Y.

          1p.

Querschnitt
          See Wittner, Victor

Princeton University Library
          See Samuels, Lee 19 Dec 1950

Quinlan, Grace
          See Otis

Prio-Socarras, Carlos ?

Cable   [27 Jan 1954, New York]

          1p.

[Quintana], Juanito (aficionado, Hotel
                      Quintana)

TLS   17 June 1927, Pamplona

          2pp., w/envelope

Purwitsky, Hilda

Cable   [26 Jan 1954, Capetown]

          1p.

Quintana, Juanito

TLS   23 May 1931, Pamplona

          2pp.

[Quintana], Juanito

TLS   25 June 1931, Pamplona

           2pp., w/envelope

[Quintana], Juanito

ALS   21 Nov 1934, Pamplona

           2pp.

[Quintana], Juanito

TLS   13 July 1932, Pamplona

           3pp., w/newspaper clipping and
           photographs, and envelope

Quintana, Juanito

TLS .   30 July 1938, Toulouse

           1p.

[Quintana], Juanito

TLS   2 June 1933, Pamplona
           2pp.

Quintana, Juanito

TLS   6 Jan 1939, Toulouse

           2pp., w/envelope

[Quintana], Juanito

ALS   21 July 1933.

           3pp., w/newspaper clipping

[Quintana], Juanito

ALS   26 Apr 1954, San Sebastian

           2pp.

[Quintana], Juanito

ALS   26 June 1934, Pamplona

           2pp.

[Quintana], Juanito

TLS   20 July 1956, San Sebastian

           1p., w/newspaper clipping and
           envelope

[Quintana], Juanito

ALS   22 Sept 1959, Madrid

      2pp.

[Quintana], Juanito

ALS   14 Nov 1960, San Sebastian

      3pp., w/envelope

Quintana, Juan

Visiting card bearing ANS Juanito, w/newspaper clipping and envelope postmarked 25 Feb 1960, San Sebastian

[Quintana], Juanito

ALS   17 Dec 1960, San Sebastian

      2pp., w/envelope bearing EH notes

[Quintana], Juanito

ALS   1 Apr 1960, San Sebastian

      2pp., w/newspaper clippings and envelope bearing EH note

[Quintana, Juanito]

Newspaper clippings and envelope postmarked 29 Dec 1960, San Sebastian

[Quintana], Juanito

ALS   17 May [1960], San Sebastian

      2pp., w/envelope bearing EH note

[Quintana], Juanito

ALS   14 Jan [1961], San Sebastian

      2pp., w/newspaper clipping and envelope bearing EH note

[Quintana], Juanito

ALS   7 Oct [1960], San Sebastian

      2pp., w/ALS Juanito, 29 Oct, to Bill, TLS de V____, 4 Oct 1960, Pamplona, to Quintana, photographs, newspaper clippings, and envelope

[Quintana], Juanito

ALS   14 Feb [1961], San Sebastian

      2pp., w/envelope bearing EH notes

[Quintana], Juanito

ALS   2 July 1961, San Sebastian

2pp., w/envelope

[Quintanilla], Luis

ALS   [10 Sept 1933]

1p., w/envelope

Quintanilla, [Jose] (chief of counter-espionage in Spain)

ALS   [c. 2 May 1937]

1p.

[Quintanilla], Luis

ALS   27 July 1934

6pp. bearing art work

Quintanilla, Jose

TLS   6 Oct 1937, Valencia

1p.

[Quintanilla], Luis

Cable   22 Sept 1934, Madrid

1p., w/confirmation

Quintanilla, Jose

TLS   26 Feb 1938, Barcelona

2pp.

[Quintanilla], Luis

ALS   13 Mar [1935], Madrid

7pp., w/photograph and envelope bearing EH note

[Quintanilla], Luis (artist, friend)

ALS   30 Aug [1933]

6pp. bearing art work

[Quintanilla], Luis

ALS   30 Mar 1935, Madrid

3pp.

Quintanilla, Luis
ALS   30 Mar 1935, Madrid, "Al
marinero Hearne"
1p.

[Quintanilla], Luis
Cable   [18 Apr 1938], N.Y.
1p.

[Quintanilla], Luis
ALSFrag
[c. 12 Apr 1935]
last page only, 1p.

[Quintanilla], Luis
Cable   [29 Apr 1938], N.Y.
1p.

[Quintanilla], Luis
ALS   25 Apr 1935
4pp.

[Quintanilla], Luis
Cable from Luis Sara Gerald [Murphy]
[2 May 1938], N.Y.
1p.

Quintanilla, Luis
ANS on TLS Preteceille, [M. E.] Ojier, 13 Mar
1937, Paris, to Rafael Vidiella
1p.

[Quintanilla], Luis
ALS   18 [July 1938, N.Y.]
2pp., w/envelope

Quintanilla, [Luis]
ANS on TLS Preteceille, [M. E.] Ojier, 13 Mar
1937, Paris, to Jose Ma. Aguirre
1p.

[Quintanilla], Luis
ALS   [1938], <u>M.S. Lafayette</u>
2pp.

[Quintanilla], Luis

ALS   1 Dec [1940], Kansas City

       2pp., w/envelope

Rains Galleries
     See Smith, William H., Jr.

[Quintanilla], Luis

ALS   9 Aug [1960], Paris

       1p., w/envelope

[Rakow, William] (friend, Office of Naval Attache, Havana)

ALS Willie

       3 July 1953, Havana

       2pp., w/envelope

[Hemingway, Pauline]

TLS   [a. 22 June 1937]

       1p.

[Rakow, William]

ALS Willie

       4 Aug 1953, Havana

       3pp., w/newspaper clipping

Quintanilla, Luis
     See also Caresse Crosby   16 Sept 1931

[Rakow, William]

ALS Willie

       29 Apr 1954, Havana

       2pp., w/envelope bearing EH note and photograph

Radway, Fred (writer)

TMsS, titled "Mayday"

       Apr 1961, Nanuet, N.Y.

       9pp., w/envelope bearing EH note

[Rakow, William]

TLS Willie

       24 May 1954, Havana

       2pp., w/envelope bearing EH note

Ramsdell, Evelyn (friend)

ALS   [Dec 1919], Petoskey

           6pp., w/envlope

Ranke, Col. H. V.

                    See Perkins, 9 May 1936

[Ramsdell, Lumen] (friend)

AL   Monday [27 Dec 1920]

           4pp., w/envelope

Ratcliff, Kathryn L.   (Oak Park student)

ALS   3 Feb 1920, Oak Park

           2pp., w/envelope

[Ramsdell, Lumen]

AL   [2 Jan 1921, Petoskey]

           2pp., w/envelope

Ratero, Manuel Tamanes

Visiting card w/ANS Manuel

                    undated

                    1p.

[Ramsdell, Lumen]

TLS Doc

           21 Jan [1927], Detroit

           2pp., w/envelope

Rawlings, Marjorie Kinnan (author, friend)

TLS   1 Aug [1936], Hawthorn, Florida

           3pp., w/envelope bearing EH note

Randall, Dave (librarian)

TLS   16 June 1960, Bloomington, Indiana

           1p., w/address-leaf

R[awlings], Marjorie K[innan]

TLS   [2 Sept 1936], Hawthorn

           5pp., w/envelope

Read, Alden Calmer (Ned Calmer's daughter)

ALS   24 Feb [1957], Upper Montclair,
          N.J.

          2pp.

Rees, O. M.

          See Strater, Henry 9 Apr 1932

Redbook

          See Balmer, Edwin

Reeves, Harrison (newspaperman)

TLS   18 Oct 1937, N.Y.

          2pp.

Redman, Laura P. (EH's parents' acquaintance)

ALS   28 Nov 1926, Baltimore, to
          Clarence and Grace Hall
          Hemingway

          3pp., w/envelope

Regler, Gustav (Spanish Civil War comrade)

ALS   18 Dec 1937, Montrouge

          1p., w/envelope bearing EH note

Reed, Ysabel (Oak Park student, reader)

TLS   [8 Nov 1929, Jefferson City, Mo.]

          1p., w/envelope bearing EH note

[Regler], Gustav

ALS   [14 Apr 1938], N.Y.

          4pp., w/envelope

Rees, [O. M.] (white hunter)

Cable [27 Jan 1954, Nairobi]

          1p.

[Regler], Gustav

ALS   8 Jan 1939, Montrouge

          2pp.

[Regler], Gustav

TLS   27 Oct 1940, Mexico City

2pp., w/envelope

Reissig, Herman F.
          See North American Committee to
          Aid Spanish Democracy.

Regler, Gustav
          See Losey, Joseph 30 Mar 1938

Remenyi, Joseph (anthologist)

TLS   3 Oct 1934, Cleveland

1p.

Reilly, John R. (military man, reader)

ALS   30 June 1961, Winnetka, Ill.

2pp., w/enclosure and envelope

Remenyi, Joseph

TLS   11 Oct 1934, Cleveland

1p.

Reinheimer, Howard E. (lawyer)

TLS   18 May 1938, N.Y.

1p.,w/enclosure

Revai
          See Curtis Brown 31 Jan 1934

Reinheimer, Howard E.
          See Reynolds, Paul 21 Jan 1930

Reves, H. Fontaine

ALS   [18 May 1935, Chicago]

2pp., w/address-leaf

Reynolds, Paul R. (literary agent)

TLS   12 Aug 1929, N.Y., to Maxwell E. Perkins

      1p. bearing ANS Max

Reynolds, Paul R.
      See Fitzgerald, F. Scott
      12 Aug 1926

Reynolds, Paul R.

TLS   30 Aug 1929, N.Y.

      1p.

Reynolds, Quentin (editor, author)

Cable from Quentin Reynolds and John O'Hara

      6 Nov 1935, N.Y.

      1p.

Reynolds, Paul R.

TLS   21 Jan 1930, N.Y.

      3pp., wTLS Reinheimer, Howard E., 21 Jan 1930, N.Y., to EH, 2pp.

Reynolds, Quentin

Cable   7 Dec 1936, N.Y.

      1p.

Reynolds, Paul R.

TLS   23 June 1931, N.Y.

      1p.

[Reynolds, Quentin]

TLS Quent

      [Dec 1936], N.Y.

      2pp.

Reynolds, Paul R., Jr.

TLS   30 June 1931, N.Y.

      1p.

[Reynolds], Quent[in]

TLS   20 Jan 1939, New York

      1p.

Richards, Ira (congratulator)
ANS Ira

      29 Oct 1954, New York

      1 p. bearing EH note

[Ritz], Charles (Ritz Hotel)
TLS   19 Oct [1950], Paris

      1p. bearing EH note

Richardson, Dorothy (author)
ALS   [23] July 1924, London

     1p., w/envelope

[Ritz], Charles
TLS   [3 Feb 1951], Paris, to MH

     1p., w/enclosure

Richmond, Watts (fishing acquaintance)
TLS   28 Apr 1936, Buffalo

     1p.

[Ritz], Charles
Cable   3 Feb 1951, Paris, to MH

     1p.

Rinehart
     See Bledsoe, Thomas A.
     Hobbs, Ronald
     Samuels, Lee 22 Sept 1952

[Ritz], Charles
A Post Card S

     [23 July 1951, Lonsdal, Norway]

     bearing EH note

[Ritz, Madame Cesar]
AN on a visiting card

     [1956]

     1p.

[Ritz], Charles
TLS   [16] Oct 1951, Paris, to EH/MH

     2pp. bearing EH note

[Ritz], Charles
TLS   11 Mar 1952, Paris
             2pp. bearing EH note

[Ritz], Charles
ANS   7 Oct 1958, Paris
             1p.

[Ritz], Charles
TLS   1 Dec 1952, Paris
             2pp. bearing EH note, w/photograph

[Ritz, Charles]
Cable   [27 Oct 1959], Paris
             1p.

[Ritz], Charles
ALS   Sat [1954], Paris, to MH
             3pp.

Rivero, M. M. (travel agent, Spanish Civil
                  War patriot)
TLS   1 Jan 1938, Madrid
             1p.

[Ritz], Charles
ALS   23 Apr 1954, Paris
             2pp.

Robilant, Carlo (friend)
ALS   3 Aug 1949, Venice
             2pp., w/envelope bearing EH note

[Ritz], Charles
TLS   2 Nov 1956, Paris
             1p.

Robilant, Carlo
ALS   13 June 1950, Venice
             2pp., w/enclosures

[Robilant], Carlo

ALS   6 Feb 1951, Venice

             2pp., w/newspaper clipping and
             envelope bearing EH note

Robinson, Jimmy (<u>Sports</u> <u>Afield</u>)

TL   15 May [1958], to EH/MH

             1p., w/TLS Pat[rick Hemingway],
             24 Apr 1958, Arusha, to Jimmy,
             TLS Jack [Dow], 20 May 1958,
             Saint Paul, to Lloyd Dalzell, and
             envelope bearing EH note

[Robilant], Carlo

Cable   [25 Jan 1954, Codroipo]

             1p.

Robinson, Jimmy

TL   5 Aug [1958], Minneapolis

             1p., w/TLS Pat[rick Hemingway],
             30 July [1958], Arusha, to Jimmy,
             and envelope

Robilant, Caroline

Cable [26 Jan 1954, Bethesda, Maryland], to
       EH/MH

             1p.

Robinson, Layhmond (<u>New</u> <u>York</u> <u>Times</u>)

TLS   7 Aug 1958, N.Y.

             1p., w/newspaper clipping and
             envelope

Robin, Philip T. (driver of car for F. P.
              Stockbridge of the Wells Building?)

ALS   29 July 1921, Oakville, Ont[ario],
             to F. P. Stockbridge

             4pp., w/enclosure and envelope

Robles, Jose (Dos Passos' Spanish translator)

ALS   8 Dec 1931, Baltimore

             2pp.

Robin, Philip T.

ALS   2 Aug 1921, New York, to F. P.
             Stockbridge

             1p.

Roca & Casuso, Carlos (fishing acquaintance)

TLS   22 Apr 1935, Havana

             1p., w/photograph and envelope

Roca & Casuso, Carlos

TLS   6 May 1935, Havana

    1p.

Rodman, Selden

TLS   19 Nov 1932, N.Y.

    1p.

Roces,

    See Ivens, Joris   undated

Rodman, Selden

ANS   13 Apr 1959, Oakland

    1p., w/enclosures

Rodell, Marie F.

    See Brague, Harry   8 May 1959

Rodriguez, Jose   (Pilar crewman)

ALS   1 Sept 1936, Miami

    3pp.

Rodman, Selden   (author, editor)

ALS   9 Mar 1932, Paris

    1p.

Rodriguez, Jose

ALS   18 Sept 1936, Miami

    1p.

Rodman, Selden

TLS   9 Aug 1952, Oakland, N.J.

    1p., w/copy of Selden's letter to
    Lillian Ross, 8 Aug 1952

Rodriguez, Jose

ALS   5 Oct 1936, Miami, to MH

    2pp.

Roeder, Ralph (League of American Writers)
TLS   28 Nov 1938, N.Y.
             1p. bearing EH notes

Rohrbach, [Henri and Marie] (femme de manage)
ALS H. Rohrbach
             26 Dec 1926, Paris, to EH, Pauline,
             and Bumby
             1p., w/envelope

Roeder, Ralph
TLS   1 Mar 1939, N.Y.
             1p.

Rohrbach, [Henri and Marie]
A Post Card S Tonton and Marie Cocotte
             [11 Aug 1927], Mur, to Bumby

Rogers, Hubert (artist, reader Toronto
                         acquaintance)
TLS   13 July 1934, Santa Fe
             1p.

[Rohrbach, Henri and Marie]
A Post Card S Tonton and Marie
             undated, Mur, to Hadley

[Rogers, William P.] (Deputy Attorney General)
Copy of a letter
             10 Apr 1957, Washington, to EH
             [Robert] Frost, and [T.S.] Eliot
             1p.

[Rolfe], Ed[win] (Spanish Civil War colleague)
TLS   5 June 1953, Los Angeles
             1p.

Rohm, Bob (fishing acquaintance)
Cable   20 Mar 1936, Miami Beach
             1p. bearing EH draft reply

Rolnicke noviny (Czechoslovakian newspaper)
    See Svetova Literatura

Romaine, Paul (Cassanova Bookseller)

TLS   11 Dec 1931, Milwaukee
                2pp.

Roman, Erl

TLS Erl
                19 Aug 1936, Miami
                1p.

Romaine, Paul

Cable   3 Jan 1932, Milwaukee
                1p.

Roman, Erl

TLS Erl
                28 Sept 1936, Miami
                1p.

Romaine, Paul

TLS   27 June 1932, Milwaukee
                1p.

[Roman, Erl]

"Angler's Notes" by Erl Roman, newspaper
clipping, undated

Roman, Erl (editor, fisherman)

TL   27 May 1935, Miami
                1p.

Romm, W. (Izvetia)

TLS   29 July 1934, N.Y.
                1p.

[Roman], Erl

TLS   29 Aug 1935, N.Y.
                1p., w/TLS Mrs. Oliver C. Grinnel,
                27 Aug 1935, N.Y.

Roosevelt, Eleanor (First Lady, stateswoman)

ALS   28 Feb [1940], Golden Beach
                1p., w/envelope

Root, Waverley Lewis (newspaperman)

TLS   17 June 1927, [Paris]

             1p., w/envelope

[Ross], Lillian (author, friend)

TLS   16 and 17 June 1949

             3pp.

Rorty, James
          See New Masses

[Ross], Lillian

TLS   14 July 1949

             2pp. bearing EH note

Rose, W. K.
          See Brague, Harry 3 Feb 1961

Ross, Lillian

Cable   20 July [1949], N.Y.

             1p.

Rosenfeld, Paul
          See The American Caravan
          See Pound, Dorothy 8 Dec 1926

[Ross], Lillian

TLS   27 July 1949

             2pp.

Ross, [Harold] (The New Yorker)

Cable   [26 Sept 1929], New York, to
               Dorothy Parker

             1p.

[Ross], Lillian

TLS   1 Aug 1949

             1p.

[Ross], Lillian

TLS   5 Aug 1949

             2pp. bearing EH note, w/newspaper
             clipping

[Ross], Lillian

TLS   14 Sept 1949

             2pp. bearing EH note, w/ALS
             Robert S. Klein, undated, Madrid,
             to Ross

[Ross], Lillian

TLS   11 Aug 1949

             1p. bearing EH note

[Ross], Lillian

TLS   24 Sept 1949

             2pp. bearing E^H note

[Ross], Lillian

TLS   15 Aug 1949

             3pp. bearing EH note, w/newspaper
             clipping

[Ross], Lillian

TLS   3 Oct 1949

             2pp.

[Ross], Lillian

TLS   16 Aug 1949

             1p., w/newspaper clippings

[Ross], Lillian

TLS   14 Oct 1949, [N.Y.]

             2pp., w/envelope bearing EH notes

[Ross], Lillian

TLS   24 Aug 1949

             4pp. bearing EH note

[Ross], Lillian

TLS   24 Oct 1949

             1p. bearing EH note, w/newspaper
             clipping

[Ross], Lillian

TLS   29 Oct 1949

      2pp. bearing EH note

[Ross], Lillian

A Post Card S

      [12 Mar 1950], Hollywood by the Sea, Florida

      1p. bearing EH note

[Ross], Lillian

TLS   31 Oct 1949

      1p. bearing EH note, w/enclosure

[Ross], Lillian

TLS   22 Mar 1950

      2pp. bearing EH note

[Ross], Lillian

TLS   9 Nov 1949

      1p. bearing EH note

[Ross], Lillian

TLS   14 Apr 1950

      2pp. bearing EH note , w/TN from Walter Bernstein

[Ross], Lillian

TLS   7 Dec 1949

      1p. bearing EH note

[Ross], Lillian

TLS   17 Apr 1950

      1p. bearing EH note

[Ross], Lillian

TLS   14 Dec 1949

      1p. bearing EH note

[Ross], Lillian

TLS   22 Apr 1950

      3pp. bearing EH note

[Ross], Lillian

TLS   26 Apr 1950

            1p.

[Ross], Lillian

TLS   20 June 1950, [N.Y.]

            2pp. bearing EH note

[Ross], Lillian

TLS   5 May 1950, [New York]

            2pp. bearing EH note

[Ross], Lillian

TLS   29 June 1950

            2pp. bearing EH note

[Ross], Lillian

TL^S 12 May 1950

            1p.

[Ross], Lillian

TL^S 6 July 1950

            2pp. bearing EH note, w/photograph

[Ross], Lillian

TLS   29 May 1950

            3pp. bearing EH note

[Ross], Lillian

TLS   14 July 1950, to MH

            1p.

[Ross], Lillian

TLS   12 June 1950

            2pp. bearing EH note

[Ross], Lillian

TLS   20 July 1950

            2pp., w/birthday greeting

[Ross], Lillian

TLS Hopalong Lillian

8 Aug 1950, Beverly Hills

3pp. bearing EH note

[Ross, Lillian]

TLS Hotspur

28 Oct 1950, Beverly Hills

3pp., w/envelope bearing EH note

[Ross], Lillian

TLS   17 Aug 1950, Beverly Hills

2pp.

[Ross], Lillian

TLS   11 Nov 1950

2pp. bearing EH note

[Ross], Lillian

ANS   Sat [17 Aug 1950], Beverly Hills

1p., w/photographs

[Ross], Lillian

TLS   9 Dec [1950], Beverly Hills

3pp., w/photograph

[Ross], Lillian

TLS   4 Sept 1950, Beverly Hills

2pp. bearing EH note

[Ross], Lillian

TLS   18 Dec 1950

3pp.

[Ross], Lillian

TLS   17 Oct 1950, [Los Angeles]

2pp., w/envelope bearing EH note

[Ross], Lillian

TLS   10 Jan 1951, [Hollywood]

2pp. bearing EH note

[Ross], Lillian

TLS   14 Feb 1951, [Beverly Hills]

2pp. bearing EH note

[Ross], Lillian

TLS   10 July 1951

2pp. bearing EH note, w/photograph
and newspaper clipping

[Ross], Lillian

TLS   23 Apr 1951, Beverly Hills

3pp. bearing EH note

[Ross], Lillian

TLS   24 Sept 1951, [Los Angeles]

3pp. bearing EH note

[Ross], Lillian

TLS   24 Apr 1951, [Beverly Hills]

2pp. bearing EH note

[Ross], Lillian

TLS   19 Nov 1951, [New York]

1p. bearing EH note

[Ross], Lillian

TLS   21 May 1951, [Beverly Hills]

2pp. bearing EH note

[Ross], Lillian

TLS   18 Dec 1951

2pp. bearing EH note

[Ross], Lillian

TLS   6 June 1951, [Beverly Hills]

2pp. bearing EH note, w/photographs

[Ross], Lillian

TLS   29 Feb 1952

2pp. bearing EH note

[Ross], Lillian

TLS 24 Mar 1952

    1p. bearing EH note

[Ross], Lillian

A Post Card S

    [19 July 1952], Aspen

    bearing EH note

[Ross], Lillian

TLS 24 Apr 1952

    2pp. bearing EH note

[Ross], Lillian

ALS 15 Aug 1952, Aspen

    1p.

[Ross], Lillian

TLS 16 June 1952

    2pp. bearing EH note

[Ross], Lillian

ALS 19 Aug 1952, Aspen

    2pp. bearing EH note

[Ross], Lillian

TLS 24 June 1952, to MH

    1p.

[Ross], Lillian

ALS 29 Aug 1952, Aspen

    2pp. bearing EH note

[Ross], Lillian

TLS 24 June 1952

    1p. bearing EH note

[Ross], Lillian

TLS 18 Nov 1952

    2pp. bearing EH note

[Ross], Lillian

TLS   19 Nov 1952

             1p. bearing EH note

[Ross], Lillian

TLS   19 Jan 1953

             1p. bearing EH note

[Ross], Lillian

TLS   2 Dec 1952, [N.Y.]

             1p. bearing EH note

[Ross], Lillian

TLS   27 Jan 1953, to MH

             1p., bearing MH notes

[Ross], Lillian

TLS   3 Dec 1952

             2pp. bearing EH note

[Ross], Lillian

TLS   14 Jan 1954, to EH/MH

             2pp.

[Ross], Lillian

TLS   9 Dec 1952

             1p. bearing EH note, w/newspaper
             clipping

[Ross], Lillian

TLS   25 Jan 1954, to EH/MH

             1p. bearing MH notes

[Ross], Lillian

TLS   11 Jan 1953, [New York]

             2pp. bearing EH note

[Ross], Lillian

TLS   26 Jan 1954, to EH/MH

             1p.

[Ross], Lillian

TLS   28 Mar 1955, to EH/MH

      2pp.

Ross, Lillian

      See Rodman, Selden   9 Aug 1952

[Ross], Lillian

TLS   14 Apr 1955, to EH/MH

      2pp.

Rottenburger, Joseph   (congratulator)

TLS   2 Nov 1954, New York

      1p. bearing EH note

[Ross], Lillian

TLS   6 Feb 1957, to EH/MH

      1p.

Rousseau, Theodore

      See Mencken, H. L.   14 Mar 1928

[Ross], Lillian

TLS   17 Nov 1958

      1p.

Roux, Christian

ALS   5 Mar 1958, Lyon

      2pp., w/ALS C. Roux, to MH, and envelope

[Ross], Lillian

TLS   [18 Nov 1958], to EH/MH

      1p.

Roux, Christian

TLS C. Roux

      20 Apr 1956, Lyon

      2pp., w/ALS C. Roux, to MH, 2pp., w/envelope

[Rowe], Reggie (friend)

TLS   [1955], San Miguel Allende, to EH/
          MH

          1p.

Rowohlt [Verlag]

Cable   12 Apr 1932, Berlin

          1p.

Rowell, George P.
         See American Red Cross

Rowohlt Verlag

Statement

          30 July 1936, Berlin

          1p.

Rowohlt Verlag

Cable   [21 Oct 1920], Berlin

          2pp.

Rowohlt Verlag

TLS Ernest Rowohlt

          8 Oct 1936, Berlin

          1p.

Rowohlt [Verlag]

Cable   [21 Oct 1929], Berlin, to Dr. Goll

          1p.

Rowohlt Verlag

Cable   [25 Jan 1954, Hamburg]

          1p.

Rowohlt Verlag

TLS Ernst Rowohlt

          28 Dec 1931, Berlin

          1p.

Rowohlt Verlag
         See Baker, Carlos   6 Dec 1959

Ruark, Robert (columnist, friend)

TLS Bob

3 Nov 1954, Palamos

1p., w/envelope bearing EH note

Rudge, Olga

See Pound, Ezra 17 Nov 1933

Ruark, Robert

TNS Bob

3 Nov [1954], Palamos

1p., w/typescript of Timely One,
3pp., and envelope bearing EH note

Russell, Ena Grunewald (daughter of Henry the
Dutchman Grunewald)

Cable   15 June 1960, Washington

1p.

Rubboli, Sandro

TLS   28 Dec 1954, Milan

1p., w/envelope

Russell, Peter (editor)

TLS   11 Mar 1950, London

1p. bearing EH note, w/address-leaf

Rubinstein Nash & Co.

See Jonathan Cape 5 Oct 1938

Rutherford, Hugo (sport fisherman)

TLS   15 Sept 1934, Allamuchy

1p.

Rudge, Olga (pianist, Ezra Pound's friend)

ALS   13 Mar 1950, Siena

14pp., w/enclosure

Rutherford, Hugo

See Blixen, Eva Von

Saez-Gonzalez, Juan Manuel (reader)

TLS   3 Oct 1956, Madrid

           1p., w/photograph and envelope
           bearing EH notes

[Sampson, Harold H.] (friend)

ALS Sam

              10 Sept 1918, Dallas

              4pp., w/envelope

Saint-Gaudens, Homer
          See Peirce, Waldo 3 Dec 1934

[Sampson, Harold H.]

TLS Sam

              8 Apr 1932, Birmingham, Alabama

              1p.

Salinger, J. D. (author)

TLS Jerry Salinger

          [27 July 1946, Nurnberg]

          2pp., w/envelope

Samuels, Lee (bibliographer, collector)

TLS "L.S."

              4 May 1950, Havana

              1p. bearing EH note

Salon d'Automne
          See Peirce, Waldo 11 Feb 1930

Samuels, Lee

ALS "L.S."

              Friday [16 June 1950], Havana

              1p. bearing EH note

Salt Water Anglers of America
          See Roman, Erl

Samuels, Lee

TLS Lee

              8 Nov 1950, N.Y.

              1p. bearing EH note

Samuels, Lee

TLS Lee

17 Nov 1950, N.Y.

1p. bearing EH note

Samuels, Lee

TLS Lee

5 Apr 1951, N.Y.

1p. bearing EH note, w/copy of a
letter from Herbert Cahoon, 3 Apr
1951, N.Y., to Samuels, and copy of
a letter from Lewis M. Stark,
3 Apr 1951, N.Y., to Samuels

Samuels, Lee

TLS Lee

19 Dec 1950, N.Y.

1p. bearing EH note, w/copy of
letter from Julian P. Boyd, 15 Dec
1950, Princeton, to Samuels

Samuels, Lee

TLS Lee

1 May 1951, N.Y.

1p. bearing EH note

Samuels, Lee

TLS "LS"

2 Jan 1951, N.Y.

1p. bearing EH note, w/copy of a
letter from Ralph A. Beals, 29 Dec
1950, N.Y., to Samuels

Samuels, Lee

TLS Lee

14 May 1951, N.Y.

1p. bearing EH note

Samuels, Lee

ANS "L"

[6 Feb 1951], Havana

1p. bearing EH note, w/newspaper
clippings

Samuels, Lee

ALS "L"

6 Aug [1951], Havana

1p., w/enclosures and envelope

Samuels, Lee

TLS Lee

3 Apr 1951, N.Y.

1p. bearing EH note

Samuels, Lee

ANS "L"

Monday [12 Nov 1951], Havana

1p. bearing EH note

Samuels, Lee
ALS "L"

20 Mar [1952], Havana

1p. bearing EH note

Samuels, Lee
TLS "L"

30 Oct 1952, N.Y.

1p. bearing EH note

Samuels, Lee
ANS "L"

31 July [1952], Havana

1p. bearing EH note, w/enclosures

Samuels, Lee
ANS "L"

Saturday [22 Nov 1952], Havana

1p. bearing EH note , w/enclosure

Samuels, Lee
TLS Lee

4 Sept 1952, N.Y.

1p. bearing EH note

Samuels, Lee
TLS

26 Mar 1953, Havana

1p. bearing EH note, w/TLS Bertin
Perez, 25 Mar 1953, Havana, to
Samuels

Samuels, Lee
TLS "L"

22 Sept 1952, N.Y.

1p. bearing EH note, w/TLcc from
Samuels to Rinehart & Co., 22 Sept
1952

Samuels, Lee
TLS Lee

5 Jan 1955, Havana

1p., w/copies of letters and
documents concerning the will of
Gustavus A. Pfeiffer

Samuels, Lee
ALS "L"

25 Sept [1952], N.Y.

1p. bearing EH note

Samuels, Lee
TLS "L"

6 Sept 1957, Havana

1p., w/enclosure

Samuels, Lee
TLS "L"

        19 Sept 1957, Havana

        1p.

[Samuels, Lee]
TLS "L"

        9 Jan 1961, Hollywood, to EH/MH

        1p.

Samuels, Lee
ANS "L"

        [Dec 1958], Havana

        1p., w/copy of TLS Marstan [Drake],
        12 Dec 1958, London, to Samuels,
        and envelope bearing EH note

[Samuels], Lee
TLS   3 Mar 1961, Hollywood, to EH/MH

        3pp., w/envelope bearing EH note

Samuels, Lee
TLS Lee

        30 Apr 1959, Havana

        1p.

[Samuels, Lee]
List of EH books and articles

        undated

        8pp.

[Samuels], Lee
TLS   11 Sept [1960], Hollywood, Florida

        1p. bearing EH note

Samuelson, Arnold (writer, companion on _Pilar_)
TLS Arnold

        [15 May 1935], Minneapolis

        1p., w/envelope

[Samuels, Lee]
TLS "L"

        [1961], Hollywood, Florida

        1p.

[Samuelson], Arnold
TLS   [8 Aug 1935], Minneapolis

        1p., w/envelope

[Samuelson], Arnold
ALS   [19 Aug 1935], White Earth, N.D.
             6pp., w/envelope

[Samuelson], Arnold
ALS   undated
             2pp.

[Samuelson], Arnold
TLS   [30 Oct 1935], Minneapolis
             1p., w/envelope

Sanborn, Paul C. (sport fisherman)
TLS Paul
             23 July 1936, Boston
             1p.

[Samuelson], Arnold
TLS   [28 Apr 1936], Minneapolis
             1p., w/envelope

[Sanchez], Gracielita   (congratulator)
ALS Gracielita
             30 Oct 1954, Isla de Pinos, Cuba
             2pp. bearing EH and MH notes

[Samuelson], Arnold
TL   26 July [1936], Minneapolis
             1p., w/envelope

[Sanchez], Julio (sportsman, friend)
ALS   22 Dec [1936]
             2pp.

[Samuelson], Arnold
TN   [23 Jan 1937], Minneapolis
             1p., w/envelope

Sanchez, Thorvald (sportsman, friend)
TLS   12 Feb 1935, Havana
             2pp.

Sanchez, Thorvald

ALS   undated, Havana

             1p.

[Sanford, James S.]   (Ernest's nephew
                       Marcelline's son)

ALS Jim

             31 July 1951, Great Lakes, Ill.

             2pp. bearing EH note

[Sandburg], Carl   (poet, author)

ANS   1p., w/Typescript "Carl Sandburg
             for the Producer's Showcase Over-
             seas Press Club, NBC, Dec 13, 1954"
             and tearsheets from Poetry of his
             essay on Ezra Pound, w/envelope
             postmarked 4 June 1955, Flat Rock,
             N.C.

Sanford, John E.   (EH's nephew, Marcelline's son)

TLS   13 Apr 1952, New Haven, Conn.

             3pp. bearing EH note

Sanders, Ros   (friend)

A Post Card S

             11 June [1929, Vienna]

[Sanford, Marcelline HEMINGWAY]   (sister)

A Post Card S Marc Ivory

             [6 Sept 1917, Oak Park]

             1p.

Sandomierska, Adam Tarn   (translator)

Cable   17 Dec 1955, Warsaw

             1p.

[Sanford, Marcelline HEMINGWAY]

A Post Card S "The Iverian"

             [18 Sept 1917], Oberlin, Ohio

[Sanford], Carol   (Ernest's niece, Marcelline's
                    daughter)

ALS   [2 June 1932, Detroit]

             1p., w/enclosure and envelope

[Sanford], Marc[elline HEMINGWAY]

ALS   [12 Oct 1917], Oberlin

             4pp., w/envelope

[Sanford, Marcelline HEMINGWAY]
ALS Ivory

        11 May 1918, [Oak Park]

        2pp., w/envelope

[Sanford], Marc[elline HEMINGWAY]
ALS   24 Oct 1918, Chicago

        8pp., w/envelope

[Sanford], Marcelline [HEMINGWAY]
ALS Ivory Marcelline

        5 July 1918, Oak Park

        8pp.

[Sanford], Marcelinne [HEMINGWAY]
ALS   25 Nov 1918, Chicago

        4pp., w/envelope

[Sanford], Marcelline [HEMINGWAY]
A Post Card S

        27 July 1918, Williams Bay, Wisc.

[Sanford], Marc[elline HEMINGWAY]
ALS   2 Jan 1919, Oak Park

        8pp., w/envelope

[Sanford], Marc[elline HEMINGWAY]
ALS Marc/Iverian

        [24 Aug 1918], Oak Park

        12pp., w/envelope

[Sanford], Marc[elline HEMINGWAY]
ALS Marc

        17 May [1921], Winnetka, Ill.

        2pp., w/envelope postmarked
Evnaston, Ill.

[Sanford], Marc[elline HEMINGWAY]
ALS   2 Oct 1918, Chicago

        8pp., w/envelope, w/art work

[Sanford], Marcelline [HEMINGWAY]
Cable   23 July 1921, Portsmouth, N.H.

        1p.

[Sanford], Marcelline [HEMINGWAY]

ALS   16 Aug 1921, Concord, N.H.

        6pp., w/envelope

SANFORD, Marcelline [Hemingway]

ALS Marcelline

        25 Sept [1925], Detroit, to Hadley/ Bumby

        2pp., w/photograph and envelope

[SANFORD, Marcelline Hemingway]

Newspaper clippings on Marcelline's wedding

        [Jan 1923]

[SANFORD], Marcelline [Hemingway]

ALS   7 Feb 1927, Detroit

        4pp., w/envelope

[SANFORD], Marc[elline Hemingway]

ALS   20 Oct [1923], Oak Park

        2pp., w/envelope

[SANFORD], Marc[elline Hemingway]

ALS Marc

        20 Feb [1928], Detroit, to EH/ Pauline

        4pp., w/newspaper clipping and envelope

SANFORD, [Marcelline Hemingway]

ALS Mazween

        17 Dec 1923, Detroit, to Hadley

        2pp., w/envelope

[SANFORD], Marc[elline Hemingway]

A Post Card S

        14 June 1928, 20 hours out from Cherbourg

        W/envelope

SANFORD, Marcelline [Hemingway]

ALS   4 Jan 1924, Detroit, to EH/Hadley

        2pp., w/ALS Sunny, 4 Jan [1924], Detroit, to EH/Hadley/Bumby, and photographs and envelope

---

SANFORD, Marcelline Hemingway

ALS Masween

        2 July 1928, Saint Jean de Luz

        4pp., w/envelope

[SANFORD], Marcelline [Hemingway]

ALS   3 Jan [1930], Detroit

           5pp., w/envelope

SANFORD, Marc[elline Hemingway]

ALS Marc

           17 June [1935], Detroit

           2pp., w/photographs and envelope

[SANFORD, Marcelline Hemingway]

ALS "MHS"

           2 Jan 1933, Oak Park, to EH/
           Pauline

           4pp., w/envelope

SANFORD, Marc[elline Hemingway]

ALS   8 Jan 1937, Detroit

           2pp., w/envelope

[SANFORD], Marcelline Hemingway

ALS   20 Dec [1933], Oak Park, to EH/
           Pauline

           3pp., w/envelope

[SANFORD], Marcelline Hemingway

ALS   9 Sept 1943, River Forest, Ill.

           2pp.

[SANFORD], Marcelline [Hemingway]

ALS   31 Aug 1934, Detroit

           8pp., w/photographs and envelope

SANFORD, Marcelline [Hemingway]

ALS   7 Apr 1945, Grosse Point Farms,
           Michigan

           4pp., w/envelope

[SANFORD], Marcelline [Hemingway]

ALS   26 Dec [1934, Detroit], to EH/
           Pauline

           4pp., w/envelope

[SANFORD, Marcelline Hemingway]

ANS MHS

           9 Oct 1950, Grosse Point Farms

           1p. bearing EH note, w/newspaper
           clipping

SANFORD, Marcelline [Hemingway]

ALS   21 Jan 1951, Grosse Point Farms,
to MH

2pp.

SANFORD, Marcelline [Hemingway]

ALS   21 July 1954, Petoskey

2pp., w/envelope bearing EH note

[SANFORD], Marcelline [Hemingway]

ALS   2 Oct 1951, Grosse Point Farms

1p., w/envelope

[SANFORD], Marcelline [Hemingway]

ANS   [22 Mar 1955, Grosse Point]

1p., on Post Card from James
D. Realty, 15 Mar 1955, St.
Petersburg, to Grace H.
Hemingway

[SANFORD], Marcelline [Hemingway]

TLS   26 Jan 1952, Grosse Point Farms

2pp. bearing EH note, w/newspaper
clipping

SANFORD, Marcelline [Hemingway]

ALS   10 Jan 1961, Grosse Pointe

2pp., w/envelope

[SANFORD], Marcelline [Hemingway]

TLS   5 Sept 1952, Petoskey

1p. bearing EH note

[SANFORD, Marcelline Hemingway]

ALS Sterling [Sanford]

17 Jan 1974, Grosse Pointe, to MH

1p.

SANFORD, Marcelline Hemingway

ALS Marc

23 Dec 1952, Grosse Point Farms

2pp. bearing EH note

[SANFORD], Marcelline [Hemingway]

ALS   undated [1930's]

2pp.

SANFORD, Marcelline [Hemingway]

ALS   30 Jan [1930's], Detroit, to EH/ Pauline

        2pp., w/envelope

Sargint, [H. J. J.] (North American Newspaper Alliance)

Cable   [18 Mar 1937], London

        1p.

[SANFORD], Marcelline [Hemingway]

ALS   undated, Chicago

        4pp.

Sargint, [H. J. J.]

Cable   [12 Apr 1937], London

        1p.

[SANFORD, Marcelline Hemingway]

    Photograph

Sargint, [H. J. J.]

Cable   [16 Apr 1937], London

        1p.

Sanford, Marcelline Hemingway
    See Hemingway, Leicester
    Summer 1938

Sargint, [H. J. J.]

Cable   20 Apr 1937, London

        1p.

Saragat, Giuseppe

Cable   [26 Jan 1954, Rome]

        1p.

Sargint, [H. J. J.]

Cable   [1 May 1937], London

        1p.

Sargint, [H. J. J.]
Cable   [10 May 1937], London
          1p.

Sargint, [H. J. J.]
Cable   15 Apr 1938, London
          1p.

Sargint, H. J. J.
TLS   23 Aug 1937, London
          2pp.

Sargint, [H. J. J.]
Cable   19 Apr 1938, London
          1p.

Sargint, H. J. J.
TLS   24 Aug 1937, London
          1p.

Sargint, [H. J. J.]
Cable   24 Apr 1938, London 29 24 2354
          1p.

Sargint, H. J. J.
TLS   1 Sept 1937, London
          1p.

Sargint, [H. J. J.]
Cable   24 Apr 1938, London   25 24 0725
          1p.

Sargint, [H. J. J.]
Cable   [8 Apr 1938], London
          1p.

Sargint, [H. J. J.]
Cable   [29 Apr 1938], London
          1p.

Sargint, [H. J. J.]

Cable   [9 May 1938], London

        1p., 2 copies

Saroyan, [William]

TLS Bill Saroyan

        18 Jan 1936, San Francisco

        4pp.

Sargint, [H. J. J.]

Cable   [10 May 1938], London

        1p.

Saturday Evening Post

Cable from W. T. Martin

        9 Mar 1938, Philadelphia

        1p.

Sargint, [H. J. J.]

Cable   [11 May 1938], London

        1p.

Saturday Review

      See Canby, Henry Seidel

Saroyan, W[illiam]

TLS   16 Dec 1934, San Francisco

        5pp.

[Savage], C. Bayley (friend)

ALS   4 July 1918, Oak Park

        11pp., w/envelope

Saroyan, W[illiam]

TLS   2 Jan 1935, San Francisco

        5pp.

Savage, C. Bayley

Cable   25 Sept 1935, Miami

        1p.

Savage, J. S.

Cable   12 July 1938, Cleveland

               1p.

[Saviers], George

ALS George and Pat

               Tuesday [13 June 1961], Denver

               1p., w/envelope bearing EH note

[Saviers], George (friend, doctor)

TLS   14 June 1960, Sun Valley, to EH/MH

               1p.

Saviers, George
               See Lanham, Buck 2 Jan 1961

[Saviers], George

ALS   22 July [1960], Sun Valley, to EH/
               MH

               2pp.

[Saxon], Don (U.S. Naval Liaison Office)

TLS   29 June 1943, Nuevitas

               1p.

Saviers, George

TLS George

               6 Sept 1960, Sun Valley, to MH

               1p.

Schafer, Ned
               See Farrington, Selwyn K.
               27 July 1936
               See Lerner, Michael
               30 July 1937

[Saviers], George

Cable   13 Jan 1961, Sun Valley

               1p.

Schauer, Konrad
               See Strater, Henry 24 Feb 1932
               3 Mar 1932
               8 Apr 1932

Scheer, Pearl and Fred

Xmas greeting from Pearl, Fred Scheer and the Boys

      undated

[Schneider], Isidor

ALS   [11 June 1926, N.Y.]

     5pp., w/envelope bearing EH note, and newspaper clipping

---

Schlesinger, Eleanor

Cable   18 June 1928, Port Washington, N.Y.

     1p.

[Schneider], Isidor

ALS   [5 Aug 1926, N.Y.]

     6pp., w/photograph, newspaper clipping and envelope bearing EH note

---

Schlesinger, Eleanor

Cable   22 June 1928, Port Washington

     1p.

[Schneider], Isidor

ALS   [Nov 1926]

     5pp.

Schneck, Jerome M. (reader, doctor)

TLS   11 Apr 1960, N.Y.

     1p.

[Schneider], Isidor

ALS   [8 Mar 1927, N.Y.]

     2pp., w/envelope

[Schneider], Isidor (Boni & Liveright, friend)

ALS   [8 Apr 1926, N.Y.]

     2pp., w/envelope

Schneider, Isidor

     See also Boni & Liveright

Schoenthal, Inge
Cable   [29 Jan 1954, Rio de Janeiro]
        1p.

Schwartzman, William   (shipmate)
ALS   23 June 1938, Miami Beach
        3pp.

Schrank, Robert   (newspaperman)
ALS Bob Schrank
        19 Jan 1961, Minneapolis
        1p.

Schwary, Didier
                    See Agence Litteraire
                        Internatione

Schutz Forlag
TLS Herman Wolsgaard Iversen
        29 Apr 1936, Copenhagen
        1p.

Scott, Edward W.
                See Pessino, Pedro Sanchez

[Schutz Forlag]
Cable from J. H. Schultz
        [26 Jan 1954, Copenhagen], to EH/MH
        1p.

Scribner, Charles, [Sr.] (publisher, friend)
TLS   31 Mar 1933, N.Y.
        1p., w/envelope

Schwartz, Jerome   (Key Books)
TLS   23 Dec 1953, N.Y.
        1p.

Scribner, Charles, [Sr.]
TLS Charlie
        1 Sept 1936, N.Y.
        1p.

[Scribner, Charles, Sr.]
ALS Charlie

[Dec 1940]

4pp.

Scribner, Charles, [Sr.]
ALS Charlie

28 Aug 1948, Far Hills

6pp.

Scribner, Charles, [Sr.]
ALS Charlie

[10 Sept 1945], Far Hills, N.J.

6pp., w/envelope

Scribner, Charles, [Sr.]
TLS Charlie

13 May 1949, N.Y.

2pp. bearing EH note

Scribner, Charles, [Sr.]
TLS Charlie

9 July 1947, N.Y.

2pp., w/newspaper clipping and envelope

Scribner, Charles, [Sr.]
TLS Charlie

19 May 1949, N.Y.

2pp.

Scribner, Charles, [Sr.]
TLS Charlie

9 June 1948, N.Y.

3pp. bearing EH note

Scribner, Charles, [Sr.]
T/ALS Charlie

6 June 1949, N.Y.

6pp.

Scribner, Charles, [Sr.]
T/ALS Charlie

6 Aug 1948, N.Y.

4pp.

Scribner, Charles, [Sr.]
TLS Charlie

9 June 1949, N.Y.

1p., w/TLS F. B. Adams, 8 June 1949, N.Y., to Scribner

Scribner, Charles, [Sr.]
T/ALS Chas

       20 June 1949, N.Y.
       3pp. bearing EH note

Scribner, Charles, [Sr.]
TLS Charlie

       22 Aug 1949, N.Y.
       2pp. bearing EH note

[Scribner, Charles, Sr.]
Cable   2 Aug 1949, N.Y.
       1p.

Scribner, Charles, [Sr.]
TLS Chas

       25 Aug 1949, N.Y.
       2pp.

Scribner, Charles, [Sr.]
T/ALS Charlie

       10 Aug 1949, N.Y.
       5pp.

Scribner, Charles, [Sr.]
TLS   26 Aug 1949, N.Y.
       1p.

Scribner, Charles, [Sr.]
T/ALS Charlie

       15 Aug 1949, N.Y.
       4pp.

[Scribner, Charles, Sr.]
ALS Charlie

       27 Aug 1949, [Far Hills]
       7pp.

Scribner, Charles, [Sr.]
TLS Charlie

       18 Aug 1949, N.Y.
       1p., w/book store bills

Scribner, Charles, [Sr.]
TLS Charlie

       29 Aug 1949, N.Y.
       4pp.

Scribner, Charles, [Sr.]

T/ALS Charles

                31 Aug 1949, N.Y.

                6pp.

[Scribner, Charles, Sr.]

ALS Charlie

                21 Sept 1949, Nantucket

                4pp.

Scribner, Charles, [Sr.]

TLS Charlie--Fragment

                6 Sept 1949, N.Y.

                3pp. only

[Scribner, Charles, Sr.]

TLS Ian Ballantine

                23 Sept 1949, N.Y., to Scribner

                1p.

Scribner, Charles, [Sr.]

T/ALS Charlie

                7 Sept 1949, N.Y.

                4pp.

Scribner, Charles, [Sr.]

ALS Charlie

                Saturday P.M. [24 Sept 1949], N.Y.

                5pp.

Scribner, Charles, [Sr.]

T/ALS Chas

                12 Sept 1949, N.Y.

                3pp.

Scribner, Charles, [Sr.]

TLS Charlie

                28 Sept 1949, N.Y.

                3pp.

Scribner, Charles, [Sr.]

TLS Chas

                14 Sept 1949, N.Y.

                4pp.

Scribner, Charles, [Sr.]

TLS Charlie

                29 Sept 1949, N.Y.

                2pp., w/carbon of a Scribner letter
                29 Sept 1949, to Hotchner, and
                envelope bearing EH note

Scribner, Charles, [Sr.]

ALS Charlie

30 Sept 1949, [Far Hills, N.J.]

4pp., w/envelope bearing EH note

[Scribner, Charles, Sr.]

Cable   28 Oct 1949, N.Y.

1p.

Scribner, Charles, [Sr.]

T/ALS Charlie

13 Oct 1949, N.Y.

4pp., w/enclosure and correspondence between F. G. Alletson Cook of London and Scribner, and envelope bearing EH note

---

Scribner, Charles, [Sr.]

TLS CS (secretary?)

31 Oct 1949, N.Y.

3pp. bearing EH note

Scribner, Charles, Sr.

T/ALS   17 Oct 1949

8pp., w/copies of Scribner's letters, 17 Oct 1949, to Jonathan Cape and Ralph Thompson, and envelope bearing EH note

---

Scribner, Charles, [Sr.]

TLS Chas

2 Nov 1949, N.Y.

1p. bearing EH note

Scribner, Charles, [Sr.]

A/TLS Charlie

Thursday P.M. [20 and 21 Oct 1949], N.Y.

6pp., w/envelope bearing EH note

Scribner, Charles, [Sr.]

TLS Chas

8 Nov 1949, N.Y.

2pp.

Scribner, Charles, [Sr.]

T/ALS Charlie

25 Oct 1949, N.Y.

4pp., w/enclosure

[Scribner, Charles, Sr.]

Correspondence between A. P. Watt & Son and Scribner, 10 Nov, 14 Nov 1949, London, and N.Y.

2pp.

Scribner, Charles, [Sr.]
T/ALS Charlie
　　　　23 Nov 1949, N.Y.
　　　　8pp.

Scirnber, Charles, [Sr.]
ALS Chas
　　　　15 July 1950, Far Hills, N.J.
　　　　2pp.

Scribner, Charles, [Sr.]
T/ALS Charlie
　　　　9 Dec 1949, N.Y.
　　　　4pp. bearing EH note

[Scribner, Charles, Sr.]
Cable　　　7 Aug [1950], N.Y.
　　　　1p.

[Scribner, Charles, Sr.]
ALS Chas
　　　　21 Apr 1950, S.S. America
　　　　6pp. bearing EH note

[Scribner, Charles, Sr.]
ALS Chas
　　　　15 Oct 1950, Far Hills
　　　　4pp., w/newspaper clippings and
　　　　envelope bearing EH note

[Scribner, Charles, Sr.]
Cable　　　2 May [1950], N.Y.
　　　　1p.

Scribner, Charles, [Sr.]
T/ALS Chas
　　　　16 Oct 1950, N.Y.
　　　　5pp., w/newspaper clippings and
　　　　envelope bearing EH note

Scribner, Charles, [Sr.]
TLS Chas
　　　　1 June 1950, N.Y.
　　　　1p., w/book jacket for ARIT

Scribner, Charles, [Sr.]
T/ALS Chas
　　　　18 Oct 1950, N.Y.
　　　　2pp., w/envelope

[Scribner, Charles, Sr.]
ALS Chas

      21 Oct 1950, Far Hills

      2pp., w/newspaper clipping and
      envelope bearing EH note

[Scribner, Charles, Sr.]
ALS Charlie

      21 Feb 1951, R. M. S. Mauretania,
      to MH

      6pp.

[Scribner, Charles, Sr.]
ALS Chas

      27 Oct 1950, Far Hills

      2pp., w/newspaper clippings and
      envelope bearing EH note

Scribner, Charles, [Sr.]
ALS Charlie

      18 Aug 1951, Far Hills, to MH

      4pp.

Scribner, Charles, [Sr.]
ALS Chas

      31 Oct 1950, Far Hills

      4pp., w/newspaper clipping and
      envelope bearing EH note

Scribner, Charles, Sr.
      See Jonathan Cape 26 Oct 1949
                          27 Oct 1949
        Thompson, Ralph
                          25 Oct 1949

Scribner, Charles, [Sr.]
ALS Charlie

      15 July 1950, Far Hills, to MH
      3pp.

[Scribner], Charles
Cable   [4 Feb 1951], Paris, to MH

      1p. bearing MH draft reply

[Scribner, Charles, Sr.]
Cable   4 Oct [1951], N.Y.

      1p.

Scribner, Charles, Jr. (publisher)
Memo of Agreement S Scribner, EH

      19 May 1952

      4pp.

Scribner, Charles, [Jr.]
TLS Charlie
                29 Aug 1952, N.Y.
                2pp.

Scribner, Charles, [Jr.]
TLS Charlie
                13 Mar 1957, N.Y.
                2pp.

Scribner, Charles, [Jr.]
TLS Charlie
                3 Oct 1952, N.Y.
                1p., w/envelope

Scribner, Charles, [Jr.]
TLS Charlie
                20 May 1958, N.Y.
                1p. bearing EH note

Scribner, Charles, Jr.
Cable   [25 Jan 1954, New York]
        1p.

Scribner, Charles, Jr.
Cable   15 Aug 1958, N.Y.
                1p. bearing EH draft reply

Scribner, Charles, [Jr.]
ALS Charlie
                28 Aug 1956, N.Y.
                1p. bearing EH notes

Scribner, Charles, [Jr.
TLS   15 Sept 1958, N.Y.
                1p. bearing EH draft reply

[Scribner, Charles, Jr.]
T/ANS Charlie
                1 Feb 1957
                1p.

Scribner, Charles, [Jr.]
TLS Charlie
                6 Mar 1959, N.Y.
                2pp. bearing EH note

Scribner, Charles, [Jr.]

TLS Charlie

7 Apr 1959, N.Y.

1p., w/copies of correspondence
between William M. Gibson and
Elizabeth Youngstrom, Jan-Apr 1959,
and between Scribner's and
Macmillan.

Scribner, Charles, [Jr.]

TLS Charlie

24 June 1959, N.Y.

1p.

Scribner, Charles, [Jr.]

TLS Charlie

16 Apr 1959, N.Y.

1p.

Scribner, Charles, [Jr.]

TLS Charlie

1 July 1959, N.Y.

1p., w/unsigned duplicate of
letter

Scribner, Charles, [Jr.]

TLS Charlie

27 May 1959, N.Y.

1p. bearing EH notes

Scribner, Charles, [Jr.]

TLS Charlie

14 Aug 1959, N.Y.

2pp. bearing EH note, w/newspaper
clippings

Scribner, Charles, [Jr.]

TLS Charlie

12 June 1959, N.Y.

2pp., w/newspaper clipping

Scribner, Charles, [Jr.]

TLS Charlie

24 Sept 1959, N.Y.

1p. bearing EH note, w/
correspondence between Sam Boal
and Elizabeth Youngstom, Sept 1959
and between Boal and Scribner,
Sept 1959

Scribner, Charles, [Jr.]

TLS Charlie

24 June 1959, N.Y.

2pp.

Scribner, Charles, [Jr.]

TLS Charlie

21 Dec 1959, N.Y.

1p., w/envelope bearing EH note

Scribner, Charles, [Jr.]
TLS Charlie

        15 Feb 1960, N.Y.

        1p., w/envelope

Scribner, Charles, [Jr.]
TLS Charlie

        1 July 1960, N.Y.

        1p. bearing EH note

Scribner, Charles, [Jr.]
TLS Charlie

        23 Mar 1960, N.Y.

        1p.

Scribner, Charles, [Jr.]
TLS Charlie

        15 Aug 1960, N.Y.

        1p.

Scribner, Charles, [Jr.]
TLS Charlie

        22 Apr 1960, N.Y.

        1p., w/envelope

Scribner, Charles, [Jr.]
Book orders for 21 Nov 1950 through 30 Mar 1960

        [18 Aug 1960, N.Y.]

        7pp., w/envelope bearing EH note

Scribner, Charles, [Jr.]
TLS Charlie

        8 June 1960, N.Y.

        1p., w/envelope bearing EH note

Scribner, Charles, [Jr.]
Cable   [23 Aug 1960], N.Y.

        1p. bearing EH note

Scribner, Charles, [Jr.]
TLS Charlie

        20 June 1960, N.Y.

        2pp. bearing EH note

Scribner, Charles, [Jr.]
Cable   [28 Aug 1960], N.Y.

        1p.

Scribner, Charles, [Jr.]

TLS Charlie

19 Oct 1960, N.Y.

1p. bearing EH draft reply, w/TLS
New American Library, to Scribner,
bearing EH notes

Charles Scribner's Sons
See Horne, William D.
19 Nov 1928
Plimpton, George
4 Mar 1961
Perkins, Maxwell
Meyer, Wallace
Brague, Harry
Darrow, Whitney
Dashiell, Alfred S.

Scribner, Charles, [Jr.]

TLS Charlie

6 Jan 1961, N.Y.

1p., w/copies of correspondence
between Scribners and Oliver &
Boyd, Ltd., 6 Dec 1960 through
6 Jan 1960, and envelope bearing
EH note

[Scribner], Vera (Charles, Sr.'s wife)

Cable   12 Feb [1952], N.Y.

1p.

Scribner, Charles, [Jr.]

TLS Charlie

30 Jan 1961, N.Y.

1p., w/envelope bearing EH note

[Scribner], Vera

ALS   26 Feb [1952],

8pp., w/envelope bearing EH note

Scribner, Charles, [Jr.]

ALS Charlie

7 June 1961, N.Y.

2pp., w/envelope

Scribner, Vera
See Ivancich, Gianfranco
12 Feb 1952

Scribner, Charles, [Jr.]

TLS Charlie

23 June 1961, N.Y.

1p., w/envelope

Scribner's Book Store
See Kropotkin, Igor
Wilcox, C. W.

Scribner's Magazine
TLS Jo H. Chamberlin
                30 Dec 1937, N.Y.
                1p.

Seldes, George
Cable   23 Feb 1938, N.Y.
               1p. bearing EH draft reply

Scribner's Magazine
        See Bridges, Robert
            Causs, Katherine
            Eleanor Earl
            Dashiell, Alfred S.

Seldes, George
TLS   35 Feb [1938, N.Y.]
               3pp., w/envelope

Sedgwich, Ellery
        See The Atlantic Monthly
            Medical Bureau to Aid
            Spanish Democracy
            Perkins, Maxwell 9 Mar 1927

Seldes, George
TLS   Noon Monday, undated, Paris
               1p.

Seeley, [Coles Van Brunt, Jr.] (W.W. I
                                colleague)
A Post Card S
                17 Oct 1918, [Turin]

Selligman, Joseph
        See Pflaum

Seldes, George (journalist, Ken)
A Post Card S George Seldes and Alma Lexcher (?)
        [Nov 1926], S.S. President Roosevelt
        [New York]

Serravalli, Luigi (poet)
TL   28 Apr 19[6]1, Merano
               1p., w/envelope

Seward, William W., Jr. (professor, author, friend)
TLS   19 Aug 1943, Surry, Virginia
           2pp.

Seward, William W., Jr.
TLS   20 Apr 1950, Norfolk
           1p.

Seward, William W., Jr.
TLS   8 Feb 1944, Forsyth, Georgia
           2pp.

Seward, William W., Jr.
TLS   12 Nov 1950, Norfolk
           1p. bearing EH note

Seward, William W., Jr.
TLS   23 Aug 1948, Norfolk, Va.
           1p. bearing EH note

Seward, William W., Jr.
TLS   3 Sept 1951, Norfolk
           1p.

Seward, William W., Jr.
TLS   27 June 1949, Norfolk
           1p.

Seward, William W., Jr.
TLS   1 Dec 1952, Norfolk
           1p. bearing EH note

Seward, William W., Jr.
TLS   3 Nov1949, Norfolk
           1p. bearing EH note

Seward, William W., Jr.
TLS   2 Mar 1953, Norfolk
           1p. bearing EH note, w/newspaper clipping

Seward, [William W., Jr.]

TLS Bill

16 Jan 1958, Norfolk

1p.

Shakespeare and Co.

See Beach, Sylvia

Seward, [William W., Jr.]

TLS Bill

1 Mar 1959, Norfolk

1p., w/envelope bearing EH notes

[Shaw, Carleton] (friend)

ALS Corp

19 June 1919, Toledo

2pp., w/envelope

Seward, [William W., Jr.]

TLS Bill

20 Feb 1960

1p., w/envelope

Shaw, Emmett

See Jenkins, Howell   11 Aug 1918

Seward, [William W., Jr.]

TLS Bill

28 Apr 1960, Norfolk

1p., w/TLS Howard Gwaltney, 27 Apr 1960, Smithfield, Va., to Seward

---

Shaw, James E. (reader)

TLS   10 Aug [1934], St. Petersburg

1p., w/envelope

Seward, [William W., Jr.]

TLS Bill

31 May 1960, Norfolk

1p.

Sheaffer Pen Co.

See Pfeiffer, Paul M.

10 Jan 1930

[Sheean, J. Vincent]   (writer, Spanish Civil
                              War comrade)

TLS "JVS"

        24Feb [1938], Washington

        1p.

[Shevlin, Thomas H.]

Cable   22 Feb 1936, Acapulco

        1p.

Sheean, [J.] V[incent]

ALS   14 Sept [1938], Dresden

        3pp.

[Shevlin, Thomas H.]

ALS Tommy

        8 Aug [1936], Catcay

        4pp., w/photograph and envelope
        postmarked 13 Aug 1936, N.Y.,
        bearing EH note

Shelton, Earl (reader)

TLS   16 May 1931, San Quentin

        1p. bearing EH note

[Shevlin, Thomas H.]

ALS Tommy

        21 Oct [1936], Pasadena, California,
        to EH/Pauline

        8pp., w/envelope

[Shevlin], Lorraine [Tommy's wife, friend)

ALS   [c. Aug 1936], Catcay

        4pp.

Shevlin, [Thomas H.]

Cable   7 Feb 1937, Palm Beach

        1p.

[Shevlin, Thomas H.]

Cable   23 Nov 1935, Bimini

        1p.

Shevlin, [Thomas H.]

Cable   [25 Dec 1937], to EH/Pauline

        1p.

Shevlin,[Thomas H.]

Cable   24 June 1938, Catcay

              1p.

[Shevlin, Thomas H.]   (sportsman, friend)

ALS Tommy

              24 July [1938], Catcay, Bahamas

              6pp.

[Shevlin, Thomas H.]

ALS Tommy

              11 Jan 1961, Tallahassee

              3pp.

Shields, Bernice (acquaintance)

TLS   25 Mar 1960, Channelview, Texas

              1p., w/newspaper clipping and
              envelope

Shipman, [Evan] (friend)

Cable   [15 Dec 1925], Boury en Vexin

              1p.

[Shipman], Evan

ALS   Saturday [1927], Paris

              1p.

[Shipman], Evan

ALS   28 Sept [1927], Plainfield, NH

              4pp.

[Shipman], Evan

ALS   Wednesday [8 Feb 1928, Paris]

              1p., w/envelope

[Shipman], Evan

ALS   Saturday [18 Feb 1928], Senlis

              2pp., w/envelope

[Shipman], Evan

ALS   6 June 1928, Boury [en Vixen]

              2pp., w/envelope

[Shipman], Evan

Cable   8 July 1928, N.Y.

          1p.

[Shipman], Evan

ALS   Thursday [13 Dec 1928, NY]

        2pp., w/newspaper clipping and envelope

[Shipman], Evan

ALS   5 Aug [1928, Plainfield]

        4pp., w/envelope

[Shipman], Evan

ALS   Friday [18 Jan 1929, NY]

        1p., w/envelope

[Shipman], Evan

ALS   29 Aug [1928, Plainfield]

        6pp., w/envelope

[Shipman], Evan

ALS   Thursday [Feb 1929, NY]

        2pp.

[Shipman], Evan

ALS   Thursday [4 Oct 1928, Plainfield]

        2pp., w/envelope

[Shipman], Evan

ALS   15 Feb [1929, NY]

        1p.

[Shipman], Evan

ALS   Tuesday [20 Nov 1928, NY]

        3pp., w/typescript of "Les Sydalises" w/notes by Shipman and envelope

---

[Shipman], Evan

ALS   20 June 1929, [Plainfield]

        4pp.

[Shipman], Evan

ALS   19 Feb 1930, Keswick, Va.

      1p., w/envelope

[Shipman], Evan

ALS   Monday [28 Jan 1935, NY]

      3pp., w/envelope

[Shipman], Evan

ALS   5 May [1930, Keswick]

      2pp., w/envelope

[Shipman], Evan

Cable   16 Sept 1935, NY

      1p.

[Shipman], Evan

ALS   22 Jan 1932, Boury en Vixen

      3pp., w/typescript of "Mazzepa"
bearing EH notes

[Shipman], Evan

Cable   24 Sept 1935, NY

      1p.

[Shipman], Evan

ALS   Wednesday [10 May 1933], R.M.S.
Orcoma

      3pp., w/enclosure and envelope

[Shipman], Evan

Cable   20 Feb 1937, NY

      1p.

[Shipman], Evan

ALS   Wednesday [Dec 1934, Key West]

      2pp.

[Shipman], Evan

TLS   21 Oct 1937

      2pp.

[Shipman], Evan

TLS   14 Mar 1938

             2pp.

[Shipman], Evan

ALS   Wednesday [25 Oct 1950], Keswick

             3pp., w/envelope both bearing
             EH notes

[Shipman], Evan

TLS   21 June 1931

             9pp.

[Shipman], Evan

ALS   Sunday [29 Oct 1950], Keswick

             6pp., wholograph of "Les Cydalises'

[Shipman], Evan

T/ALS   8 Feb [1937], NY

             3pp., w/typescripts of "Three for
             the Summer" and "Verses for Now"

[Shipman], Evan

TLS   Sunday [26 Nov 1950]

             3pp. bearing EH note

[Shipman], Evan

TLS   17 Jan 1944

             6pp.

[Shipman], Evan

ALS   Monday [11 June 1951]

             4pp.

[Shipman], Evan

TLS   23 Apr [1950]

             2pp., w/typescript of "Protest"
             bearing Shipman notes, newspaper
             clipping and envelope

[Shipman], Evan

Cable   3 Sept 1956, La Jolla, California

             1p.

Shipman, Evan
        See also Horne, William D.
                27 Feb 1937

[Shoemaker, Elizabeth]

ALS Liz

                Sun [5 Dec 1920, Petoskey]

                12pp., w/envelope

[Shipman], Garey (Evan's wife)

ALS   [1 Jan 1935], NY

                2pp., w/envelope bearing EH note

[Shoemaker, Elizabeth]

ALS Liz

                Friday [24 Dec 1920, Petoskey]

                9pp., w/envelope

Shiras, George Peter (reader)

TLS   16 Apr 1953

                2pp.

[Shoemaker, Elizabeth]

ALS Eliz

                9 Jan 1921, [Petoskey]

                6pp., w/envelope

[Shoemaker, Elizabeth] (friend)

ALS Liz

                [25 Oct 1920, Petoskey]

                8pp., w/envelope

[Shoemaker, Elizabeth]

ALS Liz

                Sunday morn [16 Jan 1921, Petoskey]

                8pp., w/envelope

[Shoemaker, Elizabeth]

ALS Liz

                Thursday Armistice Day [11 Nov
                1920, Petoskey]

                4pp., w/envelope

[Shoemaker, Elizabeth]

ALS Eliz

                23 Jan 1921, [Petoskey]

                6pp., w/envelope

[Shoemaker, Elizabeth]

ALS Elis

Blue Sunday [6 Feb 1921, Petoskey]

8pp., w/envelope

Shumlin, Herman
See Ingersoll, Ralph McA.

[Shoemaker, Elizabeth]

ALS Eliz

[2 May 1921, Petoskey

8pp., w/envelope

Sicre, [Ricardo] (friend)

Cable   27 May 1958, Madrid

1p.

[Shoemaker, Elizabeth]

ALS Eliz

Saturday [7 May 1921, Petoskey]

10pp., w/envelope

Sicre, [Ricardo]

Cable   [16 Sept 1960], Malaga

1p.

Shor, Baby and Toots (restaurateur)

Cable [25 Jan 1954, New York]

1p.

[Sicre, Ricardo]

Address noted by MH

1p.

Shumlin, Herman (The Spanish Earth)

TLS   28 Jan 1939, N.Y.

2pp.

Sidley, Thelma
See Mowrer, Hadley Hemingway
4 July 1935

Sidley, William
    See Mowrer, Hadley Hemingway
        4 July 1935

Silvester, J. M.

TLS   1 Dec 1937, Nairobi

      1p., w/enclosures

Sidley, William D. (rancher, friend)

TLS Bill

      26 Aug 1936, Encampment, Wyoming

      1p.

Simmons, Isabelle
    See Godolphin, Isabelle Simmons

Sill, Fred

TLS   4 May 1960, [Sicily]

      1p., w/envelope

Simmons, Zolmon
    See Jenkins, Howell 11 Aug 1918

Sillen, Samuel (editor, _Masses & Mainstream_)

TLS mimeograph

      20 Apr 1950, NY

      1p., w/An open letter by Ilya
      Ehrenburg

Simon and Schuster, Inc.
    See Fadiman, Clifton

Silvester, J. M. (East African Professional
              Hunters' Association)

TLS   30 Apr 1936, Nairobi

      2pp.

Simonov, Konstantin (author)

ALS   25/26 June 1946

      12pp. bearing EH note, translated,
      transcribed, and forwarded w/ALS
      Bernard Koten, 5 July 1946, 2pp.

Sims, Joseph P.
TLS   4 Feb 1935, Philadelphia
           1p.

Sims, Joseph P. (sports fisherman)
TLS   18 May 1935, Philadelphia
           1p., w/enclosure

Sircar, Joy Charan (reader)
TLS   27 Apr 1956, Calcutta
           1p.

Skelley, J. Leo
           See American Red Cross

Slocombe, George (correspondent, author)
ALS   27 Nov [1929], Paris
           1p.

Smart, David A. (Esquire, Ken)
TLS Dave
           4 Mar 1938, Chicago
           1p.

Smart, David A.
TLS Dave
           10 Mar 1938, Chicago
           2pp.

[Smart, David A.]
Cable   [29 Mar 1938], Chicago
           1p.

Smart, David A.
TLS Dave
           5 Apr 1938, Chicago
           2pp.

[Smart, David A.]
TLS Dave
           6 Apr 1938, Chicago
           1p.

[Smart, David A.]
TLS Dave
              12 May 1938, Chicago
              2pp., w/enclosure

[Smart, David A.]
TLS Dave
              30 June 19[38], Chicago
              1p.

Smart, David A.
TLS Dave
              16 May 1938, Chicago
              1p.

Smart, David A.
TLS Dave
              18 July 1938, Chicago
              1p.

[Smart, David A.]
Cable   31 May 1938, Chicago
              1p.

Smart, David A.
TLS Dave
              7 Nov 1938, Chicago
              1p.

Smart, [David A.]
Cable   10 June 1938, Chicago
              1p.

Smart, David A.
         See Gingrich, Arnold   18 May 1938

[Smart, David A.]
Cable   14 June 1938, Chicago
              1p.

Smith, Bernard (editor)
     See New Masses

Smith, Chard [Powers]
ALS   New Years [1 Jan 1927, Paris]
           2pp., w/envelope

Smith, [Robert]   (reader)
TLS Bob Smith
                undated, NY
                1p.

Smith, Charles (journalist)
Cable   [25 Jan 1954, London], to MH
           1p.

[Smith, W.] Hall (hunting friend)
TLS   [13 Sept 1927], Kansas City
           2pp., w/envelope bearing EH note

[Smith, Ernest] (friend)
ALS Ern
           8 Sept 1920, Toronto
           2pp., w/envelope

Smith, [W.] Hall
ALS   Thanksgiving [29 Nov 1928, NY]
           1p., w/envelope

Smith, Frances
        See Bacon, Frances Smith

[Smith, W.] Hall
ALS   [10 Oct 1933], Kansas City
           1p., w/envelope

Smith, Jessica (_Soviet_ _Russia_ _Today_)
TLS   4 Sept 1936, NY
           1p.

[Smith, William B.] (friend)
TLS Bill
                [Apr 1918], Columbia, Missouri
                1p.

[Smith, William B.]

TLS Bill

    It's Monday night if that interests you, where else would I be but at 1506 Rosie [Apr 1918, Columbia]

2pp.

[Smith, William B.]

ALS Ye Master

    11 June 1918, [Horton's] Bay, [Michigan]

4pp.

[Smith, William B.]

TLS Bill

    Saturn's Day at eight thirty [Apr 1918, Columbia]

2pp.

[Smith, William B.]

ALS Ye Master

    22 June 1918, [Horton's] Bay

4pp.

[Smith, William B.]

TLS Bill

    Near Supper, at the underwood [5 Apr 1918, Columbia]

1p., w/envelope

[Smith, William B.]

ALS Ye Master

    30 June 1918, [Boyne City], The Bay

4pp., w/envelope

[Smith, William B.]

ALS Bill

    27 Apr 1918, Columbia

2pp.

[Smith, William B.]

ALS Ye Master Biologist

    7 July 1918, Horton's Bay

4pp.

[Smith, William B.]

ALS "M.B"

    5 June 1918, The Bay [Boyne City, Michigan]

4pp., w/envelope

[Smith, William B.]

ALS Ye Master

    8 Aug 1918, The Bay [Boyne City]

8pp., w/envelope

[Smith, William B.]
ALS Ye Master

        18 Aug 1918, The Bay [Boyne City]

        4pp., w/envelope

[Smith, William B.]
TLS Ye Master

        17 Dec 1918, St. Louis

        1p., w/envelope

[Smith, William B.]
ALS Master Biologist

        27 Aug 1918, Boston

        5pp., w/envelope

[Smith, William B.]
ALS Ye Master

        3 Jan 1919, St. Louis

        4pp., w/envelope

[Smith, William B.]
ALS Ye Master

        11 Sept 1918, [Boston]

        6pp., w/envelope

[Smith, William B.]
TLS Ye Master

        1 Feb 1919, St. Louis

        1p.

[Smith, William B.]
ALS Ye Master

        7 Oct 1918, [Cambridge, Mass]

        4pp., w/envelope

[Smith, William B.]
TLS Ye Master

        19 Feb 1919, [St. Louis]

        1p.

[Smith, William B.]
ALS Ye Master

        27 Oct 1918, Boston

        3pp.

Smith, William B.
TLS Ye Master

        19 Mar 1919, St. Louis

        2pp.

[Smith, William B.]
TLS Ye Master
      19 Apr 1919, St. Louis
      1p., w/envelope

[Smith, William B.]
ALS Bill
      8 Oct 1919, [Horton's] Bay
      2pp., w/envelope

[Smith, William B.]
TLS Ye Master
      23 Apr [1919]
      1p.

[Smith, William B.]
ALS Garcon
      21 Oct 1919, St. Louis
      5pp.

[Smith, William B.]
TLS Ye Barterer
      29 Apr 1919, St. Louis
      1p.

[Smith, William B.]
TLS Kellner
      7 Nov 1919, St. Louis
      7pp., w/envelope

[Smith, William B.]
ALS Ye Master
      19 May 1919, The Bay [Horton's Bay]
      2pp.

[Smith, William B.]
ALS Kellneroff
      13 Nov 1919, St. Louis
      7pp.

[Smith, William B.]
TLS Garcon
      2 Oct 1919, [St. Louis]
      1p., w/envelope

[Smith, William B.]
TLS Garcon
      [14 Nov 1919, St. Louis]
      1p., w/envelope

[Smith, William B.]
ALS Kimmer-Ellner

16 Nov 1919, [St. Louis]
4pp., w/envelope

Smith, William B.
TLS Garcon

25 Jan 1920, St. Louis
2pp.

Smith, [William B.]
ALS   14 Dec 1919, [St. Louis]
4pp., w/envelope

[Smith, William B.]
TLS Kellner

[26 Jan 1920], St. Louis
2pp., w/envelope

[Smith, William B.]
ALS Kellner

15 Dec 1919, St. Louis
4pp., w/envelope

[Smith, William B.]
ALS Kellner

[1 Feb 1920], St. Louis
4pp., w/envelope

[Smith, William B.]
ALS Garcon, WBS

27 Dec 1919, St. Louis
6pp., w/envelope

[Smith, William B.]
ALS Kellner

4 Feb 1920, [St. Louis]
1p., w/envelope

[Smith, William B.]
ALS Garcon

[24 Jan 1920], St. Louis
5pp., w/envelope bearing EH note

[Smith, William B.]
ALS Kellner

8 Feb 1920, St. Louis
4pp., w/envelope

[Smith, William B.]
ALS Kimmer ·Ellner
        25 Feb 1920, [St. Louis]
        4pp., w/envelope

Smith, Will[iam] B.
TLS   7 Apr 1920, Chicago
        2pp.

[Smith, William B.]
ALS Kellneroff
        3 Mar 1920, St. Louis
        2pp., w/envelope

Smith, [William B.]
ALS Smith--not the Beamer
        8 Apr 1920, [St. Louis]
        2pp., w/envelope

[Smith, William B.]
TLS Kellner
        5 Mar 1920, St. Louis
        1p., w/envelope

[Smith, William B.]
AL   15 Apr 1920, [St. Louis]
        2pp., w/envelope

Smith, [William B.]
ALS Immer Smith
        10 Mar 1920, St. Louis
        6pp., w/envelope bearing EH notes

[Smith, William B.]
ALS Kelner
        19 Apr 1920, [St. Louis]
        1p., w/envelope

[Smith, William B.]
ALS Smithelberry
        27 Mar 1920, [St. Louis]
        3pp., w/envelope

[Smith, William B.]
ALS Lekner
        [4 May 1920, St. Louis]
        1p., w/envelope

[Smith, William B.]

TL   [1]8 May 1920, [St. Louis]

      1p., w/envelope

[Smith], Will[iam B.]

TLS H. Will

      16 Nov 1920, St. Louis

      1p.

Smith, [William B.]

ALS Immer Smith

      20 May 1920, [St. Louis]

      1p., w/envelope

[Smith], Will[iam B.]

TLS   The cile of a Saturday night after the movies [13 Feb 1921, St. Louis]

      1p., w/envelope

[Smith, William B.]

ALS Kellner

      [May 1920, St. Louis]

      2pp.

[Smith], Will[iam B.]

ALS   Sabbath day, [May/June 1921], [Horton] Bay

      4 pp.

[Smith], Will[iam B.]

ALS   21 Oct 1920, [St. Louis]

      2pp., w/envelope

[Smith, William B.]

TLS Kellner

      The Bay Thursday. at noon. [June/ July 1921, Horton Bay]

      2 pp.

      donor JH

[Smith,] Will[iam B.]

ALS H. Will

      2 Nov 1920, St. Louis

      4pp.

[Smith], Will[iam B.]

TLS Honest Will

      27 June 1921

      2pp.

[Smith, William B.]

TLS Honest Will/H. Will

> After the massacre. Gaw. [July 1921]
>
> 2 pp.

[Smith], Will[iam B.]

ALS H. Will

> 21 Nov 1924, Chicago
>
> 2pp., w/envelope

Smith, Will[iam] B.

TLS Garcon/Will

> 7 July 1921, St. Louis
>
> 2pp.

Smith, T. R. (editor, Boni and Liveright)

Cable   [[11 Nov 1929], New York
>
> 1p.

[Smith], Will[iam B.]

TLS Honest Will

> Monday Nooning just past [Aug 1921,
> Horton's] The Bay
>
> 2pp.

[Smith, William B.]

TLS Kellner

> 22 Nov [1925], Provincetown
>
> 2pp., w/envelope

[Smith, William B.]

ALS Garcon

> of a Thursday afternoon mid-way
> in the St. Mary's river [9 Aug
> 1921, Sault Ste. Marie]
>
> 3pp., w/envelope

[Smith], Will[iam B.]

ALS H. Will

> 15 Dec 1925, [Boston]
>
> 2pp., w/envelope

[Smith], Will[iam B.]

TLS H. Will

> Friday--in less that 24 hours a
> male will KNOW [June 1921]
>
> 3pp.

[Smith, William B.]

TLS H. Will

> [16 July 1926], Provincetown
>
> 2pp., w/envelope

[Smith, William B.]
TLS Kellner

24 Oct 1926, Provincetown
1p., w/envelope

[Smith], Will[iam B.]
ALS H. Will

20 Aug 1927, [Long] Beach
3pp.

[Smith, William B.]
ALS Kellner

[Dec 1926], Provincetown
2pp., w/envelope

[Smith], Will[iam B.]
TLS H. Will

15 Sept 1927, Chicago
2pp., w/envelope

[Smith], Will[iam B.]
TLS H. Will

19 May 1927, Provincetown
2pp., w/envelope bearing EH note

[Smith], Will[iam B.]
TLS H. Will

25 Sept 1927, Chicago
2pp., w/newspaper clipping and
envelope

[Smith], Will[iam B.]
TLS H. Will

15 June 1927, Provincetown
2pp.

[Smith], Will[iam B.]
TLS H. Will

10 Nov [1927], Provincetown
2pp., w/envelope

[Smith, William B.]
ALS Kellner

13 Aug 1927, Long Beach, Indiana
2pp., w/envelope

[Smith], Will[iam B.]
TLS H. Will

2 Feb [1928], Provincetown
1p., w/envelope bearing EH note

[Smith], Will[iam B.]
TLS H. Will
             17 Apr 1928, P-Town, Mass
             2pp.

Smith, William H., Jr. (Rains Galleries)
TLS   15 Sept 1936, NY
             1p.

[Smith], Will[iam B.]
TLS H. Will
             28 July 1929, Horton Bay
             2pp., w/envelope bearing EH note

Smith, [Yeremya Kenley] (friend)
TLS Y. K. Smith
             [2 Oct 1921]
             2pp.

[Smith], Will[iam B.]
TLS H. Will
             5 Oct 1929, Provincetown
             2pp.

[Smith, Yeremya Kenley]
ALS RMcN
             undated, to Y. K. [Smith]
             3pp.

[Smith], Will[iam B.]
TLS H. Will
             12 Jan 1951, Arlington, Va.
             1p. bearing EH note

Smythe,
Cable   [27 Jan 1954, Mombassa]
             1p.

Smith, William B.
        See Hopkins, Charles 4 May 1918
            Williams, Stanley

Smyth, Joseph Hilton   (journalist)
ALS   29 Mar 1927, Paris
             2pp.

[Smith], Will[iam B.]
TLS H. Will
       17 Apr 1928, P-Town, Mass
       2pp.

Smith, William H., Jr. (Rains Galleries)
TLS   15 Sept 1936, NY
       1p.

[Smith], Will[iam B.]
TLS H. Will
       28 July 1929, Horton Bay
       2pp., w/envelope bearing EH note

Smith, [Yeremya Kenley] (friend)
TLS Y. K. Smith
       [2 Oct 1921]
       2pp.

[Smith], Will[iam B.]
TLS H. Will
       5 Oct 1929, Provincetown
       2pp.

[Smith, Yeremya Kenley]
ALS RMcN
       undated, to Y. K. [Smith]
       3pp.

[Smith], Will[iam B.]
TLS H. Will
       12 Jan 1951, Arlington, Va.
       1p. bearing EH note

Smythe,
Cable [27 Jan 1954, Mombassa]
       1p.

Smith, William B.
     See Hopkins, Charles 4 May 1918
       Williams, Stanley

Smyth, Joseph Hilton (journalist)
ALS   29 Mar 1927, Paris
       2pp.

Repeats previous page

Smyth, Joseph Hilton

TLS   19 July 1938, NY

          1p.

Sommers, Francois
          See also Ritz, Charles   3 Feb 1951,
                                        to MH

Snevily, Henry M.
          See Wheeler, John   4 Dec 1936

Sommers, Lt. Col. Martin
          See Colliers

Solano, Solita
          See Flanner, Janet   22 Nov 1933

Southard, A[ddison]   (U.S. Foreign Service,
                              shipmate)

TLS   25 Jan [1934], Addis Ababa

          2pp.

Soby, James Thrall (art critic, editor)

Invitation from Mr. and Mrs. Soby

          [12 Apr 1959], New Canaan, Conn.

          1p.

Soviet Russia Today
          See Smith, Jessica

Sommer, Francois (author)

TLS F. Sommer

          20 Dec 1950, Paris

          1p., w/envelope bearing EH note

Sovietland

Cable from Baratov

          28 Oct 1938, Moscow

          2pp.

[Spanish Civil War]

Cable from William Mangold, Spanish Information Bureau

[2 Apr 1937], NY

1p.

[Spanish Civil War]

TLS Douglas Jacobs, American Relief Ship for Spain

18 July 1938, NY

1p.

[Spanish Civil War]

Cable from Playbox

[21 Apr 1937], London

1p.

[Spanish Civil War]

Cable from David McKelvy White, Friends of the Abraham Lincoln Brigade

31 Aug 1938, NY

1p.

[Spanish Civil War]

TLS Norman Lee, Spanish Medical Aid Committee of Montreal

27 May 1937, Montreal

1p.

[Spanish Civil War]

Official papers, signed, stamped, and dated from 30 Apr 1937 through 31 May 1938, from El Comisario General de Investigacion y Vigilancia, Embajada de Espana en Paris, El Director General de Seguridad, Cuartel General del Ejercito del Este, etc.

17pp.

[Spanish Civil War]

Cable from Fernand de los Rios, Spanish Ambassador

28 Jan 1938, Washington, D.C.

1p.

[Spanish Civil War]

Announcement from the American League Against War and Fascism

undated, Los Angeles

2pp.

[Spanish Civil War]

Cable from Harry Schechner, Club Hemingway

2 June 1938, NY

1p.

Spender, Stephen (poet)

ALS   undated, London

2pp., w/envelope

Spicehandler, Daniel (author)
TLS   22 May 1960, NY
                    1p., w/envelope

[Spiegel], Clara
TLS   2 Oct 1952, Sun Valley
                    1p. bearing EH note

[Spiegel], Clara (friend)
ALS   Wednesday [1940], Highland Park
              6pp.

[Spiegel], Clara
ALS   27 May 1960, Chicago, to EH/MH
                    4pp. bearing MH note

[Spiegel], Clara
ALS   3 Apr [1940], Highland Park, Ill.
                    6pp.

[Spiegel], Clara
TLS   15 July 1960, Sun Valley
                    2pp. bearing MH notes

[Spiegel], Clara
TLS   28 Oct 1949, Highland Park, Ill.,
              to EH/MH
              2pp.

[Spiegel], Clara
ALS   4 Oct 1960, Nairobi, to EH/MH
                    1p., w/address-leaf

[Spiegel], Clara
ALS   [3 Oct 1946], Highland Park
              3pp., w/envelope and enclosure

[Spiegel], Clara
TLS   16 Oct 1952, Sun Valley, to MH
                    2pp.

[Spiegel], Clara

ALS   21 May 1960, Chicago, to MH

        3pp.

Sprigg, T. Stanhope (Christopher Sprigg
          Memorial Ambulance Fund)

TLS   27 July 1937, London

        2pp.

Spiegel, Fred (W.W. I comrade, Clara's
            husband)

TLS   4 Apr 1940, Chicago

        1p.

Sproul, Kathleen (reader, Carol Hemingway's
            college professor)

TLS   10 Sept 1950, NY

        2pp.

Spiegel, Fred
        See also Brumback, Theodore
                1 Sept 1918

Stagg, Fred
        See Peirce, Waldo 12 July 1959

Sports Afield
        See Edge, Bob

Stahl, John M. (Sears-Roebuck Agricultural
              Foundation)

TLS   22 Dec 1926, Chicago

        1p., w/envelope

Sports Illustrated
        See Time-Life
           Wallace, Henry

Stahle, Nils K.
        See Nobel Foundation

Stawisky, Lotte (reader)
ALS   21 July 1938, NY
                2pp.

[Steffens, Lincoln]
ALS Stef
                21 Nov 1924, San Remo, Italy
                1p., w/envelope

Steeholm, Hardy (Book Council of America)
TLS   6 Mar 1939, Salt Point, NY
                1p.

Steffens, Lincoln
TLS   11 Oct 1928, Carmel, California
                2pp., w/envelope

[Steffens, Lincoln]   (author)
TLS Stef
                9 Dec 1922, Paris
                2pp.

Steffens, Lincoln
TLS   23 Oct 1928, Carmel
                1p., w/ALS Ella [Winter] on
                verso, and envelope

[Steffens, Lincoln]
TLS Stef
                20 June 1924, Alassio, Italy
                1p.

Stein, Gertrude (friend, author)
ALS   [Mar 1922, Paris]
                1p.

[Steffens], Lincoln
ALS Lincoln Stef
                30 June 1924, Alassio
                1p., w/envelope

[Stein, Gertrude]
ALS "G.S"
                [6 Mar 1923, Paris]
                1p., w/envelope

Stein, Gertrude

ALS   [Nov 1923, Paris]

           2pp., w/newspaper clipping

Stein, Gertrude
           See also Gallup, Donald C.

Stein, Gertrude

ALS   [11 July 1924, Paris]

           3pp., w/envelope

Steinbeck, John (author)

ALS   [23 Jan 1929], Los Gatos,
           California

           1p., w/envelope

Stein, Gertrude

ALS   [13 Aug 1924], Belley

           2pp., w/envelope

Steinhilber, Richard H. (psychiatrist)

ALS Dick

           28 Jan 1961, [Rochester]

           2pp., w/envelope bearing EH note

Stein, Gertrude

ALS   [17 Aug 1924], Belley

           6pp., w/envelope

Stephenson, Betty
           See Hemingway, Pauline 1 Dec 1926

Stein, Gertrude

ALS   [18 Sept 1924], Belley

           6pp., w/envelope

Sternberg, Martin L. A.
           See Foundation for the Deaf, Inc.

Stevens, Robert D.   (Library of Congress)

TLS   14 Feb 1961, Washington, D.C.

        1p., w/envelope bearing EH note

[Stewart], Don[ald Ogden]

TLS   31 Aug [1928, Chatham, Mass.]

        2pp., w/envelope

Stevenson, M[arcus] O.   (W. W. II colleague)

Cable   undated

        1p.

Stewart, Donald Ogden

Cable   16 June 1937, N.Y.

        1p.

[Stewart], Allan   (sport fisherman, American
            Foreign Servcie)

TLS   28 June 1956, San Jose, Costa
        Rica, to EH/MH

        1p., w/newspaper clippings and
        envelope

Stewart, Donald Ogden

TLS   1 Feb 1938, NY

        1p.

Stewart, [Donald Ogden]   (author, friend)

Cable   [late Feb 1925], NY

        1p.

Stille, Erik   (congratulator)

ALS   1 Nov 1954, Stockholm, Sweden

        2pp. bearing EH note

[Stewart], Don[ald Ogden]

TLS   29 Aug [1927], South Bristol,
        Maine

        2pp. bearing ANS Beatrice, w/
        envelope

Stitt, Ralph   (Paramount Pictures)

Cable   30 Nov 1932, NY

        1p.

Stitt, Ralph

Cable   [Dec 1932], NY

        1p.

[Stoneman, William]   (journalist, United
                        Nations)

TLS Bill

        10 Feb 1947, Lake Success, NY, to
        EH/MH

        2pp.

Stitt, Ralph

Cable   6 Dec 1932, Yonkers

        1p.

Storm, P. L.   (Oak Park neighbor)

ALS   30 Sept 1917, Chicago

        4pp.

Stone, George Winchester, Jr.   (Modern
               Language Association)

TLS   23 Jan 1961, NY

        1p.

[Storm], P. L.

ALS   [28 Oct 1918, Chicago]

        4pp., w/envelope bearing ANS
        [Caroline] Bayley

Stone, George Winchester
       See Baker, Carlos   28 Nov 1960

Stout, Rex
       See Author's League of America

Stone, Martin
       See Time-Life   8 Aug 1952

Stowe, Leland   (congratulator)

ALS   29 Oct 1954, New York
        1p. bearing EH note

Straby, Ake   (congratulator)
ALS   31 Oct 1954, Orebro, Sweden
            1p. bearing EH note

[Stater, Henry]
ALS Mike
            [1 Nov 1926], NY
            8pp., w/envelope

[Strater, Henry]
ALS Mike
            19 May [1923, NY]
            4pp.

[Strater, Henry]
ALS Mike
            16 Feb [1927], N.Y.
            2pp., w/envelope

[Strater, Henry] (sportsman, friend, artist)
ALS Mike
            5 Nov [1923], Paris
            4pp.

[Strater, Henry]
ALS Mike
            2 Apr [1927], NY
            3pp., w/envelope

[Strater, Henry]
ALS Mike
            [18 May 1926, Paris]
            2pp., w/envelope

[Strater, Henry]
ALS Mike
            28 Jan 1928, [NY]
            2pp., w/envelope

[Strater, Henry]
ALS Mike
            12 June 1926, NY
            2pp., w/envelope bearing EH note

[Strater, Henry]
ALS Mike
            25 Apr [1928], NY
            4pp., w/envelope bearing EH note

Strater, H[enry]
Envelope only postmarked 19 May 1928, NY

[Strater, Henry]
ALS Mike
                    9 Jan 1929, [NY]
                    3pp., w/envelope

[Strater, Henry]
ALS Mike
                    24 Aug 1928, Ogunquit, Maine
                    5pp.

[Strater, Henry]
AL   26 June 1929, Ogunquit
               5pp., w/envelope bearing EH notes

[Strater, Henry]
ALS Mike
                    28 Oct 1928, Ogunquit, Maine
                    3pp., w/envelope postmakred
                    29 Oct 1928, NY

[Strater, Henry]
Cable   25 Feb 1930, Philadelphia
               1p.

[Strater, Henry]
ALS Mike
                    Wednesday [21 Nov 1928], NY
                    2pp., w/photograph and envelope

[Strater, Henry]
ALS Mike
                    [11 Apr 1930, NY]
                    2pp., w/envelope

[Strater, Henry]
ALS Mike
                    8 Dec [1928, NY]
                    3pp., w/envelope

[Strater, Henry]
ALS Mike
                    4 May 1930, [NY]
                    8pp., w/envelope

[Strater, Henry]

ALS Mike

18 May [1930], NY

9pp. bearing art work,
w/photograph

[Strater, Henry]

ALS Joe [Joseph Howe]

28 Jan 1932, Pasadena, California,
to Charlie [Ellis]

4pp.

[Strater, Henry]

ALS Mike

30 Apr 1931, NY

5pp., w/envelope

[Strater, Henry]

ALS Mike

1 Feb 1932, NY

4pp.

[Strater, Henry]

ALS Mike

24 July 1931, Ogunquit

8pp., w/envelope

[Strater, Henry]

TLS Mike

19 Feb 1931 [1932], NY

2pp., w/enclosure

[Strater, Henry]

ALS Mike

11 Dec [1931], NY

6pp.

[Strater, Henry]

ALS Mike

24 Feb 1932, NY

3pp., w/TLS Konrad Schauer,
23 Feb 1932, NY, to Strater

[Strater, Henry]

TLS William N. Beach

6 Jan 1932, NY, to Strater

2pp.

[Strater, Henry]

TLS George G. Carey, Jr.

25 Feb 1932, Baltimore, to
Strater

2pp.

[Strater, Henry]
TLS Konrad Schauer
     3 Mar 1932, NY, to Strater
     1p., w/enclosure

[Strater, Henry]
ALS Mike
     13 Apr 1932, [NY]
     1p.

[Strater, Henry]
ALS George G. Carey, Jr.
     3 Mar 1932, Baltimore, to Strater
     2pp., w/enclosure

[Strater, Henry]
ALS George Carey
     11 May 1932, Baltimore, to Strater
     1p.

[Strater, Henry]
ALS Mike
     8 Apr 1932, NY
     5pp., w/enclosure and envelope

[Strater, Henry]
ALS Mike
     17 May [1932], NY
     3pp., w/envelope

[Strater, Henry]
TLS Konrad Schauer
     29 Mar 1932, NY, to Strater
     1p., w/envelope postmarked
     8 Apr 1932, NY

[Strater, Henry]
ALS J. A. Hunter
     16 Sept 1932, Nairobi, to Strater
     2pp. bearing Note by Strater

[Strater, Henry]
TLS O. M. Rees
     9 Apr 1932, Nairobi, to Strater
     2pp.

[Strater, Henry]
ALS Mike
     29 June [1933], Ogunquit
     9pp., w/envelope bearing EH note

[Strater, Henry]
TLS Mike
21 June 1934, Ogunquit
3pp., w/envelope

[Strater, Henry]
ALS Mike
16 Aug 1936, Ogunquit
8pp., w/envelope

[Strater, Henry]
TLS Mike
14 Sept 1934, Ogunquit
2pp., w/photograph and envelope

Strater, Henry
See also Beach, Sylvia 7 Aug 1935
Pfeiffer, Gustavus A.
1 Apr 1932

[Strater, Henry]
TLS Mike
Thursday [Nov 1934?], West Palm
Beach, Florida
3pp.

[Strater], Maggie (Mike Strater's wife)
ALS   25 Feb [1929], NY, to EH/Pauline
3pp., w/envelope

Strater, [Henry]
TLS Mike
9 Nov [1934], N.Y.
2pp., w/envelope bearing EH note

[Streit], Clarence (editor, correspondent)
TLS   30 July 1929, Geneva
1p., w/envelope

[Strater, Henry]
ALS Mike
14 Sept 1935, NY
4pp.

Strode, Hudson (author)
ALS   28 Sept 1934, University,
Alabama
2pp., w/envelope

Strode, Hudson
ALS   17 Dec 1934, University
             2pp.

Stuart-Ferguson, M. (librarian)
TLS   1 Aug 1936, London
             1p.

Strong, L. A. G. (anthologist)
TLS   6 July 1923, Oxford
             1p.

Sturm, Jus[tin] (sculptor)
ALS   30 July 1934, Westport
             2pp.

Strong, Rupert (writer)
ALS   5 May 1936, Birkenhead
             6pp., w/envelope

Sturm, Jus[tin]
ALS   7 Sept 1934, Westport
             2pp.

Stuart, Isobel (reader)
ALS   5 Apr 1935, Medford, Oregon
             2pp.,w/envelope

Suchy, Arthur B. (map publisher)
TLS   18 July 1939, Cleveland
             1p., w/enclosure

Stuart, [Robert] (writer)
TLS Bob Stuart
             16 Sept 1949, Clear Lake, Iowa
             1p., w/envelope bearing EH note

Sullivan, [J. B. "Sully"] (friend)
Cable from The Sullivans
             15 Dec 1937, Key West
             1p. bearing EH cable draft

Sulzberger, C. L. (New York Times)

TLS   14 June 1951, Paris

         2pp.

Sweeny, Charles

TLS   3 Sept 1952, Mrray, Utah

         1p. bearing EH note

Sunday Worker
       See North, Joseph

Sweeny, Charles

TLS   14 Sept 1952, Murray

         3pp. bearing ANS Dorothy and EH note

Svetova Literatura (World Literature magazine)

Three Letters

     1. TLS Frantisek Necasek and Jan Rezac, 23 Nov 1959, Praha, Czechoslovakia, 1p.
     2. TL from Leopold Podstupka, editor of Rolnicke noviny, 24 Nov 1959, Bratislava, Czechoslovakia, 1p., to Alfred Rice.
     3. TLS L. Podstupka, 24 Nov 1959, Bratislava, Czechoslovakia, 1p.

     Total 3pp., w/forwarding envelope bearing notes

Sweeny, Charles

TLS   25 Oct 1952, Murray

         1p. bearing EH note

Swain, Richard J. (writer)

ALS Dick Swain

         10 Sept 1957, Victoria, British Columbia

         1p., w/enclosure and newspaper clipping

Sweeny, Charles

TLS   3 Nov 1952, Murray, to MH

         1p.

Sweeny, Charles (military man, friend)

TLS   31 Aug 1937, Paris

         1p.

Sweeny, Charles

TLS   7 Nov 1952, Murray, to MH

         1p.

Sweeny, Charles

TLS   26 June 1953, Murray, to MH

          1p. bearing MH notes

Sweeny, Charles

TLS   25 Mar 1954, Murray

       1p.

[Sweeny, Charles]

ALS "C.S."

       2 Dec 1954, Murray

       4pp., w/enclosures, and envelope

Swope, Herbert Bayard (newspaperman)

TLS "H.B.S."

       2 Sept 1952, NY

       1p. bearing EH note

Swope, Herbert Bayard

TLS "H.B.S."

       26 Jan 1954, NY

       1p., w/envelope

Swope, Herbert Bayard

TLS "H.B.S."

       9 Apr 1954, NY

       1p., w/envelope

S[ylvester], Harry (writer, friend)

TLS   7 July 1936, Wellfleet, Mass.

       1p.

Sylvester, Harry

TLS   2 Aug 1936, Wellfleet

       1p., w/correpondence between
       Robert Daubney and Sylvester

[Sylvester, Harry]

Galley of a letter to the editor written by
Sylvester w/ANS Betty Heeling

       [post 11 Nov 1936]

       1p.

Sylvester, Harry

TLS   19 Dec 1936, Brooklyn

       3pp.

Sylvester, Harry

TLS   1 Feb 1937, Provincetown

           2pp.

Sylvester, Harry

TLS   21 July 1937, Provincetown, to
           Pauline

           1p., w/envelope

S[ylvester], Harry

TLS   11 Feb 1937, Provincetown

           2pp.

Sylvester, Harry

TLS   24 Apr 1938, Ascutney, Vermont

           2pp., w/envelope

Sylvester, Harry

TLS   22 Feb 1937, Provincetown

           1p.

[Sylvester], Rita (Harry's wife)

TLS   1 July 1938, Wellfleet, to Pauline

           2pp.

Sylvester, Harry

TLS   3 Apr 1937, Key West

           1p.

Taggard, Genevieve (author)

ALS   20 May 1926, NY

           3pp., w/envelope

Sylvester, Harry

TLS   2 July 1937, Provincetown, to
           Pauline

           1p., w/envelope

Talbot   ?   (friend)

Cable   19 Feb 1932, Miami

           1p.

Talbot   ?
Cable   19 July 1933, Chicago
                1p.

Tass
Cable   6 Feb 1937, NY
                1p.

Talbot   ?
ALS   15 Apr [1935], Washington
                2pp., w/photographs and envelope

[Tate, Allen] (critic, poet)
ALS "A.T."
                16 Apr 1930, Clarksville, Tenn.
                1p., w/envelope

Talbot   ?
ALS   29 June n.y., Chicago
                5pp. bearing EH note

[Tate], Allen
ALS   17 May [1930], Clarksville
                1p.

Tapatco, American Pad and Textile Co.
        See Baker, Charles H., Jr.

[Tate], Caroline (author, wife of Allen)
TLS   16 May [1930], Clarksville, to
                Pauline
                1p.

Tarassenkoff, An. (editor of <u>Znamya</u>)
TLS   9 Oct 1936
                1p.

Taylor, Alexander (American tourist in Cuba)
TLS Alex
                28 June 1960, NY, to the Editor,
                <u>N.Y. World Telegram and Sun</u>, w/
                ANS "AT"
                3pp.

Taylor, Harvey (literary manager and advisor,
                 publisher, collector)

TLS   15 Mar 1932, NY

             1p.

Temple, Mildred

TLS   22 June 1927, London

             2pp., w/envelope

Taylor, K. P. A.   (doctor)

ALS   19 July 1933, Havana

             2pp., w/envelope

Terris, Tom

TLS   3 June [1936], N.Y.

             1p., w/EH draft reply on verso

Teague, Arthur N. (W.W. II colleague)

TLS Art Teague

             29 July 1951, Mount Washington,
             N.H.

             2pp. bearing EH note

[Teter], Dan (friend)

TLS Florence and Dan

             27 Feb 1960, Friday Harbor,
             Washington, to EH/MH

             1p. bearing MH notes

Tedford, John H. (Red Cross colleague)

TLS   [31 Mar 1930], Boston

             3pp., w/envelope

[Teter], Florence (Dan's wife, friend)

ALS   10 Aug [1960], Friday Harbor,
             Washington, to EH/MH

             1p. bearing MH notes

Temple, Mildred (International Magazine Co.)

TLS   15 June 1927, London

             1p.

The Tetzelis

Cable   [25 Jan 1954, Havana]

             1p.

Texas Heritage Foundation
    See Brague, Harry 24 July 1958
                        7 Oct 1958

Theisen, Earl

TLS Ty

        23 Aug 1955, Los Angeles, to EH/MH

        1p. bearing MH note

Theatre National de Belgique

TLS M. Huisman

        18 Oct 1947, Brussels

        1p.

Theisen, Earl

TLS Ty

        24 June 1959, Los Angeles, to EH/MH

        1p.

[Theisen, Earl] (photographer)

ALS Ty

        15 Jan 1954, Los Angeles

        3pp., w/envelope bearing EH note

Theisen, Earl
    See Meyer, Wallace 8 Feb 1954

Theisen, Earl

TLS Ty

        22 July 1954, Los Angeles

        1p.

<u>This Week Magazine</u>
    See Hotchner, A. E. 13 July 1953

[Theisen, Earl]

TLS Ty

        6 Dec 1954, Los Angeles, to EH/MH

        1p. bearing MH note

Thomas, Virgil (composer)

ALS   22 Mar [1927], Paris

        2pp., w/envelope bearing EH notes

[Thompson], Charles (friend)
ALS   12 June 1928, Key West
           2pp.

[Thompson], Charles
ALS   16 May 1936, Key West
           2pp.

[Thompson], Charles
ALS   26 July 1929, Key West
           4pp., w/envelope bearing EH note

[Thompson], Charles
ALS   [3 Sept 1936], Key West
           2pp., w/envelope

[Thompson], Charles
ALS   5 Nov 1929, Key West
           6pp., w/envelope bearing EH notes

Thompson, Edward K.
           See Time-Life

[Thompson], Charles
ALS   5 Oct 1933, Key West
           7pp.

Thompson, Lorine (wife of Charles)
Cable   3 May 1932, Key West, to Charles
           1p.

[Thompson], Charles
ALS   17 Oct 1933, Key WEst
           2pp.

[Thompson], Lorine
Cable   21 May 1932, Key West
           1p.

[Thompson], Lorine

ALS   [1928], Key West, to Pauline

      6pp., w/envelope

Thompson, William Boyce
    See Horne, William D., Jr.
               22 July 1918

[Thompson], Lorine

ALS   Sunday AM [Dec 1937], to Pauline

      20pp., w/newspaper clipping

Thompson, [Robert]

TLS Bob

      11 Nov 1944, Hdqters, Third
      Infantry Division

      3pp.

Thompson, Lorine
    See Hemingway, Pauline 25 Oct 1928
                    to others

Thompson, W. O. (book collector)

TLS   17 Apr 1959, Turlock, California

      2pp.

Thompson, Ralph (*The Times*)

TLS   25 Oct 1949, Sheffield, to
      [Charles Scribner]

      1p.

Thompson, W. S. (Grand Trunk Railway System)

TLS   2 Oct 1923, Montreal

      1p., w/envelope

Thompson, Ralph
    See Scribner, Charles, Sr.
              17 Oct 1949

[Thomson, A. E.] (W.W. I colleague)

ALS Tommy

      22 Feb 1919, Buffalo

      4pp., w/envelope

Three Mountain Press
See Bird, William

Time-Life

TLS Daniel Longwell

15 Aug 1952, NY

1p., w/copy of TLS W[illiam]
S[omerset] Maugham, 13 Aug 1952,
Ouchy-Lausanne, to Longwell

Time-Life

TLS Henry R. Luce

28 Feb 1930, NY

1p. bearing EH note

Time-Life

Cable from Don Burke

5 Sept [1952], NY

2pp.

Time-Life

Cable from [John C.] Manthorp

[summer 1937], NY
2pp.

Time-Life

TLS Daniel Longwell

20 Oct 1952, NY, to Mary

1p. bearing MH note

Time-Life

TLS John C. Manthorp

6 July 1937, NY

1p.

Time-Life

TLS Sid[ney L. James]

23 May 1953, N.Y.

2pp., w/envelope

Time-Life

TLS Daniel Longwell

8 Aug 1952, NY

2pp., w/enclosure and TLS Martin
Stone, 4 Aug 1952, NY, to Longwell

Time-Life

TLS Edward K. Thompson

20 Dec 1954, NY

1p.

Time-Life

TLS Dick [Richard W.] Johnston

14 Nov 1955, N.Y.

1p. bearing EH note

Time-Life

Cable from Sidney L. James

[3 Aug 1959], NY

1p.

Time-Life

Cable from Sid [J]ames

22 Nov 1955, NY

1p. bearing MH notes

Time-Life

Cable from Sidney James

[7 Aug 1959], NY

1p.

Time-Life

Cable from Sid James

[late July 1959], NY

1p.

Time-Life

Cable from Will Lang

[8 Aug 1959], Paris, to MH

3pp.

Time-Life

Cable from Sid James

7 July 1959, NY

1p.

Time-Life

Cable from Edward [K. Thompson]

[8 Aug 1959]

1p.

Time-Life

Cable from Sid James

17 July 1959, NY

2pp.

Time-Life

Cable from [Edward K.] Thompson

[11 Aug 1959], NY

1p.

Time-Life

Telex from [William] Lang

       12 Aug 1959, to Time, Inc.

       1p.

Time-Life

TLS Bill [Lang]

       Wednesday [Sept 1959], Paris

       1p.

Time-Life

Cable from Ed K. [Thompson]

       [13 Aug 1959], NY, to Bill Lang

       1p.

Time-Life

TLS Bill [Lang]

       18 Sept [1959], Paris

       1p.

Time-Life

TLS Sid[ney L. James]

       13 Aug 1959, NY

       2pp., w/newspaper clipping

Time-Life

Telex from Blashill

       1 Oct 1959, to Lang/Orshevsky

       1p.

Time-Life

TLS Will [Lang]

       29 Aug 1959, Paris

       1p.

Time-Life

Cable from Ed Thompson

       29 Oct 1959, NY

       1p.

Time-Life

Cable from Will Lang

       [Sept 1959, Madrid]

       1p.

Time-Life

TLS Ralph Graves

       3 Nov 1959, NY

       1p., w/enclosure

Time-Life

TLS Bill [Lang]

21 Jan 1960, Paris

1p.

Time-Life

Cable from Bill [Lang]

8 Mar [1960], Paris

4pp.

Time-Life

TLS Bill [Lang]

10 Feb 1960, NY

1p.

Time-Life

Cable from Ed Thompson

11 Mar 1960, NY

1p.

Time-Life

TLS Natalie Kosek

11 Feb 1960, NY

1p.

Time-Life

Cable from Ed Thompson

14 Apr 1960, NY

1p. bearing EH draft reply

Time-Life

Cable from Bill [Lang]

1 Mar [1960], Paris

3pp.

Time-Life

TLS Bill [Lang]

19 Apr 1960, Paris

2pp.

Time-Life

Cable from Ed Thompson

1 Mar 1960, NY

1p. bearing EH notes

Time-Life

TLS Ed Thompson

20 May 1960, NY

1p.

Time-Life

Typescript of correspondence w/EH from 7 July 1959 through 2 June 1960

18pp.

Time-Life

Cable   26 Aug 1960

1p.

Time-Life

Cable from Bill [Lang]

15 Aug 1960

2pp.

[Time-Life]

Cable from Bill [Nathan] Davis

[Sept 1960, to John] Blashill

1p.

Time-Life

Cable from Bill [Lang]

[16 Aug 1960], Malaga to Bill [Nathan] Davis

1p.

Time-Life

Cable from Blashill

[Sept 1960]

1p.

Time-Life

Cable from Ed Thompson

[17 Aug 1960], NY

1p.

Time-Life

TLS Sid[ney L, James]

2 Sept 1960, NY

1p., w/copy of ALS to James from his daughter and envelope bearing EH note

---

Time-Life

Cable from John Blashill

[20 Aug 1960], San Sebastian

2pp.

Time-Life

Cable from Ralph Graves

[19 Sept 1960], NY

1p.

Time-Life
TLS Bill [Lang]
        20 Sept 1960, Paris
        1p., w/envelope

Time-Life
Cable from William P. Gray
        [22 Oct 1960, NY]
        1p.

Time-Life
Cable from Dede Fetter
        [21 Sept 1960], NY
        3pp.

Time-Life
Cable from Tom Dozier penciled by EH
        [c. Nov 1960]
        6pp.

Time-Life
Transcript of Cable
        26 Sept 1960
        1p.

Time-Life
TLS Tom Dozier
        8 Nov 1960, New York
        1p., w/enclosure

Time-Life
Cable from Dozier
        27 Sept 1960, to Blashill
        1p.

Time-Life
TLS Ed[ward K. Thompson]
        10 Nov 1960, NY
        1p., w/envelope

Time-Life
Cable from [John] Blashill
        29 Sept 1960, Madrid
        1p.

Time-Life
TLS Bill [Lang]
        5 June [1961], Paris
        1p., w/envelope

Time-Life
      See Hayward, Leland   25 Apr 1958
                            14 July 1958
                            29 July 1958
      Manning, Robert

Titus, Edward W.

TLS E. W. Titus

                  26 Nov 1929, Paris

                  1p.

Time Magzine
      See Barrett, Peter

Tobias, T. D. (W.W.I colleague)

ALS   4 Aug 1918, Rome

               2pp., w/envelope

Tinker, F[rank] G., Jr. (American volunteer
            aviator, Spanish Civil War)

ALS   8 Oct 1937, De Witt, Arkansas

            2pp.

Toronto Star
            See Bone, John

Tisdall, Hans
      See Scribner, Charles, Sr.
            1 June 1950

Toronto Weekly Star

PL   9 June 1921

        1p.

Titus, Edward W. (publisher)

TLS E. W. Titus

            4 Oct 1929, Paris

            1p.

Toronto Writers' Club

TLS Elton Johnson

            19 Nov 1923, Toronto

            1p., w/envelope

Torresan, Juan Osvaldo   (congratulator)

TLS   29 Oct 1954, Argentia.

           1p. bearing EH note

Train, Arthur   (author, National Institute of
                Arts and Letters)

ALS   20 Dec 1934, [NY]

           3pp., w/envelope

Towne, Charles Hanson   (<u>Harper's Bazaar</u>)

TLS   5 Feb 1927, Paris

           1p., w/envelope bearing EH note

Trait D'Union Press

TLS Jean Jarden

           12 Jan 1938, Paris

           2pp., w/envelope

Townsend, Paul   (sport fisherman)

TLS   15 Aug 1935, Washington

           1p., w/newspaper clipping

<u>Transatlantic</u> <u>Review</u>

ALS Natalie Clifford Barney

           5 Apr n.y., [Paris], to [Ford
           Madox Ford]

           2pp.

[Townsend], Roger O.   (friend)

TLS   20 June 1946, Alamogordo, NM, to
           EH/MH

           2pp., w/envelope

<u>Transatlantic</u> <u>Review</u>

Newspaper clipping, w/envelope

           undated

[Tracy], Spence[r]   (actor)

Cable   [26 Jan 1954, Beverly Hills]

           1p.

<u>Transatlantic</u> <u>Review</u>

Miscellaneous typescripts, proofs, and
drawings

           12pp.

transition
        See Jolas, Eugene
            Hickok, Guy 2 Jan 1928

Troutman, Ivy

ALS   Wednesday, undated, [NY]

            4pp.

Tregaskis, Richard (reader)

TLS Dick

            18 Sept 1957, Costa Mesa,
            California

            1p.

Ture Magazine
        See Barrett, Peter

Trik, Carl H. (W.W. I colleague)

ALS   13 Mar a933, Columbus, Ohio

            8pp., w/envelope bearing EH note

Tunney, Gene [James Joseph] (heavyweight
                            champion, friend)

TLS Gene

            7 Jan 1958, NY

            1p., w/newspaper clipping and
            envelope bearing EH note

Trout, Robert (newsman)

TLS Bob

            25 Jan 1954, to MH

            1p. bearing MH note

Tunney, Gene [James Joseph]

TLS Gene

            14 Dec 1959

            1p.

[Troutman], Ivy

ALS   Tuesday [21 June 1938, NY]

            3pp., w/envelope

Tunney, Gene
        See also Baker, Carlos 2 Feb 1961

22nd Infantry Association
    See Lanham, Charles Trueman
        22 Aug 1947
        24 Aug 1948
         7 Aug 1949

United States Information Agency
TLS George V. Allen

        2 Apr 1959, Washington

    2pp.

Twysden, Lady Duff (friend)
ANS Duff

        [June 1925, Paris]

        1p.

United States Information Agency
TLS Dick [Richard G. Cushing]

        2 Apr 1959, Washington

        1p.

Twysden, [Lady] Duff
ALS   [Sept-Oct 1925], Paris

        2pp., w/envelope

United States Naval Liaison Office,
Nuevitas, Cuba
      See Miller, George J.

Unge, Catharina von (reader)
ALS   1 Dec [1958], Stockholm

        1p., w/address-leaf

Untermeyer, Louis (author)
TLS   5 June 1932, Elizabethtown, NY

        1p.

United Press
Cable   [25 Jan 1954, London]

        1p.

Untermeyer, Samuel
      See Non-Sectarian Anti-Nazi League

Van Dongen
See Peirce, Waldo 11Feb 1930

[Vandersluis], Art (Mary's friend)

TLS   22 Nov [1947, Bemidji, Minn.],
             to EH/MH

             7pp.

Valentine, O. C. (Oxford University Press)

ALS   4 Mar 1927, London

             2pp.

[Vandersluis], Art

TLS   9 Mar 1952, Bemidji, to EH/MH

             3pp.

Vallejo, Juan (shipmate on The Gripsholm)

ALS   1 May 1934, Bilbao

             2pp., w/newspaper clipping and
             envelope bearing EH note

[Vandersluis], Art

TLS   3 Apr 1955, to EH/MH

             2pp.

Vallejo, Maria (shipmate on The Gripsholm)

ALS   28 Nov 1938, [Madrid]

             4pp., w/envelope bearing MH note

[Vanderwicken, Edwin and Martha] (friends)

Cable   19 Mar 1946

             1p.

[Vallejo], Maria

ALS   7 Feb 1939, [Madrid]

             4pp.

Van Dongen, Helen
See Ivens, Joris 24 Jan 1938
                   8 June 1938
                  11 Feb 1938

Van Doren, Carl
    See Literary Guild of America

Vanity Fair
TLS Lewis [Galantiere]

    7 Mar 1927, NY

    1p., w/newspaper clipping and
    envelope

Van Doren, Irita
    See New York Herald Tribune

Vanity Fair
TLS Donald Freeman

    23 Mar 1932, NY

    1p.

VanGundy, E. (reader)
TLS   7 Sept 1933, Kansas City

    1p. bearing EH note

Vanity Fair
    See also Crowninshield, Frank

Van Gundy, E.
TLS   26 Oct 1933, Kansas City

    2pp.

Varley, H. L. (The Literary Society)
TLS   5 Feb 1956, Amherst, Mass.

    1p., w/envelope bearing EH notes

Vanity Fair
TLS Lewis Galantiere

    6 Jan 1927, NY

    1p., w/envelope bearing EH note

Verband Deutscher Sportfischer e. V. (German
    Sportsfishermen)
TLS Arthur Kobes

    20 Dec 1958, Hamburg, Germany

    1p., w/enclosure and translations

Veteran's Association of the American Red
Cross in Italy
　　　　See Mac Donald, Elsie　30 Apr 1933

Vidiella, Rafael
　　　　See Quintanilla, Luis　13 Mar 1937

Vezelay, Paule　(friend, friend of Masson)
ALS　　　7 Nov [1933], Paris
　　　1p., w/envelope

[Viertel], Peter　(friend, screenplay writer)
TLS　　　31 May 1948
　　　2pp.

Vezelay, Paule
ALS　　　Friday [Nov 1933], Paris
　　　1p., w/envelope

[Viertel], Peter
TLS　　　16 June 1948
　　　3pp.

Vezelay, Paule
　　　　See Masson, Andre

[Viertel], Peter
TLS　　　4 July 1948
　　　2pp.

Vickery, Howard F.　(newspaperman)
TLS Vick
　　　[Jan 1935], Pittsburgh
　　　1p.

[Viertel], Peter
TLS　　　30 Aug 1948
　　　1p.

[Viertel], Peter

TLS   1 May 1949, [Malibu, California]

2pp., w/envelope

[Viertel], Peter

TLS   22 Sept 1953, [Paris]

2pp., w/envelope

[Viertel], Peter

TLS   17 July 1949, [Beverly Hills]

2pp., w/address corner of
envelope

[Viertel], Peter

TLS   21 Apr 1954, St. Jean de Luz

1p., w/envelope

[Viertel], Peter

TLS   31 Aug 1949, [Malibu]

2pp., w/envelope fragment bearing
address

[Viertel], Peter

ALS   19 Sept 1954

3pp.

[Viertel], Peter

TLS   10 Oct 1949, [Malibu Beach]

1p., w/envelope bearing EH notes

[Viertel], Peter

TLS   31 Oct 1954, Donadea, Co. Kildare

4pp., w/envelope bearing EH note

[Viertel], Peter

ALS   23 July 1953

3pp.

[Viertel], Peter

TLS   6 Mar 1955, [Klosters]

1p., w/envelope bearing EH note

[Viertel], Peter

TLS   22 Mar 1955, [Donadea]
           2pp., w/envelope bearing EH note

[Viertel], Peter

TLS   7 Oct 1956
           1p.

[Viertel], Peter

TLS   29 Apr 1955, [Los Angeles]
           1p., w/envelope bearing EH note

[Viertel], Peter

TLS   26 Oct [1956], Paris
           1p., w/envelope bearing EH note

[Viertel], Peter

TLS   6 Aug 1955, [Biarritz La Negresse]
           3pp., w/envelope bearing EH note

[Viertel], Peter

TLS   31 Oct 1956, Paris
           2pp., w/envelope

[Viertel], Peter

TLS   18 Dec 1955, [Paris]
           2pp., w/envelope bearing EH note

[Viertel], Peter

Cable   [8 Nov 1956], Loughrea, [Ireland]
           1p.

[Viertel], Peter

TLS   12 Aug [1956], Paris
           3pp., w/envelope both bearing
           EH notes

[Viertel], Peter

TLS   12 Nov 1956, Dublin, to EH/MH
           1p., w/envelope

[Viertel], Peter

TLS   [31 May 1957], Mexico [City]

             2pp., w/envelope

[Viertel], Peter

ALS   18 May 1961, [Klosters]

             2pp., w/envelope

[Viertel], Peter

TLS   4 Sept 1957

             2pp.

Viertel, Peter
                    See Dominguin 29 Sept 1955

[Viertel], Peter

TLS   13 Nov 1957, [Courtown, Kilcock,
             Co. Kildare

             2pp., w/envelope and enclosure

Vila Fuentes, Gaspar

TLS G. Vila Fuentes

             16 May 1959, Jativa, Spain

             1p.

[Viertel], Peter

TLS   [15 May 1958], Vienna

             3pp., w/envelope

Villarreal, Rene   (household employee)

ALS   15 Sept 1956, San Francisco de
             Paula, to EH/MH

             2pp.

[Viertel], Peter

TLS   8 Dec 1958, [Madrid]

             2pp., w/envelope bearing EH note

Villarreal, Rene

ALS   5 Mar 1961, San Francisco de
             Paula, to EH/MH

             2pp.

Vincenzo, Bellia Pier (W.W. I associate)
TLS   9 Feb 1920, Torino
             2pp., w/envelope

Wald, Jerry
TLS   30 Jan 1961, Beverly Hills
             1p. bearing EH notes

[Vittorini], Elio   (author)
Cable   [26 Jan 1954, Milan]
             1p.

[Walker, G. A.] (friend)
A Post Card S Weeg
             13 Dec 1919, S. Bethlehem, Pa.

Voight, F. A. (reader)
TLS "FV"
             22 Jan 1939, London
             1p.

[Walker, G. A.]
TLS Weege
             17 Feb 1921, Olivet, Mich.
             1p.

Voila
TLS [Florent] Fels
             19 Dec 1934, Paris
             1p.

Wallace, Henry (Sports Illustrated)
TLS   22 Nov 1955, Havana
             1p.

Wald, Jerry (Twentieth Century Fox)
TLS   8 June 1960, Beverly Hills
             1p., w/envelope

Wallack, N. N. (book collector)
TLS   4 May 1936, Washington
             1p.

[Walsh], Ernest (This Quarter)

ANS, on verso of p. 1 of EH letter dated
24 Mar [1925]

   1p.

Walton, William (journalist, friend)

TLS   15 July [1945], Walton's Bavarian
           Retreat, to EH/MH

           3pp., w/envelope

[Walsh], Ernest

TLS   9 Jan 1926, Grasse, France

           1p.

[Walton, William]

TL   10 Sept [1946], to EH/MH

           2pp.

Walsh, Richard J. (The John Day Company)

TLS   28 Sept 1949

           1p. bearing EH note

[Walton, William]

TLS Willy

           29 July [1951], Oaxaca, Mexico,
           to EH/MH

           1p. bearing EH note

Walter, Raymond
         See New York Times

Ward, T. H. (friend)

ALS Mike

           14 June 1948, Washington

           4pp., w/envelope bearing EH notes

Walton, [William]

TLS   5 Apr [1945], NY, to MH

           1p.

[Ward, T. H.]

TLS Mike

           4 Oct 1949

           3pp.

[Ward, T. H.]
TLS Mike

8 June 1950
1p. bearing EH note

Watson, E. M. (reader)
ALS   [7 Aug 1929], Buffalo
1p., w/envelope bearing EH note

Warner Brothers
    See Lerner, Michael 30 Oct 1943

Watt, A. P. & Son
    See Scribner, Charles 10 Nov 1949
                           14 Nov 1949

Wartels, Nat (Crown Publishers)
TLS Nat

10 Jan 1961, N.Y.
2pp. bearing EH note

Weaver, John V. A. (writer)
TLS   2 Oct 1929, Hollywood
1p. bearing EH note

Waters, Harold (writer)
TL   18 Jan 1937, Fort Lauderdale
2pp.

Weaver, [John V. A.]
TLS   23 Apr [1936], Beverly Hills
2pp., w/envelope

Waters, Harold
TLS   26 Feb 1938, Fort Lauderdale
1p.

[Weaver, Leland Stanford]
ALS Chub

20 Mar 1931, Red Lodge, Montana
2pp.

[Weaver, Leland Stanford] (ranch hand, friend)
ALS Chub

        12 Aug 1931, Bert Wallace R[anch]
        3pp.

Weidman, Jerome (author)
TLS   8 Apr 1949, Westport, Conn.
        1p.

Webb, Coop
Cable   7 Jan 1936, Miami
        1p.

Weiss, Swifty
      See Jenkins, Howell 11 Aug 1918

Weber, Dr. H. L.
      See Hemingway, Clarence E. 13 June 1921

Weissberger, Jose A. (Spanish Civil War
                 comrade)
ALS   [1937, NY]
        4pp.

Weeks, Edward
      See Atlantic Monthly

Weissberger, [Jose A.]
Cable   20 July 1937, NY
        1p.

Webb, Jon Edgar (Works Progress Administration)
TLS   31 Oct n.y., [NY]
        1p.

Weissberger, [Jose A.]
Cable   27 July [1937]
        1p.

Weissberger, [Jose A.]

TLS   4 Nov 1937, NY

             1p.

Westinghouse Broadcasting Co.
             See Aldrich, David

Wells, James R.
             See Peirce, Waldo   21 Mar 1929

Westminster Magazine
             See England, Robert D.

Werner, M. R. (correspondent, author)

TLS Werner

             19 Oct 1929, NY

             1p.

Wheaton, Bill and Bunny

Cable   undated, Paris

             1p. bearing EH notes

Wertheim, Barbara (Spanish Civil War comrade)

TLS   19 Jan [1939, NY]

             1p., w/enclosure and envelope

Wheeler, John N. (North American Newspaper
                        Alliance)

TLS   25 Nov 1936, NY

             1p.

Wescott, Glenway (author, National Institute
                        of Arts and Letters)

TLS   23 Dec 1960, NY

             2pp., w/envelope both bearing
             EH notes

[Wheeler, John N.]

TLS Henry M. Snevily

             4 Dec 1936, NY

             1p.

Wheeler, John N.

TLS   18 Dec 1936, NY

         1p., w/newspaper clipping

Wheeler, John N.

TLS   24 Nov 1937, NY

         1p.

Wheeler, John N.

TLS   8 June 1937, NY

         2pp.

[Wheeler, John N.]

Cable   [8 Jan 1938], N.Y.

         1p.

Wheeler, John N.

TLS   8 June 1937, NY, to Whom It May
Concern

         1p.

Wheeler, John [N.]

TLS   27 Feb 1938, Miami Beach

         1p.

[Wheeler, John N.]

Cable   5 Aug 1937, NY

         1p. bearing EH note

Wheeler, John N.

TLS "J.N.W."

         31 May 1938, NY

         2pp., w/newspaper clipping and
memo to Wheeler from [Bertram G.]
Zilmer, 31 May 1938

Wheeler, John N.

TLS   10 Aug 1937, NY

         1p.

Wheeler, John N.

TLS "J.N.W."

         2 June 1938, NY

         1p.

Wheeler, John N.
TLS "J.N.W."
          14 June 1938, NY
          2pp.

Wheeler, John N.
TLS "J.N.W."
          15 Nov 1938, NY
          2pp.

Wheeler, John N.
TLS "J.N.W."
          20 June 1938, NY
          1p.

Wheeler, John N.
TLS "J.N.W."
          15 Nov 1938, NY
          1p.

Wheeler, John N.
TLS "J.N.W."
          28 June 1938, NY
          1p.

Wheeler, John N.
TLS   1 June 1939, NY
          1p.

Wheeler, John N.
T.S "J.N.W."
          20 July 1938, NY
          1p., w/TLS from The New York Times
7 July 1938, Paris, to Philip
Carr

Wheeler, John N.
Copy of a TL
          7 Sept 1956
          1p.

Wheeler, John N.
T.S "J.N.W."
          26 Oct 1938, NY
          1p. bearing EH note

Wheeler, John N.
TLS John
          13 Sept 1956, NY
          1p.

Wheeler, John [N.]

Cable   [1 Aug 1959], NY

          1p.

Wheeler, John N.

TLS   11 May 1965, NY, to MH

          1p.

Wheeler, John [N.]

Cable   [2 Aug 1959], NY

          1p.

White, Bob

Cable   [13 Nov 1929], Piggott

          1p.

Wheeler, John N.

TLS John

          6 Aug 1959, NY

          1p. bearing EH note

White, Helen (wife of Bud White)

ALS Helen

          Monday [Jan 1932], Kansas City,
          to Pauline

          6pp.

Wheeler, John [N.]

Cable   7 Aug 1959, NY

          1p.

White, Helen

ALS Helen

          Friday [21 May 1932], Kansas
          City, to Pauline

          6pp., w/envelope

Wheeler, John [N.]

TLS   8 Dec 1960, NY.

          1p., w/copy of a TL, 19 Oct 1960,
          to EH, and envelope bearing EH
          note

White, [Helen]

Envelope only

          8 Sept 1952, Paris, to EH/MH

White, Raymond B. (lumber manufacturer, cousin?)
TLS R. B. White
        26 Dec 1929, Kansas City
        1p., w/newspaper clipping

[White, Raymond B.]
ALS Bud
        [23 May 1932, Kansas City]
        3pp., w/enclosure and envelope

White, Raymond B.
TLS Bud
        7 Jan 1932, Kansas City
        1p., w/enclosure

White, Raymond B.
ALS Bud
        25 Nov 1932, Kansas City
        2pp.

White, Raymond B.
TLS by secretary
        5 Feb 1932, Kansas City
        1p.

White, Raymond B.
ALS Bud
        19 Mar 1934, Kansas City
        2pp.

[White, Raymond B.]
Cable   16 Apr 1932, Kansas City
        1p.

White, Trumbell (journalist, neighbor in Michigan)
TLS   21 Apr 1932, NY
        2pp.

White, Raymond B.
TLS Bud
        10 May 1932, Kansas City
        2pp.

White, Trumbell
TLS   9 Apr 1934, NY
        1p.

White, Trumbell
Cable   26 Apr 1934, NY
                    1p.

Wilcox, C. W.
ALS   undated, NY
                    2pp.

Wickware, Mary
          See *Partisan Review*

[Wilder], Thornton (author)
A Post Card S
          [28 June 1926], Speculator, NY

Wilcox, C. W. (Scribner's Book Store)
ALS   [1 Sept 1936], NY
                    2pp., w/envelope

Wilder, Thornton
ALS   9 Nov 1926, Munich
                    4pp., w/envelope

[Wilcox, C. W.]
ALS C.W.W.
                    [Nov 1949], NY
                    2pp.

[Wilder], Thornton
ALS   22 Nov 1926, Paris
                    4pp., w/envelope

[Wilcox, C. W.]
Envelope only
                    [7 Dec 1956, NY]
                    bearing E^n note

[Wilder], Thornton
ALS   10 Jan 1927, Juan-les-Pins
                    4pp., w/envelope bearing EH note

[Wilder], Thornton

ALS   15 Feb 1927, [New Haven]

        4pp., w/envelope

[Wilder, Thornton]

ALS Thornt

             Friday noon [20 Sept 1929], Oxford

             3pp., w/envelope

[Wilder, Thornton]

ALS John Wiley

        Sunday [Apr 1927], Paris

        2pp., w/ALS Thornton Wilder, 3 Apr 1927, New Haven, to EH, 2pp., w/envelope

---

[Wilder, Thornton]

ALS "T.W."

        [Mar 1933]

        4pp.

[Wilder, Thornton]

ALS Tipton Blish

        5 Jan 1928, [Paris]

        2pp., w/ALS Thornton 7 Dec 1927, Lawrenceville, N.Y., to EH, 2pp., w/envelope

---

[Wilder], Thornton

ALS   13 Mar 1935, Chicago

        1p., w/TLS George Morgenstern, [24 Mar 1935], Miami, to EH, 1p., w/envelope

---

[Wilder, Thornton]

ALS "T.W."

        Tuesday [Mar 1928, Paris], to EH/ Pauline

        2pp.

[Wilder], Thornton

ALS   1 Mar 1938, NY

        8pp., w/envelope

Wilder, Thornton

ALS Thornt

        20 June 1928, Lawrenceville

        1p., w/envelope

Wiley, John
      See Wilder, Thornton Apr 1927

Wiley, John and Irene (diplomat)
Cable   18 Mar 1939, Washington
          1p.

Williams, Joe (newspaperman)
TLS   [18 Apr 1935, NY]
          1p., w/envelope

Willard, Irina Soulpayrac (<u>International Observer</u>)
ALS   undated, NY
          3pp.

Williams, John D. (producer)
ALS   4 Oct 1938, NY
          4pp.

Willert, Paul (friend)
TLS   26 Oct [1938], NY
          1p.

Williams, John D.
ALS   11 Oct 1938, NY
          4pp.

[Willert], Paul
TLS   21 July [1939], London
          1p., w/envelope

Williams, Stanley T. (author)
ALS Ura [Ursula Hemingway Jepson]
          [16 July 1952],
          2pp., w/ALS Stanley T. Williams,
          13 July 1952, South Dennis, Mass.,
          to Jepson, TLS Stanley T. Williams
          2 Aug 1952, Hamden, Conn., to
          Jepson, w/excerpt from EH to
          William B. Smith, 4 Mar 1925

William Morris Agency
          See Geller, James J.

[Williams, T. Norman] (friend)
TLS Tubby
          Sunday night [1918], St. Louis
          2pp.

[Williams, T. Norman]

TLS Tubby

        Wednesday [8 May 1918, St. Louis]

        3pp., w/envelope

[Williams], Taylor

ALS   6 July 1953, Sun Valley, to EH/MH

       1p., w/carbons of corresondence
between Taylor and Abercrombie
& Fitch

[Williams, T. Norman]

TLS Tubby

        Friday [5 Dec 1919, Chicago]

        15pp., w/envelope

Williams, William Carlos (author)

TLS Bill

        23 June 1927, Rutherford, N.J.

        1p., w/envelope

[Williams, T. Norman]

TLS Tubstein

        Thursday [26 Feb 1920], Chicago

        1p., w/newspaper clippings and
envelope

Williams, William Carlos

TLS Bill

        Easter Sunday

        1p. bearing EH note

Williams, T. Norman (Tubby)
    See Hemingway, Clarence E. 23 July 1918
       Hemingway, Grace Hall   25 July 1918

Williams, William Carlos
    See Cowley, Malcolm 9 June 1937

[Williams], Taylor (friend)

ALS   6 June 1952, Sun Valley, to EH/MH

      1p.

Wilson, Dale (Kansas City Star)

TLS   24 Nov [1919], Kansas City

      2pp., w/envelope

Wilson, [Earl] (columnist)
Cable   [25 Jan 1954, New York]
         1p.

Wilson, Edmund
TLS   4 May 1927, NY
            1p.

[Wilson], Earl
TLS   9 Nov 1955, to EH/MH
            1p., w/newspaper clipping

Wilson, Edmund
TLS   18 May 1927, NY
            1p.

Wilson, Earl
TLS Earl
            7 Aug 1958, [NY]
            1p., w/newspaper clippings and
            envelope

Wilson, Edmund
TLS "E.W."
            29 Feb 1932, NY, to Dos Passos
            2pp.

Wilson, Edmund (editor, The New Republic)
TLS   20 Oct 1926, NY
            1p.,w/envelope

Wiman, Dwight Deere
        See Perkins, Maxwell E.   3 Dec 1926

Wilson, Edmund
TLS   7 Jan 1927, NY
            1p., w/EH notes on verso

Winchell, Walter (newsman)
TLS Walter
            25 Jan 1954, NY
            2pp., w/forwarding letter

Winter, Ella (author, wife of Lincoln
                        Steffens)

ALS   11 Jan 1927, [Sache]

             1p., w/envelope

Wister, Owen (author)

ALS   5 Aug 1928, Shell, Wyoming

             1p.

Winter, Ella

ALS   26 Aug [1927], Carmel, Califronia

             4pp., w/TLS F. J. Smith, to Winter,
             and TLS Robert Joyce Tasker to
             Smith

Wister, Owen

ALS   13 Sept 1928, Bryn Mawr, Pa.

             2pp.

Winter, Ella

ALS   26 Sept 1936, Carmel

             1p., w/photograph and envelope
             bearing EH note

Wister, Owen

ALS   17 Oct 1928, Geneva

             3pp., w/envelope

Winter, Ella

ALS   17 Feb [1937], Hollywood

             2pp., w/envelope

[Wister, Owen]

ANS "O.W.", on newspaper clipping

                        w/envelope postmarked 22 Oct 1928,
                        Paris

Winter, Ella
                        See Steffens, Lincoln 23 Oct 1928

Wister, Owen

Typescript of a statement beginning "Ernest
Hemingway's book is many jumps of seven league
boots ahead. . ."

             [1929]

             1p.

Wister, Owen
ALS   27 Feb 1929, Bryn Mawr
     2pp., w/envelope

[Wister, Owen]
ALS Nuncle
     12 Feb 1936, Bryn Mawr
     5pp.

Wister, Owen
ALS   25 Feb 1929
     1p.

Witte, E. P. (writer)
TLS   15 Aug 1934, Tulsa, Oklahoma
     2pp.

Wister, Owen
ALS   8 Mar 1929, Bryn Mawr
     2pp.

Wittner, Victor (Der Querschnitt)
TLS   24 Oct 1938, Zurich
     1p.

[Wister, Owen]
ALS "O.W."
     17 Mar 1929, Bryn Mawr
     2pp., w/envelope

Wolf, Robert (writer, husband of Genevieve
     Taggard)
ALS   24 Aug 1926, New Preston, Conn.
     3pp., w/envelope

Wister, Owen
ALS "O.W."
     8 Dec 1935
     2pp.

Wolfe, William
     See Jenkins, Howell 11 Aug 1918

Wood, Jasper L. (publisher)

TLS   2 June 1938, Cleveland

            1p.

Wyckoff, Irma

            See Perkins, Maxwell E.   21 July 1938

Wood, Jasper

Cable   16 June 1938, Cleveland

            1p.

Wynne, Gerrald W. (reader)

ALS   2 Dec [1926], Washington

            4pp., w/envelope

[Wood, Jasper]

Cable from Lehman Wood

            19 July 1938, Cleveland

            1p.

Yallahy, Beatrice (journalism student)

TLS   17 June 1946, Columbia, Missouri

            1p. bearing EH notes

Woodward, H. L. (sport fisherman)

TLS   27 July 1933, Havana

            1p.

Y.M.C.A.

TLS Arthur M. LeWald

            21 July 1919, Great Lakes, Ill.

            1p.

Woodward, H. L.

TLS   11 Feb 1935, Havana

            2pp., w/copy of a letter from
            Leonard E. Brownson, Jr., to
            Woodward

Yohalem, George (reader)

ALS   28 Feb n.y., Hollwood

            2pp.

Yorke, Selina (?)
See Peirce, Waldo 11 Mar 1932

Young, Philip

TLS   26 June 1952, Ramapo

             2pp. bearing EH note

Young, Philip (literary critic, writer)

TLS   1 Mar 1952, NY

             2pp. bearing EH note

Young, Philip

TLS   4 July 1952, Ramapo

             1p. bearing EH note

Young, Philip

TLS   23 May 1952, NY

             2pp. bearing EH note

Young, Phil[ip]

TLS   5 Oct 1952, Bronx

             1p. bearing EH note

Young, Philip

ALS   28 May 1952, Ramapo, NY

             2pp. bearing EH note

Young, W. F.

TL   25 May 1920, Oak Park

             1p.

Young, Philip

TLS   10 June 1952, Ramapo

             2pp. bearing EH note

Youngstrom, Elizabeth
See Scribner, Charles, Jr.
          7 Apr 1959
          24 Sept 1959

[Zaphiro], Denis (game warden, friend)

TLS   22 July 1954, Kajiado

2pp.

Zaphiro, Denis

TLS   31 May 1957, Kajiado

2pp., w/address-leaf

[Zaphiro], Denis

TLS   31 July 1954, Kajiado, to MH

1p.

[Zaphiro], Denis

TLS   7 July [1958], Kajiado

2pp., w/envelope

Zaphiro, Denis

TLS   20 Sept 1954, Kajiado, to Bill
[William Lowe]

1p.

[Zaphiro], Denis

ALS   3 Aug 1959, Kajiado, to EH/MH

3pp. bearing MH note

[Zaphiro], Denis

TLS   21 Mar 1955, Kajiado

1p.

Zielinski, Bronislaw (Polish translator)

TLS B. Zielinski

        6 Feb 1957, Warsaw

        2pp.

Zaphiro, Denis

TLS   6 Jan 1956, Kajiado

1p., w/address-leaf

[Zielinski, Bronislaw]

ALS Old Wolf from Warsaw

        14 Dec 1958, NY

        2pp., w/newspaper clipping and
        envelope bearing EH note

[Zielinski, Bronislaw]
ALS Bron

10 Apr 1960, Warsaw
2pp., w/photograph and envelope

[Zielinski, Bronislaw]
ALS Bron

1 May 1960, Warsaw
1p., w/photographs and envelope

Zielinski, Bronislaw
See Harry Brague 7 Oct 1958

Ziffren, Lester (writer, newsman)
TLS Ziff

27 Feb 1934, Madrid
2pp.

Ziff[ren, Lester]
TLS   28 Apr 1934, Madrid
5pp. bearing EH note

Ziff[ren, Lester]
TLS   5 July 1934, Madrid
3pp.

Ziff[ren, Lester]
TLS   31 July 1934, Madrid
2pp.

Ziff[ren, Lester]
TLS   3 Sept 1934, Madrid
2pp.

Ziff[ren, Lester]
Cable   19 Oct 1934, Madrid
1p.

Ziff[ren, Lester]
TLS   1 Nov 1934, Madrid
1p.

Ziff[ren, Lester]
TLS Ziff

                30 Dec 1934, Madrid
                2pp.

Ziffren, Lester
TLS Ziff

                7 Feb 1937, Rock Island, Ill.
                1p.

Ziff[ren, Lester]
TLS   11 Mar 1935, Madrid
                3pp.

Ziff[ren, Lester]
TLS   18 Feb 1937, Rock Island
                3pp., w/carbon

Ziff[ren, Lester]
TLS Ziff

                11 June 1935, Madrid
                3pp.

Ziff[ren, Lester]
Cable   18 Feb 1937, Davenport, Iowa
                1p.

[Ziffren, Lester]
Cable from Giffren

                14 Feb 1936, Madrid
                1p.

Ziffren, Lester
TLS Ziff

                30 June 1937, Beverly Hills
                1p.

Ziff[ren, Lester]
Cable   30 July 1936, Madrid
                1p.

Ziffren, Lester
TLS Ziff

                9 Feb 1939, NY
                1p.

Zilmer, Bertram G.

TLS   3 May 1937, NY, to Pauline

          1p.

Zilmer, Bertram G.

TLS   27 Apr 1938, NY, to Pauline

          1p.

Zilmer, Bertram G.   (North American Newspaper Alliance)

TLS   13 Aug 1937, NY

          1p.

Zilmer, Bertram G.

TLS   20 May 1938, NY, to Pauline

          1p.

Zilmer, Bertram G.

TLS   1 Feb 1938, NY

          1p.

Zilmer, Bertram G.

TLS   23 May 1938, NY, to Pauline

          1p.

Zilmer, Bertram G.

TLS   18 Mar 1938, NY

          1p.

Zilmer, Bertram G.

     See Wheeler, John   31 May 1938

Zilmer, Bertram G.

TLS   15 Apr 1938, NY, to Pauline

          1p.

[Zinneman], Fred   (director)

TLS   4 Nov 1955

          2pp.

Z[inneman], Fred
TLS   13 Jan 1956, [Los Angeles]
          3pp., w/envelope bearing EH note

Unidentified
ALS Molly
          Sunday noon [16 Oct 1916?, Aurora, New York]
          6pp., w/envelope
          see als 1 Sept 1916--unidentified

[Zinneman], Fred
TLS   20 Aug 1956
          2pp. bearing EH note

Unidentified
ALS "One gut Cordes"
          27 Sept 1916, Wyoming
          4pp., w/envelope
          see also 16 Oct 1916--unidentified

[Zinneman], Fred
TLS   11 Oct 1957, to EH/MH
          2pp

Unidentified
ALS Bill
          16 Oct 1916, Wyoming, Ohio
          4pp., w/envelope
          see also 27 Sept 1916--unidentified

Znamya
       See Tarassenkov, An.

Unidentified
A Post Card S "The Wild Cat"
          [16 Aug 1918, Rome]

Unidentified
ALS Molly
          Thursday [1 Sept 1916, LaCrosse, Wisconsin]
          3pp., w/envelope bearing EH notes
          see also 16 Oct 1916--unidentified

Unidentified
ALS ?
          18 Dec 1920, Clovis, New Mexico
          4pp.

Unidentified

ALS Dorothy

  23 May [1924], Paris, to Hadley

  4pp. w/2 envelopes, 1 of which bears
Hadley's notes

Unidentified

ANS Noel

   [13 Dec 1929, Paris]

   1p., w/address-leaf

   see also 6 Dec 1929--unidentified

Unidentified

ALS Muggie

  [c. 29 Dec 1925]

  2pp. w/envelope

Unidentified

ALS ?

   26 Feb 1930

   3pp.

Unidentified

A Post Card S

   [2 Feb 1928, Kansas City]

Unidentified

ALS No tips

   [August 1933], M.V. "Reina del
Pacifico"

   2pp.

Unidentified

ANS Noel

   [6 Dec 1929, Paris]

   1p., w/address-leaf

   see also 13 Dec 1929--unidentified

Unidentified

A Postcard S D____, G____, & B____

   17 Feb 1936, Oaxaca, [Mexico]

   1p.

Unidentified

TLS Percy   (New York Evening Post)

  13 Dec 1929, New York

  1p.

Unidentified

Cable unsigned

   23 July 1936, Bimini

   1p.

Unidentified
Cable unsigned

       25 July 1936, Cat Cay

       1p.

Unidentified
ALS Archie

       13 May [1938], Englewood,
       Englefield Green, Surrey

       4pp.

       see also 5 Apr 1938--Unidentified

Unidentified
TLS H____?

       27 May 1937, Winchester, N.H.

       2pp.

Unidentified
ALS Archie

       5 Apr [1938], White's

       2pp.

       see also 13 May 1938--Unidentified

Unidentified
ALS Charles

       17 Feb 1938, New York

       3pp.

Unidentified
A Post Card S ?

       14 Feb 1941, Lasto [di Rocca, Belluno],
       to Per de Grandi Elisa

       2pp.

Unidentified
ALS John

       1 Mar 1938, New York

       2pp.

Unidentified
Xmas Card S Marion C.

       [c. Dec 1943]

       1p.

Unidentified
Cable   [22 Mar 1938, New York]

       1p.

Unidentified
A Post Card S ?

       5 Aug 1950, B[illin]gs, Mont.

Unidentified
ALS Patricia

        8 Sept 1952, Paris, to EH/MH
        2pp.

Unidentified
Cable from Alec

        [26 Jan 1954, Nairobi], to EH/MH
        1p.

Unidentified
TLS Ramon (Cuban friend, art gallery)
        9 Sept 1952, to Dear Friends [EH/MH]
        1p. bearing EH note

Unidentified
Cable from Cookie

        [26 Jan 1954, Homestead]
        1p.

Unidentified
Cable from Dorothy/Charlie

        [25 Jan 1954, Holladay, Utah]
        1p.

Unidentified
ALS Maria ?

        28 Jan 1954, Vienna
        1p., w/newspaper clipping

Unidentified
Cable from Adrian/Betty

        [26 Jan 1954, Havana]
        1p.

Unidentified
ALS   4 Nov 1954
        1p.

Unidentified
Cable from Marita

        [25 Jan 1954, Rome], to EH/MH
        1p.

Unidentified
ALS   ?

        23 Mar 1955, New York
        2pp., w/envelope bearing EH notes

Unidentified

TLS Rodrigo R_____   (congratulator)

2 Nov 1956, Madrid

1p.

Unidentified

ALS Charles

undated, Paris

1p.

Unidentified

ANS ?   [1950's], Paris

1p. drawing and invitation
acceptance on Ritz Hotel letterhead

Unidentified

ALS H_____?

Tuesday, Varadero, Cuba

2pp.

Unidentified

ANS ?

14 Jan 1957, Paris, to EH/MH

1p. drawing and thank you on
Ritz Hotel letterhead

Unidentified

TLS "RB"

undated, beginning "Of course I
should follow. . ."

3pp.

Unidentified

TL Fragment

17 Apr 1959, Chapel Hill

3pp. only

Unidentified

ANS   ?

[1 Jan] n.y., on notepaper of
"1er Bataillon Etranger de
Parachutistes"

1p.

Unidentified

TLS Balle

5 May n.y.

1p.

Unidentified

Cable from H

[30 May 19?], Paris

1p.

Unidentified
ALS J___

      undated, Havana

      1p.

Unidentified
AL   undated, Madrid

      1p. w/envelope

Unidentified
TL Fragment

      undated, beginning "and not too
commonplace. . ."

      1p. only

Unidentified
AN   undated, Madrid, to Encatado

      1p.

Unidentified
ANS   11 [Dec n.y.], Venice, to Cher Monsieur

      1p.

Photographs

Box #	Description and Folder Titles	Box #	Description and Folder Titles

1 Clarence E. Hemingway's Photographs, 1888–1903

Photographs (glass plates) taken by EH's father, portraying his travels, friends, and associates, the vicinity of Oak Park, Illinois, and elsewhere. Arranged by subject.

    C. E. H's friends
      1888–1891
      Oberlin College
    Great Smoky Mountains, 1891
    Oak Park, city views
    Country views
    Walloon Lake, Henry Bacon's barn
      raising, 1903
    Microscope photos

Early Years, 1899–1921

EH, members of his family, their friends, activities and other subjects. Includes photos of locales associated with Hemingway's youth. Arranged by subject first, and chronologically therein.

    EH, portrait photos, 1899–1904
    Oak Park
      CEH family, 1901–1919
      EH and sisters, c. 1900–1906
      EH and Marcelline, 1916
      EH and Leicester, 1919–1921
      EH
      EH with friends
      Hemingway house, Kenilworth
        Avenue
    Walloon Lake
      CEH family, 1899–1906. 2 folders
      EH, hunting, c. 1913
      EH with sisters and friends, c. 1915
      EH, fishing, 1916
      EH, 1919
      Windemere Cottage, 1919
      Grace Cottage, 1919
    Horton Bay, Dilworths, 1918
    Michigan
      Upper peninsula views
      Fishing trips, 1915, 1916. 2 folders
      Fishing
    Canoe trip, Des Plaines River
    Camping trip with schoolfriends

1

    EH with Bill Smith and Charles Hopkins,
      1919
    EH with Hadley, courtship, c. 1921
    Marriage to Hadley Richardson, 9/3/21
    Hall and Hancock ancestors

2

    Anson T. Hemingway and family
    Clarence E. Hemingway, 1899–1924
    Grace Hall Hemingway
    Clarence E. and Grace Hall Hemingway,
      1930 s
    Marcelline Hemingway
    Ursula Hemingway
    Madelaine "Sunny" Hemingway
    Leicester Hemingway
    Leicester Hemingway's Caribbean
      voyage, 11/34. 2 folders
    Sporting events, 1915
    EH's classmates, Oak Park
    EH's friends
    Oak Park, unidentified people
    Unidentified people

Paris Years, 1922–1930

Photos of EH, his wives Hadley and Pauline, children and friends. The photos document Hemingway's activities—particularly his trips—in Europe. Arranged chronologically first, then by subject.

    Black Forest, Germany, EH and Hadley,
      8/22
    Chamby, Switzerland, EH and Hadley,
      1922
    Ronda, Spain, EH, Bill Bird, Bob
      McAlmon, 1923
    Madrid, corrida, EH, others, 1923
    Paris
      EH with Hadley and Bumby, 1924
      Hadley, Bumby, Gertrude Stein and
        Alice B. Toklas, 1924
    Pamplona
      EH, Hadley and others, c. 1925
      "The Amateurs," 1925
      Corridas. 2 folders
    Schruns, Austria
      EH, Hadley, Pauline Pfeiffer,
        others, 1925/6
      EH, Hadley, Bumby, others, 1926
    Pamplona, EH, Hadley, Pauline, Murphys, 1926

| Box # | Description and Folder Titles | Box # | Description and Folder Titles |

2 Paris Years, 1922–1930 (cont.)

Gstaad, Switzerland, EH, Pauline,
 others, 1927
San Sebastian, EH, Pauline, Waldo
 Peirce, 1927
Spain
 EH, with Sidney Franklin, 1929
 EH, Sidney Franklin, and others,
  picnic
 Corridas, EH and Pauline
Pamplona
EH
EH and Hadley
Hadley

3

Bumby
EH and Pauline
Pauline
Patrick
City and country views
Sporting events, Italy and France
Boxers
Maine, photos by Waldo Peirce
Quebec, photos by Waldo Peirce

Wars, 1917–1945

Photos of EH and others, and scenes of various countries visited by Hemingway during various wars. Arranged chronologically by war, and then by subject.

World War I
 Italy, EH & others
 A. R. C. ambulances
 Italian Front. 4 folders
Spanish Civil War
 S. S. Paris, EH with Sidney
  Franklin, 1937
 EH in Spain. 2 folders
 Martha Gellhorn
 EH with Martha
 Scenes. 4 folders
Sino-Japanese War
 S. S. Matsonia, EH, Martha,
  others, 1941
 EH, Martha in Hawaii, 1941
 EH, Martha in China

4

World War II
 EH in France, 1944
 EH with Patrick
 Mary Welsh
 EH, Mary in France
 Scenes in France, 1944
 Liberation of Paris—souvenir photos

Key West Years, 1928–1939

Photos of EH, his family and their friends, and their activities—primarily deep sea fishing—while residing in Key West. Also includes photos of Hemingway and others in other areas. Arranged by locale first, and then by subject. Dates are noted when possible.

Key West
 EH, Waldo Peirce, others, fishing,
  1928. 2 folders
 EH & Pauline
 Pauline
 EH's sons
 EH with parents
 EH with unidentified
 EH's house
 Hurricane aftermath, 9/35
 Anita, EH and others, with catch, 1933
 Pilar, in berth, 1936
Dry Marquesas, hunting, 1929
Piggott, Arkansas, EH's Sons
Havana Harbor
 Anita, EH, others, 1932, 1933. 2 folders
 EH, Sidney Franklin, others, 7/34
 EH, others with silver marlin, 1934
 EH, others with blue marlin, 1934
 EH, others with marlin, 1934
 Pilar
  Underway
  EH, others with striped marlin,
   1939. 2 folders
  EH, others with black marlin
  EH, others with blue marlin
  EH's associates with various fish
Cojimar, Cuba
 EH, others
 Pauline
 Market fishermen, 1934
Cuba
 Native fishing boats & crews, 1933, 1934
 Coastline views

Box #   *Description and Folder Titles*   Box #   *Description and Folder Titles*

5   Key West Years, 1928–1939 (cont.)

Bimini
    EH, Pauline, others
    Pauline, children, arrival via seaplane, 4/35
    Pauline, 1935
    Pauline, others
    EH, boxing 1935
    EH, others, aboard *Pilar* & ashore
    EH, Pauline, others with shark, 6/35
    EH, Pauline, sons & others with marlin, 1935
    EH, others with marlin, 1935. 4 folders
    EH, sons with tuna, 1935
    EH, others with various tunas
    Cat Cay, EH, others with marlin, 1935. 2 folders
    Pilar and crew, 1935
    Native fishermen
    Native celebrations
    Views, 1936, 1932
Anita
    Dos Passos, 1932
    EH, Pauline, others, 1933
    Bumby, others with fish, c. 1932
    Bumby, others
    EH, others, fishing
Anita/Pilar, aground
Pilar
    Underway
    EH
    EH, Pauline, others, 1/36, 6/36
    EH, Bumby, others
    EH, Bumby, others with tommy gun, 1935
    Pauline, 1934
    Pauline, others

6
    Bumby, others
    EH, others chasing whales, 1934. 2 folders
    EH, others, fishing, 1934. 2 folders
    EH, others with sailfish, 1934
    Carlos & crew, c. 1934
    School of porpoises
    Other boats off Bimini
    EH, portrait photos
Dos Passos
Photo story on baiting hooks
Photos sent to EH

6   Wyoming, 1928–1937
Photos of EH, his family, and their activities during vacation trips to this state. Arranged by subject.

    EH & Pauline, fishing, Oct–Nov 1928
    Nordquist's Ranch, hunting, 1932 & undated.   2 folders

Idaho, 1939–1961
Photos of EH, his wives Martha and Mary, his sons and friends, and their activities during vacations spent at Sun Valley and elsewhere, and while residing in Ketchum. Arranged chronologically first, and then by subject.

Sun Valley
    EH, Martha Gellhorn, others, 1939
    EH & Martha, 1940
    Martha, 1940
    EH, Martha & EH's sons, 1940
    EH, friends, 1940
Pahsimeroi Valley, antelope hunt, 9/26/40
EH, Martha, sons, pheasant hunting, 10/40
EH, Gary Cooper, duck hunting at Silver Creek, 10/16/40
EH, Martha hunting at Middle Fork, Salmon River, c. 10/40
EH, hunting with Robert Capa for LIFE Magazine, 1940
Gary Cooper, 1940
EH with mule deer hunters, 1940
EH's sons, c. 1941
Richardson's Ranch, EH with Gregory, 1941

7
Pahsimeroi Valley, antelope hunt, 9/26/41
EH, Gregory, duck hunting, 10/41
EH, Martha, Patrick, Gregory, duck hunting, 10/41
Free's Farm, rabbit pest drive, 11/41
Stutter's Farm, ridge duck hunting, 1941
EH, Patrick, c. 1946
Free's Farm, EH, others, pheasant hunting, 1947

Box #	Description and Folder Titles	Box #	Description and Folder Titles

7 Idaho, 1939–1961 (cont.)

    EH, Mary, others, hunting, c. 1946–1958.
      3 folders
    EH, others, hunting, 1959, 1960
    EH, others, picnic, 1959
    Silver Creek, magpie shooting
    Purdy's Ranch, duck hunting, 1960
    Trail Creek Cabin
      Various parties, 1939–1941
      Cooper's get-acquainted party, 1940
      Party for Nin Van Guilder, 1940
      Pre-wedding party for EH & Martha,
        11/14/40
      Parties, 1946. 2 folders
      New Year's Eve party, 1947/8
    Heiss house, EH, Bron Zielinski, 1958
    Ketchum, EH's home
    EH
    Mary
    EH with Gary Cooper
    EH with Jane Russell
    EH and friends
    EH's associates
    Dietrich, Idaho, EH, Mary at post office
    Sun Valley & vicinity, views
    Sun Valley, Beatie's Cabin, 1959

8 Africa, 1933/4, 1953/4

Photos of EH and his wives Pauline and Mary
on safari. Arranged by subject.

    EH, Pauline on safari, 1933/4
    Enroute to Africa, 1953
    EH, Mary on safari
      Thiessen's contact sheets
      Mary's contact sheets
    EH with Patrick
    EH, Mary with game. 2 folders
    EH, Mary in camp. 2 folders
    EH, Mary with natives. 2 folders
    Plane crash (wreckage)

Europe, 1948–1959

Photos of EH, Mary Hemingway, and their
friends during Hemingway's trips to and
through Europe. Arranged chronologically
first, then by subject.

8

    S. S. Jagiello
      EH, Mary, others, Genoa, 9/48
      EH, Mary, others, enroute to Cuba,
        4/49–5/49
    S. S. Ile de France
      EH, Mary, others, enroute to France
        11/49
      EH, Mary, others, enroute to U. S. A.,
        3/50
    S. S. Flandre, EH, Mary, others, enroute
      to France, 6/53
    S. S. Africa, EH, Mary, others, enroute to
      Italy, 3/54
    S. S. Francesco Morosini, EH, others,
      Curaçao, 1954
    S. S. Ile de France
      EH, others, enroute to France, 1956
      EH, Mary, others, enroute to U. S. A.,
        6/57
    S. S. Constitution, EH, Mary, others,
      Algeciras, 1959
    S. S. Liberté, EH, Mary, others, enroute to
      U. S. A., 1959
    Venice
      Gritti Palace, EH, others, 10/48
      EH & Mary, 1949, 1950
      Harry's Bar, EH, others, 1949
      Adriana Ivancich

9

    City views
    Snowstorm scenes, 1/28/50
    Torcello, Italy
      EH, Mary, others, 11/48
      EH, others, hunting
      EH poses for a bust, 12/48
      EH—photo story by Interfoto, 1948
      Views of island and lagoon
    Latisana, Italy, Franchetti's Preserve, EH,
      others, hunting, 12/48
    Cortina, Italy
      EH, Mary, others. 2 folders
      Views
    Stresa, EH
    Milan, EH, others
    Italy/France, EH, Mary, others, auto
      trips. 3 folders
    Paris
    Photos sent to EH

Box #	Description and Folder Titles	Box #	Description and Folder Titles

9 Cuba Years, 1939–1960

Photos of EH, his wives Martha and Mary, his sons, friends and others at Hemingway's finca in Cuba and elsewhere. Also documented are EH's activities, especially deep sea fishing with his family and friends. Arranged by subject and therein chronologically.

Finca Vigia
EH, Martha, sons
EH's sons
EH, 1940–45. 2 folders
EH with his cats

10
Mary
EH & Mary (color), 1946
EH & Mary
EH, Mary, & sons
EH, Mary, with EH's sisters & children
EH, Mary with Leonard Lyons, 1952
Wedding, Jensen-Houck, 4/30/52
EH, Mary, Spencer Tracy & others, 1953
Nobel Prize celebration, 1954
LOOK photo story, EH, Mary, others, 1956
EH, Mary, with Kid Tunero
EH, Mary, others
Dinners, EH, Mary, others
EH is awarded a medal
EH with Buck Lanham
EH with U. S. military personnel, 1946–1959
EH with Basque pelota players
EH, others, hunting
EH, others
EH with Black Dog
Various guests. 2 folders
Margaux Hemingway
Native children
Cats. 3 folders
Cats (notes by EH)

11
Interior views
Exterior views. 2 folders
Pilar
Underway
Martha
EH, sons, others, fishing, c. 1940
EH & Mary
EH (color), 5/46, c. 9/51. 2 folders

11
EH's birthday, 7/21/51?
EH
Mary
Gianfranco Ivancich
Taylor Williams
EH, Bruces, others, fishing
EH, others, fishing
EH, others
Fighting fish
Views of the sea
Havana Harbor
Pilar, EH, others with marlin, c. 1948
Pilar, EH, others
Pilar at anchor (color), 1946
"The Tin Kid," Mary, others, c. 1947
Havana, EH awards fishing trophies
Paraiso
Pilar, EH, Mary, others
EH, others, picnic
Pilar at anchor, views
"The Tin Kid," Mary
Club de Cazadores
EH, Martha, sons, others
Martha
EH, others
Mary, others
EH, Martha aboard Leicester's sailboat, 1939
Puerto Rico, Martha, 8/1/42
Martha, portrait photos
Pauline, Patrick and Gregory
San Francisco, Mary, Pauline, 1947
EH, Patrick, Gregory, unidentified plane terminal

12
New York City
EH, Martha, others
Stork Club
EH, Martha, others
EH & Mary
EH, others
Filming "The Old Man and the Sea"
EH, Mary, others, c. 1955
Cabo Blanco, Peru, EH, others, filming marlin, 4/56. 2 folders
Spencer Tracy, stills
EH portrait photos
Havana
EH visits the Ringling Bros. Circus, 1952, 1953

Box #	Description and Folder Titles	Box #	Description and Folder Titles

12 Cuba Years, 1939–1960 (cont.)

La Florida, EH, Mary, others
EH, Mary, miscellaneous clubs
EH, Mary with the Duke and Duchess of Windsor
EH, others, hunting
Mary. 2 folders
EH with natives, net fishing, c. 1950 s
EH with natives
EH with unidentified people
EH's sons
Bumby
Patrick
Adriana Ivancich
Cojimar, Cuba, fishermen, 1953
Native festivals
Native fishermen, netcasting
Havana Harbor, views
Cuba, views
Photos sent to EH

13 Spain, 1953–1960

Photos of EH, Mary and friends during trips to Spain. Included are photos of various corridas attended by Hemingway and his associates. Arranged chronologically first and then by subject.

San Idelfonso, EH, Mary, others, 1953
Escorial, Tienta, EH, Ava Gardner, Dominguín, 1954
Robert Jordan's Bridge, EH, Mary, others, 1954
Logroño, corrida, EH, Mary, 9/21/56
Calatayud, EH, Mary, others, 10/56
Zaragoza, corrida, Ordoñez, 10/56
Corrida, EH, Mary, 1956
MH's contacts, 1959
Aranjuez, corrida, EH, Mary, others, 1959
Bayona, corrida, EH, others, 1959
Bilbao, corridas, EH, Davis, others, 1959, 1960
Pamplona, EH, 7/59
Ronda, corrida, c. 1959
Valencia, corrida, EH, Mary, others, 1959. 2 folders

13

Corridas
   EH, Mary, others. 11 folders
   Bullfighters & bulls (MH's photos). 2 folders
EH
EH with Ordoñez, 1959
EH, others, accident, Aranjuez, 1959
EH, Mary, others
Buck Lanham

14

Touring Spain, Views. 3 folders
Santa Pola, EH, Davis, others, 1959
Malaga, views
Madrid, radio interviews, 5/23/59
La Consula
   EH
   EH, others
   Luncheon
      EH, Ordoñez, 1959
      EH, Mary, others, 1959. 2 folders
   Swimming pool, EH, Ordoñez, others, 1959
   EH, Mary, Davis, others, 1959
   EH's 60th birthday, 7/21/59
   Annie Davis
   Davis Children, 1959
   Views, 1959
Gondarez' finca
   EH, Mary, others, 1959
   EH, Mary, others, hunting. 2 folders
Malaga, EH, others, picnic, 1959
Antonio Ordoñez
Costa del Sol, Ordoñez, others
Ordoñez' ranch, EH, others, 1959. 2 folders

15 Spain: Death in the Afternoon

Photos of various corridas, collected by Hemingway for use in his book, *Death in the Afternoon*. Arranged by subject.

Corridas. 14 folders

16

Sidney Franklin, various corridas
Madrid, corridas
Pamplona, Feria
San Sebastian, corrida
Seville, corrida
Toledo, corrida

Box #	Description and Folder Titles	Box #	Description and Folder Titles

17 Spain: The Dangerous Summer

Photos of various corridas (perhaps) sent to Hemingway by photographers. Included are some LIFE photos used in Hemingway's three-part article, entitled "The Dangerous Summer." Arranged alphabetically by city/town and thereafter by subject.

> Aranjuez, corridas, 1958, 1959
> Badajoz, corridas, 1958, 1959
> Bayona, corrida, 1959
> Bilbao, corridas, 1952–1958
> Burgos, corrida
> El Escorial, corrida, 1959
> Granada, corrida, 1957
> Guadalajara, corridas, 1952, 1958
> Jerez de la Frontera, corridas, 1954, 1958
> Logroño, corridas, 1954–1959
> Madrid, corridas, 1953–1959. 3 folders
> Malaga, corridas, 1952–1959
> Palencia, corridas, 1953, 1954
> Palma de Majorca, corrida, 1959
> Pamplona, corridas, 1954–1959. 3 folders
> Puerto de Santa Maria, corrida, 1953
> Salamanca, corridas, 1957–1959
> San Sebastian, corridas, 1957–1959
> Segovia, corrida, 1953
> Seville, 1952–1958. 3 folders

> Seville, 1959. 3 folders
> Talavera de la Reina, corrida, 1956
> Toledo, corridas, 1955, 1957
> Valencia, corridas, 1952–1959. 9 folders
> Valladolid, corridas, 1953–1959
> Vista Alegre, corrida, 1959
> Vitoria, corrida, 1958
> Zaragoza, corridas, 1957–1958
> Corridas, unidentified. 3 folders
> Antonio Ordoñez, various corridas
> Luis Miguel Dominguín, various corridas
> Paco Camino, various corridas
> Finca de Don Carlos Nuñes, 1954
> Bullfighters—sketches

18 Miscellany

Miscellaneous photos and prints sent to EH or members of his family. Also photos removed from EH's correspondence files. Arranged by subject.

18

> Sketches of EH
> Photos sent to Bumby
> Hall Hemingway—paintings
> Prints & posters
> Portrait photos—unidentified
> Unidentified places
> Photos from EH's correspondence

19 Oversized Photographs

Arrangement corresponds to that of the preceding boxes.

EARLY YEARS

> Oak Park, football teams
> Carol Hemingway

PARIS YEARS

> EH, portrait photos
> EH, Pauline, corrida
> Photos sent to EH

KEY WEST YEARS

> Key West, Pauline
> St. Louis, Patrick
> Havana Harbor, EH with sailfish
> Bimini, *Pilar* underway
> Photos sent to EH

IDAHO

> EH and Martha
> EH hunting with Robert Capa for LIFE
> EH and friends
> EH, Mary in Ketchum
> Sun Valley vicinity, geese feeding

AFRICA

> EH, Pauline on safari
> LOOK photos—article, 1/26/54

Box #	Description and Folder Titles	Box #	Description and Folder Titles

19 Oversized Photographs (cont.)

EUROPE

Torcello, EH

CUBA

EH, portrait photos
Mary, portrait photos
Finca Vigia
   EH
   EH and Mary
   Mary
Havana Harbor, *Pilar* underway
Cabo Blanco, filming marlin for "The
   Old Man and the Sea"
Club de Cazadores
Bumby
Photos sent to EH

SPAIN

EH with Hotchner
Bayona, corrida, EH, others
Logroño, corrida, EH
Zaragoza, corrida, EH
EH with Dominguín and Ordoñez
Dominguín and Ordoñez

MISCELLANY

Sketches of EH
Pamplona, dedication of a bust of
   EH, 1968
Photos sent to EH

20T Color Transparencies, 1953–1960
Photos taken by Mary Hemingway of EH,
their activities and their friends, while on
safari in East Africa, 1953–4, travelling
through Europe, vacationing in Idaho, and
elsewhere. Arrangement corresponds to that
of the preceding boxes.

20T AFRICA

EH, others in camp
EH, others with game
EH, others with natives

21T EH, others
Views

22T Views
Egypt, views

CUBA

Finca Vigia
   EH
   Interior views
   Exterior views
Pilar, EH, others
Views

SPAIN

San Idelfonso, EH, others
Robert Jordan's Bridge
EH
Corridas
La Consula, EH, others

23T La Consula, EH, others
Ordoñez' ranch

EUROPE

Torcello, EH, others
Auto trips
   EH
   Views
Venice
   EH
   Views

IDAHO

EH, others
Views

UNIDENTIFIED PLACE

Newspaper
Clippings

Brady, William
  The Lad at 16 years
  Daily News:
  Nov 12, 1916

                    1916

[Hemingway, Ernest]
  Glaring Lights May Return
  Kansas City Star
  25 Oct 1917

                    EH   25 Oct 1917

Scouts Hold Up Returns
Kansas City Star
[1917]?,

                    1917

Hemingway, Ernest
  Negro Methodists Meeting Here
  Little Hope for Chief Vaughn
  Kansas City Star
  25 Oct 1917

                    EH   25 Oct 1917

Mrs. Miller Hall: Pioneer Woman Passes
Away After Years of Faithful Service as
Mother and Religious Teacher

Oak Park, Oak Leaves
2 June 1917

                    1917

[Hemingway, Ernest]
  Cheap Coal
  Kansas City Star
  3 Dec 1917

                    1917
  donor: E. R. Hagemann (typescript)

Joke Is Warlike

23 June 1917

                    1917

[Hemingway, Ernest]
  Have Plenty of Coal Now: Supply on
  Kansas Side is Greater tnan the Demand
  Kansas City Star
  3 Dec 1917

                    1917
  donor: E. R. Hagemann (typescript)

A Line O' Type or Two
Chicago Daily Tribune
17 Sept 1917

              Hemingway, Clarence E.
              18 Sept 1917 (oversize)

[Hemingway, Ernest]
  Cheap Coal Is Plentiful
  Kansas City Times
  4 Dec 1917

                    1917
  donor: E. R. Hagemann (typescript)

[Hemingway, Ernest]

    Kansas Side Dealers to Meet

    Kansas City Times

    4 Dec 1917

               1917

donor: E. R. Hagemann (typescript)

---

photo: Lt. Hemingway Convalescing from 237 Wounds, Being Driven Around Milan by an Italian Officer

[1918]

               1918

[Hemingway, Ernest]

    Bowman Still Avoids Jail

    Kansas City Star

    5 Dec 1917

               1917

donor: E. R. Hagemann (typescript)

Two Are Killed, Four Wounded, Three Missing

[1918]

               1918
               original--Grandparents'
               Scrapbook

[Hemingway, Ernest]

    A Note Hints at Suicide

    Kansas City Times

    5 Dec 1917

               1917

donor: E. R. Hagemann (typescript)

Wounded American Hero

[1918]

               1918
               original -- Grandparents'
               Scrapbook

    The Meaning of Pain

    British Weekly

    [1918]

               1918
               original--Grandparents'
               Scrapbook

[Hemingway, Ernest]

    Fire Destroy's 3 Firms

    Kansas City Star

    26 Jan 1918

               1918

donor: E. R. Hagemann (typescript)

---

photo: Lieut. E. M. Hemingway taking an airing in Milan, Italy

[1918]

               1918
               original--Grandparents'
               Scrapbook

[Hemingway, Ernest]

    Alec Left With the Cubs

    Kansas City Star

    [Mar 1918]

               EH 14 Mar 1918

[Hemingway, Ernest]

Hospital Clerk Let Out

Kansas City Star

[Mar 1918]

EH   14 Mar 1918

Dave Dent Loves Tanks

Kansas City Star

21 Apr 1918

1918

[Hemingway, Ernest]

Slay a Laundry Guard

Kansas City Star

[12 Mar 1918]

EH   14 Mar 1918

cartoon

Hemingway, Grace Hall
8 May 1918

Tank Corps Wants Men Who Are Fighting Mad

[New York Globe]

[4 Apr 1918]

1918

Sixteen Leave for Italy to Drive Army Ambulances

Chicago Daily Tribune

12 May 1918

Hemingway, Clarence E.
15 May 1918 &
1918
   original--Grandparents'
   Scrapbook

Newburn and Hemingway Go to Italy

18 May 1918

1918
original--Grandparents'
Scrapbook

Go Together from the Star to the Italian Front

Kansas City Star

13 May 1918

1918 &
Grandparents' Scrapbook

[Hemingway, Ernest]

Six Men Became Tankers

Kansas City Star

[17 Apr 1918]

1918

Following is a letter from Arthur C. Newburn. . .

[9 June 1918]

1918
original--Grandparents'
Scrapbook

cartoon

Hemingway, Grace Hall
23 June 1918

All Italy Honors America

Kansas City Star

14 July 1918

Kollenborn, Roy
3 Sept 1918

Kingsley, Charles

Be not anxious. . .

Hemingway, Grace Hall
23 June 1918

Honors for the Kansas City Man

[16 July 1918]

Kollenborn, Roy
3 Sept 1918

Kingsley, Charles

The Days of Real Sport

Hemingway, Grace Hall
23 June 1918

Wounded Oak Park Boy Cited for Medal

[16 July 1918]

1918
original--Grandparents'
Scrapbook

Win Four Mile Line

Chicago Daily Tribune

5 July 1918

1918

Newspaper Man Survives 200 Battle Wounds

New York Evening Telegram

17 July 1918

Brumback, Theodore
8 Aug 1918
&
1918

Wounded on Italy Front

Kansas City Star

14 July 1918

Kollernborn, Roy
3 Sept 1918

---

3 Dead, 6 Hurt, 3 Missing, City's Share
of Glory

Chicago Daily Tribune

17 July 1918

Hemingway, Anson T.
19 July 1918--oversize
& 1918
& Grandparents' Scrapbook

Valor Cross to Hemingway

Kansas City Times

[17 July 1918]

Kollenborn, Roy
3 Sept 1918

Kollenborn, Roy
Baker

Clippings by the two above

Kollenborn, Roy   3 Sept 1918

Hemingway Wounded, to be Rewarded for Valor

20 July 1918

1918
original--Grandparents'
Scrapbook

With our Wounded

7 Sept 1918

1918
original--Grandparents'
Scrapbook

Italy Rewards 21 Ambulance Men for Red Cross

[Tribune]

[20 July 1918]

1918
original--Grandparents'
Scrapbook

Going Back to the Front

Kansas City Star

Hale, Juddy   21 Sept 1918

Lardner, Ring

"E'en War So Grim Refuses to Dim Humor of Him"
"Lardner Meets Horrors in the Wake of War"

Bagley, Caroline   Aug 1918

Von Pot and Von Kettle

Hemingway, Grace Hall
30 Sept 1918

"Some of These Day's We'll Learn to Apply the Same Lessons at Home"
"Our Boy"

Hemingway, Grace Hall
5 Aug 1918

Wounded 227 Times

[Oak Leaves]

5 Oct 1918

1918
original--Grandparents'
Scrapbook

Lo Sportsman

Giornale Di Sport Ippico   Milan, Italy

9 Oct 1918

        1918

War Cross for Ted Brumback

Kansas City Star

1 Dec 1918

        1918

First Congregational Church Program

Oak Park, Illinois

13 Oct 1918

      Hemingway, Clarence E.
      13 Oct 1918

"The Spice of Life"
"Fading Festivities"
"Experiments as They Are Done"
A Cartoon

      Hemingway, Grace Hall
      11 June 1918

Oak Park Boy Shot to Pieces Jokes about It

[23 Oct 1918]

    1918
    original--Grandparents'
    Scrapbook

To My Mother

[1919]

    1919
    original--Grandparents'
    Scrapbook

Lieut. E. M. Hemingway sends
interesting picture. . .

16 Nov 1918

    1918
    original--Grandparents'
    Scrapbook

Lieut. Arthur Newburn Home from Overseas

[Jan 1919]

    1919
    original--Grandparents'
    Scrapbook

Chicago Flyer Survives Fall of 5,000 Feet

Chicago Daily Tribune

16 Nov 1918

      1918

Yankee Punctured by 227 Pieces of
Austrian Shrapnel

[Jan 1919]

    1919
    original--Grandparents'
    Scrapbook

Man with 227 Wounds Returns from Italy

24 Jan 1919

1919
original--Grandparents'
Scrapbook

Heroes Back Loaded Down With Medals
New York American
22 Jan 1919

1919

Gibraltar Chronicle and Official Gazette
9 Jan 1919

1919

341st Went in Fight After 4 Weeks
Training
Chicago Daily Tribune
22 Jan 1919

1919

Lieutenant Hemingway Is on His Way Home

[11 Jan 1919]

1919
original--Grandparents'
Scrapbook

Yankee Red Cross Man With 237 Wound
Scars Wins Italian War Cross

New York Evening World
22 Jan 1919

1919

Reynolds, Dorothy
Lieut Hemingway's Visit
Oak Park Hawthorne [School] Reporter
21 Feb 1919

1919

Dean, Roselle
First Lieutenant Hemingway
The Oak Parker
1 Feb 1919

1919 &
Grandparents' Scrapbook

Got 227 Wounds Says Ambulance Driver
[Kansas City]
22 Jan 1919

1919

Real Old World Festival

22 Feb 1919

1919
original--Grandparents'
Scrapbook

Dean, Roselle

France, Italy and America

The Oak Parker

[24 Feb 1919]

    1919
    original--Grandparents'
    Scrapbook

Hemingway to Fish Then Work

[26 Mar 1919]

    1919
    original--Grandparents'
    Scrapbook

Beware Propaganda

1 Mar 1919

    1919
    original--Grandparents'
    Scrapbook

Winged Victory Edition

Chicago Herald Examiner

21 Apr 1919

    1919

From Italian Front

[14 Mar 1919]

    1919
    original--Grandparents'
    Scrapbook

Fishin'

    Hemingway, Clarence E.
    5 June 1919

Lt. Hemingway Talks

22 Mar 1919

    1919
    original--Grandparents'
    Scrapbook

Jack Elkhorn's Elbow Grease Philosophy

    Hemingway, Clarence E.
    5 June 1919

War Hero to Address Club

[25 Mar 1919]

    1919
    original--Grandparents'
    Scrapbook

Mrs. Tom Thumb Dies, Aged 77, in Massachusetts

    Hemingway, Adelaide
    26 Nov 1919

Missouri Poet Stars in New Spiker Drama

Kansas City

Williams, T. Norman
26 Feb 1920

Hemingway, Ernest

Toronto Women Who Went to the Prize Fights
Applauded the Rough Stuff

Toronto Star

15 May 1920

Star Scrapbook, p. 2

Triangle--Job in War Builds Love
Triangle

Kansas City

Williams, T. Norman
26 Feb 1920

Hemingway, Ernest

It's Time to Bury the Hamilton Gag,
Comedians Have Worked it to Death

Toronto Star

12 June 1920

Star Scrapbook, p. 3

Hemingway, Ernest

How to be Popular in Peace Though a
Slacker in War

Toronto Staf

"30 Mar 1920" (Hanneman dates this
article 13 Mar 1920)

Star Scrapbook, p. 1

Hemingway, Ernest

A Fight With a 20-Pound Trout

Toronto Star

20 Nov 1920

Star Scrapbook, p. 3

Hemingway, Ernest

Sporting Mayor at Boxing Bouts

Toronto Star

13 Mar 1920

Star Scrapbook, p. 1

Hemingway, Ernest

Our Confidential Vacation Guide

Toronto Star

21 May 1921

Star Scrabook, p. 4

Hemingway, Ernest

Store Thieves Use Three Tricks

Toronto Star

3 Apr 1920

Star Scrapbook, p. 2

Hemingway, Ernest

Gun-Men's Wild Political War On in Chicago

Toronto Star

28 May 1921

Star Scrapbook, p. 4

Hemingway, Ernest

   The Super-man Myth

   "25 June 1921"

             Star Scrapbook, p. 5

Chicago Arrivals in Paris

[1922]

          1922
          original--Grandparent's
          Scrapbook

Hemingway, Ernest

   Chicago Never Wetter Than It Is To-day

   Toronto Star

   2 July 1921

             Star Scrapbook, p. 5

Forest Reserve Yearbook Out; Demand Is Heavy

[1922]

          1922

Hemingway, Ernest

   Cheap Nitrates Will Mean Cheaper Bread

   Toronto Star

   12 Nov 1921

             Star Scrapbook, p. 6

Shop-Talk: Bouquets from the Dolomites. . . Begins Today

Toronto Star

[Mar 1922]

             Star Scrapbook, p. 34

Chicago Greets Italy's Hero As Her Own Today

Chicago Sunday Tribune

[20 Nov 1921]

             Star Scrapbook, p. 47

Hemingway, Ernest

   The Mecca of Fakers Is French Capital

   Toronto Star

   [25 Mar 1922]

             Star Scrapbook, p. 6

Hemingway, Ernest

   On Weddynge Gifts

   Toronto Star

   17 Dec 1921

             Star Scrapbook, oversize

Shop-Talk   ". . . Ernest Hemingway, a comparatively new. . ."

Toronto Star

[Apr 1922]

             Star Scrapbook, p. 33

Hemingway, Ernest

Much-Feared Man Is Monsieur Deibler

Toronto Star

[1 Apr 1922]

Star Scrapbook, p. 7

Hemingway, Ernest

Tchitcherin At It Again: Wants Japs Excluded

Toronto Star

11 Apr 1922

Star Scrapbook, p. 10

Hemingway, Ernest

95,000 Now Wearing the Legion of Honor

Toronto Star

[1 Apr 1922]

Star Scrapbook, p. 7

Mowrer, Paul Scott

Britain and France Are In Close Accord

[11 Apr 1922]

Star Scrapbook, p. 28

Hemingway, Ernest

Anti-Alcohol League Is Active in France

Toronto Star

[8 Apr 1922]

Star Scrapbook, p. 7

Hemingway, Ernest

Picked Sharpshooters Patrol Genoa Streets

Toronto Star

[13 Apr 1922]

Star Scrapbook, p. 8 and p. 50

Hemingway, Ernest

Russian Mission to Genoa Hedged Around by Guards

Toronto Star

[10 Apr 1922]

Star Scrapbook, p. 9

Hemingway, Ernest

Russian Claims to Offset Allies

Toronto Star

[15 Apr 1922]

Star Scrapbook, p. 11

Hemingway, Ernest

World Economic Conference Opens in Genoa

Toronto Star

10 Apr 1922

Star Scrapbook, p. 9

Hemingway, Ernest

French Politeness

Toronto Star

[15 Apr 1922]

Star Scrapbook, p. 8

Hemingway, Ernest

Genoa Scrubs Up For Peace Parley

Toronto Star

[16 Apr 1922]

       Star Scrapbook, p. 13

Hemingway, Ernest

Two Russian Girls the Best Looking at Genoa Parley

Toronto Star

[24 Apr 1922] (dateline is 10 Apr)

       Star Scrapbook, p. 10

Hemingway, Ernest

Interpreters Make or Mar Speeches at Genoa Party

Toronto Star

[16 Apr 1922]

       Star Scrapbook, p. 13

Hemingway, Ernest

Schober of Austria, at Genoa, Looks Every Inch a Chancellor

Toronto Star

[25 Apr 1922]

       Star Scrapbook, p. 11

Hemingway, Ernest

Barthou, Like a Smith Brother, Crosses Hissing Tchitcherin

Toronto Star

[18 Apr 1922]

       Star Scrapbook, p. 11

Hemingway, Ernest

Russian Delegates at Genoa Appear Not to be of This World

Toronto Star

[27 Apr 1922]

       Star Scrapbook, p. 12

Hemingway, Ernest

Regarded by Allies as German Cunning

Toronto Star

[18 Apr 1922]

       Star Scrapbook, p. 13

Hemingway, Ernest

Getting a Hot Bath an Adventure in Genoa

Toronto Star

[2 May 1922]

       Star Scrapbook, p. 14

Genoa Conference after Big Storm Now Emerges into Smoother Waters

New York Herald, European Edition (entire front page)

22 Apr 1922

       1922

Hemingway, Ernest

Russian Delegation Well Guarded at Genoa

Toronto Star

[4 May 1922]

       Star Scrapbook, p. 12

Hemingway, Ernest

There Are Great Fish in the Rhone Canal

Toronto Star

[10 June 1922]

Star Scrapbook, p. 14

Hemingway, Ernest

Rug Vendor Is Fixture in Parisian Life

Toronto Star

[12 Aug 1922]

Star Scrapbook, p. 16

Hemingway, Ernest

There are Great Fish in the Rhone Canal

Toronto Star

[10 June 1922]

Star Scrapbook, p. 14

Hemingway, Ernest

Old Order Changeth in Alsace-Lorraine

Toronto Star

[26 Aug 1922]

Star Scrapbook, p. 17

Hemingway, Ernest

'Pot-Shot Patriots' Unpopluar in Italy

Toronto Star

[24 June 1922]

Star Scrapbook, p. 15

Hemingway, Ernest

Takes to the Water, Solves Float Problem

Toronto Star

[26 Aug 1922]

Star Scrapbook, p. 17

Hemingway, Ernest

A Veteran Visits Old Front, Wishes He Had Stayed Away

Toronto Star

[22 July 1922]

Star Scrapbook, p. 15

Hemingway, Ernest

Germans Are Doggedly Sullen Or Desparate Over the Mark

Toronto Star

1 Sept 1922

Star Scrapbook, p. 19

Hemingway, Ernest

Latest Drink Scandal Now Agitates Paris

Toronto Star

[12 Aug 1922]

Star Scrapbook, p. 16

Hemingway, Ernest

Once Over Permit Obstacle, Fishing in Baden Perfect

Toronto Star

[2 Sept 1922]

Star Scrapbook, p. 18

Hemingway, Ernest

   German Inn-Keepers Rough Dealing with
"Auslanders"

Toronto Star

5 Sept 1922

                Star Scrapbook, p. 20

Hemingway, Ernest

   Turk Red Crescent Propaganda Agency

Toronto Star

[4 Oct 1922]

                Star Scrapbook, p. 51

Hemingway, Ernest

   A Paris-to-Strasburg Flight Shows Living
Cubist Picture

Toronto Star

[9 Sept 1922]

                Star Scrapbook, p. 18

---

pages 1 and 2

New York Journal

4 Oct 1922

                Star Scrapbook
                oversize

Hemingway, Ernest

   Crossing to Germany Is Way to Make Money

Toronto Star

[19 Sept 1922]

                Star Scrapbook, p. 19

Hadley, John [Ernest Hemigway]

   Progress . . . Being Made at Meeting

[5 Oct 1922][?]

                Star Scrapbook, p. 21

Hemingway, Ernest

   Hubby Dines First, Wife Gets Crumbs!

Toronto Star

[30 Sept 1922]

                Star Scrapbook, p. 63

Hadley, John [Ernest Hemingway]

   Allies and Turks Plan Early Peace Conference

Pittsburgh Press

[5 Oct 1922]

                Star Scrapbook, p. 22

Hemingway, Ernest

   Riots Are Frequent Throughout Germany

Toronto Star

[30 Sept 1922]

                Star Scrapbook, p. 63

Kemalists Fire Upon Destroyer at Aivaly

[5 Oct 1922]

                Star Scrapbook, p. 44

Hadley, John [Ernest Hemingway]

The Near East armistice conference. . .

Chicago American

[6 Oct 1922]

Star Scrapbook, p. 21

Hemingway, Ernest

Balkans Look Like Ontario, A Picture of Peace, Not War

Toronto Star

[16 Oct 1922]

Star Scrapbook, p. 53

Hadley, John [Ernest Hemingway]

Peace Parley Will Start Again Sunday or Monday, Is Report

Washington Times

[6 Oct 1922]

Star Scrapbook, p. 23

Hadley, John [Ernest Hemingway]

Turkish Soldiers Cross to Europe

[16 Oct 1922]

Star Scrapbook, p. 25

Hemingway, Ernest

Hamid Bey Wears Shirt Tucked in When Seen by Star

Toronto Star

[9 Oct 1922]

Star Scrapbook, p. 54

Hadley, John [Ernest Hemingway]

Turks Cross Bosphorus to Police Thrace

Washington Times

[16 Oct 1922]

Star Scrapbook, p. 23

Hadley, John [Ernest Hemingway]

Turkish Cavalry and Infantry Reported Moving Northward

Washington Times

[9 Oct 1922]

Star Scrapbook, p. 21

Hemingway, Ernest

Constantinople, Dirty White, Not Glistening and Sinister

Toronto Star

[18 Oct 1922]

Star Scrapbook, p. 49

Turk Women Delay Peace

[11 Oct 1922]

Star Scrapbook, p. 45

Hemingway, Ernest

Constantinople Cut-Throats Await Chance for an Orgy

Toronto Star

[19 Oct 1922]

Star Scrapbook, p. 49

Hemingway, Ernest

A Silent, Ghastly Procession Wends Way from Thrace

Toronto Star

20 Oct 1922

Star Scrapbook, p. 53

Hemingway, Ernest

Kemal Has Afghans Ready to Make Trouble for Britain

Toronto Star

31 Oct 1922

Star Scrapbook p.54

Hemingway, Ernest

Russia to Spoil the French Game with Kemalists

Toronto Star

[23 Oct 1922]

Star Scrapbook, p. 51

Hadley, John   [Ernest Hemingway]

Constantinople Faces Dry Time Under Kemal

Washington Times

10 Nov 1922

Star scrapbook, loose

Hemingway, Ernest

Turks Beginning to Show Distrust of Kemal Pasha

Toronto Star

[24 Oct 1922]

Star Scrapbook, p. 52

Hadley, John   [Ernest Hemingway]

Kemal's Lone Submarine Plays Pirate in Black Sea as British Hunt It

Washington Times

10 Nov 1922

Star scrapbook, loose

Hemingway, Ernest

Censor Too "Thorough" in the Near East Crisis

Toronto Star

[25 Oct 1922]

Star Scrapbook, p. 51

Hadley, John   [Ernest Hemingway]

Turkish Submarine Plays Pirate

Boston-American

10 Nov [1922]

Star Scrapbook p.25

Hemingway, Ernest

"Old Constan" in True Light Is Tough Town

Toronto Star

[28 Oct 1922]

Star Scrapbook, p. 52

Hemingway, Ernest

Refugee Procession is Scene of Horror

Toronto Daily Star

14 Nov 1922

1922

One Who Knew Him
  Mustapha Kemal

22 Nov 1922

    1922

Hadley, John [Ernest Hemingway]
  Soviets Refuse Minor Role in Parley

[28 Nov 1922]

    Star Scrapbook, p. 22

Hadley, John [Ernest Hemingway]
  Allies to Render Turks Helpless in Thrade

24 Nov [1922]

    Star Scrapbook p.24

Hadley, John [Ernest Hemingway]
  Pact Couples Exodus of Million

[2 Dec 1922]

    Star Scrapbook, p. 23

Hadley, John [Ernest Hemingway]
  Bar Army from Boundary of Thrade

24 Nov [1922]

    Star Scrapbook p.22

Hadley, John [Ernest Hemingway]
  Great Exodus in Near East is Under Way
  Syracuse American
  3 Dec 1922

    Star Scrapbook, loose

Open Door in East Insisted on by U.S.,
Child Says

[25 Nov 1922]

    Star Scrapbook, p. 45

Hadley, John [Ernest Hemingway]
  Turks Tie Up Peace Meet
  Washington Times
  5 Dec 1922

    Star Scrapbook, loose

Hadley, John [Ernest Hemingway]
  Britain Victor in Battle for Oil

[27 Nov 1922]

    Star Scrapbook, p. 24

Hadley, John [Ernest Hemingway]
  Lausanne Meet Deadlocked by Russ Plan

[5 Dec 1922]

    Star Scrapbook, p. 23

Hadley, John

    Russia's Plea to Give Turks Dardenelles Denounced

    San Francisco Call and Post

    [6 Dec 1922]

                Star Scrapbook, p. 24

Turks Accept Straits Plan of Allies

The Atlanta Georgian

8 Dec

---

    pp. 1 and 2

    Boston American

    6 Dec 1922

                Star Scrapbook, loose

Turks Accept Straits Plan of Allies

The Atlanta Georgian

[8 Dec 1922]

                Star Scrapbook, p. 44

---

    pp. 1 and 2

    Syracuse Telegram

    6 Dec 1922

                Star Scrapbook, loose

Turks Balking at Allies' Proposal

[20 Dec 1922]

                Star Scrapbook, p. 44

Hadley, John [Ernest Hemingway]

    Turkey Yields to Demands of Allies on Straits

    San Francisco Call and Post

    [8 Dec 1922]

                Star Scrapbook, p. 24

[Hemingway, Ernest]

    I Like Americans

    Toronto Star

    [1923]

                Star Scrapbook p.35

Hadley, John [Ernest Hemingway]

    Turks Agree to U.S.-Allied Policy

    [8 Dec 1922]

                Star Scrapbook, p. 23

[Hemingway, Ernest]

    I Like Canadians

    Toronto Star

    [1923]

                Star Scrapbook p.35

No Room In Canada For European Reds
Preacher Maintains

[1923]

Star Scrapbook p.38

Hemingway, Ernest

Gaudy Uniform Is Tchitcherin's Weakness,
A "Chocolate Soldier" of the Soviet Army

Toronto Star

[10 Feb 1923]

Star Scrapbook p.56

Miss Hemingway's Marriage Notable Event
in Oak Park

Chicago Daily Tribune

3 Jan 1923

Sanford, Marcelline
3 Jan 1923

Mrs. Anson Hemingway. Pioneer Woman of
Oak Park, Native of Illinois and Mother
of Distinguished Family, Passes Away

Oak Leaves

10 Feb 1923

Star Scrapbook p.48

John Barber White Dead

Kansas City Star

[5 Jan 1923]

1923

French Financiers Review Situation

[22 Feb 1923]

Star Scrapbook, p. 45

Hemingway-Sanford (wedding announcement
of Marcelline Hemingway)

Oak Leaves

6 Jan 1923

Marcelline Sanford
6 Jan 1923

Two Revolutions Are Likely If Germany
Suffers Collapse

Toronto Star

7 Mar 1923

Star Scrapbook p.64

Hemingway, Ernest

Mussolini, Europe's Prize Bluffer More
Like Battomley Than Napoleon

Toronto Star

27 Jan 1923

Star Scrapbook p.55

Will France Have a King Again?

Toronto Star

13 Mar 1923

Star Scrapbook p.30

Why Is France in the Ruhr?

Toronto Star

[1 Apr 1923]

Star Scrapbook, p. 45

Hemingway, Ernest

A Brave Belgian Lady Shuts Up German Hater

Toronto Star

[28 Apr 1923]

Star Scrapbook p.60

Shop Talk. Something About Ernest M. Hemingway, Who is Taking the Lid off Europe

Toronto Star

14 Apr 1923

Star Scrapbook p.35

An attempt has been made. . .

[May 1923]

Star Scrapbook, p. 45

Hemingway, Ernest

French Royalist Party Most Solidly Organized

Toronto Star

18 Apr 1923

1923

Hemingway, Ernest

Getting Into Germany Quite A Job, Nowadays

Toronto Star

[2 May 1923]

Star Scrapbook p.61

Hemingway, Ernest

Government Pays For News In French Papers

Toronto Star

21 Apr 1923

Star Scrapbook p.61

Hemingway, Ernest

Quite Easy To Spend A Million, If In Marks

Toronto Star

5 May 1923

Star Scrapbook p.59

Hemingway, Ernest

Ruhr Commercial War Question of Bankruptcy

Toronto Star

25 Apr 1923

1923

Hemingway, Ernest

Amateur Starvers Keep Out of View in Germany

Toronto Star

[9 May 1923]

1923

Hemingway, Ernest

Hate in Occupied Zone A Real Concrete
Thing

Toronto Star

[12 May 1923]

Star Scrapbook p.58

"La Boxe a Paris La reouvertune de la
Salle Wagram sera a soir celle de la
saison pugislistique." On Larry Gains

4 Sept 1923

William Bird
4 Sept 1923

Hemingway, Ernest

French Register Speed When Movies are on
Job

Toronto Star

[16 May 1923]

Star Scrapbook p.57

Education Physique: Comment un nez-vous?

c.4 Sept 1923

William Bird
4 Sept 1923

Jones, Uwellyn

Love and Other Forms of Electronic Energy
(Review of Edwin H. Lewis White Lightning)

Chicago Evening Post

1 June 1923

Grace Hemingway
4 July 1923

Larry Gains est il poids 1 orerd?

c. 4 Sept 1923

William Bird
4 Sept 1923

Lord and Lady Cranworth

[Sept 1923]

Star Scrapbook p.38

Larry Gains vanquer de Jouriee va
recoutner Mathieu

c. 4 Sept 1923

William Bird
4 Sept 1923

Shop Talk. . . Ernest Hemingway, who
writes the lead feature. . .

Toronto Star

[Sept 1923]

Star Scrapbook p.33

Offer Sir Donald Soviet Railroads, Won't
Take Them

Toronto Star

10 Sept 1923

Star Scrapbook p.30

Aided by Smoke Screen Convicts Break
From Pen

[10 Sept 1923]

1923

Moscow Theater Company Will Not Come
To Toronto

[Oct 1923]

Star Scrapbook p.38

[Hemingway, Ernest]

Kingston Convicts Still At Large

Toronto Star

11 Sept 1923

Star Scrapbook p.30

Hemingway, Ernest

Little Welshman Lands, Anxious to Play
Golf

Toronto Star

5 Oct 1923

Star Scrapbook p.65

[Hemingway, Ernest]

Convicts Break Away From Swamp Refuge

Toronto Star

[11 Sept 1923]

Star Scrapbook p.40
P.41, p.42

Hemingway, Ernest

Lloyd George Up Early As Big Liner
Arrives

Toronto Star

5 Oct 1923

Star Scrapbook p.66

Hemingway, Ernest

King Business in Europe Isn't What It
Used To Be

Toronto Star Weekly

15 Sept 1923

Star Scrapbook p.31,32

---

2 pages of advertisements from a Toronto
newspaper

5 Oct 1923

Star Scrapbook

Hemingway, Ernest

Tossed About On Land Like Ships In A
Storm

Toronto Star

25 Sept 1923

1923

Hungarian Statesman Delighted With Loan

Toronto Daily Star

[15 Oct 1923]

Star Scrapbook p.31

Hungarian Statesman in Toronto

Toronto Daily Star

18 Oct 1923

Star Scrapbook p.31,32

Hemingway, Ernest

More Game to Shoot in Crowded Europe
Than in Ontario. Forests and Animals
Are Really Protected Over There.

Toronto Star

3 Nov 1923

1923

Nem, Nem, Soha! No, No, Never! Cries
Hungarian

Toronto Star

18 Oct 1923

Star Scrapbook p.32

---

pages 1 & 2

Toronto Star

10 Nov 1923

Star Scrapbook, loose

Hemingway, Ernest

Bull Fighting Is Not A Sport - It Is A
Tragedy

Toronto Star

20 Oct 1923

Star Scrapbook, loose
& 1923

2pp of advertisements

Toronto Star

10 Nov 1923

Star Scrapbook, loose

Fifth Generation of Family Lives On
Old Canadian Manor

Toronto Star

20 Oct 1923

Star Scrapbook p.38

---

fragment of p. 1 & 2

Toronto Daily Star

15 Nov 1923

Star Scrapbook, loose

Hemingway, Ernest

World Series of Bull Fighting a Mad
Whirling Carnival

Toronto Star Weekly

27 Oct 1923

Star Scrapbook

Hemingway, Ernest

Trout Fishing All Across Europe
Spain Has the Best, Then Germany

Toronto Star

17 Nov 1923

1923

Hadley, John [Ernest Hemingway]

    Cheer Up! The Lakes Aren't Going Dry
High Up and Low Down Is Just Their Habit

    Toronto Star Weekly

    [17 Nov 1923]

              Star Scrapbook p.26

Stein, Gertrude

    Three Stories and Ten Poems

    Paris Chicago Tribune

    27 Nov 1923

             Stein, Gertrude
             6 Mar 1923

Hemingway, Ernest

    The Sport of Kings

    The Big Dance on the Hill

    Toronto Star

    24 Nov 1923

             Star Scrapbook,
             loose

    Premier King Returns, Old World Needs
New

    Toronto Star

    [30 Nov 1923]

             Star Scrapbook, p. 43

Hemingway, Ernest

    Tancredo is Dead

    Toronto Star Weekly

    24 Nov 1923

             Toronto Scrapbook p.29

Hemingway, Ernest

    Fifty-Ton Doors Laugh at Robbers Tools,
Bank Vaults Defy Scientific Cracksmen

    Toronto Star

    1 Dec 1923

             Star Scrapbook, loose

Jackson, Peter

    Wild Gastronomic Adventures of a Gourmet,
Eating Sea Slugs, Snails, Octopus, etc.
for Fun

    Toronto Star

    24 Nov 1923

             Star Scrapbook, loose

Hadley, John [Ernest Hemingway]

    German Marks Make Last Stand as Real
Money in Toronto's 'Ward'

    Toronto Star

    8 Dec 1923

             Star Scrapbook, loose

    Learns to Commune With the Fairies, Now
Wins the $40,000 Nobel Prize

    Toronto Star Weekly

    [24 Nov 1923]

             Star Scrapbook p.36

Hemingway, Ernest

    Night Life in Europe a Disease/Constanti-
nople's Most Hectic

    Toronto Star

    15 Dec 1923

             Star Scrapbook, loose

Hadley, John [Ernest Hemingway]

Dose Whole City's Water Supply to Cure
Goiter by Mass Medication

Toronto Star Weekly

[15 Dec 1923]

Star Scrapbook, p. 25

Hemingway, Ernest

Weird, Wild Adventures of Some of Our
Modern Amateur Imposters

Toronto Star

29 Dec 1923

Star Scrapbook, loose

Williams, Howard

Real Buffalo Hunting Out West Back in the
Sixties/Toronto Man Knows Old Days of the

Toronto Star

15 Dec 1923

Star Scrapbook, loose

New York Times Book Review, entire section

30 Dec 1923

1923

Toronto 'Red'Children Don't Know Santa
Claus

Toronto Star

22 Dec 1923

Star Scrapbook, loose

Hemingway, Ernest

Ski-er's Only Escape from Alpine
Avalanche is to Swim! Snow Slides Off
Mountains as Fast as Off Roof of House

Toronto Star

12 Jan 1924

1924

Hemingway, Ernest

Toronto Is Biggest Betting Place in North
America / 10,000 People Bet $100,000 on
Horses Every Day (and pages 23 through 29)

Toronto Star
29 Dec 1923

Star Scrapbook, loose

St. George's Gazette (entire edition)

29 Feb 1924

1924

Hadley, John [Ernest Hemingway]

Wild New Year's Even Gone Forever/Only
Ghost of 1914 Remains

Toronto Star

29 Dec 1923

Star Scrapbook, loose

Entire Sunday Magazine Section (w/one
clipping missing)

Paris, Chicago Tribune and New York Daily
News

11 May 1924

1924

Bull Gores 2 Yanks Acting as Toreadores

[29 July 1924]

1924

Hickok, Guy

Hemingway First Lives Wild Stories, Then He Writes Them

Brooklyn Eagle

17 May 1925

Hickok, Guy   17 May 1925

New York Herald (European Edition), entire paper

5 Aug 1924

1924

Seligmann, Herbert

In Our Time

New York City Sun

17 Oct 1925

EH: 20 Nov [1925, Paris] oversize

Wilson, Edmund

Mr. Hemingway's Dry Points

[Dial]

[Oct 1924]

in our time

In Our Time.   Short stories of contemporary life. . .

Boston Transcript

18 Nov 1925

In Our Time

---

pp. 23 and 24

Toronto Star

11 Oct 1924

Star Scrapbbok, loose

C.L.

Books: In Our Time

Register of Hotel Penn

21 Nov 1925

In Our Time

Crawford, Nelson Antrim

A Little Book by Ernest Hemingway Shows Promise

Kansas City Star

20 Dec 1924

Hemingway, Clarence E.
8 Mar 1925 (oversize)
& Three Stories and Ten Poems

Rosenfeld, Paul

Tough Earth

The New Republic

25 Nov 1925

3 copies

In Our Time

Plum, Mary
A New Chicago Writer
Chicago Post
27 Nov 1925

In Our Time

Kaufman, S. Jay
Round the Town
New York Telegram
1 Dec 1925

In Our Time

Edwin Balmer's Wife is Burned
Chicago Tribune
29 Nov 1925

Hemingway, Clarence E.
2 Dec 1925

Lewis, Sinclair
Manhattan at Last
Saturday Review of Literature
5 Dec 1925

1925

In Our Time. Fifteen short stories. . .
N.Y. Book Review
Dec 1925

In Our Time

In Our Time. Here is a book. . .
Cleveland Plaindealer
6 Dec 1925

In Our Time

In Our Time. Sketches which show. . ."
N.Y. Bookman
Dec 1925

In Our Time

L.H.R.
In Our Time
Parkersburg, W. Va. News
6 Dec 1925

In Our Time

In Our Time. With a striking economy. . .
N.Y. Book Review Digest
Dec 1925

In Our Time

In the Modern Manner
Newark Evening News
8 Dec 1925

In Our Time

American Art from Soil

Kansas City Star

10 Dec 1925

     1925

Ernest Hemingway, the author. . .

Hartford Times

26 Dec 1925

     1925

Schuyler, Ashley

 Another American Discovers the Acid in
the Language

 Kansas City Star

 12 Dec 1925

    In Our Time

In 'Contemporary Reminiscences' published
. . .

Oklahoma City Oklahoman

13 Dec 1925

     1925

2 copies

From a Paris Letter

New York Telegram

16 Dec 1925

    1925

New York Herald (European Edition),
entire paper

22 Dec 1925

     1925

O'Brien, Edward J.

 The Best Short Stories

 Boston Transcript

 19 Dec 1925

    1925

H.B.

 One approaches that widely heralded
volume of short stories by Ernest. . .

 [1926]

    In Our Time

The new writers, with the exception. . .

Parkersburg, W. Va., News

20 Dec 1925

    1925

L.B.

 Revista de Revistas

 Orientaciones

 [1926]

     1926

It is rare to find a writer. . .

[Toledo Times]

[1926]

Torrents of Spring

Reims Reclame des Habitants

Johnston, Dorothy M.
Jan 1926

Roll of Honor

Boston Evening Transcript

1926

1926

Shinkman, Paul

Latin Quarter Notes

Johnston, Dorothy M.
Jan 1926

The Torrents of Spring. Ernest Hemingway,
whom. . .

[New York Evening Post]

[1926]

Torrents of Spring

American Author Living in Paris Writes
New Book

St. Louis Globe Democrat

2 Jan 1926

In Our Time

Walsh, Ernest

The Cheapest Book I Ever Read

[1926]

Torrents of Spring S.B.,
p. 27

Digby, Kenelm

Two books. . .

Minneapolis Tribune

3 Jan 1926

1926

Who's Who Abroad--George Waller Parker

Johnston, Dorothy M.
Jan 1926

With a Bookworm

Minneapolis Journal

3 Jan 1926

1926

Bromfield, Louis

    Life here is luxurious and cheap. . .

    New York Evening Post

    9 Jan 1926

                1926

In Our Time. The author of this book. . .

Omaha World-Herald

10 Jan 1926

              In Our Time

Digby, Kenelm

    The Literary Lobby

    Buffalo News

    9 Jan 1926

                1926

Taylor, Warren

    Chiselled Prose Found in Fiction of
    Hemingway

    Nashville Tennessean

    10 Jan 1926

              In Our Time

Digby, Kenelm

    The Literary Lobby

    New York Post

    9 Jan 1926

                1926

H.B.

    Books on Our Table

    New York Post

    11 Jan 1926

                1926

    Author Discusses Writing a Novel

    Richmond Dispatch

    10 Jan 1926

                1926

In Our Time. Short Stories.

New York Outlook

13 Jan 1926

              In Our Time

    How Hemingway Works

    Omaha World-Herald

    10 Jan 1926

            In Our Time

2 copies

H.B.

    Books on Our Table

    New York Post

    14 Jan 1926

              1926

Newman, Frances
    In Our Time
    Atlanta Journal
    24 Jan 1926
                    In Our Time

Charles Scribner's Sons announce for
spring. . ."
Newark Evening News
27 Mar 1926
                    Torrents of Spring S.B.,
                    p. 1

In Our Time. With a striking economy. . .
New York Book Review Digest
Feb 1926
                    In Our Time

Several authors. . ."
Chicago News
31 Mar 1926
                    Torrents of Spring S.B.,
                    p. 1

Lighter Fiction
N.Y. Brentano's Book Chat
Feb 1926
                    Torrents of Spring S.B.,
                    p. 65

Book Note
Toledo Times
4 Apr 1926
                    Torrents of Spring S.B.,
                    p. 1

Ho, For the Toreador
Brooklyn Eagle
8 Feb 1926
                    Sun Also Rises

Charles Scribner's Sons announce. . .
Toledo News Bee
23 Apr 1926
                    Torrents of Spring

Linati, Carlo
    Racconti in verde e sole
    Milan Corriere della Sera
    4 Mar 1926
                    1926

Charles Scribner's Sons announce. . .
Johnstown, Pa., Democrat
26 Apr 1926
                    Torrents of Spring S.B.,
                    p. 1

Of all the work by the young men. . .

New York Bookman

May 1926

    In Our Time

General Reading: Notable Books

New Orleans Times-Picayune

9 May 1926

     Torrents of Spring S.B.,
     p. 1

Before Ernest Hemingway's novel 'The Sun
Also Rises'. . .

Minneapolis Tribune

2 May 1926

     Torrents of Spring S.B.,
     p. 1

General Reading

Omaha News

23 May 1926

     Torrents of Spring S.B.,
     p. 1

Books on Our Table

New York Evening Post

2 May 1926

     Torrents of Spring S.B.,
     p. 3

Books on Our Table

New York Evening Post

24 May 1926

     Torrents of Spring

In Our Time. There must be something. . .

Portland Oregonian

2 May 1926

    In Our Time

2 copies

Hansen, Harry

 An American Parody

New York World

30 May 1926

     Torrents of Spring S.B.,
     p. 2
     & Torrents of Spring

And Eugene O'Neill couldn't. . .

N.Y. Saturday Review of Literature

8 May 1926

     Torrents of Spring S.B.,
     p. 1

. . . Up and to the office. . .

[June 1926]

     Torrents of Spring

Books on Our Table

New York Evening Post

1 June 1926

Torrents of Spring S.B.,
p. 4

New Parody Lacks the With and Humor
Expected

Boston Globe

5 June 1926

Torrents of Spring S.B.,
p. 3

Walfon, Edith H.

Chicago School Parodied

Springfield, Mass., Evening Union

4 June 1926

Torrents of Spring

Torrents of Spring.   The author himself. . .

Publishers' Weekly

5 June 1926

Torrents of Spring S.B.,
p. 3

The Cruise of the Colleen Dawn. . .

New York Evening Post

5 June 1926

Torrents of Spring S.B.,
p. 2

Torrents of Spring.   A fantastic series
of. . .

Boston Transcript

5 June 1926

Torrents of Spring S.B.,
p. 3

Digby, Kenelm

The national prize. . .

New York Evening Post

5 June 1926

Torrents of Spring S.B.,
p. 2

Walton, Edith H.

'Chicago School' Parodied

The Springfield Union

5 June 1926

Torrents of Spring S.B.,
p. 4

Digby, Kenelm

Ernest Hemingway has parodied. . .

Buffalo News

6 June 1926

Torrents of Spring S.B.,
p. 3

Fiction

New York Herald Tribune

6 June 1926

Torrents of Spring S.B.
p. 5

Mott, Frank Luther

The Short Story of Today

Des Moines Register

6 June 1926

In Our Time

Torrents of Spring. The clever quips. . .

Argonaut

9 June 1926

Torrents of Spring

Roedder, Karsten

The Book Parade

Brooklyn Citizen

6 June 1926

Torrents of Spring S.B.,
p. 5

Hansen, Harry

An American Parody: Ernest Hemingway
Tries to Reduce Sherwood Anderson to the
Absurd

Sunday Morning World

10 June 1926

See Schneider, Isidore
11 June 1926

Torrents of Spring. A novel in honor. . .

New York Times

6 June 1926

Torrents of Spring S.B.,
p. 4

The Torrents of Spring: Something in the
way. . .

Milwaukee Journal

11 June 1926

Torrents of Spring S.B.,
p. 4

Torrents of Spring. Ernest Hemingway, who
in serious moments. . .

Portland, Maine, Express

8 June 1926

Torrents of Spring S.B.,
p. 5

F.P.A.

The Conning Tower

New York World

12 June 1926

Torrents of Spring S.B.,
p. 8

A Spring Scoffer

Chicago News

9 June 1926

Torrents of Spring S.B.,
p. 4

Boyd, Ernest

Readers and Writers

The Independent

12 June 1926

Torrents of Spring S.B.,
p. 6
& Torrents of Spring

Hammond, Bray

    Torrents of Spring

    New York Sun

    12 June 1926

                 Torrents of Spring S.B.,
                 p. 5

Photo: Ernest Hemingway is the author. . .

Columbus Dispatch

13 June 1926

                 Torrents of Spring S.B.,
                 p. 11

Laughing at Authors: The Torrents of Spring

Cincinnati Enquirer

12 June 1926

                 Torrents of Spring

Mr. Hemingway Writes Some High-Spirited Nonsense

The New York Times Book Review

13 June 1926

                 Torrents of Spring S.B.,
                 p. 7

W.Y.

    The Torrents of Spring

    New York Post

    12 June 1926

                 Torrents of Spring S.B.,
                 p. 8
                 & Torrents of Spring

Pages in Waiting

Louisville Herald

13 June 1926

                 Torrents of Spring S.B.,
                 p. 6

Burlesque: The Torrents of Spring

Columbus Dispatch

13 June 1926

                 Torrents of Spring

Rennels, Mary

    Critic Looks at Critic's Latest Book

    Cleveland Times

    13 June 1926

                 Torrents of Spring S.B.,
                 p. 9

Digny, Kenelm

    Ernest Hemingway has parodied. . .

    Minneapolis Tribune

    13 June 1926

                 Torrents of Spring S.B.,
                 p. 2-3 loose

It is so rare. . .

Toledo Times

13 June 1926

                 Torrents of Spring S.B.,
                 p. 8

Sherwood Anderson the Latest Victim to
Feel the Keen Axe of the Parodist

Hartford Courant

13 June 1926

Torrents of Spring S.B.,
p. 9

The Torrents of Spring. This is the
story. . .

Columbus Dispatch

13 June 1926

Torrents of Spring S.B.,
p. 9

The Torrents of Spring

Memphis Commercial Appeal

13 June 1926

Torrents of Spring S.B.,
p. 6

F.P.A.

The Conning Tower

New Bedford Mercury

14 June 1926

Torrents of Spring S.B.,
pp. 8-9 loose and 49

The Torrents of Spring. A burlesque
subtitled. . .

Wheeling Register

13 June 1926

Torrents of Spring S.B.,
p. 10

Horan, Kenneth

The Torrents of Spring

Chicago Journal of Commerce

14 June 1926

Torrents of Spring S.B.,
p. 10

The Torrents of Spring. It must have
been. . .

San Francisco Chronicle

13 June 1926

Torrents of Spring

Photo: Ernest Hemingway is the author. . .

Chicago Evening Post Literary Review

18 June 1926

Torrents of Spring S.B.,
p. 32

Torrents of Spring. This is another of. . .

Washington Post

13 June 1926

Torrents of Spring S.B.,
p. 7

Jones, Llewellyn

Worst Literary Outrage in Years

Chicago Post

18 June 1926

Torrents of Spring S.B.,
p. 11

To read joyously. . .

Dayton News

18 June 1926

Torrents of Spring S.B.,
p. 12

The Torrents of Spring. When Barry
Pain wrote . . .

Cleveland Plaindealer

20 June 1926

Torrents of Spring

Laughing at Authors

Cincinnati Enquirer

19 June 1926

Torrents of Spring

The Torrents of Spring. The story of
Yogi. . .

Detroit News

20 June 1926

Torrents of Spring

2 copies

A Literary Skit

San Francisco Bulletin

19 June 1926

Torrents of Spring S.B.,
p. 10

Torrents of Spring. It used to be
said. . .

Portland [Oregon] Journal

20 June 1926

Torrents of Spring

Highly Specialized

Louisville Courier Journal

20 June 1926

Torrents of Spring S.B.,
p. 11

The Torrents of Spring. A somewhat. . .

Rochester Democrat Chronicle

20 June 1926

Torrents of Spring

J.G.N.

Effective Criticism in a Burlesque Novel

Kansas City Journal-Post

Torrents of Spring

Tenscher, Lorna Jane

Books in Silhouette

Oklahoma City News

22 June 1926

Torrents of Spring S.B.,
p. 10

Torrents of Spring. This is a small. . .

Cincinnati Wester Christian Advocate

22 June 1926

    Torrents of Spring

Recommended for Your Week-End

Boston Herald

26 June 1926

    Torrents of Spring S.B.,
    p. 12

Ernest Hemingway Joins the Chicago School
of Literature

Milwaukee Journal

25 June 1926

    Torrents of Spring S.B.,
    p. 10

Snyder, Ruth

A Minute or Two with Books

New York Evening World

26 June 1926

    Torrents of Spring

You probably would enjoy a warm weather
laugh. . .

Toledo News Bee

25 June 1926

    Torrents of Spring S.B.,
    p. 17

Torrents of Spring. Having no end of
fun. . .

Boston Herald

26 June 1926

    Torrents of Spring

Four New Novels Deal with Intrigue,
Mystery, the Supernatural, and Parody

Newark News

26 June 1926

    Torrents of Spring S.B.,
    p. 12
    & Torrents of Spring

J.B.C.

A Take-off on Anderson

South Bend Tribune

27 June 1926

    Torrents of Spring S.B.,
    p. 12

Hemingway Writes an Anderson Book

Cincinnati Times-Star

26 June 1926

    Torrents of Spring S.B.,
    p. 13

A Clever Burlesque

Buffalo Times

27 June 1926

    Torrents of Spring, S.B.,
    p. 13
    & Torrents of Spring

Photo: Ernest Hemingway is the author. . .

St. Paul News

27 June 1926

Torrents of Spring S.B.,
p. 12

The Torrents of Spring. A satire on Sherwood Anderson. . .

Literary Digest

July 1926

Torrents of Spring S.B.,
p. 19

Smith, Maude Sumner

Do you read many new books? . .

Omaha News

27 June 1926

Torrents of Spring S.B.,
p. 13

Gray, James

The World of Art, Books and Drama

St. Paul Dispatch

2 July 1926

Torrents of Spring S.B.,
p. 14
& Torrents of Spring

Stark, George W.

Perilous Petoskey

Detroit News

27 June 1926

Torrents of Spring S.B.,
p. 15

Chicagoan Writes Romantic Novel That's Very Funny

Chicago Tribune

3 July 1926

Torrents of Spring S.B.,
p. 15

Ten Days Labor

Providence Journal

27 June 1926

Torrents of Spring S.B.,
p. 15

W.E.H.

The Torrents of Spring

Boston Evening Transcript

3 July 1926

Torrents of Spring S.B.,
p. 13
& Torrents of Spring

Disrespectful

Cleveland Time Magazine

28 June 1926

Torrents of Spring S.B.,
p. 11

Yust, Walter

Hemingway Novel After Manner of 'Dark Laughter'

Philadelphia Public Ledger

3 July 1926

Torrents of Spring S.B.,
p. 14

The above literary criticism is
offered. . .

Brooklyn Eagle

7 July 1926

        Torrents of Spring S.B.,
        p. 17

Poking Fun at Modernism

New Orleans Times-Picayune

11 July 1926

        Torrents of Spring S.B.,
        p. 15
        & Torrents of Spring

Ernest Hemingway has done something. . .

Town Topics

8 July 1926

        Torrents of Spring S.B.,
        p. 14

Alert Readers

Time

12 July 1926

        Torrents of Spring S.B.,
        p. 14

Torrents of Spring. Mr. Sherwood Anderson
has been. . .

Harrisburg News

9 July 1926

        Torrents of Spring S.B.,
        p. 16

Ernest Hemingway, author of The Torrents
of Spring has gone to Pamplona. . .

Johnstown, Pa., Democrat

12 July 1926

        Torrents of Spring S.B.,
        p. 32

Dreary Fooling a la Sherwood Anderson

Louisville Herald

11 July 1926

        Torrents of Spring S.B.,
        p. 14
        & Torrents of Spring

Burlesque

Indianapolis News

14 July 1926

        Torrents of Spring S.B.,
        p. 14

Petrolia, Astul

  A Parody with a Chuckle to Every Line

Tulsa Tribune

11 July 1926

        Torrents of Spring S.B.,
        p. 16

Photo: Ernest Hemingway, author of In
Our Time. . .

Philadelphia Inquirer

17 July 1926

        Torrents of Spring S.B.,
        p. 32

Ernest Hemingway, author of The Torrents
of Spring has gone to Pamplona. . .

Cincinatti Enquirer

17 July 1926

        Torrents of Spring S.B.,
        p. 32

The Torrents of Spring by Ernest
Hemingway can't be generally. . .

New Haven Courier

17 July 1926

        Torrents of Spring S.B.,
        p. 17

Ernest Hemingway goes to Pamplona. . .

New York Evening Post

17 July 1926

        Torrents of Spring S.B.,
        p. 32

Ernest Hemingway, author of Torrents of
Spring. . .

Dayton News

18 July 1926

        Torrents of Spring S.B.,
        p. 16

In The Torrents of Spring the author. . .

Charleston Post

17 July 1926

        Torrents of Spring S.B.,
        p. 16

Ernest Hemingway, author of The Torrents
of Spring has gone to Pamplona. . .

Haverill, Mass., Gazette

18 July 1926

        Torrents of Spring S.B.,
        p. 32

Paul Rosenfeld writes that he and a
group. . .

Buffalo News

17 July 1926

        Torrents of Spring S.B.,
        p. 32

Latimer, Margery

A Burlesque of Sherwood Anderson

New York Herald Tribune

18 July 1926

        Torrents of Spring S.B.,
        p. 18
        & Torrents of Spring

The Torrents of Spring. Here is a
rioutous. . .

Des Moines Capital

17 July 1926

        Torrents of Spring S.B.,
        p. 16

Leslie, L. C.

Hemingway Book Like Typewriter Gone Loco
on Bet

Denver News

18 July 1926

        Torrents of Spring S.B.,
        p. 16
        & Torrents of Spring

Leek, John

    None is Safe from a Parodist

    Oklahoma City Oklahoman

    19 July 1926

            Torrents of Spring S.B.,
            p. 24

Latimer, Margery

    Burlesque

    Minneapolis Journal

    25 July 1926

            Torrents of Spring

Ernest Hemingway, author of The Torrents
of Spring, has gone to Pamplona. . .

    Helena, Mont., Independent

    21 July 1926

            Torrents of Spring S.B.,
            p. 32

Paul Rosenfeld writes that. . .

    Minneapolis Tribune

    25 July 1926

            Sun Also Rises

Ernest Hemingway, author of The Torrents
of Spring. . .

    San Francisco Argonaut

    24 July 1926

            Sun Also Rises
            & Torrents of Spring S.B.,
            p. 32

West, Richard S., Jr.

    Dark Laughter is Satirized in The Torrents
    of Spring

    Nashville Tennessean

    25 July 1926

            Torrents of Spring S.B.,
            p. 19

Ernest Hemingway, author of The Torrents
of Spring has gone to Pamplona. . .

    Toledo Blade

    25 July 1926

            Torrents of Spring S.B.,
            p. 32

Ernest Hemingway in The Torrents of
Spring burlesques. . .

    New Bedford Mercury

    26 July 1926

            Torrents of Spring S.B.,
            p. 17

Good Fun

    Oakland Tribune

    25 July 1926

            Schneider, Isidore
            5 Aug 1926
            & Torrents of Spring
            S.B., p. 19
            & Torrents of Spring

Tate, Allen

    The Spirituality of Roughnecks

    Nation

    28 July 1926

            Torrents of Spring S.B.,
            p. 19
            & Torrents of Spring

S.K.R.

The Torrents of Spring.

Los Angeles Saturday Night

31 July 1926

Torrents of Spring S.B.,
p. 18

The Torrents of Spring. Written with a
laudable intention. . .

McNaughts Monthly

Aug 1926

Torrents of Spring S.B.,
p. 22

Torrents of Spring. Mr. Hemingway is one
of the young writers. . .

New York Saturday Review of Literature

31 July 1926

Schneider, Isidore
5 Aug 1926
& Torrents of Spring
S.B., p. 17

The Torrents of Spring. The author
has left. . .

Salem, Oregon, Larent

Aug 1926

Torrents of Spring S.B.,
p. 23

Touchstone

Ernest Hemingway's Torrents of Spring is
burlesque. . .

New Yorker

31 July 1926

Torrents of Spring S.B.,
p. 17

Hemingway, Ernest. Torrents of Spring.
Torrents of Spring is an amusing. . .

New York Book Review Digest

Aug 1926

Torrents of Spring S.B.,
p. 23
& Torrents of Spring

Vachel Lindsay now rejoices in a
daughter. . .

New York Saturday Review of Literature

31 July 1926

Torrents of Spring S.B.,
p. 32

Currie, George

The Chicago Peril

Waterbury Republican

1 Aug 1926

Torrents of Spring S.B.,
p. 21

Ernest Hemingway who is absolutely
modernistic. . .

McNaughts Monthly

Aug 1926

Torrents of Spring S.B.,
p. 22

The Torrents of Spring. Billing his
effort. . .

Ft. Worth Star-Telegram

1 Aug 1926

Torrents of Spring S.B.,
p. 18

Ultra-Modern Tale

Rochester Democrat Chronicle

1 Aug 1926

Torrents of Spring S.B.,
p. 18 and 20

Dear Old Hemingway

Honolulu Star Bulletin

7 Aug 1926

Torrents of Spring S.B.,
p. 32

Snyder, Ruth

Ernest Hemingway is Ed Wynn of
Literature

Galviston Tribune

Schneider, Isidore
5 Aug 1926

Hemingway Burlesques a Certain School
of Fiction

Kansas City Star

7 Aug 1926

Torrents of Spring S.B.,
p. 20
& Torrents of Spring

West, Richard S., Jr.

Dark Laughter is Satirized in The
Torrents of Spring

Los Angeles Sun

Schneider, Isidore
5 Aug 1926

The Torrents of Spring. Somebody will
have to toss a coin. . .

Los Angeles Record

7 Aug 1926

Torrents of Spring S.B.,
p. 20
& Torrents of Spring

Anderson a la Mode

Downers Grove, Ill., Reporter

6 Aug 1926

Torrents of Spring S.B.,
p. 20

Ernest Hemingway, author of The Torrents
of Spring has gone to Pamplona. . .

St. Paul News

8 Aug 1926

Torrents of Spring S.B.,
pp. 32 & 33

Callaghan, Morley

Introducing Ernest Hemingway

Saturday Night

7 Aug 1926

Callaghan, Morley
12 Aug 1926

Ernest Hemingway, author of The Torrents
of Spring. . .

Haverill, Mass., Gazette

13 Aug 1926

Sun Also Rises

Ultra-Modern Tale

Rochester Democrat Chronicle

1 Aug 1926

Torrents of Spring S.B.,
p. 18 and 20

Dear Old Hemingway

Honolulu Star Bulletin

7 Aug 1926

Torrents of Spring S.B.,
p. 32

Snyder, Ruth

Ernest Hemingway is Ed Wynn of
Literature

Galviston Tribune

Schneider, Isidore
5 Aug 1926

Hemingway Burlesques a Certain School
of Fiction

Kansas City Star

7 Aug 1926

Torrents of Spring S.B.,
p. 20
& Torrents of Spring

West, Richard S., Jr.

Dark Laughter is Satirized in The
Torrents of Spring

Los Angeles Sun

Schneider, Isidore
5 Aug 1926

The Torrents of Spring. Somebody will
have to toss a coin. . .

Los Angeles Record

7 Aug 1926

Torrents of Spring S.B.,
p. 20
& Torrents of Spring

Anderson a la Mode

Downers Grove, Ill., Reporter

6 Aug 1926

Torrents of Spring S.B.,
p. 20

Ernest Hemingway, author of The Torrents
of Spring has gone to Pamplona. . .

St. Paul News

8 Aug 1926

Torrents of Spring S.B.,
pp. 32 & 33

Callaghan, Morley

Introducing Ernest Hemingway

Saturday Night

7 Aug 1926

Callaghan, Morley
12 Aug 1926

Ernest Hemingway, author of The Torrents
of Spring. . .

Haverill, Mass., Gazette

13 Aug 1926

Sun Also Rises

Repeats previous page

Burlesque and Parody

Worcester Telegram

15 Aug 1926

Torrents of Spring S.B.,
p. 21
& Torrents of Spring

Small, Harold A.

Chicago School of Literature Takes
Ducking From Parodist

San Francisco Chronicle

22 Aug 1926

Torrents of Spring S.B.,
p. 23
& Torrents of Spring

Eden Phillpotts, who writes more books in
a year. . .

Providence Journal

15 Aug 1926

Torrents of Spring S.B.,
p. 33

The Torrents of Spring. A howling
farce. . .

Oklahoma City Oklahoman

22 Aug 1926

Torrents of Spring S.B.,
p. 20 & p. 21

Ernest Hemingway, author of Torrents of
Spring has been

Providence Journal

15 Aug 1926

Torrents of Spring S.B.,
p. 21

Weeks, Howard

Burlesque

Detroit Free Press

22 Aug 1926

Torrents of Spring S.B.,
p. 22

The Torrents of Spring is a romantic. . .

Beaumont, Texas, Enterprise

15 Aug 1926

Torrents of Spring S.B.,
p. 21

The Phoenician

Ernest Hemingway's first novel The Sun
Also Rises. . .

New York Saturday Review of Literature

28 Aug 1926

Torrents of Spring S.B.,
p. 33,
& Sun Also Rises

Ernest Hemingway's new novel. . .

Cleveland Plaindealer

22 Aug 1926

Torrents of Spring S.B.,
p. 32
& Torrents of Spring

Torrents of Spring Parodies Anderson

Philadelphia Record

28 Aug 1926

Torrents of Spring S.B.,
p. 21
& Torrents of Spring

An Anderson Parody

Springfield Republican

29 Aug 1926

Torrents of Spring S.B.,
p. 21
& Torrents of Spring

The Golden Dancer

San Francisco Chronicle

5 Sept 1926

Torrents of Spring S.B.,
p. 22

Photo: Very, very funny!

Cleveland Times

29 Aug 1926

Torrents of Spring S.B.,
p. 33

The Torrents of Spring. Torrents of
words. . .

Miami Herald

5 Sept 1926

Torrents of Spring S.B.,
p. 24

Ernest Hemingway in his Torrents of
Spring . . .

New York Brentano's Book Chat

Seot 1926--Oct 1926

Torrents of Spring S.B.,
p. 24

Brickell, Herschel

Paris Overrun with American Writers

New York Post

11 Sept 1926

Torrents of Spring S.B.,
p. 25-26

Ernest Hemingway is absolutely
modernistic. . .

McNaught's Monthly

Sept 1926

Torrents of Spring

Short Stories of Distinction

Des Moines Register

12 Sept 1926

In Our Time

The Torrents of Spring. A parody
novel. . .

New York Bookman

Sept 1926

Torrents of Spring S.B.,
p. 24
& Torrents of Spring

Morris, Lawrence S.

Frolicking on Olympus

The New Republic

15 Sept 1926

Torrents of Spring S.B.,
p. 24
& Torrents of Spring

The Torrents of Spring. A Romantic Novel
in Honor of the Passing of a Great Race

Outlook

15 Sept 1926

    Torrents of Spring

Anderson's Newest Book

New Orleans Tribune

10 Oct 1926

    Torrents of Spring S.B.,
    p. 29

The Torrents of Spring. This book, which
one. . .

Portland Oregonian

19 Sept 1926

    Torrents of Spring S.B.,
    p. 26
    Torrents of Spring

Advertisement for Ulysses in Two Worlds
Monthly, also mentioning Hemingway as
a writer appearing in the publication

The Nation

18 Oct 1926

    1926

Torrents

St. Petersburg Times

26 Sept 1926

    Torrents of Spring S.B.,
    p. 29

Scribners announces a new novel by Ernest
Hemingway. . .

New York Sun
Minneapolis Tribune

16 Oct 1926

    Torrents of Spring S.B.,
    p. 34

Mason, Thomas L.

 We are Bigger, but are we Funnier?

The Literary Digest: International Book
Review

Oct 1926

    Torrents of Spring S.B.,
    p. 28

Roedder, Karsten

 The Book Parade

 Brooklyn Citizen

 21 Oct 1926

    Sun Also Rises

Forthcoming Books--Fiction

New York Times

3 Oct 1926

    Torrents of Spring S.B.,
    p. 35

Ernest Hemingway and His Inebriates in
Paris

Milwaukee Journal

22 Oct 1926

    Sun Also Rises
    & Torrents of Spring S.B.,
    p. 33

Hall Hemingway Exhibit

The Oak Parker

22 Oct 1926

Hemingway, Grace Hall
31 Oct 1926-- oversize

Sherwood Anderson's Notebook

Charleston Post

23 Oct 1926

Torrents of Spring S.B.,
p. 29

MacDonal, Norman

French-English, English-French

Springfield, Mass., Evening Union

22 Oct 1926

Torrents of Spring S.B.,
p. 33

Sherwood Anderson's notebook. . .

Charleston Post

23 Oct 1926

Torrents of Spring S.B.
p. 29

Hansen, Harry

The First Reader: Library Lore

New York World

23 Oct 1926

Torrents of Spring S.B.,
p. 36

The Sun Also Rises. A story of life. . .

Boston Transcript

23 Oct 1926

Torrents of Spring S.B.,
p. 33
& Sun Also Rises

Kiddish Ha-Shem. By Sholem Ash. . .

New York Evening Post

23 Oct 1926

Torrents of Spring S.B.,
p. 34

. . . Vanity of vanities, saith the
preacher. . .

Philadelphia Inquirer

23 Oct 1926

Sun Also Rises

Our first thought this week. . .

New York Saturday Review of Literature

23 Oct 1926

Torrents of Spring S.B.,
p. 34

With the appearances of Porgy. . .

Philadelphia Inquirer

23 Oct 1926

Torrents of Spring S.B.,
p. 39

Yust, Walter

For those who find books an adventure. . .

New York Evening Post

23 Oct 1926

Torrents of Spring S.B.,
p. 34

The Sun Also Rises. Mr. Hemingway, who
so successfully. . .

Richmond Dispatch

25 Oct 1926

Torrents of Spring S.B.,
p. 35

G.R.C.

Cheering Cop Life's Nostrum

Cleveland Times

24 Oct 1926

Torrents of Spring S.B.,
p. 36

The Sun Also Arises

Brooklyn Eagle

27 Oct 1926

Torrents of Spring S.B.,
p. 37
& Sun Also Rises

I.M.P.

Turns with a Bookworm

New York Herald Tribune

24 Oct 1926

Torrents of Spring S.B.,
p. 35

Heustis, Bertha

Lecutre at Hollywood Public Library

28 Oct 1926

Sun Also Rises

The Sun Also Rises. A novel by. . .

Savanah News

24 Oct 1926

Torrents of Spring S.B.,
p. 39

Books on our Table

New York Evening Post

29 Oct 1926

Torrents of Spring S.B.,
p. 34
& Sun Also Rises

The Sun Also Rises. In paris, La vie. . .

San Francisco Chronicle

24 Oct 1926

Torrents of Spring S.B.,
p. 35

Digby, Kenelm

The Literary Lobby

New York Evening Post

30 Oct 1926

Torrents of Spring S.B.,
p. 39

Photo: Ernest Hemingway, Author of
The Sun Also Rises

Springfield Evening Union
30 Oct 1926

Torrents of Spring S.B.,
p. 37

The Torrents of Spring. This book,
sub-titled. . .

Charleston Post
30 Oct 1926

Torrents of Spring S.B.,
p. 27

Ford Hails Joyce Sanest in World

New York Evening Sun
30 Oct 1926

1926

We are disappointed however in Ernest
Hemingway's. . .

Buffalo News
30 Oct 1926

Torrents of Spring S.B.,
p. 36

Pity the Poor Expatriate

Milwaukee Journal
30 Oct 1926

Torrents of Spring S.B.,
p. 37
& Sun Also Rise

We have been looking through a beautiful
book. . .

New York Saturday Review of Literature
30 Oct 1926

Torrents of Spring S.B.,
p. 36
& Sun Also Rises

Study in Futility
Cincinnati Enquirer
30 Oct 1926

Torrents of Spring S.B.,
p. 38
& Sun Also Rises

. . . The wise ones are telling us. . .

Publishers' Weekly
30 Oct 1926

1926

The Sun Also Rises, by Ernest Hemingway,
author of . . .

Cincinnati Times Star
30 Oct 1926

Torrents of Spring S.B.,
p. 37
& Sun Also Rises

Cartoon: Ernest Hemingway

New York World
31 Oct 1926

Torrents of Spring S.B.,
p. 38

Photo: Ernest Hemingway, through the
Scribners. . .

Columbus Dispatch

31 Oct 1926

> Torrents of Spring S.B.,
> p. 43

Some authors whose. . .

The World

31 Oct 1926

> 1926

Photo: Ernest Hemingway. With the
publication

St. Paul News

31 Oct 1926

> Torrents of Spring S.B.,
> p. 38

There is always a bright boy of
American letters. . .

Minneapolis Journal

31 Oct 1926

> Torrents of Spring S.B.,
> p. 38

Aiken, Conrad

> Expatriates

> New York Herald Tribune Books

> 31 Oct 1926

>> Torrents of Spring S.B.,
>> p. 41
>> & Sun Also Rises

A Nautical Dance

> Hemingway, Grace Hall
> 31 Oct 1926

Roedeer, Karsten

> The Book Parade

> Brooklyn Citizen

> 31 Oct 1926

>> Torrents of Spring S.B.,
>> p. 40
>> & Sun Also Rises

Charles Scribner's Sons believe that
standards. . .

Literary Digest Book Review

Nov 1926

> Torrents of Spring S.B.,
> p. 56

Marital Tragedy

New York Times

31 Oct 1926

> Sun Also Rises

Intelligentsiana: Ernest Hemingway has a
suggestion for you. . .

McNaughts Monthly

Nov 1926

> 1926

Kaufman, S. Jay

    Round the Town

    New York Telegram

    1 Nov 1926

               Torrents of Spring S.B.,
               p. 30

Rascoe, Burton

    Diversity in the Younger Set

    New York Sun

    6 Nov 1926 (not 7 Nov 1926)

               Torrents of Spring S.B.,
               p. 42
               & Torrents of Spring

Rascoe, Burton

    The Book of the Week

    Middletown, N.Y., Herald

    1 Nov 1926

               Sun Also Rises

K.J.W.

    The Sun Also Rises

    Boston Transcript

    6 Nov 1926

               Torrents of Spring S.B.,
               p. 40
               & Sun Also Rises

Ernest Hemingway describes a Spanish
bull fight. . .

    New York Evening Post

    2 Nov 1926

               Torrents of Spring S.B.,
               p. 58

About a year ago, was it, appeared a
satirical yarn. . .

    Providence Journal

    7 Nov 1926

               Torrents of Spring S.B.,
               p. 43

Sayler, Oliver M.

    A very different tale of . . .

    Footlight & Lamplight

    4 Nov 1926

               Bridges, Robert
               11 Nov 1926
               & Torrents of Spring S.B.,
               p. 43

Ernest Hemingway has found out. . .

    Oklahoma City Oklahoman

    7 Nov 1926

               Torrents of Spring S.B.,
               pp. 26 & 42

    The World of Art, Books, and Drama

    St. Paul Dispatch

    5 Nov 1926

               Torrents of Spring S.B.,
               p. 56

Clever Story Well Done

    Richmond Times Dispatch

    7 Nov 1926

               Torrents of Spring S.B.,
               p. 43

Rascoe, Burton

The Book of the Week

Charleston, W.Va., Gazette
Evansville Courier
Seattle Times

7 Nov 1926

Torrents of Spring S.B.,
p. 43
& Sun Also Rises

A story of the . . .

Wheeling Register

7 Nov 1926

Sun Also Rises

Sun Also Rises--An Amazing Book

Hartford Courant

7 Nov 1926

Sun Also Rises

E.L.P., Jr.

The Torrents of Spring

Johnstown, Pa., Democrat

8 Nov 1926

Torrents of Spring S.B.,
p. 29

The Sun Also Rises. Ernest Hemingway
published two. . .

Utica Observer-Dispatch

7 Nov 1926

Torrents of Spring S.B.,
p. 44

Rascoe, Burton

The Daybook of a New Yorker

Seattle Times

8 Nov 1926

Torrents of Spring, S.B.,
p. 45

The Sun Also Rises. A story of the
American. . .

Cleveland

7 Nov 1926

Torrents of Spring S.B.,
p. 43

D.A.

Book Stuff--In Which we Swat Realism

Emporia Gazette

10 Nov 1926

Torrents of Spring S.B.,
p. 44

The Sun Also Rises. We conclude the
term. . .

Portland, Oregon, Journal

7 Nov 1926

Torrents of Spring S.B.,
p. 45

E.B.

The Sun Also Rises

Los Angeles Record

13 Nov 1926

Torrents of Spring S.B.,
p. 46

Some New Publications

Saturday Review of Literature

13 Nov 1926

Pound, Ezra
2 Dec 1926--oversize

He Writes Bit of Realistic Fiction
Hemingway Book Is Masterpiece

Cleveland Plain Dealer

14 Nov 1926

Torrents of Spring S.B.,
p. 47
& Sun Also Rises

Wine, Bullfights and the Loves of Lost
Generation

Philadelphia Public Ledger

13 Nov 1926

Torrents of Spring S.B.,
p. 45

It is pleasant to note our friend. . .

Hartford Courant

14 Nov 1926

Torrents of Spring S.B.,
pp. 44 & 46

Photo: Ernest Hemingway, who's recently
published. . .

Omaha Bee

14 Nov 1926

Torrents of Spring S.B.,
p. 46

Pens First Novel

Dallas Times

14 Nov 1926

Torrents of Spring S.B.,
p. 46

Expatriates in Paris

Rochester Democrat Chronicle

14 Nov 1926

Torrents of Spring S.B.,
p. 45 & 47

Salpeter, Henry

Ford M. Ford Discusses Letters

New York World

14 Nov 1926

Torrents of Spring S.B.,
p. 47

Gorman, Herbert S.

Hemingway Keeps His Promise

New York World

14 Nov 1926

Torrents of Spring S.B.,
p. 50
& Sun Also Rises

Stark, George W.

Now, Go Back to Burlesque

Detroit News

14 Nov 1926

Torrents of Spring S.B.,
p. 46

The Sun Also Rises. A well told story. . .
Boston Post
14 Nov 1926

       Torrents of Spring S.B.,
       p. 45
       & Sun Also Rises

Brown, Heywood
   It Seems to Me
   New York World
   19 Nov 1926

       Torrents of Spring S.B.,
       pp. 48-49
       & Vanity Fair, 7 Mar 1927
       & Sun Also Rises

You'll Not Be Bored by this Book
Toledo Times
14 Nov 1926

       Torrents of Spring S.B.,
       p. 48
       & Sun Also Rises

F.P.A.
   The Conning Tower
   New York World
   30 Nov 1926

       1926

Story of Some Young Americans in Europe
Boston Globe
15 Nov 1926

       Torrents of Spring S.B.,
       pp. 47 & 48

Boyd, Ernest
   Readers and Writers
   Concord, N.H., Independent
   20 Nov 1926

       Sun Also Rises

The Sun Also Rises. A story of life. . .
Boston Evening Transcript
17 Nov 1926

       Torrents of Spring S.B.,
       p. 48

Boyd, Ernest
   Readers and Writers
   New York Independent Weekly Review
   20 Nov 1926

       Torrents of Spring, S.B.,
       p. 51

Torrents of Spring: A series of
fantastic. . .
Boston Evening Transcript
17 Nov 1926

       Torrents of Spring

Brown, Heywood
   It Seems to Me
   New York World
   20 Nov 1926

       Torrents of Spring S.B.,
       p. 49

The Sun Also Rises, by Ernest Hemingway, is a new novel. . .

New Yorker

20 Nov 1926

Torrents of Spring S.B., p. 52

One of the best is the new book. . .

Buffalo Courier

22 Nov 1926

Torrents of Spring S.B., p. 52

Ernest Hemingway also came in for discussion. . .

New York Tribune

21 Nov 1926

Torrents of Spring S.B., p. 49

Wednesday November 17--To the office. . .

New Bedford Mercury

22 Nov 1926

Torrents of Spring S.B., p. 49

I.M.P.

Turns with a Bookworm

New York Herald Tribune

21 Nov 1926

Torrents of Spring S.B., p. 50

Some Things Also Sink

New York Commercial

23 Nov 1926

Sun Also Rises

The Sun Also Rises. Ernest Hemingway's first novel. . .

Atlanta Journal

21 Nov 1926

Torrents of Spring S.B., p. 51
& Sun Also Rises

Brickell, Herschel

Books on Our Table: A. G. Gardiner Sketches 37 Personalities

New York Evening Post

24 Nov 1926

Torrents of Spring S.B., p. 53

Hansen, Harry

The inclusion of The All-Star Literary Vaudeville. . .

22 Nov 1926

In Our Time

The Sun Also Rises. In his book Ernest. . .

Stamford Advocate

24 Nov 1926

Torrents of Spring S.B., p. 52

Ernest Hemingway, who has become a
Parisian. . .

New York Telegraph

25 Nov 1926

       Torrents of Spring S.B.,
       p. 52

Ernest Hemingwa's colorful description. . .

St. Louis Post Dispatch

27 Nov 1926

       Torrents of Spring S.B.,
       p. 54
       & Sun Also Rises

Brickell, Herschel

    Books on Our Table: Microscope Upon
    the Lost Generation

    New York Evening Post

    26 Nov 1926

           Torrents of Spring S.B.,
           p. 53
           & Sun Also Rises

Hemingway Seems Out of Focus in The
Sun Also Rises

Chicago Daily Tribune

27 Nov 1926

       Musselman, Morris,
       27 Nov 1926
       & Hemingway, Grace Hall,
       4 Dec 1926
       & Torrents of Spring S.B.,
           p. 53
           & Sun Also Rises

Raymond, Holden

    The Newest Fiction: A Lost Generation

    Chicago Evening Post Literary Review

    26 Nov 1926

        Musselman, Morris
        27 Nov 1926
        & Torrents of Spring S.B.,
        p. 54
        & Sun Also Rises

It is related that Ernest Hemingway's
accurate. . .

Cincinnati Enquirer

27 Nov 1926

       Torrents of Spring S.B.,
       p. 53
       & Sun Also Rises

Brickell, Herschel

    Books on Our Table

    New York Evening Post

    27 Nov 1926

        Torrents of Spring S.B.,
        p. 55

Our Hard New World

San Francisco Argonaut

27 Nov 1926

       Sun Also Rises

Ernest Hemingway describes a Spanish
bull fight. . .

New York Evening Post

27 Nov 1926

       Torrents of Spring S.B.,
       p. 53
       & Sun Also Rises

Shenton, Edward

    Open Letter to Writer of The Sun Also
    Rises

    Philadelphia Record

    27 Nov 1926

        Torrents of Spring S.B.,
        p. 54
        & Sun Also Rises

Two novels I have enjoyed. . .

New York Evening Post

27 Nov 1926

Torrents of Spring S.B.,
p. 52

Pace, T. Bernard

The Style That Tells

Ashville Times

28 Nov 1926

Torrents of Spring S.B.,
p. 55
& Sun Also Rises

Ernest Hemingway's accurate and colorful
description. . .

Wheeling Register

28 Nov 1926

Torrents of Spring S.B.,
p. 55

The Patient Sun

New Orleans Times-Picayune

28 Nov 1926

Sun Also Rises

Ernest Hemingway's publishers advise
us. . ,

New York Tribune

28 Nov 1926

Torrents of Spring S.B.,
p. 56

Seeking Sensations

Springfield, Mass., Union

28 Nov 1926

Torrents of Spring S.B.,
p. 55
& Sun Also Rises

Photo: Ernest Hemingway wrote The Sun
Also Rises

Dayton News

28 Nov 1926

Torrents of Spring S.B.,
p. 54

When Ernest Hemingway writes about
bullfighting. . .

New York Times

28 Nov 1926

Torrents of Spring S.B.,
p. 55

A Fighting Author

Des Moines Register

28 Nov 1926

Sun Also Rises

K.H.

Cafe et Liqueuers

Chicago Journal of Commerce

29 Nov 1926

Torrents of Spring S.B.,
p. 27

Stagg, Hunter

A Swift Novel of Gertrude Stein's Lost Generation

Richmond News Leader

29 Nov 1926

Torrents of Spring S.B., p. 55

Of Ernest Hemingway's The Sun Also Rises. . .

Sioux City Journal

1 Dec 1926

Torrents of Spring S.B., p. 57

Brickell, Herschel

Books on Our Table

New York Post

30 Nov 1926

Torrents of Spring S.B., p. 56
& Sun Also Rises

The Sun Also Rises. Ever since Mr. Hemingway's . . .

Pasadena Star News

1 Dec 1926

Torrents of Spring S.B., p. 67

Rose, Stuart

Of Post-War Days in Paris

New York Book Review

Dec 1926

Sun Also Rises

Kandel, Aben

A Novel with Pulse-Beat

New York American

3 Dec 1926

Sun Also Rises

The Sun Also Rises. We are introduced. . .

New York Book Review Digest

Dec 1926

Torrents of Spring S.B., p. 56
& Sun Also Rises

The Sun Also Rises. A group of . . .

Milwaukee Journal

3 Dec 1926

Torrents of Spring S.B., p. 57

The Sun Also Rises. Deals with a group. . .

McNaughts Monthly

Dec 1926

Torrents of Spring S.B., p. 56

Americans in Paris Only to Have Good Time

St. Louis Globe Democrat

5 Dec 1926

Torrents of Spring S.B., p. 57
& Torrents of Spring

Schuyler, Ashley

Hemingway Leads Young Ineffectuals Through Europe

Kansas City Star

11 Dec 1926

Hemingway, Clarence E.,
13 Dec 1926
& Sun Also Rises

. . . Victor Llona, the famous French critic. . .

Charleston, S.C., Post

4 Dec 1926

1926

Schuyler, Ashley

Hemingway Leads Young Ineffectuals Through Europe

St. Louis Star

4 Dec 1926

Torrents of Spring S.B.,
p. 57

F.Q.E.

Give Us Air

Witchita Beacon

5 Dec 1926

Torrents of Spring S.B.,
p. 57
& Sun Also Rises

Benet, William Rose

The Time of Man. . .

Saturday Review of Literature

4 Dec 1926

Torrents of Spring S.B.,
p. 58

Ernest Hemingway, author of In Our Time. . .

New Orleans Times-Picayune

5 Dec 1926

Torrents of Spring S.B.,
p. 59

Other of this season's novels of unusual distinction. . .

New York Sun

4 Dec 1926

Torrents of Spring S.B.,
pp. 57 & 67

Ernest Hemingway in The Sun Also Rises. . .

New York Times

5 Dec 1926

Torrents of Spring S.B.,
p. 58

Sun Also Rises. A brilliant study. . .

New Yorker

4 Dec 1926

Sun Also Rises

Realism of Life Stabs Hemingway

San Francisco Chronicle

5 Dec 1926

Torrents of Spring S.B.,
p. 58

The Sophisticate

Cleveland Times

5 Dec 1926

Torrents of Spring S.B.,
p. 58

Ho, For the Toreador

Brooklyn Eagle

8 Dec 1926

Torrents of Spring S.B.,
p. 59

Ernest Hemingway's accurate and
colorful . . .

Johnstown, Pa., Democrat

6 Dec 1926

Sun Also Rises

George, Lloyd

The Book Cellar

Chicago Post

10 Dec 1926

Torrents of Spring S.B.,
p. 61

G.C.H.

Rebel Against Chicagoans

Waterbury Republican

6 Dec 1926

Torrents of Spring S.B.,
p. 60

A.R.F. of Johnstown, Pa. asks for a
list. . .

New York Post

11 Dec 1926

Torrents of Spring S.B.,
pp. 29 & 67

Ernest Hemingway.   Natural phenomena
interest. . .

Chicago News

8 Dec 1926

Torrents of Spring S.B.,
p. 59

Chase, Cleveland B.

Out of Little, Much

Saturday Review of Literature

11 Dec 1926

Torrents of Spring S.B.,
p. 60
& Sun Also Rises

Currie, George

Passed in Review

Brooklyn Eagle

8 Dec 1926

Torrents of Spring S.B.,
p. 59

Ernest Hemingway in the Arena

Boston Transcript

11 Dec 1926

Sun Also Rises

Photo: Ernest Hemingway, the young
satirist. . .

Philadelphia Inquirer

11 Dec 1926

Torrents of Spring S.B.,
p. 58

Conley, Walter

The Sun Also Rises

Dayton News

12 Dec 1926

Torrents of Spring S.B.,
p. 63

Other But Lesser Favorites

New York Evening World

11 Dec 1926

Torrents of Spring S.B.,
p. 59
& Sun Also Rises

Ernest Hemingway describes a Spanish
bull fight. . .

Minneapolis Tribune

12 Dec 1926

Torrents of Spring S.B.,
p. 58

Entire paper except for one clipping

The Paris Times

11 Dec 1926

1926

Ernest Hemingway who impressed the
discriminating. . .

Oakland Tribune

12 Dec 1926

Torrents of Spring S.B.,
p. 59
& Sun Also Rises

The Sun Also Rises. A brilliant study. . .

New Yorker

11 Dec 1926

Torrents of Spring S.B.,
p. 59

S.E.F.

The Sun Also Rises

Miami News

12 Dec 1926

Torrents of Spring S.B.,
p. 61
& Sun Also Rises

But the committee may surprise us. . .

Brooklyn Citizen

12 Dec 1926

Torrents of Spring S.B.,
p. 60

Roedder, Karstan

The Book Parade

Brooklyn Citizen

12 Dec 1926

Sun Also Rises

The Sun Also Rises. In the Sun Also Rises. . .

Kalamzaoo Gazette

12 Dec 1926

> Torrents of Spring S.B.,
> p. 61
> & Sun Also Rises

The Sun Also Rises. The characters are of that group. . .

Portland, Maine, Express

14 Dec 1926

> Torrents of Spring S.B.,
> p. 67
> & Sun Also Rises

The Sun Also Rises. It has neither beginning. . .

Portalnd Oregonian

12 Dec 1926

> Torrents of Spring S.B.,
> p. 61

Broun, Heywood

It Seems to Me

New Bedford Mercury

15 Dec 1926

> Torrents of Spring S.B.,
> p. 64

The Sun Also Rises. When we laid this book. . .

Minneapolis Tribune

12 Dec 1926

> Torrents of Spring S.B.,
> p. 61
> & Sun Also Rises

Patterson, H. A. S.

A Coming Celebrity

Princeton Literary Observer

15 Dec 1926

> Torrents of Spring S.B.,
> p. 63

Weeks, Howard

Hemingway at his Best

Detroit Free Press

12 Dec 1926

> Torrents of Spring S.B.,
> p. 62
> & Sun Also Rises

The Sun Also Rises. Ernest Hemingway's philosophy. . .

Indianapolis News

15 Dec 1926

> Torrents of Spring S.B.,
> p. 60

Broun, Heywood

It Seems to Me

New York World

14 Dec 1926

> Torrents of Spring S.B.,
> p. 64

Tate, Allen

Hard Boiled

New York Nation

15 Dec 1926

> Torrents of Spring S.B.,
> p. 64

Benet, William Rose

    The Time of Man. . .

    Saturday Review of Literature

    18 Dec 1926

              Torrents of Spring S.B.,
              p. 62

Ernest Hemingway Does Excellent Work

Louisville Journal-Courier

19 Dec 1926

              Torrents of Spring S.B.,
              p. 71

Best Short Stories of the Last Year

Cincinnati Times

18 Dec 1926

           The Undefeated

Ernest Hemingway's accurate and colorful. . .

Columbis, Ohio, Dispatch

19 Dec 1926

           Sun Also Rises

Ernest Hemingway, who writes about bull fighting. . .

New York Evening World

           Torrents of Spring S.B.,
           p. 62

Starrett, Vincent

    The Best Short Stories of 1926

    New York World

    19 Dec 1926

              The Undefeated

Erratum: The following paragraph was omitted. . .

Saturday Review of Literature

18 Dec 1926

           Torrents of Spring S.B.,
           p. 62

The Sun Also Rises. Traveling madly from. . .

Scranton Scrantonian

19 Dec 1926

           Torrents of Spring S.B.,
           p. 63
           & Sun Also Rises

Morley, Christopher

    Bread and Quercuses

    Saturday Review of Literature

    18 Dec 1926

            Sun Also Rises

Young Ineffectuals Wrecked by War Theme of Hemingway Story

Sioux City Journal

19 Dec 1926

           Torrents of Spring S.B.,
           p. 63

Brickell, Herschel

Books on Our Table

New York Evening Post

20 Dec 1926

The Undefeated

A Variety of Novels

St. Paul News

26 Dec 1926

Torrents of Spring S.B.,
p. 65

Morris, Lawrence

Warfare in Man and Among Men

New Republic

22 Dec 1926

Torrents of Spring S.B.,
p. 75

The Best Short Stories

St. Louis Post-Dispatch

27 Dec 1926

The Undefeated

A Grand Book

Hartford Times

24 Dec 1926

Torrents of Spring S.B.,
p. 67

Preston, Keith

Paris Life Palls on Exiled Americans

Chicago News

29 Dec 1926

Torrents of Spring S.B.,
p. 65

. . . As to Ernest Hemingway's 'The
Undefeated' . . .

Galveston News

26 Dec 1926

The Undefeated

They Want to Know

New Republic

29 Dec 1926

Torrents of Spring S.B.,
p. 68

McNeill, Warren A.

The Best Short Stories of 1926 and the
Yearbook of the American Short Story

Richmond, Virginia, Times-Dispatch

26 Dec 1926

The Undefeated

F.P.A.

The Conning Tower

New York World

31 Dec 1926

1926

Decadent Characters

Newark Evening News

31 Dec 1926

                    Torrents of Spring S.B.,
                    p. 67

Burnham, David

    The Sun Continues to Rise

    Princeton Literary Observer

    [1927]

                Men Without Women

Dog's Barking Saves Lives of 103 Mountain Climbers

International Tribune

                Johnston, Dorothy M.
                31 Dec 1926

Ernest Hemingway Shown at His Best

Hartford Courant

[1927]

                Men Without Women

Hazlitt, Henry

    Only the Best, You Know

    New York Evening Sun

    31 Dec 1926

                The Undefeated

[Farrar, John]

    . . . Mr. Hemingway is still brutal. . .

    [Bookman]

    [1927]

                Men Without Women

Barone, Amico J.

    Hemingway's Short Stories

    Springfield, Massachusetts, Union

    [1927]

                Men Without Women

A.W.J.

    Transcribes Life

    Wichita Beacon

    [1927]

                Men Without Women

Book Chatter

Brentano's

[1927]

                Men Without Women

Books on Our Table

[1927]

                Sun Also Rises

Nelson, Frederic

This Remarkable Hemingway

Hartford Times

[1927]

          Men Without Women

Anderson, Emily B.

The Sun Also Rises

New York Junior League Bulletin

Jan 1927

          Torrents of Spring S.B.,
          p. 66

O. Henry Memorial Prizes Awarded

[1927]

          1927

Mr. Hemingway, we are informed, has. . .

McNaughts

Jan 1927

          1927

Rose, Stuart

With Lively Dialog

Bowker Book Review

[1927]

          Men Without Women

The Sun Also Rises. A novel of futility. .

New York Bookman

Jan 1927

          Torrents of Spring S.B.,
          p. 65

Russell, Holis

Hemingway Story Has Many Unusual Turns

Oklahoma City Daily Oklahoman

[1927]

          Men Without Women

The Sun Also Rises. If to report
correctly. . .

Camden Dial

Jan 1927

          Torrents of Spring S.B.,
          p. 66

Speaking of Books

The Spur

[1927]

          Men Without Women

On the other hand, Carl Van Vechten's. . .

Cincinnati Enquirer

1 Jan 1927

          Torrents of Spring S.B.,
          p. 65

J.U.S.

O'Brien's Best Stories

Cincinnati Enquirer

1 Jan 1927

The Undefeated

Taylor, Warren

The Sun Also Rises Presents Achievement
in Prose Fiction

Nashville Tennessean

2 Jan 1927

Torrents of Spring S.B.,
p. 66

The Sun Also Rises. A brilliant study. . .

New Yorker

1 Jan 1927

Torrents of Spring S.B.,
p. 65

The Sun Also Rises. The story of a lost. . .

Atlanta Journal

2 Jan 1927

Torrents of Spring S.B.,
p. 69

Crawford, John W.

Three More Anthologies of 'Best' Stories

New York Times

2 Jan 1927

The Undefeated

Boxing Regarded as Too Brutal in Soviet
Russia

Pound, Ezra   5 Jan 1927

Best American Stories

Atlanta Journal

2 Jan 1927

The Undefeated

Newman, Frances

Before the Bombardment

New York Evening Post

8 Jan 1927

1927

The following brief reviews. . .

Atlanta Journal

2 Jan 1927

Torrents of Spring S.B.,
p. 67

The Sun Also Rises. A brilliant study. . .

New Yorker

8 Jan 1927

Torrents of Spring S.B.,
p. 66

The Sun Also Rises. Like our beloved
Corra Harris

Easton, Pennsylvania, Express

8 Jan 1927

              Torrents of Spring S.B.,
              p. 69

A.S.

The Sun Also Rises. This is a
brilliantly. . .

Cincinnati Commercial Tribune

9 Jan 1927

              Torrents of Spring S.B.,
              pp. 68 & 69

We are still bullish on 'Revelry'. . .

Hartford Times

8 Jan 1927

              Torrents of Spring S.B.,
              p. 69

The Six Best Sellers

New York Herald Tribuen

9 Jan 1927

              Torrents of Spring S.B.,
              p. 69

All About Bull Fighting

South Bend Tribune

9 Jan 1927

              Torrents of Spring S.B.,
              p. 69

The Sun Also Rises. This novel belongs
in the big class. . .

Washington Star

9 Jan 1927

              Torrents of Spring S.B.,
              pp. 67 & 69

Best Sellers in City and Country

New York World

9 Jan 1927

              Torrents of Spring S.B.,
              p. 69

The Height of Babbitry

Chicago News

12 Jan 1927

              Torrents of Spring S.B.,
              p. 67 & 70

McClenahan, R. F.

   Our First Near-Winners

   Des Moines Register

   9 Jan 1927

              Torrents of Spring S.B.,
              p. 66

Baird Leonard, who reviews books for
Life. . .

Hartford Times

15 Jan 1927

              Torrents of Spring S.B.,
              p. 71

Ernest Hemingway.   In Paris

Buffalo News

15 Jan 1927

Torrents of Spring S.B.,
p. 71

Kronenberger, Louis

Short Stories.   The Best Short Stories of
1927

New York Herald Tribune

16 Jan 1927

The Undefeated

I have no quarrel with the selection. . .

Saturday Review of Literature

15 Jan 1927

The Undefeated

Metropolitan Best Sellers

Providence Journal

16 Jan 1927

Torrents of Spring S.B.,
p. 71

The Sun Also Rises.   A brilliant study. . .

New Yorker

15 Jan 1927

Torrents of Spring S.B.,
p. 69

O'Brien, Denis

Sophisticates Subject of Novel

Seattle Post Intelligencer

16 Jan 1927

Torrents of Spring S.B.,
p. 73

We recommend. . .

Easton, Pennsylvania, Express

15 Jan 1927

Torrents of Spring S.B.,
p. 71

Ross, Crystal

Ernest Hemingway, Expatriate

Dallas News

16 Jan 1927

Torrents of Spring S.B.,
pp. 72 & 73

Broun, Heywood

It Seems to Me

New York World

16 Jan 1927

Torrents of Spring S.B.,
p. 70

Never allow a book review to influence
you. . .

Post

18 Jan 1927

Torrents of Spring S.B.,
p. 71
& Hemingway, Grace Hall
21 Jan 1927

Broun, Heywood

It Seems to Me

New York World

20 Jan 1927

Torrents of Spring S.B.,
p. 70

---

advertisement: The Sun Also Rises

New York Times Book Review

23 Jan 1927

Pound, Ezra 15 Feb 1927

Ernest Hemingway Writes a Novel

New Haven Courier

21 Jan 1927

Torrents of Spring S.B.,
p. 76

America's 'Best': Review of O'Brien
Collection

Minneapolis Journal

23 Jan 1927

The Undefeated

House, Jay E.

On Second Thought

Philadelphia Public Ledger

21 Jan 1927

Torrents of Spring S.B.,
pp. 73 & 74

The Best Short Stories of 1926 and the
Year Book of the American Short Story

Charlotte Observer

23 Jan 1927

The Undefeated

Putnam, Samuel

Here and There

21 Jan 1927

Torrents of Spring S.B.,
p. 74

Book Tastes of Omahans Differ Widely

Omaha News

23 Jan 1927

Torrents of Spring S.B.,
p. 76

The Sun Also Rises. A brilliant study. . .

New Yorker

22 Jan 1927

Torrents of Spring S.B.,
p. 74

Booth Tarkington Takes Lead

New York World

23 Jan 1927

Torrents of Spring S.B.,
p. 71

Current Books Which Lead in Popular Favor

Seattle Times

23 Jan 1927

Torrents of Spring S.B.,
p. 71

Marshall, Marguerite Mooers

The Woman of It

New York Evening World

25 Jan 1927

Torrents of Spring S.B.,
p. 77

Ernest Hemingway's accurate and colorful
description. . .

Dayton News

23 Jan 1927

Torrents of Spring S.B.,
p. 71

The Sun Also Rises is a novel. . .

Attleboro Sun

27 Jan 1927

Torrents of Spring S.B.,
p. 77

Keith Preston is moved to verse. . .

New York World

23 Jan 1927

Torrents of Spring S.B.,
p. 76

Author's Wife Given Divorce

New York American

29 Jan 1927

1927

Newman, Frances

The Sun Also Rises

Atlanta Journal

23 Jan 1927

Torrents of Spring S.B.,
p. 76

H.B.

Ernest Hemingway was described. . .

Buffalo News

29 Jan 1927

1927

Roan, Tom

The Best Short Stories of 1926 and the
Year Book of the American Short Story

Seattle Post Intelligencer

23 Jan 1927

The Undefeated

'Salty' seems to have been. . .

Philadelphia Record

29 Jan 1927

Torrents of Spring S.B.,
p. 75

The Sun Also Rises. A brilliant study. . .

New Yorker

29 Jan 1927

Torrents of Spring S.B.,
p. 75

Novel Wins Fame for Him

Dallas Times

30 Jan 1927

Torrents of Spring S.B.,
p. 77

Ernest Hemingway. There was a time. . .

Cleveland Times

30 Jan 1927

Torrents of Spring S.B.,
p. 78

Rascoe, Burton

The Day Book of a New Yorker

Peoria Transcript

31 Jan 1927

Torrents of Spring S.B.,
p. 78

It is evident that the growing success. . .

Raleigh News

30 Jan 1927

Torrents of Spring S.B.,
p. 75

Marshall, Margaret M.

Intelligent Women Tired of 'Peaches,'
Asserts Writer

Denver News

2 Feb 1927

Sun Also Rises

Metropolitan Best Sellers

Providence Journal

30 Jan 1927

Torrents of Spring S.B.,
p. 74

We were astonished when reading. . .

Sioux City Journal

2 Feb 1927

Sun Also Rises

Moralists can have a dandy. . .

San Francisco Chronicle

30 Jan 1927

Sun Also Rises

Celebrating in Sinny Spain

Columbus, Ohio, Citizen

4 Feb 1927

Sun Also Rises

First Novel a Success
Columbus, Ohio, Dispatch
6 Feb 1927
                    Sun Also Rises

The fifth printing of Ernest. . .
Philadelphia Inquirer
12 Feb 1927
                    Sun Also Rises

The Sun Also Rises. Every sentence. . .
New Haven Times-Leader
7 Feb 1927
                    Sun Also Rises

Perhaps you don't like woodcuts. . .
Louisville Herald
13 Feb 1927
                    Sun Also Rises

The Sun Also Rises. This is no book
for Priscillas. . .
Montclair Times
9 Feb 1927
                    Sun Also Rises

Ernest Hemingway: There was a time. . .
Toledo Times
13 Feb 1927
                    Sun Also Rises

Brief-Case Notes
New York Evening Post
12 Feb 1927
                    Sun Also Rises

A review 'The Exile' which is to be. . .
Johnstown, Pennsylvania, Democrat
14 Feb 1927
                    1927

Photo: Ernest Hemingway, author of . . .
New York Graphic
12 Feb 1927
                    Sun Also Rises

Sketches of 'Little Old New York'
Middletown, N.Y., Journal
14 Feb 1927
                    Sun Also Rises

Brickell, Herschel
    Books on Our Table
    New York Evening Post
    15 Feb 1927
                    Sun Also Rises

The Six Best Sellers
New York Herald-Tribune
20 Feb 1927
                    Sun Also Rises

O'Brien Judges the 1926 Short Story Crop
Milwaukee Journal
19 Feb 1927
                    The Undefeated

The Yale News reports that Ernest. . .
Cincinnati Enquirer
26 Feb 1927
                    Sun Also Rises

Not so long ago it was remarked. . .
Buffalo News
19 Feb 1927
                    Sun Also Rises

A Glamorous Novel
Buffalo Times
27 Feb 1927
                    Sun Also Rises

Galantiere, Lewis
    Ballet Mecanique to Din Ears of New York
    New York World
    20 Feb 1927
                    1927

New Stylists to the Fore
Los Angeles Times
27 Feb 1927
                    Sun Also Rises

Hemingway's Novel is for Sophisticate
Tulsa World
20 Feb 1927
                    Sun Also Rises

This Novelist is Also a Bull Fighter
Minneapolis Journal
Dallas News
27 Feb 1927
                    Sun Also Rises

Mulder, Arnold
    A Post War Picture of Despair
    Saginaw, Michigan, New-Courier
    2 Mar 1927
            Sun Also Rises

Pew, Marlen
    Shop Talk at Thirty
    Editor and Publisher
    16 Apr 1927
            1927

    The Youngest Bullfighters
    Chicago Sunday Tribune
    6 Mar 1927
           Hemingway, Grace Hall
           6 Mar 1927

Hemingway, Ernest
    Der Boxer
    Frankfurter Zeitung
    17 Apr 1927
            1927

Mrs. Hadley Richardson Hemingway of. . .

[Apr 1927]
           Mowrer, Hadley R. Hemingway
           13 Aug 1927
3 clippings

Hemingway, Ernest
    Italy--1927
    The New Republic
    18 May 1927
            1927

Barton, Bruce
    In writing this I am thinking of . . .
    [Atlantic Monthly]
    [Apr 1927]
           Sun Also Rises

Hemingway, Ernest
    Das Ende von Etwas
    Frankfurter Zeitung
    22 May 1927
            1927

Hemingway, Ernest
    Indianisches Lager
    Franfurter Zeitung
    10 Apr 1927
           1927

Kingsley, Charles
    Mr. Hemingway's Stories
    London Nation
    11 June 1927
           Hickok, Guy   26 July 1927

Gould, Gerald

New Novels. Mothers and Daughters.
Fiesta by Ernest Hemingway

London Observer

12 June 1927

Sun Also Rises

---

cartoon

Mowrer, Hadley R. Hemingway
13 Aug 1927

Robles Pazos, J.

Libros Yankis 'The Sun Also Rises'

Miro, Jean   21 June 1927

Muir, Edwin

Fiction

The Nation & Athenaeum

2 July 1927

Mowrer, Hadley Hemingway R.
13 Aug 1927

Sun Also Rises in Atlantic

San Francisco Chronicle

17 July 1927

Mowrer, Hadley R. Hemingway
13 Aug 1927

Stein, Gertrude

Photo

Mowrer, Hadley R. Hemingway
13 Aug 1927

Fiesta

Hickok, Guy   25 July 1927

Sacco and Vanzetti Executed

Springfield, Massachusetts, Republican

23 Aug 1927

1927

The Bull Turns the Tables in the Ring:
Gavira

Mowrer, Hadley R. Hemingway
13 Aug 1927

Writes Another (Nancy Hoyt)

Perkins, Maxwell E.
31 Aug 1927

4 Ears, 2 Bull Tail, Rare Honor for
Toreador

New York Graphic

              Murphy, Gerald
              24 Sept 1927

Ernest Hemingway and the Method of the
Searchlight

New York Evening Sun

14 Oct 1927

              Men Without Women

[Dempsey-Tunney Fight]

American Sports

              Smith, William
              25 Sept 1927

H.T.C.

    Book of the Week: Men Without Women

    Philadelphia Record

    15 Oct 1927

              Men Without Women

Art Exhibition Receives Ovation

Oak Park, Oak Parker

27 Oct 1927

              Hemingway, Grace Hall
              9 Oct 1927--oversize

Distinctive Short Stories

Philadelphia Record

15 Oct 1927

              Men Without Women

Walpole, Hugh

    London Letter: September

    New York Herald-Tribune

    9 Oct 1927

              Men Without Women

Ernest Hemingway is an Unusually Fine
Photographer

Philadelphia Public Ledger

15 Oct 1927

              Men Without Women

---

photo: The Pioneer of the New Literary
Canons: Gertrude Stein

              Mowrer, Hadley R. Hemingway
              13 Oct 1927

Hutchison, Percy

    Mr. Hemingway Shows Himself a Master
    Craftsman in the Short Story

    New York Times Book Review

    16 Oct 1927

              Men Without Women

Gray, James

Hemingway Again

St. Paul Dispatch

17 Oct 1927

Men Without Women

A Notable Group

Louisville Herald

23 Oct 1927

Men Without Women

Brickell, Herschel

Two Collections of Good Stories

New York Evening Post

18 Oct 1927

Men Without Women

Stories Without Heroines

Buffalo Times

23 Oct 1927

Men Without Women

Currie, George

Passed in Review

Brooklyn Eagle

19 Oct 1927

Men Without Women

Men Without Women. The Stories

Time Magazine

24 Oct 1927

Men Without Women

Men Without Women. It is unlikely that. . .

Milwaukee Journal

22 Oct 1927

Men Without Women

Horan, Kenneth

Men Without Women

Chicago Journal of Commerce

25 Oct 1927

Men Without Women

G.V.B.

Bits of Life: Men Without Women

Denver News

23 Oct 1927

Men Without Women

F.P.A.

The Conning Tower: The Importance of
Discovering Ernest

Fitzgerald, F. Scott
25 Oct 1927--oversize

Stagg, Hunter

    Galley Sheets in the Wind

    Sacramento Union

    28 Oct 1927

              Men Without Women

Vivid Sketches

Columbus, Ohio, Dispatch

30 Oct 1927

              Men Without Women

March, J. M.

    A Book of Hemingway's Admirable Short
    Stories

    29 Oct 1927

              Men Without Women

Unrestrained He-ness

St. Louis Post-Dispatch

3 Nov 1927

              Men Without Women

Constant Reader

    Reading and Writing

    New Yorker

    29 Oct 1927

              Torrents of Spring S.B.,
              p. 64
              & Men Without Women

Zorn, Gremin

    We Have With Us Today

    Jamaica, N.Y., Times

    5 Nov 1927

              Men Without Women

Men Without Women. Ernest Hemingway is. . .

Fargo Forum

30 Oct 1927

              Men Without Women

G.V.B.

    Bits of Life

    Akron News

    6 Nov 1927

              Men Without Women

Small, Harold A.

    Between the Lines

    San Francisco Chronicle

    30 Oct 1927

              Men Without Women

Beck, Clyde

    Short Stories in Three Keys

    Detroit News

    6 Nov 1927

              Men Without Women

Dabney, Crystal Ross

Ernest Hemingway's Short Stories are
Pattern of Stark Simplicity

6 Nov 1927

Men Without Women

Hemingway's Short Stories

Omaha World-Herald

13 Nov 1927

Men Without Women

Ellis, Roland, Jr.

Hemingway's Sketches

Macon Telegraph

6 Nov 1927

Men Without Women

Krutch, Joseph Wood

Books: The End of Art

The Nation

16 Nov 1927

Men Without Women

Men Without Women by Ernest Hemingway

Oakland Tribune

6 Nov 1927

Men Without Women

Teuscher, Lorna Jane

Books in Silhouette

16 Nov 1927

Men Without Women

Duplex

Not in the Least Like O'Henry

Jacksonville Times-Union

6 Nov 1927

Men Without Women

Davis, George

He Writes About Men, No Women

Cleveland Press

19 Nov 1927

Men Without Women

Ballou, Robert O.

Modern Short Stories from Two Points of
View

Chicago News

9 Nov 1927

Men Without Women

Mostly Men

Newark Evening News

19 Nov 1927

Men Without Women

S.K.R.

    Men Without Women

    Los Angeles Saturday Night

    19 Nov 1927

          Men Without Women

Sans Women

    St. Paul News

    20 Nov 1927

          Men Without Women

Ranft, Joseph L.

    Ernest Hemingway: A Rising Star in the
    Short-Story Firmament

    Baltimore Sun

    19 Nov 1927

          Men Without Women

Connolly, Cyril

    New Novels

    The New Statesman

    26 Nov 1927

          Lewis, Wyndham
          28 Nov 1927

Unusual Feature in 13 Stories of Men

Boston Globe

19 Nov 1927

          Men Without Women

New Novels

London The New Statesman

26 Nov 1927

          Men Without Women

Men Without Women: Mr. Hemingway's
Short Stories of Life in the Raw

Springfield, Massachusetts, Republican

20 Nov 1927

          Men Without Women

Men Without Women. Here are thirteen
stories. . .

Charlotte, N.C., Observer

27 Nov 1927

          Men Without Women

Salpeter, Harry

    Wandering Novelist

    New York World

    20 Nov 1927

          1927

Prescott, Charlotte Hubbard

    Short Stories Seclected from the Work of
    Three Master Craftsmen

    Sioux City Sunday [Journal]

    27 Nov 1927

          Men Without Women

Those who expected fine things of. . .

New Orleans Times Picayune

27 Nov 1927

Men Without Women

Wilson, Edmund

The Sportsman's Tragedy

The New Republic

14 Dec 1927

Men Without Women

Weeks, Howard

Hemingway's Literary Stature Increases
with His New Collection

Detroit Free Press

27 Nov 1927

Men Without Women

Smyth, Joseph Hilton

He Drank with Them, Played with Them, Wrote
a Book about Them

Boston Globe

18 Dec 1927

1927

When Ernest Hemingway writes. . .

New York Times

28 Nov 1927

Sun Also Rises

Alvarez Jusue, Aurelio

Defensa del Toro

Pound, Ezra   26 Dec 1927

Mother of Four Becomes Artist / Wins
Notice for Portraits at 52

Lynchburg Advance

30 Nov 1927

1927

Photo: Ernest Hemingway. The author
of. . .

New York

1928

1928

The Literary Landscape: Ernest Hemingway's
Stories

North American Review

Dec 1927

Men Without Women

The Fixer: A Story of Colonial Life (in the
manner of one of the foremost American
writers)

Transition, no. 10, pp. 113-117

Hickok, Guy 2 Jan 1928

The Nattion's Honor Roll for 1927

The Nation

4 Jan 1928

Men Without Women

Fiction. There is probably. . .

New York Plain Talk

Mar 1928

Men Without Women

O. Henry Prize Winners Named at Arts Dinner

New York Herald Tribune

20 Jan 1928

MacDonald, Elsie
20 Jan 1928

McIntyre, O. O.

It seems to me the most widely. . .

Jepson, Ursula Hemingway
15 Mar 1928

Indian Exiles Found Hungry in Hovel Here

Detroit

19 Feb 1928

Sanford, Marcelline H.
20 Feb 1928

Ōvitt, Leonore

Ernest Hemingway One of Ours

Oak Park, Oak Parker

29 June 1928

Hemingway, Clarence E.
2 July 1928--oversize

Illinois Artist is Guest at Studio Tea

Glendale News

22 Feb 1928

Hemingway, Grace Hall
11 Mar 1928

Hansen, Harry

The First Reader

Chicago Daily Journal

2 July 1928

Hemingway, Clarence E.
2 July 1928

Art Career Begins at 52

Kansas City Star

28 Feb 1928

Hemingway, Grace Hall
11 Mar 1928--oversize

Hobo Tendencies of Rich Dr. How Divorce Grounds

New York Herald Tribune

Peirce, Waldo 2 July 1928

Presque Isle Party Goes after Restigouche Whales

Bangor Daily News

26 July 1928

Peirce, Waldo 28 July 1928

In Chicago

[Sept 1928]

Hemingway, Grace Hall
21 Sept 1928

Shipman, Evan

Trotting in France

[American Horse Breeder]

8 Aug 1928

Shipman, Evan 13 Dec 1928

Cinquante mille dollars, par Ernest Hemingway, traduit de l'anglais. . .

[Semaine a Paris]

[14 Sept 1928]

Fifty Grand Scrapbook, p. 2

Round Three in the Fight Film Serial

Bangor Daily Commercial

20 Aug 1928

Peirce, Waldo 12 Sept 1928

Women Leaders in Oak Park / Many Attend Hemingway Exhibit

Oak Park Times

27 Sept 1928

Hemingway, Grace Hall
5 Oct 1928

Grace Hall Hemingway's New Pictures to Be on View This Weekend

Oak Park, Oak Parker

21 Sept 1928

Hemingway, Grace Hall
24 Sept 1928--oversize

Ovitt, Leonore

A Contribution to American Art

Oak Park, Oak Parkder

28 Sept 1928

Hemingway, Grace Hall
5 Oct 1928--oversize

Grace Hall Hemingway issued invitations. . .

Oak Park, Oak Leaves

[Sept 1928]

Hemingway, Grace Hall
5 Oct 1928

Grace Hall Hemingway issued invitations. . .

Oak Park, Oak Leaves

Hemingway, Grace Hall
5 Oct 1928

Rose, Don

Making a Modern Critic Out of a Sensitive Soul

New York Herald Tribune, Paris

21 Oct 1928

Wister, Owen 22 Oct 1928

Toreador is Banned for Beating Up Critic

21 Dec 1928

Fitzgerald, F. Scott
28 Dec 1928

Shipman, Evan

Racing in France

American Horse Breeder

7 Nov 1928

Shipman, Evan 13 Dec 1928

A Farewell to Arms. Up Boston way. . .

[1929]

Farewell to Arms

Dr. Hemingway, Writer's Father, Ends Own Life

Chicago

[Dec] 1928

1928

Migod, a Letter!

Life

1929

1929

Clarence E. Hemingway, M.D.

[Dec] 1928

1928

Soskin, William

Books on Our Table

New York Post

[1929]

Scrapbook

Blackmur, R. P.

Am Not Prince Hamlet Nor Was Meant to Be

Hound and Horn

MacLeish, Archibald
17 Dec 1928

Llona, Victor

Lettres Etrangeres

La Nouvelle Revue Francaise

[1 Jan 1929]

Fifty Grand Scrapbook, p. 1

Llona, Victor

Une Rectification

[Mercure de France]

[15 Jan 1929]

Fifty Grand Scrapbook, p. 7

Other highlights in the May issue. . .

Dallas News

12 May 1929

Scrapbook

Announcement of Morley Callaghan's Strange
Fugitive

The Majestic Daily

4 Feb 1929

Pfeiffer, Gustavus A.
5 Feb 1929

The first installment of Ernest. . .

South Bend News Times

19 May 1929

Scrapbook

Ernest Hemingway. Cinquante mille
dollars. Six contes--on osarait. . .

[Tribune]

[Mar 1929]

Fifty Grand Scrapbook, p. 7

Scribner's

Salt Lake Tribune

26 May 1929

Scrapbook

Miraculous Bambino

Time

Musselman, Morris
4 Mar 1929

Mighty Oak From Little Acorn

Wilmington Evening Journal

4 June 1929

Fitzgerald, F. Scott
4 June 1929--oversize

Beardshear, William M.

Sport the Law Bars

Denver News

1 May 1929

Scrapbook

Goulding, Stuart D.

Books, Men and Things

Bayonne, N.J., Evening News

7 June 1929

Scrapbook

. . .Also Arises, that the coarseness is introduced. . .

Newark News

8 June 1929

       Scrapbook

Ernest Hemingway, whose new novel, A Farewell. . .

Denver News

19 July 1929

       Scrapbook

Ernest Hemingway contributes a valentine. . .

Chicago Tribune

13 June 1929

       Scrapbook

Hansen, Harry

    The First Reader

    Tulsa Tribune

    21 July 1929

       Scrapbook

[Hickok, Guy]

    Brooklyn Bull Fighter the Toast of Spain after Sensational Debut There

    Brooklyn Daily Eagle

    26 June 1929

       Hickok, Guy July 1929

Periodical Plums

Springfield, Illinois, Journal

28 July 1929

       Scrapbook

There are No Old Wives' Tales

Evansville, Indiana, Courier & Journal

30 June 1929

       Scrapbook

Very little has come from the Russians. . .

Charleston, West Virginia, Gazette

28 July 1929

       Scrapbook

Hemingway's Art Matched Only by Defoe's He Says

Tulsa Tribune

7 July 1929

       Scrapbook

Le Lutecien

    L'engouement continue pour cette Amerique qui. . .

    [Comoedie]

    [30 July 1929]

       Fifty Grand Scrapbook, p. 2

Ernest Hemingway est ne dans l'Illinois
(Etats Unis). . .

[Ind. Luxembourgeoise]

[Aug 1929]

   Fifty Grand Scrapbook, p. 2

Cinquante mille dollars. Hemingway, jeune
et inconnu. . .

[Intransigeant]

[22 Aug 1929]

   Fifty Grand Scrapbook, p. 2

The Call to Arms Episode in Boston

Evansville, Indiana, Courier & Journal

4 Aug 1929

   Scrapbook

Bofa, Gus

 50,000 Dollars par Ernest Hemingway
 traduit par Ott et Weymer

 [Crapouillot]

 [1 Sept 1929]

   Fifty Grand Scrapbook, p. 2

Chaudun, Fernand

 A la Nouvelle Revue Francaise on
 announce. . .

 [Rumeur]

 [5 Aug 1929]

   Fifty Grand Scrapbook, p. 2

Cinquante mille dollars. Recueil de
dix contes. . .

[Le Cri des Peuples]

[5 Sept 1929]

   Fifty Grand Scrapbook, p. 2

Serial Pleases Elsewhere

Tulsa Tribune

11 Aug 1929

   Scrapbook

Cohn, Gene

 And there is Ernest Hemingway. . .

 Fairmount, West Virginia, Virginian

 8 Sept 1929

   Scrapbook

Cinquante Mille Dollars. Nouveau venu
pour le public. . .

[Dernieres Nouvelles]

[15 Aug 1929]

   Fifty Grand Scrapbook, p. 2

Peu de romanciers reussissent dans. . .

[Revue Mondiale]

[15 Sept 1929]

   Fifty Grand Scrapbook, p. 3

Which reminds us that a dozen versions. . .

Richmond, Virginia, News Leader

15 Sept 1929

Scrapbook

Broun, Heywood

It Seems to Me

New York Telegram

28 Sept 1929

Scrapbook
& Farewell to Arms

The First Reader

Greensboro News

16 Sept

Scrapbook

Butcher, Fanny

Here is Genius, Critic Declares of Hemingway

Chicago Tribune

28 Sept 1929

Hemingway, Grace Hall
5 Oct 1929--oversize
& Scrapbook
& Farewell to Arms

Hansen, Harry

The First Reader

New York World

27 Sept 1929

Scrapbook
& Farewell to Arms

Farewell to Arms. Against the background
of. . .

Boston Herald

28 Sept 1929

Scrapbook

Paterson, Isabel

Readers and Other Things

New York Herald Tribune

27 Sept 1929

Scrapbook

A Farewell to Arms, and Liam O'Flaherty's
The House of Gold

Philadelphia Inquirer

28 Sept 1929

Scrapbook

Soskin, William

Books on Our Table

New York Evening Post

27 Sept 1929

Farewell to Arms

Love in War is the theme. . .

Boston Evening Transcript

28 Sept 1929

Scrapbook

Hazlitt, Henry

In a Farewell to Arms Ernest Hemingway
Grows as a Novelist

New York Sun

28 Sept 1929

       Scrapbook

Farewell to Arms. A story of love in
war. . .

San Francisco Chronicle

29 Sept 1929

       Scrapbook

What Boston Banned

Newark News

28 Sept 1929

       Scrapbook

Freeman Lincoln, son of Cape Cod
Chronicler, Follows in Father's Footsteps
-- But at His Own Gait

Philadelphia Record

29 Sept 1929

       Scrapbook

Books of the Week

Louisville Journal

29 Sept 1929

       Scrapbook

Hutchison, Percy

Farewell to Arms. Love and War in the
Pages of Mr. Hemingway

New York Times Book Review

29 Sept 1929

       Farewell to Arms

Butcher, Fanny

Here is Genius, Crutic Declares

Chicago [Daily Tribune]

[29 Sept] 1929

       Farewell to Arms

Lustig, Norman

Books

Brooklyn Citizen

29 Sept 1929

       Scrapbook

Farewell to Arms. Hemingway's novel of
the war in. . . .

Denver News

29 Sept 1929

       Scrapbook

Pinckard, H. R.

Ernest Hemingway's New Novel Easily
Suprases All His Previous Writings

Huntington, West Virginia, Advertiser

29 Sept 1929

       Scrapbook

Present Day American Stories
Kansas City Journal
29 Sept 1929
          Scrapbook

Gorman, Herbert
     War Novels are Popular
     Book Review
     Oct 1929
               Scrapbook

Buenzod, Emmanuel
     Encore un ronancier americain
     [Gazette de Lausanne]
     [30 Sept 1929]
               Fifty Grand Scrapbook, p. 3

And there is Ernest Hemingway who has
created. . .
Lancaster, Ohio, Gazette
1 Oct 1929
          . Scrapbook

Neihardt, John G.
     Of Making Many Books
     St. Louis Post Dispatch
     30 Sept 1929
               Scrapbook

Farewell to Arms. Disillusioned by war,
a young American. . .
New York Herald Tribune
1 Oct 1929
          Scrapbook

Ernest Hemingway est de la race. . .
[Revue Nouvelle]
[Oct 1929]
          Fifty Grand Scrapbook, p. 4

So we were pleased to learn. . .
New York Herald Tribune
1 Oct 1929
          Scrapbook

Of Hemingway the Shakespearean scholar. . .
Worlds Work
Oct 1929
          Scrapbook

Currie, George
     Passed in Review
     Brooklyn Daily Eagle
     2 Oct 1929
               Farewell to Arms

Gordon, Lewis

    Notes and Prefaces

    Richmond, Virginia, News Courier

    2 Oct 1929

            Scrapbook

A Masterpiece of Tragic Experience

Chicago Journal of Commerce

5 Oct 1929

            Scrapbook

Farewell to Arms. Elizabeth Toms adds an
illuminating critical footnote. . .

New York Herald Tribune

4 Oct 1929

            Scrapbook

Of War, Wine and Women

Boston Herald

5 Oct 1929

            Farewell to Arms

F.H.

    Books

    Beverly Hills Script

    5 October 1929

            Scrapbook

Sturgis-Jones, Marion

    Young War Volunteer Bids Farewell to Arms
Only to Greet Death Face to Face

    Philadelphia Inquirer

    5 Oct 1929 [29 Oct 1929]

            Scrapbook (misdated?)
            & Farewell to Arms

Hemingway's Novel Coming Up to the Lead

New York World

5 Oct 1929

            Scrapbook

War is Background for Superb Novel

Davenport, Iowa, Times

5 Oct 1929

            Scrapbook

Love and War in Hemingway's New Novel,
Farewell to Arms

Milwaukee Journal

5 Oct 1929

            Scrapbook

Aswell, James

    Critic Lavishes Praise on New Hemingway
Novel

    Richmond, Virginia, Times Dispatch

    6 Oct 1929

            Scrapbook

Beardshear, William M.

A Farewell to Arms

Denver News

6 Oct 1929

Scrapbook

Robinson, Ted

Living Figures Writhe on Hemingway's Pages as His Stark Art Tears at You

Cleveland Plain Dealer

6 Oct 1929

Scrapbook

Bryan, Wright

Present Day American Stories

Atlanta Journal

6 Oct 1929

Scrapbook

Variety Features Latest Books of Favorite Authors

Mansfield, Ohio, News

6 Oct 1929

Scrapbook

Cowley, Malcolm

Not Yet Demobilized

New York Herald Tribune

6 Oct 1929

Scrapbook
& Farewell to Arms

Hemingway and Others

Martinsburg, West Virginia, Journal

7 Oct 1929

Scrapbook

Near Winners

Des Moines Register

6 Oct 1929

Scrapbook

Love and War When Italian Front Wavered

Portland, Maine, Express

7 Oct 1929

Scrapbook

On behalf of those readers . . . can't stand. . .

New York World

6 Oct 1929

Scrapbook

[Hemingway, Ernest]

Le Village Indien

[Humanite]

[8 Oct 1929]

Fifty Grand Scrapbook, p. 5

de Regnier, Henri

    J'ai a signaler aussi, de M. Ernest. . .

    [Figaro]

    [9 Oct 1929]

            Fifty Grand Scrapbook, p. 4

Hemingway's War

    Akron Journal

    11 Oct 1929

            Scrapbook

Matthews, T. S.

    Nothing Ever Happens to the Brave

    The New Republic

    9 Oct 1929

          Scrapbook

          & Farewell to Arms

Jones, Llewellyn

    Hemingway at His Best

    Chicago Evening Post

    11 Oct 1929

            Scrapbook

Best Sellers

    Cleveland Press

    10 Oct 1929

          Scrapbook

McNulty, John

    Some Say Indecent Others Romance

    Columbus Citizen

    11 Oct 1929

           Scrapbook

Farewell to Arms. Ernest Hemingway's
new opus A Farewell to Arms. . .

    Kalamazoo Gazette

    10 Oct 1929

          Scrapbook

J.G.C.

    First Seller

    Erie, Pennsylvania, Times

    12 Oct 1929

           Scrapbook

Modern Novelists who Succeed in Gaining
the Attention of Those who Love Excellent
Stories

    Dayton News

    10 Oct 1929

          Scrapbook

Canby, Henry Seidel

    Story of the Brave

    Saturday Review of Literature

    12 Oct 1929

           Scrapbook
           & Farewell to Arms

    Galleys also

C.L.H.

    War and the Boys

    Emporia Gazette

    12 Oct 1929

        Scrapbook

A.W.S.

    Present-Day American Stories

    New Yorker

    12 Oct 1929

        Scrapbook

Ernest Hemingway. The Ernest Hemingway disciples. . .

    Youngstown, Ohio, Vindicator

    12 Oct 1929

        Scrapbook

White, Paul

    Bound to Be Read

    St. Petersburg

    [12 Oct 1929]

        Farewell to Arms

Ernest Hemingway Has Novel Story of War

    Rochester Times-Union

    12 Oct 1929

        Scrapbook

Campbell, Isabell

    Farewell to Arms Tells of Love in Time of War

    Oklahoma City Oklahoma

    13 Oct 1929

        Scrapbook

Photo: Ernest Hemingway. Tender and hard boiled. . .

    Youngstown, Ohio, Express

    12 Oct 1929

        Scrapbook

Capers, Julian, Jr.

    Love and War are Basic Elements of New Hemingway Novel

    Dallas Morning News

    13 Oct 1929

        Capers, Julian, Jr.
        16 Oct 1929
        & Scrapbook

Jackson, Joseph Henry

    Books on the Table

    San Francisco Argonaut

    12 Oct 1929

        Scrapbook

Chrischilles, T. N.

    The Week's Winner

    Des Moines Register

    13 Oct 1929

        Scrapbook

Daniel, Frank
A Farewell to Arms
Atlanta Journal
13 Oct 1929
Scrapbook

Hansen, Harry
New Hemingway Novel
Detroit Free Press
13 Oct 1929
Scrapbook

A Farewell to Arms comes very near. . .
New Orleans Picayune
13 Oct 1929
Scrapbook

Hemingway
Oakland Tribune
13 Oct 1929
Scrapbook

Farewell to Arms. Mr. Hemingway's
fierce and vital. . .
Hartford Courant
13 Oct 1929
Scrapbook

Hemingway Improves
Minneapolis Journal
13 Oct 1929
Scrapbook

Farewell to Arms. This novel of love in
war stirs up. . .
Burlington Free Press
13 Oct 1929
Scrapbook

R.D.L.
Hemingway's Latest A Farewell to Arms
Columbus, Ohio, Dispatch
13 Oct 1929
Scrapbook

For our own part, there is a. . .
Ponca City, Oklahoma, News
13 Oct 1929
Scrapbook

Renwood, Barry M.
War Romance Has Poignant Scenes
Columbus, Ohio, State Journal
13 Oct 1929
Scrapbook

Small, Harold A.

    Between the Lines

    San Francisco Chronicle

    13 Oct 1929

            Scrapbook

Paltangall, Jo

    Hemingway on Love and War

    Portland, Maine, News

    13 Oct 1929

            Scrapbook

F.M.W.

    War Theme in Hemingway's Brilliant Novel

    Wichita Beacon

    13 Oct 1929

            Scrapbook

A.W.S.

    Farewell to Arms: This novel by the
    most outstanding. . .

    Daytone Beach Journal

    16 Oct 1929

            Scrapbook

White, Paul W.

    Bound to be Read

    Nebraska City News Press

    13 Oct 1929

            Scrapbook

Cinquante mille dollars par Ernest
Hemingway: Six nouvelles. . .

    [Cri du Jour]

    [18 Oct 1929]

            Fifty Grand Scrapbook, p. 4

White, Paul W.

    Farewell to Arms. Ernest Hemingway's A
    Farewell to Arms is a. . .

    Philadelphia Press

    13 Oct 1929

            Scrapbook

Rousseaux, Andre

    Les Jeunes Americaines

    [Candide]

    [18 Oct 1929]

            Fifty Grand Scrapbook, p. 6

Cosgrove, Elizabeth Williams

    Book Worm

    Muskogee Democrat

    15 Oct 1929

            Scrapbook

A.C.

    Farewell to Arms. Echoes from the Great
    War in Ernest Hemingway's Novel

    Boston Evening Transcript

    19 Oct 1929

            Scrapbook

Caparetto Retreat of 1917 Is Background
for Romance

Columbus, Missouri, Missourian

19 Oct 1929

Scrapbook

Farewell to Arms. A great love story. . .

Cleveland News

20 Oct 1929

Scrapbook

In a few brief sentences. . .

New York World

19 Oct 1929

Scrapbook

Photo: A new camera study of. . .

Pittsburgh Press

20 Oct 1929

Scrapbook

Photo: Popular

Wichita Beacon

19 Oct 1929

Scrapbook

John McClure of the New Orleans. . .

Savannah News

20 Oct 1929

Scrapbook

G.C.

Hemingway's Latest Opus

Albany Knickerbocker Express

20 Oct 1929

Scrapbook

Photo: New Book

Winston-Salem Sentinel

20 Oct 1929

Scrapbook--p. 8

The Critic's Almanac

Memphis Appeal

20 Oct 1929

Scrapbook

Parsons, Margaret Getchell

Non-Bostonians May Read Hemingway

Worcester Telegram

20 Oct 1929

Scrapbook

Skinner, Macie

Forces of War Shape Destinies in New World

Rockford, Illinois, Star

20 Oct 1929

Scrapbook

Two New and Important Novels

Des Moines Register

20 Oct. 1929

Scrapbook

Those peculiar people who look. . .

Buffalo Times

20 Oct 1929

Scrapbook

Ernest Hemingway's Farewell to Arms has been approved. . .

Mobile Register

21 Oct 1929

Scrapbook

A Tragedy of Humanity

Toledo News

20 Oct 1929

Scrapbook

Koch, A.

The Bookworm: A Review of Happenings in the World of Books

The Playgoer

Hemingway, Grace Hall
25 Oct 1929

Travel Topics: Work of Authors Will Bring Us Many Notables

Cleveland News

20 Oct 1929

Scrapbook

A Farewell to Arms Commended by Walpole

Lansing Journal

25 Oct 1929

Scrapbook

Photo and cartoon: Two Authors and a Book Jacket

Los Angeles Times

20 Oct 1929

Scrapbook

In a few brief sentences. . .

Greensboro News

25 Oct 1929

Scrapbook

. . . Italian Front, by Ernest
Hemingway. . .
Yale University Alumni Monthly
25 Oct 1929

Scrapbook

A War Story
Greensboro Record
26 Oct 1929

Scrapbook

A novel of love in war time which. . .
Yale University Alumni Monthly
25 Oct 1929

Scrapbook

All's Fair
Ft. Wayne Journal Gazette
27 Oct 1929

Scrapbook

Carew, Harold D.
Hemingway's New War Novel
Pasadena Star News
26 Oct 1929

Scrapbook

Farewell to Arms. A great love story. . .
Cleveland News
27 Oct 1929

Scrapbook

Gives New Life with Meaning to Old Words
New York Sun
26 Oct 1929

Scrapbook

Miller, Mary M.
She's Afraid So
Des Moines Register
27 Oct 1929

Scrapbook

Needham, Wilbur
Books
Los Angeles Saturday Night
26 Oct 1929

Scrapbook

Said a bookseller: See that stack. . .
Memphis Appeal
27 Oct 1929

Scrapbook--p. 101

Steffens, Bob
    Books and Bookmen
    Akron Times
    27 Oct 1929
        Scrapbook

Ghent, Sarge
    War-Distorted Passions
    Clearfield, Iowa Progress
    29 Oct 1929
        Scrapbook

War As it Really Is
Rochester Democrat Chronicle
27 Oct 1929
    Scrapbook

Fadiman, Clifton P.
    A Fine American Novel
    Nation
    30 Oct 1929
        Scrapbook

Doubt, Peter
    Farewell to Arms
    Green Bay Press-Gazette
    28 Oct 1929
        Scrapbook

A Farewell to Arms by Ernest Hemingway
by far the most enchanting. . .
Brooklyn Daily Eagle
30 Oct 1929
    Scrapbook

We do not like it at all. . .
Fort Dodge, Iowa, Messenger
28 Oct 1929
    Scrapbook

In strange contrast, out of the. . .
Atlantic Monthly
Nov 1929
    Scrapbook

Erenst Hemingway's new novel A Farewell
to Arms has. . .
Northfield, Massachusetts, News
29 Oct 1929
    Scrapbook

War in the Hospitals
North American Review
Nov 1929
    Scrapbook

B.E.

Hemingway's Best Seller

Cedar Rapids Gazette

1 Nov 1929

Scrapbook

C.T.

Hemingway's Latest Establishes Him in
Literary Firmament

Tulsa Tribune

3 Nov 1929

Scrapbook

Photo: Ernest Hemingway, whose latest
literary offering. . .

Cleveland Press

2 Nov 1929

Scrapbook

Photo: Wins Point

Huntington, West Virginia, Advertiser

3 Nov 1929

Scrapbook

D.D.

The Critic's Almanac: Perfect Behavior

Memphis Appeal

3 Nov 1929

Scrapbook

Caroll, Raymond G.

Paris Day by Day

Philadelphia Public Leader

[4 Nov 1929]

Scrapbook·

Hemingway's Experience

Mansfield, Ohio, News

3 Nov 1929

Scrapbook

Hartley, Alice E.

Chat About Books

Morgantown, West Virginia, New Democrat

5 Nov 1929

Scrapbook

No Single Best Seller is Outstanding

Baltimore Sun

[3 Nov 1929]

Scrapbook

Hemingway. Fortunately it no. . .

San Diego Sun

6 Nov 1929

Scrapbook

Hasty Glance at Current Taste
Beverly Hills Script
[7 Nov 1929]
                Scrapbook

From Mrs. Millea
Des Moines Register
10 Nov 1929
                Scrapbook

James Weber Linn, who accounts for. . .
Chicago News
7 Nov 1929
                Scrapbook

Kresensky, Raymond
    Near-Winners
    Des Moines Tribune
    10 Nov 1929
                Scrapbook

H.F.V.
    Farewell to Arms
    San Francisco News
    9 Nov 1929
                Scrapbook

Well, Major Alex
    Hemingway's War Story Masterly
    Albany Knickerbocker Press
    10 Nov 1929
                Scrapbook

B.E.
    Hemingway's Best Seller
    Cedar Rapids Gazette
    10 Nov 1929
                Scrapbook

Farewell to Arms. Hemingway more than
fulfills. . .
Dayton Herald
11 Nov 1929
                Scrapbook

Farewell to Arms. The story of a love
affair. . .
Savannah News
10 Nov 1929
                Scrapbook

Surpasses Himself
Buffalo News
12 Nov 1929
                Scrapbook

Werner, B. E.

    Manner unter sich

    Deutsche Allgemeine Zeitung

    12 Nov 1929

        1929

    The War's Interminableness

    Kansas City Star

    16 Nov 1929

        Scrapbook

Davis, Lambert

    Farewell to Arms. Ernest Hemingway might
    be expected. . .

    Fredericksburg Star

    13 Nov 1929

        Scrapbook

    Farewell to Arms. Love story surrounded
    by the war. . .

    Cleveland News

    17 Nov 1929

        Scrapbook

    Ernest Hemingway's threatened disagreement
    with. . .

    Brooklyn Daily Eagle

    13 Nov 1929

        Scrapbook

    There is the new Ernest Hemingway
    opus. . .

    Oklahoma City News

    19 Nov 1929

        Scrapbook

Alexander, Norman

    Books and Things

    Newton Centre, Massachusetts, Town Crier

    15 Nov 1929

        Scrapbook

    Romance: Farewell to Arms

    Everyman

    21 Nov 1929

        Scrapbook

    New Books You May Like

    Los Angeles Record

    15 Nov 1929

        Scrapbook

Hall, Norman Alexander

    Books and Things

    Newton Center, Massachusetts, Town Crier

    22 Nov 1929

        Scrapbook

Book Reviews
New Haven Journal-Courier
23 Nov 1929
    Scrapbook

Looby, Mike T.
Hemingway's New Book Is War Romance
Ft. Worth Telegram
24 Nov 1929
    Scrapbook

Photo: Ernest Hemingway, author. . .
Buffalo Evening News
23 Nov 1929
    Scrapbook

Reviews: A Farewell to Arms
Book Review Digest
[24 Nov 1929]
    Scrapbook

Ernest Hemingway
Toledo Times
24 Nov 1929
    Scrapbook

Turns With a Bookworm
New York Herald Tribune
24 Nov 1929
    Scrapbook

Farewell to Arms. Ernest Hemingway has
given us. . .
Pittsburgh Sun-Telegram
24 Nov 1929
    Scrapbook

The War Novel
Baltimore Morning Sun
24 Nov 1929
    Scrapbook

From Indianapolis, Ind.: Why is
everybody. . .
Wheeling Register
24 Nov 1929
    Scrapbook

Some Italian Novels
Times Literary Supplement
28 Nov 1929
    1929

Farewell to Arms. Another war story,
which however uses the war. . .

Ft. Wayne News-Sentinel

30 Nov 1929

Scrapbook

Farewell to Arms. A great love story. . .

Toledo Times

1 Dec 1929

Scrapbook

The Prize Winner

Sioux City Journal

30 Nov 1929

Scrapbook

Farewell to Arms. One's reaction to
A Farewell. . .

Lexington, Kentucky, Herald

1 Dec 1929

Scrapbook

J.L.S.

William Wingshot Looks at a Critic

Philadelphia Record

30 Nov 1929

Scrapbook

Farewell to Arms. Perhaps no other book
this fall. . .

Tulsa World

1 Dec 1929

Scrapbook

Tragic Love Upon Background of War

Mobile Press

30 Nov 1929

Scrapbook

Prof. John F. Frederick of the. . .

Cedar Rapids Gazette

1 Dec 1929

Scrapbook

Priestly, J. B.

Farewell to Arms. Ernest Hemingway's A
Farewell. . .

Now and Then

Dec 1929

Scrapbook

Salemson, Harold J.

Memento. Quelques etudes fort. . .

[Mercure de France]

[1 Dec 1929]

Fifty Grand Scrapbook, p. 6

Buenzod, Emmanuel

Ernest Hemingway: Cinquante mille dollars

[Revue de Beneve]

[4 Dec 1929]

Fifty Grand Scrapbook, p. 6

Farewell to Arms. The moving love. . .

New York Post

7 Dec 1929

Scrapbook

New Books

Spencer, West Virginia, Times Record

4 Dec 1929

Scrapbook

Farewell to Arms. Special limited edition of. . .

New York Post

7 Dec 1929

Scrapbook

Individual

Santa Monica Saturday Sunset

6 Dec 1929

Scrapbook

If you would give one of the. . .

Camden, N.J., Courier

7 Dec 1929

Scrapbook

Cunningham, E. F.

Farewell to Arms Keen Human Analysis

Wilmington Every Evening

7 Dec 1929

Scrapbook

J.P.

Reader Rises to Defense of Ernest Hemingway in Book Page Congroversy

Philadelphia Record

7 Dec 1929

Scrapbook

Entree's

Milwaukee Journal

7 Dec 1929

Scrapbook

E.E.S.

A Farewell to Arms

Topeka Capitol

7 Dec 1929

Scrapbook

Photo: Author of One of the Most
Significant of All Novels Today

Birmingham Age-Herald
Birmingham News

8 Dec 1929

Scrapbook

Curtis, William

Some Recent Books

MacDonald, Elsie
15 Dec 1929

Long, Ted

War Novel by Ernest Hemingway Not to Be
Read by Squeamish

Salt Lake City Telegram

8 Dec 1929

Scrapbook

Mrs. Wharton, Chic Sale Books Among
Favorites

MacDonald, Elsie
15 Dec 1929

Most widely discussed of the newest. . .

Winston-Salem Sentinel

8 Dec 1929

Scrapbook

Week's Best Sellers as Compiled by
Brentano's

MacDonald, Elsie
15 Dec 1929

Farewell to Arms. With a few exceptions
the best books. . .

Quincy, Massachusetts, Patriot Ledger

11 Dec 1929

Scrapbook

We note that Hemingway's A Farewell to
Arms. . .

Buffalo Times

15 Dec 1929

Scrapbook

Farewell to Arms. One doesn't know
whether this is the farewell. . .

Cincinnati Enquirer

14 Dec 1929

Scrapbook

What books of the year are. . .

[New York] Herald Tribune

15 Dec 1929

Scrapbook

Spener, Wilheim

    Ein Dichter, der sein metier beherricht

    Das Unferhaltungsblatt

    18 Dec 1929

            1929

Caroline Bancroft, who writes. . .

Sioux City Journal

24 Dec 1929

          Scrapbook

Heywood Broun insists that. . .

Beverly Hills Script

21 Dec 1929

          Scrapbook

Roberts, Bessie K.

    Books Preferred

    Fort Wayne Journal-Gazette

          White, Raymond B.
          26 Dec 1929

I'd like a copy of that book. . .

Portland, Maine, Express

21 Dec 1929

          Scrapbook

Rennels, Mary

    Now that book publishing is over for
    1929. . .

    New York Telegram

    27 Dec 1929

          Scrapbook

Best seller lists from Baker and
Taylor's. . .

Pawhauska, Oklahoma, Capital

22 Dec 1929

          Scrapbook

White, Paul W.

    Recent Books

    Roanoke World News

    27 Dec 1929

          Scrapbook

Farewell to Arms. Alternate episodes
of love and war. . .

Wheeling Register

22 Dec 1929

          Scrapbook

Farewell to Arms.   This war love story. . .

Downieville, California, Messenger

28 Dec 1929

          Scrapbook

Fiction: A Farewell to Arms by. . .

Baltimore Evening News

28 Dec 1929

Scrapbook

Swinnerton, Frank

Kipling III, Conan Doyle, Too: Other News

Hemingway, Grace Hall
29 Dec 1929

Hughes, Richard

Ernest Hemingway's A Farewell to Arms is just. . .

Chicago Tribune

28 Dec 1929

Scrapbook

There is the Hollywood Revue. . .

Cedar Rapids Gazette

29 Dec 1929

Scrapbook

Photo: Representing those whose stories. . .

Portland, Maine, Express

28 Dec 1929

Scrapbook

White, Paul W.

This is a self-imposed task. . .

St. Joseph Gazette

24 Dec 1929

Scrapbook

Best Sellers

Oak Park, Illinois

Hemingway, Grace Hall
29 Dec 1929

Whether the flood of war. . .

New York Post

31 Dec 1929

Scrapbook

Survey of Best Sellers Published in Year '29

Grand Junction, Colorado, Sentinel

29 Dec 1929

Scrapbook

The Library of the Quarter

Yale Review

Winter 1930

Scrapbook

Lundbergh, Holger

 A Farewell to Arms

 Knott Knotes

 Jan 1930

    Scrapbook

Ernest Hemingway's A Farewell to Arms is
to be. . .

Burlington, Vermont, Free Press

4 Jan 1930

    Scrapbook

 Trust the younger generation

 Virginia Quarterly Review

 Jan 1930

    Scrapbook

The rumor is that Laurence Stallings. . .

Mansfield, Ohio, News

6 Jan 1930

    Scrapbook

Salt, Syd S.

 What Next

 New World Monthly

 Jan 1930

    Scrapbook--p. 48

Soskin, William

 Books on Our Table

 New York Post

 7 Jan 1930

    Scrapbook

 A Farewell to Arms by Ernest Hemingway
has. . .

Akron Journal

3 Jan 1930

    Scrapbook

At Illinois Artists' Exhibit

    Hemingway, Grace Hall
    9 Jan 1930

 Lucky Hemingway

 Camden, N.J., Courier

 4 Jan 1930

    Scrapbook

Ernest Hemingway has written his. . .

Burlington, Vermont, Free Press

11 Jan 1930

    Scrapbook

Such is the narrative skill and power revealed in. . .

Buffalo Times

12 Jan 1930

Scrapbook

Turns With a Bookworm

[New York] Herald Tribune

19 Jan 1930

Scrapbook

Grantham, Katherine E.

Love Among World War's Harsh Facts

Charlotte, N.C., News

12 Jan 1930

Scrapbook

Farewell is Fiction

Columbus, Ohio, Citizen

24 Jan 1930

Scrapbook

Ernest Hemingway's latest best seller. . .

Lorain, Ohio, Journal

17 Jan 1930

Scrapbook

The Echo, published by students. . .

Watsonville, Cal, Register

25 Jan 1930

Scrapbook

The Bookshelf of a Worlking Man

The Weekly People

18 Jan 1930

Farewell to Arms

Farewell to Arms. In a sason flooded with mediocre. . .

Jackson, Mississippi, Clarion-Ledger

26 Jan 1930

Scrapbook

Photo: Ernest Hemingway, whose story The Undefeated. . .

Detroit Free Press

19 Jan 1930

Scrapbook

Floyd, W. F.

The Book Corner

Laguna Beach South Coast News

31 Jan 1930

Scrapbook

Vulgarity in Fiction

Carnegie Magazine

Feb 1930

        Scrapbook

Huston, McCready

Under the title Great Modern Short. . .

South Bend News Times

9 Feb 1930

        Scrapbook

Readers of Ernest Hemingway's A Farewell
to Arms. . .

Saturday Review of Literature

1 Feb 1930

        Scrapbok

Ernest Hemingway's first novel The
Sun. . .

Portland, Maine, Express

8 Feb 1930

        Scrapbook

The Hemingways

Des Moines Register

2 Feb 1930

        Scrapbook

The Sun Also Rises, Ernest Hemingway's
first novel. . .

Portsmouth, Ohio, Sun

9 Feb 1930

        Scrapbook

Hemingway Says It's Fiction

Santa Monica Outlook

2 Feb 1930

        Scrapbook

Braxmeier, Frederic

Under the Reading Lamp

Manitowoc, Wisconsin, Times

11 Feb 1930

        Scrapbook

Ernest Hemingway's first novel The Sun
Also Rises. . .

New York Times

9 Feb 1930

        Scrapbook

The Sun Also Rises Ernest Hemingway's
first novel. . .

Youngstown, Ohio, Telegram

15 Feb 1930

        Scrapbook

The Phoenix Nest

Saturday Review of Literature

15 Feb 1930

        Scrapbook

The Sun Also Rises Ernest Hemingway's first novel. . .

Pensacola Journal

2 Mar 1930

        Scrapbook

The Sun Also Rises Ernest Hemingway's first novel. . .

Cincinnati Times Star

18 Feb 1930

        Scrapbook

Sun Also Rises. Ernest Hemingway was a war correspondent. . .

Troy Record

7 Mar 1930

        Scrapbook

Rises now a critic to find five distinct literary. . .

Denver News

23 Feb 1930

        Scrapbook

Two excellent pieces of writing. . .

Youngstown, Ohio, Telegram

8 Mar 1930

        Scrapbook

It is surprising with what ease. . .

Buffalo Times

23 Feb 1930

        Scrapbook

Beardshear, William M.

Three Modern Library Additions

Denver News

9 Mar 1930

        Scrapbook

One-sex plays. A rarity, yes. . .

Tulsa Tribune

2 Mar 1930

        Scrapbook

Farewell to Arms. This is not the first nor yet the last. . .

Lowell, Massachusetts, Sun-Telegram

9 Mar 1930

        Scrapbook

Hemingway in Cheap Edition
Trenton Times
9 Mar 1930
            Scrapbook

The Sun Also Rises, Ernest Hemingway's
first novel. . .
Fort Dodge, Iowa, Messenger
12 Mar 1930
            Scrapbook

Hemingway Writes Upon Bull, Fighting
Buffalo Times
9 Mar 1930
            Scrapbook

Pity the Picador
Chicago News
13 Mar 1930
            Scrapbook

Mansell, Darrel
    The Sun Also Rises
    Canton, Ohio, Repository
    9 Mar 1930
            Scrapbook

The initials I.M.P. which are. . .
Buffalo Times
16 Mar 1930
            Scrapbook

Story Says U.S. Inconsistent
New Bedford Standard
9 Mar 1930
            Scrapbook

Modern Library
Savannah, Georgia, News
16 Mar 1930
            Scrapbook

R.L.V.
    A Timely Reprint
    Syracuse Post-Standard
    9 Mar 1930
            Scrapbook

Sun Also Rises. One of the successful
novels. . .
Springfield, Ohio, Sun
16 Mar 1930
            Scrapbook

Two more widely varied and yet interesting. . .

Palm Beach Post

16 Mar 1930

Scrapbook

Photo: Ernest Hemingway

San Jose Mercury-Herald

23 Mar 1930

Scrapbook

We note with mild amazement. . .

Buffalo Times

16 Mar 1930

Scrapbook

The Sun Also Rises by Ernest Hemingway. . .

Davenport Democrat

23 Mar 1930

Scrapbook

Sam Y.

Book Worm

Muskogee Democrat

18 Mar 1930

Scrapbook

Sun Also Rises. This was Hemingway's first successful novel. . .

Tampa Tribune

23 Mar 1930

Scrapbook

Modern Library Reprints

Newark News

22 Mar 1930

Scrapbook

H.R.P.

Modern Library Adds New Books

Huntington, W.Va., Advertiser

30 Mar 1930

Scrapbook

About Gloria

Cleveland News

23 Mar 1930

Scrapbook

Scribner's remarks that after having been banned. . .

Holyoke, Massachusetts, Transcript

2 Apr 1930

Scrapbook

The Sun Also Rises, the book which. . .
Sacramento Bee
5 Apr 1930

Scrapbook

Censorship Is a Local Issue
[New York] Herald Tribune
30 Apr 1930

Scrapbook

Hanser, Richard
Book Chat
Buffalo Times
13 Apr 1930

Scrapbook

Censorship
Cleveland Heights Dispatch
1 May 1930

Scrapbook

Valuable Additions to Modern Library
San Jose Mercury Herald
13 Apr 1930

Scrapbook

Cheaper Reading
Seminole, Oklahoma, News
3 May 1930

Scrapbook

Farewell to Arms. Not strictly speaking
a new. . .
Washington Star
27 Apr 1930

Scrapbook

A Farewell to Arms by Ernest Hemingway
which. . .
Dayton News
4 May 1930

Scrapbook

War Book That Is Different
Rhinelander, Wisconsin, News
29 Apr 1930

Scrapbook

The Phoenix Nest
Saturday Review of Literature
10 May 1930

Scrapbook

Ban Boots Books

Wilmington, N.C., Star

11 May 1930

Scrapbook

Photo: Margaret Anderson and a Few Fellow
Rebels in Literature

New York World

25 May 1930

Scrapbook

Cooper, Carolyn

Farewell to Arms

Silver City, New Mexico, Independent

13 May 1930

Scrapbook

A Farewell to Arms by Ernest Hemingway
which. . .

Winston-Salem Sentinel

25 May 1930

Scrapbook

Lucky Strike advertisement avec Foujita

Peirce, Waldo
15 May 1930

Farewell to Arms. I want to go on
record. . .

Oklahoma City News

6 June 1930

Scrapbook

Pladner Domine Huat, Mais C'est a
L'Americaine que les juges donnent la
decision

Le Miroir des Sports

Peirce, Waldo
15 May 1930--oversize

Taylor, Harry

Intense Naive

Manchester, New Hampshire, Leader

14 June 1930

Scrapbook

Behind the Backs of Books and Authors

New York Telegram

16 May 1930

Scrapbook

Farewell to Arms. I do not know whether
this is a good book. . .

Richmond, Virginia, Times Dispatch

15 June 1930

Scrapbook

Sun Also Rises. The Modern Library, New York, presents. . .

Buffalo Courier-Express

15 June 1930

    Scrapbook

Hollingsworth, Ann

    Just Speaking of Books

    Ardmore, Oklahoma, Ardmoreite

    29 June 1930

    Scrapbook

The Trhee Day Blow by Hemingway is. . .

Hartford Courant

22 June 1930

    Scrapbook

Books: An item about Lawrence Stalling's. . .

Wasp

5 July 1930

    Scrapbook

Bouquet for Mr. Hemingway

Milwaukee Sentinel

25 June 1930

    Scrapbook

American Firsts

Chicago Evening Post

11 July 1930

    Scrapbook

M.S.M.

    Hugh Walpole's Latest Novel

    Holyoke Transcript

    28 June 1930

    Scrapbook

Farewell to Arms Is Disillusioning

Tulsa Tribune

13 July 1930

    Scrapbook

Detective stories are popular. . .

Cedar Rapids Gazette

29 June 1930

    Scrapbook

Lawrence Stallings is reported to have said. . .

Beloit News

17 July 1930

    Scrapbook

Hansen, Harry
The First Reader
New York World
22 July 1930
Scrapbook

Remembering the pitiful and poignant. . .
Buffalo Times
10 Aug 1930
Scrapbook

Hemingway and Others
Oshkosh Northwestern
26 July 1930
Scrapbook

Also the fact interests us that in. . .
Ridgewood, New York, Herald
15 Aug 1930
Scrapbook

Davis, Elrick B.
Old Southwest
Cleveland Press
2 Aug 1930
Scrapbook

The midsummer fiction number of Scribner's
is. . .
Waterbury, Connecticut, Republican
24 Aug 1930
Scrapbook

Davis, Elrick B.
The Whipping Breathes of American Soil
Buffalo Times
3 Aug 1930
Scrapbook

Mike Writes for Children
San Francisco Call
26 Aug 1930
Scrapbook

In 1926, when that little known. . .
Cedar Rapids Gazette
10 Aug 1930
Scrapbook

There are times when it seems to. . .
San Francisco Call
26 Aug 1930
Scrapbook

One of the differences between Ernest
Hemingway and. . .

Waterbury, Connecticut, Republican

31 Aug 1930

Scrapbook

Hansen, Harry

The First Reader

New York World

15 Oct 1930

Scrapbook

Hemingway Now a Broadway Name

Waterbury, Connecticut, Repbulican

7 Sept 1930

Scrapbook

Charles Scribner's Sons will reissue. . .

Dayton News

24 Oct 1930

Scrapbook

The Phoenix Nest

Saturday Review of Literature

20 Sept 1930

Scrapbook

The Book Survey

Burlington, Vermont, News

1 Nov 1930

Scrapbook

Way of All Literati

Akron Journal

22 Sept 1930

Scrapbook

A.R.

In Our Time. In Our Time is a
collection of. . .

Miami Herald

2 Nov 1930

Scrapbook

Busy Broadway Week Featured by Variety

New Haven Register

28 Sept 1930

Scrapbook

Dramatic and Colorful

Chicago Journal of Commerce

8 Nov 1930

Scrapbook

M.S.O.

Hemingway's Stories Appear in New Edition

Philadelphia Record

8 Nov 1930

Scrapbook

V.S.

Hemingway's First Book Republished

Buffalo Times

9 Nov 1930

Scrapbook

Stevens, Marjorie

Hemingway--Early View

San Francisco Argonaut

8 Nov 1930

Scrapbook

Ernest Hemingway's first book In Our. . .

Buffalo Evening News

14 Nov 1930

Scrapbook

C.F.

In Our Time

Pittsburg Press

9 Nov 1930

Scrapbook

In Our Time. In Our Time is a. . .

Denver News

16 Nov 1930

Scrapbook

In Our Time. This collection of. . .

Washington Post

9 Nov 1930

Scrapbook

Redman, Ben Ray

Old Wine in New Bottles

[New York] Herald Tribune

16 Nov 1930

Scrapbook

In Our Time. Hemingway, author of. . .

Columbus, Ohio, Dispatch

9 Nov 1930

Scrapbook

Early Hemingway

Portland, Maine, Express

22 Nov 1930

Scrapbook

F.S.

    In Our Time
    Dayton News
    23 Nov 1930
              Scrapbook

Hemingway Tells Group of Stories
Marion, Ohio, Star
8 Dec 1930
              Scrapbook

F.S.

    First Hemingway Stories Reprinted
    Raleigh Observer
    23 Nov 1930
              Scrapbook

Farewell to Arms by Ernest Hemingway in which. . .
Brooklyn Daily Star
11 Dec 1930
              Scrapbook

W.W.V.

    In Our Time
    Waterbury, Connecticut, Republican
    23 Nov 1930
              Scrapbook

A Walden Catalog
Chicago Evening Post
12 Dec 1930
              Scrapbook

Hemingway's Stories
Springfield, Mass., Republican
30 Nov 1930
              Scrapbook

Hemingway Reprint Gives Graphic Tales
Oakland Tribune
14 Dec 1930
              Scrapbook

There are some volumes of short. . .
Atlantic Monthly
Dec 1930
              Scrapbook

Between Lines
Enid, Oklahoma, News
21 Dec 1930
              Scrapbook

Glenn, Mary

    English 1930

    Tulsa World

    21 Dec 1930

        Scrapbook

In Our Time. For the reader who. . .

Portland, Maine, News

3 Jan 1931

        Scrapbook

Farewell to Arms. Strong Lines on the experiences. . .

Jacksonville Times Union

22 Dec 1930

        Scrapbook

Young Hemingway also will give us. . .

Colorado Springs Gazette

3 Jan 1931

        Scrapbook

The most remarkable sale. . .

Grand Junction, Colorado, Sentinel

29 Dec 1930

        Scrapbook

Stallings, Laurence

    The Book of the Day

    New York Sun

    12 Jan 1931

        Scrapbook

Paterson, Isabel

    Books and Other Things

    [New York] Herald Tribune

    31 Dec 1930

        Scrapbook

K.S.B.

    Reprints of Hemingway

    Louisville Journal

    25 Jan 1931

        Scrapbook

Wildes, Harry Emerson

    Of Making Many Books

    Philadelphia Public Ledger

    [1931]

        Scrapbook

Author! Author!

New York Post

8 Feb 1931

        Scrapbook

The First Reader

New York World

16 Feb 1931

      Scrapbook

M.O.

    Kat

    Berliner Morgenpost

    2 Sept 1931

        1931

Deutsches Theater

Berliner Lokal-Anzeiger

2 Sept 1931

    1931

Werner, B. E.

    Kat

    Deutsche Allgemeine Zeitung

    2 Sept 1931

        1931

Falk, Norbert

    Zuckmayer-Hilpert: Kat; Hemingways Roman
    im Deutschen Theater

    B. Z. Mittag

    2 Sept 1931

        1931

Hemingway

Jersey City Journal

31 Oct 1931

      Scrapbook

Jacobs, Monty

    Kat im Deutschen Theater: Hemingway in
    Zuckmayers Buhnenform

    Berlin Vossischen Zeitung

    2 Sept 1931

        1931

Highly commendable is Ernest. . .

Milwaukee Journal

28 Nov 1931

      Scrapbook

Kerr, Alfred

    Zuckmayer und Hilpert: Kat

    Berliner Tageblatt

    2 Sept 1931

        1931

Ernest Hemingway has written to his
publishers. . .

Burlingame, N.J., Enterprise

30 Nov 1931

      Scrapbook

Among the November Births

Kansas City Research Hospital Bulletin

Dec 1931

1931

Pacifist Bull Snubs Terrible Toreador

Brooklyn Daily Eagle

23 Feb 1932

Hickok, Guy
9 Mar 1932

Sixty Years Later

Cleveland Press

1 Dec 1931

Scrapbook

On the jacket of the German edition. . .

Wasp

5 Mar 1932

Scrapbook

In Our Time. The second edition. . .

Oklahoma City Oklahoman

24 Jan 1932

Scrapbook

Lazaneff, Pierre

Francis Charles

Apres-Midi

11 Mar 1932

Hickok, Guy
9 Mar 1932

Mackall, Leonard L.

Notes for Bibliophiles

[New York] Herald Tribune

31 Jan 1932

Scrapbook

Geagan, Bill

Fishermen Attend Early Breakfast Despite
Heavy Rain

[Bangor Daily News]

[Apr 1932]

Peirce, Waldo
2 Apr 1932

Ernest Hemingway's A Farewell to Arms. . .

Lewsiton, Maine, Sun

5 Feb 1932

Scrapbook

Heavy Rains Fail to Dampen Pomp and
Ceremony as Famous Bangor Salmon Pool's
1932 Season is Opened

Bangor Daily News

2 Apr 1932

Peirce, Waldo
2 Apr 1932--oversize

William Faulkner's new novel Light in. . .
New York Sun
5 Apr 1932
                    Scrapbook

Wagner, Charles A.
    Books
    New York Mirror
    25 May 1932
                    Scrapbook

Ernest Hemingway is rumored by. . .
Advertising and Selling
14 Apr 1932
            Bird, William
            Apr 1932

O'Meara, Jack
    Ernest Hemingway has published. . .
    Lorain, Ohio, Journal
    3 June 1932
                    Scrapbook, p. 84

Hansen, Harry
    The First Reader
    Greensboro, N.C.
    18 Apr 1932
                Scrapbook

Malone, Joseph Alan
    Book Reviews
    Mt. Kisco, N.Y., Times
    10 June 1932
                    Scrapbook

Towne, Charles Hanson
    A Number of Things
    New York American
    20 Apr 1932
            Peirce, Waldo
            22 Apr 1932--oversize

Ernest Hemingway Collection
Philadelphia Record
19 June 1932
                Scrapbook

Whereas all the aforementioned authors. . .
Translation of article in Der Dame

            Pfeiffer, Gustavus A.
            23 May 1932

Polgar, Alfred
    Der Neue Hemingway
    Berliner Tageblatt
    [July 1932]
                Pfeiffer, Gustavus A.
                7 Oct 1932

Hesse, Otto Ernst

Hemmingway: In unserer Zeit; Dos Passos: Auf den Trummern

B. Z. am Mittag

4 July 1932

Pfeiffer, Gustavus A.
7 Oct 1932

Knight, Eric M.

Anxious to Fight Bulls? Take Hemingway's Advice

Philadelphia Public Ledger

[Sept 1932] ?

Scrapbook

Miscelanea Taurina

Quintana, Juanito
13 July 1932

Author! Author!

New York Post

[6] Sept 1932

Scrapbook

Paterson, Isabel

Books and Things

[New York] Herald Tribune

15 July 1932

Scrapbook

Cartoon: The Bullfighters' Historian

New York Post

22 Sept 1932

Scrapbook

Weiss, Ernst

In unserer Zeit: Zu dem neuen Erzahlungsand von Hemingway

Berliner Borsen-Courier

17 July 1932

Pfeiffer, Gustavus A.
7 Oct 1932

Gannett, Lewis

Books and Things

New York Herald Tribune

23 Sept 1932

Scrapbook

Glancing again at the new catalogue...

Jacksonville Times-Union

7 Aug 1932

Scrapbook

Hansen, Harry

The First Reader

New York World Telegram

23 Sept 1932

Scrapbook

Soskin, William

Reading and Writing

New York Post

23 Sept 1932

Scrapbook

Duffus, R. L.

Hemingway Now Writes of Bull-fighting as an Art

New York Times

25 Sept 1932

Scrapbook

Baker, Charlotte

Writing is Linked with Bullfighting Hemingway Finds

Buffalo Evening News

24 Sept 1932

Scrapbook

Polsky, T. E.

Bullfights are Described in Ernest Hemingway's Death in the Afternoon

Akron Press

25 Sept 1932

Scrapbook

Maslin, Marshall

That Bull Fight Book Penned by Hemingway

San Francisco Call

24 Sept 1932

Scrapbook

Robinson, Ted

Bully Book by Hemingway Gores All Notions That Bullfighting is Brutal

Cleveland Plain Dealer

25 Sept 1932

Scrapbook

C.B.

The Lance of the Matador

Jacksonville Times Union

25 Sept 1930

Scrapbook

All About Bull Fighting

Chicago News

28 Sept 1932

Scrapbook

Brickell, Herschel

What Bullfighting Means to the Spaniard

[New York] Herald Tribune

25 Sept 1932

Scrapbook

Author! Author!

New York Post

28 Sept 1932

Scrapbook

Gannett, Lewis

Books and Other Things

Cleveland News

29 Sept 1932

Scrapbook

Ernest Hemingway's new book is a. . .

Oakland Tribune

1 Oct 1932

Scrapbook

Jones, Llewellyn

Bullfighting Is All You Thought and More

Chicago Evening Post

30 Sept 1932

Scrapbook

Smith, H. Allen

Bound to Be Read

Hollywood Citizen

1 Oct 1932

Scrapbook

R.A.

Hemingway On Bullfights

Cincinnati Enquirer

1 Oct 1932

Scrapbook

Stallings, Laurence

Books of the Week

Youngstown, Ohio, Vindicator

1 Oct 1932

Scrapbook

The Conning Tower

[New York] Herald Tribune

1 Oct 1932

Scrapbook

Adams, John R.

New Hemingway Story Increases Writer's Prestige

San Diego Union

2 Oct 1932

Scrapbook

Death in the Afternoon by Ernest Hemingway (Scribners) will... .

Chicago Herald Examiner

1 Oct 1932

Scrapbook

A Book About Bullfighters

New York News

2 Oct 1932

Scrapbook

Ernest Hemingway has written Death in. . .
Peoria Star
2 Oct 1932
            Scrapbook

Two weeks before the. . .
High Point, N.C., Enterprise
2 Oct 1932
            Scrapbook

Ernest Hemingway's new volume entitled
Death in. . .
Madison, Wisconsin, Journal
2 Oct 1932
            Scrapbook

Until today the bullfighting part. . .
Pittsburgh Press
2 Oct 1932
            Scrapbook

Pope, J. S.
      Death in the Afternoon
      Atlanta Journal
      2 Oct 1932
            Scrapbook

Miller, Max
      Books and Authors
      San Diego Sun
      3 Oct 1932
            Scrapbook

Sees High Art in Bullfight Drama
Mansfield, Ohio, News
2 Oct 1932
            Scrapbook

Chatton, Bruce
      High Art in Bull Fight Ritual
      Knoxville, Tennessee, Sentinel
      5 Oct 1932
            Scrapbook

Selby, John
      Scanned in Brief
      New Orleans Item
      2 Oct 1932
            Scrapbook

Death in the Afternoon. There is
almost. . .
Indianapolis News
8 Oct 1932
            Scrapbook

MacDonald, Claire

New Hemingway Book Interesting

San Jose News

8 Oct 1932

Scrapbook

Hemingway Writes About Bull Fights

Marion, Ohio, Star

15 Oct 1932

Scrapbook

Death in the Afternoon. Those readers who enjoyed. . .

Middletown, Ohio, Journal

9 Oct 1932

Scrapbook

Davidson, Gustav

Book Reviews

New York Mirror

18 Oct 1932

Scrapbook

Processional

Ft. Wayne Journal-Gazette

9 Oct 1932

Scrapbook

Author! Author!

New York Post

19 Oct 1932

Scrapbook

Publishers are announcing some. . .

Evanston, Illinois, News Index

11 Oct 1932

Scrapbook

Ford, Lillian C.

Hemingway Celebrates Bull Fighting As an Art

Los Angeles Times

23 Oct 1932

Scrapbook

Towne, Charles Hanson

A Number of Things

New York American

11 Oct 1932

Scrapbook

WADI

Author Graphs

Cleveland Plain Dealer

23 Oct 1932

Scrapbook

Path of the Bull
Rochester Democrat-Chronicle
23 Oct 1932
        Scrapbook

Fernandez de Castro, Jose Antonio
    Pescando Agujas con Hemingway
    Havana Diario de la Marina
    28 May 1933
            1933

Davis, Elrick B.
    Bullfighting is Analyzed by Hemingway
    Cleveland Press
    24 Oct 1932
            Scrapbook

Hansen, Harry
    The First Reader
    New York World Telegram
    28 Oct 1933
            Scrapbook

Jackson, Joseph Henry
    Death in the Afternoon is Graphically
    Told Story of Bull Fighting
    San Francisco Chronicle
    24 Oct 1932
            Scrapbook

Photo: Hemingway and His Record Catch
    Chicago Tribune
    28 Oct 1933
            Scrapbook

Shelton, Wilson E.
    The Bookshelf
    Beverly Hills Bulletin
    27 Oct 1932
            Scrapbook

Knight, Eric M.
    Winner Take Nothing
    Philadelphia Public Ledger
    28 Oct 1933
            Scrapbook

Gessler, Clifford
    Hemingway Explains Old Spanish Custom
    Honolulu Star-Bulletin
    29 Oct 1932
            Scrapbook

Thurber
    Cartoon
    New Yorker
    29 Oct 1932
            Musselman, Morris
            29 Oct 1932

It is first made graphic to. . .

Atlantic Monthly

Nov 1932

        Scrapbook

The Lost Generation

Paramount Magazine

18 Nov 1932

        Scrapbook

Book Shelves

Bakersfield Californian

8 Nov 1932

        Scrapbook

A Farewell to Arms. Paramount
Producers displayed. . .

Paramount Magazine

18 Nov 1932

        Scrapbook

Hicks, Granville

    Bulls and Bottles

    The Nation

    9 Nov 1932

        Death in the Afternoon

Turns With a Bookworm

[New York] Herald Tribune

20 Nov 1932

        Scrapbook

Doyle, Edward D.

    A Book a Week

    San Francisco University Foghorn

    10 Nov 1932

        Scrapbook

Ben Daschepsky, president of the
Spanish Club at City College. . .

New York Sun

21 Nov 1932

        Scrapbook

Ernest Hemingway Retorts to the
Reviewer of The New Yorker

New York World Telegram

11 Nov 1932

        Scrapbook

Death in the Afternoon deals with. . .

Memphis Appeal

27 Nov 1932

        Scrapbook

The Book Boat

[New York] Herald Tribune

28 Nov 1932

        Scrapbook

Crowe, Regina

    Farewell to Arms, Hemingway Story,
    Triumph for Film Art

    New York American

    9 Dec 1932

              Pfeiffer, Gustavus A.
              9 Dec 1932

Smith, H. Allen

    The New Books

    San Fernando Sun

    29 Nov 1932

        Scrapbook

Death in the Afternon. . . and after
on of our. . .

West Los Angeles Independent

9 Dec 1932

        Scrapbook

Bliss, H. Bond

    This is Bullish. Death in the
    Afternoon

    Memphis Appeal

    4 Dec 1932

        Scrapbook

Johnaseson, Bland

    Farewell to Arms' Masterpiece.
    Hemingway's Story Made into Film of
    Beauty, Exquisite, Noble

    New York Daily Mirror

    9 Dec 1932

              Pfeiffer, Gustavus A.
              9 Dec 1932

Advertisement for the movie A Farewell
to Arms

New York Times

8 Dec 1932

        Pfeiffer, Gustavus A.
        9 Dec 1932

Hall, Mordaunt

    The Screen: Helen Hayes, Gary Cooper
    and Adolphe Manjou in a Film of
    Hemingway's Farewell to Arms

    New York Times

    9 Dec 1932

              Pfeiffer, Gustavus A.
              9 Dec 1932

Celebrities at Premiere of A Farewell
to Arms at Criterion Theatre

New York Evening Journal

9 Dec 1932

        Pfeiffer, Gustavus A.
        9 Dec 1932

Pelswick, Rose

    Happy Ending Not Shown in N.Y. Premiere
    of Hemingway's Farewell to Arms

    New York Evening Journal

    9 Dec 1932

              Pfeiffer, Gustavus A.
              9 Dec 1932

Hansen, Harry

The First Reader

New York World Telegram

9 Dec 1932

Scrapbook

Hansen, Harry

The First Reader

San Francisco News

15 Dec 1932

Scrapbook

Thirer, Irene

Farewell to Arms: Poignant Picture

New York Daily News

Pfeiffer, Gustavus A.
9 Dec 1932

Ernest Hemingway has asked his publishers
Charles Scribner's Sons. . .

Washington Post

23 Dec 1932

Scrapbook

Watts, Richard, Jr.

On the Screen: A Farewell to Arms--
Criterion

9 Dec 1932

Pfeiffer, Gustavus A.
9 Dec 1932

The saga of the bull fights. . . .

Washington Post

23 Dec 1932

Scrapbook

Author! Author!

New York Post

13 Dec 1932

Scrapbook

Death in the Afternoon. Taste is pitted
against. . .

Santa Ana, California, Register

31 Dec 1932

Scrapbook

Ernest Hemingway tells his publishers. . .

New York Sun

13 Dec 1932

Scrapbook

Smith, Agnes

The Last Word

New York American

31 Dec 1932

Scrapbook

American Writers Highly Praised by
Thomas Mann

New York

19 Feb 1933

1933

Books: Unpegged Pound

Time

20 Mar 1933

1933

The House of Books announces God Rest You
Merry Gentlemen

New York Sun

23 Feb 1933

Scrapbook

Ernest Hemingway has just written a new
short story. . .

New York Times

7 April 1933

Scrapbook

Perhaps Ernest Hemingway's Death in. . .

New York Sun

1 Mar 1933

Sorapbook

[Stewart, Mrs. D. Ogden]

Smart Clothers for Race Going

[27 Apr 1933]

Hemingway, Pauline
28 Apr 1933

First of three new short stories. . .

Cleveland Press

7 Mar 1933

Scrapbook

Wife of Famous Author Joins Husband Here

Havana American News

3 May 1933

1933

Ernest Hemingway has asked his
publishers. . .

Dayton News

10 Mar 1933

Scrapbook

The Modern Library has added. . .

New York Mirror

4 May 1933

Scrapbook

Among winners in an annual contest. . .
Time Magazine
8 May 1933

　　　　1933

A 271 Pound Tuna Caught in Maine
New York Herald Tribune
July 1933

　　　　Perkins, Maxwell E.
　　　　2 Aug 1933

Topics of the Times [Excerpt]
New York Times
27 May 1933

　　　　1933

Davisons Bag Elephants for Akeley Hall. . .
New York Times
[Aug 1933]

　　　　Pfeiffer, Gustavus A.
　　　　14 Aug 1933

Eastman, Max
　　Bull in the Afternoon
　　The New Republic
　　7 June 1933

　　　　MacLeish, Archibald
　　　　7 June 1933--oversize

Last Fall the Messrs Charles Scribner's. . .
Brooklyn Daily Eagle
6 Aug 1933

　　　　Scrapbook

Horwill, Herbert
　　News and Views of Literary London
　　New York Times
　　18 June 1933

　　　　Scrapbook

Hauled It in With a 16-Ounce Rod
New York Sun
10 Aug 1933

　　　　Pfeiffer, Gustavus A.
　　　　14 Aug 1933

La Corrida du 15 Juillet a Pamplona

21 July 1933

　　　　Quintana, Juanito
　　　　21 July 1933

Gen. Machado Out
Havana Post--entire paper
12 Aug 1933

　　　　1933

Hemingway, Ernest

    Marlin Off The Morro

    Esquire

    Autumn 1933

            EH Magazine, p. 2

Poore, C. G.

    Ernest Hemingway's Story of His African Safari

    New York Times

    27 Oct 1933

            Scrapbook

Bromfield, Louis

    Gertrude Stein, Experimenter with Words

    New York Herald Tribune Books

    3 Sept 1933

            1933

Butcher, Fanny

    Short Stories Still Live as Works of Art

    Chicago Tribune

    28 Oct 1933

            Scrapbook

    Staging Bullfights with Toreadors in Automobiles

    St. Louis Post Dispatch

    16 Sept 1933

            1933

    Photo: Proud fisherman in Cuba. . .

    New York Post

    28 Oct 1933

            Scrapbook

Horan, Embrey

    Reviewing the New Books and the Talkies

    Dalton North Georgia Citizen

    19 Oct 1933

            Scrapbook

Gregory, Horace

    Ernest Hemingway Has Put on Maturity

    [New York] Herald Tribune

    29 Oct 1933

            Scrapbook

Gannett, Lewis

    Books and Things

    [New York] Herald Tribune

    27 Oct 1933

            Scrapbook

Soskin, William

    Reading and Writing

    New York Post

    31 Oct 1933

            Scrapbook

Winner Take Nothing. Ernest Hemingway stepped into the limelight. . .

Madison, Wisconisn, Times

1 Nov. 1933

       Scrapbook

Kronenberger, Louis

    Hemingway's New Stories and Other Recent Works of Fiction

    New York Times

    5 Nov 1933

       Scrapbook
       & Winner Take Nothing

J.R.

    Hemingway's Gamy Dishes

    Cincinnati Enquirer

    4 Nov 1933

       Scrapbook

Winner Take Nothing. For the first. . .

Milwaukee Sentinel

5 Nov 1933

       Scrapbook

Bingham, Harry

    News and Reviews

    Louisville Journal

    5 Nov 1933

       Scrapbook

Winner Take Nothing. In my musings. . .

Springfield, Ohio, Sun

5 Nov 1933

       Scrapbook

Erskine, John

    The Hollow Life

    Brooklyn Daily Eagle

    5 Nov 1933

       Scrapbook

Hemingway Hits the Skids

Chicago News

8 Nov 1933

       Scrapbook

Incandescent Brilliance

Los Angeles Times

5 Nov 1933

       Scrapbook

Towne, Charles Hanson

    A Number of Things

    New York American

    9 Nov 1933

       Scrapbook

Hemingway Again Presents Volume of Short Stories

Milwaukee Journal

11 Nov 1933

Scrapbook

Winner Take Nothing. Hemingway has had so. . .

Beverly Hills Bulletin

16 Nov 1933

Scrapbook

Douglas, Marjorie Stoneman

Pity and Terror

Miami Herald

12 Nov 1933

Scrapbook

The Daily Book Review

Dayton Herald

22 Nov 1933

Scrapbook

Robinson, Ted

Public Will Learn to Like Books of Short Stories if Our Best Writers Insist

Cleveland Plain Dealer

12 Nov 1933

Scrapbook

Pinckard, H. R.

Here are New Short Stories by Hemingway

Huntington, W. Va., Advertiser

26 Nov 1933

Scrapbook

Winner Take Nothing. Here are fourteen short. . .

Atlanta Journal

12 Nov 1933

Scrapbook

Patten, John A.

Winner Take Nothing

Chatanooga Times

3 Dec 1933

Scrapbook

Onlooker

Jimmy Is Here

London Daily Mail

15 Nov 1933

1933

Another short story writer who is. . .

Columbia, S.C., State

10 Dec 1933

Scrapbook

Another short story writer who is. . .
Raleigh, N.C., News
10 Dec 1933
       Scrapbook

Winner Take Nothing. Pointing out. . .
Memphis Appeal
7 Jan 1934
       Scrapbook

Smith, Martha M.
   Winner Take Nothing
   Green Bay Press-Gazette
   16 Dec 1933
       Scrapbook

McKee, Ruth E.
   Winner Take Nothing
   Honolulu Star-Bulletin
   13 Jan 1934
       Scrapbook

Ernest Hemingway Bound for Africa
Charlotte, N.C., News
17 Dec 1933
       Scrapbook

Ernest Hemingway Becomes a Catholic
Chicago Herald & Examiner
21 Jan 1934
       Miller, Madelaine H.
       9 Mar 1934

Walley, Harold R.
   The Book Worm's Turn
   Columbus, Ohio, State Journal
   20 Dec 1933
       Scrapbook

Hemingway, Ernest
   A Paris Letter
   Esquire
   Feb 1934
       EH Magazine, p. 8

Hemingway, Ernest
   The Friend of Spain
   Esquire
   Jan 1934
       EH Magazine, p. 6

Hemingway on War
[Memphis]
[5 Feb 1934]
       Hickok, Guy
       5 Feb 1934

Hansen, Harry

The First Reader

[New York] World Telegram

17 Mar 1934

1934

Hickok, Guy

Sitting Down is the Best Way to Shoot a Lion, Take if From Ernest Hemingway Who Knows

Brooklyn Daily Eagle

25 Apr 1934

1934

Ernest Hemingway's Short Novel

Davenport, Louisiana, Democrat

18 Mar 1934

Scrapbook

Tengo una curiosa de la epoca de mi mejor forma de boxeador

Vallejo, Juan
1 May 1934

Hemingway, Ernest

a.d. in Africa

Esquire

April 1934

EH Magazine, p. 10

Liebling, A. J.

He Starts a Short Story; Bingo a Novel and a Nobel Prize, Thomas Mann Moans

New York World Telegram

29 May 1934

1934

Perpetual Members

New Orleans, The Southern Jesuit

Apr/May 1934

1934

Hemingway, Ernest

Shootism versus Sport

Esquire

June 1934

EH Magazine, p. 12

Wiener, Willard L.

Hepburn Back from Paris, Homesick

New York Evening Journal

4 Apr 1934

1934

Morris, Lloyd

Art is Not Enough. Will Our Bull-Fighting Man of Letters. . .

Brooklyn Daily Eagle

3 June 1934

Scrapbook

Hemingway, Ernest

Notes on Dangerous Game

Esquire

July 1934

EH Magazine, p. 14

Hemingway, Ernest

Out in the Stream

Esquire

Aug 1934

EH Magazine, p. 16

Photo: The Hemingways on Land and Sea

Vanity Fair

July 1934

1934

Sullivan, Ed

Broadway: Behind the Scenes

[New York] Daily News

17 Aug 1934

Gingrich, Arnold
20 Aug 1934/28 Aug 1934

There isn't anything about the...

Chicago Tribune

7 July 1934

Scrapbook

Broun, Heywood

It Seems to Me

Ernest Hemingway's A Farewell to Arms

New York World Telegram

18 Aug 1934

Farewell to Arms

Sunday--A letter from Arnold Samuleson, former...

Minneapolis Tribune

15 July 1934

Scrapbook

It's about time someone wrote in defense of dirty words...

Springfield, Massachusetts, Evening Union

18 Aug 1934

Gingrich, Arnold
28 Aug 1934

Notes from Esquire

Atlanta Constitution

29 July 1934

Scrapbook

Broun, Heywood

It Seems to Me

Youngstown, Ohio, Telegram

20 Aug 1934

Gingrich, Arnold
28 Aug 1934/22 Aug 1934

Broun, Heywood
   It Seems to Me
   Bridgeport, Connecticut, Post
20 Aug 1934
         Scrapbook

Hemingway, Ernest
   Defense of Dirty Words
   Esquire
   Sept 1934
               EH Magazine, p. 18

Hemingway's Salvo

[20 Aug 1934]

         Gingrich, Arnold
         28 Aug 1934

Julio Hidalgo, the port pilot. . .
Havana Post
8 Sept 1934
               Griggs, Nonie
               8 Sept 1934

Dirty Words
Birmigham, Alabama, Age Herald
20 Aug 1934
         Gingrich, Arnold
         28 Aug 1934

Hemingway Gets Spearfish
Miami Herald

               Hemingway, Pauline
               15 Sept 1934

September Esquire
Keene, N.H., Sentinel
25 Aug 1934
         Scrapbook

Whopper
New York Daily News
25 Sept 1934
               Pfeiffer, Gustavus A.
               25 Sept 1934

The Conning Tower
New York Herald Tribune
28 Aug 1934
         Gingrich, Arnold
         4 Sept 1934

Hemingway, Ernest
   Genio after Josie
   Esquire
   Oct 1934
               EH Magazine, p. 20

Cain, James M.

    Ring Lardner

                 Gingrich, Arnold
                 1 Oct 1934

A Rebel Spanish Etcher

New York Times

22 Nov 1934

                 Perkins, Maxwell E.
                 28 Nov 1934

The Time Has Come, the Walrus Said

Arkansas Gazette Magazine

[Oct 1934]

                 Gingrich, Arnold
                 22 Oct 1934

Ernest Hemingway, author of A Farewell to Arms. . .

Burlington, Vermont, Free Press

24 Nov 1934

                 Scrapbook

O'Brine, Jack

    Cuban Fishing Highly Praised by Hemingway

    Havana Post

    26 Oct 1934

                 1934

Hemingway, Ernest

    Old Newsman Writes

    Esquire

    Dec 1934

                 EH Magazine, p. 21

Between the Leaves. Are Critics Coyotes?

New York Sun

15 Nov 1934

              Scrapbook

Art: Quintanilla in Madrid's Jail; . Etchings in New York

Newsweek

1 Dec 1934

                 1934

Book Marks for Today. Ernest Hemingway and John Dos Passos. . .

New York World Telegram

20 Nov 1934

              Scrapbook

Ernest Hemingway has some hard words. . .

New York American

1 Dec 1934

              Scrapbook

Los Grabados de Luis Quintanilla han
Obtenido un Extraordinario exito en
Norteamerica

Heraldo de Madrid

12 Dec 1934

1934

A New Hemingway Story

New York Sun

[1935]

Scrapbook, p. 102

Two great figures of modern literature. . .

Philadelphia Inquirer

16 Dec 1934

1934

Roman, Erl

Angler's Notes

[1935-1936]

Roman, Erl

Book Notes. An essay by Ernest. . .

New York Times

[1935]

1935

With the linotyper tapping out. . .

[New York] Herald Tribune

[1935]

Scrapbook, p. 102

Chamberlain, John

Books of the Time

New York Times

[1935]

Scrapbook, p. 102

Hemingway, Ernest

Notes on Life and Letters

Esquire

Jan 1935

EH Magazine, p. 86

The New Books

Philadelphia Public Ledger

[1935]

Scrapbook, p. 103

Hemingway, Ernest

Remembering Shooting-Flying

Esquire

Feb 1935

EH Magazine, p. 22

Atherton, Gertrude

Advice to Young Writers

New York American

11 Feb 1935

MacBride, Burt
27 Mar 1935

St. Francis River Levees Give Way

[16 Mar 1935]

Pfeiffer, Karl
18 Mar 1935

Hallam-Hipwell, Hermine

El toreo y Mr. Hemingway

Buenos Aires La Nacion

17 Feb 1935

1935

Hemingway, Ernest

The Sights of Whitehead Street

Esquire

Apr 1935

EH Magazine, p. 26

Marlow, James

Gertrude Stein Does Not Repeat--It's Just
the Way People Talk

New Orleans Times-Picayune

19 Feb 1935

McGrath, Thomas
28 Feb 1935

Hemingway to Fish

[Jacksonville]

[15 Apr 1935]

Capers, Julian
15 Apr 1935

Hemingway, Ernest

Sailfish off Mombasa

Esquire

Mar 1935

EH Magazine, p. 24

Ernest Hemingway's Green Hills of. . .

Chattanooga News

22 Apr 1935

Scrapbook, p. 102

Vice Wires Bared Thieves Dishonor

[New York] Daily News

7 Mar 1935

Calmer, Ned
25 Mar 1935--oversize

Hemingway, Ernest

a.d. Southern Style

Esquire

May 1935

EH Magazine, p. 28

Ernest Hemingway who spent a year. . .
Richmond, Virginia, News-Leader
6 May 1935

Scrapbook

Record Catch: copy of typescript of news
release plus copy of letter from GAP to
New York Times, 7 June 1935

Pfeiffer, Gustavus A.
7 June 1935

Greenfield, George

Wood, Field and Stream

[New York Times]

[13 May 1935]

1935

Book Notes
New York Times
15 June 1935

1935

Roman, Erl

Angler's Notes

[26 May 1935]

1935

Entire edition
Mansfield, Ohio, The New Day
15 June 1935

1935

Hemingway, Ernest

On Being Shot Again

Esquire

June 1935

EH Magazine, p. 30

The Author's Best Fishing Story
New York Times
16 June 1935

MacBride, Burt
20 June 1935
& 1935

photo: Record Catch

[1 June 1935]

1935

Reel Fish
New York Daily News
21 June 1935

Pfeiffer, Gustavus A.
21 June 1935--to Pauline

Roman, Erl

Angler's Notes

Miami Herald

22 June 1935

1935

Linn, Robert

Viva Hemingway

The Beacon

Townsend, Paul
15 Aug 1935

Hemingway, Ernest

The President Vanquishes

Esquire

July 1935

EH Magazine, p. 32

Hemingway, Ernest

Notes on the Next War

Esquire

Sept 1935

EH Magazine, p. 36

Photo: Four Giant Marlin Displayed at
One Time in Bimini

[28 July 1935]

1935

National Affairs: Catastrophe

Time

Sept 1935

1935

Hemingway, Ernest

He Who Gets Slap Happy

Esquire

Aug 1935

EH Magazine, p. 34

Lincoln Steffens Speaking

Carmel, California, Pacific Weekly

28 Sept 1935

1935

Academy Sponsor of 24 Expeditions

New York Times

4 Aug 1935

1935

Hemingway, Ernest

Monologue to the Maestro

Esquire

Oct 1935

EH Magazine, p. 38

Brickell, Hirschel

Ernest Hemingway Tells the Tale of an
African Hunting Trip

New York Post

[Oct 1935]

Scrapbook

Butcher, Fanny

The Book Week Has a Special Appeal to Men

Chicago Tribune

26 Oct 1935

Scrapbook
& Green Hills of Africa

Patterson, Alicia

The Book of the Week

New York News

[Oct 1935]

Scrapbook

DeVoto, Bernard

Hemingway in the Valley

Saturday Review

26 Oct 1935

Scrapbook

Chamberlain, John

Books of the Times

New York Times

25 Oct 1935

Green Hills of Africa

Gannett, Lewis

Books and Things

[New York] Herald Tribune

26 Oct 1935

Scrapbook

Grey, James C.

Books This Week

New York Sun

25 Oct 1935

Scrapbook

A.L.C.

Green Hills of Africa

Miami News

27 Oct 1935

Scrapbook

Africa: Book Hemingway Wrote So He Could
Rejoin the Lions

Newsweek

26 Oct 1935

Scrapbook

A few years ago. . .

Charlotte, N.C., News

27 Oct 1935

Scrapbook

Hemingway's Latest Book Tells of Hunting in Africa

Charlotte, N.C., Observer

27 Oct 1935

Scrapbook

Hemingway in Africa

Newark News

[Nov 1935][2].

Scrapbook

Van Doren, Carl

Ernest Hemingway, Singing in Africa

[New York] Herald Tribune

27 Oct 1935

Scrapbook

Soskin, William

Reading & Writing. Realism Over Africa

New York American

[Nov 1935][2],

Scrapbook

Hemingway, Leicester

Hemingway Reviews Hemingway

Chicago News

30 Oct 1935

Scrapbook

Foster, Willis

With P.O.M. to Darkest Africa

San Francisco Argonaut

1 Nov 1935

Scrapbook

Perry, H. Allan

Hemingway Leaves Literature for Africa

Boston Evening Transcript

30 Oct 1935

Scrapbook

Catton, Bruce

Hemingway Goes on a Hunting Trip and Writes a Book

Gastonia, S.C., Gazette

2 Nov 1935

Scrapbook

Hemingway, Ernest

The Malady of Power

Esquire

Nov 1935

EH Magazine, p. 40

An African Safari

Chicago Journal of Commerce

2 Nov 1935

Scrapbook

Daniel, Frank

Green Hills of Africa

Atlanta Journal

3 Nov 1935

Scrapbook

The Shape of a Country

Miami Herald

3 Nov 1935

Scrapbook

Keys, Joseph

Second Glances

Charlotte, N.C., News

3 Nov 1935

Scrapbook

Turns with a Bookworm

[New York] Herald Tribune

3 Nov 1935

Scrapbook

A.M.

Hemingway, in Africa, a Blend of Sport and Art

Milwaukee Journal

3 Nov 1935

Scrapbook

MacDonald, Claire

The Book Parade

San Jose News

9 Nov 1935

Scrapbook

The New Books

San Francisco Chronicle

3 Nov 1935

Scrapbook

Ernest Hemingway, unquestionably one. . .

New Orleans Picayune

10 Nov 1935

Scrapbook

J.S.

Hemingway is Writer on Africa

Lexington, Kentucky, Herald

3 Nov 1935

Scrapbook

Grant, Luis F.

Green Hills of Africa

San Jose Mercury-Herald

10 Nov 1935

Scrapbook

Lee, B. Virginia

Hemingway Writes of Big Game Hunting in Africa

Fresno Bee & Republican

10 Nov 1935

Scrapbook

Hansen, Harry

The First Reader

New York World Telegram

11 Nov 1935

Scrapbook

M.M.

Big-Game Hunting

Los Angeles Times

10 Nov 1935

Scrapbook

Mr. Hemingway Hunts the Kudu

San Diego Sun

16 Nov 1935

Scrapbook

Miller, Max

Hemingway Book Theme is Boring

San Fiego Union

16 Nov 1935

Scrapbook

F.S.H.

In Lyrical Prose He Describes Hunting Trip

Richmond, Virginia, Times-Dispatch

17 Nov 1935

Scrapbook

B.S.

Mr. Simba is a Bit Squeamish

Winston-Salem Sentinel

10 Nov 1935

Scrapbook

In Green Hills of Africa, Ernest. . .

Charlotte, N.C., Observer

17 Nov 1935

Scrapbook

Catton, Bruce

A Book a Day

Sarasota, Florida, Tribune

11 Nov 1935

Scrapbook

Mebane, Betty and John

Books and Authors

High Point, N.C., Enterprise

17 Nov 1935

Scrapbook

Kendall, Paul M.
    Books to Own
    Bristol, Virginia, Herald-Courier
    18 Nov 1935
            Scrapbook

Green Hills of Africa. Mr. Hemingway has
a deceptively. . .
New Haven Journal-Courier
28 Nov 1935
            Scrapbook

Maslin, Marshall
    All of Us
    San Jose Mercury-Herald
    18 Nov 1935
            Scrapbook

Hemingway, Ernest
    Million Dollar Fright
    Esquire
    Dec 1935
            EH Magazine, p. 42

Hall, Owene Lynch
    Books
    Chattanooga News
    21 Nov 1935
            Scrapbook

Dear Santa letter signed Ernie Hemingway
California Arts
Dec 1935
            Scrapbook

Kendall, Paul M.
    Books
    Rosslyn, Virginia, Chronicle
    22 Nov 1929 [1935]
            Scrapbook

Green Hills of Africa. Ernest Hemingway
went into. . .
Harpers
Dec 1935
            Scrapbook

Metz, Virginia Dongall
    Green Hills of Africa
    Bronxville, N.Y., Press
    27 Nov 1935
            Scrapbook

Hemingway, Ernest. Green Hills of Africa.
Account of a hunting. . .
Book Review Digest
[Dec 1935] -
            Scrapbook

Bull, Eula Sealey

Ernest Hemingway's Africa

Jacksonville Times-Union

1 Dec 1935

Scrapbook

People who admire Ernest Hemingway and collectors. . .

Savannah, Georgia, News

8 Dec 1935

Scrapbook

Ernest Hemingway's Green Hills of Africa, the story of. . .

New York Times

1 Dec 1935

Scrapbook

Turns with a Bookworm

[New York] Herald Tribune

15 Dec 1935

Scrapbook

Green Hills of Africa. Hunting in the country. . .

[New York] Herald Tribune

1 Dec 1935

Scrapbook

On the Bookshelf

Greenwich, Connecticut, Graphic

17 Dec 1935

Scrapbook

Green Hills of Africa. Mr. Hemingway hunts the elusive. . .

New York Evening Post

3 Dec 1935

Scrapbook

Brickell, Herschel

Trend of Public Opinion Shown in Selections from Magazines Made into Excellent Volume

New York Post

[1936]

Scrapbook

Several weeks ago I reviewed. . .

Columbus, Ohio, State Journal

4 Dec 1935

Scrapbook

Hemingway, Ernest

Wings Always Over Africa

Esquire

Jan 1936

EH Magazine, p. 44

To Have and Have Not. When it comes. . .
Harpers
Jan 1936².

      Scrapbook

Hemingway, Ernest
   On the Blue Water
   Esquire
   Apr 1936

      EH Magazine, p. 48

Hemingway's latest, The Green Hills. . .
Daytona Beach News
12 Jan 1936

      Scrapbook

While Ernest Hemingway's Green Hills. . .
Santa Barbara News
2 Feb 1936

      Scrapbook, p. 102

American Words
Saturday Review of Literature
18 Jan 1936

      Scrapbook

Kendall, Paul M.
   Books to Own
   Drakes Branch, Virginia, Gazette
   6 Feb 1936

      Scrapbook

Hemingway in Africa
Lorain, Ohio, Journal
19 Jan 1936

      Scrapbook

Boastful Record of African Hunt
Hartford Courant
15 Mar 1936

      Scrapbook

Hemingway, Ernest
   The Tradesman's Return
   Esquire
   Feb 1936

      EH Magazine, p. 46

C.J.P.
   Hills of Africa
   Raleigh, N.C., Observer
   26 Mar 1936

      Scrapbook

The Compleat Collector

Saturday Review of Literature

11 Apr 1936

      Scrapbook

McIntyre, O. O.

    Writer of New York Day by Day Reports
    Ernest Hemingway's Home in Key West,
    Fla., Has Become a Literary Mecca

    [2 June 1936]

           1936

Flower, Desmond

    Green Hills and Dark Valleys

    London Observer

    19 Apr 1936

        Green Hills of Africa

Cuban News Week

16 June 1936

        Greer, Abner
        20 June 1936

Hemingway, Ernest

    There She Breaches

    Esquire

    May 1936

        EH Magazine, p. 50

Hemingway's Fine Book

Richmond Times-Dispatch

        Gregory, Duke
        23 June 1936

A Farewell to Arms by Ernest Hemingway
will be published. . .

Winston-Salem Sentinel

20 May 1936

      Scrapbook

Photo: Zeppelin Passenger

New York World Telegram

        Pfeiffer, Gustavus A.
        16 July 1936

McIntyre, O. O.

    New York Day by Day

    Miami Daily News

    2 June 1936

        1936

Turns with a Bookworm

[New York] Herald Tribune

9 Aug 1936

      Scrapbook

Ernest Hemingway is now in Montana. . .

Buffalo Evening News

13 Aug 1936

      Scrapbook

Piscatorial

         Farrington, Selwyn K.
         24 Sept 1936

Green Hills of Africa. Ernest Hemingway is probably the most recent. . .

Rocky Mount, N.C., Telegram

22 Aug 1936

      Scrapbook

Bishop, John Peale

    Homage to Hemingway

    The New Republic

    11 Nov 1936

         1936

Ernest Hemingway is Writing Book on Dude Ranches

Helena, Montana, Independent

25 Aug 1936

      1936

Trullinger, Ray

    New Big Fish Club is Organized, But It's Awfully Hard to Crash

    New York World Telegram

    23 Nov 1936

         Farrington, Selwyn K.
         4 Dec 1936

Baroness Plans Stockholm Hop

New York Sun

27 Aug 1936

         Pfeiffer, Gustavus A.
         28 Aug 1936

Brawley, Jack

    Angler and Hunter

    New York American

    24 Nov 1936

         Farrington, Selwyn K.
         4 Dec 1936

Markahm Plane Ends Seal Flight in Nova Scotia Crash

         Pfeiffer, Gustavus A.
         8 Sept 1936

Stillman, Donald

    Rod and Gun

    New York Herald Tribune

    24 Nov 1936

         Farrington, Selwyn K.
         4 Dec 1936

Phillips, J. D.

Cuba is Anxious in Civil-Army Rift; Talks of President's Resignation

New York Times

[18 Dec 1936]

Wheeler, John N.
18 Dec 1936

Rio Tinto Company Limited

[London] Times

30 Apr 1937

1937

Barnes, Howard

On The Screen. Spain in Flames

[1937]

1937

Hemingway, Ernest

Hemingway Reports Spain

The New Republic

5 May 1937

EH Magazine, p. 88

Betrothal Announced. [Madelaine Hemingway to Kenneth Sinclair Mainland]

[Chicago Daily News]

[c. Jan 1937]

Hemingway, Grace Hall
6 Jan 1937

If Ernest Hemingway had been conscripted into the. . .

Santa Monica Outlook

13 May 1937

Scrapbook

To Have and Have Not. There's no way to find. . .

Scribner

Jan 1937

Scrapbook

H.H.

He's 1936 Short Story Master

Pittsburgh Press

6 June 1937

Scrapbook

Hemingway, Ernest

Brihuega Likened by Hemingway to Victory on World War Scale

New York Times

29 Mar 1937

1937

Hansen, Harry

The First Reader

New York World Telegram

[Oct 1935]

Scrapbook

Hemingway, Ernest

Fascism is a Lie

New Masses

22 June 1937

Ingersoll, Ralph McA.
9 July 1937

The fall list of Scribner's. . .

Watertown, N.Y., Times

27 Aug 1937

Scrapbook

English '37

Saturday Review of Literature

3 July 1937

Scrapbook

To Have and Have Not is to be the title of. . .

Boston Evening Transcript

28 Aug 1937

Scrapbook

Writers in Spain Subject of Article

New Bedford Standard

1 Aug 1937

Scrapbook

Ernest Hemingway, and, incidentally, the publishing. . .

El Paso Times

29 Aug 1937

Scrapbook

Broun, Heywood

It Seems to Me

Hemingway, Pauline
17 Aug 1937

Oct. 25 has been set by Scribner's. . .

New Bedford Standard

29 Aug 1937

Scrapbook

Fighter-Editor

Evanston, Illinois, News-Index

19 Aug 1937

Scrapbook

Hemingway Novel

Springfield, Mass., Republican

12 Sept 1937

Scrapbook

October 15 has been set by Scribner's
Sons as. . .

San Francisco Argonaut

24 Sept 1937

Scrapbook

Brickell, Herschel

Ernest Hemingway Explores Key West Sector
in Another Novel of Blood and Guts School

New York Post

15 Oct 1937

Scrapbook

To Have and Have Not. The first novel
in eight. . .

Scribners

Oct 1937

Scrapbook

Ernest Hemingway's New Novel

Santa Monica Outlook

15 Oct 1937

Scrapbook

Photo: New Hemingway Book

Winston-Salem, N.C., Sentinel

3 Oct 1937

Scrapbook

Gannet, Lewis

Books and Things.

[New York] Herald Tribune

15 Oct 1937

Scrapbook

Photo: New Book Soon

New Bedford, Standard

10 Oct 1937

Scrapbook

Hansen, Harry

The First Reader

New York World Telegram

15 Oct 1937

Scrapbook

Selby, John

The Literary Guidepost

Bridgeport, Connecticut, Telegram

12 Oct 1937

Scrapbook

Poore, Charles

Books of the Times

New York Times

15 Oct 1937

To Have and Have Not
& Scrapbook

Brickell, Herschel

    Hemingway's Novel Poor Piece of Work

    Philadelphia Record

    16 Oct 1937

        Scrapbook

Smith, Theodore

    Realism Lives in Newest Book by Hemingway

    San Francisco News

    16 Oct 1937

        Scrapbook

Butcher, Fanny

    Horror Packed into New Novel by Hemingway

    Chicago Tribune

    16 Oct 1937

        Scrapbook

Stevens, George

    Two Kinds of Love

    Saturday Review of Literature

    16 Oct 1937

        Scrapbook

    Chief Hair-On-His-Chest. . .

    Portland, Maine, Express

    16 Oct 1937

        Scrapbook

    Struggle for Life

    Easton, Pa., Express

    16 Oct 1937

        Scrapbook

    Death Goes Round 'n' Round

    San Francisco Call

    16 Oct 1937

        Scrapbook

[DeVoto, Bernard]

    Tiger, Tiger!

    Saturday Review of Literature

    16 Oct 1937

        Scrapbook

McFee, William

    William McFee Inquires Where is Hemingway Going?

    New York Sun

    16 Oct 1937

        Scrapbook

Adams, Donald

    Ernest Hemingway's First Novel in Eight Years

    New York Times

    17 Oct 1937

        Scrapbook

Dine, Josef C.

    Builds Story About Rum Runner

    Worcester, Mass., Telegram

    17 Oct 1937

        Scrapbook

Hemingway Writes Preface for Book by
Paris Barman

    Charlotte, N.C., Observer

    17 Oct 1937

        Scrapbook

First Hemingway Novel in 8 Years Shows
Strength and Gripping Drama

    Buffalo Sunday Times

    17 Oct 1937

        Scrapbook

Kazin, Alfred

    Hemingway's First Book on His Own People

    [New York] Herald Tribune

    17 Oct 1937

        Scrapbook

B.K.H.

    The Importance of Being Ernest Hemingway
is Plain

    Providence, R.I., Journal

    17 Oct 1937

        Scrapbook

Montgomery, John

    Hemingway Novel

    Memphis Appeal

    17 Oct 1937

        Scrapbook

Hansen, Harry

    Carpentry

    Greensboro, N.C., News

    17 Oct 1937

        Scrapbook

Patterson, Alicia

    The Best of the Wekk

    New York News

    17 Oct 1937

        Scrapbook

Hemingway Writes for Those Who Can Take It

    Brooklyn Daily Eagle

    17 Oct 1937

        Scrapbook

Robinson, Ted

    Hemingway's To Have and Have Not is
Called Most Violent Book Imaginable

    Cleveland Plain Dealer

    17 Oct 1937

        Scrapbook

Selby, John

Hemingway's Latest Novel Taxes Reader's Patience

Charlotte, N.C., Observer

17 Oct 1937

Scrapbook

The First Reader. Divided Opinion

Greensboro, N.C., News

20 Oct 1937

Scrapbook

Smith, Russell

Hemingway Tips the Scales

Washington Post

17 Oct 1937

Scrapbook

I Love Me Theme

Riverside, California, Press

21 Oct 1937

Scrapbook

Warwick, Ray

To Have and Have Not

Atlanta Journal

17 Oct 1937

Scrapbook

Book Reviews

Greensburg, Pa., Review

22 Oct 1937

Scrapbook

March, Michael

Page After Page

Brooklyn Citizen

18 Oct 1937

Scrapbook

Darrow, Mary

Books Authors

Glendale, California, News-Press

22 Oct 1937

Scrapbook

Jackson, Joseph Henry

A Bookman's Notebook

San Francisco Chronicle

19 Oct 1937

Scrapbook

Berry, Lee

This World of Books

Pittsburgh Post Gazette

23 Oct 1937

Scrapbook

Fadiman Speaks on Books, Good and Not
So Good

Bridgeport, Connecticut, Times-Star

23 Oct 1937

Scrapbook

Broun, Heywood

Mr. Broun Splits Some Noted Hairs

Charlotte, N.C., News

24 Oct 1937

Scrapbook

Sonnichsen, C. L.

Hemingway Uses the Dregs

El Paso, Texas, Herald-Post

23 Oct 1937

Scrapbook

Bugbee, Willis

Admirers of Unabashed Masculinity Will
Enjoy Hemingway's Latest

Dayton Journal

24 Oct 1937

Scrapbook

Summers, Richard

Junior League's Literary Rambles

Tucson Citizen

23 Oct 1937

Scrapbook

A.M.F.

Key West Comes to Live in New Hemingway
Novel

24 Oct 1937

Scrapbook

To Have and Have Not. This is by. . .

Boston Herald

23 Oct 1937

Scrapbook

Florida Boatman Hero of Sea Saga by
E. Hemingway

New Bedford Standard

24 Oct 1937

Scrapbook

S. W.

Mr. Hemingway Turns Preacher

Philadelphia Inquirer

23 Oct 1937

Scrapbook

Gannett, Lewis

They Die Fast in New Hemingway Thriller

Oakland, California, Tribune

24 Oct 1937

Scrapbook

Goldstein, Albert

    If you are poised. . .

    New Orleans Times-Picayune

    24 Oct 1937

        Scrapbook

Selby, John

    Blood, Action--Hemingway

    Rochester Democrat and Chronicle

    24 Oct 1937

        Scrapbook

Hansen, Harry

    Mr. Hemingway Again

    Pittsburgh Press

    24 Oct 1937

        Scrapbook

Sheridan, Mary

    A Wisconsin Slant on New Books and Their Writers

    Madison Journal

    24 Oct 1937

        Scrapbook

Lutz, Mark

    Hemingway Writes of He-Men

    Richmond, Virginia, Times-Dispatch

    24 Oct 1937

        Scrapbook

This Must Be The Place

    Birmingham, Alabama, News

    24 Oct 1937

        Scrapbook

Merlin, Milton

    Hemingway Writes of Smugglers

    Los Angeles Times

    24 Oct 1937

        Scrapbook

Whether or not you are a devotee of Ernest Hemingway. . .

    Buffalo Courier-Express

    24 Oct 1937

        Scrapbook

Miller, Max

    Reviewer Complains of Novel's Crudity

    San Diego Union

    24 Oct 1937

        Scrapbook

Garrard, Maxine

    Ernest Hemingway in Hemingway Fashion Writes Virile and Realistic Novel of Life in the Keys of Florida

    Columbus, Georgia, Enquirer-Sun

    25 Oct 1937

Brought to Book

New Haven Journal-Courier

26 Oct 1937

Scrapbook

S.W.

Ernest Hemingway Writes for Stage

Philadelphia Inquirer

28 Oct 1937

Scrapbook

Dunton, Edith K.

To Have and Have Not

Rutland, Vermont, Herald

26 Oct 1937

Scrapbook

The Answer to Old Age

Chicago Journal of Commerce

30 Oct 1937

Scrapbook

Berry, Lee

This World of Books

Toledo Blade

27 Oct 1937

Scrapbook

Conley, Meredith

Bookmarks

Plainfield, N.H., Courier-News

30 Oct 1937

Scrapbook

Book Review

Middletown, Connecticut, Press

28 Oct 1937

Scrapbook

MacDonald, Claire

The Book Parade

San Jose News

30 Oct 1937

Scrapbook

C.M.

To Have and Have Not

Mansfield, Ohio, Journal

28 Oct 1937

Scrapbook

Schriftgiesser, Edward B.

The Struggle Between the Haves and Have Nots

Boston Evening Transcript

30 Oct 1937

Scrapbook

Straubel, James

Powerful Book by Hemingway

Green Bay Press-Gazette

30 Oct 1937

Scrapbook

Bound to be Read

Lodi, California, News-Sentinel

4 Nov 1937

Scrapbook

J.F.

Ernest Hemingway's Realism Makes Simple
Story Exceptionally Good

San Diego Sun

31 Oct 1937

Scrapbook

Slaughter in the Sun

San Francisco Argonaut

5 Nov 1937

Scrapbook

Hemingway, Ernest. To Have and Have Not

Book Review Digest

[Nov 1937]

Scrapbook

Wheeler, H. E.

Any book by Ernest Hemingway. . .
[Title is cut: "Between. . ."]

Lowell, Massachusetts, Leader

5 Nov 1937

Scrapbook

To Have and Have Not. Mr. Hemingway's
first novel in. . .

Scribners

Nov 1937

Scrapbook

H. H. & H.

Books in Town

Brattleboro Reformer

6 Nov 1937

Scrapbook

To Have and Have Not. To Have and Have
Not is Ernest Hemingway's first. . .

Newport News Press

2 Nov 1937

Scrapbook

The Literary Supplement also gives. . .

Boston Evening Transcript

6 Nov 1937

Scrapbook

Paul, Elliot

Hemingway and the Critics

The Saturday Review of Literature

6 Nov 1937

Scrapbook

Pinckard, H. R.

Hemingway Enters Field of Sociology

Huntington, West Virginia, Advertiser

7 Nov 1937

Scrapbook

The Book Nook

West Palm Beach Post

7 Nov 1937

Scrapbook

To Have and Have Not. There are a few interesting facts. . .

Durham, N.C., Herald

7 Nov 1937

Scrapbook

Book Shows Trend of Leftist Writers

Oakland, California, Tribune

7 Nov 1937

Scrapbook

Turns with a Bookworm

[New York] Herald Tribune

7 Nov 1937

Scrapbook

Concha, Key West and the Yachting Fraternity

Miami Herald

7 Nov 1937

Scrapbook

Morse, Edrie Ann

Book Review

Altoona, Pennsylvania, Tribune

8 Nov 1937

Scrapbook

Goldstein, Albert

Serious readers of reviews. . .

New Orleans Times-Picayune

7 Nov 1937

Scrapbook

Hood, Florence L.

To Have and Have Not

Birmingham, Alabama, Post

10 Nov 1937

Scrapbook

Brickell, Herschel

More about Mr. Hemingway and the Reviews
of his Novel, Echoes of Which Keep Right
On

New York Post

11 Nov 1937

Scrapbook

J.T.

Fast-Moving Story Based on Spanish War

San Diego, California, Sun

14 Nov 1937

Scrapbook

Gould, William Jay

Books

Arlington, Virginia, Chronicle

12 Nov 1937

Scrapbook

R. W. L.

To Have and Have Not

Lewiston, Maine, Sun

19 Nov 1937

Scrapbook

E.M.

Battling over Hemingway

Raleigh, N.C., Observer

14 Nov 1937

Scrapbook

M.H.B.

To Have and Have Not

El Paso Times

21 Nov 1937

Scrapbook

New Hemingway Novel

Boston Post

14 Nov 1937

Scrapbook

J.S.C.

To Have Not Seems to be the Lot of Mr.
Hemingway

Birmingham, Alabama, News

21 Nov 1937

Scrapbook

Recent Fiction

Knoxville Sentinel

14 Nov 1937

Scrapbook

Sibyl C. Hayes

To Have and Have Not

San Jose, California, Mercury-Herald

21 Nov 1937

Scrapbook

Snell, George

New Phases of Author's Talent Noted

Salt Lake Tribune

21 Nov 1937

Scrapbook

Key West Youth Commits Another Act of Thievery

Thompson, Lorine
Dec 1937--to Pauline

Bready, Lowell

On the Library Shelf

Pacific Grove, California, Tide

26 Nov 1937

Scrapbook

Peabody-Latimer Nuptial Event Here This Morning

Thompson, Lorine
Dec 1937--to Pauline

McOlure, Robert B.

I have just read. . .

Santa Monica Outlook

26 Nov 1937

Scrapbook

Social Calendar

Thompson, Lorine
Dec 1937--to Pauline

We have heard of authors who. . .

Boston Evening Transcript

27 Nov 1937

Scrapbook

To Have and Have Not. Mr. Hemingway, the Hair-Apparent. . .

Mercury

Dec 1937

Scrapbook

Hemingway: Historian or Novelist

New York World Telegram

28 Nov 1940

Scrapbook

Ernest Hemingway's first novel. . .

New York Times

1 Dec 1937

Scrapbook

Somehow it seems appropriate to start. . .
New York Sun
3 Dec 1937

    Scrapbook

Then, or course, there is the. . .
Oakland, California, Post-Enquirer
11 Dec 1937

    Scrapbook

The Browser has observed. . .
Lawrence, Massachusetts, Eagle
4 Dec 1937

    Scrapbook

Clayton, Robert
Hemingway on Soap Box
Chattanooga Times
12 Dec 1937

    Scrapbook

To Have and Have Not. Hemingway writes
about. . .
[New York] Herald Tribune
6 Dec 1937

    Scrapbook

Hemingway, Stark, Bold
Honolulu Advertiser
12 Dec 1937

    Scrapbook

To Have and Have Not. Episodic saga. . .
North Adams, Massachusetts, Transcript
9 Dec 1937

    Scrapbook

When book writers write reviews. . .
New Orleans Picayune
12 Dec 1937

    Scrapbook

A Tough Hombre
Manchester, N.H., Union & Leader
11 Dec 1937

    Scrapbook

To Have and Have Not was Ernest. . .
Columbus, Georgia, Inquirer-Sun
13 Dec 1937

    Scrapbook

A Tough Hombre

Manchester, N.H., Union & Leader

13 Dec 1937

    Scrapbook

Notes

Shreveport Times

19 Dec 1937

    Scrapbook

Weinstock, Matt

  Town Talk

  Los Angeles Daily News

  15 Dec 1937

    Drus, Paul
    16 Dec 1937

Ernest Hemingway, according to a. . .

Miami Herald

26 Dec 1937

    Scrapbook

Lowe, Katherine Rice

  In the World of Books

  Nashville Tennessean

  16 Dec 1937

    Scrapbook

To Have and Have Not. Probably Ernest
Hemingway delivered. . .

Huntington, West Virginia, Advertiser

26 Dec 1937

    Scrapbook

Shocker

Toledo Blade

16 Dec 1937

    Scrapbook

Ennis, Martha

  To Have and Have Not

  Los Angeles Westwood Hills News Press

  31 Dec 1937

    Scrapbook

Ernest Hemingway's To Have and to. . .

Milwaukee News

19 Dec 1937

    Scrapbook

Nielsen, Svend Aage

  Samtale med Ernest Hemingway

[1938]

    1938

Rascoe, Burton

    Esquirer's Five-Minute Shelf

    Esquire

    Jan 1938

        Scrapbook

Hemingway Writes Play

Green Bay Press-Gazette

8 Jan 1938

        Scrapbook

Ernest Hemingway Writes from Madrid

Philadelphia Record

1 Jan 1938

        Scrapbook

Hemingway, Ernest

    Hemingway Reports Spain

    The New Republic

    13 Jan 1938

        EH Magazine, p. 85

Ernest Hemingway Creates Discussion

Greensboro, N.C., News

2 Jan 1938

        Scrapbook

Maslin, Marshall

    The Browser Talks of Books

    Lawrence, Massachusetts, Eagle

    15 Jan 1938

        Scrapbook

Let us take, however. . .

Washington Star

2 Jan 1938

        Scrapbook

Reynolds, Rossi

    Between the Covers

    Stockton, California, Record

    15 Jan 1938

        Scrapbook

Bound to be Read

Lodi, California, News-Sentinel

8 Jan 1938

        Scrapbook

To Have and Have Not. To Have and Have
Not is a man's book. . .

Madison Times

16 Jan 1938

        Scrapbook

Sobol, Louis

The Voice of Broadway

Los Angleles Evening Herald & Express

31 Jan 1938

    Drus, Paul
    2 Feb 1938

The second book of fiction. . .

Greenwich, Connecticut, Press

17 Mar 1938

    Scrapbook

Miss Madelaine Hemingway, daughter. . .

Oak Park Oak Leaves

3 Feb 1938

    Hemingway, Grace Hall
    4 Feb 1938--oversize

Thomas, Alan

The Bystander Bookshelf

The Bystander

23 March 1938

    1938

Spain and her Lessor. of War is Nineteenth Century Topic

Oak Park Oak Leaves

3 Feb 1938

    Hemingway, Grace Hall
    4 Feb 1938

The distinguished Spanish artist. . .

Savannah Press

2 Apr 1938

    Scrapbook

Photo: Live's Pictures

Life

    Burton, Harry Payne
    4 Feb 1938

From Modern Age Books, Inc.

Script

2 Apr 1938

    Scrapbook

To Have and Have Not, Ernest Hemingway first full. . .

Dalton, Georgia, News

10 Feb 1938

    Scrapbook

Hemingway, Ernest

The Time Now, The Place Spain

Ken

7 Apr 1938

    EH Magazine, p. 52
    & 1938

P.F.

A Vivid Record of War's Realities
Preserved by Hemingway and Crane

Kansas City Star

18 Apr 1938

Farewell to Arms

Hemingway, Ernest

Hemingway Reports Spain

The New Republic

27 Apr 1938

EH Magazine, p. 90

Marcantonio, Victor

Readers' Forum. Hemingway and the Italians

New Masses

19 Apr 1938

1938

Hemingway, Ernest

The Cardinal Picks a Winner

Ken

5 May 1938

EH Magazine, p. 56
& 1938

Hemingway, Ernest

Dying Well or Badly

Ken

21 Apr 1938

EH Magazine, p. 54
& 1938

When 400 New York state women's.... .

Time

9 May 1938

Scrapbook

At the end of this month. . ."
New York Times

24 Apr 1938

Scrapbook

Pegler, Westbrook

Fair Enough

New York Times

17 May 1938

Wheeler, John
31 May 1938

Guns and Castanets will be the title. . .
New York Times

24 Apr 1938

Scrapbook

Hemingway, Ernest

The Old Man at the Bridge

Ken

19 May 1938

EH Magazine, p. 58
& 1938

Hemingway, Ernest

   United We Fall Upon Ken

   Ken

   2 June 1938

        EH Magazine, p. 59
        & 1938

James, Edwin L.

   Franco Slowly Pushes Loyalist Armies Back

   [New York Times]

   [18 June] 1938

        1938

Hemingway, Ernest

   Hemingway Reports Spain

   The New Republic

   8 June 1938

        EH Magazine, p. 92

Cash, W. J.

   The Censors and Those Little Words

   Charlotte, N.C., News

   19 June 1938

        Scrapbook

Ernest Hemingway's Play. . .

Nashville Banner

8 June 1938

     Scrapbook

Case to Be Tried on Its Merits

Publishers' Weekly

25 June 1938

        Perkins, Maxwell E.
        1 July 1938

On June 15 the Savage Press. . .

Raleigh Observer

12 June 1938

      Scrapbook

Nielsen, Svend Aage

   Med en vafldsskribent over Atlanten

   Goteborgs-Postens

   25 June 1938

        1938

Hemingway, Ernest

   H. M.'s Loyal State Department

   Ken

   16 June 1938

        EH Magazine, p. 60
        & 1938

Hemingway, Ernest

   Treachery in Aragon

   Ken

   30 June 1938

        EH Magazine, p. 61
        & 1938

Hemingway, Ernest

    Call for Greatness

    Ken

    14 July 1938

            EH Magazine, p. 62
            & 1938

Blythe, LeGette

    Former Charlotte Student Publishes
    New Hemingway

    Charlotte Observer

    31 July 1938

            Scrapbook

Barron, Mark

    Hemingway's Play on Spain Being Studied

    New Haven Register

    24 July 1938

            Scrapbook

    The Fifth Column, a play by. . .

    New Orelans Picayune

    31 July 1935

            Scrapbook

Gardner, Jennie B.

    Book Ends

    Memphis Appeal

    24 July 1938

            Scrapbook

Robertson, Jack

    The Spanish Earth

    Winston-Salem Sentinel

    7 Aug 1938

            Scrapbook

Hemingway, Ernest

    My Pal the Gorilla Gargantua

    Ken

    28 July 1938

            EH Magazine, p. 63
            & 1938

    The Spanish Earth. The Hemingway
    sound. . .

    New Yorker

    8 Aug 1938

            Scrapbook

    Spanish Earth. This contains in. . .

    White Plains Times

    29 July 1938

            Scrapbook

Hemingway, Ernest

    A Program for U.S. Realism

    Ken

    11 Aug 1938

            EH Magazine, p. 64
            & 1938

S.N.

Mussolini Offers Hemingway a Kick in the Pants

Chicago News

17 Aug 1938

Scrapbook

A Bookman's Notebook

San Francisco Chronicle

3 Sept 1938

Scrapbook

Simon & Schuster have on their fall. . .

New York Times

21 Aug 1938

Scrapbook

Hemingway, Ernest

False News to the President

Ken

8 Sept 1938

EH Magazine, p. 66

Hemingway, Ernest

Good Generals Hug the Line

Ken

26 Aug 1938

EH Magazine, p. 65 & 1938

Hemingway, Ernest

Fresh Air on an Inside Story

Ken

22 Sept 1938

EH Magazine, p. 67

Ernest Hemingway is finally on his way to Spain. . .

New York Post

25 Aug 1938

1938

Hemingway's New Major Work

New York Post

4 Oct 1938

Scrapbook

Ernest Hemingway, as we reported. . .

Nashville Tennessean

28 Aug 1938

Scrapbook

Hemingway Tells How He Wrote Spanish War Play

Charlotte Observer

8 Oct 1938

Scrapbook

Cameron, May

    Books on Our Table

    New York Post

    14 Oct 1938

        Scrapbook

Campbell, Priscilla

    Written under Fire in Madrid

    Worcester, Massachusetts, Telegram

    Oct 1938

        Scrapbook

Gannett, Lewis

    Books and Things

    [New York] Herald Tribune

    14 Oct 1938

        Scrapbook

Goldstein, Albert

    Making his bow as playwright. . .

    New Orleans Times-Picayune

    16 Oct 1938

        Scrapbook

Poore, Charles

    Books of the Times

    New York Times

    14 Oct 1938

        Scrapbook
        & First 49 Stories

Kazin, Alfred

    What Spain Has Made of Ernest Hemingway

    [New York] Herald Tribune

    16 Oct 1938

        Scrapbook

    Every year that hairy-chested he-man
    among men. . .

    Portland, Maine, Express

    15 Oct 1938

        Scrapbook

    New Hemingway Collection Contains Forceful
    Play about Spain

    Akron Beacon Journal

    16 Oct 1938

        Scrapbook

    War, Death, Love a la Hemingway

    San Francisco Call

    15 Oct 1938

        Scrapbook

Roberts, Carl

    The Fifth Column

    Dayton News

    16 Oct 1938

        Scrapbook

Baker, Dorothy

Forty-Nine Great Stories, a Play from Hemingway

Boston Transcript

17 Oct 1938

Scrapbook

If you see your favorite library. . .

Concord, N.H., Monitor

21 Oct 1938

Scrapbook

Dramatist of Violence

Time

17 Oct 1938

Scrapbook

Scribner's will release Ernest. . .

San Francisco Argonaut

21 Oct 1938

Scrapbook

Hemingway Gives Flavor of War

New York World Telegram

17 Oct 1938

Scrapbook

Complete Hemingway

Brooklyn Daily Eagle

22 Oct 1938

Scrapbook

Selby, John

The Literary Guidepost

Pensacola Journal

17 Oct 1938

Scrapbook

Fadiman, Clifton

News from the Ernest Hemingway Front. . .

New Yorker

22 Oct 1938

Scrapbook

North, Sterling

Book of the Week. The Fifth Column

Chicago News

19 Oct 1938

Scrapbook

Hemingway Turns Playwright: Spain Is Drama's Scene

Pasadena Star News

22 Oct 1938

Scrapbook

Violence: Forget the Ernest. . .

Pittsburgh Post-Gazette

22 Oct 1938

        Scrapbook

Turns with a Bookworm

[New York] Herald Tribune

23 Oct 1938

        Scrapbook

The Fifth Column and the First Forty-Nine
by Ernest Hemingway brings for. . .

Buffalo Courier-Express

23 Oct 1938

        Scrapbook

Yarns and Play by Hemingway

Hartford Courant

23 Oct 1938

        Scrapbook

Jack, Peter Monro

    Hemingway's Play and Stories

    New York Times

    23 Oct 1938

        Scrapbook

Books. Ernest Hemingway's new play. . .

Sharon, Pennsylvania, Herald

27 Oct 1938

        Scrapbook

Myrick, Susan

    The Fifth Column

    Macon Times

    23 Oct 1938

        Scrapbook

Ernest Hemingway's The Fifth Column and
First Forty-Nine Stories is a collection
of all. . .

New York Times

28 Oct 1938

        Scrapbook

Robinson, Ted

    Hemingway's New Book

    Cleveland Plain Dealer

    23 Oct 1938

        Scrapbook

Capsule Reviews

Philadelphia Record

29 Oct 1938

        Scrapbook

Sonnichsen, C. L.

Hemingway Under Fire

El Paso Herald-Post

29 Oct 1938

Scrapbook

W. N.

Hemingway's Madrid Play and All His Tales

Los Angeles Times

30 Oct 1938

Scrapbook

Ernest Hemingway, Britain Contribute Short Story Books

New Haven Register

30 Oct 1938

Scrapbook

Rand, Christopher

Hairy-Chested Prose in Review

San Francisco Chronicle

30 Oct 1938

Scrapbook

The Fifth Column. The Fifth Column is a play. . .

Atlanta Journal

30 Oct 1938

Scrapbook

Thomas, Gwyn

From an Oft-Bombed Hotel, Ernest Hemingway's Play

Rochester Democrat-Chronicle

30 Oct 1938

Scrapbook

Hemingway No Playwright

Charlotte Observer

30 Oct 1938

Scrapbook

Beatty, Richmond Croom

Strong Reading

Nashville Banner

2 Nov 1938

Scrapbook

Hemingway Play, Stories Placed in One Volume

Springfield, Ohio, News

30 Oct 1938

Scrapbook

Catton, Bruce

A Book a Day

Columbia, S.C., Record

2 Nov 1938

Scrapbook

Catton, Bruce

    Greenville, S.C., Piedmont

    2 Nov 1938

        Scrapbook

Kelliher, Beatrice E.

    War Novels Influence Object of Speculation

    New Haven Register

    6 Nov 1938

        Scrapbook

    Hemingway's Play and Short Stories

    Santa Monica Outlook

    4 Nov 1938

        Scrapbook

    Realist Drama of Spanish War

    Youngstown, Ohio, Vindicator

    6 Nov 1938

        Scrapbook

Catton, Bruce

    Rebels Pounded at His Heart

    Pottsville, Pennsylvania, Journal

    5 Nov 1938

        Scrapbook

    Ernest Hemingway's new play. . .

    Tucson Star

    13 Nov 1938

        Scrapbook

Sheridan, Mary

    Hemingway

    Madison Journal

    6 Nov 1938

        Scrapbook

Pinckard, H. R.

    The Fifth Column Tells about Madrid in Wartime

    Huntington, West Virginia, Advertiser

    13 Nov 1938

        Scrapbook

Blythe, LeGette

    Hemingway Writes Play on Spanish Loyalists Fight on Fascist Spies

    Charlotte Observer

    6 Nov 1938

        Scrapbook

    Rebels Pounded at His Heart

    San Diego Sun

    13 Nov 1938

        Scrapbook

Warren, Josephine

Ernest Hemingway's first full-length play. . .

Knoxville, Tennessee, Sentinel

13 Nov 1938

Scrapbook

The Fifth Column and the First Forty-Nine Stories. Hirsute Hemingway

Richmond, Virginia, News-Leader

24 Nov 1938

Scrapbook

Going a bit abroad. . .

Santa Monica Topics

17 Nov 1938

Scrapbook

The Hoax Andalusian

San Francisco Argonaut

25 Nov 1938

Scrapbook

Hemingway's Play

Savannah News

20 Nov 1938

Scrapbook

A Play and 49 Short Stories

Boston Post

27 Nov 1938

Scrapbook

E.K.B.

The Fifth Column and the First Forty-Nine Stories

Providence Journal

20 Nov 1938

Scrapbook

The Fifth Column. Ernest Hemingway wrote his new war play. . .

Harpers

Dec 1938

Scrapbook

Morgan, Dale

Story-Teller Hemingway Takes Playwright's Role

Salt Lake Tribune

20 Nov 1938

Scrapbook

All of Ernest Hemingway's. . .

New York Times

3 Dec 1938

Scrapbook

American Novelettes

Chicago Tribune

3 Dec 1938

Scrapbook

The Spanish Earth. The sound track. . .

New Yorker

10 Dec 1938

Scrapbook

The Fifth Column and the First Forty-Nine
Stories. Collection of all. . .

[New York] Herald Tribune

4 Dec 1938

Scrapbook

Whiteside, Burns

Recent Books I Have Liked

Oakland, California, Post-Enquirer

10 Dec 1938

Scrapbook

Brode, Robert

Bites off Too Much

Brooklyn Daily Eagle

8 Dec 1938

Scrapbook

The Fifth Column and the First Forty-Nine
Stories. This is Hemingway's. . .

Santa Monica Outlook

16 Dec 1938

Scrapbook

In fiction we have added. . .

Pacific Grove, California, Tide

9 Dec 1938

Scrapbook

The Fifth Column and the First Forty-Nine
Stories. This is Hemingway's

Youngstown, Ohio, Vindicator

18 Dec 1938

Scrapbook

Hemingway Returns

Boston Herald

10 Dec 1938

Scrapbook

The Fifth Column. Unless you are. . .

New Orleans Picayune

18 Dec 1938

Scrapbook

Abernethy, Cecil

    Has Double Interest

    Chattanooga Times

    18 Dec 1938

          Scrapbook

Cassandra

    Books

    Middlebury, Vermont, Register

    6 Jan 1939

          Scrapbook

    On the other hand. . .

    New Yorker

    24 Dec 1938

          Scrapbook

    Ernest Hemingway's The Fifth Column. . .

    Pittsburgh Press

    8 Jan 1939

          Scrapbook

Greene, Marion Austin

    Death at All Hours--Daily and Sunday

    Richmond, Virginia, Times Dispatch

    25 Dec 1938

          Scrapbook

Hemingway, Ernest

    The Next Outbreak of Peace

    Ken

    12 Jan 1939

          EH Magazine, p. 68

    The Fifth Column and the First Forty-Nine Stories. The Fifth Column is a three-act play. . .

    Greenwich, Connecticut, Press

    29 Dec 1938

          Scrapbook

    Although belatedly, this is a reminder that. . .

    Brooklyn Citizen

    13 Jan 1939

          Scrapbook

    The Fifth Column and the First Forty-Nine Stories was written in Madrid. . .

    Rutland, Vermont, Herald

    3 Jan 1939

          Scrapbook

Hutchens, John K.

    Hemingway in Madrid, a Dozen Years Afterward

    Boston Evening Transcript

    14 Jan 1939

          Scrapbook

Catton, Bruce

New Intensity in Hemingway

Toledo Times

29 Jan 1939

Scrapbook

3 Writers, Artist Tell About Spain

Columbus, Ohio, Citizen

14 May 1939

Scrapbook

M.M.

Hemingway Writes Play

San Diego Union

15 Jan 1939

Scrapbook

Very Jolly Fisherman

Gastonia, N.C., Gazette

3 June 1939

Scrapbook

Idle Rich & Points South Dept.

Philadephia Record

11 Feb 1939

Scrapbook

But there is, alas, a con for every
pro. . .

Winston-Salem Sentinel

1 Oct 1939

Scrapbook

The Fifth Column and the First Forty-Nine
Stories by Ernest Hemingway contains. . .

Dayton News

12 Feb 1939

Scrapbook

The American who delves into the
intricacies. . .

Corry, Pennsylvania, Journal

7 Oct 1939

Scrapbook

The Fifth Column and the First Forty-Nine
Stories is Mr. Hemingway's full. . .

Mercury

March 1939

Scrapbook

Ernest Hemingway, a leader of a. . .

Burlington, Vermont, Free Press

14 Oct 1939

Scrapbook

Mowrer, Edgar Ansel
    35 Plane Passengers Marooned in Azores
    St. Louis Post-Dispatch
    Dec 1939

                1939

Ernest Hemingwai Is in Cuba
New Orleans Item
5 May 1940

            Scrapbook

Ernest Hemingway's play. . .
Akron Journal
4 Feb 1940

            Scrapbook

Grauer, Otto C.
    Back of Books
    Buffalo Courier-Express
    5 May 1940

                Scrapbook

Hemingway's Play
Santa Barbara News
18 Feb 1940

            Scrapbook

Scribners report that they. . .
El Paso Times
5 May 1940

            Scrapbook

Book Notes
[New York] Herald Tribune
26 Apr 1940

            Scrapbook

New Hemingway Novel Manuscript Is
Received
Gastonia, N.C., Gazette
11 May 1940

            Scrapbook

Burns, Ben
    In the Breeze
    San Francisco People's World
    3 May 1940

                Scrapbook

Ernest Hemingway is reported. . .
New York Times
12 May 1940

            Scrapbook

Tropic Adventures
Akron Journal
12 May 1940
       Scrapbook

Book Chat
Burlington, Vermont, Free Press
25 May 1940
       Scrapbook

Scribners has in hand the. . .
Chicago Tribune
15 May 1940
       Scrapbook

Turns with a Bookworm
[New York] Herald Tribune
2 June 1940
       Scrapbook

A new book is promised soon. . .
Springfield, Mass., News
16 May 1940
       Scrapbook

Charles Scribner's Sons have just. . .
San Francisco Argonaut
7 June 1940
       Scrapbook

A new book about present-day. . .
New Orleans Picayune
19 May 1940
       Scrapbook

Ernest Hemingway's new novel is. . .
Portland, Maine, Express
8 June 1940
       Scrapbook

Burns, Ben
    Literary World Awaits Hemingway's New Novel
    San Francisco People's World
    23 May 1940
       Scrapbook'

Ernest Hemingway's new novel is. . .
Portland, Maine, Press-Express
8 June 1940
       Scrapbook

News about another manuscript. . .
New York Times
10 June 1940
Scrapbook

Munroe, Bob
Hemingway Sees Tough Job Ahead for Hitler
Miami Daily News
24 July 1940
1940

A new novel by Ernest Hemingway. . .
Red Bluff, California, News
15 June 1940
Scrapbook

Photo: Ernest Hemingway
Charlotte, N.C., Observer
4 Aug 1940
Scrapbook

M.M.
Play Rewritten
Los Angeles Times
23 June 1940
Scrapbook

Ernest Hemingway has also finished. . .
High Point, N.C., Enterprise
4 Aug 1940
Scrapbook

But of course you know. . .
Red Bluff, California, News
29 June 1940
Scrapbook

Ernest Hemingway is said to have. . .
Burlington, Vermont, Free Press
10 Aug 1940
Scrapbook

The Fifth Column. Hemingway's original text. . .
[New York] Herald Tribune
14 July 1940
Scrapbook

Twice as long as. . .
Buffalo News
10 Aug 1940
Scrapbook

Damon Runyon writes that. . .

Memphis Appeal

11 Aug 1940

Scrapbook

Ernest Hemingway has delivered. . .

Chicago Tribune

21 Aug 1940

Scrapbook

Hemingway Writes New, Lengthy Novel

Akron Journal

11 Aug 1940

Scrapbook

Burns, Ben

Book Notes. Hemingway's Newest Book on Spain Hailed as His Best Work

San Francisco People's World

21 Aug 1940

Scrapbook

---

van Gelder, Robert

Ernest Hemingway Talks of Work and War

New York Times

11 Aug 1940

Scrapbook

Burns, Ben

Book Marks: John Steinbeck Writes a Book about Fish--Finds It Tough Going

San Francisco People's World

7 Aug 1940

Scrapbook

Ernest Hemingway has finished his new. . .

Wasp

16 Aug 1940

Scrapbook

Ernest Hemingway, novelist and fisherman, has been appointed. . .

New York Times

25 Aug 1940

Scrapbook

Turns with a Bookworm

[New York] Herald Tribune

18 Aug 1940

Scrapbook

Turns with a Bookworm

[New York] Herald Tribune

25 Aug 1940

Scrapbook

Ernest Hemingway has finished. . .
New Orleans Picayune
1 Sept 1940

    Scrapbook

Iddon, Don

    Don Iddon's Diary
    Paris, Continental Daily Mail
    14 Sept 1940

        1940

The new Ernest Hemingway novel. . .
New York Times
6 Sept 1940

    Scrapbook

Photo: For Whom the Bell Tolls
New York Times
22 Sept 1940

    Scrapbook

More about Books and Authors
Columbus, Georgia, Ledger
9 Sept 1940

    Scrapbook

Scribner's has some promising. . .
Richmond, Virginia, Times-Dispatch
22 Sept 1940

    Scrapbook

News of Books and Authors
Columbis, Georgia, Inquirer-Sun
9 Sept 1940

    Scrapbook

Ernest Hemingway has finished. . .
San Francisco Argonaut
27 Sept 1940

    Scrapbook

Book of the Month
Hartford Times
14 Sept 1940

    Scrapbook

Hemingway Described by Max Perkins
New York World Telegram
27 Sept 1940

    Scrapbook

Ernest Hemingway's new novel. . .

Raleigh, N.C., Observer

29 Sept 1940

Scrapbook

For Whom the Bell Tolls. November choice of. . .

Chicago Tribune

2 Oct 1940

Scrapbook

Ernest Hemingway's new novel. . .

Syracuse Herald

29 Sept 1940

Scrapbook

Ernest Hemingway's new novel. . .

Boston Evening Transcript

6 Oct 1940

Scrapbook

War Literature Is Enriched by Regler Volume

Dallas Times-Herald

29 Sept 1940

Scrapbook

The ways of the creator. . .

Buffalo Courier-Express

6 Oct 1940

Scrapbook

Chamberlain, John

Hemingway Tells How Men Meet Death

[New York] Herald Tribune

29 Sept 1940

Scrapbook

Headlining this day. . .

Saturday Review of Literature

12 Oct 1940

Scrapbook

Perkins, Max

Ernest Hemingway

Book of the Month Club News

Oct 1940

Scrapbook

Cartoon: Book is Chosen

New Bedford Standard

13 Oct 1940

Scrapbook

Photo: The Double Check
New Bedford Standard
13 Oct 1940
      Scrapbook

Prominent in October fiction. . .
Salt Lake Tribune
13 Oct 1940
      Scrapbook

Ernest Hemingway's new novel. . .
Madison, Wisconsin, Journal
13 Oct 1940
      Scrapbook

For Whom the Bell Tolls. The Book-of-
the-Month. . .
Cleveland News
14 Oct 1940
      Scrapbook

Grauer, Otto C.
    Back of Books
    Buffalo Sun Courier-Express
    13 Oct 1940
      Scrapbook

The first printing of Ernest. . .
Kenne, N.H., Sentinel
19 Oct 1940
      Scrapbook

Hemingway Got Writing Start on Newspaper
Columbia, S.C., State
13 Oct 1940
      Scrapbook

Photo: A recent photograph of. . .
Buffalo News
19 Oct 1940
      Scrapbook

Maxwell Perkins of Scribners. . .
Raleigh, N.C., Observer
13 Oct 1940
      Scrapbook

J.S.
A New and Mellower Hemingway Writes
a Novel of Worth
Gastonia, N.C., Gazette
19 Oct 1940
      Scrapbook

Nicholas, Louis

    Hemingway on Spanish War: Story of AP

    Philadelphia Record

    20 Oct 1940

        Scrapbook

Block, Maurine

    Ernest Hemingway Gets Back in Stride

    Dallas Times-Herald

    20 Oct 1940

        Scrapbook

    October 21: Ernest Hemingway's long
novel. . .

    New Orleans Picayune

    20 Oct 1940

        Scrapbook

Bower, Helen C.

    Masterly Spanish Novel Is Hemingway
Come-Back

    Detroit Free Press

    20 Oct 1940

        Scrapbook

Adams, J. Donald

    The New Novel by Hemingway

    New York Times

    20 Oct 1940

        Scrapbook

    For Whom the Bell Tolls. This new
novel of. . .

    Knoxville Journal

    20 Oct 1940

        Scrapbook

B.B.

    Hemingway's Latest Is His Best

    Richmond, Virginia, Times-Dispatch

    20 Oct 1940

        Scrapbook

    It is not enough to say. . .

    Detroit News

    20 Oct 1940

        Scrapbook

Beals, Helen

    War Story of Terrific Impact

    Worcester Telegram

    20 Oct 1940

        Scrapbook

Parker, Dorothy

    Mr. Hemingway's Finest Story Yet

    New York, PM

    20 Oct 1940

        Scrapbook

Turns with a Bookworm
[New York] Herald Tribune
20 Oct 1940
      Scrapbook

Robinson, Ted
    Hemingway's New Novel Is His Best
    Cleveland Plain-Dealer
    21 Oct 1940
         Scrapbook

Appel, David H.
    Book of the Week
    Cleveland News
    21 Oct 1940
         Scrapbook

Thompson, Ralph
    Books of the Times
    New York Times
    21 Oct 1940
         Scrapbook

Death in Spain
Time
21 Oct 1940
      Scrapbook

Gannett, Lewis
    Books and Things
    [New York] Herald Tribune
    22 Oct 1940
         Scrapbook

Hansen, Harry
    The First Reader
    New York World Telegram
    21 Oct 1940
         Scrapbook

Butcher, Fanny
    Man's Emotions Throb in Novel by
    Hemingway
    Chicago Tribune
    23 Oct 1940
         Scrapbook

Hemingway's Spanish War
Newsweek
21 Oct 1940
      Scrapbook

Ernest Hemingway, whose new. . .
Chicago Tribune
23 Oct 1940
      Scrapbook

Ernest Hemingway Writes His Most
Distinguished Work

Chicago News

23 Oct 1940

Scrapbook

Berry, Lee

This World of Books

Toledo Blade

26 Oct 1940

Scrapbook

Hyde, Fred G.

Book of the Week: Novel of War in
Spain Is Hemingway's Finest

Philadelphia Inquirer

23 Oct 1940

Scrapbook

Book Chat

Burlington, Vermont, Free Press

26 Oct 1940

Scrapbook

For Whom the Bell Tolls. Away from
the Spanish. . .

Newark, N.J., News

24 Oct 1940

Scrapbook

Cheney, Robert J.

Books and Book Folk

Portland, Maine, Express

26 Oct 1940

Scrapbook

Tooill, Kenneth D.

For Whom the Bell Tolls

Columbus, Ohio, State-Journal

24 Oct 1940

Scrapbook

Ernest Hemingway Cross the Bridge

New Yorker

26 Oct 1940

Scrapbook

Davis, Clyde Brion

You Must Open This by Dec. 25

Buffalo News

25 Oct 1940

Scrapbook

Ernest Hemingway's new novel. . .

Middletown Press

26 Oct 1940

Scrapbook

For Whom the Bell Tolls. A powerful
and moving. . .

Ssturday Review of Literature

26 Oct 1940

      Scrapbook

Molloy, Robert

    The Book of the Day

    New York Sun

    26 Oct 1940

      Scrapbook

For Whom the Bell Tolls. This new
novel of. . .

Corry, Pennsylvania, Journal

26 Oct 1940

      Scrapbook

Murray, George M.

    On the Bookshelf

    Greenwich Times

    26 Oct 1940

      Scrapbook

Hemingway's Return to Arms

Oakland, California, Post-Enquirer

26 Oct 1940

      Scrapbook

Murray, Marian

    Splendid Novel of Spain's War by
    Hemingway

    Hartford Times

    26 Oct 1940

      Scrapbook

Jones, Howard Mumford

    The Soul of Spain

    Saturday Review of Literature

    26 Oct 1940

      Scrapbook

Stupendous Novel

Kenne Sentinel

26 Oct 1940

      Scrapbook

Lee, Charles

    Hemingway's Finest Novel: For Whom
    the Bell Tolls

    Boston Herald

    26 Oct 1940

      Scrapbook

After the summer doldrums. . .

Palm Beach Post

27 Oct 1940

      Scrapbook

Archer, Ward

Ernest Hemingway's New Novel Acclaimed
as His Best So Far

Memphis Appeal

27 Oct 1940

Scrapbook

Books o. . . .: The new book by
Ernest. . .

Buffalo Sunday Courier-Express

27 Oct 1940

Scrapbook

Bell, Malcolm, Jr.

War Again the Theme of Hemingway's Novel

Savannah News

27 Oct 1940

Scrapbook

Dennis, Frank L.

The Gong Tormented Scene

Washington Post

27 Oct 1940

Scrapbook

Ben Dixon MacNeill reports. . .

Raleigh, N.C., Observer

27 Oct 1940

Scrapbook

For Whom the Bell Tolls. American
readers have. . .

Montgomery Journal

27 Oct 1940

Scrapbook

The Book of the Month Club. . .

New York Times

27 Oct 1940

Scrapbook

Fretwell, M. E.

Hemingway's Great Novel

Jacksonville Times-Union

27 Oct 1940

Scrapbook

The Book of the Week

New York News

27 Oct 1940

Scrapbook

Grimes, George

Hemingway's Best Work

Omaha World Herald

27 Oct 1940

Scrapbook

Hatcher, Harlan

    Hemingway's New Book Powerful, Deeply Moving

    Columbus, Ohio, Citizen

    27 Oct 1940

        Scrapbook

Jackson, Joseph Henry

    Books and Their Writers: Hemingway's Great Novel of the Spanish War

    San Francisco Chronicle

    27 Oct 1940

        Scrapbook

    Hemingway's Latest Novel

    Baltimore Sun

    27 Oct 1940

        Scrapbook

King, Art

    Hemingway Writes of War Incident

    Winston-Salem Sentinel

    27 Oct 1940

        Scrapbook

    Hemingway's Latest Novel Proves His Mature Talent

    Akron Beacon

    27 Oct 1940

        Scrapbook

W.A.M.

    A Frank, Beautiful, Effective Novel

    Nashville Tennessean

    27 Oct 1940

        Scrapbook

    Hemingway's Power in Finer Revelation

    Springfield, Mass., Republican

    27 Oct 1940

        Scrapbook

Merlin, Milton

    American in Spain Fights Fascist Horde for His Life

    Los Angeles Times

    27 Oct 1940

        Scrapbook

    Hemingway Tolls the Bell, but Too Long

    Hartford Courant

    27 Oct 1940

        Scrapbook

Miller, Max

    Hemingway Regains Mastery as Novelist

    San Diego Union

    27 Oct 1946

        Scrapbook

Novels

PM

27 Oct 1940

Scrapbook

Selby, John

Simple, Beautiful Prose Based on Spain's War

Rochester, N.Y., Democrat and Chronicle

27 Oct 1940

Scrapbook

H.P.

Hemingway Attains His Full Stature

New Bedford Standard

27 Oct 1940

Scrapbook

Somebody should tell Jay Dratler. . .

Akron Journal

27 Oct 1940

Scrapbook

F.M.S.

Hemingway's New Novel a Work of Vigor, Beauty

Milwaukee Journal

27 Oct 1940

Scrapbook

Ernest Hemingway's novel For. . .

Suffolk, Virginia, New-Herald

28 Oct 1940

Scrapbook

Selby, John

Ernest Hemingway Produces Novel of American in Spain

New Haven Register

27 Oct 1940

Scrapbook

Latest Books

Elmira, N.Y., Advertiser

28 Oct 1940

Scrapbook

Selby, John

For Whom the Bell Tolls

Milwaukee Sentinel

27 Oct 1940

Scrapbook

The critics seem to be unaminous. . .

San Francisco People's World

30 Oct 1940

Scrapbook

Anthony Wells in collaboration with Steve Nelson

Books of the Shelf

San Francisco People's World

30 Oct 1940

        Scrapbook

J.I.T., Jr.

    Hemingway Writes First Great Novel about the Second World War

    Boston Globe

    1 Nov 1940

        Scrapbook

Highlights in New Books

Bakersfield Californian

31 Oct 1940

        Scrapbook

Author! Author!

Saturday Review of Literature

2 Nov 1940

        Scrapbook

One Elizabethan poem by John Donne not only. . .

Eve [?] Journal

31 Oct 1947

        Scrapbook

Boie, Mildred

    Tragic Segment from Tragic War

    Boston Evening Transcript

    2 Nov 1940

        Scrapbook

Chamberlain, John

    The New Books

    [Nov 1940]

        Scrapbook

Chappell, John O., Jr.

    Adventure, Love, Death

    Cincinnati Enquirer

    2 Nov 1940

        Scrapbook

The great principle expressed by John Donne. . .

New York Times

1 Nov 1940

        Scrapbook

For Whom the Bell Tolls. A novel of wartime. . .

Burlington, Vermont, Free Press

2 Nov 1940

        Scrapbook

Anthony Wells in collaboration with Steve Nelson

Books of the Shelf

San Francisco People's World

30 Oct 1940

Scrapbook

J.I.T., Jr.

Hemingway Writes First Great Novel about the Second World War

Boston Globe

1 Nov 1940

Scrapbook

Highlights in New Books

Bakersfield Californian

31 Oct 1940

Scrapbook

Author! Author!

Saturday Review of Literature

2 Nov 1940

Scrapbook

One Elizabethan poem by John Donne not only. . .

Eve [?] Journal

31 Oct 1947

Scrapbook

Boie, Mildred

Tragic Segment from Tragic War

Boston Evening Transcript

2 Nov 1940

Scrapbook

Chamberlain, John

The New Books

[Nov 1940]

Scrapbook

Chappell, John O., Jr.

Adventure, Love, Death

Cincinnati Enquirer

2 Nov 1940

Scrapbook

The great principle expressed by John Donne. . .

New York Times

1 Nov 1940

Scrapbook

For Whom the Bell Tolls. A novel of wartime. . .

Burlington, Vermont, Free Press

2 Nov 1940

Scrapbook

Repeats previous page

Thompson, Morton

NNW: Books

Hollywood Citizen News

2 Nov 1940

Scrapbook

For Whom the Bell Tolls is being received. . .

Dayton News

3 Nov 1940

Scrapbook

Bender, Naomi

Ernest Hemingway Rises

Miami Herald

3 Nov 1940

Scrapbook

Goldstein, Albert

Ernest Hemingway's new book. . .

New Orleans Picayune

3 Nov 1940

Scrapbook

Benet, Stephen Vincent and Rosemary

Ernest Hemingway: Byron of Our Day

[New York] Herald Tribune

3 Nov 1940

Scrapbook

Lee, Charles

Hemingway's For Whom the Bell Tolls

Philadelphia Record

3 Nov 1940

Scrapbook

The Book Nook

West Palm Beach Post

3 Nov 1940

Scrapbook

Lowrey, Jacob H.

Hemingway Uses Trilogy of Life, Love and Death to Surpass His Own High Mark

Columbia, S.C., State

3 Nov 1940

Scrapbook

Books of the House: Hemingway Turns to Spanish War as Subject for Powerful Novel

Miami News

3 Nov 1940

Scrapbook

For Whom the Bell Tolls. As good as ever. . .

New York Times

4 Nov 1940

Scrapbook

More becomes known about. . .

New York Times

5 Nov 1940

    Scrapbook

Note on the Margin

San Francisco Chronicle

8 Nov 1940

    Scrapbook

Burns, Ben

    Critics Disagree on Merits of For
    Whom the Bell Tolls

    San Francisco People's World

    6 Nov 1940

        Scrapbook

Arfield, Eugene

    Ernest Hemingway has received. . .

    Saturday Review of Literature

    9 Nov 1940

        Scrapbook

Ray, Pauline

    Book Review

    Alameda, California, Times-Star

    6 Nov 1940

        Scrapbook

Latest Books

Salinas Index-Journal

9 Nov 1940

    Scrapbook

New Fiction

Great Barrington, Massachusetts, Courier

7 Nov 1940

    Scrapbook

The while Ernest Hemingway's new. . .

Burlington, Vermont, Free Press

9 Nov 1940

    Scrapbook

Miller, Mary Thomas

    Books on the Table

    San Francisco Argonaut

    8 Nov 1940

        Scrapbook

Paging

Toledo Times

10 Nov 1940

    Scrapbook

Rhodes, Arthur

Passed in Review

Brooklyn Daily Eagle

10 Nov 1940

Scrapbook

Hemingway's Great American Novel

Milwaukee Post

14 Nov 1940

Scrapbook

Roberts, C. V.

Hemingway Lets Down Followers

Dayton News

10 Nov 1940

Scrapbook

March, Michael

Page after Page

Brooklyn Citizen

15 Nov 1940

Scrapbook

Tobias, Rowena W.

Author Makes a Comeback

Charleston, S.C., News

10 Nov 1940

Scrapbook

Carew, Harold D.

Men in Days of Battle

Pasadena Star-News

16 Nov 1940

Scrapbook

Walker, Christin

Book of the Week

Columbus, Ohio, Dispatch

10 Nov 1940

Scrapbook

Ernest Hemingway's For Whom the Bell Tolls has. . .

Buffalo News

16 Nov 1940

Scrapbook

The way in which. . .

New York Times

11 Nov 1940

Scrapbook

Ernest Hemingway's For Whom the Bell Tolls was. . .

Portland, Maine, Press-Herald

16 Nov 1940

Scrapbook

Addison, Jr.

    Worst Pun of the Year

    Philadelphia Record

    17 Nov 1940

        Scrapbook

    For Whom the Bell Tolls, Ernest
    Hemingway's new novel. . .

    New Orleans Picayune

    17 Nov 1940

        Scrapbook

Bradshaw, Michael

    Hemingway's New Novel Enduring
    Literature

    Dayton Herald

    17 Nov 1940

        Scrapbook

Northrop, Mary

    Says Hemingway Hugely Overrated

    Charlotte, N.C., News

    17 Nov 1940

        Scrapbook

B.C.

    For Whom the Bell Tolls.

    Tucson Star

    17 Nov 1940

        Scrapbook

Roberts, Mary-Carter

    New Hemingway Novel Is Seen as Summing
    Up of Views on Spanish War

    Washington Star

    17 Nov 1940

        Scrapbook

Clayton, Robert

    Ernest Hemingway Achieves Rare Triumph
    in a Story of the Spanish Civil War

    Chattanooga Times

    17 Nov 1940

        Scrapbook

    For Whom the Bell Tolls. The story
    of four. . .

    Greenwood, S.C., Index-Journal

    18 Nov 1940

        Scrapbook

    Ernest Hemingway has just. . .

    [New York] Herald Tribune

    17 Nov 1940

        Scrapbook

    Latest Hemingway Novel Captures
    Sprirt of War

    Stanford University Daily

    20 Nov 1940

        Scrapbook

Author Takes Writer for Third Wife

[c. 22 Nov 1940]

1940

Photo: Ernest Hemingway, whose. . .

Miami News

24 Nov 1940

Scrapbook

Owens, Olga

Books All Gossip

Boston Evening Transcript

23 Nov 1940

Scrapbook

Reader's Guide: With Christmas a month away. . .

New Orleans Picayune

24 Nov 1940

Scrapbook

W.R.B.

Criticis. of Hemingway Novel Draws Severe Rebuke of Reader

Charlotte, N.C., News

24 Nov 1940

Scrapbook

. . .ave read one book in the last few. . .

New York World Telegram

26 Nov 1940

Scrapbook

Ellingson, H. K.

Hemingway Comes Back

Colorado Springs Gazette

24 Nov 1940

For Whom the Bell Tolls

Burns, Ben

Lower-Priced Books May Result from New Process Used in Printing For Whom the Bell Tolls

San Francisco People's World

27 Nov 1940

Scrapbook

Ernest Hemingway's Latest

Boston Post

24 Nov 1940

Scrapbook

An Open Letter to Hemingway from the Lincoln Brigade Vets

San Francisco People's World

27 Nov 1940

Scrapbook

Hemingway: Historian or Novelist?

New York World Telegram

28 Nov 1940

      Scrapbook (see 1937)

For Whom the Bell Tolls. The story
of four days. . .

Clearfield, Pennsylvania Progress

30 Nov 1940

      Scrapbook

For Whom the Bell Tolls. The story
of four days. . .

Cle[arfi]eld, Pennsylvania, Times

[2]9 Nov 1940

      Scrapbook

Rascoe, Burton

    Wolfe, Farrell and Hemingway

    Mercury

    Dec 1940

      Scrapbook

Many writers way they dislike. . .

Chester, Pennsylvania, Times

29 Nov 1940

      Scrapbook

Hemingway, Ernest. For Whom the Bell
Tolls. A story of love and war. . .

Wilson Bulletin

Dec 1940

      Scrapbook

Bonner, Ruth Hard

    Books in Town: Young American Teacher
    Blows up Spanish Bridge

    Brattleboro, Vermont, Reformer

    30 Nov 1940

      Scrapbook

Ernest Hemingway's For Whom. . .

Syracuse, N.Y., Herald

1 Dec 1940

      Scrapbook

Ernest Hemingway is receiving
extravagant. . .

Script

30 Nov 1940

      Scrapbook

Photo: Ernest Hemingway's magnificent
novel. . .

[New York] Herald Tribune

1 Dec 1940

      Scrapbook

For Whom the Bell Tolls. Of death
and dignity in Spain. . .

[New York] Herald Tribune

1 Dec 1940

Scrapbook

Three days in a man's life. . .

Pittsburgh Press

1 Dec 1940

Scrapbook

For Whom the Bell Tolls. Two years in
the writing

New York PM

1 Dec 1940

Scrapbook

Hansen, Harry

The First Reader

New York World Telegram

2 Dec 1940

Scrapbook

Gardner, Jennie B.

Book Ends

Memphis Appeal

1 Dec 1940

Scrapbook

For Whom the Bell Tolls: is a
passionate. . .

Cleveland Press

3 Dec 1940

Scrapbook

In my opinion, they are all. . .

Philadelphia Record

1 Dec 1940

Scrapbook

Authors of Ten Best Novels

Chicago Tribune

4 Dec 1940

Scrapbook

Moreland, John

Hemingway at His Best

Oakland, California, Tribune

1 Dec 1940

Scrapbook

Ernest Hemingway, whose new novel. . .

Chicago Tribune

4 Dec 1940

Scrapbook

The Inquiring Reporter

Chicago Tribune

4 Dec 1940

      Scrapbook

Books Our Reviewers Are Giving for
Christmas

Saturday Review of Literature

7 Dec 1940

      Scrapbook

Like Ernest Hemingway's great. . .

Chicago Tribune

4 Dec 1940

      Scrapbook

The Browser

    Bookends

    Lawrence, Massachusetts, Eagle

7 Dec 1940

      Scrapbook

I am told. . .

Lawrence, Massachusetts, Tribune

6 Dec 1940

      Scrapbook

But if you've got. . .

Red Bluffs, California, News

7 Dec 1940

      Scrapbook

November Book-of-the-Month

Vacaville, California, Reporter

6 Dec 1940

      Scrapbook

Ernest Hemingway's superb and. . .

Buffalo News

7 Dec 1940

      Scrapbook

Slaten, Dr. A. W.

    A Book a Day

    Honolulu Star-Bulletin

6 Dec 1940

      Scrapbook

Novels of Contemporary Life

Hartford Times

7 Dec 1940

      Scrapbook

Exercise in Hindsight

Knoxville, Tennessee, Journal

8 Dec 1940

    Scrapbook

Novelist Drops Cuss Words from New Best Seller

Lansing Journal

8 Dec 1940

    Scrapbook

For Whom the Bell Tolls. Enough copies. . .

San Francisco People's World

8 Dec 1940

    Scrapbook (Sept 1940)

Suggested Reading

Memphis Appeal

8 Dec 1940

    Scrapbook

---

1. For Whom the Bell Tolls: heads the list. . .

New Haven Register

8 Dec 1940

    Scrapbook

War on the Literary Fronts

Philadelphia Record

8 Dec 1940

    Scrapbook

For Whom the Bell Tolls: perhaps this is. . .

Columbis, Ohio, Dispatch

8 Dec 1940

    Scrapbook

For Whom the Bell Tolls, by Ernest Hemingway, author. . .

Columbus, Georgia, Inquirer-Sun

9 Dec 1940

    Scrapbook

Last-minute note on the season's best-selling. . .

New York PM

8 Dec 1940

    Scrapbook

For Whom the Bell Tolls, by Ernest Hemingway, author. . .

Columbus, Georgia, Ledger

9 Dec 1940

    Scrapbook

By any reckoning, the new Hemingway novel, For. . .

New York Sun

11 Dec 1940

Scrapbook

Ernest Hemingway has been rebuked in an. . .

Saturday Review of Literature

14 Dec 1940

Scrapbook

Even though he's a married man again. . .

San Francisco People's World

11 Dec 1940

Scrapbook

For Whom the Bell Tolls. A vigorous tale. . .

San Francisco News

14 Dec 1940

Scrapbook

For Whom the Bell Tolls, by Ernest Hemingway, the best. . .

Chicago News

11 Dec 1940

Scrapbook

Hansen, Harry

The First Reader

New York World Telegram

14 Dec 1940

Scrapbook

Ernest Hemingway and his recent bride. . .

Watertown, N.Y., Times

13 Dec 1940

Scrapbook

If you know somebody who insists. . .

Oakland, California, Post-Enquirer

14 Dec 1940

Scrapbook

Ernest Hemingway and Martha. . .

Keene, N.H., Sentinel

14 Dec 1940

Scrapbook

Ernest Hemingway's For Whom the Bell Tolls in the. . .

Milwaukee Sentinel

15 Dec 1940

Scrapbook

Ernest Hemingway's For Whom the Bell
Tolls is the. . .

Youngstown, Ohio, Vindicator

15 Dec 1940

        Scrapbook

Of Trains and Books

Raleigh, N.C., Observer

15 Dec 1940

        Scrapbook

For those whose reading. . .

El Paso Times

15 Dec 1940

        Scrapbook (see 7 Dec)

On the whole I have found. . .

Columbus, Ohio, Citizen

15 Dec 1940

        Scrapbook

Photo: For Whom the Bell Tolls.
Hemingway has. . .

Oakland, California, Tribune

15 Dec 1940

        Scrapbook

Shortly after Ernest Hemingway and
Martha. . .

Buffalo Courier-Express

15 Dec 1940

        Scrapbook

Hemingway's For Whom the Bell Tolls:
Certainly one. . .

New Orleans Picayune

15 Dec 1940

        Scrapbook

For Whom the Bell Tolls. The greatest
novel of the. . .

New York News

15 Dec 1940

        Scrapbook

Here's Peek at Some National Best
Sellers

Charlotte, N.C., Observer

15 Dec 1940

        Scrapbook

Without question Ernest Hemingway. . .

Emporium, Pennsylvania, Press

19 Dec 1940

        Scrapbook

Ernest Hemingway and his bride. . .

Worcester, Mass., Gazette

20 Dec 1940

    Scrapbook

Burns, Ben

    Book Notes: More Condemnation for
    Author / Hemingway's Untrue Tale of
    Spain

    San Francisco People's World

    26 Dec 1941

        Scrapbook

We have yet to meet a man who. . .

Red Bluff, California, News

21 Dec 1940

    Scrapbook

Ernest Hemingway and Martha Gelhorn,
who. . .

Wasp

27 Dec 1940

    Scrapbook

It pleases the Bookworm. . .

San Francisco Call Bulletin

21 Dec 1940

    Scrapbook

Murray, George M.

    On the Bookshelf

    Greenwich, Connecticut, Time

    28 Dec 1940

        Scrapbook

Britton, Beverly

    Balancing the Books

    Richmond, Virginia, Times-Dispatch

    22 Dec 1940

        Scrapbook

Bonner, Mrs. J. W.

    The Literary World

    St. Petersburg Times

    29 Dec 1940

        Scrapbook

This might be entitled. . .

Pittsburgh Sun-Telegram

22 Dec 1940

    Scrapbook

Ernest Hemingway's For Whom the Bell
Tolls. . .

Washington Star

29 Dec 1940

    Scrapbook

Novels
Columbia, S.C., State
29 Dec 1940
        Scrapbook

Novels Fall Short, Too
Port Arthur, Texas, News
5 Jan 1941
        Scrapbook

H.A.W.
    Book Fog
    Trenton Times
    29 Dec 1940
        Scrapbook

The following list of titles. . .
Rockville Center, N.Y., News Owl
10 Jan 1941
        Scrapbook

Novels of the Year
New York World Telegram
30 Dec 1940
        Scrapbook

When Ernest Hemingway has a success. . .
Lawrence, Mass., Eagle
11 Jan 1941
        Scrapbook

Novels of the Year
Greensboro News
3 Jan 1941
        Scrapbook

Establishing something of a record. . .
Atlanta Constitution
19 Jan 1941
        Scrapbook

When Ernest Hemingway has a success. . .
San Francisco Call
4 Jan 1941
        Scrapbook

I.N.S.
The 'Cussing' By Hemingway
Akron Journal
19 Jan 1941
        Scrapbook

Turns with a Bookworm

[New York] Herald Tribune

19 Jan 1941

Scrapbook

For Whom the Bell Tolls. The story of four. . .

Palatka, Florida, News

29 Jan 1941

Scrapbook

New Books at Library Here

Dover, N.H., Democrat

20 Jan 1941

Scrapbook

Hemingway Booms Donne

Newark, N.J., News

1 Feb 1941

Scrapbook

The Bookworm

A very nice lady told. . .

San Francisco Call

25 Jan 1941

Scrapbook

Readers pretend to be. . .

Lawrence, Mass., Eagle

1 Feb 1941

Scrapbook

Ernest Hemingway, author. . .

Concord, N.C., Tribune

26 Jan 1941

Scrapbook

Clearing the Desk

El Paso Times

2 Feb 1941

Scrapbook

Books -- Authors

New York Times

27 Jan 1941

Scrapbook

Ernest Hemingway is, or. . .

New York Times

2 Feb 1941

Scrapbook

Hemingways Are Expecting Big Show in Orient
Honolulu Nippu Fiji
5 Feb 1941

1941

With the arrival. . .
Keene, N.H., Sentinel
8 Feb 1941

Scrapbook

Ernest Hemingway and his wife. . .
Worcester, Mass., Gazette
7 Feb 1941

Scrapbook

After all these years. . .
New York Times
9 Feb 1941

Scrapbook

Ernest Hemingway, whose. . .
Boston Traveler
7 Feb 1941

Scrapbook

Bell Tolls Makes Unknown Poet a Best Seller
Columbus, Ohio, Citizen
9 Feb 1941

Scrapbook

Blom, Frans
Hemingway and Spanish
Saturday Review of Literature
8 Feb 1941

Scrapbook

Ernest Hemingway's For Whom the Bell. . .
Charlotte, N.C., News
9 Feb 1941

Scrapbook

For Whom the Bell Tolls has now reached. . .
Boston Herald
8 Feb 1941

Scrapbook

Ernest Hemingway's For Whom the Bell. . .
Trenton Times
9 Feb 1941

Scrapbook

Graver, Otto C.

Back of Books

Buffalo Courier-Express

9 Feb 1941

Scrapbook

Ernest Hemingway performed both. . .

Watertown, N.Y., Times

14 Feb 1941

Scrapbook

Hemingway Hits 500,000; Starts for Far East

Charlotte, N.C., Observer

9 Feb 1941

Scrapbook

A.D.B.

It may interest you. . .

Boston Herald

15 Feb 1941

Scrapbook

Watching that Hemingway book. . .

Hartford Courant

9 Feb 1941

Scrapbook

During a recent interview. . .

Keene, N.H., Sentinel

15 Feb 1941

Scrapbook

With the arrival. . .

Jacksonville Times-Union

9 Feb 1941

Scrapbook

For Whom the Bell Tolls Heads Editors' Book Poll

Lewsiton, Maine, Journal

15 Feb 1941

Scrapbook

Hemingway--For Whom the Bell Tolls: A story of Spain

Newport, R.I., News

13 Feb 1941

Scrapbook

The Hard Way. . .

New Orleans Picayune

16 Feb 1941

Scrapbook

Picking a Year's Books
Springfield, Mass., Republican
16 Feb 1941
    Scrapbook

Hlavaty, Ann
   Book Reviews
   So. Milwaukee Voice
   27 Feb 1941
       Scrapbook

Of living quality books. . .
Placerville, California, Republican
17 Feb 1941
    Scrapbook

First Person Singular
Atlantic Monthly
March 1941
    Scrapbook

It's being over-Donne department. . .
Memphis Appeal
23 Feb 1941
    Scrapbook

For Whom the Bell Tolls. A novel. . .
Raleigh, N.C., Observer
2 Mar 1941
    Scrapbook

Pippett, Roger
   News of Books
   New York PM
   23 Feb 1941
       Scrapbook

Record in Sales Volume Set by Hemingway
Novel
Chicago Tribune
2 Mar 1941
    Scrapbook

Ernest Hemingway, author of For. . .
Sommersworth, N.H., Free Press
27 Feb 1941
    Scrapbook

Ernest Hemingway's For Whom the Bell
Tolls has. . .
Chester, Pa., Times
3 Mar 1941
    Scrapbook

For Whom the Bell Tolls. A novel of
the. . .
Claremont, N.H., Eagle
7 Mar 1941
  Scrapbook

Ernest Hemingway's novel For Whom. . .
Trenton Times
23 Mar 1941
  Scrapbook

Sales of Ernest Hemingway's. . .
San Francisco Argonaut
7 Mar 1941
  Scrapbook

Photo: Pacific Interlude
Winston-Salem Sentinel
23 Mar 1941
  Scrapbook

The popularity of. . .
San Francisco Call
8 Mar 1941
  Scrapbook

Gresham, Bessie P.
 Book Review
 Oakland Fruitvale Journal
27 Mar 1941
  Scrapbook

Keller, Jack
 Romance of the Civil War
 Columbus, Ohio, Citizen
16 Mar 1941
  Scrapbook

Sales of Ernest Hemingway's. . .
Vacaville, California, Reporter
28 Mar 1941
  Scrapbook

You never can tell. . .
[New York] Herald Tribune
16 Mar 1941
  Scrapbook

One book never reviewed by me. . .
Providence, R.I., Journal
30 Mar 1941
  Scrapbook

Brown, Thelma

    Charles Scribner's Sons. For Whom the Bell Tolls. . .

    News and Views

    April 1941

        Scrapbook

Ernest Hemingway's For Whom the Bell Tolls has led. . .

Lawrence, Mass., Tribune

18 Apr 1941

        Scrapbook

Hemingway Sales a Record

Chicago Tribune

2 Apr 1941

        Scrapbook

Horwill, Herbert W.

    News and Views of Literary London

    20 Apr 1941

        Scrapbook

That short quotation from John Donne. . .

Cincinnati Times-Star

7 Apr 1941

        Scrapbook

Pulitzer Prize Awards Shock Literate America

Chicago News

7 May 1941

        Scrapbook

Book Marks

San Francisco People's World

9 Apr 1941

        Scrapbook

Bell Tolls for Pulitzer Prizes

Detroit Free Press

11 May 1941

        Scrapbook

Thompson, Mrs. Jane R.

    For Whom the Bell Tolls

    Arroyo Grande, California, Herald-Record

    11 Apr 1941

        Scrapbook

Prize Novel Award Omission Puzzle

Miami Herald

11 May 1941

        Scrapbook

Ernest Hemingway's novel. . .
Columbus, Ohio, Dispatch
16 May 1941
        Scrapbook

Spring book notes. . .
Boston Post
25 May 1941
        Scrapbook

Chit-chatter: Surprises to. . .
Red Bluff, California, News
17 May 1941
        Scrapbook

In speaking of Hemingway's. . .
Pittsburgh Press
1 June 1941
        Scrapbook

Ernest Hemingway has advised. . .
New York Times
19 May 1941
        Scrapbook

Back from China comes. . .
Worcester, Mass., Gazette
6 June 1941
        Scrapbook

Homeward Bound
Chelsea, Mass., Records
24 May 1941
        Scrapbook

Ernest Hemingway and his wife. . .
Memphis Appeal
8 June 1941
        Scrapbook

Charles Scribner's Sons received
word. . .
Curham, N.C., Herald
25 May 1941
        Scrapbook

Hemingway Is Home
New Bedford, Mass., Standard
8 June 1941
        Scrapbook

E. P. Dutton and Co. say that even. . .

Savannah News

15 June 1941

Scrapbook

Peter

Terminando con Score Cerrado se Anoto
Rodrigo Diaz por Quinta Vez el Campeonato
Nacional de Pichon

Diario de la Marina

26 July 1942

1942

Now a word about. . .

Merced, California, Sun Star

21 June 1941

Scrapbook

Bauza, P. Martinez

Palabras: Goliat-David

[17 Aug 1942]

1942

Appel, David H.

Calfornia Novelists Reviewed

Cleveland News

7 July 1941

Scrapbook

Photo: Gigi Hemingway, con solo 11
anos. . .

17 Aug [1942]

1942

Crown Publishers tell us that Ernest
Hemingway's Men at War. . .

Publishers Weekly

2 Jan 1942

Men at War

donor: Matthew Bruccoli

Particularly and grimly appropriate
this year is. . .

Cincinnati Enquirer

12 Dec 1942

donor: Matthew Bruccoli

Kilgallen, Dorothy

The $64 Questions

New York American

9 Feb 1942

1942

donor: Matthew Bruccoli

Men at War. This volume contains. . .

Nashville Banner

16 Dec 1942

Men at War

donor: Matthew Bruccoli

Carew, Harold D.

    Stories of Men at War

    Pasadena Star News

    19 Dec 1942

               Men at War

donor: Matthew Bruccoli

    Promotion for Ernest Hemingway's
    anthology. . .

    Publishers Weekly

    30 Jan 1943

               1943

donor: Matthew Bruccoli

Balch, Jack

    At the Movies: For Whom Bell Tolls a
    Film Masterpiece

    [1943]

               1943

    Men at War. An anthology of the best
    war. . .

    Raleigh, N.C., Observer

    14 Feb 1943

               1943

donor: Matthew Bruccoli

    Men at War. The best stories written
    about war from earliest times. . .

    New York American News Journal

    Jan 1943

               Men at War

donor: Matthew Bruccoli

Cameron, Kate

    Tale of Spanish War and Love at Rivoli

    New York

    [July 1943]

               1943

    American Authors Popular in Russia

    New York Times

    7 Jan 1943

               1943

donor: Matthew Bruccoli

Cook, Alton

    The Movies: For Whom the Bell Tolls Leans
    Too Heavily on Its Dialogue

    [July 1943]

               1943

    Mr. Hemingway Gets a Plucking

    New York PM

    28 Jan 1943

               1943

donor: Matthew Bruccoli

Creelman, Eileen

    The New Movie. For Whom the Bell Tolls,
    Melodrama with a Background of Spanish
    Civil War

    New York

    [July 1943]

               1943

McManus, John T.

The Tongue-Tied Bell Tolls Dully

New York

[July 1943]

1943

Mortimer, Lee

The Movies. For Whom Bell Tolls
Stupendous Film

New York Daily Mirror

15 July 1943

1943

Pelswick, Rose

For Whom Bell Tolls Opens at the Rivoli

[July 1943]

1943

Solar, Antonio G.

Notas del Club de Cazadores del Cerro

Caza y Pesca

Sept 1943

1943

Winsten, Archer

Archer Winsten's Review of For Whom the
Bell Tolls

[New York] Post

[July 1943]

1943

Carlton Cinema: For Whom the Bell Tolls

London Times

11 Oct 1943

1943

Barnes, Howard

On the Screen

New York Herald Tribune

15 July 1943

1943

Dixon, Campbell

For Whom the Bell Tolls

London Daily Telegram

11 Oct 1943

1943

Crowther, Bosley

The Screen in Review. For Whom the Bell
Tolls a Drama from the Hemingway Novel

[15 July 1943]

1943

L500,000 Film Builds Two Stars

London Daily Express

11 Oct 1943

1943

Rust, William

    For Whom the Bell Tolls

    Philadelphia Worker

    11 Oct 1943

        1943

Hemingway, Ernest

    Voyage to Victory

    Colliers

        EH Magazine, p. 69

Tabori, Paul

    Best Film in Years

    Daily Mail

    11 Oct 1943

        1943

Cowley, Malcolm

    Book in Review. Hemingway at Midnight

    The New Republic

    14 Aug 1944

        1944

Whitley, Reg

    Bell Tolls Now with an Accent on Love

    Daily Mirror

    11 Oct 1943

        1943

Hemingway, Ernest

    London Fights the Robots

    Colliers

    19 Aug 1944

        EH Magazine, p. 72

Winnington, Richard

    Hemingway's Spanish War Film Comes to
    Town

    London News Chronicle

    11 Oct 1943

        1943

    Paris est Délivéré

    Paris l'Aube

    25 Aug 1944

        1944

    People

    Life Magazine

    26 June 1944

        1944

    Paris Republicain Acclame DeGaulle

    Paris Le Populaire

    26 Aug 1944

        1944

Hinckner, Michel

La Romancier American Hemingway est a Paris

Combat

29 Aug 1944

1944

Hemingway, Ernest

The G.I. and the General, w/EH note

4 Nov 1944

EH Magazine, p. 80

Cowley, Malcolm

Notes for a Hemingway Omnibus

Saturday Review of Literature

23 Sept 1944

1944

Hemingway, Ernest

War in the Siegfried Line

Colliers

18 Nov 1944

EH Magazine, p. 82

Hemingway, Ernest

Battle for Paris

Colliers

30 Sept 1944

EH Magazine, p. 74
& 1944

Guck, Homer

Chicago Letter. Mary Welsh, of Time Magazine writes. . .

Lake Linden, Michigan, Native Copper Times

1946

1946

Hemingway, Ernest

How We Came to Paris

Colliers

7 Oct 1944

EH Magazine, p. 76

Photo: Ernest Hemingway, novelist and war correspondence. . .

[Mar 1946]

1946

The Stars and Stripes   (entire paper)

1 Nov 1944

1944

Hemingway Wed in Havana to Mary Welsh

[Mar 1946]

1946

Photo: His Fourth

[Mar 1946]
           1946

Photo: Wedding Bells
Chicago American
7 Mar 1946
           1946

Hemingway Crowding Peggy Joyce's Record

[Mar 1946]
           1946

Photos and mixed captions on EH/MH
wedding and the lion in the Los Angeles
circus
Palm Beach Times
23 Mar 1946
                 Pinnell, Charles H.
                 24 Mar 1946

Photo: Ernest Hemingway and Miss Mary
Welsh. . .
Miami Herald
16 Mar 1946
           1946

They Like to Wear Beards
Parade, Detroit Free Press
2 June 1946
           1946

Honeymooners
Havana
17 Mar 1946
           1946

Ernest Hemingway Has Soft Spot in Heart
For This City
[New Orleans] Times-Picayune
13 Aug 1946
           1946

Photo: The Smart Set

[Mar 1946]
           1946

Harrington, Mary
     They Call Him Papa
     New York Post
     28 Sept 1946
           1946

Guests in the Hemingway House

New York Daily Mirror

10 Mar 1947

1947

Condecorado el gran escritor americano
Ernest Hemingway con la Medalla de Bronce
de los E.U.

Diario de la Marina

14 June 1947

1947

Stevens, Ashton

Settling the Case of a Self-Made Widow

Chicago Herald American

2 May 1947

1947

Photo: Condecoradad con la Estrella de
Bronce de los Estados Unidos

14 June 1947

1947

Stevens, Ashton

When Pat Covici Sent Sam Putnam to Paris

[Chicago Herald American

18 May 1947

1947

Cartoon by Jicky

London News Chronicle

17 June 1947

Scribner, Charles, Sr.
9 July 1947

Fitzgerald, Adeline

At the Moment

Chicago Sun

14 May 1947

1947

Mary Hemingway's GI Hairdo Occasions
Stir at Sun Valley

Boise Statesman

18 Jan 1948

1948

Babcock, Frederic

Among the Authors

Chicago Sunday Tribune

1 June 1947

1947

Butcher, Fanny

The Literary Spotlight

30 Mar 1948

1948

Thalia

Saints' Days in Cuba Are Days of Gaiety and Entertainment

30 Mar 1948

1948

Powell, Dawn

Speaking of the Younger Generation

Harper's Bazaar

Aug 1949

Ross, Lillian. 15 Aug 1949

Cowley, Malcolm

A Portrait of Mister Papa

Life

10 Jan 1949

Scrapbook 54, p. 38
& 1949

Hacket, Francis

Hemingway: A Farewell to Arms

Saturday Review

6 Aug 1949

Ross, Lillian 5 Aug 1949

Creel, Dess Gowdy

Hemingway Has Shown Steady Growth

Charleston, S.C., News & Courier

29 Mar 1949

Hemingway, Pauline B.
15 Dec 1950

Powell, Dawn

Reader Left Parched in McCarthy Oasis

New York Post Home News

14 Aug 1949

Ross, Lillian 15 Aug 1949

Gober, William, Jr.

Cabell, 70, Hits Lorelei of Literature

Los Angeles Times

17 Apr 1949

1949

(bearing ANS Sam)

Gill, Brendan

The O'Hara Report and the Wit of Miss McCarthy

The New Yorker

20 Aug 1949

Ross, Lillian 16 Aug 1949

[Geismar, Maxwell]

Position of Hemingway--Part II

New York [Times Book] Review

31 July 1949

1949

Cannon, Jimmy

Rocky K.O.d Fusari and Persecution Complex

New York Post Home News

15 Sept 1949

Hotchner, A. E.
28 Sept 1949

Hemingway Novel Slated for March

New York Times

13 Oct 1949

1949

Operation on Waldo Peirce is Considered

19 Apr 1950

Browne, Kenneth H.
1 May 1950

Dempsey, David

In and Out of Books

New York Times Book Review

23 Oct 1949

Ross, Lillian   24 Oct 1949

Barnes, Howard

On the Screen

New York Herald Tribune

Shipman, Evan   23 Apr 1950

New Novel Due from Hemingway

Lanham, Charles T.
26 Oct 1949

G.N.

Sono io il Vecchio del Mare ma Hemingway
e un uomo senza parola

Tempo

7 June 1950

1950

New Novel Due from Hemingway

Lanham, Charles T.
30 Oct 1949

Williams, Tennessee

A Writer's Quest for a Parnassus

New York Times

13 Aug 1950

1950

Title Defender

Newsweek

Plummer, William L.
12 Apr 1950

Entire edition

John O'London's Weekly

18 Aug 1950

1950

Hemingway Novel Slated for March
New York Times
13 Oct 1949
                    1949

Operation on Waldo Peirce is Considered

19 Apr 1950

            Browne, Kenneth H.
            1 May 1950

Dempsey, David
    In and Out of Books
    New York Times Book Review
23 Oct 1949
            Ross, Lillian   24 Oct 1949

Barnes, Howard
    On the Screen
    New York Herald Tribune

            Shipman, Evan   23 Apr 1950

New Novel Due from Hemingway

            Lanham, Charles T.
            26 Oct 1949

G.N.
    Sono io il Vecchio del Mare ma Hemingway
    e un uomo senza parola
    Tempo
    7 June 1950
                    1950

New Novel Due from Hemingway

            Lanham, Charles T.
            30 Oct 1949

Williams, Tennessee
    A Writer's Quest for a Parnassus
    New York Times
    13 Aug 1950
                    1950

Title Defender
Newsweek

            Plummer, William L.
            12 Apr 1950

Entire edition
John O'London's Weekly
18 Aug 1950
                1950

Bedell, W. D.

    Across the River and Into the Trees

    Houston Post

    10 Sept 1950

        Across the River

On the Ropes
& Hemingway Is Bitter about Nobody--
But His Colonel Is

Time

11 Sept 1950

        Across the River

O'Hara, John

    Across the River and into the Trees

    New York Times Book Review

    10 Sept 1950

        Across the River

Breit, Harvey

    Talk with Mr. Hemingway

    New York Times Book Review

    17 Sept 1950

        1950

Paul, Elliot

    Thanks to Ernest

    Providence, R.I., Sunday Journal

    10 Sept 1950

        Across the River

Hemingway: Pro and Con

Nashville Tennessean

17 Sept 1950

        1950

donor: Matthew Bruccoli

Sandroff, Ivan

    Our World Runs Short

    Worcester, Mass., Telegram

    10 Sept 1950

        Across the River

Hoyt, Elizabeth North

    The Colonel

    Cedar Rapids Gazette

    17 Sept 1950

        Across the River

Seward, William W., Jr.

    A Brooding Awareness of the Tragic
    Marks Hemingway's Return to Writing

    Norfolk Virginian-Pilot

    10 Sept 1950

        Across the River

Fantasy Under the Trees (Now We are
Fifty)

Punch (England)

20 Sept 1950

        Scribner, Charles, Sr.
        16 Oct 1950

Babcock, Frederic

Among the Authors

Chicago Sunday Tribune

24 Sept 1950

Across the River

Rugoff, Milton

Much Smoke, Some Sparks

New York Herald Tribune Book Review

15 Oct 1950

Scribner, Charles, Sr.
15 Oct 1950

McGill, Ralph

Bearing as if with Tongs

5 Oct 1950

1950

Galbraith, John K.

Side Glances

20 Oct 1950

Scribner, Charles, Sr.
21 Oct 1950

Obituary: Wesley Dilworth

Detroit News

9 Oct 1950

Sanford, Marcelline Hemingway
9 Oct 1950

Markfield, Wallace

Hemingway's Articulate Ox

The New-Leader

21 Oct 1950

Scribner, Charles, Sr.
27 Oct 1950

Clune, Henry W.

Seen and Heard

Rochester Democratic and Chronicle

12 Oct 1950

Scribner, Charles, Sr.
16 Oct 1950

Poore, Charles

Books of the Times

New York Times

26 Oct 1940

Scribner, Charles, Sr.
27 Oct 1950

Hicks, Granville

The Critics Have Never Been Easy on
Ernest Hemingway

New York Times Book Review

15 Oct 1950

Scribner, Charles, Sr.
15 Oct 1950

Waugh, Evelyn

The Case of Mr. Hemingway

Commonweal

3 Nov 1950

Scribner, Charles, Sr.
31 Oct 1950

Author's Nephew Gets Exciting Call

Miller, Madelaine H. M.
14 Nov 1950

Ferrer Musical to Star Baker
New York Daily News
31 Jan 1951

Samuels, Lee 6 Feb 1951

McGill, Ralph
Faulkner's Nobel Prize

14 Nov 1950

1950

McCord, Bert
News of the Theatre: South Atlantic
New York Herald Tribune
31 Jan 1951

Samuels, Lee 6 Feb 1951

McGill, Ralph
The Agony and the Sweat

[15 Oct 1950]

1950

Robilant, Carlo di
Hemingway et Venezia

[Feb 1951]

Robilant, Carlo di
6 Feb 1951

Gary Cooper Arrives
Havana Post
30 Dec 1950

1950

Hare, Lionel
The Fabulous Mr. Hemingway
Illustrated
10 Feb 1951

1951

Hemingway, Mary
Girl at Sea
Cosmopolitan
[1951]

1951

Johnson, Erskine
[A column mentioning Ernest Hemingway]
Los Angeles Daily News
25 Apr 1951

Cowley, Malcolm 8 June 1951

Desastre Aereo

Havana Prensa Libra

26 Apr 1951

1951

Rosetahl, Sherwin H.

Protection without Statutory Copyright

Authors League News

July 1951

Cowley, Malcolm   3 Nov 1951

Baker, Carlos

25 Years of a Hemingway Classic

New York Times Book Review

29 Apr 1951

Baker, Carlos   4 May 1951

Drinks on Monty

Life Magazine

Cochran, James   18 July 1951

Mrs. Hemingway, Mother of the Novelist, Dies

[June 1951]

1951

Pauline Hemingway, 55, Second Wife of Hemingway

New York Herald Tribune

2 Oct 1951

1951

Services in Illinois for Writer's Mother

[June 1951]

1951

Ruark, Robert

Hemingway's New Novel Puts Papa Back on Beam

[1952]

Old Man and the Sea

Johnson, Erskine

Exclusively Yours

Los Angeles Daily News

11 June 1951

Ross, Lillian   10 July 1951

Lyons, Leonard

In this Corner: Havana, Cuba

Minneapolis Star

12 Jan 1952

1952

Cranston, Herbert

When Hemingway Earned Half a Cent a Word
on The Toronto Star

New York Herald Tribune Book Review

13 Jan 1952

Baker, Carlos 12 Jan 1952
Fenton, Charles 10 Jan 1952

Obituary: Mark Murphy

[4 Aug 1952]

Hotchner, A. E. 4 Aug 1952

Downing, Margot

He Wrote Better in School Says
Hemingway's Mother

Sanford, Marcelline H.
26 Jan 1952

McCaslin, Walt

New Kind of Hemingway

Dayton Daily News

24 Aug 1952

Old Man Scrapbook, p. 26

Photo: [Mary Hemingway and others]

Havana Herald

20 Sept 1952

1952

Bradley, Van Allen

Astonishing and Superb

Chicago Daily News

28 Aug 1952

Old Man Scrapbook, p. 26

Cuban Dictator with the People

Time

21 Apr 1952

1952

Chase, William D.

Author Tries Again after Producing
Literary Fiasco

28 Aug 1952

Old Man Scrapbook, p. 45

Canby, Henry Seidel

The Old Man and the Sea

Book of the Month Club Bulletin

Aug 1952

Davis, Hassoldt 6 Aug 1952
& Old Man and the Sea

Hill, Bob

Looking at Books

Spokane Chronicle

28 Aug 1952

Old Man Scrapbook, p. 46

Hutchens, John K.

Books and Things

New York Herald Tribune

28 Aug 1952

Old Man Scrapbook, p. 4

Ruark, Robert C.

A Line to the Heart

New York World Telegram

28 Aug 1952

Old Man Scrapbook, p. 47

The Old Man and the Sea. Take heart,
says Ernest. . .

Michigan City News-Disptach

28 Aug 1952

Old Man Scrapbook, p. 41

Brown, Cecil

Good Evening, Everyone

CBS Broadcast

29 Aug 1952

Old Man Scrapbook, p. 88

O'Neil, Frank

Books in the News: Hemingway's Itsy
Bitsy Novel Shows Champ at Top of Classic
Form

Cleveland News

28 Aug 1952

Old Man Scrapbook, p. 18

Cannon, Jimmy

The essence of courage is a well-kept
secret. . .

New York Post

29 Aug 1952

Old Man Scrapbook, p. 37

Prescott, Orville

Books of the Times

New York Times

28 Aug 1952

Old Man Scrapbook, p. 8

This Is San Francisco

San Francisco KCBS radio broadcast

29 Aug 1952

Old Man Scrapbook, p. 84

Rogers, W. G.

The Old Man and the Sea, by Ernest
Hemingway

Associated Press

28 Aug 1952

Old Man Scrapbook, p. 22

We have seen an advance copy of Ernest
Hemingway's new. . .

Dallas Neiman-Marcus Point of View

29 Aug 1952

Old Man Scrapbook, p. 18

Courage, Will and Spirit Glorified in a New Novel

Council Bluffs, Iowa, Nonpareil

30 Aug 1952

    Old Man Scrapbook, p. 78

Bond, Alice Dixon

    A New Classic Makes Its Bos Eleven Days Before Book Store Publication

    Boston Herald

    31 Aug 1952

        Old Man Scrapbook, p. 50

T.L.H.

    Hemingway Shows Old Power, Pictures Elemental Struggle

    Hartford, Connecticut, Times

    30 Aug 1952

        Old Man Scrapbook, p. 75

Dilley, Ray

    Hemingway Work Appears in Magazine, Book Issue

    Savannah News

    31 Aug 1952

        Old Man Scrapbook, p. 53

Scott, Eward

    Interesting if True. Real Cubans Just Like the White Sox

    Havan Post

    30 Aug 1952

        Old Man and the Sea

Dwight, Ogden G.

    The Master Touch

    Des Moines Sunday Register

    31 Aug 1952

        Old Man Scrapbook, p. 7

Bedell, W.D.

    Hemingway--An Old Man, a New Mood

    Houston Post

    31 Aug 1952

        Old Man Scrapbook, p. 30

V.P.H.

    Hemingway Writes Profoundly Moving Novel

    Omaha World-Herald

    31 Aug 1952

        Old Man Scrapbook, p. 48

Williams, Ernest E.

    Hemingway Package Startles Book World

    Fort Wayne News-Sentinel

    30 Aug 1952

        Old Man Scrapbook, p. 51

    Hemingway Story

    San Antonio Express

    31 Aug 1952

        Old Man Scrapbook, p. 66

Jenkins, Jan

A Hemingway Fish of Literary Fortune

Raleigh, N.C., News and Observer

31 Aug 1952

Old Man Scrapbook, p. 77

Putcamp, Luise, Jr.

Hemingway, Old Man, Win Triumph Over
Literary, if Not Real, Sharks

Dallas Times Herald

31 Aug 1952

Old Man Scrapbook, p. 33

Kennedy, Paul M.

An American Classic

Boston Globe

31 Aug 1952

Old Man Scrapbook, p. 31

Ross, Thomas W.

The Power of Old Hemingway

Colorado Springs Free Press

31 Aug 1952

Old Man Scrapbook, p. 49

Lipscomb, Anna

Book Notes

Beaumont Enterprise

31 Aug 1952

Old Man Scrapbook, p. 86

Sann, Paul

Across the River and into the Sea

New York Post

31 Aug 1952

Old Man Scrapbook, p. 36

C.O.

Old Man and the Sea: Hemingway Makes
Triumphal Return

Charlotte Observer

31 Aug 1952

Old Man Scrapbook, p. 52

Sprague, E. J.

Death and Affirmation

Colorado Springs Free Press

31 Aug 1952

Old Man Scrapbook, p. 50

O'Neill, Lois Decker

Looks at Books

Louisville Courier-Journal

31 Aug 1952

Old Man Scrapbook, p. 42

Tinkle, Lon

Reading and Writing: Now Hemingway's
Ancient Mariner: The Old Man and The Old
Master

Dalas News

31 Aug 1952

Old Man Scrapbook, p. 57

Wilson, Earl

 A Letter from Ernest Hemingway

 New York Post

 31 Aug 1952

   Old Man Scrapbook, p. 34

Ernest Hemingway. His new book The Old. . .

Vogue

Sept 1952

   Old Man and the Sea
   & Old Man Scrapbook, p. 41

Pickrel, Paul

 Outstanding Novels

 Yale Review

 Autumn 1952

   Old Man Scrapbook, p. 27

The Francis Jarman Show

Durham, N.C., WDNC, WDNC-FM radio
broadcast

[Sept 1952]

   Old Man Scrapbook, p. 88

Adamson, Hans Christian

 The Old Man and the Sea

 Columbia Scholastic Press Advisers
 Association

 [Sept 1952]

   Old Man Scrapbook, p. 16

Kinnaird, Clark

 The Old Man and the Sea

 King Features Syndicate

 [Sept 1952]

   Old Man Scrapbook, p. 23

Breit, Harvey

 The Old Man and the Sea

 The Nation

 [Sept 1952]

   Old Man Scrapbook, p. 43

Lagard, Gerald

 Hemingway Hero Fights Great Fish

 Long Beach Press

 [Sept 1952]

   Old Man Scrapbook, p. 79

Clune, Henry W.

 Seen and Heard: A Salutory Thing

 Rochester, N.Y., Democrat-Chronicle

 [Sept 1952]

   Old Man Scrapbook, p. 67

Rave Dept.: Go-Getter Copy of The Old
Man and the Sea

Writers' Newsletter

[Sept 1952]

   Old Man Scrapbook, p. 24

Weeks, Edward

    Hemingway at His Best

    The Atlantic Bookshelf

    Sept 1952

        Old Man Scrapbook, p. 22

Lerner, Max

    Old Man

    New York Post

    4 Sept 1952

        Old Man Scrapbook, p. 38

Blatchford, Nicholas

    The Endless Pursuit of Manliness

    Washington, D.C., News

    1 Sept 1952

        Old Man Scrapbook, p. 64

Lissner, Will

    The Old Man and the Sea

    The Catholic Messenger

    4 Sept 1952

        Old Man Scrapbook, p. 75

Walbridge, Earle F.

    Hemingway, Ernest, The Old Man and the Sea

    Library Journal

    1 Sept 1952

        Old Man Scrapbook, p. 11

The Old Man and the Sea. The story of an old. . .

    Publishers Weekly

    4 Sept 1952

        Old Man Scrapbook, p. 51

Newest Hemingway Ranks with His Best

Springfield, Mass., News

2 Sept 1952

        Old Man Scrapbook, p. 78

Barley, Rex

    Old Man Triumphs

    Los Angeles Daily Mirror

    5 Sept 1952

        Old Man Scrapbook, p. 3

Barnett, Chuck A. & Seymour Reit

    Niggling at Papa's Lines

    New York Post

    4 Sept 1952

        Old Man Scrapbook, p. 36

Douglas, Mary Stahlman

    Hemingway Hooks a Winner

    Nashville Banner

    5 Sept 1952

        Old Man Scrapbook, p. 63

Meyer, Lewis

The Values We Live By

Tulsa KTUL

5 Sept 1952

Old Man Scrapbook, p. 69

Leach, Joseph

The Old Man and the Sea

El Paso Herald

6 Sept 1952

Old Man Scrapbook, p. 31

Baker, Carlos

The Marvel Who Must Die: The Old
Man and the Sea

Saturday Review

6 Sept 1952

Old Man and the Sea
& Old Man Scrapbook, p. 15

The Old Man and the Sea, by Ernest
Hemingway, shows. . .

New Yorker

6 Sept 1952

Old Man Scrapbook, p. 20

Deacon, William Arthur

Hemingway Deals Tenderly with Aged Cuban
Fisherman

Toronto Globe and Mail

6 Sept 1952

Old Man Scrapbook, p. 73

Saunders, Bob

The Punch Is There: Still the Champion

Charlotte News

6 Sept 1952

Old Man Scrapbook, p. 53

Death Duel with Spearfish in Latest
Hemingway Opus

Toronto Star

6 Sept 1952

Old Man Scrapbook, p. 74

Smith, Harrison

There are only three characters. . .

Saturday Review: Book Service for
Newspapers

6 Sept 1952

Old Man Scrapbook, p. 17

Ernest Hemingway has written his greatest
story. . .

New York Morning Telegraph

6 Sept 1952

Old Man Scrapbook, p. 58

At Ease with the Authors

Lansing State Journal

7 Sept 1952

Old Man Scrapbook, p. 64

Barker, William J.

The Old Champ Can Still Write

Denver Post

7 Sept 1952

Old Man Scrapbook, p. 91

Connolly, Cyril

New Fiction: Mr. Hemingway's Golden Tale

London Times

7 Sept 1952

Old Man and the Sea
& Old Man Scrapbook, p. 72

Breit, Harvey

Talk with Ernest Hemingway

New York Times Book Review

7 Sept 1952

Old Man Scrapbook, p. 9

Cowley, Malcolm

Book Review: Hemingway's Novel Has the
Rich Simplicity of a Classic

New York Herald Tribune

7 Sept 1952

Old Man Scrapbook, p. 1

Butcher, Fanny

Hemingway at His Incomparable Best

Chicago Sunday Tribune

7 Sept 1952

Old Man Scrapbook, p. 11

Cross, Leslie

Mr. Hemingway and the Big Fish

Milwaukee Journal

7 Sept 1952

Old Man Scrapbook, p. 44

Cogburn, Anne

Hemingway's Classic Tragedy Emerges

Atlanta Constitution

7 Sept 1952

Old Man Scrapbook, p. 32

Dobbier, Maurice

Hemingway's Great Suspenseful Story

Providence, R.I., Journal

7 Sept 1952

Old Man Scrapbook, p. 71

Davis, Robert Gorham

Hemingway's Tragic Fisherman

New York Times Book Review

7 Sept 1952

Old Man Scrapbook, p. 5

Evers, Karl J.

Hemingway's New Novel Great in Its
Simplicity

Knoxville News-Sentinel

7 Sept 1952

Old Man Scrapbook, p. 25

Foot, Robert O.

    Hemingway Himself Again

    Pasadena Star News

    7 Sept 1952

                Old Man Scrapbook, p. 28

Kogan, Herman

    Another Hemingway Masterpiece

    Chicago Sun-Times

    7 Sept 1952

                Old Man Scrapbook, p. 29

Heyberg, Max

    Hemingway Fuzzy but Still Among Greatest

    Newark, N.J., News

    7 Sept 1952

                Old Man Scrapbook, p. 83

Leigh, Michael

    The Old Man and the Sea

    Pensacola, Florida, News Journal

    7 Sept 1952

                Old Man Scrapbook, p. 83

Jackson, Joseph Henry

    Hemingway at His Best in a Story of a Fisherman and His Catch

    San Francisco Chronicle

    7 Sept 1952

                Old Man Scrapbook, p. 12

Maner, William

    Hemingway Wins Praise on Old Man

    Richmond, Virginia, Times-Dispatch

    7 Sept 1952

                Old Man Scrapbook, p. 34

Kirschten, Ernest

    A Junior Moby Dick

    St. Louis Post-Dispatch

    7 Sept 1952

                Old Man Scrapbook, p. 59

Meyer, Lewis

    Hemingway Writes Masterful Story

    Tulsa World

    7 Sept 1952

                Old Man Scrapbook, p. 13

Kofold, Jack

    Hemingway Proves Again He Is a Story Man

    Miami Herald

    7 Sept 1952

                Old Man Scrapbook, p. 62

Monroe, Harold

    Hemingway's Latest Tells of Man-Nature Sturggle

    Fort Worth Star

    7 Sept 1952

                Old Man Scrapbook, p. 62

Muir, Edwin

Two Novelists

London Observer

7 Sept 1952

Old Man Scrapbook, p. 72

Perkins, Robert L.

One Man's Pegasus: Don't Miss Hemingway's Latest

Denver Rocky Mountain News

7 Sept 1952

Old Man Scrapbook, p. 56

Myers, Sim

This Week's Feature Book: The Old Hemingway Returns to Create Greatest Masterpiece

Lubbock, Texas, Avalanche-Journal

7 Sept 1952

Old Man Scrapbook, p. 85

Seward, William W., Jr.

Hemingway: The Sea, a Marlin and Man

Norfolk Virginian-Pilot

7 Sept 1952

Old Man Scrapbook, p. 82

North, Sterling

Hemingway's New Book Has Deep Meaning

Buffalo Courier Express

7 Sept 1952

Old Man Scrapbook, p. 80

Tinkle, Lon

Reading and Writing: Papa Hemingway Is, and We Repeat, Again Writing at Top of His Form

Dallas Morning News

7 Sept 1952

Old Man Scrapbook, p. 58

The Old Man and the Sea. Regardless of what. . .

Orlando Sentinel-Sun

7 Sept 1952

Old Man Scrapbook, p. 81

Webster, Harvey Curtis

Looks at Books

Louisville, Kentucky, Courier-Journal

7 Sept 1952

Old Man Scrapbook, p. 40

Parsons, Margaret

Never Alone on the Sea

Worcester, Mass., Telegram

7 Sept 1952

Old Man Scrapbook, p. 38

Yeiser, Frederick

Some of the Recent Fiction

Cincinnati Enquirer

7 Sept 1952

Old Man Scrapbook, p. 37

Book of the Week: The Old Man and the Sea
Quick
8 Sept 1952
                    Old Man Scrapbook, p. 45

The Old Man and the Sea. A long short
story. . .
Virginia Kirkus Bulletin
8 Sept 1952

                    Old Man Scrapbook, p. 46

Clean and Straight
Time
8 Sept 1952
                    Old Man Scrapbook, p. 21

Price, Emerson
Hemingway's Yarn Not That Good
Cleveland Press
9 Sept 1952
                    Old Man Scrapbook, p. 56

Industry! Hemingway's Gimmick
Newsweek
8 Sept 1952
                    Old Man Scrapbook, p. 66

Wilson, Earl
Hemingway Tells of Yen for His Adopted
Homeland
Havana Herald
10 Sept 1952
                    Old Man and the Sea

Lunstrom, Richard H., S.J.
    The Old Man and the Sea
    Catholic Review Service
    8 Sept 1952
                    Old Man Scrapbook, p. 87

Book of the Week: The Old Man and the Sea
Jet
11 Sept 1952
                    Old Man Scrapbook, p. 59

Manchester, William
    Hemingway's Story of Man and Marlin
    Baltimore Sun
    8 Sept 1952
                    Old Man Scrapbook, p. 78

Dean, Edith
    From a Woman's Corner: Man's Grandeurs and
    Sea's Power
    Fort Worth Press
    11 Sept 1952
                    Old Man Scrapbook, p. 68

Hormel, Olive Deane

    The Artist and the Millions

    Christian Science Monitor

    11 Sept 1952

          Old Man Scrapbook, p. 24

Cody, Ernest

    Books: A Minority Report

    Columbus, Ohio, Dispatch

    14 Sept 1952

          Old Man Scrapbook, p. 79

N.H.

    Book Shelf: The Old Man and the Sea

    Catholic Review

    12 Sept 1952

          Old Man Scrapbook, p. 39

Klein, Francis A.

    Books--What's New

    St. Louis Globe-Democrat

    14 Sept 1952

          Old Man Scrapbook, p. 60

Sharpe, Marjorie Bright

    Ladies in the News

    San Bernardino, California, KITO radio
    broadcast

    12 Sept 1952

          Old Man Scrapbook, p. 87

Patrick, Corbin

    Book Nook: Hemingway in Form

    Indianapolis Star

    14 Sept 1952

          Old Man Scrapbook, p. 60

Gardiner, Harold C.

    Pathetic Fallacy

    America

    13 Sept 1952

          Old Man Scrapbook, p. 33

Sherman, John K.

    Hemingway's Story of Old Fisherman Is a
    Triumph of Rugged Simplicity

    Minneapolis Tribune

    14 Sept 1952

          Old Man Scrapbook, p. 65

Hofson, Laura

    Trade Winds. With everybody spewing. . .

    Saturday Review

    13 Sept 1952

          Old Man Scrapbook, p. 19

Smith, Stan

    Woods and Waters

    New York Sunday News

    14 Sept 1952

          Old Man Scrapbook, p. 61

Spearman, Walter

The Literary Lantern: With The Old Man
and The Sea Hemingway Regains Lost Stature

Asheville, N.C., Citizen-Times

14 Sept 1952

Old Man Scrapbook, p. 80

Webster, Harvey Curtis

Hemingway's Saga of Futility

New Leader

22 Sept 1952

Old Man Scrapbook, p. 93

Webb, Walter Prescott

Hemingway Hassle: Webb, DeGolyer, et Al.

Dallas News

14 Sept 1952

Old Man Scrapbook, p. 92

Scott, Edward

Interesting if True: The Champions

Havana Post

25 Sept 1952

Old Man and theSea

Spicehandler, Miriam

Book Front: The Old Man and the Sea

Justice

15 Sept 1952

Old Man Scrapbook, p. 86

The Old Man and the Sea. For all the
grade-school. . .

Holiday

Oct 1952

Old Man Scrapbook, p. 20

Krim, Seymour

Ernest Hemingway: Valor and Defeat

Commonweal

19 Sept 1952

Old Man Scrapbook, p. 54

Parsons, Louella O.

Hemingway's Magic Touch

Cosmopolitan

Oct 1952

1952

Adams, J. Donald

Speaking of Books

New York Times

21 Sept 1952

Old Man Scrapbook, p. 94

North, Sterling

Sterling North Reviews the Books

[3 Oct 1952]

1952 &
North, Sterling 3 Oct 1952

Booth, Richard W.

Ennui in the Afternoon, or What Papa
Never Told Me

The Daily Princetonian

3 Nov 1952

Baker, Carlos 7 Nov 1952

Books I Have Liked

Dec 1952

Ross, Lillian 9 Dec 1952

Ritz, Charles

J'ai vecu avec Hemingway: Le Vieil Home
et la Mer dans les eaux des Caraibes

Paris-presse-l'intransigeant

29 Nov 1952

Old Man and the Sea

Pryor, Thomas M.

Hollywood Canvas

[New York Times]

[18 Jan 1953]

Hayward, Leland 11 Feb 1953

Smith, Virginia Beck

The Old Man and the Sea

Extension

Dec 1952

The Old Man and the Sea

Guernsey, Otis L., Jr.

The Elusive Art of a Hollywood Director

[New York Herald Tribune]

[25 Jan 1953]

Hayward, Leland 11 Feb 1953

Photo: To Join the 7th Army

The Stars and Stripes

4 Dec 1952

Barrett, John 4 Dec 1952

Weiler, A. H.

On the Local Scene

New York Times

25 Jan 1953

Hayward, Leland 11 Feb 1953

Photo: What Chicago Wears

Chicago Daily News

10 Dec 1952

Miller, Madelaine Hemingway
11 Dec 1952

Green, Abel

Tri-Dimension's Hectic Race: Don't Wanna
Get Left at the Post

Variety

28 Jan 1953

Hayward, Leland 11 Feb 1953

Beer, Thomas

    Death at 5:45 P.M.

    American Spectator--entire edition

    Feb 1933

          1933

Lyons, Leonard

    The Lyons Den

    New York Post

    10 Feb 1953

          1953

Crowther, Bosley

    Images in Space

    [New York Times]

    [8 Feb 1953]

        Hayward, Leland 11 Feb 1953

Drive-Ins Shaping Up As 3-D Era's Orphan
Annies; Screen, Light Problems

[Variety]

[11 Feb 1953]

        Hayward, Leland 11 Feb 1953

Lyons, Leonard

    The Lyons Den

    New York Post

    8 Feb 1953

          1953

(Copies for the entire week were sent to EH
by the New York Post, envelope dated 16 Feb 1953

Lyons, Leonard

    The Lyons Den

    New York Post

    11 Feb 1953

          1953

Pryor, Thomas M.

    Hollywood Uproar

    New York Times

    8 Feb 1953

        Hayward, Leland, 11 Feb 1953

Parsons, Luella

    Spencer Tracy Out on Top in Scramble for
    Acting Plum

    New York Journal American

    11 Feb 1953

          1953

Lyons, Leonard

    The Lyons Den

    New York Post

    9 Feb 1953

          1953

Writers Also Will Have to Script Their
Stuff in 3-D-Arthur Scwartz

[Variety]--and other articles from same #
[11 Feb 1953]

        Hayward, Leland 11 Feb 1953

Pelswick, Rose

3 Dimension at the Rialto

New York Journal American

11 Feb 1953

Hayward, Leland   11 Feb 1953

Guernsey, Otis L., Jr.

The 3-Dimension Fever Grips Hollywood

New York Herald Tribune

[15 Feb 1953]

Hayward, Leland   11 Feb 1953

H.H.T.

Tri·orama Program of Four Short Subjects
Illustrating a Stereoscopic. . .

New York Times

11 Feb 1953

Hayward, Leland   11 Feb 1953

Poore, Charles

Books of the Times

New York Times

26 Feb 1953

1953

Lyons, Leonard

The Lyons Den

New York Post

12 Feb 1953

1953

Seward, William W., Jr.

Recent Critical Volumne Examines
Hemingway

Norfolk Virginian-Pilot

1 Mar 1953

Seward, William W., Jr.
2 Mar 1953

Lyons, Leonard

The Lyons Den

New York Post

13 Feb 1953

1953

Gran Recepcion en la Embagada Britanica

Havana Diario de la Marina

2 Mar 1953

1953

Pryor, Thomas M.

Hemingway Novel Is Eyed for Screen

New York Times

14 Feb 1953

1953

Hemingway Wins Pulitzer Award

[4 May 1953]

1953

Williams, Verne O.

UM Scientist Near Solution of The Great Tuna Mystery

Miami Daily News

17 May 1953

1953

Lyons, Leonard

A Day in Town with Hemingway

Minneapolis Star

9 July 1953

1953

Scott, Edward

Interesting if True: The Mountain that Went to Elizabeth

Havana

2 June 1953

1953

For those who like their reading in short jumps. . .

Paterson, N.J., Call

25 July 1953

Scrapbook 54, p. 45

Concurso Internacional de Pesca en Opcion al Trofeo Hemingway

Havana

9 June 1953

1953

Fugitive Rebels Begin to Surrender to Army

[Aug 1953]

Rakow, William

Lyons, Leonard

The Lyons Den: A Day in Town with Hemingway

New York Post

26 June 1953

1953

Linklater, Eric

My marks and scars I carry with me

Aug 1953

Scrapbook 54, p. 37

Ernest Culled and Collected

Los Angeles Mirror

3 July 1953

Scrapbook 54, p. 44

Wagenknecht, Edward

A Collection of Hemingway

[Chicago Tribune]

[Aug 1953]

Scrapbook 54, p. 44

Walbridge, Earle

    Ernest Hemingway. A Hemingway Reader

    [Aug 1953]

        Scrapbook 54, p. 45

Gribben, J. C.

    Collections: The Hemingway Reader

    Cincinnati Enquirer

    30 Aug 1953

        Scrapbook 54, p. 43

Buchwald, Art

    Europe's Lighter Side: For Whom the
    Bloody Marys Toll

    Paris New York Herald Tribune

    5 Aug 1953

        1953

    The Hemingway Reader

    St. Louis Globe Democrat

    30 Aug 1953

        Scrapbook 54, p. 43

J.B.

    TV Poses No Serious Threat while
    Hemingway is Active

    Charlotte, N.C., Observer

    23 Aug 1953

        Scrapbook 54, p. 45

Herzberg, Max

    Impressive Collection of Hemingway's Work

    Newark Evening News

    30 Aug 1953

        Scrapbook 54, p. 43

Brady, Charles A.

    Ernest Hemingway, When He's Good, Is
    Incomparable

    Buffalo Evening News

    29 Aug 1953

        Scrapbook 54, p. 43

Johnson, Dick

    Hemingway? Fine and True

    Dallas Daily Times Herald

    30 Aug 1953

        Scrapbook 54, p. 43

Campbell, Don

    Hemingway Reader Sure to Evoke
    Controversies

    Indianapolis Star

    30 Aug 1953

        Scrapbook 54, p. 42

Morrissey, Ralph

    Under the Green Lamp: Chronicle of Modern
    Chivalry

    Nashville Tennessean

    30 Aug 1953

        Scrapbook 54, p. 42

Murray, Don

Ernest Hemingway Reader Planned for Pleasures

Boston Sunday Herald

30 Aug 1953

Scrapbook 54, p. 45

Smith, Ted

The Hemingway Reader

[31 Aug 1953]

Scrapbook 54, p. 44

Sandrof, Ivan

Best of the Old Maestro

Worcester, Mass., Sun-Telegram

30 Aug 1953

Scrapbook 54, p. 41

Hemingway, Mary

Living with a Genius!

London, The Modern Woman

Sept 1953

1953

Washburn, Beatrice

Books in Review

Miami Herald

30 Aug 1953

Scrapbook 54, p. 42

O'Neill, Frank

Here's a Load of Hemingway

Cleveland News

1 Sept 1953

Scrapbook 54, p. 43

Gannett, Lewis

Book Review

New York Herald Tribune

31 Aug 1953

Scrapbook 54, p. 45

Learning, Delmar

Midwestern Book Shelf

5 Sept 1953

Scrapbook 54, p. 45

Prescott, Orville

Books of the Times

New York Times

31 Aug 1953

Scrapbook 54, p. 46

A Few Introductory Remarks

Providence, R.I., Sun-Journal

6 Sept 1953

Scrapbook 54, p. 41

Davis, Evangeline

    A Fine New Hemingway Collection

    Greensboro, N.C., Daily News

    6 Sept 1953

            Scrapbook 54, p. 41

Photo: At a Small Party. . .

Detroit Free Press

12 Oct 1953

            Scrapbook 54, p. 34

Porterfield, Waldon

    A Hemingway Anthology

    Milwaukee Journal

    6 Sept 1953

            Scrapbook 54, p. 45

Celler, Emanuel

    The Book and Censor

    ALA Bulletin

    Nov 1953

            Scrapbook 54, p. 35

Farrell, James T.

    Guadagnamo Troppo!

    Epoca

    13 Sept 1953

            Scrapbook 54, p. 21

Molleson

    Quentin Reynolds Duped

    [New York Herald Tribune]

    [15 Nov 1953]

            Scrapbook 54, p. 40-41

F.T.K.

    The Hemingway Reader

    Long Beach, Indiania, Press Telegram

    16 Sept 1953

            Scrapbook 54, p. 42

Molleson, John

    Man Who Talked Too Much: Money Back for
    Hoax Book Buyers

    16 Nov [1953]

            Scrapbook 54, p. 41

    Sterling North Reviews the Books

    [New York] World Telegram

    22 Sept 1953

            Scrapbook 54, p. 43

    Gran Acusacion de Braden

    [El Pais]

    [23 Dec 1953]

            Scrapbook 54, p. 40

Salve a Cuba, dice Braden

[Manana]

[28 Dec 1953]

Scrapbook 54, p. 40

Williams, Tennessee

A Writer's Quest for a Parnassus

New York Times

13 Aug 1950

1950

Title Defender

Newsweek

Plummer, William L.
12 Apr 1950

Entire edition

John O'London's Weekly

18 Aug 1950

1950

Operation on Waldo Peirce is Considered

19 Apr 1950

Browne, Kenneth H.
1 May 1950

Bedell, W. D.

Across the River and Into the Trees

Houston Post

10 Sept 1950

Across the River

Barnes, Howard

On the Screen

New York Herald Tribune

Shipman, Evan   23 Apr 1950

O'Hara, John

Across the River and into the Trees

New York Times Book Review

10 Sept 1950

Across the River

G.N.

Sono io il Vecchio del Mare ma Hemingway
e un uomo senza parola

Tempo

7 June 1950

1950

Paul, Elliot

Thanks to Ernest

Providence, R.I., Sunday Journal

10 Sept 1950

Across the River

Sandroff, Ivan

    Our World Runs Short

    Worcester, Mass., Telegram

    10 Sept 1950

        Across the River

Hoyt, Elizabeth North

    The Colonel

    Cedar Rapids Gazette

    17 Sept 1950

        Across the River

Seward, William W., Jr.

    A Brooding Awareness of the Tragic
    Marks Hemingway's Return to Writing

    Norfolk Virginian-Pilot

    10 Sept 1950

        Across the River

Fantasy Under the Trees (Now We are
Fifty)

Punch (England)

20 Sept 1950

        Scribner, Charles, Sr.
        16 Oct 1950

On the Ropes
& Hemingway Is Bitter about Nobody--
But His Colonel Is

Time

11 Sept 1950

        Across the River

Babcock, Frederic

    Among the Authors

    Chicago Sunday Tribune

    24 Sept 1950

        Across the River

Breit, Harvey

    Talk with Mr. Hemingway

    New York Times Book Review

    17 Sept 1950

        1950

McGill, Ralph

    Bearing as if with Tongs

    5 Oct 1950

        1950

Hemingway: Pro and Con

Nashville Tennessean

17 Sept 1950

        1950

donor: Matthew Bruccoli

Obituary: Wesley Dilworth

Detroit News

9 Oct 1950

        Sanford, Marcelline Hemingway
        9 Oct 1950

Clune, Henry W.

Seen and Heard

Rochester Democratic and Chronicle

12 Oct 1950

Scribner, Charles, Sr.
16 Oct 1950

Poore, Charles

Books of the Times

New York Times

26 Oct 1940

Scribner, Charles, Sr.
27 Oct 1950

Hicks, Granville

The Critics Have Never Been Easy on
Ernest Hemingway

New York Times Book Review

15 Oct 1950

Scribner, Charles, Sr.
15 Oct 1950

Waugh, Evelyn

The Case of Mr. Hemingway

Commonweal

3 Nov 1950

Scribner, Charles, Sr.
31 Oct 1950

Rugoff, Milton

Much Smoke, Some Sparks

New York Herald Tribune Book Review

15 Oct 1950

Scribner, Charles, Sr.
15 Oct 1950

Author's Nephew Gets Exciting Call

Miller, Madelaine H. M.
14 Nov 1950

Galbraith, John K.

Side Glances

20 Oct 1950

Scribner, Charles, Sr.
21 Oct 1950

McGill, Ralph

Faulkner's Nobel Prize

14 Nov 1950

1950

Markfield, Wallace

Hemingway's Articulate Ox

The New-Leader

21 Oct 1950

Scribner, Charles, Sr.
27 Oct 1950

McGill, Ralph

The Agony and the Sweat

[15 Oct 1950]

1950

Gary Cooper Arrives
Havana Post
30 Dec 1950

    1950

Hare, Lionel
    The Fabulous Mr. Hemingway
    Illustrated
    10 Feb 1951

        1951

Hemingway, Mary
    Girl at Sea
Cosmopolitan
[1951]

    1951

Johnson, Erskine
    [A column mentioning Ernest Hemingway]
    Los Angeles Daily News
    25 Apr 1951
            Cowley, Malcolm   8 June 1951

Ferrer Musical to Star Baker
New York Daily News
31 Jan 1951
        Samuels, Lee   6 Feb 1951

Desastre Aereo
Havana Prensa Libra
26 Apr 1951

        1951

McCord, Bert
    News of the Theatre: South Atlantic
    New York Herald Tribune
    31 Jan 1951
            Samuels, Lee   6 Feb 1951

Baker, Carlos
    25 Years of a Hemingway Classic
    New York Times Book Review
    29 Apr 1951
            Baker, Carlos   4 May 1951

Robilant, Carlo di
    Hemingway et Venezia

    [Feb 1951]
            Robilant, Carlo di
            6 Feb 1951

Mrs. Hemingway, Mother of the Novelist, Dies

    [June 1951]
                1951

Services in Illinois for Writer's Mother

[June 1951]

1951

Ruark, Robert

Hemingway's New Novel Puts Papa Back on Beam

[1952]

Old Man and the Sea

Johnson, Erskine

Exclusively Yours

Los Angeles Daily News

11 June 1951

Ross, Lillian   10 July 1951

Lyons, Leonard

In this Corner: Havana, Cuba

Minneapolis Star

12 Jan 1952

1952

Rosetahl, Sherwin H.

Protection without Statutory Copyright

Authors League News

July 1951

Cowley, Malcolm   3 Nov 1951

Cranston, Herbert

When Hemingway Earned Half a Cent a Word on The Toronto Star

New York Herald Tribune Book Review

13 Jan 1952

Baker, Carlos 12 Jan 1952
Fenton, Charles 10 Jan 1952

Drinks on Monty

Life Magazine

Cochran, James   18 July 1951

Downing, Margot

He Wrote Better in School Says Hemingway's Mother

Sanford, Marcelline H.
26 Jan 1952

Pauline Hemingway, 55, Second Wife of Hemingway

New York Herald Tribune

2 Oct 1951

1951

Photo: [Mary Hemingway and others]

Havana Herald

20 Sept 1952

1952

Cuban Dictator with the People

Time

21 Apr 1952

1952

Chase, William D.

Author Tries Again after Producing
Literary Fiasco

28 Aug 1952

Old Man Scrapbook, p. 45

Canby, Henry Seidel

The Old Man and the Sea

Book of the Month Club Bulletin

Aug 1952

Davis, Hassoldt 6 Aug 1952
& Old Man and the Sea

Hill, Bob

Looking at Books

Spokane Chronicle

28 Aug 1952

Old Man Scrapbook, p. 46

Obituary: Mark Murphy

[4 Aug 1952]

Hotchner, A. E. 4 Aug 1952

Hutchens, John K.

Books and Things

New York Herald Tribune

28 Aug 1952

Old Man Scrapbook, p. 4

McCaslin, Walt

New Kind of Hemingway

Dayton Daily News

24 Aug 1952

Old Man Scrapbook, p. 26

The Old Man and the Sea. Take heart,
says Ernest. . .

Michigan City News-Disptach

28 Aug 1952

Old Man Scrapbook, p. 41

Bradley, Van Allen

Astonishing and Superb

Chicago Daily News

28 Aug 1952

Old Man Scrapbook, p. 26

O'Neil, Frank

Books in the News: Hemingway's Itsy
Bitsy Novel Shows Champ at Top of Classic
Form

Cleveland News

28 Aug 1952

Old Man Scrapbook, p. 18

Prescott, Orville

    Books of the Times

    New York Times

    28 Aug 1952

        Old Man Scrapbook, p. 8

This Is San Francisco

San Francisco KCBS radio broadcast

29 Aug 1952

    Old Man Scrapbook, p. 84

Rogers, W. G.

    The Old Man and the Sea, by Ernest
    Hemingway

    Associated Press

    28 Aug 1952

        Old Man Scrapbook, p. 22

We have seen an advance copy of Ernest
Hemingway's new. . .

Dallas Neiman-Marcus Point of View

29 Aug 1952

    Old Man Scrapbook, p. 18

Ruark, Robert C.

    A Line to the Heart

    New York World Telegram

    28 Aug 1952

        Old Man Scrapbook, p. 47

Courage, Will and Spirit Glorified in a
New Novel

Council Bluffs, Iowa, Nonpareil

30 Aug 1952

    Old Man Scrapbook, p. 78

Brown, Cecil

    Good Evening, Everyone

    CBS Broadcast

    29 Aug 1952

        Old Man Scrapbook, p. 88

T.L.H.

    Hemingway Shows Old Power, Pictures
    Elemental Struggle

    Hartford, Connecticut, Times

    30 Aug 1952

        Old Man Scrapbook, p. 75

Cannon, Jimmy

    The essence of courage is a well-kept
    secret. . .

    New York Post

    29 Aug 1952

        Old Man Scrapbook, p. 37

Scott, Eward

    Interesting if True. Real Cubans Just
    Like the White Sox

    Havan Post

    30 Aug 1952

        Old Man and the Sea

Bedell, W.D.

    Hemingway--An Old Man, a New Mood

    Houston Post

    31 Aug 1952

        Old Man Scrapbook, p. 30

V.P.H.

    Hemingway Writes Profoundly Moving Novel

    Omaha World-Herald

    31 Aug 1952

        Old Man Scrapbook, p. 48

Williams, Ernest E.

    Hemingway Package Startles Book World

    Fort Wayne News-Sentinel

    30 Aug 1952

        Old Man Scrapbook, p. 51

Hemingway Story

San Antonio Express

31 Aug 1952

        Old Man Scrapbook, p. 66

Bond, Alice Dixon

    A New Classic Makes Its Bos Eleven Days
    Before Book Store Publication

    Boston Herald

    31 Aug 1952

        Old Man Scrapbook, p. 50

Jenkins, Jan

    A Hemingway Fish of Literary Fortune

    Raleigh, N.C., News and Observer

    31 Aug 1952

        Old Man Scrapbook, p. 77

Dilley, Ray

    Hemingway Work Appears in Magazine,
    Book Issue

    Savannah News

    31 Aug 1952

        Old Man Scrapbook, p. 53

Kennedy, Paul M.

    An American Classic

    Boston Globe

    31 Aug 1952

        Old Man Scrapbook, p. 31

Dwight, Ogden G.

    The Master Touch

    Des Moines Sunday Register

    31 Aug 1952

        Old Man Scrapbook, p. 7

Lipscomb, Anna

    Book Notes

    Beaumont Enterprise

    31 Aug 1952

        Old Man Scrapbook, p. 86

C.O.

Old Man and the Sea: Hemingway Makes
Triumphal Return

Charlotte Observer

31 Aug 1952

Old Man Scrapbook, p. 52

Sprague, E. J.

Death and Affirmation

Colorado Springs Free Press

31 Aug 1952

Old Man Scrapbook, p. 50

O'Neill, Lois Decker

Looks at Books

Louisville Courier-Journal

31 Aug 1952

Old Man Scrapbook, p. 42

Tinkle, Lon

Reading and Writing: Now Hemingway's
Ancient Mariner: The Old Man and The Old
Master

Dalas News

31 Aug 1952

Old Man Scrapbook, p. 57

Putcamp, Luise, Jr.

Hemingway, Old Man, Win Triumph Over
Literary, if Not Real, Sharks

Dallas Times Herald

31 Aug 1952

Old Man Scrapbook, p. 33

Wilson, Earl

A Letter from Ernest Hemingway

New York Post

31 Aug 1952

Old Man Scrapbook, p. 34

Ross, Thomas W.

The Power of Old Hemingway

Colorado Springs Free Press

31 Aug 1952

Old Man Scrapbook, p. 49

Pickrel, Paul

Outstanding Novels

Yale Review

Autumn 1952

Old Man Scrapbook, p. 27

Sann, Paul

Across the River and into the Sea

New York Post

31 Aug 1952

Old Man Scrapbook, p. 36

Adamson, Hans Christian

The Old Man and the Sea

Columbia Scholastic Press Advisers
Association

[Sept 1952]

Old Man Scrapbook, p. 16

Breit, Harvey

    The Old Man and the Sea

    The Nation

    [Sept 1952]

                Old Man Scrapbook, p. 43

Lagard, Gerald

    Hemingway Hero Fights Great Fish

    Long Beach Press

    [Sept 1952]

                Old Man Scrapbook, p. 79

Clune, Henry W.

    Seen and Heard: A Salutory Thing

    Rochester, N.Y., Democrat-Chronicle

    [Sept 1952]

                Old Man Scrapbook, p. 67

    Rave Dept.: Go-Getter Copy of The Old Man and the Sea

    Writers' Newsletter

    [Sept 1952]

                Old Man Scrapbook, p. 24

Ernest Hemingway. His new book The Old. . .

    Vogue

    Sept 1952

                Old Man and the Sea
                & Old Man Scrapbook, p. 41

Weeks, Edward

    Hemingway at His Best

    The Atlantic Bookshelf

    Sept 1952

                Old Man Scrapbook, p. 22

The Francis Jarman Show

    Durham, N.C., WDNC, WDNC-FM radio broadcast

    [Sept 1952]

                Old Man Scrapbook, p. 88

Blatchford, Nicholas

    The Endless Pursuit of Manliness

    Washington, D.C., News

    1 Sept 1952

                Old Man Scrapbook, p. 64

Kinnaird, Clark

    The Old Man and the Sea

    King Features Syndicate

    [Sept 1952]

                Old Man Scrapbook, p. 23

Walbridge, Earle F.

    Hemingway, Ernest, The Old Man and the Sea

    Library Journal

    1 Sept 1952

                Old Man Scrapbook, p. 11

Newest Hemingway Ranks with His Best
Springfield, Mass., News
2 Sept 1952

>> Old Man Scrapbook, p. 78

Barley, Rex
>> Old Man Triumphs
>> Los Angeles Daily Mirror
>> 5 Sept 1952

>>> Old Man Scrapbook, p. 3

Barnett, Chuck A. & Seymour Reit
>> Niggling at Papa's Lines
>> New York Post
>> 4 Sept 1952

>>> Old Man Scrapbook, p. 36

Douglas, Mary Stahlman
>> Hemingway Hooks a Winner
>> Nashville Banner
>> 5 Sept 1952

>>> Old Man Scrapbook, p. 63

Lerner, Max
>> Old Man
>> New York Post
>> 4 Sept 1952

>>> Old Man Scrapbook, p. 38

Meyer, Lewis
>> The Values We Live By
>> Tulsa KTUL
>> 5 Sept 1952

>>> Old Man Scrapbook, p. 69

Lissner, Will
>> The Old Man and the Sea
>> The Catholic Messenger
>> 4 Sept 1952

>>> Old Man Scrapbook, p. 75

Baker, Carlos
>> The Marvel Who Must Die: The Old
>> Man and the Sea
>> Saturday Review
>> 6 Sept 1952

>>> Old Man and the Sea
>>> & Old Man Scrapbook, p. 15

The Old Man and the Sea. The story
of an old. . .
Publishers Weekly
4 Sept 1952

>> Old Man Scrapbook, p. 51

Deacon, William Arthur
>> Hemingway Deals Tenderly with Aged Cuban
>> Fisherman
>> Toronto Globe and Mail
>> 6 Sept 1952

>>> Old Man Scrapbook, p. 73

Death Duel with Spearfish in Latest
Hemingway Opus

Toronto Star

6 Sept 1952

      Old Man Scrapbook, p. 74

Smith, Harrison

    There are only three characters. . .

    Saturday Review: Book Service for
    Newspapers

    6 Sept 1952

        Old Man Scrapbook, p. 17

Ernest Hemingway has written his greatest
story. . .

New York Morning Telegraph

6 Sept 1952

      Old Man Scrapbook, p. 58

At Ease with the Authors

Lansing State Journal

7 Sept 1952

      Old Man Scrapbook, p. 64

Leach, Joseph

    The Old Man and the Sea

    El Paso Herald

    6 Sept 1952

        Old Man Scrapbook, p. 31

Flanagan, Barbara

    Hemingway Wife Grand Says Bronko

    Minneapolis Tribune

    1954

        1954

The Old Man and the Sea, by Ernest
Hemingway, shows. . .

New Yorker

6 Sept 1952

      Old Man Scrapbook, p. 20

Forse Hemingway nemmeno sa che il capote
lo odia

Le Ore

[1954]

      Scrapbook 54, p. 16

Saunders, Bob

    The Punch Is There: Still the Champion

    Charlotte News

    6 Sept 1952

        Old Man Scrapbook, p. 53

Glauri, Aldo

    Le Nove Vite di Hemingway

    [1954]

        Scrapbook 54, p. 5

Hemingway, Ernest
    Partita di Caccia
    Tempo
    [1954]
            Scrapbook 54, p. 2

Vittorini, Elio
    Ne Aveva Parlato con Vittorini

    [1954]
            Scrapbook 54, p. 7

Najera
    Ernest Hemingway in Tolosa

    [1954]
            Scrapbook 54, p. 43

Zaldivar, Rodolfo Rodriquez
    Hemingway en la Havana
    Bohemia
    [1954]
            1954

Nella Bassa Friulana e nat il penultimo
romanzo di Hemingway

    [1954]
            Scrapbook 54, p. 8

Accidente en Uganda
Cartelei
[Jan 54]
            Zebra Scrapbook, p. 2

Photo: Hemingway, un den sich ein. . .

    [1954]
            Scrapbook 54, p. 21

Aparecen Ilesos el Novelista Hemingway
y su Esposa

    [Jan 1954]
            Scrapbook 54, p. 24

H.R.
    Por el doblan las campanas

    [Jan 1954]
            Scrapbook 54, p. 60

Attorno ad Hemingway Barrivano gli Elefanti
Oggi
[Jan 1954]
            Scrapbook 54, p. 10

Author and wife worlds better
[Tanganyika] Standard
[Jan 1954]

> Antelope Scrapbook, p. 41

Every once in a while I find myself. . .

[Jan 1954]

> Antelope Scrapbook, p. 11

Brush with Death

[Jan 1954]

> Antelope Scrapbook, p. 12

Gardner, Hy
> Early Bird Coast to Coast

[Jan 1954]

> Antelope Scrapbook, p. 12

Cartoon: There were the Hemingways. . .

[Jan 1954]

> Antelope Scrapbook, p. 29

Hemingway he vivido como en sus novelas,
una gran aventura
Madrid
[Jan 1954]

> Scrapbook 54, p. 72

Ernest Hemingway mit dem Flugzeug
abgesturzt

[Jan 1954]

> Scrapbook 54, p. 4

Hemingway Jolts Out of Jungles--by Auto

[Jan 1954]

> Scrapbook 54, p. 63

Ernest Hemingway seemed to have a
premonition. . .

[Jan 1954]

> Antelope Scrapbook, p. 11

Hemingway Lives to Write Again

[Jan 1954]

> Antelope Scrapbook, p. 28

Hemingway Luck Prevails Again

[Jan 1954]

Antelope Scrapbook, p. 29

Kinnear, Michael

E Rususcitato come Prevedeva

[Jan 1954]

Scrapbook 54, p. 7

Hemingway Party Safe

[Uganda Herald]

[Jan 1954]

Antelope Scrapbook, p. 41

Man Talking to Himself

[Jan 1954]

Antelope Scrapbook, p. 11

Hemingway Suffers Only Arm Injury as
Result of Crash in Lion Country

[Jan 1954]

Antelope Scrapbook, p. 29

The Midnight Earl--Ernest Hemingway's Big
Book

[Jan 1954]

Antelope Scrapbook, p. 12

Hemingway Tells of Two Air Crashes

London [Daily Telegraph]

[Jan 1954]

Antelope Scrapbook, p. 40

Mr. Hemingway, the novelist, and. . .

London Times Weekly Review

[Jan 1954]

Antelope Scrapbook, p. 40

Hemingway Ubersteht Zwei
Fugzengabsturze

Westdeutsche Allgemeine

[Jan 1954]

Scrapbook 54, p. 63

Mr. Hemingway Keeps to Pilot He Started With

[Jan 1954]

Antelope Scrapbook, p. 42

Mr. Hemingway Will Watch for Elephants
on Way Home

[Jan 1954]

        Antelope Scrapbook, p. 42

Der Recke in Bett

[Jan 54]

        Scrapbook 54, p. 19

One of the outstanding features. . .

[Jan 1954]

        Scrapbook 54, p. 12

Salvado Hemingway

[Jan 1954]

        Antelope Scrapbook, p. 46

Photo: El accidénto viaje de Hemingway
por Africa

[Jan 1954]

        Zebra Scrapbook, p. 4

Sullivan, Ed

    Little Old New York: Men and Maids and
    Stuff

[Jan 1954]

        Antelope Scrapbook, p. 12

Photo: Luck Still With Him

New York Times

[Jan 1954]

        Antelope Scrapbook, p. 31

Sullivan, Ed

    Little Old New York: Talk of the Town

[Jan 1954]

        Antelope Scrapbook, p. 19

H.R.

    Por el doblan las campanas--con Ernesto
Hemingway

[Jan 1954]

        Antelope Scrapbook, p. 48

Teed, Dexter

    Press Digest: Herald Tribune: President
    Eisenhower. . .

[Jan 1954]

        Antelops Scrapbook, p. 15

U.S. Author Arrives by Car in Entebbe
E[ast] A[frica], Standard
[Jan 1954]

Antelope Scrapbook, p. 43

Ernest Hemingway Missing in Africa after
Plane Crash
San Diego Union
[24 Jan 1954]

1954

Walker, Danton

Broadway Beat: Igor Gonzeski. . .

[Jan 1954]

Antelope Scrapbook, p. 11

Hemingway desaparece en un accidente
Telefono
[24 Jan 1954]

Scrapbook 54, p. 4 and 12

Winchell, Walter

Thanks for the Plug Pome
New York Mirror
[Jan 1954]

Antelope Scrapbook, p. 16

Hemingway Falece Num Acidente de Aviao

[24 Jan 1954]

Scrapbook 54, p. 56

Yardley

Cartoon: Reports of My Death Are
Greatly Exaggerated

[Jan 1954]

Antelope Scrapbook, p. 30

Arece en la Selva del a Ernest
Hemingway
Havana Crisol
25 Jan 1954

Antelope Scrapbook, p. 50

. . .A former Fort Frances border
resident. . .
Winnipeg Tribune
[16 Jan 1954]

1954

Author and Wife on Way Out of African Wilds

[25 Jan 1954]

Scrapbook 54, p. 54

Author in Real Thriller: Hemingways Safe
in 2 Crashes

[San Antonio Light]

[25 Jan 1954]

Scrapbook 54, p. 62

Ernest Hemingway Missing in Jungle Plane

London Daily Mail

25 Jan 1954

1954

Baker, Russell W.

London Press Overlooks Durability of
Hemingway

[25 Jan 1954]

Antelope Scrapbook, p. 19

Ernest Hemingway Feared Dead in Air Crash

San Francisco Examiner

25 Jan 1954

Scrapbook 54, p. 17

La Ciudad y el Mundo

El Espectador

25 Jan 1954

Scrapbook 54, p. 36

Ernest Hemingway, Wife Reported Killed in
Crash

Brooklyn Daily

25 Jan 1954

Scrapbook 54, p. 51

Ernest Hemingway and Wife Missing in Crash
in Africa

New York Herald Tribune

25 Jan 1954

Ernest Hemingway y su esposa resultan
ilesos de un accidente africana

[25 Jan 1954]

Scrapbook 54, p. 26

Ernest Hemingway and Wife Missing in Crash
in Africa
Biography of a Foremost American Writer
Mrs. Hemingway Made Name as War Reporter

New York Herald Tribune

25 Jan 1954

Antelope Scrapbook, p. 3
& Scrapbook 54, p. 30, 35, and 6

Ernie's Life Charmed: Sister

[25 Jan 1954]

Scrapbook 54, p. 60

Author in Real Thriller: Hemingways Safe in 2 Crashes

[San Antonio Light]

[25 Jan 1954]

Scrapbook 54, p. 62

Ernest Hemingway Missing in Jungle Plane

London Daily Mail

25 Jan 1954

1954

Baker, Russell W.

London Press Overlooks Durability of Hemingway

[25 Jan 1954]

Antelope Scrapbook, p. 19

Ernest Hemingway Feared Dead in Air Crash

San Francisco Examiner

25 Jan 1954

Scrapbook 54, p. 17

La Ciudad y el Mundo

El Espectador

25 Jan 1954

Scrapbook 54, p. 36

Ernest Hemingway, Wife Reported Killed in Crash

Brooklyn Daily

25 Jan 1954

Scrapbook 54, p. 51

Ernest Hemingway and Wife Missing in Crash in Africa

New York Herald Tribune

25 Jan 1954

Ernest Hemingway y su esposa resultan ilesos de un accidente africana

[25 Jan 1954]

Scrapbook 54, p. 26

Ernest Hemingway and Wife Missing in Crash in Africa
Biography of a Foremost American Writer
Mrs. Hemingway Made Name as War Reporter

New York Herald Tribune

25 Jan 1954

Antelope Scrapbook, p. 3
& Scrapbook 54, p. 30, 35, and 6'

Ernie's Life Charmed: Sister

[25 Jan 1954]

Scrapbook 54, p. 60

Repeats previous page

Author in Real Thriller: Hemingways Safe
in 2 Crashes

[San Antonio Light]

[25 Jan 1954]

Scrapbook 54, p. 62

Ernest Hemingway Missing in Jungle Plane

London Daily Mail

25 Jan 1954

1954

Baker, Russell W.

London Press Overlooks Durability of
Hemingway

[25 Jan 1954]

Antelope Scrapbook, p. 19

Ernest Hemingway Feared Dead in Air Crash

San Francisco Examiner

25 Jan 1954

Scrapbook 54, p. 17

La Ciudad y el Mundo

El Espectador

25 Jan 1954

Scrapbook 54, p. 36

Ernest Hemingway, Wife Reported Killed in
Crash

Brooklyn Daily

25 Jan 1954

Scrapbook 54, p. 51

Ernest Hemingway and Wife Missing in Crash
in Africa

New York Herald Tribune

25 Jan 1954

Ernest Hemingway y su esposa resultan
ilesos de un accidente africana

[25 Jan 1954]

Scrapbook 54, p. 26

Ernest Hemingway and Wife Missing in Crash
in Africa
Biography of a Foremost American Writer
Mrs. Hemingway Made Name as War Reporter

New York Herald Tribune

25 Jan 1954

Antelope Scrapbook, p. 3
& Scrapbook 54, p. 30, 35, and 6⁹

Ernie's Life Charmed: Sister

[25 Jan 1954]

Scrapbook 54, p. 60

Repeats previous page

Find Hemingway Safe in Crash
Hemingway Missing in Flight
Circles Above Plane, Doubts Anyone Died

New York Daily Mirror

25 Jan 1954

Antelope Scrapbook, p. 34

Hemingway and His Wife Crash in Africa;
Plane Is Seen in Jungle, No Word on Fate

New York Times

25 Jan 1954

Antelope Scrapbook, p. 14
& Scrapbook 54, p. 48

Hallado Ileso Ernest Hemingway--Hemingway
Escapo de Milagro a la Muerte

Havana El Pais

25 Jan 1954

Antelope Scrapbook, p. 45

Hemingway and Wife Are Reported Safe
After Two Plane Crashes in East Africa

[New York Times]

[25 Jan 1954]

Antelope Scrapbook, p. 26

Headline only: Aparecio Ernest Hemingway

Havana Mediodia

25 Jan 1954

Scrapbook 54, p. 24

Hemingway and Wife Lost in Africa Crash

New York Daily Mirror

25 Jan 1954

Antelope Scrapbook, p. 5

Headline and Photo: Hemingway OK in 2
Crashes

Brooklyn Eagle

25 Jan 1954

Scrapbook 54, p. 56

Hemingway and Wife Survive Two Jungle
Plane Crashes

New York World Telegram

25 Jan 1954

Antelope Scrapbook, p. 20
& Scrapbook 54, p. 58

Hemingway Abgesturzt

[25 Jan 1954]

Scrapbook 54, p. 4

Hemingway Feared Dead in Africa Plane
Smashup

[Idaho Statesman]

[25 Jan 1954]

Antelope Scrapbook, p. 6

Find Hemingway Safe in Crash
Hemingway Missing in Flight
Circles Above Plane, Doubts Anyone Died

New York Daily Mirror

25 Jan 1954

      Antelope Scrapbook, p. 34

Hemingway and His Wife Crash in Africa;
Plane Is Seen in Jungle, No Word on Fate

New York Times

25 Jan 1954

      Antelope Scrapbook, p. 14
      & Scrapbook 54, p. 48

Hallado Ileso Ernest Hemingway--Hemingway
Escapo de Milagro a la Muerte

Havana El Pais

25 Jan 1954

      Antelope Scrapbook, p. 45

Hemingway and Wife Are Reported Safe
After Two Plane Crashes in East Africa

[New York Times]

[25 Jan 1954]

      Antelope Scrapbook, p. 26

Headline only: Aparecio Ernest Hemingway

Havana Mediodia

25 Jan 1954

      Scrapbook 54, p. 24

Hemingway and Wife Lost in Africa Crash

New York Daily Mirror

25 Jan 1954

      Antelope Scrapbook, p. 5

Headline and Photo: Hemingway OK in 2
Crashes

Brooklyn Eagle

25 Jan 1954

      Scrapbook 54, p. 56

Hemingway and Wife Survive Two Jungle
Plane Crashes

New York World Telegram

25 Jan 1954

      Antelope Scrapbook, p. 20
      & Scrapbook 54, p. 58

Hemingway Abgesturzt

[25 Jan 1954]

      Scrapbook 54, p. 4

Hemingway Feared Dead in Africa Plane
Smashup

[Idaho Statesman]

[25 Jan 1954]

      Antelope Scrapbook, p. 6

Repeats previous page

Find Hemingway Safe in Crash
Hemingway Missing in Flight
Circles Above Plane, Doubts Anyone Died

New York Daily Mirror

25 Jan 1954

Antelope Scrapbook, p. 34

Hemingway and His Wife Crash in Africa;
Plane Is Seen in Jungle, No Word on Fate

New York Times

25 Jan 1954

Antelope Scrapbook, p. 14
& Scrapbook 54, p. 48

Hallado Ileso Ernest Hemingway--Hemingway
Escapo de Milagro a la Muerte

Havana El Pais

25 Jan 1954

Antelope Scrapbook, p. 45

Hemingway and Wife Are Reported Safe
After Two Plane Crashes in East Africa

[New York Times]

[25 Jan 1954]

Antelope Scrapbook, p. 26

Headline only: Aparecio Ernest Hemingway

Havana Mediodia

25 Jan 1954

Scrapbook 54, p. 24

Hemingway and Wife Lost in Africa Crash

New York Daily Mirror

25 Jan 1954

Antelope Scrapbook, p. 5

Headline and Photo: Hemingway OK in 2
Crashes

Brooklyn Eagle

25 Jan 1954

Scrapbook 54, p. 56

Hemingway and Wife Survive Two Jungle
Plane Crashes

New York World Telegram

25 Jan 1954

Antelope Scrapbook, p. 20
& Scrapbook 54, p. 58

Hemingway Abgesturzt

[25 Jan 1954]

Scrapbook 54, p. 4

Hemingway Feared Dead in Africa Plane
Smashup

[Idaho Statesman]

[25 Jan 1954]

Antelope Scrapbook, p. 6

Repeats previous page

Hemingway Feared Dead in Crash: Wife Also
Aboard Wrecked Plane in African Wilderness
Lef Life He Loved in Key West Years

Miami Herald

25 Jan 1954

Antelope Scrapbook, p. 8

Hemingway Nephews Knew All the Time
Adventure Story Author Would Come Through

Washington, D.C., Star

25 Jan 1954

Scrapbook 54, p. 25

Hemingway Feared Dead in Nile Air Crash

New York Daily News

25 Jan 1954--City Edition

Antelope Scrapbook, p. 2

Hemingway Plane Down in Jungles
Hemingway's Latest Tells of East Africa

Dallas Morning News

25 Jan 1954

Scrapbook 54, p. 29

Hemingway Feared Missing

[Tanganyika Standard]

[25 Jan 1954]

Antelope Scrapbook, p. 41

Hemingway racconte i suoi incontri con la
morte

[Epoca]

[25 Jan 1954]

Scrapbook 54, p. 11

Hemingway gerettet

[25 Jan 1954]

Scrapbook 54, p. 26

Hemingway og hans kone laver!

[Dagbladet]

[25 Jan 1954]

Scrapbook 54, p. 64

Hemingway in Jungle Air Crash

Cleveland Plain Dealer

25 Jan 1954

Bryan, John E. 11 Aug 1954

Hemingway Safe after Two Crashes
Hemingway and His Wife Unharmed
Two Plane Crashes in Africa
Fans Hail Hemingway as Invulnerable Papa
(See Earl Wilson, 25 Jan 1954)

New York Post

25 Jan 1954

Antelope Scrapbook, p. 25
& Scrapbook 54, p. 25

Hemingways Safe in Jungle: Author's Arm
Hurt in 2 Plane Crashes
Hemingway Often Braved Death with Joy

New York World Telegram

25 Jan 1954

        Antelope Scrapbook, p. 21

Hemingways OK in Crashes

25 Jan 1954

        Scrapbook 54, p. 60

Hemingways Alive: Survive Two Plane
Mishaps in Africa

Nashville Banner

[25 Jan 1954]

        Antelope Scrapbook, p. 27

Hemingway's Plane Crashes in Nile Jungle:
Intact Craft Leaves Hope He, Wife Lived

Atlanta Constitution

25 Jan 1954

        Scrapbook 54, p. 18

Hemingways Escape Death

Brooklyn Eagle

25 Jan 1954

        Scrapbook 54, p. 52 and p. 49

Hemingway's Plane in Crash!
A Farewell to Hemingway
Fear Hemingway Dead in Crash
Hemingway, Wife Missing in Africa Crash
(see Robert Parker, 25 Jan 1954)

New York Daily News

25 Jan 1954--Late Edition
        Antelope Scrapbook, p. 1 and p. 7
        & Scrapbook 54, p. 65

Hemingways Escape 2 Africa Air Crashes

Chicago Daily Sun-Times

25 Jan 1954

        Scrapbook 54, p. 63

Headline and Photo:
Hemingways Safe! Survive 2 Plane Crashes
Hemingway Saga--On Safari in Africa Before
Air Crash

New York Journal American

25 Jan 1954

        Antelope Scrapbook, p. 9 and 37
        & Scrapbook 54, p. 53

Hemingways Feared Africa Crash Victims:
Wrecked Plane Seen Near Nile

Chicago Daily Sun-Times

25 Jan 1954

        Scrapbook 54, p. 61

Hemingways Safely Out of Jungle
He Tells of Luck After Two Crashes

[New York Herald Tribune]

[25 Jan 1954]

        Antelope Scrapbook, p. 23

Hemingways Survive Crashes: Famed Writer
Unhurt: Wife Suffers Injury

Dallas Daily Times Herald

25 Jan 1954

        Scrapbook 54, p. 27

McGill, Ralph

    Death in the Afternoon

    [Atlanta Constitution]

    [25 Jan 1954]

        Scrapbook 54, p. 13

Hemingway Wife Missing: Planes' Wreckage
Sighted in Africa
Book Told How He Loved Africa

Wisconsin State Journal

25 Jan 1954

    1954

Mondodori, Alberto

    L'Ultima avventura

    [25 Jan 1954]

        Scrapbook 54, p. 19

Lancaster, Chris

    Hemingway e perito in un incidente aereo?

    [25 Jan 1954]

        Scrapbook 54, p. 4

Morto Hemingway in un desastro aereo

[25 Jan 1954]

        Scrapbook 54, p. 19

Lyons, Leonard

    The Lyons Den: Papa--I Hope It's Not True

    New York Post

    25 Jan 1954

        Antelope Scrapbook, p. 17
        & 1954

Mrs. Ernest Hemingway in Uganda Air Crash

[East Africa] Standard

[25 Jan 1954]

        Antelope Scrapbook, p. 42

El matrimonio Hemingway salio ileso de un
accidente de aviacion

[25 Jan 1954]

        Antelope Scrapbook, p. 48

Parker, Robert

    Violence Has Marked His Writing and His Life

    New York Daily News

    25 Jan 1954

        Antelope Scrapbook, p. 17
        & Scrapbook 54, p. 65

Photo: Escape Clean

[New York] Daily News

25 Jan 1954

1954

Snell, David

Hemingway Often Braved Death with Joy

New York World Telegram

25 Jan 1954

Antelope Scrapbook, p. 21
& Scrapbook 54, p. 59

Report from Africa: Hemingway, Wife Killed
in Air Crash
Hemingway Feared Dead in Africa Crash
(see Fred Zepp, 25 Jan 1954)

New York Mirror

25 Jan 1954

Antelope Scrapbook, p. 4
& Scrapbook 54, p. 57

Temese Por Hemingway

Havana Alerto

25 Jan 1954

Antelope Scrapbook, p. 51
& Zebra Scrapbook, p. 5

Salvos Hemingway y su esposa en dos
accidentes de aviacion casi consecutivos
en Africa

[Havana] Avance

25 Jan 1954

Scrapbook 54, p. 26, 28, and 33

Welt in Sorge um Hemingway

Frankische Tagespost

25 Jan 1954

Scrapbook 54, p. 12

Das Schicksal Hemingways noch ungewiB

Weiner Kurier

25 Jan 1954

Scrapbook 54, p. 32

Wilson, Earl

Fans Hail Hemingway as Invulnerable Papa

New York Post

25 Jan 1954

Antelope Scrapbook, p. 25
Scrapbook 54, p. 55

Schriftsteller Hemingway todlich
verungluckt

25 Jan 1954

Scrapbook 54, p. 32

Wilson, Earl

It Happened Last Night

[New York Post]

[25 Jan 1954]

Antelope Scrapbook, p. 13

Writer, Wife Use Auto for Return to Civilization

[25 Jan 1954]

Scrapbook 54, p. 54

Books Explain the Headlines
Paterson, N.J., News
26 Jan 1954

Scrapbook 54, p. 54

Zepp, Fred
Last Meeting with an Old Friend
New York Daily Mirror
25 Jan 1954

Antelope Scrapbook, p. 4
Scrapbook 54, p. 57

Borum, Bill
Sports: Up to But Not Over the River
New York Journal American
26 Jan 1954

Antelope Scrapbook, p. 18

Zwei Flugzengunfalle uberlebt

[25 Jan 1954]

Scrapbook 54, p. 26

Causo intensa satifaccion la notice de que Hemingway y su esposa se habian salvado
Havana Diario de la Marina
26 Jan 1954

Zebra Scrapbook, p. 3

Los accidentes de aviacion
Havana Informacion
26 Jan 1954

Scrapbook 54, p. 47

Considine, Bob
Happy Birthday, General
New York Journal American
26 Jan 1954

Scrapbook 54, p. 51

Aparecio Herido Hemingway
Manana
26 Jan 1954

Scrapbook 54, p. 24

Editorials: Two Miracles in a Day
Dr. Hemingway, I Believe
[Havana Post]
[26 Jan 1954]

Antelope Scrapbook, p. 13
& Scrapbook 54, p. 19

Esta Vivo

Havana El Mundo

26 Jan 1954

Zebra Scrapbook, p. 1

Hemingway in Fine Spirits

New York [Daily Mirror]

[26 Jan 1954]

Antelope Scrapbook, p. 30

Hemingway, Ernest

Safari

Look Magazine

[26 Jan 1954]

Scrapbook 54, p. 22

Hemingway Out of the Jungle, Arm Hurt

New York Times

26 Jan 1954

Antelope Scrapbook, p. 24
& Scrapbook 54, p. 53

Happy Ending

Dayton News

26 Jan 1954

Scrapbook 54, p. 61

Hemingway Safe after 2 Plane Crashes

New York Daily Worker

26 Jan 1954

Scrapbook 54, p. 20

Hemingway, Ernest

Safari advertising material

Look Magazine

[26 Jan 1954]

Scrapbook 54, p. 31. 8, 9,
14 and 15
& 1954

Hemingway Feeling Fine; Gin and Bananas
Prove It

[New York] Daily News

26 Jan 1954

Antelope Scrapbook, p. 33
& Scrapbook 54, p. 49

Hemingway, His Luck She's Running Good

New York Post

26 Jan 1954

Antelope Scrapbook, p. 26
& Scrapbook 54, p. 54

Hemingways gute Laune blieb erhalten

Wiener Kurier

26 Jan 1954

Scrapbook 54, p. 32

Hemingways Survive 2nd Plane Crash
San Francisco People's World
26 Jan 1954

   Scrapbook 54, p. 20

The House of Culture
Dayton Journal Herald
26 Jan 1954

   Scrapbook 54, p. 47

Hemingway's Safe, In the Tradition
Cleveland News
26 Jan 1954

   Scrapbook 54, p. 54

Ileso de dos Accidentes Aereos Hemingway
Herida su Esposa
Havana [Excelsior]
26 Jan 1954

   Antelope Scrapbook, p. 46-47

A Hemingway Story
Southbridge, Mass., News
26 Jan 1954

   Scrapbook 54, p. 45

Ilesos el escritor y su esposa Mary Welsh
Prensa Libre
26 Jan 1954

   Scrapbook 54, p. 28

Hemingway, the Durable
Glen Falls, N.Y., Post-Star
26 Jan 1954

   Scrapbook 54, p. 44

Kupcinet
 Kup's Column
 Chicago Sun-Times
 26 Jan 1954

   Scrapbook 54, p. 60

Hemingway to Do Book on His Narrow Escape
New York World-Telegram and Sun
26 Jan 1954

   Scrapbook 54, p. 27 and 50
   & Antelope Scrapbook, p. 29

McGill, Ralph
 Life in the Afternoon
 Atlanta [Constitution]
 26 Jan 1954

   Scrapbook 54, p. 13

My Luck, She Runs Very Good
Brooklyn Eagle
26 Jan 1954
> Scrapbook 54, p. 55

Photo: Primera Foto de Hemingway Herido

[26 Jan 1954]
> Antelope Scrapbook, p. 46

Not the Hemingway Manner
Toledo Blade
26 Jan 1954
> Scrapbook 54, p. 51

Photo: Salvados mila grosamente
Havana Ataja Diario Cubano
26 Jan 1954
> Antelope Scrapbook, p. 44

Papa's Fickle Friend
Pittsburg Post-Gazette
26 Jan 1954
> Scrapbook 54, p. 44

Photo: Writer Alive
Brooklyn Daily
26 Jan 1954
> Scrapbook 54, p. 17

Photo: Alive and Quipping
New York Daily Mirror
[26 Jan 1954]
> Antelope Scrapbook, p. 36

Resulto Ileso en el Accidente el Famoso
Escrito E. Hemingway
Havana La Campana
26 Jan 1954
> Zebra Scrapbook, p. 1

Photo: 1st Photo of Hemingway After Rescue
[New York Journal-American
[26 Jan 1954]
> Antelope Scrapbook, p. 32

Rugged Hemingway to Resume Safari
New York Journal-American
26 Jan 1954
> Scrapbook 54, p. 47

Stranger Than Fiction

Harrisburg, PA, Patriot

26 Jan 1954

      Scrapbook 54, p. 54

Photo: Another Hemingway Climax--End of
Air Thriller Chapter

New York Journal American

27 Jan 1954

      Scrapbook 54, p. 50
      & Antelope Scrapbook, p. 39

Waiting for Injured Wife to Rest

New York Journal-American

26 Jan 1954

      Antelope Scrapbook, p. 31 & 32

Photo: Hemingways Bag a Leopard

Trenton, NJ, Times

27 Jan 1954

      Scrapbook 54, p. 44

Hemingway Refuses to Sell Crash Story

New York Post

27 Jan 1954

      Scrapbook 54, p. 46
      & Antelope Scrapbook, p. 38

Photo: Hemingways Rest after Plane
Crack-Ups

New York Herald Tribune

27 Jan 1954

      Scrapbook 54, p. 12
      & Antelope Scrapbook, p. 38

Hobson, Laura Z.

    To the Ladies: Lives to Read His Own
    Obits

    New York Journal American

    27 Jan 1954

        Scrapbook 54, p. 53
        & Antelope Scrapbook, p. 10

Photo: The Importance of Being Ernest
(Hemingway)

New York Daily News

27 Jan 1954

      Scrapbook 54, p. 47
      & Antelope Scrapbook, p. 38

Photo: After Close Call in African Wilds

27 Jan 1954

      Scrapbook 54, p. 48

Photo: Time to Relax

New York Post

27 Jan 1954

      Antelope Scrapbook, p. 38

Snoring and Jungle Elephants
Milwaukee Journal
27 Jan 1954

> Scrapbook 54, p. 13

Hemingway will keine Absturz-Story

[28 Jan 1954]

> Scrapbook 54, p. 26

Sobol, Louis
New York Calvacade: Tribute to a Good Guy
New York Journal American
[27 Jan 1954]

> Antelope Scrapbook, p. 10

Intefering Ibises
Watertown, N.Y., Times
28 Jan 1954

> Scrapbook 54, p. 24

Storybook Stuff
Cincinnati Enquirer
27 Jan 1954

> Scrapbook 54, p. 33

Mr. Ernest Hemingway Will Fly to Coast
Nairobi
28 Jan 1954

> Scrapbook 54, p. 54
> & Antelope Scrapbook, p. 43

Hemingway
Gallatin, Tenn., Examiner
28 Jan 1954

> Scrapbook 54, p. 12

Photo: Ernie's Luck. . .
Jefferson, Indiana, News
28 Jan 1954

> Scrapbook 54, p. 48

Hemingway to Fly to Nairobi
New York Times
28 Jan 1954

> Scrapbook 54, p. 12

Schacht, Beulah
Take It from Beulah: Her Confusion's Ernest
St. Louis Globe-Democrat
28 Jan 1954

> Scrapbook 54, p. 25

Winchell, Walter

    Of New York: Author! Author!

    Buffalo Courier Express

    28 Jan 1954

            Antelope Scrapbook, p. 16

Tired Hemingway in Nairobi

New York Times

29 Jan 1954

            Scrapbook 54, p. 54

    Class Will Tell

    Washington, D.C., Times-Herald

    29 Jan 1954

            Scrapbook 54, p. 44

Ernest Hemingway, Wife Survive Two Air Crashes

Publisher's Weekly

30 Jan 1954

            Scrapbook 54, p. 52

    Ernest Hemingway, the American author. . .

    Princess Anne, Maryland, Marylander and Herald

    29 Jan 1954

            Scrapbook 54, p. 20

Hemingway Sent to Bed by Physician

New York World-Telegram and Sun

30 Jan 1954

            Scrapbook 54, p. 12

    Keine Angst vorm Fliegen

    [29 Jan 1954]

            Scrapbook 54, p. 26

Photo: Makes It

New York Journal American

30 Jan 1954

            Antelope Scrapbook, p. 35

Scott, Ernest

    Interesting if True: Those Snows of Kilimanjaro

    Havana Post

    29 Jan 1954

            Antelope Scrapbook, p. 18

Laird, Landon

    About Town: A few nights ago. . .

    Kansas City Times

    30 Jan 1954

            Scrapbook 54, p. 13

Hemingway Resting from Delayed Shock
Brooklyn Eagle
31 Jan 1954
        Scrapbook 54, p. 44

H.A.
    Photo: Hemingway, um den sich ein. . .

    [Feb 1954]
            Scrapbook 54, p. 21

Nach dem Todessturz- erkrankt

[31 Jan 1954]
        Scrapbook 54, p. 32

Novelist Ernest Hemingway
Time Magazine
1 Feb 1954
            Scrapbook 54, p. 46

Ruark, Robert
    Perfect Eptiaph for Hemingway
    Tampa [Herald]
    [31 Jan 1954]
                1954

Only His Heroes Die
Newsweek
1 Feb 1954
            Scrapbook 54, p. 51

Sobol, Louis
    Calendar of a Gothamite
    [New York Journal American]
    [31 Jan 1954]
            Antelope Scrapbook, p. 35

Photo: Now He Must Rest
New York Journal American
1 Feb 1954
            Antelope Scrapbook, p. 28

What They Said: Ernest Hemingway (after
surviving. . .
[New York Post]
[31 Jan 1954]
        Antelope Scrapbook, p. 15

Ruark, Robert C.
    The Unkillable Hemingway
    [San Francisco News]
    [1 Feb 1954]
            Antelope Scrapbook, p. 15
            & Scrapbook 54, p. 34

Wales

    Odd Lots and Broken Sizes

    Nieman-Marcus Point of View

    1 Feb 1954

                Scrapbook 54, p. 36

Walker, Danton

    Broadway: Incidental Intelligence

    New York Daily News

    6 Feb 1954

                Scrapbook 54, p. 49

Winchell, Walter

    Of New York: Man About Town

    [New York Mirror]

    [1 Feb 1954]

                Antelope Scrapbook, p. 16

Lyons, Leonard

    The Lyons Den: Broadway Gazette

    New York Post

    11 Feb 1954

                Scrapbook 54, p. 47

Hemingway ist wutend

    2 Feb 1954

                Zebra Scrapbook, p. 3

Photo: For Whom No Bell Tolled!

Picture Post

[13 Feb 1954]

                Scrapbook 54, p. 29

Hemingway-Grobes Tamtam

Der Spiegel

3 Feb 1954

                Antelope Scrapbook, p. 49

Rose, Billy

    Pitching Horseshoes: Minority Report on
    Papa

    [New York Mirror]

    [15 Feb 1954]

                Scrapbook 54, p. 18

Photo: Survive Two Crashes

Martinsville, Indiana, Reporter

4 Feb 1954

                Scrapbook 54, p. 50

McDermott, William F.

    McDermott's Mailbag: Financial Editor
    Recalls Visit with Hemingway and His
    Tremendous Capacity for Friendship

    Cleveland Plain Dealer

    22 Feb 1954

                Bryan, John E. 11 Aug 1954

Photo: Mister Papa a Venezia

[Mar 1954]

      Scrapbook 54, p. 29

Hemingway e Stanco
Venezia
April [1954]

      Scrapbook 54, p. 71

Premio di 1000 dollari per Hemingway
L'arrivo della svedesse Martha Toren

[Mar 1954]

      Scrapbook 54, p. 20

Maldini, Sergio
   Incontro a Venezia con Hemingway

[Apr 1954]?

      Scrapbook 54, p. 42

Todisco, Alfredo
   Hemingway a Venezia--Combate Contro
   Le Iene

[Mar 1954]

      Scrapbook 54, p. 23

Photo: Hemingway ospite del Friuli

[Apr 1954]

      Scrapbook 54, p. 34

Hemingway e a Venezia

23 Mar 1954

      Scrapbook 54, p. 20

Photo: Incontro con zio Ernesto

[Apr 1954]

      Scrapbook 54, p. 34

Bertoldi, Silvio
   Mister Papa a Venezia

[25 Mar 1954]

      Scrapbook 54, p. 20

Tutti mi chiamano Bionda
Milan [Tempo]
[8 Apr 1954]

      Scrapbook 54, p. 22

Photo: Ernest Hemingway fotografate

Settimo Giorno

8 Apr 1954

Scrapbook 54, p. 17

Hemingway, Ernest

Mes aventures dans le brousse africaine IV

Le Figaro

13 Apr 1954

Scrapbook 54, p. 66

Soncini, Italo

Bottecchia Razza Piave: Mister Papa sa di Ciclismo

La Gazetta

8 Apr 1954

1954

Hemingway, Ernest

The Great Novelist's Own Story of His Two African Plane Crashes

London Sunday Express

18 Apr 1954

Scrapbook 54, p. 79

Hemingway, Ernest

Hemingway's Own Story

London The Sunday Express

11 Apr 1954

Scrapbook 54, p. 67

Hemingway, Ernest

Il Regalo di Natale

Tempo

22 Apr 1954

Scrapbook 54, pp. 68 & 74

Al Friuli in una Breve Tappa--
Hemingway Dispensa Sorrisi Autografi

Messaggero Veneto Domenica

11 Apr 1954

Antelope Scrapbook, loose

Hemingway, Ernest

Mes aventures dans la brousse africaine V

Le Figaro

22 Apr 1954

Scrapbook 54, p. 77

C.S.

Il Grande Romanziese Americano si Trova in Friuli

Il Gazzettino Domenica

11 Apr 1954

Antelope Scrapbook, loose

Hemingway, Ernest

The Vice of Reading Your Own Obituaries

London Sunday Express

25 Apr 1954

Scrapbook 54, p. 78

Hemingway, Ernest

Mes aventures dans la brousse africaine
VII

Le Figaro

28 Apr 1954

Scrapbook 54, p. 75

Corriere Della Sera

Milan

28 May 1954

Scrapbook 54, p. 64-65

Hemingway, Ernest

Mes aventrues dans la brousse africaine
VIII

Le Figaro

29 Apr 1954

Scrapbook 54, p. 76

Blakeley, H. W.

D Plus Ten Years

Combat Forces Journal

July 1954

National 4th Division Assoc.

Sanchez Cobos, M.

Entrevista del Dia

Madrid

[May 1954]

Scrapbook 54, p. 72-73

En la Embajada del Canada

Havana

25 July 1954

1954

Hemingway's Secret Inuries Nearly
Killed Him

[14 May 1954]

1954

Ernest Hemingway's School Days

Chicago

Aug 1954

1954

Photo: Hemingway en La Voz de Madrid

[20 May 1954]

1954

Medal for Hemingway

Chicago Timely Events

3 Aug 1954

1954

Photo: Exotica y Artistica Foto

[Sept-Oct 1954]

1954

Crawford, Ollie

Headline Hopping: Ernest Hemingway wins Nobel. . .

[Oct 1954]

Scrapbook 54, p. 36-37

Ruark, Robert C.

Heads I Win

New York World Telegram

15 Sept 1954

Lowe, William, 15 Sept 1954

Ernest Hemingway Wins a Well-Deserved Honor

Atlanta Journal

[Oct 1954]

Scrapbook 54, p. 82

Cinema Newsreel

Time

27 Sept 1954

Lowe, William 20 Sept 1954

Hemingway Gets Award

Miami Herald

[Oct 1954]

Scrapbook 54, p. 80

American Ernest Hemingway Wins Nobel Prize for Literature

Providence, R.I. Evening Bulletin

[Oct 1954]

Scrapbook 54, p. 84

Hemingway Nobel Winner for Old Man and the Sea

New York Herald Tribune

[Oct 1954]

Scrapbook 54, p. 82

Campoamor, Fernando C.

Este es un premio Nobel para Cuba

[Diario Nacional]

[Oct 1954]

Scrapbook 54, p. 98

Hemingway Wins Nobel Prize for '54

[Oct 1954]

1954

Hemingway y Los Picadores
Alerta
[Oct 1954]

Scrapbook 54, p. 101

The Old Man Gets His Prize
Shelby Daily Star
[Oct 1954]

Scrapbook 54, p. 83

Literature is Richer for the Old Man
Courier-Journal
[Oct 1954]

Scrapbook 54, p. 85

Parajon, Mario
Me Siento Cubano, Hemingway

[Oct 1954]

Scrapbook 54, p. 100

Lo que se premia es un himno a la
reciedumbre de los hombres de la costa
Norte

[Oct/Dec 1954]

Scrapbook 54, p. 98-99

Photo: Hemingway, Premio Nobel
Diario de la Marina
[Oct 1954]

Scrapbook 54, p. 100

Mr. ...ingway's Prize

[Oct 1954]

Scrapbook 54, p. 81

El Premio Nobel a Hemingway

[Oct 1954]

Scrapbook 54, p. 96

No acudira Hemingway a recibir el Premio
Nobel
El Crisol
[Oct 1954]

Scrapbook 54, p. 98

Los Premios Nobel: Otorgado a Hemingway
el Literatura para ete ano
Informacion
[Oct 1954]

Scrapbook 54, p. 99

Montale, Eugenio

    Hemingway premio Nobel per la litteratura

    Corriere della Sera

    [18 Oct 1954]

            Ivancich, Adriana 2 Nov 1954

U.S. Novelist Hemingway Wins Nobel Prize for Literature

Washington, D.C., Evening Star

28 Oct 1954

            Scrapbook 54, p. 118-119

    Hemingway Obtiene el Premio Nobel de Literatura

    [Madrid] ABC

    20 Oct 1954

            Chicote, Pedro 29 Oct 1954

Assegnato a Hemingway

Il Gazzettino

29 Oct 1954

            Ivancich, Adriana 2 Nov 1954

Scarpetta, J. G.

    Ernest Hemingway es el. . .

    [Pueblo]

    [27 Oct 1954]

            Scrapbook 54, p. 96

Hemingway Is Winner of Nobel Literature Prize

New York Times

29 Oct 1954

            Scrapbook 54, p. 80 & 1954

News Bulletins
AP17 Ernest Hemingway, North. . .
AP18 The Academy selected. . .
AP29 Hemingway, whose adventurous. . .
AP30 Previous North American Nobel. . .

28 Oct 1954

        1954

Matthews, Herbert L.

    Winner Rules Out Trip to Stockholm

    New York Times

    [29 Oct 1954]

            Scrapbook 54, p. 81

Obtuvo E. Hemingway el Premio Nobel

[El Pais]

[28 Oct 1954]

            Scrapbook 54, p. 96

Hemingway: Premio Nobel de Literatura

Havana Prensa Libre

[29 Oct 1954]

            Scrapbook 54, p. 97

Hemingway Receives Recognition Long Due

[Atlanta Constitution]

[29 Oct 1954]

> Scrapbook 54, p. 83

Hemingway Prize

Salt Lake Tribune

30 Oct 1954

> Sweeney, Charles 2 Dec 1954

Hemingway Debts Get Part of Nobel Prize

Chicago Daily Tribune

29 Oct 1954

> 1954

Picart, Jose M.

> Ernest Hemingway y el Nobel
>
> Havana [El Pais]
>
> [30 Oct 1954]
>
> > Scrapbook 54, p. 101

McGill, Ralph

> The Old Man and the Sea
>
> Atlanta Constitution
>
> [29 Oct 1954]
>
> > Scrapbook 54, p. 83

Nobel Prize for Hemingway

[Milwaukee Journal]

[1 Nov 1954]

> Scrapbook 54, p. 84

Poore, Charles

> Hemingway's Quality Built on a Stern Apprenticeship
>
> [New York Times]
>
> [29 Oct 1954]
>
> > Scrapbook 54, p. 81

Breit, Harvey

> The Sun Also Rises in Stockholm
>
> New York Times Book Review
>
> 7 Nov 1954
>
> > Scrapbook 54, p. 85

Summerlin, Sam

> Hemingway Reels in Nobel Prize with The Old Man and the Sea
>
> [Atlanta Constitution]
>
> [29 Oct 1954]
>
> > Scrapbook 54, p. 83

Hemingway, Mary

> I Won't Worry
>
> Miami Daily News--This Week Magazine
>
> 7 Nob 1954
>
> > 1954

Brock, Ray
    A Letter from Ernest Hemingway
    Life Magazine
    8 Nov 1954
            1954

An American Storyteller
Time Magazine
13 Dec 1954
        1954

The Old Man Lands Biggest Catch
Life
8 Nov 1954
        1954

. . . In Stockholm, Sweden, King Gustav VI
Adolph handed out. . .

[Dec 1954]
        1954

Smith, Norman
    Hemingway: premio Nobel
    Havana Prensa Libre
    11 Nov 1954
            1954

Cookson, Clive
    My Meeting with Mr. Hemingway

    [1955]
                1955
    JFK Collection

Sullivan, Ed
    Ed Sullivan Speaking
    [New York Herald Tribune]
    26 Nov [1954]
            1954

Sandburg, Carl
    The Work of Ezra Pound
    Poetry

            Sandburg, Carl 1955

Envoy Accepts Nobel Award for Hemingway

[10 Dec 1954]
        1954

Bull Gores Bandillero
New York Post
10 Jan 1955
        Hotchner, A. E. 25 May 1955

Breit, Harvey

    A Walk with Faulkner

    New York Times

    30 Jan 1955

        McEvoy, J. P.

[Hemingway, Mary, John O'Hara, Malcolm Cowley, John Groth, et al.]

    Who the Hell is Hemingway?

    True

    [Feb 1956]

                1956

    donor: Alfred Rice

Dietrich, Marlene

    The Most Fascinating May I Know

    New York Herald Tribune

    13 Feb 1955

           1955

Wilson, Earl

    It Happened Last Night: Hemingway in Bed 40 Days but Whips Hepatitis Virus

    [New York Post]

    6 Feb 1956

           1956

Hemingway, Ernest

    Great Blue River: True Takes You Fishing with Ernest Hemingway

    [True]

    [Apr 1955]

        1955

Wilson, Earl

    It Happened Last Night. . . Ernest Hemingway, who read. . .

    New York Post

    8 Feb 1956

           1956

Wilson, Earl

    It Happened Last Night: Hemingway, Writing Good, About to Bank Another Book

    New York Post

    9 Nov 1955

        Wilson, Earl   9 Nov 1955

Mailer, Norman

    Quickly, a Column for Slow Readers

    [New York] Village Voice

    28 Mar 1956

           1956

    Right Thing Gets Hemingway to Let Tracy Film Book

    [1956]

        1956

Mallin, Jay

    Hemingway: America's No. 1 He-Man

    Modern Man

    June 1956

        1956

Big One Didn't Get Away
Tico Times
8 June 1956

        Stewart, Allan 28 June 1956

Ernest Hemingway, Nobel prize winning. . .
New York Catholic News
25 Aug 1956

        1956

At his home in Cuba, Author Ernest. . .
Time
18 June 1956

        1956

Kiley, Jed

    Hemingway: A Title Bout in Ten Rounds,
    Round 1 and Round 2

    Playboy

    September 1956

        1956

Torres, Emmanuel Mora

    Un Coloso en Una Cuerdo

    La Nacion

    22 June 1956

        Stewart, Allan 28 June 1956

Hemingway, Ernest

    A Personal Picture Story by Ernest
    Hemingway

    Look

    4 Sept 1956

        1956

Las Corridas de feria en Bilbao

        Quintana, Juanito 20 July 1956

Leaving behind his Cuban finca, 25 cats. . .
Time Magazine
10 Sept 1956

        1956

Mirilla

    Tiro, Caza y Pesca

    Rio de la Marina

    15 Aug 1956

        1956

Kiley, Jed

    Hemingway: A Title Bout in Ten Rounds
    Round 3

    Playboy

    [Oct 1956]

        1956

Campaigning: To students of Scotland
University of Glasgow who want to elect
grizzled Ernest. . .

Newsweek

29 Oct 1956

1956

McKinney, J. Cartin

Zanuck Tackles Sun with Imagination

[1957]

1957

People

Time

29 Oct 1956

1956

When I say, there is no story. . .

Bulletin

Jan 1957

Across the River

Kiley, Jed

Hemingway: A Title Bout in Ten Rounds
Rounds 4 and 5

Playboy

[Nov 1956]

1956

Kiley, Jed

Hemingway: A Title Bout in Ten Rounds
Round 7

Playboy

[Mar 1957]

1957

Kiley, Jed

Hemingway: A Title Bout in Ten Rounds
Round 6

Playboy

[Dec 1956]

1956

Kiley, Jed

Hemingway: A Title Bout in Ten Rounds
Round 8

Playboy

[Apr 1957]

1957

Buchwald, Art

Hemingway Again in the Fight News

New York Herald Tribune

[1957]

1957

MacLean, Robert

An Afternoon with Papa Hemingway

Bachelor

May 1957

1957

Wilson, Earl

    A Visit with Papa

    New York Post

    26 May 1957

          1957

Born July 21, 1899, in Oak Park. . .

Victoria, B.C., Canada Sunday Times

          Swain, Richard   10 Sept 1957

---

clipping fragment on EH films

          Hotchner, A.E. 26 June 1957

Lawrenson, Helen

    Shooting The Sun with Ava

    Esquire

    Oct 1957

          1957

Kiley, Jed

    Hemingway: A Title Bout in Ten Rounds
    Round 9

    Playboy

    [Aug 1957]

          1957

Hemingway, Ernest

    Two Tales of Darkness

    Atlantic Monthly

    Nov 1957

          1957

James, T. F.

    Hemingway at Work

    Cosmopolitan

    8 Aug 1957

          1957

Meyer, Charles R.

    Hemingway and the Pilar

    Popular Boating Magazine

    Nov 1957

          1957

Kiley, Jed

    Hemingway: A Title Bout in Ten Rounds
    Round 10

    Playboy

    [Sept 1957]

          1957

Coppola, Jo

    The View from Here

    New York Post

    11 Nov 1957

          Hotchner, A. E. 14 Nov 1957

R.F.S.

    Hemingway's Adams

    New York Times

    11 Nov 1957

        Hotchner, A. E. 14 Nov 1957

Behind the Scenes: It's Hemingway's Year

Newsweek

16 Dec 1957

        1957

    Tele Follow-Up Comment

    Variety

    13 Nov 1957

        Hotchner, A. E. 14 Nov 1957

Movies: Behind the Scenes: It's Hemingway's Year

Newsweek

16 Dec 1957

        1957

Boal, San

    The Hemingway I Know

    [Gentleman]

    [Dec 1957]

        1957

Hemingways in Old Man and Sea

[1958]

        1958

Lyons, Leonard

    The Lyons Den

    New York Post

    11 Dec 1957

        1957

Kemp, Tom

    The Fishing Times of a Great Author

    Fisherman Magazine

    Jan 1958

        1958

    Ernest Hemingway

    Atlantic

    12 Dec 1957

        1957

Talese, Guy

    Tunney Floored by James Joyce's Prose

    New York Times

    6 Jan 1958

        Tunney, James Joseph
        7 Jan 1958

[Selznick, David O.]

To: Whom It May Concern
From: David O. Selznick
Subject: Making a Movie

Life Magazine

17 Mar 1958

1958

Aronowitz, Alfred

The Author Also Rises

New York Post

7 Aug 1958

Wilson, Earl   7 Aug 1958

Plimpton, George

The Art of Fiction XXI: Ernest Hemingway

Paris Review

Spring 1958

1958

Robinson, Layhmond

Hemingway Says He Will Drop Suit

New York Times

7 Aug 1958

Robinson, Layhmond
7 Aug 1958

Books: Hemingway. . . He Writes in an Icy Mood

Newsweek

21 Apr 1958

1958

People: Author Ernest Hemingway was bullmad. . .

Time

18 Aug 1958

1958

Ernest Hemingway: Rogue of Distinction

Rogue Magazine

May 1958

1958

People: The Same Old Papa

Newsweek

18 Aug 1958

1958

McKnight, Gerald

How Writers Work. . . London

[Cosmopolitan]

[Aug 1958]

1958

Beatty, Jr., Jerome

Ernest Hemingway vs. Esquire

Saturday Review

23 Aug 1958

1958

Machlin, Milt

    Hemingway Talking

    Argosy

    Sept 1958

        1958

Offer by Hemingway Romises $1000 to Pole
for Translating Green Hills

New York Times

3 Dec 1958

    Zielinski, Bronislaw
    4 Dec 1958

Powers, Ormund

    Paragraphs

    Orland Sentinel

    10 Sept 1958

        Wilson, Earl 7 Aug 1958

O'Flaherty, Terrence

    Hemingway, Meet the Monster

    San Francisco Chronicle

    [Mar 1959]

        1959

Knight, Arthur

    The Old Man on the Screen

    Saturday Review

    4 Oct 1958

        1958

Fragment: . . . from the
Lost Generation. . .

[New York Post]

[9 Mar 1959]

        1959

Schier, Ernie

    Happy Ending to a Fish Story

    Philadelphia Bulletin

    12 Oct 1958

        1958

Williams, Bob

    On the Air

    New York Post

    27 Mar 1959

        1959

    Girl Seduced Atop 65-Ft. Flagpole

    New York Herald Tribune

    23 Oct 1958

        Brague, Harry
        23 Oct 1958

Harris, Phil

    Papa-San, Mama-San brighten Local Scene

    Sarasota, Florida, News

    2 Apr 1959

        1959

Oil by Waldo Peirce, Bulls at Pamplona
Tucson Daily Citizen
4 Apr 1959

        Peirce, Waldo 13 Jan 1960

Crosby, John
    John Crosby on TV: The Son Rises
    New York Herald Tribune
    [8 June 1959]
        1959

Eastman, Max
    The Great and Small in Ernest Hemingway
    Saturday Review
    4 Apr 1959
        1959

Rubiera
    Tercera Corrida de la Feria de Burgos
    Arriba
    1 July 1959
        Davis, Nathan
        18 Mar 1960

Castro Biopic via Jerry Wald

28 Apr [1959]
        Hotchner, A. E. 13 May 1959

Sotos, Jesús
    Hemingway nos dijo ayer en Burgos: Miro
    al Arlanzón desde el puente de San Pueblo
    no para escribir, sino para adorar
    Burgos, La Voz de Castilla
    1 July 1959
        Davis, Nathan
        25 Mar 1960

Ernest Hemingway's son Gregory. . .

[May 1959]
        Bruce, T. Otto 19 Nov 1959

Boal, Sam
    The Old Man and the Truth
    Escapade
    Aug 1959
        1959

Crosby, John
    Afternoon with the Bulls
    New York Herald Tribune
    [June 1959]
        Scribner, Charles, Jr.
        12 June 1959

Matador Throne is Vacant in Spain
New York Times
9 Aug 1959
        Time-Life 13 Aug 1959

Claro, Don

A Bayonne Grande Journee d'Ordonez
Dominguin Excellent

Bayonne Basque-Eclair

17 Aug 1959

Quintana, Juanito 1 Apr 1960

Cousins, Norman

For Whom the Bells Ring

Saturday Review

22 Aug 1959

Scribner, Charles, Jr.
14 Aug 1959

Hemingway to Do a Book about Spanish
Bullfighter

New York Herald Tribune

18 Aug 1959

Scribner, Charles, Jr.
14 Aug 1959

Scwartz, Delmore

The Fiction of Ernest Hemingway

Perspectives USA, #13

Autumn 1959

1959

Lyons, Leonard

The Lyons Den

New York Post

19 Aug 1959

1959

Ditzel, Paul

Ernest Hemingway's Private War with
Adolph Hitler

Man's

Sept 1959

1959

Sueiro, Daniel

Hemingway o la Solidaridad

Madrid, ABC

19 Aug 1959

1959

Appendix

New York Times Book Review

4 Oct 1959

Brague, Harry 2 Oct 1959

Claro, Don

Apres la Corrida du 16 aout a Bayonne,
du Grand Dominguin

Bayonne Basque Eclair

20 Aug 1959

Quintana, Juanito
1 Apr 1960

Clark, Sir Kenneth

Bernard Berenson: The Poor Scholar Who
Captured the Intellectual World

[London] Times

11 Oct 1959

1959

Hemingway to Moscow

Havana Post

18 Oct 1959

1959

Renuncian un comandante de la Fuerza
Aerea y un teniente del grupo)-22
Ciro Redondo, INRA

Havana Avance

16 Jan 1960

1960

Hotchner, A. E.

    Hemingway Talks to American Youth

    This Week Magazine

    18 Oct 1959

1959

Anderson, Jack

    Hemingway Play--Brutal but Effective

    [Miami Herald]

    [30 Jan 1960]

1960

[Lyons, Leonard]

    [The Lyons Den]: Support: One of
    Ernest Hemingway's. . .

    [New York Post]

    [21 Oct 1959]

1959

Baer, Atra

    Hemingway's Prose Stronger Than Any Stage

    New York Journal American

    30 Jan 1960

            Hotchner, A. E. 30 Jan 1960
            & 1960

Photo: Ernest (Papa). . .

Daily News

3 Nov 1959

1959

Bakal, Sid

    TV Review: Electra Playhouse

    New York Herald Tribune

    30 Jan 1960

            Hotchner, A. E. 30 Jan 1960
            & 1960

. . . Joe Blumenfeld, California. . .

Variety

[Jan 1960]

        Hotchner, A. E. 30 Jan 1960

Gross, Ben

    What's On?

    New York Daily News

    30 Jan 1960

            Hotchner, A. E. 30 Jan 1960
            & 1960

H.V.H.

Fifth Column Full of Smoke, Gunfire

[New York World Telegram]

[30 Jan 1960]

1960

Kenny, Nick

Art Murray's Party Is a Ball

[New York Daily Mirror]

[2 Feb 1960]

1960

B.S.

5th Column Effective on TV

[L.I. Press]

[30 Jan 1960]

1960

Les

The Fifth Column

Variety

[3 Feb 1960]

Hotchner, A. E.   10 Feb 1960
& 1960

TV: The Fifth Column

New York Times

30 Jan 1960

Hotchner, A. E.   30 Jan 1960
& 1960

Kirkley, Donald

Look and Listen

Baltimore Sun

1 Feb 1960

Hotchner, A. E.   10 Feb 1960

Machlin, Milt

Hemingway and the World's Phoniest Sport

Argosy

Feb 1960

1960

The TV Scene

Los Angeles Times

1 Feb 1960

Hotchner, A. E.   10 Feb 1960

[Delativer, Barbara]

The Fifth Column

1 Feb 1960

1960

Photo: Toast to Peace

Mesa Tribune

11 Feb 1960

Browne, Ken   12 Feb 1960

Norteamericanos e ingleses ante las
inquietudes de Shanti Andrea

Quintana, Juanito
25 Feb 1960

Gross, Ben

What's On?

[New York Daily News]

[26 Mar 1960]

1960

Hemingway Playhouse

[Newsday]

[3 Mar 1960]

1960

Ross, Don

Television Review

[New York Herald Tribune]

[26 Mar 1960]

1960

[Roberts, Bill]

Celebrities

Houston Press

Shields, Bernice
25 Mar 1960

R.F.S.

The Snows of Kilimanjaro Presented

[New York Times]

[26 Mar 1960]

1960

Areilza disertara en el Cocherito el mismo
dia de la corrida extraordinaria E Invitara
a los actos al embajador de Estados Unidos
y a Hemingway

El Correo Espanol--El Pueblo Vasco

26 Mar 1960

Dunabeita, Juan 29 Mar 1960

Theater News: Hemingway Adapter Using
8 Works in Dramatization

New York Herald Tribune

26 Mar 1960

1960

Baer, Atra

Theme and Cast Are Great--But Snows a
Frost

[New York Journal]

[26 Mar 1960]

1960

Kilimanjaro Dull and Cluttered

[Long Island Press]

[27 Mar 1960]

1960

The televersion of Ernest Hemingway's The
Snows. . .

[New York Daily Mirror]

[27 Mar 1960]

1960

Daniel, Dan

1961 Seen End of IL's Ties in Castro
Land

New York World Telegram and Sun

28 June 1960

1960

Harry Dies Again in Kilimanjaro

[New York World Telegram]

[28 Mar 1960]

1960

Radio Estocolmo Dijo Esta Manana que
Habia Muerto E. Hemingway en Espana

Madrid Pueblo
8 Aug 1960

1960

Les (McCann-Erickson)

The Snows of Kilimanjaro

Variety

30 Mar 1960

1960

El de Buenavista

Les Corridas des 15 et 16 Aout

Bayonne, Le Republicain du Sud-Ouest

17 Aug 1959

Quintana, Juanito   1 Apr 1960

F. DeB.

The Hemingway Specials

[TV Guide].

23 Apr 1960

Hotchner, A. E.   20 Apr 1960

Cayetano

Quintana, Juanito   7 Oct 1960

Guevara, Luis

Hemingway Habla a Manana

Manana

[25 May 1960]

Gonzalez Silva, Manuel
26 May 1960

Cayetano Ordonez

Quintana, Juanito   7 Oct 1960

Daley, Robert
    Ordonez Now the No. 1 Man in Bullfighting
    New York Times
    [13 Oct 1960]
            Brague, Harry   31 Oct 1960

Photo: Un Christmas para ustedes

            Ordonez, Antonio 8 Dec 1960

Ordonez Desmiente a Dominguin
Excelsior
11 Nov 1960
            Ordonez, Antonio 11 Nov 1960

Popelin, Claude
    Le Bombe H.
    Nimes Toros
    1 Dec 1960
            Quintana, Juanito 29 Dec 1960

[Mujica, Manuel (Don Acho)]
    Fue Manolete un Gran Torero?
    [La Prensa]
    [c. Dec 1960]
                1960

Salipe
    Tercio de Toros
    Gaceta Ilustrada

            Quintana, Juanito
            29 Dec 1960

Giraldo, Iader
    Hemingway no es Novelista
    El Espectador

            Ordonez, Antonio 8 Dec 1960

Tolosa, Paco
    Hemingway Fait Rebondir Le Conflit
    D'Orgueils Dominguin-Ordonez
    Paris L'Equipe
    2 Dec 1960
            Quantana, Juanito
            29 Dec 1960

Hemingway no es Novelista Afrima Luis
Miguel en Bogota

            Ordonez, Antonio 8 Dec 1960

Hemingway Will Leave Mayo's Soon

[1961]
                1961

Hemingway Is Patient at Mayo Clinic

Minneapolis Tribune

11 Jan 1961

1961

Hemingway Eyes Hunting Trip Jan. 20

St. Paul

13 Jan 1961

1961

Ernest Hemingway Under Treatment at Mayo
Clinic

Chicago Tribune

11 Jan 1961

1961

Hemingway Enfermo, en Tratamiento en una
Clinica de Minnesota

Quintana, Juanito
14 Jan 1961

Mystery Patient: Novelist Hemingway
Hiding in Mayo Clinic

11 Jan 1961

1961

Hemingway Going to Inauguration? No
Comment

Rochester Post Bulletin

18 Jan 1961

1961

Official Statement--Ernest Hemingway Being
Treated for Hypertension

Rochester Post-Bulletin

11 Jan 1961

1961

. . . The new patient at the Mayo. . .

Time

20 Jan 1961

1961

Spain's aging (34) Matador Luis Miguel
Dominguin. . .

Briggs, Ellis O. 11 Jan 1961

Sickname: The white-bearded patient. . .

Newsweek

23 Jan 1961

1961

Hutchens, John K.

Hemingway and His Critics

New York Herald Tribune

31 Mar 1961

Brague, Harry   31 Mar 1961

Simple Farewell to Hemingway

Newsday

7 July 1961

1961

Murphy, Michael

Ernest Miller Hemingway

Inland

Spring 1961

1961

JFK Collection

Author Left Manuscripts

New Bedford, Mass., Sunday Standard-Times

9 July 1961

1961

donor: Isabel Gattorno

Rev. Msgr. Daniel Sullivan, pastor of the
church and the priest who gave Cooper. . .

Mowrer, Hadley R. H.
20 May 1961

Curtis, Francis M.

Hemingway Told Acushnet Artist Death
Like Knockout

New Bedford, Mass., Sunday Standard-Times

9 July 1961

1961

donor: Isabel Gattorno

Ernest Hemingway's Health is Improved

Boston Herald

1 June 1961

1961

JFK Collection

Village Artist Remembers Ernesto

New York, The Villager

13 July 1961

1961

donor: Isabel Gattorno

Ernest Hemingway. The Super-Man Myth

Toronto Star

25 June 1921

Star Scrapbook, p. 5

Howe, Irving

Hemingway: The Conquest of Panic

The New Republic

24 July 1961

1961

JFK Collection

Maiorana, Ronald

Hemingway Wrote His Will in Legal Style

New York Times

25 Aug 1961

1961

Campbell, Colin

Trio of Hemingway Portraits

Boston Christian Science Monitor

16 Aug 1962

1962

donor: Matthew Bruccoli

The Snows of Kilimanjaro and Other Stories

Wichita Falls, Texas, Times

3 Sept 1961

Snows of Kilimanjaro

donor: Matthew Bruccoli

Poore, Charles

When people asked Ernest Hemingway's. . .

New York Times

16 Aug 1962

1962

donor: Matthew Bruccoli

Ernest Hemingway: The Man and His Work (advertisment)

25 Sept [1961]

1961

Fouser, Donald B.

Ho Hum Hemingway

Worcester, Mass., Telegram

19 Aug 1962

1962

donor: Matthew Bruccoli

Sherman, Thomas B.

Reading and Writing

Literary News

1 Apr 1962

1962

E.A.L.

Ernest Never Grew Up

Boston Globe

19 Aug 1962

1962

donor: Matthew Bruccoli

Kupferberg, Herbert

Daily Book Review: At the Hemingways

New York Herald Tribune

14 Aug 1962

1962

donor: Matthew Bruccoli

, Robert

At the Hemingways: A Family Portrait

Rutland, Vermont, Herald

28 Aug 1962

1962

donor: Matthew Bruccoli

Baker, Carlos

When Ernie Was Just an Eldest Brother

New York Times

2 Sept 1962

1962

donor: Matthew Bruccoli

M.E.G.

Life at the Hemingways Proves Rather Dull

New Bedford, Mass., Standard Times

18 Nov 1962

1962

donor: Matthew Bruccoli

J.S.K.

Hemingway's Family

Hartford, Conn., Catholic Transcript

13 Sept 1962

1962

donor: Matthew Bruccoli

Nolan, W. F.

A Note on Ernest Hemingway

Gamma, Vol. 1, No. 2

1963

1963

At the Hemingway's. . . is a book. . .

Burlington, Vermont, News

30 Sept 1962

1962

donor: Matthew Bruccoli

Barkham, John

Desks Cleared of Memorabilia, The Work Begins

St. Petersburg Times

19 Jan 1963

Feast Scrapbook, p. 11

D.F.K.

Books and Authors: At the Hemingways

Lewiston-Auburn, Maine, Sun

25 Oct 1962

1962

donor: Matthew Bruccoli

Markel, Helen

A Look Back, A Look Ahead

Good Housekeeping Magazine

Feb 1963

1963

JFK Collection

At the Hemingway's. . . is an account. . .

Burlington, Vermont, Free Press

7 Nov 1962

1962

donor: Matthew Bruccoli

Books and Authors

New York Times

23 Oct 1963

Feast Scrapbook, p. 5

Final Hemingway Book Due in Spring
Atlanta Journal
23 Oct 1963

Feast Scrapbook, p. 6

New Book Soon by Hemingway
San Francisco Examiner
23 Oct 1963

Feast Scrapbook, p. 6

Hemingway Book Due in Spring
Dallas Morning News
23 Oct 1963

Feast Scrapbook, p. 5

New Hemingway Book Announced
Washington Post
23 Oct 1963

Feast Scrapbook, p. 5

Hemingway Book Due Next Spring
Philadelphia Inquirer
23 Oct 1963

Feast Scrapbook, p. 6

New Hemingway Book to Appear Early in '64
Washingon, D.C., Evening Star
23 Oct 1963

Feast Scrapbook, p. 5

Hemingway Finale Due in Spring
San Francisco News-Call Bulletin
23 Oct 1963

Feast Scrapbook, p. 6

People in the News: Ezra Pound. . .
New York Journal American
23 Oct 1963

Feast Scrapbook, p. 7

Hemingway's New Book Ready
Atlanta Constitution
23 Oct 1963

Feast Scrapbook, p. 7

UPI

Book Hemingway Wrote at Death to Be
Published
Hartford, Conn., Times
23 Oct 1963

Feast Scrapbook, p. 6

The Book Corner
San Francisco Examiner
24 Oct 1963

        Feast Scrapbook, p. 7

Society by Suzy
New York Journal American
24 Oct 1963

        Feast Scrapbook, p. 6

Hemingway's Last Book Slated
Evansville, Indiana, Courier
24 Oct 1963

        Feast Scrapbook, p. 7

New Volume by Hemingway
Philadelphia Inquirer
27 Oct 1963

        Feast Scrapbook, p. 5

Names and Faces
Detroit Free Press
24 Oct 1963

        Feast Scrapbook, p. 5

Tips: Previews, Promotions, Sales
Publisher's Weekly
28 Oct 1963

        Feast Scrapbook, p. 5

People
Dayton, Ohio, News
24 Oct 1963

        Feast Scrapbook, p. 6

Hemingway's New Book
Boston Christian Science Monitor
31 Oct 1963

        Feast Scrapbook, p. 5

Plan New Book by Hemingway
Milwaukee Journal
24 Oct 1963

        Feast Scrapbook, p. 7

Another book by Ernest. . .
Cleveland Plain Dealer
3 Nov 1963

        Feast Scrapbook, p. 7

. . . The book Ernest Hemingway was. . .

Raleigh, N.C., News and Observer

3 Nov 1963

        Feast Scrapbook, p. 7

St. John, Robert

    About Books, World Reporter, Pal of
    Hemingway's, Authors 15th Book

    Phoenix Gazette

    6 Nov 1963

        Feast Scrapbook, p. 7

Doar, Harriet

    About Writers and Readers

    Charlotte, N.C., Observer

    3 Nov 1963

        Feast Scrapbook, p. 6

Hemingway's Last Book

Providence, R.I., Journal

10 Nov 1963

        Feast Scrapbook, p. 7

Mrs. Roosevelt's Christmas Book to Be
Released: . . . A memoir of Ernest. . .

St. Paul Pioneer Press

3 Nov 1963

        Feast Scrapbook, p. 7

New Hemingway

Baltimore, Maryland, Sun

10 Nov 1963

        Feast Scrapbook, p. 6

Notes on a Margin

Los Angeles Herald Examiner

3 Nov 1963

        Feast Scrapbook, p. 5

---

12 Grow Up and Gilbreths Write Again

Minneapolis Sunday Tribune

24 Nov 1963

        Feast Scrapbook, p. 5

Book Week News

New York Herald Tribune

6 Nov 1963

        Feast Scrapbook, p. 5

Breslin, Jimmy

    Papa's Sketches

    New York Herald Tribune

    10 Dec 1963

        Feast Scrapbook, p. 10

Gilroy, Harry

    Hemingway Left Variety of Works

    New York Times

    10 Dec 1963

            Feast Scrapbook, p. 10
            & 1963

Breslin, Jimmy

    Life with Papa

    Boston Globe

    15 Dec 1963

            Feast Scrapbook, p. 12

He Feared Taxes: 50 Pounds of Hemingway
Transcript in a Bank

San Francisco Chronicle

10 Dec 1963

            Feast Scrapbook, p. 10

Peckham, Stanton

    Readers' Roundup: Moveable Feast,
    Hemingway's Last, Has Advice for Skiers

    Denver Post

    15 Dec 1963

            Feast Scrapbook, p. 11

Hemingway Novel Revealed

New York Post

10 Dec 1963

            Feast Scrapbook, p. 10

Smith, Miles A.

    New Hemingway Book Coming in the Spring

    [Cleveland] Plain Dealer

    15 Dec 1963

            Feast Scrapbook, p. 12

New Book on the Way: Like Most of Us
Hemingway Disliked to Pay Taxes

Washington, D.C., Daily News

10 Dec 1963

            Feast Scrapbook, p. 11

Posthumous Hemingway

Publisher's Weekly

16 Dec 1963

            Feast Scrapbook, p. 11

People in the News: Importance of Being
Ernest

Miami News

10 Dec 1963

            Feast Scrapbook, p. 12

In and Out of Books

New York Times

22 Dec 1963

            Feast Scrapbook, p. 12

From the Bookshelf: Hemingway's
Posthumous Works

Sioux City Sunday Journal

29 Dec 1963

    Feast Scrapbook, p. 13

Newquist, Roy A.

 Books of the Week: 1964 Titles Show
 Promise

 Chicago Heights Star

 1 Jan 1964

    Feast Scrapbook, p. 13

Introducing Next Month's Books

[Publisher's Weekly]

[1964]

    Feast Scrapbook, p. 21

Dever, Joseph X.

 Society Today: Greek Shipping Queen's
 Romance Is in Full Speed

 New York World Telegram

 3 Jan 1964

    Feast Scrapbook, p. 13

Photo: Portrait of a Poet in Paris

[1964]

    Feast Scrapbook, p. 40

Hemingway

Omaha World-Herald

5 Jan 1964

    Feast Scrapbook, p. 12

Photo: The young Hemingway. . .

Saturday Review

[1964]

    Feast Scrapbook, p. 14

Lyons, Leonard

 The Lyons Den

 New York Post

 5 Jan 1964

    Feast Scrapbook, p. 12

Smith, Ruth

 Moveable Feast or Portable Bar

 Orlando Sentinel

 [1964]

    Feast Scrapbook, p. 45

Barkham, John

 A Writer's Diary

 Philadelphia Sunday Bulletin

 12 Jan 1964

    Feast Scrapbook, p. 14

50 Pounds of Hemingway

New York Newsweek

12 Jan 1964

      Feast Scrapbook, p. 14

Miss Mary Works: Little by Little into Hemingway Papers

Charlotte Observer

15 Mar 1964

      Feast Scrapbook, p. 15

Tips: Previews, Promotions, Sales

Publisher's Weekly

10 Feb 1964

      Feast Scrapbook, p. 21

Hemingway, Ernest

Paris

Life Magazine

10 Apr 1964

      Feast Scrapbook, p. 19

Montgomery, Connie

    Cuba and Central Park: Park East Personality Mary Hemingway

    Park East

    20 Feb 1964

      Feast Scrapbook, p. 14

Griffin, Lloyd W.

    Hemingway, Ernest. A Moveable Feast. Begun in 1958. . .

    1 Apr 1964

      Feast Scrapbook, p. 25

Paris and Hemingway's Spring

[Virginia Kirkus Review]

1 Mar 1964

      Feast Scrapbook, p. 25

MacGregor, Martha

    The Week in Books

    New York Post

    5 Apr 1964

      Feast Scrapbook, p. 16

Bond, Alice Dixon

    The Case for Books: Acclaim Is Won by Authors

    Boston Sunday Herald

    15 Mar 1964

      Feast Scrapbook, p. 13

Hunt, George P.

    How Hemingway Wrote A Moveable Feast

    Life Magazine

    10 Apr 1964

Buck, W. Barton

    Paris As Hemingway Could Remember It

    St. Petersburg Times

    12 Apr 1964

        Feast Scrapbook, p. 21

Orgain, Marian M.

    Hemingway Recaptures Paris of His Youth

    Houston Chronicle

    26 Apr 1964

        Feast Scrapbook, p. 50

Darack, Arthur

    Was Hemingway a Lousy Lover

    Cincinnati Enquirer

    18 Apr 1964

        Feast Scrapbook, p. 51

Tips: Previews, Promotions, Sales

Publisher's Weekly

28 Apr 1964

        Feast Scrapbook, p. 21

Tehan, Arline Boucher

    Books on Trial: Hemingway's Memoirs of
    Lost Generation in Paris

    Hartford, Conn., Times

    18 Apr 1964

        Feast Scrapbook, p. 43

Books: Ernest Hemingway's posthumous. . .

Playboy

May 1964

        Feast Scrapbook, p. 60

Cross, Leslie

    Reading and Writing: Mr. Hemingway
    Does It Again

    Milwaukee Journal

    19 Apr 1964

        Feast Scrapbook, p. 21

Geismar, Maxwell

    Books: When He Was Good

    Cosmopolitan

    May 1964

        Feast Scrapbook, p. 60

Knott, John

    Young Hemingway, Sylvia Beach and Library

    Memphis Commercial Appeal

    19 Apr 1964

        Feast Scrapbook, p. 51

A Moveable Feast: Sketches of the
Author's Life in Paris in the Twenties

Harper's Bazaar

[May 1964]

        Feast Scrapbook, p. 60

New Books: A Moveable Feast

Seventeen

May 1964

      Feast Scrapbook, p. 60

Bates, Dan

    Feast Reveals Early Hemingway

    Fort Worth Star Telegram

    3 May 1964

        Feast Scrapbook, p. 50

Pryce-Jones, Alyn

    Hemingway: Poor and Very Happy

    New York Herald Tribune

    May 1964

        Feast Scrapbook, p. 31

. Beatty, Floy W.

      Under the Green Lamp--Paris in the
      Twenties

      Nashville Tennessean

      3 May 1964

          Feast Scrapbook, p. 51

Faherty, Robert

    Memoir Bares Soul: By Hemingway: The
    Paris Tale

    Chicago Daily News

    2 May 1964

        Feast Scrapbook, p. 47

Butler, Henry

    Book Reviews: Hemingway's 5 Good Years
    in Paris

    Indianapolis Sunday Times

    3 May 1964

        Feast Scrapbook, p. 57

Smith, Miles A.

    A Backward Look

    AP Newsfeatures

    2 May 1964

        Feast Scrapbook, p. 58

Edelstein, Arthur

    Other Voices, Other Tombs

    New York Post

    3 May 1964

        Feast Scrapbook, p. 39

Wharton, Will

    Early Hemingway Days: Poor, Happy

    St. Louis Globe-Democrat

    2 May 1964

        Feast Scrapbook, p. 49

Greene, A. C.

    The Printed Page: Hemingway Detects Life

    Dallas Times Herald

    3 May 1964

        Feast Scrapbook, p. 48

Haas, Victor Paul

    From a Bookman's Notebook

    Omaha World-Herald

    3 May 1964

        Feast Scrapbook, p. 53

Kirsch, Robert R.

    Hemingway: Self-Portrait of Artist as Young Expatriate

    Los Angeles Times

    3 May 1964

        Feast Scrapbook, p. 37

Haddican, James

    Hemingway Views Paris Salad Days--Life Was Good

    New Orleans Times-Picayune

    3 May 1964

        Feast Scrapbook, p. 46

Martin, Jack

    The Book Shelf: Hemingway Looks at His Youth

    Detroit Free Press

    3 May 1964

        Feast Scrapbook, p. 49

Havighurst, Walter

    Hemingway at Sunrise

    Chicago Tribune

    3 May 1964

        Feast Scrapbook, p. 54

Moore, Harry T.

    An American in Paris

    St. Louis Post-Dispatch

    3 May 1964

        Feast Scrapbook, p. 49

Hobby, Diana

    Young Hemingway

    Houston Post

    3 May 1964

        Feast Scrapbook, p. 64

H.N.

    Book Week: Young Hemingway's Life in Paris of 20s

    Chicago Sun-Times

    3 May 1964

        Feast Scrapbook, p. 46

Hogan, William

    A Moveable Feast

    San Francisco Sunday Chronicle

    3 May 1964

        Feast Scrapbook, p. 42

Plimpton, George

    When Papa Was Apprenticing

    Washington Post

    3 May 1964

        Feast Scrapbook, p. 30

Reed, Margaret

The Pre-Dawn of World Recognition

Wichita Falls Times

3 May 1964

Feast Scrapbook, p. 47

Lerner, Max

Papa's Paris

New York Post

4 May 1964

Feast Scrapbook, p. 39

Swinson, Tom

Hemingway Paris of 20s Lives Again in Vivid Prose

Denver Rocky Mountain News

3 May 1964

Feast Scrapbook, p. 43

A Moveable Feast. Finished in 1960. . .

Publisher's Weekly

5 May 1964

Feast Scrapbook, p. 25

Wellejus

Bookshelf. If you are lucky. . .

Erie, Pa., Times-News

3 May 1964

Feast Scrapbook, p. 49

Poore, Charles

Books of the Times: Ernest Hemingway's Memoir of Paris in the Twenties

New York Times

5 May 1964

Feast Scrapbook, p. 31

Photo: The Young Author in Paris

San Francisco Sunday Chronicle

3 May 1964

Feast Scrapbook, p. 42

Rogers, W. G.

The Bookshelf: Hemingway, Paris and Happy 20s

New York World Telegram

5 May 1964

Feast Scrapbook, p. 38

Boroff, David

Papa in the Paris of the '20s: Nice and Nasty

National Observer

4 May 1964

Feast Scrapbook, p. 57

Fuller, Edmund

Reading for Pleasure: Hemingway's Paris

Wall Street Journal

7 May 1964

Feast Scrapbook, p. 38

Douglas, Mary Stahlman

    Hemingway Recalls Paris in Twenties

    Nashville Banner

    8 May 1964

        Feast Scrapbook, p. 49

Howat, Mark

    Hemingway in Love

    Bergen County, N.J., Record

    9 May 1964

        Feast Scrapbook, p. 55

Lerner, Max

    The Hemingway Book: Some Scores Paid Off

    Boston Traveler

    8 May 1964

        Feast Scrapbook, p. 53

Kauffman, Stanley

    Paris and Hemingway in the Spring

    New Republic

    9 May 1964

        Feast Scrapbook, p. 59

    When Papa Was Tatie

    Time

    8 May 1964

        Feast Scrapbook, p. 33

Kinnaird, Clark

    A Moveable Feast

    King Features

    9 May 1964

        Feast Scrapbook, p. 58

Danby-Smith, Valerie

    Reminiscence of Hemingway

    Saturday Review

    9 May 1964

        Feast Scrapbook, p. 59

La Fleche, Cuane

    Books and Authors: Memories of Paris
    Haunted Hemingway

    Albany, N.Y., Knickerbocker News

    9 May 1964

        Feast Scrapbook, p. 40

Hicks, Granville

    Oh to Be Poor in Paris

    Saturday Review

    9 May 1964

        Feast Scrapbook, p. 59

Rogers, W. G.

    Hemingway and Paris Make Fascinating
    Book

    Tucson Daily Citizen

    9 May 1964

        Feast Scrapbook, p. 41

Barmann, George

　　Paris Life in the 1920s Was Ernest for Hemingway

　　[Cleveland] Plain Dealer

　　10 May 1964

　　　　Feast Scrapbook, p. 47

Hemingway, Mary

　　The Making of the Book:　A Chronicle and a Memoir

　　New York Times Book Review

　　[10 May 1964]

　　　　Feast Scrapbook, p. 29

Bond, Alice Dixon

　　The Case for Books:　A Movealbe Feast Has Poignant Beautry

　　Boston Sunday Herald

　　10 May 1964

　　　　Feast Scrapbook, p. 52

Hunter, Anna C.

　　Sketches by Hemingway Recapture That Rare Ambience of Paris in 20s

　　Savannah Morning News

　　10 May 1964

　　　　Feast Scrapbook, p. 52

Cannell, Kathleen

　　Ernest Hemingway's Last Book

　　Providence, R.I., Journal

　　10 May 1964

　　　　Feast Scrapbook, p. 53

Laycock, Edward A.

　　Hemingway's Paris His Beginning

　　Boston Globe

　　10 May 1964

　　　　Feast Scrapbook, p. 46

Carr, Mildred L.

　　The Young Hemingway Looks at Paris

　　Greensboro Daily News

　　10 May 1964

　　　　Feast Scrapbook, p. 55

O'Leary, Theodore M.

　　Hemingway Self-Revealed:　So Splendid and So Petty

　　Kansas City Star

　　10 May 1964

　　　　Feast Scrapbook, p. 52

Galantiere, Lewis

　　There Is Never Any End to Paris

　　Baltimore News American

　　10 May 1964

　　　　Feast Scrapbook, p. 55

Plimpton, George

　　Hemingway Remembers His Paris

　　St. Petersburg Times

　　10 May 1964

　　　　Feast Scrapbook, p. 44

Poore, Charles

Sojourn in Paris: Hemingway--The Vivid
Past

Winston-Salem, N.C., Journal and Sentinel

10 May 1964

Feast Scrapbook, p. 48

Southern Accents: If you are lucky. . .

Raleigh, N.C., News and Observer

10 May 1964

Feast Scrapbook, p. 50

Rogers, W. G.

Very Poor, Very Happy, Hemingway's Years
in Paris

Philadelphia Sunday Bulletin

10 May 1964

Feast Scrapbook, p. 50

Stuart, Reece

Young Hemingway Found Paris a Feast

Des Moines Register

10 May 1964

Feast Scrapbook, p. 46

Sandroff, Ivan

Days of Wine and Roses

Worcester, Mass., Sunday Telegram

10 May 1964

Feast Scrapbook, p. 48

Thorpe, Day

Hemingway's Paris in a Vivid Memoir

Washinton, D.C., Sunday Star

10 May 1964

Feast Scrapbook, p. 52

Sherman, John K.

Hemingway Recreates Lost Generation Era in
Moveable Feast

Minneapolis Sunday Tribune

10 May 1964

Feast Scrapbook, p. 50

Wolfe, Ann F.

A True Love Letter to Hemingway's Paris

Colubus, Ohio, Dispatch

10 May 1964

Feast Scrapbook, p. 54

Sizer, Alvin V.

Hemingway's Early Paris Years: A
Fascinating Literary Memoir

New Haven Register

10 May 1964

Feast Scrapbook, p. 43

Hyman, Stanley Edgar

Ernest Hemingway with a Knife

New Leader

11 May 1964

Feast Scrapbook, p. 63
& 1964

The Torrents of Spring

Newsweek

11 May 1964

      Feast Scrapbook, p. 32

O'Neill, Joan

    Hemingway Paris a Stoic's Love

    Atlanta Journal

    17 May 1964

        Feast Scrapbook, p. 45

Wilson, W. Emerson

    Hemingway and Happy Paris Days

    Wilmington Morning News

    11 May 1964

        Feast Scrapbook, p. 53

Peckham, Stanton

    Hemingway's Recollections of Paris in
    the 20s Is Mellow, Light, Nostalgic,
    Agreeable Reading

    Denver Post

    17 May 1964

        Feast Scrapbook, p. 56

Duckworth, Lois

    A Happy Loving Young Hemingway

    Louisville Times

    12 May 1964

        Feast Scrapbook, p. 54

Baisden, Frank

    Puny, Posthumous Publication Not Saved
    by Hemingway Name

    Chattanooga Daily Times

    24 May 1964

        Feast Scrapbook, p. 50

Maddocks, Melvin

    Hemingway's Paris Legend

    Boston Christian Science Monitor

    14 May 1964

        Feast Scrapbook, p. 54

Cole, Verne

    Hemingway's Sketches of His Youth in Paris

    Fresno Bee

    24 May 1964

        Feast Scrapbook, p. 42

Barley, Rex

    Reminiscence in Posthumous Hemingway Book

    Phoenix Arizona Republic

    17 May 1964

        Feast Scrapbook, p. 41

Fiedler, Leslie A.

    A Different View of the Hemingway Legend

    Chicago Tribune

    24 May 1964

        Feast Scrapbook, p. 35

Kinnaird, Clark

A Moveable Feast

New York Journal American

24 May 1964

Feast Scrapbook, p. 38

Burger, Von Eric

Hemingways Schubladen

DieWelt der Literatur

28 May 1964

Feast Scrapbook, p. 65

Shroyer, Frederick

Hemingway's Paris Feast

Los Angeles Herald Examiner

24 May 1964

Feast Scrapbook, p. 42

De Mott, Benjamin

The Need for Watering Places

Harper's

June 1964

Feast Scrapbook, p. 62

Best Sellers of the Week

Publisher's Weekly

25 May 1964

Feast Scrapbook, p. 66

Ernest Hemingway's A Moveable. . .

Mademoiselle

June 1964

Feast Scrapbook, p. 60

Kay, Jane

How It Really Was

Quincy Patriot Ledger

26 May 1964

Feast Scrapbook, p. 56

Kazin, Alfred

Hemingway as His Own Fable

Atlantic Monthly

Feast Scrapbook, p. 62

M.A.S.

Late Hemingway Writing Shows Paris in Twenties

Kalamzoo Gazette

26 May 1964

Feast Scrapbook, p. 48

Wells, Joel

A Moveable Feast by Ernest Hemingway

Chicago Critic

June 1964

Feast Scrapbook, p. 61

Best Sellers of the Week

Publisher's Weekly

1 June 1964

      Feast Scrapbook, p. 66

Best Sellers of the Week

Publisher's Weekly

6 July 1964

      Feast Scrapbook, p. 66

Wagner, Geoffrey

    Hemingway Playing Hemingway Victim of a Manner

    The Nation

    1 June 1964

      Feast Scrapbook, p. 61

Root, William

    A Feast of Sketches Offered by Hemingway after Death

    New York Worker

    7 July 1964

      Feast Scrapbook, p. 56

Smith, Miles A.

    Books: A Moveable Feast

    El Paso Times

    7 June 1964

      Feast Scrapbook, p. 51

Best Seller List

[August 1964]

      Feast Scrapbook, p. 67

Kermode, Frank

    Hemingway's Last Novel

    New York Review of Books

    11 June 1964

      Feast Scrapbook, p. 36

Books: Bounty

Newsweek

21 Dec 1964

      Feast Scrapbook, p. 77

Chaplin, George

    Prime Reading for This Week

    Honolulu Star-Bulletin and Advertiser

    21 June 1964

      Feast Scrapbook, p. 56

Hotchner, A. E.

    Hemingway, Part II

    [New York] Post

    26 Mar 1966

        1966

JFK Collection

Manning, Robert

The Meaning of Hemingway's Achievement

Sun Valley Sun

August 1966

1966

Hemingway's Idaho

Venture

Sept 1968

1968

Taylor, Dorice

Ernest Hemingway's Sun Valley Visits

Sun Valley Sun

August 1966

1966

Wardlow, Jean

At Home with Miss Mary

Venture

Sept 1968

1968

Porterfield, Waldon R.

The Past Clings to Hemingway Home

1967

1967

Bruccoli, M. J.

Ernest Hemingway as Cub Reporter, w/reprint of EH's Battle of Raid Squads, 6 June 1918, Kansas City Star

Esquire

Dec [1968]

1968

JFK Collection

Brucker, Jerry

Azure Days in Key West: Hemingway in His Prime

Kirkwood, Missouri, Mark Twain Journal

Feb 1968

1968

Country School Trustees to Honor Hemingway

Twin Falls

1969

1969

Wolf, Jacob H.

An Unnoticed Side of Hemingway

[9 June 1968]

1968

Kann, Hans-Joachim

Audre Hannemann: Ernest Hemingway: A Comprehensive Bibliography [review]

Die Neueren Sprachen

Jan 1969

1969

donor: Hans-Joachim Kann

Kazin, Alfred

He Sensed the Disenchantment in Our Time

Chicago Tribune Book World

13 Apr 1969

1969

The Fifth Column and Four Stories

Book of the Month Club News

Fall 1969

Fifth Column

donor: Matthew Bruccoli

McCormick, John

The Sound of Hooves

Sports Illustrated

7 July 1969

1969

Murphy, Michael

Hemingway: Rod & Gun

Inland Magazine

Autumn 1969

1969

JFK Collection

The Fifth Column and Four Stories of the
Spanish Civil War. Four previously. . .

V[irginia] Kirkus Bulletin

1 Aug 1969

Fifth Column

donor: Matthew Bruccoli

Novel by Hemingway Uncovered

[Hartford, Connecticut, Times]

[c. Sept 1969]

1969

The Fifth Column and Four Stories of the
Spanish Civil War. Four previously. . .

V[irginia] Kirkus Bulletin

15 Aug 1969

Fifth Column

donor: Matthew Bruccoli

Blackstock, Walter

Transforming Ephemeral Material into
Literature

Fayetteville, N.C., Observer

7 Sept 1969

Fifth Column

donor: Matthew Bruccoli

Once Over but Lightly

Fort Worth Star

31 Aug 1969

Fifth Column

donor: Matthew Bruccoli

Seward, William W., Jr.

The Extremes of Hemingway

Norfolk, Virginia, Pilot

8 Sept 1969

Fifth Column

donor: Matthew Bruccoli

Hogan, William

    Good Old Times in the Hotel Florida

    San Francisco Chronicle

    10 Sept 1969
            Fifth Column

donor: Matthew Bruccoli

Hagemann, E. R.

    Hemingway Stories, Play Show Love for Spain

    Louisville, Kentucky, Courier Journal

    14 Sept 1969

            Fifth Column

donor: Matthew Bruccoli

Bruccoli, Matthew

    It's Not Great but It's Papa

    Chicago News

    12 Sept 1969

            Fifth Column

donor: Matthew Bruccoli

Porterfield, Waldon R.

    Still a Winner, Hemingway Returns to Portray
    a War

    Milwaukee Journal

    14 Sept 1969

            Fifth Column

donor: Matthew Bruccoli (1 copy only)

SDL

    New-Found Hemingway Boring: Rerpinted
    Maugham Refereshing

    Columbus, Ohio, Citizen Journal

    13 Sept 1969

            Fifth Column

donor: Matthew Bruccoli

Trotter, William

    Papa's Fire Rekindled

    Charlotte, N.C., Observer

    14 Sept 1969

            Fifth Column

donor: Matthew Bruccoli

Carton, Jasper, II

    A Middle-Years Collection of Ernest
    Hemingway

    Houston Chronicle

    14 Sept 1969

            Fifth Column

donor: Matthew Bruccoli

    Photo: First Fruits

    Wichita Falls, Texas, Times

    14 Sept 1969

            Fifth Column

donor: Matthew Bruccoli

Culligan, Glendy

    Books: Another Look at Hemingway

    Washington, D.C., Sunday Star

    14 Sept 1969

            Fifth Column

donor: Matthew Bruccoli

Cady, Richard E.

    Hemingway's Worst Still Good Enough

    Indianapolis Star

    21 Sept 1969

            Fifth Column

donor: Matthew Bruccoli

Harris, Lee

    Early Hemingway

    Riverside, California, Enterprise

    21 Sept 1969

        Fifth Column

donor: Matthew Bruccoli

Ernest Hemingway left a considerable
body. . .

    Fresno Register

    26 Sept 1969

        Fifth Column

donor: Matthew Bruccoli

Larson, Ray

    Fly-Weight Hemingway

    Worcester, Massachusetts, Telegram

    21 Sept 1969

        Fifth Column

donor: Matthew Bruccoli

Raymont, Henry

    Unpublished Hemingway

    Middletown, Connecticut, Press

    26 Sept 1969

          1969

JFK Collection

Young, Philip

    The Fifth Column

    New York Times

    21 Sept 1969

        Fifth Column

donor: Matthew Bruccoli

Inge, M. Thomas

    Important Addition to Canon of Author
Ernest Hemingway

    Richmond Times Dispatch

    28 Sept 1969

        Fifth Column

donor: Matthew Bruccoli

Raymont, Henry

    Hemingway Papers Yield Surprises

    [New York Times]

    [22 Sept 1969]

          1969

JFK Collection

Sudler, Barbara

    Hemingway Tells of War

    Denver Post

    28 Sept 1969

        Fifth Column

donor: Matthew Bruccoli

Raymont, Henry

    Hemingway Papers List Novel Among
Surprises

    Salt Lake City Tribune

    23 Sept 1969

          1969

JFK Collection

Cooke, Alistair

    Alistair Cooke's America: What Price
Hemingway

    Manchester & London, Guardian

    29 Sept 1969

          1969

JFK Collection

Cooke, Alistair

    Doubtful Fate of Hemingway under the
    Hammer

    Glasgow Herald

    29 Sept 1969

                            1969

JFK Collection

Wylder, Delbert

    4 Hemingway Tales Are Given New Life

    Minneapolis Tribune

    12 Oct 1969

                Fifth Column

    donor: Matthew Bruccoli

Hogan, William

    Good Old Time in the Hotel Florida

    Palos Verdes Peninsula News & Rolling
    Hills Herald

    1 Oct 1969

            Fifth Column

donor: Matthew Bruccoli

GMP

    Contains One Play, Four Stories

    Galesburg, Illinois, Register Mail

    17 Oct 1969

                Fifth Column

    donor: Matthew Bruccoli

Goldstein, Laurence

    E.H. under the Spanish Guns

    Providence, R.I., Journal

    5 Oct 1969

            Fifth Column

donor: Matthew Bruccoli

McNamara, Eugene

    The Fifth Column and Four Stories of the
    Spanish Civil War

    America

    18 Oct 1969

            Fifth Column

    donor: Matthew Bruccoli

Porte, Joel

    Saigon Could Be Today's Setting for
    Hemingway's Drama

    Boston Globe

    12 Oct 1969

            Fifth Column

donor: Matthew Bruccoli

Honig, Nat

    Unpublished Tales by Hemingway

    Garden Grove, California, Orange County
    Evening News

    19 Oct 1969

            Fifth Column

donor: Matthew Bruccoli

Smith, Goldie Capers

    More from Hemingway

    Tulsa World

    12 Oct 1969

            Fifth Column

donor: Matthew Bruccoli

    The Fifth Column . . . appears dated. . .

    El Paso Times

    20 Oct 1969

            Fifth Column

    donor: Matthew Bruccoli

Barry, Tom

    Papa's Doings

    Austin American Statesman

    26 Oct 1969

        Fifth Column

donor: Matthew Bruccoli

    Priced Write

    Chicago Daily News

    7 Nov 1969

        1969

McCormick, Jay

    Some Hemingway You May Have Missed

    Detroit News

    26 Oct 1969

        Fifth Column

donor: Matthew Bruccoli

Walker, C. J.

    Four Nuggets from Master of Great American
    Short Story

    Olympia, Washington, Olympian

    23 Nov 1969

        Fifth Column

donor: Matthew Bruccoli

Satterfield, Archie

    Hemingway and Spain: Four Civil War Tales

    Seattle Times

    26 Oct 1969

        Fifth Column

donor: Matthew Bruccoli

Martin, Judith

    The Difficult Legacy of Mrs. Ernest
    Hemingway

    Washington Post

    30 Nov 1969

        1969

JFK Collection

    The Fifth Column and Four Stories of
    the Spanish Civil War published. . .

    Playboy

    Nov 1969

        Fifth Column

donor: Matthew Bruccoli

Meacham, Harry M.

    Hemingway's Early Tales Compiled

    Richmond News Leader

    3 Dec 1969

        Fifth Column

donor: Matthew Bruccoli

Brumfield, Les

    Hemingway Tales in Collection

    New Orleans Picayune

    2 Nov 1969

        Fifth Column

donor: Matthew Bruccoli

    Hemingway's Stories Depict War

    Anderson, S.C., Independent

    7 Dec 1969

        Fifth Column

donor: Matthew Bruccoli

Paul, Kenneth

    Vintage Hemingway

    Newsweek

    10 Dec 1969

        Fifth Column

donor: Matthew Bruccoli

Latham, Aaron and Judith Martin

    Papa's Novel: Posthumous Hemingway

    Washington, D.C., Post

    [1970]

        Islands

Martin, Judith

    Hemingway Legacy Is Tough Job

    St. Paul Pioneer Press

    12 Dec 1969

        1969

Quiza, Ricardo

    Hemingway 70: Sorprendio las Villas

    [1970]

        1970

Lyons, Leonard

    The Lyons Den

    Minneapolis Star

    16 Dec 1969

        1969

Smith, Miles A.

    Hemingway Appears to Be Hero of His Posthumous Novel

    [Boston Globe]

    [1970]

        Islands

GMP

    Contains One Play, Four Stories

    Galesburg, Illinois, Register Mail

    17 Oct 1969

        Fifth Column

donor: Matthew Bruccoli

Smith, Miles

    Hemingway Novel Going into Print

    Bergan County, N. J., Record

    [1970]

        Islands

Hemingway, Mary

    Journey South to a Cold Summer

    [1970]

        1970

Wood, Sylvia

    Islands in the Stream

    [1970]

        Islands

Nicchi, Ubaldo

Cuando Doblaron las Campanas por Ernest Hemingway

Buenos Aires Clarin

17 Jan 1970

1970

The Fifth Column and Four Stories of the Spanish Civil War

Astoria, Oregon, Astorian

22 Jan 1970

Fifth Column

donor: Matthew Bruccoli

Llegó a Buenos Aires la viuda de Hemingway

Buenos Aires La Nacion

18 Jan 1970

1970

Hemingway Brindo Siempre su Apoyo a la Revolucion Cubana, Declara la Viuda del Escritor

[22 Jan 1970]

1970

Martin, Judith

Hemingway Widow Trying to Live a Life of Her Own

Los Angeles Times

18 Jan 1970

1970

Vine a la Antartica porque quería respirar aire fresco

El Magallanes

14 Feb 1970

1970

Tzigana, Tamara

Mary Hemingway Holds Papa's Memory Tight

Buenos Aires Herald

18 Jan 1970

1970

Douglas, Betsy

Mary Hemingway and Betsy Douglas in Antarctica with Idahoans on a Trip to the South Pole

Boise Idaho Statesman

8 Mar 1970

1970

Entrevista con Mary Welsh, viuda de Ernest Hemingway

[La Prensa]

[19 Jan 1970]

1970

Sheppard, Eugenia

At five minutes before. . .

[20 Mar 1970]

1970

Hemingway's Bitter-Sweet Novel: A Wifely
Preview

New York Post

28 Apr 1970

Islands

Robinet, Marta

Mary Hemingway Walks Alone Now--The
Caretaker of Papa's Legacy

Philadelphia Sunday Bulletin

19 May 1970

1970

Raymont, Henry

Book Left by Hemingway Will Be Published
in Fall

New York Times

29 Apr 1970

Islands

Barkham, John

Posthumous Books: More Due from Hemingway

Dallas News

24 May 1970

1970

New Hemingway Book to Be Printed This Fall

Los Angeles Times

29 Apr 1970

Islands

Bradshaw, Hank

Out in Hemingway Country

Field and Stream

June 1970

1970

Barkham, John

The Author Speaks

Saturday Review

9 May 1970

1970

JFK Collection

Jones, Bonnie Baird

Tourists to the South Pole

Twin Falls, Idaho, Times-News

7 June 1970

1970

Kiester, Don A.

A Life of Donne

Cleveland Plain Dealer

17 May 1970

1970

donor: Matthew Bruccoli

Barzini, Ludina

Voleva prendere Hitler con l'arpione

L'Espresso

5 July 1970

1970

Mary Hemingway y la novela del mar

Vandidates Continental

[14 July 1970]

1970

Hemingway, Mary

Ernest's Homework

Book-of-the-Month Club News

Fall 1970

Islands

Collins, Tom

Mary Hemingway: Caring for a Legacy

Chicago Today Magazine

19 July 1970

1970

Reiger, George W.

A Visit with Tommy Gifford

Salt Water Sportsman

Sept 1970

1970

Ketchum Dedicates Hemingway School

Twin Falls, Idaho, Times News

22 July 1970

1970

Hogan, William

Old Professional in Very Good Form

San Francisco Chronicle

15 Sept 1970

Islands

Hernando, Carlos

Hemingway: Un Legado Inedito

La Prensa

16 Aug 1970

1970

Powers, James

Book Reviews

Hollywood Reporter

18 Sept 1970

Islands

Fadiman, Clifton

Report

Book-of-the-Month Club News

Fall 1970

Islands

Joost, Nicholas

An Island Artist's Moment of Truth

St. Louis Globe Democrat

26-27 Sept 1970

Islands

Clement, Sarah V.

Hemingway's The Fifth Column and
Short Stories Are Reprinted

Jackson, Tenn., Sun

27 Sept 1970

Fifth Column

donor: Matthew Bruccoli

Macauley, Robie

Islands in the Stream

New York Times Book Review

4 Oct 1970

Islands

JFK Collection (1 copy only)

Barkham, John

Book of the Week

Book Service for Newspapers

3 Oct 1970

Islands

Cook, Bruce

A Posthumous Hemingway Novel Yields Both
Gold and Platitude

National Observer

15 Oct 1970

Islands

Geismar, Maxwell

Hemingway's Lost Novel: Illuminating
Self-Portrait

Chicago Sun Times

4 Oct 1970

Islands

Eye Too: . . . Miss Mary Talks. . .

Women's Wear Daily

9 Oct 1970

1970

Hanauer, Joan

Hemingway's Islands

Miami Herald
Duluth News Tribune

4 Oct 1970

Islands

Aldridge, John W.

Hemingway Between Triumph and Disaster:
Islands in the Stream

Saturday Review

10 Oct 1970

Islands

Hudson, Roy

Last Hemingway Novel Judged Literary
Milestone

Salt Lake Tribune

4 Oct 1970

Islands

Shroyer, Frederick

Ernest Hemingway's Last Writings

Los Angeles Herald-Examiner

11 Oct 1970

Islands

Kirsch, Robert

    Islands in the Stream a Worthy Addition to the Hemingway Canon

    Los Angeles Times

    18 Oct 1970

        Islands

Spong, Richard

    The Jackals vs. Papa Hemingway

    Miami Herald

    19 Nov 1970

        Islands

Salterfield, Archie

    Hemingway Legend Lives in a New Book Islands in the Stream

    Seattle Times

    18 Oct 1970

        Islands

Hughes, John W.

    Age of the Emotive Man

    New Leader

    24 Nov 1970

        Fifth Column

donor: Matthew Bruccoli

Gutkin, Lee Alan

    Fishing, Writing, Drinking

    Billings, Montana, Gazette

    15 Oct 1970

        1970

    How Not to Write a Book

    [1971]

        1971

    The Fifth Column and Four Stories of the Spanish Civil War

    Maryland

    Nov 1970

        Fifth Column

donor: Matthew Bruccoli

Kann, Hans-Joachim

    Anekdotenerzahler und Dichter

    Rheinischer Merkur

    [1971]

        Islands

donor: Hans-Joachim Kann

Evans, Walter A.

    Hemingway's Gift to Sons Jack, the Eldest Tells of Exposure to Outdoor Values

    Seattle Post-Intelligencer

    13 Nov 1970

        1970

Reich-Ranicki, Von Marcel

    Freude durch Kraft: Uber Ernest Hemingway und die Deutschen aus gegebenem Alnaf

    [1971]

        Islands

donor: Hans-Joachim Kann

Marsh, Robert C.

    In Defense of Hemingway's Islands

    Chicago Sun-Times

    7 Jan 1971

        Islands

Photo: A beaming Mrs. Hemingway. . .

St. Thomas, Virgin Islands, Home Journal

16 Apr 1971

        1971

Cancer Crusade: Mrs. Hemingway Named
Honorary Chairman

Caldwell, Idaho, News Tribune

[Apr 1971]

        1971

Fishing for a Hit Movie

New York Post

30 Apr 1971

        1971

Late Author's Widow to Aid Cancer Crusade

Nampa Idaho Free Press

1 Apr 1971

        1971

Mary Hemingway

The Lotus Club

May 1971

        1971

Hemingway's Widow Named Chairman of Cancer
Drive

Lewiston, Idaho Morning Tribune

2 Apr 1971

        1971

Bory, Jean-Louis

    Un Roman ou Hemingway Explique sa Mort

    Paris Match

    May 1971

        Islands

She Lends Her Name to Health Crusade

Boise Idaho Statesman

4 Apr 1971

        1971

San Martin, Julio

    IX Ernest Hemingway: Inauguran Hoy Torneo
de Pesca de la Aguja

    [14 May 1971]

        1971

Arce, Raúl

    Pesco el pinareño Francisco Mieres una
    Aguja Blanca de 57,5 Libras

    [16 May 1971]

          1971

Newman, M. W.

    The Earliest Ernest: A Born Genius at
    Oak Park High School

    Chicago Daily News Panorama

    31 July/1 Aug 1971

          1971

McCable, Bruce

    JFK Library Prize: Hemingway Papers

    [Boston Globe]

    [4 June 1971]

          1971

JFK Collection

Leeright, Bob

    Idaho Environment '71: Lake Chatcolet
    Destined to Die from Pollution

    Salt Lake Tribune

    18 Oct 1971

          1971

Payne, Ronald

    The Spectator

    5 May 1971

        Islands

Kolling, Fritz

    Zeit, durchlitten und durchliebt

    Die Bucherkommentare

    Nov 1971

               Islands

donor: Hans-Joachim Kann

Canby, Vincent

    Screen: Dramatic Pursuit of Elusive
    Killer Shark

    New York Times

    12 May 1971

          1971

Delvaux, Michel

    Sketches Americains (V): Rencontre avec
    Mary Hemingway

    d'Letzeburger Land

    19 Nov 1971

          1971

Starrett, Vincent

    Where's Papa: Ernest Hemingway, a
    Remembrance and Reevalutation

    Chicago Tribune Magazine

    18 July 1971

          1971

Kann, Hans-Joachim

    Baker, Carlos: Ernest Hemingway: A Life
    Story

    Kritikon Litterarum

    1972

          1972

Memorial Service Set for Anne Janss: 5 pm

[1972]

1972

Lee, Mike

On Papa's Trail

Miami Pictorial

Apr 1972

1972

Jones, Bonnie

Famous Men Donate to Potpourri

Twin Falls, Idaho, Times News

9 Jan 1972

1972

Bruccoli, Matthew J.

Return of Nick Adams

Chicago Daily News

1 Apr 1972

Nick Adams Stories

Martin, Judith

Papa, Poor Papa

Washington, D.C., Post

23 Jan 1972

1972

V.P.H.

He Had Grace Under Pressure: The Nick
Adams Stories

Omaha World Herald

3 Apr 1972

Nick Adams Stories

Brian, Denis

The Importance of Knowing Ernest

Esquire

Feb [1972]

1972

From the Book. Unpublished Hemingway:
Secrets of Papa/Nick

Detroit Free Press

12 Apr 1972

Nick Adams Stories

Shroyer, Frederick

Spring: When Batches of Good Books Bloom

Los Angeles Herald Examiner

26 Mar 1972

Nick Adams Stories

Brady, Charles A.

Nick Adams Stories--Papa at His Best

Buffalo Evening News

18 Apr 1972

Nick Adams Stories

Langford, Richard

    Books and Authors. Collection: New Evidence On Hemingway's Genius

    Deland, Florida, Sun News

    9 Apr 1972

        Nick Adams Stories

Thomas, Phil

    A Bit Frustrating: The Nick Adams Stories

    [15 Apr 1972]

        Nick Adams Stories

Barkham, John

    The Literary Scene: The Nick Adams Stories

    New York Post

    12 Apr 1972

        Nick Adams Stories

L.B.

    Nick Adams Stories Now Collected

    New Orleans Times Picayune

    16 Apr 1972

        Nick Adams Stories

Ames, Kenneth

    New Collection for Hemingway Fans: The Nick Adams Stories

    Long Beach, California, Press Telegram

    14 Apr 1972

        Nick Adams Stories

Casto, James E.

    Here's More Gold from the Hemingway Archives

    Huntington, W.Va., Herald Advertiser

    10 Apr 1972

        Nick Adams Stories

Moore, Harry T.

    Hemingway Trove, Nick Adams Back

    St. Louis Globe Democrat

    15 Apr 1972

        Nick Adams Stories

Diehl, Digby

    New Helping of Unissued Hemingway

    Los Angeles Times

    16 Apr 1972

        Nick Adams Stories

Thomas, Phil

    Adam Tales: The Nick Adams Stories

    Passaic, N.J., Herald News

    15 Apr 1972

        Nick Adams Stories

Elliott, Gerald A.

    Revealing of the Creator

    Grand Rapids Press

    16 Apr 1972

        Nick Adams Stories

Freshwater, Philip C.

    The Common Reader: Still the Master

    Sacramento Bee

    16 Apr 1972

        Nick Adams Stories

Reid, Margaret W.

    Hemingway's Fictional Self: The Nick
    Adams Stories

    Wichita Falls, Texas, Times

    16 Apr 1972

        Nick Adams Stories

Grant, Louis T.

    The Ones that Should've Got Away

    Baltimore Sun

    16 Apr 1972

        Nick Adams Stories

Thomas, Phil

    Unfinished Hemingway Frustrates The Nick
    Adams Stories

    Shreveport, Texas, Times

    16 Apr 1972

        Nick Adams Stories

Lopez, Eddie

    A Hemingway Treasure

    Fresno Bee

    16 Apr 1972

        Nick Adams Stories

    The Nick Adams Stories

    Hammond, Indiana, Times

    16 Apr 1972

        Nick Adams Stories

Maschal, Richard

    Refreshing Retrospect

    Charlotte, N.C., Observer

    16 Apr 1972

        Nick Adams Stories

P.S.P. [Peter S. Prescott]

    Big Two-Hearted Writer: The Nick Adams
    Stories

    Newsweek

    17 Apr 1972

        Nick Adams Stories

Murray, G. E.

    New Discoveries: Papa's Tales of Nick
    Adams, His Heroic Alter Ego

    Chicago Sun Times

    16 Apr 1972

        Nick Adams Stories

Barkham, John

    Returning to Nick Adams

    Middletown, Conn., Press

    18 Apr 1972

        Nick Adams Stories

Thomas, Phil

Unfinished Collection good, bad: The
Nick Adams Stories

New York Daily News

18 Apr 1972

Nick Adams Stories

Thomas, Phil

Hemingway Fragments Spoil a Good Pattern

Allentown, Pa., Chronicle

23 Apr 1972

Nick Adams Stories

Watts, Richard

Random Notes

New York Post

18 Apr 1972

Nick Adams Stories

Hemingway Reread Has Original Impact: The
Nick Adams Stories

Durham, N.C., Morning Herald

23 Apr 1972

Nick Adams Stories

King, George M.

New Light on Writer's Work, Personality:
The Nick Adams Stories

Nashville Banner

31 Apr 1972

Nick Adams Stories

Thomas, Phil

Mixed Bay of Hemingway: The Nick Adams
Stories

Anniston, Alabama, Star

23 Apr 1972

Nick Adams Stories

Donaldson, Scott

Tales Are Hemingway's Coming-of-Age Novel:
The Nick Adams Stories

Minneapolis Tribune

23 Apr 1972

Nick Adams Stories

Manning, Margaret

Nick Adams--a Reminder

Boston Globe

24 Apr 1972

Nick Adams Stories

Rubin, Louis D., Jr.

A Portrait of Nick Adams and How He
Happened

Washington, D.C., Sunday Star

23 Apr 1972

Nick Adams Stories

Wilson, W. Emerson

Adams Stories Contradict

Wilmington, Delaware, Morning News

26 Apr 1972

Nick Adams Stories

Francis, William A. C.

    Hemingway, Ernest. The Nick Adams Stories

    Best Sellers

    1 May 1972

           Nick Adams Stories

Woman Asks License for Bullfighting

Twin Falls Times-News

13 Aug 1972

          1972

Skow, John

    A Moveable Fast: The Nick Adams Stories

    Time

    1 May 1972

           Nick Adams Stories

Park Book Stalls Get Permit

New York Times

31 Aug 1972

          1972

Griggs, Richard L.

    Griggs Finally Bags a Jaguar

    Duluth News-Tribune

    2 July 1972

        1972

Abrahams, William

    Hemingway: The Poshumous Achievement:
    The Nick Adams Stories

    Atlantic

    June 1972

           Nick Adams Stories

Casey, Phil

    Janet Flanner: The Most Celebrated
    American in Paris

    Winnipeg Free Press

    22 July 1972

        1972

Mary Hemingway Donates Sound System to
Police

Blaine County, Hailey, Idaho, Wood River
Journal

31 Aug 1972

          1972

---

le Clec'h, Guy

    Inepuisable Hemingway

    [Le Figaro]

    [12 Aug 1972]

        1972

Roche, Judy

    Creative Cooking of Game Is an Adventure
    with Mary Hemingway

    Sawtooth Mountain Star

    Fall 1972

        1972

von Hoffman, Nicholas

Get the Godfather (Alias Tight Lips) Out of White House

[Salt Lake Tribune]

[5 Sept 1972]

1972

St. John, Donald

Letters: The Paris Hemingway Knew

1973

1973

JFK Collection

Clarke, Jay

Key West: A Tranquil Sense of the Past

Chicago Tribune

10 Sept 1972

1972

Cowley, Malcolm

Hemingway; The Image and the Shadow

[Horizon]

[Winter 1973]

1973

JFK Collection

Retraction Demand Released in WRJ Hemingway Charge

[Oct 1972]

1972

Barkham, John

Cowley Sees Hemingway

New York Post

4 May 1973

1973

Weaver, Margaret

Good Food and Yarns at Dave's

Cincinnati Post

4 Oct 1972

1972

(bearing TNS David and Tina)

Topor, Tom

The Suicide Story. Article V: From Monroe to Hemingway

New York Post

4 May 1973

1973

Phillips, McCandlish

Party Recalls Tallulah Bankhead Era

New York Times

10 Nov 1972

1972

World Hunting Honors Bestowed on 86-Year-Old Retired Duluthian

Mesabi, [Virginia, Minn.], Daily News

13 May 1973

1973

Hemingway, Mary

    Hemingway's Paris

    Chicago Sun-Times

    1 July 1973

            1973

Hemingway, Ernest

    On the Blue Water: A Gulf Stream Letter

    Esquire

    Oct 1973

            1973

    JFK Collection

Winakor, Bess

    Eye View

    Woman's Wear Daily

    23 Aug 1973

            1973

Hemingway, Ernest

    The Snows of Kilimanjaro

    Esquire

    Oct 1973

            1973

    JFK Collection

    Favorite Authors of Lawrence Area Students

    Lawrence, Mass., Journal

    13 Sept 1973

            1973

JFK Collection

Reynolds, Stanley

    World Needs More Hemingway, Despite Critics

    [1974]

            1974

    JFK Collection

    The Fitzgerald Hemingway Epoch

    Esquire

    Oct 1973

            1973

JFK Collection

McKercher, Bert

    C. E. "Chuck" Atkinson Dies in Phoenix Tuesday

    [Jan 1974]

            1974

Gingrich, Arnold

    Scott, Ernest and Whoever

    Esquire

    Oct 1973

            1973

JFK Collection

Wilson, Earl

    Everything Is Lovely Including the Prices

    St. Louis Dispatch

    12 Jan 1974

            1974

Gebhardt, Richard

The Old Man and the Key

Travel and Leisure Magazine

May 1974

1974

JFK Collection

Hemingway Opens Monday

Staten Island, N.Y., Advance

16 Oct 1974

1974

JFK Collection

Kirsch, Robert

The Book Report: A Rosebud that Fails to Blossom

Los Angeles Times

17 May 1974

1974

Christy, Marian

Papa was Grandpop to this Young Hemingway

Boston Globe

8 Dec 1974

1974

JFK Collection

Murphy, Michael

Hemingway: The Best of What He Had

American Way Magazine

July 1974

1974

JFK Collection

Mary Hemingway, wife of the author. . .

Boston Globe

29 Jan 1975

1975

JFK Collection

At 50, Jack Hemingway looks. . .

Newsweek

12 Aug 1974

1974

JFK Collection

Reinhold, Robert

Hemingway Papers Open for Study in a Setting that Belies their Vitality

New York Times

31 Jan 1975

1975

JFK Collection

Williams, Bob

On the Air: Fidel Castro has agreed. . .

New York Post

20 Aug 1974

1974

JFK Collection

Longworthy, David

Papa's Manuscripts Find a Home

Christian Science Monitor

3 Feb 1975

1975

JFK Collection

Breindel, Eric M.

JFK Library Opens Hemingway Files

[Harvard Crimson]

[6 Feb 1975]

1975

JFK Collection

Mary Hemingway, widow of American. . .

[Boston Globe]

[15 Mar 1975]

1975

JFK Collection

Reinhold, Robert

Hemingway's Original Papers Leave their Hideaways

Glocester, Mass., Daily Times

6 Feb 1975

1975

JFK Collection

McCable, Bruce

Ernest's Wild Ride with Scott and Zelda

[Boston Globe]

[24 Mar 1975]

1975

JFK Collection

A Hemingway Donation

Boston Globe Calendar

13 Feb 1975

1975

JFK Collection

Collins, Thomas

Looking over Hemingway's Shoulder

Newsday

4 Apr 1975

1975

JFK Collection

Moskow, Shirley

Hemingway Papers Open for Research at the Kennedy Library in Waltham

Waltham, Mass., News-Tribune

21 Feb 1975

1975

JFK Collection

Hemingway Granddaughter Weds her Burger Baron

[Newark] Sunday Star-Ledger

22 June 1975

1975

JFK Collection

Raymer, Dorothy

Conch Chowder

Key West Citizen

27 Feb 1975

1975

JFK Collection

Cohen, Sheeley

Hemingway Papers for JFK Library

[Boston] Herald Advertiser

13 July 1975

1975

JFK Collection

Cohen, Shelley

    Hemingway Papers a Feast for Fans

    Kansas City Times

    19 July 1975

               1975

JFK Collection

Christy, Marian

    Hemingway Son Had Love-Hate Bond

    [1976]

               1976

JFK Collection

Behrsing, Siegfried

    Meter Hemingway

    Die Weltbuhme

    9 Sept 1975

               1975

Hotchner, A. E.

    Papa Hemingway

    [1976]

               1976

JFK Collection

Amon, Rhoda

    Hemingway's Widow, Granddaughters Live the Good Life

    Asbury Park, N.J., Press

    19 Oot 1975

               1975

JFK Collection

Papa: A Personal Memoir by Gregory H. Hemingway, M.D.

    Book-of-the-Month Club

    [1976]

               1976

JFK Collection

Buckley, Tom

    Michener Fears Publishing Take-overs May Ground Fledgling Novelists

    New York Times

    27 Oct 1975

               1975

JFK Collection

Hemingway Libel Suit: A Footnote

    New York Times

    30 Apr 1976

               1976

JFK Collection

Hochhuth, Rolf

    Der Alte Mann und der Tod

    Zeit Magazine

    [Dec 1975]

               1975

  donor: Hans-Joachim Kann

Braem, Helmut M.

    Hochnut's Play Tod eines Jaegers Wide of the Mark

    Hamburg, German Tribune

    May 1976

               1976

JFK Collection

Christy, Marian

    A Hemingway Son Remembers Papa

    Boston Sunday Globe

    16 May 1976

              1976

JFK Collection

Ask the Globe: Q. Was Ernest Hemingway, in his play by that name. . .

    Boston Globe

    15 Aug 1976

              1976

JFK Collection

Oberbeck, S. K.

    A Paella for Papa: Hemingway in Spain by Jose Luis Castillo-Puche

    Newsweek

    27 May [1976]

              1976

JFK Collection

Locklin, Gerald and Charles Stetler

    The Hemingway Primer

    Coast

    Sept 1976

              1976

JFK Collection

Price, Reynolds

    Papa. A Personal Memoir. By Gregory H. Hemingway

    New York Times Book Review

    30 May 1976

              1976

JFK Collection

Bourjaily, Vance

    The Trials and Satisfactions of Being Mrs. Hemingway

    New York Times Book Review

    26 Sept 1976

              How It Was

JFK Collection

    Papa: A Personal Memoir by Gregory H. Hemingway, M.D. [review]

    Time

    26 July 1976

              1976

JFK Collection

Clemons, Walter

    Life with Papa

    Newsweek

    27 Sept 1976

              How It Was

JFK Collection

Lubash, Arnold H.

    Hotchner's $125,000 Libel Award Upheld

    New York Times

    3 Aug 1976

              1976

JFK Collection

Lehmann-Haupt, Christopher

    It Was Despite All

    New York Times

    27 Sept 1976

              How It Was

JFK Collection

Baker, Carlos

    Mary Hemingway's Years with Ernest

    Saturday Review

    2 Oct 1976

             How It Was

JFK Collection

Wool, Robert

    Memory of the Montafon

    New York Times

    6 Mar 1977

             How It Was

JFK Collection

Editor's Page

    The Hemingway Letters

    Saturday Review

    2 Oct 1976

             How It Was

JFK Collection

Hemingway's Cuban Haunts Lure Fans

    Greenwich, Connecticut, Time

    10 Mar 1977

                  1977

JFK Collection

More Papa

New York Post

22 Nov 1976

             1976

JFK Collection

Kazin, Alfred

    Hemingway the Painter

    New Republic

    19 Mar 1977

             1977

JFK Collection

Anderson, Jane Lee

    Miss Mary's How It Was on Living with Hemingway

    7 Dec 1976

             How It Was

JFK Collection

Leonard, John

    Books: By Force of Will: The Life and Art of Ernest Hemingway by Scott Donaldson

    New York Times

    [Apr 1977]

             1977

JFK Collection

S.L.

    Ernest Hemingway Award Goes to Darcy O'Brien

    [1977]

            1977

JFK Collection

Renata Adler Wins Hemingway Award

    Asbury Park, N.J., Press

    15 May 1977

             1977

JFK Collection

Malone, Brian

    Papa's Widow Tells It Like It IS--Or Was

    Grand Rapids, Mich., Press

    16 June 1977

           How It Was

JFK Collection

Martin, Lionel

    A Sentimental Journey for Mary Hemingway

    Washington, D.C., Post

    14 July 1977

           1977

JFK Collection

    Film on Hemingway Taking His Wife to Cuba

    [July 1977]

           1977

JFK Collection

Hemingway, Si!

    Asbury Park, N.J., Press

    17 July 1977

           1977

JFK Collection

    People in the News: Hemingway Research

    Boston Herald American

    3 July 1977

           1977

JFK Collection

Vogt, Ted and Allen Wulc

    Looking for the Way It Was

    Paris Metro

    20 July 1977

           1977

JFK Collection

Gross, Laurel

    Mary Hemingway Returns to Cuba for Film

    New York Post

    6 July 1977

           1977

JFK Collection

Baker, Russell

    The Sun Also Sets

    New York Times

    23 July 1977

           1977

JFK Collection

    Papa Remembered

    Newark, N.J., Star Ledger

    7 July 1977

           1977

JFK Collection

Daly, Maggie

    Barbara Irritates Castro

    Chicago Tribune

    27 July 1977

           1977

JFK Collection

Bradley, Jeff

    Paper Drive

    Washington Post

    11 Sept 1977

          1977

JFK Collection

Berry, Graham

    Stories We'll Always Love

    Modern Maturity

    Oct-Nov 1977

          1977

JFK Collection

Latham, Aaron

    A Farewell to Machismo

    New York Times Magazine

    16 Oct 1977

          1977

JFK Collection

    Behind the Macho Facade

    Boston Sunday Globe

    23 Oct 1977

          1977

JFK Collection

Taylor, Robert

    Papa's Psyche Plumbed Again

    [Boston Globe]

    [c. Nov 1977]

          1977

JFK Collection

Flaherty, Joe

    Muhammad Ali Meets Ernest Hemingway

    New York Times Book Review

    6 Nov 1977

          1977

JFK Collection

Guegan, Gerard

    Hemingway, l'unique

    Le Matin

    8 Nov 1977

          1977

JFK Collection

Croce, Francis A., Michael V. Korda and Anne Lambert

    The Adrogynous Hemingway: Letters to the Editor

    New York Times Magazine

    13 Nov 1977

          1977

JFK Collection

    Mrs. Cohn to Be Honored

    AB Weekly

    14 Nov 1977

          1977

JFK Collection

Walters, Ray

    Paperback Talk: How It Was

    New York Times Book Review

    27 Nov 1977

          How It Was

JFK Collection

Exhibit Recreates Magic of Expatriate
Years

University of Virginia, University
Register

1 Dec 1977

1977

JFK Collection

Wechsler, Pat

Literary Display of Greats Opens

Charlottesville, Va., Daily Progress

5 Dec 1977

1977

JFK Collection

Kelly, Brian

Here Are the Playthings and Great Works
of the Giants

Washington Star

7 Dec 1977

1977

JFK Collection

Hiss, Anthony and Sheldon Bart

Hemingway, High on the Wild by Lloyd
Arnold

New York Times Book Review

18 Dec 1977

1977

JFK Collection

We don't travel in the same circles, but
Margaux told me to come along. . .

Time

27 Feb 1978

1978

JFK Collection

Photo: Ernest Hemingway's
typescript. . .

AB Weekly

20 Mar 1978

1978

JFK Collection

At Presidential Libraries: People and
Events

On the Record (GSA)

April 1978

1978

JFK Collection

Sheppard, R. Z.

The Far Side of Friendship

Time

3 Apr 1978

1978

JFK Collection

She's just doin' what comes naturally
to a Hemingway. . .

Newsweek

10 Apr 1978

1978

JFK Collection

Wright, David

Ernest Hemingway Had Out-of-Body
Experience

National Enquirer

18 Apr 1978

1978

JFK Collection

Berg, A. Scott

    Max Perkins, Editor

    New York Times Book Review

    23 Apr 1978

           1978

JFK Collection

Haney, Daniel Q.

    A Hemingway Find in Natick

    Framingham, Mass., South Middlesex News

    15 May 1978

           1978

JFK Collection

Grumbach, Doris

    Nonfiction in Brief: Scott and Ernest by Matthew J. Bruccoli

    New York Times Book Review

    23 Apr 1978

           1978

JFK Collection

Long-forgotten Hemingway Work Discovered by Rare Book Dealer

    Greenwich, Conn., Time

    16 May 1978

           1978

JFK Collection

    Aperitif for Moveable Feast

    Bruccoli Clark News

    May 1978

           1978

JFK Collection

Abrahams, Linda

    Rare Book Dealer Wealthy by Default

    [Framingham, Mass.], South Middlesex News

    21 May 1978

           1978

JFK Collection

Walters, Ray

    Paperback Talk: By Force of Will: The Life and Art of Ernest Hemingway by Scott Donaldson

    New York Times Book Review

    14 May 1978

           1978

JFK Collection

Scott and Ernest: The Fitzgerald-Hemingway Friendship by Matthew J. Bruccoli

    ..New York Times

    21 May 1978

           1978

JFK Collection

    Comedy Traced to Hemingway

    Asbury Park, N.J., Press

    15 May 1978

           1978

JFK Collection

Main, Patricia

    Hemingway and Fitzgerald by Matthew J. Bruccoli

    Newton, Mass., Graphic

    25 May 1978

           1978

JFK Collection

Cunningham, Rip

  Recreation: Our Fisherman in Havana

  Boston Globe

  23 June 1978

      1978

JFK Collection

Manning, Margaret

  Hemingway the Man

  Boston Globe

  [25 Sept 1978]

       1978

JFK Collection

Tortorella, Karen

  Hemingway's Miss Mary

  Buffalo News Magazine

  16 July 1978

      1978

JFK Collection

Morris, Wright

  Memory, Emotion, Image

  New York Times Book Review

  13 Nov 1978

      1978

JFK Collection

Kuntz, Jenny

  Ernest Hemingway in the Smith College
  Library

  [Fall 1978]

      1978

JFK Collection

  Hemingway Hokum

  New York Times

  19 Nov 1978

      1978

JFK Collection

Nakhdjavani, Erik

  Views and Reviews: Hemingway's Connection

  Bradford, Pa.

  [Fall 1978]

      1978

JFK Collection

Phillips, Gene, S.J.

  Author's Query

  New York Times

  26 Nov 1978

      1978

JFK Collection

Burgess, Anthony

  The Importance of Ernest

  Observer

  24 Sept 1978

      1978

JFK Collection

  Hemingway's Paris by Robert E. Gadjusek

  New York Times Book Review

  3 Dec 1978

      1978

JFK Collection

Hotchner, A. E. and Gilbert Sorrentino
    Letters: Hemingway
    [New York Times]
    [17 Dec 1978]
                1978
JFK Collection

Club Starts Year with Papa Portrayal
    [Oak Park]
    [10 Jan 1979]
                1979
JFK Collection

Reynolds, Sharon M.
    In His Father's Image
    Miami Herald
    28 Dec 1978
                1978
JFK Collection

Wliz. H. Mowrer, Hemingway's First Wife
    Asbury Park Press
    25 Jan 1979
                1979
JFK Collection

Krebs, Albin
    Key West: Anyone's Place in the Sun
    New York Times Magazine
    31 Dec 1978
                1978
JFK Collection

Hemingway's First Wife Dies, Elizabeth Mowrer
    Orlando Star-Sentinel
    25 Jan 1979
                1979
JFK Collection

Q: Hasn't that much-touted movie
biography. . .
    [New York]
    [1979]
                1979
JFK Collection

Rand, Sumner
    For Hemingway Buffs
    [Crlando Star-Sentinel]
    [16 Feb 1979]
                1979
JFK Collection

Interview: Writing about Writers
    William and Mary
    Winter 1979
                1979
JFK Collection

Ober, Frank
    Ernest Hemingway Isn't Forgotten in
    Venice
    Boston Sunday Globe
    25 Feb 1979
                1979
JFK Collection

Pepe, Phil

    Hemingway Loved It, So Does Cuba

    Boston Globe

    28 Feb 1979

            1979

JFK Collection

Chutkow, Paul

    Hemingway's First-Born Son Remembers
    Life with Papa

    [Framingham, Mass], Middlesex News

    1 July 1979

            1979

JFK Collection

    Ernest Devotion

    Newark, N.J., Star Ledger

    16 Mar 1979

            1979

JFK Collection

Nathan, Paul S.

    Rights and Permissions

    [Publisher's Weekly]

    [2 July 1979]

                    How It Was

JFK Collection

Baker, Carlos

    The Sun Rose Differently

    New York Times Book Review

    18 Mar 1979

            1979

JFK Collection

Lask, Thomas

    Publishing: Scribner's to Issue
    Hemingway Letters

    [New York Times]

    [20 July 1979]

                    Letters

donor: Nancy Williams Bryant

Dong, Stella

    Hasen Wins Hemingway Award; Figures
    Suggest 1979 Rise in Published First
    Novels

    Publisher's Weekly

    11 June 1979

            1979

JFK Collection

    Names. . . Faces: Ernest Hemingway's
    letters. . .

    Boston Globe

    21 July 1979

                    How It Was

JFK Collection

Dong, Stella

    The Case of the Two First Novels; The
    Hemingway Award Reexamined

    Publisher's Weekly

    25 June 1979

            1979

JFK Collection

Dahlin, Robert

    Trade News: Hardcover Books: Hemingway
    Letters, Poems Due in Next Two Seasons

    Publisher's Weekly

    [30 July 1979]
            1979

JFK Collection

Exhibtions, Lectures and Receptions

Chapter and Verse: A Report to the
Associates of the University of Virginia
Library

August 1979

1979

JFK Collection

McGraw, James, Robert Martin and Judith W. Stein

Letters

New York Times

25 Nov 1979

1979

JFK Collection

Lask, Thomas

Book Ends: Kennedy and Roosevelt:
Hemingway the Poet

New York Times Book Review

[12 Aug 1979]

1979

JFK Collection

Sullivan, Paul

Can You Write Like Hemingway?

Boston Herald

28 Nov 1979

1979

JFK Collection

Purdum, Todd S.

Hemingway's Softer Side, Humor
Revealed in Letters

17 Aug 1979

How It Was

JFK Collection

Buck, Jerry

My Old Man Heartwarming

Asbury Park, N.J., Press

30 Nov 1979

1979

JFK Collection

Powers, John

The Old Man and the New Paris

Boston Globe Magazine

16 Sept 1979

1979

JFK Collection

Raidy, William A.

Broadway Opening: Genet Letters Lose
Their Tartness in Staging

[Newark] Star Ledger

24 Dec 1979

1979

JFK Collection

Lewis, Flora

Today's Havana: Few Reminders of a
Gaudy Past

New York Times

21 Oct 1979

1979

JFK Collection

Margaux Marries

Boston Globe

2 Jan 1980

1980

JFK Collection

Lehman-Haupt, Christopher

Books of the Times: The Last Safari by
Richard Rhodes

New York Times

26 Jan 1980

1980

JFK Collection

Dahiya, Bhim Singh

P. G. Rama Rao, Ernest Hemingway: A
Study in Narrative Technique

Indian Journal of American Studies

[July 1980]

1980

JFK Collection

A Study of Hemingway

[Madras] The Mail

22 Mar 1980

1980

JFK Collection

Negri, Gloria

Scholars to Sample Life, Recipes of
Hemingway

Boston Globe

6 July 1980

1980

JFK Collection

Ask the Globe

Boston Globe Magazine

[12 Apr 1980]

1980

JFK Collection

Fripp, Bill

Making Room for Hemingway

Boston Globe

19 July 1980

1980

JFK Collection

Style that Shows

[Calcutta Amrika Bazar Patrika]

[5 May 1980]

1980

JFK Collection

---

photo: Hemingway Room Dedicated

Washington Star

19 July 1980

1980

JFK Collection

Chopra, Sonia

The Old Man and the Legend

[New Delhi Sunday Statesman]

[4 June 1980]

1980

JFK Collection

Taylor, Robert

A Place for Hemingway

Boston Globe

21 July 1980

1980

JFK Collection

Hemingway's Paris

Sheraton

[Autumn 1980]

1980

JFK Collection

---

di Robilant, Olghina

Ernest Hemingway's Long-Ago Crush on a Venetian Girl Is Once Again the Talk of Italy

People Magazine

1 Dec 1980

1980

JFK Collection

---

photos: Jacqueline Onassis, Patrick Hemingway. . .

Wilson Library Bulletin

Sept 1980

1980

JFK Collection

They met on a cold, damp Venetian. . .

Time

1 Dec 1980

1980

JFK Collection

Hemingway, Lorian

The Young Woman and the Sea

New York Times Hemingway

21 Sept 1980

1980

JFK Collection

Plimpton, George

A Clean Well-Lighted Place

New York Review

18 Dec 1980

1980

JFK Collection

Sloan, Robin Adams

Gossip Column

Asbury Park, N.J., Press

23 Oct 1980

1980

JFK Collection

Blay, Regina

A Letters: Key West

New York Times

21 Dec 1980

1980

JFK Collection

August, Jo

Hemingway at Columbia Point: the Kennedy Library's Holdings

Wilson Library Bulletin

Dec 1980

1980

JFK Collection

Ivancich, Adriana

Letters: Hemingway's Best

Time

22 Dec 1980

1980

JFK Collection

Hayes, E. Nelson

    Papa's Letters: Something Missing

    Quincy, Massachusetts, Patriot Ledger

    1981

              Letters

JFK Collection

Howe, Irving

    Messages from a Divided Man

    New York Times Book Review

    29 Mar 1981

              Letters

JFK Collection

Meryman, Richard

    Archibald MacLeish and the Enlarged Life

    Yankee

    Jan 1981

              1981

JFK Collection

Kenner, Hugh

    Writing by Numbers: Hemingway's Letters

    Harpers

    Apr 1981

              Letters

JFK Collection

Wilk, Max

    Of Armed Services Editions I Sing

    Publishers Weekly

    2 Jan 1981

              1981

JFK Collection

Trudeau, G. B.

    Doonsbury

    Boston Sunday Globe

    5 Apr 1981

              1981

JFK Collection

Atlas, James

    The Private Hemingway from His
    Unpublished Letters, 1918-1961

    New York Times Magazine

    15 Feb 1981

              Letters

JFK Collection

Core, George

    The Self-Revealing Letters of Ernest
    Hemingway

    [Wall Street Journal]

    [7 Apr 1981]

              Letters

JFK Collection

Harris, Roger

    Letters Reveals the Two Sides of Hemingway

    [Mar 1981]

              Letters

JFK Collection

Whitman, Alden

    Hemingway's Letters Reveal Full Measure
    of a Restless Life

    [Boston] Globe

    12 Apr 1981

              Letters

JFK Collection

Kazin, Alfred

    The Battler

    New York Review

    16 Apr 1981

             Letters

JFK Collection

Morse, Jane

    Key West: Sea, Sunsets, and Sex

    Boston Sunday Globe

    1 June 1981

             1981

JFK Collection

Blowen, Michael

    Hollywood and Hemingway

    Boston Globe Calendar

    [May] 1981

             1981

JFK Collection

Leibstone, Marvin

    Twenty Years Since Hemingway's Death, a
    Time to Reflect

    Boston

    [July 1981]

             1981

JFK Collection

Oldsey, Bernard

    Papa's Private World

    The Nation

    9 May 1981

             Letters

JFK Collection

Josephs, Allen

    The Epistolary Papa

    New Boston Review

    July/August 1981

             Letters

JFK Collection

    Pulitzer Prize of 41 Didn't Go to
    Hemingway

    Newark Sunday Star Ledger

    24 May 1981

             1981

JFK Collection

Updike, John

    Hem Battles the Pack; Wins, Loses

    New Yorker

    13 July 1981

             Letters

JFK Collection

Sheed, Wilfrid

    Ernest Hemingway: Selected Letters,
    1917-1961

    Book-of-the-Month Club News

    June 1981

             Letters

JFK Collection

Lehmann-Haupt, Christopher

    A Hirsute Hemingway Eschews Respectability

    New York Times

    23 July 1981

             Letters

JFK Collection

Higgins, George

A Not-so-magnificent Obsession

[Boston Globe]

[25 July 1981]

1981

JFK Collection

Kakutani, Michiko

Be More Like Graham Greene, Dear

New York Times Book Review

16 Aug 1981

1981

JFK Collection

Marquez, Gabriel Garcia

Gabriel Garcia Marquez Meets Hemingway

New York Times Book Review

26 July 1981

1981

JFK Collection

Taylor, Robert

A Strater Retrospective: No Faces of Fame

Boston Globe Magazine

16 Aug 1981

1981

JFK Collection

Engel, Benjamin

Hemingway Letters Distort Biographer's Role, Widow Claims

New Haven Register

2 Aug 1981

Letters

donor: Frank Hills

Cecchin, Giovanni

Hemingway, un amore segreto a Torino

Stampa Sera

17 Aug 1981

1981

donor: Giovanni Cecchin

Marsh, Robert C.

Papa Hemingway Knew What He Liked

[Boston Globe]

[6 Aug 1981]

1981

JFK Collection

La Fidanzata di Hemingway Scoperta a Torino de Stampa Sera

Stampa Sera

18 Aug 1981

1981

donor: Giovanni Cecchin

Hotchner, A. E.

Ernest Hemingway: an American Original

TV Guide

15 Aug 1981

1981

JFK Collection

Grey, M. Cameron

The Last of the Bohemians

[London, Woman's Journal]

[Sept 1981]

1981

JFK Collection

Marlette, Doug

    Kudzu

    Boston Sunday Globe

    13 Sept 1981

               1981

JFK Collection

    Significa November 8, 1981: Men Who
Were Raised asGirls

    [Boston Globe] Parade

    8 Nov 1981

JFK Collection   1981

    Hanson, C. S. Larry

        Letters: The Real Story

        [New York Times Book Review]

        [27 Sept 1981]

               1981

Bauza, P. Martinez

    Palabras

               undated

    Remington, Richard S.

        Hemingway's Spain Recalled by Veteran of
Lincoln Brigade

        [Newark, N.J., Star Ledger]

        [28 Sept 1981]

               1981

donor: Mildred R. August

Bina, Bernard

    In the House Where Hemingway Lived,
Walked, and Died, His Widow Mary Tends
to His Legend

            How It Was

JFK Collection

Baker, Russell

    Sunday Observer: I Remember Papa

    New York Times Magazine

    25 Oct 1981

               1981

donor: Allan B. Goodrich

Boal, Sam

    The Hemingway I Know

               undated

Baker, Russell

    The Importance of Being Ernest

    Quincy, Massachusetts, Ledger

    26 Oct 1981

               1981

donor: Phyllis Dailey

Bourke, George

    Night Life: Place: Cuba; Setting:
Chat with Hemingway / Author Pays Full
U.S. Taxes, Faces New Levy

               undated

Burros, Marian

    Fish and Game Dinners with the [Jack and Puck] Hemingways

    Family Living

                  undated

Castillo-Puche, Jose Luis

    American de cabo a rabo

    Pueblo

    [1950's]

                  undated

Campbell, Sally S.

    A Key West House Evokes the Presence of Hemingway

    New York Times
    24 Feb 1980

             1980

JFK Collection

    The Counterfeiters

    Harvest

             Hemingway, Grace Hall
             undated

    At home with Gert and Al. . .

    [1980's]

                  undated

    Dahl Said to be Missing

    15 Feb

             Matthews, Herbert L.
             17 Feb [1950's]

Billingsley, Sherman

    U.S. Drinking Habits: Total War Changes Night Club Picture

    St. Louis Post-Dispatch

    [15 Aug 1940's]

                  undated

[Eades, Dan and Joan]

    Winner Takes Nada

    Lost Generation Journal

                  undated

    Capt. Zenon Urresti, of the Caribe, Nicaraguan flag. . .

                  undated

    Ellen Mackay's Bored Debutantes Are Satirized by Scott Fitzgerald

                  undated

Ernest Hemingway as a Catholic

The Sign

Pfeiffer, Gustavus A.
undated

Fragment headed, "One fighter invented the psychology of the body. The other man was a war machine."

undated

Estas son las Caras mas Provocodoras del Mundo

undated

Greatest Boy Actor Is a Toronto Lad

Star Scrapbook, p. 37

Exposicion de estampas de Quintanilla en el Museo de Arte Moderno

Luz

undated

Guest, Mrs. Winston

Letter: After reading that. . .

[Playboy]

undated

Fragment beginning "Quick Gary!" he said. . .

Saturday [Evening Post]

undated

Heilner, Sam

Sunday's People

undated

Fragment: . . . expedition to Matanzas with Bumby. . .

undated

Hemingway Boosts Fishing Off Cuba

[Miami Daily Herald]

undated

Hemingway, Ernest

The first panacea for a mismanaged nation. . .

undated

. . . Hemingway once tried to get a job. . .

undated

Hillinger, Charles

Buyer of Hemingway's Florida House Sells Descendents of Papa's Cats

undated

Hickok, Guy

Experts' Table Shows How Vast Are Debts to War

Brooklyn Daily Eagle

1 Feb n.y.

Hickok, Guy undated

Hlavin, Robert F.

Mary's Story [Program]

undated

Hoover, John P.

Guns, Trophies Fill Hemingway's Cuba House

[1970's]

undated

Huguenin, Jean-Rene

Une Journee avec Hemingway

[1950's]

undated

Italy Puts Idle Men to Work on Pontine Marsh

Star Scrapbook, p. 45

Jackson, Peter

Motor Cars Slaying Toronto's Splendid Old Oak Trees

Star Scrapbook, p. 27

Latin Quarter Notes

Musselman, Morris undated

Lord, Father Daniel

Ernest Hemingway as a Catholic

[The Sign]

undated

McDowell, Edwin

The Literati's Appreciation for Baseball

New York Times

undated

JFK Collection

Lyons, Leonard

Lyons Den: A Manhattan Cocktail, Wherein Sarnoff Sings and Rothstein Bets

undated

The Morning-Evening (entire edition)

Vol. XXII

undated

Madox Ford Figures in Libel Action

Transatlantic Review
undated

Munroe, Bob

Fishing Guide: Ernest Hemingway Chats Re Current Fishing Off Cuba

[Miami Daily News]

undated

Maksian, George

A Special on Hemingway

undated

. . . The new Playboy prints a letter from Mrs. Winston Guest. . .

undated

Marks Not Caused by Ill Treatment

Toronto Mail and Empire

Star Scrapbook, p. 37

New York Yachtsman Goes Back After Fish

undated

Papers Donated to Princeton

undated

Photo: Two Hemingways. . .
Boston Globe

undated

Photo: Aparecio el Hawkshaw. . .
Carteles

undated

photo: You Who've Read Ernest Hemingway's
Best Seller, Death. . .

undated

Photo: Ernest Hemingway loves to flex
his muscles. . .

undated

Qui ganera la 19 course de Six Jours a
Berlin

undated

Photo: New Soviet Gold Currency

Star Scrapbook, p. 29

Roman, Erl
       Angler's Notes
       Miami Herald

undated

photo: Quiero Mucho a Cuba

undated

Ruark, Robert
       Hero Worshiper Glad as Champ Comes Back

undated

Ryan, John

    A [Patrick] Hemingway in The Hills of
    Africa

                    undated

[Three Poems]

    In Flanders Fields by John McCrae
    The Soldier by Rupert Brooke
    I Have a Rendezvous with Death by
    Alan Seeger

                    undated

[Sagoff, Maruice]

    A Farewell to Arms by Ernest Hemingway

    Shrinklits

                    undated

. . . To return to the native American
population of Montparnasse. . .

                    undated

Shaffer, George

    Proviso Preps Beat Kankakee in Last
    Quarter

    [29 Sept, n.y. c. 1916]
                    undated

Wescott vs. Bromfield

                    Fitzgerald, F. Scott
                    undated

She Sacrifices Herself that Children
May Live

Toronto Star

            Star Scrapbook, p. 37

Winchell, Walter

    Walter Winchell on Broadway

    Boston Sunday Advertiser

                    undated

Suzy Says: Royal Gathering

                    undated

Other Material

Adaptations

Programs from foreign adaptations of
Hemingway's works, 1963 - 1972. 2 items

Art Papers: La Ferme by Miro

Various papers relating to this painting
including the exhibition program,
receipts, a reproduction, and
correspondence concerning the loan and
restoration of the painting. 33 items

Addresses

Names and addresses typed and handwritten
by EH, MH and others. undated. 19 items

Art Papers: Programs

Various programs from 1924 through 1959,
including exhibitions of Masson, Becat,
Monnier, Strater, and Jose Caballero, and
from Le Salon des Tuileries and Galerie
E. Druet. Also, the funeral announcement
for Juan Gris. 9 items

Advertisements

Brochures and catalogs from various shops
and establishments, including shops for
shoes, liquors, tea, etc. 8 items

Art Papers: Receipts and Reproductions

Receipts, reproductions and notes on art
works bought by EH, or brought to his
attention, or saved by EH, 1921-1939, and
undated. Does not include Miro's
La Ferme. 20 items

Africa

Miscellaneous materials from both safaris,
including notes on baggage, rifles, and
trophies, expenses, travel arrangements,
printed material from the East Africa
Professional Hunters' Association, EH's
honorary Game Warden card, memos on the
Mau-Mau activity, and three pages EH
manuscript on first safari, EH's amoebic
dysentery, and writings from that safari.
16 items

Art Work

Drawings of/by EH/MH. 10 items

Apartment Leases

Receipts and leases and other materials
concerning Hemingway's apartments and
rental of the Key West property,
specifically 113 rue Notre dame des
Champs, Bathurst Street, 6 rue Ferou.
11 items

Auto Papers/Driving Licenses

Parking, gas, rental receipts, receipts
from car repairs, automobile registration
and drivers licenses, 1929 - 1959.
28 items

Awards/Citations

Certificates and correspondence relating
to the Pulitzer Prize, the Award of Merit
Medal for the Novel presented by the
American Academy of Arts and Letters,
the Cavalaiere di Gran Croce al Merito,
"Bait-Bate's" Boat Cat License, etc.
1939 - 1954 and undated. 6 items

See also World War I

Book Lists

Miscellaneous Bills. Bills from stores
other than Scribner's, correspondence,
book lists, and magazine subscriptions.
1925 - 1951. 15 items

Bicycle Races

Schedules, programs, journals, and EH
notes. 1925-1933 and undated. 8 items

Book Lists

Key West House. List of books in
"Big house" in Key West, Florida.
List is numbered from 1 to 200 and
contains note to Mary [Hemingway]
"Doesn't include little house; many
more than this." 8pp.

Biography

"Ernest Heminfway - A short Biographical
Note." Typed on Finca Vigia letterhead.
Undated, but post-1953. 2pp.

Book Lists

Shipping lists. Typescript list of
books shipped from Key West to Havana.
Titles listed according to crate number
30 pp.

Book Jackets

Men Without Women -- not first edition
Free-for-All by Evan Shipman

Book Lists

Key West House. List of books
alphabetically arranged, in the
pool house and garage apartment in
Key West, Florida. Dated December
1955 and contains approximately
3,000 titles. 32pp. in binder w/
envelope

Book Lists

Scribner Book Store Bills. 1933. 3pp.
Also, copies of Scribner Bills appearing
in the correspondence files.

Book Lists

EH handwritten lists of books, and one
typed list (EH?). 3 items

Book Plates

    Ex Libris Ernest Hemingway

Books

    Bible. King James version. Oxford :
University Press, [n.d.]
    Names of Mary Dunhill Miller-Hall,
Ernest Hall, Grace Hall-Hemingway,
and Ernest Miller Hemingway embossed
on cover.

Books

    Arthur, Chester A., Jr.
       Twelve poems / by Chester A.
Arthur, Jr. -- Los Angeles: Young
& McCallister, 1927.
       12 p. ; 20 cm.

       Handwritten note and author's
signature on flyleaf.

Books

    Blake, William
       The world is mine: the story of a
modern Monte Cristo / a novel by
William Blake. -- New York : Simon
and Schuster, 1938.
       [8], viii, 741 p. ; 22 cm.

       Special limited preview edition
copy number 180 for Ernest Hemingway.

       Handwritten note and signature by
M. Lincoln   , . Schuster on cover.

Books

    Baroja, Pio
       Locuras de carnaval / Pio Baroja.
-- Madrid : Espasa-Calpe, S.A., 1937.
       291 p. ; 20 cm.

       Uncut pages.

Books

    Childers, Erskine
       The riddle of the sands: a record
of secret service / by Erskine Childers.
-- Boston : Charles E. Lauriat Co., 1935
       xi, 289 p. ; 19 cm.

       Cover: "The story of an American
yachting cruise in the North Sea."

Books

    Bazalgette, Leon
       George Grosz, l'homme & l'oeuvre /
Leon Bazalgette. --Paris : Les
Ecrivains Reunis, 1926.
       19 p., [27] leaves of plates ; 19 cm.

Books

    Cocteau, Jean
       Thomas l'imposteur / Jean Cocteau.
-- 4th ed. -- Paris : Nouvelle Revue
Francaise, 1923.
       184 p. ; 19 cm.

       Handwritten note on half title:
"A la grande Gertrude Stein son ad-
mirateur Jean Cocteau 1923"

Books

    Bergamin, Jose
       El arte de Birlibirloque / Jose
Bergamin. -- Madrid : Editorial
Plutarco, 1930.
       96, [6] p. ; 21 cm.

       Pencil marks. Uncut pages.

Books

    Foreign language editions of EH novels.
70 assorted titles in several languages.

Books

Harispe, Pierre
    Le pays Basque: histoire, langue,
civilisation / Pierre Harispe. --
Paris : Payot, 1929.
    240 p. ; 20 cm.

Books

Hemingway, Ernest
    Three stories and ten poems / Ernest
Hemingway. -- Paris : Published by Robert
McAlmon at the Contact Publishing Co.,
1923.
    [xii], 64 p. ; 18 cm.

    [First limited edition. In paper
sleeve.

Books

Hemingway, Alfred T.
    How to Make Good or Winning Your
Largest Success: A Business Man's Talks
on Personal Proficiency and Commercial
Character-Building -- The Only Success
Insurance / by Alfred T. Hemingway. --
Kansas City : Personal Proficiency Bureau,
1915
    86 p. ; 19 cm.

Inscribed "Ernest Miller Hemingway from
Alfred T. Hemingway (Uncle Tyler)
Kansas City,   Ms. June -- 1917"

Books

Hemingway, Ernest
    Today is Friday / Ernest Hemingway.
-- Englewood, NJ : As Stable Publications
1926.
    [8] p. : ill. ; 20 cm.

    Number 45 and cover of number 46 of
300 numbered copies printed.

Books

Hemingway, Ernest
    Gattorno / Ernest Hemingway. --
Havana : Ucar, Garcia y Cia, 1935.
    16 p. [38] p. of Plates ; 26 cm.

    Copy 440 of a limited edition
of 460.
    [Gift of Isabel Gattorno].

Books

Joyce, James
    Ulysses / by James Joyce. --
Paris : Shakespeare and Co., 1922.

    Unnumbered press copy.
    Unbound.
    Ernest Hemingway's signature on
cover page.

Books

Hemingway, Ernest
    In our time / by ernest hemingway.
-- Paris : Three Mountains Press, 1924.
    30, [1] p. ; 27 cm.
    Number 129 of 170 copies printed on
rives hand-made paper.
    Inscribed "To Jack, N.Y.C. '24
Hank S." and "To my good friend Ernest
Hemingway In the giver's den (study) Jack
Cowles   February 14, 1926

Books

Kiki
    Kiki's memoirs / translated from
the French by Samuel Putnam ; introduction by Ernest Hemingway. --
Paris ; Edward W. Titus, 1930.
    185 p. : ill. ; 23 cm.

Books

Hemingway, Ernest
    The Spanish Earth / Ernest Hemingway
; with an introduction by Jasper Wood ;
illustrations by Frederick K. Russell.
-- Cleveland : J.B. Savage Co., 1938.
    60 p. : ill. ; 20 cm.
    Unnumbered copy of edition of 1000
numbered copies. First issue.
    EH pencil notes pp. 19,29,31,46,47.
    Slight bookworm damage.

Books

Kluge, E.F.
    Cleveland poems / by E.F. Kluge.
-- Cleveland : Buckeye Pub. Co., 1953.
    20 p. ; 22 cm.

Books

Koestler, Arthur
    Spanish testament / by Arthur
Koestler ; with an introduction by
the Duchess of Atholl. -- London :
Victor Gollancz Ltd., 1937.
    384 p. ; 21 cm.

Books

Peers, E. Allison
    The Spanish tragedy 1930-1936:
dictatorship, republic, chaos / by
E. Allison Peers. -- New York :
Oxford Univ. Press, 1936.
    xv, 247 p. ; 23 cm.

    EH signature on flyleaf.

Books

Lafont, A.
    Toreros d'aujourd'hui / par A.
Lafont (Paco Tolosa) ; reportage
photographique effectue sous la
direction de Gil De Kermadec. --
Paris : Art Et Industrie, 1959.
    [2], 120, [5] p. : ill. ; 28 cm.

Books

Pound, Ezra
    A draft of xvi. cantos of Ezra
Pound for the beginning of a poem of
some length now first made into a book /
with initials by Henry Strater. -- Paris
Three Mountains Press, 1925.
    [33] leaves ; 39 cm.

    Number 10 (Printed for Ernest
Hemingway) of seventy on Roma paper
specially water, marked.

Books

[Loyola, Attilio]
    The captivity of the Italians in
Austria: impressions and recollections
of my captivity. -- Turin : Unione
Tipografico - Editrice Torinese, 1918.
    36 p. ; ill. ; 25 cm.

    Two copies.

Books

Quintanilla, Luis
    All the brave / by Luis Quint-
anilla ; preface by Ernest Hemingway ;
text by Elliot Paul and Jay Allen. --
New York : Modern Age Books, 1939.
    29, [91] p. : plates ; 28 cm.

Books

Marulic, Marko
    Libar v chomse usdarsi Istoria
sfete udouice Iudit u uersih haruacchi
slosena, chacho ona ubi uoiuodu Olo-
pherna posridu uoische gnegoue i
oslodobi puch israelschi od ueliche
pogibili. -- Venice, 1521 ; Facsimile
edition, Zagreb : Jugoslavenske Akademije Znanosti i Umjetnosti, 1950.
    facsim : [74] p. ; 22 cm.

Books

Reed, Chester A.
    Bird guide part 2: land birds
east of the Rockies from parrots to
bluebirds / by Chestar A. Reed. --
New York : Doubleday, Page & Co.,
1909.
    223 p. : Col. plates ; 9 X 15 cm.

    EH signature on front flyleaf.

Books

Miller, Francis Trevelyan
    Portrait life of Lincoln /
by Francis Trevelyan Miller. --
Springfield, MA : Patriot Pub. Co.,
1910.
    [10], 164 p. : ports. ; 28 cm.

    Handwritten note from Grandfather
and Grandmother Hemingway on front
flyleaf.

Books

Regler, Gustave
    La passion de Joss Fritz / Gustave
Regler. -- Paris : Editions Sociales
Internationales, 1937.
    344 p. ; 19 cm.

    EH signature pencilled on flyleaf.

Books

Sandburg, Carl
A Lincoln preface / Carl Sandburg.
-- New York : Harcourt, Brace and Co.,
1953.
16 p. ; 20 cm.

Handwritten note and signature of
author on title page. Letter from
Harcourt.

Books

Sweeny, Charles
Petain / by Charles Sweeny. --
privately printed, 1945.
36 p. ; 23 cm.

Handwritten note and author's
signature on title page

Books

Schlosser, Julius
Francisco Goya / von Julius
Schlosser. -- Leipzig : Verlag
von E.A. Seeman, 1922.
10 p. : [19] p. of plates ; 18 cm.

Books

Tavolato, Italo
Georg Grosz / Italo Tavolato. --
Rome : Editions de Valori Plastici,
1924.
13, [37] p. : ill. ; 20 cm.

Uncut pages.

Books

Stein, Gertrude
Portrait of Mabel Dodge at the
Villa Curonia / by Gertrude Stein.
-- [n.l., n.p., n.d.]
11 p. ; 20 cm.

Inside front cover: "To the two
Hemingways with much affection
Gtrde Stein."

Books

Tennant, Eleonora
Spanish journey: personal experiences of the civil war / by Eleonora
Tennant. -- London : Eyre and Spott-
iswoode, 1936.
127, [1] p. ; 20 cm.

EH signature on front flyleaf.

Books

Sweeny, Charles
Pearl Harbor / by Charles Sweeny.
-- Privately printed, 1946.
74 p. ; 22 cm.

Title page : "To Ernest God bless
him. Charles Sweeny."

Books

Velazquez y Sanchez, José
Annales del toreo: reseña histori-
ca de la lidia de reses bravas: galeria
biografica de los principales lidia-
dores / escrita por D. José Velazquez
y Sanchez. -- Segunda edicion ilustrada
-- Seville : Delgado y Comp, 1873.
317, [3] p. ; ports. plates ; 42 cm.
folio.

EH signature in ink on half title.

Books

Hemingway, Ernest
The torrents of spring: a romantic
novel in honor of the passing of a
great race / by Ernest Hemingway. --
Paris : Crosby Continental Editions,
1932.
vii, 176 p. ; 16 cm.
Title page line endings differ
from that described by Hanneman.

Books

Zoranic, Peter
Planine che zdarxe usebi pisni pete
po pastirich, pripouisti i prituori
iunachou i dechlic, i mnoge ostale
stuarti. -- Venice : Appresso D. Farri,
1569 (Facsimile edition, Zagreb :
Jugoslavenske Akademije Znanosti
i Umjetnosti, 1952).
76 leaves : facsim. ; 23 cm.

Boxing

    Announcements, tickets, programs, and
journals. 1920-1926 and undated.
10 items

Bullfight Materials

    Photographs. <u>Antonio Ordonez</u>: <u>Temporada</u>
<u>1958</u>, book of photographs.

Bullfight Materials

    Regulations for Bullfights. <u>Reglement des</u>
<u>Corridas</u>, published by Ministere de
l'Interieur on 20 Aug 1923 to take effect
1 Jan 1924. 25pp.

Bullfight Materials

    Photographs, Portraits, & Sketches.
Miscellaneous art work, sketches, pictures,
post cards, etc.

Bullfight Materials

    Schedules. Misc. typescript and holograph
bullfight schedules, listing locations,
dates, and names of matadors. 1959? and
undated

Bullfight Materials

    Clippings. On Antonio Ordonez. 1960

Bullfight Materials

    Ticket Stubs. Miscellaneous ticket stubs
for 1923, 1925, 1926, 1927, 1929, and
undated.

Bullfight Materials

    Clippings. On Luis Miguel Dominguin.
Sept 1960

Bullfight Materials

    Photographs. Photos of Antonio Ordonez
sent 10 Mar 1960 to EH. 8 photos,
2 newspaper clippings, w/envelope.

Bullfight Materials

    Clippings. On Luis Miguel Dominguin and
Antonio Ordonez

Bullfight Materials

    Clippings. Ordonez, Antonio. "Hemingway and I" (undated, after 1961). Sent from Gig [Gregory Hemingway] to MH

Bullfight Materials

    Spanish Newspapers

      ABC: 1 May 1924
           22 May 1924
           6 Aug 1925

Bullfight Materials

    Miscellaneous newspaper clippings sent in Jan 1961 from Juanito Quintana to EH.

Bullfight Materials

    Spanish Newspapers.

      El Eco Taurino: 3 Nov 1927

Bullfight Materials

    Programs. Aranjuez:

        1926

Bullfight Materials

    Spanish Newspapers.

      La Fiesta Brava: 7 Apr 1933

Bullfight Materials

    Programs. Madrid:

        1923
        1926

Bullfight Materials

    Spanish Newspapers

      Gaceta Ilustrada: 20 July 1959
               29 Aug 1959
                8 Aug 1959

oversize

Bullfight Materials

    Programs. Pamplona:

        1924
        1933
        1934

Bullfight Materials

    Spanish Newspapers

      La Lidia: 6 June 1892
             15 Aug 1892
             24 Oct 1887
              4 Nov 1889
             25 Nov 1889
             16 June 1920

oversize

Bullfight Materials

    Spanish Newspapers

        <u>El Pensamiento Navarro</u>: 14 July 1959

oversize

Bullfight Materials

    Spanish Newspapers

        <u>Toreros y Toros</u>: 3 June 1923
                      10 June 1923
                      23 Mar 1924
                      30 Mar 1924

Bullfight Materials

    Spanish Newspapers

        <u>Pueblo</u>: 6 July 1959 (frag -- article on
                       Antonio Ordonez)

oversize

Bullfight Materials

    Spanish Newspapers

        <u>El Universal</u>: 7 Feb 1927 (frag)

oversize

Bullfight Materials

    Spanish Newspapers

        El Ruedo: 25 June 1959
                 9 July 1959 (2)
               16 July 1959 (2)
               23 July 1959

oversize

Bullfight Materials

    Spanish Newspapers

        <u>La Voz de Navarra</u>: 11 July 1923
                             4 July 1927 (frag)

oversize

Bullfight Materials

    Spanish Newspapers

        Sangre y Arena: 23 Apr 1924
                        28 May 1924
                        25 June 1924
                        9 July 1924

    (fragments)

oversize

Bullfight Materials

    Spanish Newspapers

        <u>Zig Zag</u>: 19 July 1923
                  9 Aug 1924
                  27 Sept 1924

Bullfight Materials

    Spanish Newspapers

        El Sol: 7 Feb 1927 (frag)

oversize

Bullfight Materials

    Spanish Newspapers. Miscellaneous
    clippings

    see oversize also

Bullfight Materials

    French Newspapers

        Le Journal du Midi: 26 Apr 1924 (frag)

oversize

Bullfight Materials

    Journals

        Madrid: Tauro: 5 July 1923

Bullfight Materials

    French Newspapers

        Le Toril:

15 May 1926	1 Nov 1926	22 Oct 1927
22 May 1926	4 Dec 1926	24 Dec 1927
14 Aug 1926	8 Jan 1927	18 Feb 1928
21 Aug 1926	1 Mar 1927	7 Apr 1928
4 Sept 1926	2 Apr 1927	
11 Sept 1926	9 Apr 1927	
18 Sept 1926	23 Apr 1927	
2 Oct 1926		

oversize

Bullfight Materials

    Journals

        Madrid, El Toreo: 30 July 1923

Bullfight Materials

    French Newspapers

        Le Torero: 27 Apr 1924 (2)
                  7 Sept 1924
                  21 Sept 1924

oversize

Bullfight Materials

    Journals

        Mexico City, El Eco Taurino: 10 Feb 1927

Bullfight Materials

    Journals

        Barcelona, La Corrida: 21 June 1923

Bullfight Materials

    Journals

        Valencia, Album Torino: July 1959

Bullfight Materials

    Journals

        Madrid, Sol y Sombra: 5 July 1923
                      12 July 1923
                      20 Mar 1924
                      29 May 1924
                      18 Sept 1924

Bullfight Materials

    Miscellaneous Bullfight Publications

Church Papers

Programs, directories and other materials. 1896 - 1928. 5 items

Cuban Affairs

EH pencil and ink notes on Cuba and Dr. Castro. 3 items

Chinese Magic Squares

EH pencil notes and diagrams on Chinese Magic Squares. Undated, on verso of Standard Parts Company of Cleveland letterhead. 6pp.

Customs

Official forms and correspondence concerning customs in the U.S., Cuba, France, and Spain. 1932 - 1959 and undated. 8 items

Club Cards and U.S. Identity Cards

Various membership and identification cards including Toronto YMCA, Societe de Peche, Biscayne Bay Yacht Club, Idaho Liquor Consumer's Permit, etc. 1920-1961 and undated. 20 items

Entertaining

List of Invitados al Fiesta de Ernesto. 1p.

Cooperative Commonwealth

Memos and other materials. Sept 1920 - Feb 1921. 10 items

Envelopes

Miscellaneous empty envelopes from unknown correspondents, some bearing EH notes about responses. 1919 - 1961 and undated. 21 items

Court

Subpoena to appear before the District Court for the Western District of Missouri, dated 23 Apr 1918. 1 item

Envelopes

Envelopes and folders, bearing notes by EH and MH which formerly held manuscripts and correspondence. Box bearing word count from Islands in the Stream. 23 items

Finca Papers

    Typewritten notes on repairs and servant's assignments, w/annotations. 5pp,

Genealogies

    Randall-Hall Genealogy prepared by Harold E. Board

Fishing Licenses

    Licenses for EH, Pauline, and Pat Guthrie, and correspondence relating to them. 1924 - 1946. 16 items

High School

    Chemistry Notebooks
    1. Beginning "Test for Sugar", w/EH pencil annotations. 17pp.
    2. Exercise Book. Collection of exercises, written by EH, and graded. 85pp.

Fishing Notes

    EH and Pauline notes on fishing tackle, fishing logs, and other notes on fishing. Typewritten log running from April to June 13 recording fishing experiences in Cuban waters with Bud, Charles, Joe, Pauline, Helen, Jane, Bra, Carlos, Carol, and others (13pp. w/carbon). Also notes on Bimini in another hand. 13 items

High School

    Notes
    1. Class notes and assignments for English, chemistry, Latin, history
    2. Notes passed to class-mates

    63pp.

Fishing Papers

    Printed materials on the Hemingway Trophy, record catches, competitions, fish in Cuban waters, and Tycoon Tackle, papers from the University of Miami Marine Laboratory, and handwritten (unknown hand) notes on same. 14 items

High School Papers

    Class Day program, 13 June 1917
    Diploma, 14 June 1917

Foreign Language

    French, Spanish and Basque language pamphlets, and notes on French grammar in unknown hand. 4 items

High School Writings

    See #286a, 623a, 672.5, 717c, 859, 257

Horse Racing

Programs and EH notes, 1922 - 1925 and undated. 3 items

Identity Papers -- Foreign

Various identity cards from Italy, France, Spain, England, etc., for EH, Pauline, and MH. Also printed material. 1923 - 1956. 9 items

Hotel Receipts

Receipts for EH and family and friends, 1923 - 1957 and undated. 32 items

Inventories

EH notes on contents of black and brown bags [c. 1960], a list of "MSS Missing [post 1956], contents of "Square Leather Bag left at 1 E. 62nd" [c. 1960], list of 9 pieces of luggage, and a typed shopping/packing list. 5 items

Hunting Licenses

Licenses and club cards for EH, Pauline, and MH, 1919 - 1946 and undated. 16 items

Invitations/Tickets

1923 and undated. 4 items

Hunting Papers

Printed materials on Le Tir aux Pigeons, 1926 - 1933, and EH notes on "Ammo," and receipt from the Academy of Natural Sciences for trophies, 1935. 5 items

Ketchum House

House bill, 1958. 1 item

Ice Patrol

Pencil notes by EH on "International Service of ice observation and ice patrol." 6pp.

Journals

EH journal for August 12 and August 13 [1928?], mentioning Kate [Smith] and [John] Dos Passos, O.W. [Owen Wister], and Bill Horne, 3pp. EH calendar for Jan - March 1956. 2 items

Key West House

    Receipt for repairs, 27 Mar 1957. 2 items

Manuscripts -- Not EH

Baker, Carlos

    Typescript of chapter 1, "The Slopes of Montparnasse" and chapter 11, "The River and the Trees," from Hemingway: <u>Writer as Artist</u>, sent to EH, 1 Oct 1951. 60pp., w/envelope

---

Lectures

    Data on speeches given by Ernest Hemingway, 1919. 5 items

---

Manuscripts -- Not EH

Bahr, Jerome

    Hello Lover, 5pp.
    NRA Day, 27pp.
    Tonight There Is Rain, 27pp.
    Twilight for the Dead, 23pp., w/ALS dated 1 May 1936
    Wooden Box, 16pp.

Licenses to Bear Arms

    Certificates and papers relating to bearing arms in Cuba and Belgium, 1950 and undated 4 items

---

Manuscripts -- Not EH

Callaghan, Morley

    A Girl with Ambition, 11pp.
    Along with Youth, 46pp.
    Amuck in the Bush, 10pp.
    I Should Have Been a Preacher, 12pp.
    Last Spring They Came Over, 12pp.
    On the Way Home, 3pp.
    Things, 9pp.

Lottery Tickets

    Spain
        Loteria Nacional: Sorteo 20 de 1923
                       Sorteo 19 de 1924
                       Sorteo 21 de 1927

    4 items

Manuscripts -- Not EH

Calmer, Edgar

    Intimate Chronicle, 4pp.

Manuscripts -- Not EH

Author Unknown

    Typescripts of two sections of a work on fishing:

  1. Section IX: The West Coast of Florida. Uncorrected carbon w/EH's L-Bar-T Ranch address penciled-in by EH on first page 7pp.
  2. Section 12: Bermuda. W/EH pencil corrections. 6pp.

Manuscripts -- Not EH

Charters, Jimmy

    <u>This Must Be the Place</u>. Fragments on Pat and Duff, Louise Bryant, Lawrence Vail, Lena Hutchins, Djuna Barnes, Francis Musgrave, Buffy Glasgow and Graham Taylor, Flossie Martin, and Michael Arlen. 16pp.

Manuscripts -- Not EH

Dos Passos, John

Luis Quintanilla Catalogue. Typescript draft w/ink corrections and signed. 2pp. Also, two carbon copies.

Manuscripts -- Not EH

Mann, Klaus

Ernest Hemingway. Translated from German by Klaus Mann for Wolgang Hellmert, 4pp.

Manuscripts -- Not EH

Ford, Ford Madox

No More Parades. Settinc oopy. Typescript w/pencil corrections and printer's marks. In binder with label that reads: "No More Parades / Paris 31/10/24 / Guermantes 25/4/25 / M.S. the property of F. M. Ford / Guermantes, pres Lagny, S. et M. / France 316pp. W/ALS ?, 5 June 1925, [London], to Mrs. Palmer, 1p., w/envelope, and also w/newspaper clipping on The Mausoleum Co. of America, The ⌐ World, 4 May 1925.

Manuscripts -- Not EH

Mowrer, Hadley RICHARDSON Hemingway

Miscellaneous handwritten notes, poems and manuscript, including a diary entry for 27 Aug 1933, 23pp.

Manuscripts -- Not EH

Heinz, W. C.

I'm Sorry, Eddie, 32pp. (Appeared in Cosmopolitan, 10 Feb 1948)

Manuscripts -- Not EH

Musselman, Morris McNeil

Camouflage (a Play in Four Acts), 5pp.

Manuscripts -- Not EH

Hemingway, Grace Hall

Heritage. (Family History). 28pp.

Manuscripts -- Not EH

Seaver, Edwin

Readers and Writers. A review of The Fifth Column and the First Forty-Nine Stories for WQXR, 20 Oct 1938, 3pp.

Manuscripts -- Not EH

Mackintosh, Alastair

Untitled typescript of personal experiences sent to EH, 21 Dec 1956. 73pp., w/envelope

Manuscripts -- Not EH

Stuart, Lee

Que Pasa en Cuba?, 38pp.

Manuscripts -- Not EH

Sweeny, Charles

　　　Review: This Is Pearl! by Walter Millis,
4pp.

Map

　　　Canadian Arctic Expedition
　　　Department of the Naval Service Canadian
Arctic Expedition: Discoveries in the Arctic
Sea, 1913-1914 and 1917-1918. Positions Deduced
and Mapped by the Geodetic Survey of Canada,
31 July 1920
　　　Department of the Naval Service Key Map of
Canadian Arctic Expedition: Discoveries in the
Arctic Sea, 1913-1918. Positions Deduced and
Mapped by the Geodetic Service of Canada,
undated

Manuscripts -- Not EH

Wildman, Gerald

　　　Half, Fish, Fish that You Were, 4pp.

Map

　　　France. Cartes Taride pour Cyclistes et
Automobilistes. Pyrenees, Section Est, No. 21.
Published by A. Taride, no date

Manuscripts -- Not EH

Miscellaneous manuscripts/ authors unknown.

Map

　　　France. Evreux, Elbeuf, Louviers. Road Map
Sheet No. 26. Drafting and Reproduction by
654th Engineers, First U.S. Army, 1944. First
edition, August 1944

Map
　　　Asia Minor, Syria & Mesopatamia, New Map
of. Published by Geographia, Ltd., London,
1914

Map

　　　France. Fragments: "This one shows how to
get out of Chantilly to come to Aumont. . .And
this one shows how to get out of Senlis.

Map
　　　"Battle of Luxembourg 16-24 Dec 1944."
Composite of U.S. Army, 1944 terrain maps,
w/accompanying hand drawn maps (3).

Map

　　　France. Institut Geographique National
　　　Merlun, No. 65, May 1943
　　　Paris, No. 48. Fragment

Map

France. Maps compiled from air photographs on a control provided by existing French Triangulation. Publisher/date?
Gauray, Sheet No. 31/14 S.E., Aug 1943
Tessy, Sheet no. 34/14 S.W., July 1943
31/12 N.E., Jan 1944, fragment
34/12 N.W., Jan 1944, fragment

Map

Grand Rapids and Indiana Railway, undated

Map

France: Michelin
Sorties de Paris, No. 100, undated, fragment
Environs de Paris, undated
Environs de Paris. Ou aller le dimanche. No. 95, Foret de Fontainebleau, undated, fragment
Paris-Nord, No. 88, undated
Fragment w/Chartres

Map

Longfield Farm. Plot plan of North Part of Lot One, Section 10 T33N R.6W., Michigan, Mrs. C. E. Hemingway, Prop. D. C. Nettleton, Surveyor, July 1905. W/envelope addressed to EH from Grace Hall Hemingway, 4 Aug 1946.

Map

France. Nouvelle Carte de la Foret de Rambouillet. Published by Girard et Berrere, 1942

Map

Paris. Plan de Paris. Published by A. Leconte, undated

Map

France. Topographical Maps publsihed by U.S. War Office. Reproduced at the Ordnance Survey 1944 from French 1:50,000 map
Bruyeres, Sheet No. XXXV-18, 1930
St. Die, Sheet No. XXXVI-17, 1928
Rambervillers, undated

Map

Paris. Autobus, Tramways, Bateaux Lignes de Banlieue. Published by the Societe des Transports en Commun de la Region Parisienne

Map

Germany. Terrain maps, published by U.S. Army, 1944, copied from German maps, dated below
Buir, Sheet 5105, 1940
Duren, Sheet 5104, 1940
Lendersdorf, Sheet 5204, 1941 (fragment also)
Stolberg, Sheet 5203, 1939
Trier, Sheet T.1   ?
Sheet 5303, 1941, fragment
Sheet 5304, 1939, fragment
Sheet 5205, 1934, fragment

Map

Paris Seen in Four Days. Published by L. Guilmin, undated. W/Nouveau Plan de Paris Monumental

Map

    Rome. Nuovissima Pianta di Roma.
Stabilimento Tipo-Litografico del Genic Civile,
1918

Map

    Spain. Visite Espana. Published by the
Banco de Bilbao, Madrid

Map

    Switzerland. Suisse Carte du Touriste.
Published by the Agence Officielle des Chemins
de Fer Federaux, Paris. 1916

Map

    Texas. Road map published by Gulf, undated

Map

    Trench Maps
      France Sheet 51B N.W., Edition 5 A
      France Sheet 51B S.W. Edition 5 A
      France Bullecourt 51B S.W. 4 Edition 2 A
plus fragment
      Zillebeke Sheets 28 N.W. 4 & N.E. 3
(parts of). Edition 5 A

Map

    USA. Road maps published by the American
Automobile Association
      North Central States, [1930]
      South Central States, 1946

Map

    USA. Standard Oil Road Maps
      Eastern United States, 1956
      Georgia, Alabama, 1957
      Highway Map, North Central Section of the
United States, undated

Menus

    Menus from Banquet in honor of
Generalissimo Diaz by the Italians of
Chicago, 20 Nov 1921; Concours Hippique,
Lucerne, 4 July 1925; Gritti Palace-Hotel,
Venice, 20 Oct 1948; and take-out menus.
5 items

Messages

    Telephone messages and numbers in EH,
MH, and unidentified hands, undated.
3 items

Miscellaneous Publications

    The Alleanza Nazionale, documents of
the second Italian risorgimento. Paris
1931.

    Pamphlet.

Miscellaneous Publications

Argosy Book Stores, Inc. catalogue of first editions (#67) including two Hemingway listings on page 14.

Miscellaneous Publications

Brown, John
Hemingway / par John Brown. -- France : Firmin-Didot, 1961.

Unbound, uncut galley proof.

Miscellaneous Publications

Bel Esprit. Privately circulated announcement of a subscription fund for T.S. Eliot.

Miscellaneous Publications

Burand, Tony, [ed.]
La peche du tout gros. -- Paris : Editions Camille Rousset, 1947.
Ritz, Charles C.
"Aux prises avec les 'tout gros'"
p. 3-5

Photograph of EH p.4
Handwritten note in ink by Charles
C. Ritz on flyleaf.

Miscellaneous Publications

Boni & Liveright publications announcement catalog. 1927

Pencil markings

Miscellaneous Publications

Charles Scribner's Sons publications catalog, Fall 1962.

Miscellaneous Publications

Bragdon, Clifford
"Suffer little children."
Short story torn from The Midland magazine (Vol.16, No.2, March-April, 1930).

Miscellaneous Publications

Desnos, Robert
Les sans cou. -- Paris, 1934.

Handwritten note and signature of author on flyleaf.

Miscellaneous Publications

Braque, Georges, et al.
Testimony against Gertrude Stein. -- The Hague : Servire Press, Feb 1935.

Statements by Georges Braque, Eugene Jolas, Maria Jolas, Henri Matisse, Andre Salmon, Tristan Tzara.

Miscellaneous Publications

Devoe, Alan
The Naturalist's Christmas. -- New York.

Inscribed "To Ernest Hemingway -- in admiration Alan Devoe. 7 December 1929"

Miscellaneous Publications

An exhibition of sculpture by Jo Davidson
for the benefit of the Spanish Children's
Milk Fund, The Arden Gallery, New York
18 Nov - 3 Dec [1938]

Hemingway, Ernest
"Milton Wolff" p. 22

Miscellaneous Publications

[Joyce, James]
Extracts from Press Notices of Ulysses by
James Joyce. Printed by Leveridge & Co.,
Harlesden, N.W.

Miscellaneous Publications

Famous verse manuscripts: facsimiles of
original manuscripts as submitted to
Poetry.

Pamphlet.

Miscellaneous Publications

The Kansas City Star. Style Book

Inscribed "To Ernest Hemingway from Pete
Wellington with affection." on cover

Miscellaneous Publications

The Fifth Column. Playbill from the
Alvin Theatre, NY, March 25, 1940.

Miscellaneous Publications

Lewis, Robert W., Jr. and Max Westbrook
    The Snows of Kilimanjaro: Collated
and Annotated. Reprinted from The Texas
Quarterly, Spring 1970.

Inscribed "For Mary Hemingway, with good
wishes. Max Westbrook & Robert Lewis"
on cover.

Miscellaneous Publications

"If this be treason......" Printed for
Olga Rudge by Tip. Nuova, Siena, Italy,
January 1948

    33 p. ; 22 cm.

Miscellaneous Publications

Lyle & Davidson, Ltd. (London) list
(# 19) of military and naval books.

    Handwritten note on cover. Marked
throughout.

Miscellaneous Publications

[Joyce, James]
Anna Livia Plurabelle. Text by James
Joyce, Music by Hazel Felman. Chicago:
Argus Book Shop. Edition limited to 350
numbered copies. Unnumbered Review Copy.
Ross, Martin. Music and James Joyce to
accompany Anna Livia Plurabelle by Hazel
Felman. Chicago: Argus Book Shop, 1936.

Miscellaneous Publications

Noble de Navarra, D. Carlos III el. V
Centenario de la Publicacion del Privilegio
de la Union. -- Pamplona : Artes Graficas,
1923.

Miscellaneous Publications

    Petticoat power. Talk given at the
Parlor Lecture Club, Fresno, California, April 12, 1928.

      Signature of [?] Curtin on p.[1].
Handwritten note in ink on cover.

Miscellaneous Publications

    Quintanilla: An Exhibition of Drawings of
the War in Spain. The Museum of Modern
Art, New York, March 1938.

Hemingway, Ernest
  [Preface]
W/invitation to the opening of the exhibit

Miscellaneous Publications

    [Pound, Ezra]
"The cantos of Ezra Pound: some testi-
monies by Ernest Hemingway..." [et al].

EH testimonial p. 13

Miscellaneous Publications

    Stein, Gertrude
      "Descriptions of literature"
May, 1926.

      Uncut pamphlet. Number 117 of
two hundred numbered copies.

Miscellaneous Publications

    [Pound, Ezra]. ~~Harcourt, Brace and Co.~~
sampler from The Letters of Ezra Pound 1907-
1941.

EH notations on front cover.

Miscellaneous Publications

    Stein, Gertrude
      "An elucidation" From Transition
April 1927.

Miscellaneous Publications

    Quintanilla. Pierre Matisse Gallery,
New York, 20 Nov - 4 Dec [1934]

Hemingway, Ernest
  [Appraisal]
Dos Passos, John
  [Appraisal]

Miscellaneous Publications

    [Stein, Gertrude]
Book promotion advertisements for The
Making of Americans, and A Book
Concluding With As a Wife Has a Cow

Miscellaneous Publications

    [Quintanilla, Luis]
Book promotion advertisements for La
Carcel por Dentro: Cincuenta dibujos de
Luis Quintanilla. Madrid: Editorial
Espana, 1935

Miscellaneous Publications

    Steinbach, Reuben
      Offprints of "On English Usage"
(Feb 1929) ; "The Misrelated Construc-
tions" (Feb 1930) ; and "English As
Some Teach It" (Aug 1930). Reprinted
from American Speech.

Miscellaneous Publications

    Tropical fish handbook. -- Dayton, Ohio :
L.D. Sauer, 1933.

Miscellaneous Publications

    W. Heffer & Sons, Ltd. catalog of
secondhand and antiquarian books
(Catalog # 719).

    Markings on cover and in listings.

Miscellaneous Publications

    U.S. Dept. of Commerce
      Pilot rules for certain inland
waters of the Atlantic and Pacific
coasts and of the coast of the Gulf
of Mexico. July 1933.
    [2], 39 p. ; 23 cm.

Money

    Foreign currency. 16 items

Miscellaneous Publications

    U.S. Office of Civil and Defense Mobil-
      ization
      Facts about fallout protection. --
Washington, D.C. : Govt. Print. Off.,
April 1958.

    EH note to MH in ink on cover.

Movies

    EH pencil notes on 20th Century Fox,
undated [1950's]. 1p.

Miscellaneous Publications

    Viereck, Peter
      "Pure poetry, impure politics, and
Ezra Pound." Reprint from Commentary
June 1951.

Movies -- The Old Man and the Sea

    EH pencil notes on The Old Man and the
Sea, w/cable draft to Leland Hayward and
other notes on verso. [c. 5 July 1957].
2pp.

Miscellaneous Publications

    Wescott, Glenway
      Miss Moore's observations / by
Glenway Wescott.

    [4] p. ; 18 cm.

    pamphlet.

Music

    Program "Serata in onore degli ufficiali
'Delle Armate Alleate'", 11 Dec 1918.
1 item.

Notebook   1913

Account book 1913; lists daily
expenditures from May 11 through
June 16. Lists items such as
hair cut, pop corn, tackle, pictures,
car fare, lunch, etc. Lists money
received from May 11 through May 30.
Ink. 5pp.

Notebook   1924 Jan-Dec

Diary 1924; lists expenditures,
departures and arrival dates for
misc trips, and numerous references
to the activities of EH's cats.
pencil and pen. 20pp.

Notebook   1915 Mar 21

Pocket Account Book. Inventory
of Personal Property of Ernest
Hemingway. Includes list of
personal items along with 3pp.
of EH's goals and desires in
life.   6pp.

orig --

Notebook   1927 May

Date book for marriage to Pauline.
pencil. 13pp.

Notebook   1915 - 1916

Webster Notebook # 5585. Notes
on Cicero, lists and plans for
Moose River Trip, and list of
expenses from Sept 6 to Oct 1915.
24pp.

orig --

Notebook   1929 July 24 - Aug 8

Bullfight program notebook with
pencil notes in Spanish. Notebook
printed title "Feria de Julio:
Programa de Festejos".
7 pp w/notes

Notebook   1916 June 10 – June 17

Camping trip with Lewis Clarahan
from Onekama along the Manistee
River to Bear Creek. Describes
trip and weather, along with list
of materials brought. pencil.
21pp. w/notes

Notebook   [1930's]

Inventory of personal property
[currency - francs]; and list of
daily expenditures [currency -
pesetas] from Aug 7 through Aug 11;
and list of items to be brought on
fishing trip. Business card inserted.
ink and pencil. 21pp. w/notes

Notebook   1922 April

Account book; lists daily
expenditures and misc. notes
from April 1 through April 30.
Notes from stay in Constantinople
covering war between Greece and
Turkey. pencil. 53pp.

Notebook   1930-1934

Fishing book; lists fishing trips
and describes destinations, type
of catch, weights and lengths of
catches, flies or bait used, crew,
and weather conditions. pencil
and pen 16pp.

original on display in Hemingway
Room

Notebook   1930-1934

Hunting book; lists hunting trips and describes the game shot, names of persons on trip, location of trip, and sightings of animals. pencil and pen. 27pp.

original on display in Hemingway Room

Notebook   26 Apr - 28 May 1932

"Fishing Log / H.M.S. Anita." Written both by EH and Pauline in Western Union Cable Blanks pad. pp. 1082. 40pp.

Notebook   1933 Jan 25 - May 15

Calendar 1933. Used as boating log listing outings from Jan 25 through May 15. Describes locations, crew, weather conditions, fish caught, and activities such as the completion of a story. pen and pencil. 61pp. w/notes

---

Notebook   1933 Feb 22

Calendar 1933. Used as a notebook with one log entry on Feb 22 for a boating trip. Notes on prices for various sizes of misc fish. pencil. 6pp. w/notes

---

Notebook   1933 Apr 12 - July 16

Record Book. Used as boat log for "Cuba Trip 1933". pencil.

Notebook   1936 Feb 4 - July 17

Calendar 1936. Used as fishing log primarily between Feb 4 through July 17. Contains w/in cover: 3pp. of 1938 calendar, calling card of Cap. Luis J. Sastre, and a receipt from Algibe "Dos Hermanos" de Jose Vazquez. pencil

---

Notebook   1937

Barclay pad. Notes for The Spanish Earth. pencil. 12pp.

Notebook   1939 Apr 7 - Aug 12

Calendar 1939. Used as fishing log primarily between Apr 7 through Aug 12, containing notes as "worked on novel." Contains 7 fragments w/in its covers: lists, notes, receipts. pencil.

Notebook   [1941-1942]

Blocks para Calculos No. 4034. Notes for Men at War, beginning "Each piece should include enough so that a man reading it knows who the people are and what it is about." Contains quotations from Shakespeare, Plato, American political figures, etc. Pencil. 34pp.

Notebook   [1942]

Leather bound calendar for 1941 w/EH's name on front cover. Log for Pilar during World War II Caribbean activities. 113pp.

Notebook   1945 – 1949

Log of the Pilar for various trips,
w/entries by EH, MH and "R.O.T." ?
pp. 1-174. 19pp.

Notebook   Undated

3" x 5" lined paper notebook.
Used for school notes.
26pp.

orig --

Notebook   1951

Stock holdings, writing exercises,
and notes, handwritten in ledger.
Entry dated Mar 7, 1951 lists
stock holdings.   Writing exercises
titled "Early Summer", "Christian
Kitty", and "Goats".   pencil and
pen.   11pp.

MS 70-114

Notebook   Undated

No. 3/100. Spiral notebook w/ blue
cover containing drafts of a few
lines, beginning "The plain trees
journey over the road. . ." ink
and pencil. 6pp.

Notebook   1955   Aug

Block para Calculos No. 4034 1/2.
Notes on renting and purchasing
boats and equipment for the filming
fishing sequences for The Old Man
and the Sea. ink and pencil. 2pp.

Notebook   Undated

8" x 4" graph paper notebook w/
black cover. Includes name of
Ernest Waxey, numerical figures,
and three brief lines. Pressed
leaf and flower inserted. Stamp
on inside cover - B.H.V. 1F.45
ink and pencil. 2pp.

Notebook   1959 Nov 12 – Nov 19

Spiral notebook listing EH's trip
from Key West to Ketchum; includes
date and time of departure and
arrival of misc cities, and the
prices paid for gasoline during
the trip. pencil and pen. 7pp.
w/notes.

Notebook   Undated

Scratch pad on bullfighting;
w/note for names and histories
of picadores and bandeulleros.
pen. 2pp w/notes.

Notebook   1960

Block para Calculos No. 4036 1/2.
Headed "Notes The Dangerous
Summer -- Letter Thompson Life"
11pp. of notes on Antonio Ordonez,
Luis Miguel, A.E. Hotchner, etc.
9pp. of draft letter to Edward
Thompson Life on the writing of
"A Dangerous Summer." Ink and
pencil.

Notebook   undated

Scratch Book No. 4034. Notes on
war, beginning "war as a way of
life." pencil. 4pp.

Notebook   Undated

Standard School Series. Used as
fishing log, May 11 - June 8.
Includes notes on Key West house
and expenses. Note on Thompson
Fish Company receipt inserted.
pencil. 24pp.

Objects

Gott Mit Uns belt buckle

Notebooks   Undated

L'Incroyable 100 pages Cahier.
Blank notebook.

Objects

Leather Pouch

Notes

Miscellaneous notes written by EH, Pauline,
MH, unknown, and also typed. Includes
some expenses, addresses, lists, date book,
"a key to the understanding of Hemingway's
genius," and other. 22 items

Objects

Medal. Club Nautico Internacional de la
Habana, 1949

Objects

Baby spoon. W/initials "EMH" engraved
on curved handle.

Objects

Medal. "Loggia Cristofaro / Colombo
Unione Siciliana No. 15. In box

Objects

Feathers

Objects

Medal. "San Cristobal / Gbnd, Provincial
de la Habana / Comision de Turismo."
On verso: "Premio a la Constancia la
honradez y la Prudencia siendo Gbndor
Francisco R. Batista y Zaldivar."

Objects

    Medal. "Pedro Romero"
    On verso: "Il Centenario Ronda: 1754 -
    1954."

Objects

    Stripes and patches. 2 items

Objects

    Medallion. Flandre: Compagnie Generale
    Transatlantique

Objects

    Wallet. Containing: Safe Driver Reward,
    AAA cards (1947-1948), money bearing notes,
    photos of John Hemingway, business cards,
    receipts, Certificate of Identity of
    Noncombatant (1944), 22nd Infantry Associa-
    tion Card (1951), driver's license and
    registration (1946-1947), War Department
    identification card (1944), etc.

Objects

    Nazi war cross pin

Objects

    Wallet, green, empty

Objects.

    Photo holder, empty.

Objects

    Wood carving w/shell hat

Objects

    Shell case w/257 Roberts Super-X shells

Objects

    Watches. 3 items

Objects

World War I medals. 5 items

Passport   1930

John Hadley N. Hemingway dated 13 June 1930.

Passport   1921

Ernest Miller Hemingway "accompanied by his wife Hadley" dated 26 Nov 1921.

Passport   1931

Ernest Miller Hemingway dated 16 Apr 1931.

Passport   1923

Ernest Miller Hemingway "accompanied by his wife, Hadley and minor son, John H. -----" dated 20 Dec 1923. W/loose photograph of Hadley

---

Passport   1958

Ernest Miller Hemingway dated 19 Sept 1958. In case also including International Certificates of Vaccination, "PAPA's LUGGAGE CONTENTS", Idaho Non-Resident Bird License for Carmen Ordonez (1959), American Express card, a bull-fight schedule for August and September 1959, business cards, cash register receipts, directions, and a note from MH: "Love, Health, and Happiness to my Big Sweetheart."

Passport   1926

Ernest M. Hemingway, dated 6 Jan 1926, amended to include his son John Hadley Nicanor Hemingway

---

Periodicals

ALMANACH DU CHASSEUR (1930)

Passport   1926

Pauline Marie Pfeiffer dated 10 Dec 1926

Periodicals

AMERYKA (No.49, 1960)

Fisher, William J.
  "Hemingway's search for an honest morality" (pp. 2-8)

Periodicals

THE ATLANTIC (Vol.152, No.2, Aug 1933)

Stein, Gertrude
"Ernest Hemingway and the post-war
decade" (pp.197-208)

Periodicals

IL CARROCCIO (Vol.9, No.1, Jan 1919)

Periodicals

BIFUR (Sept 1929)

Hemingway, Ernest
"Les collines sont comme des
elephants blancs" (pp. [54]-60)

Pages uncut.

Periodicals

COMMERCE (Autumn 1926)

Pencil notes on front and back
covers. Note inserted p.17.

Periodicals

THE BOOKMAN (Vol.70, No.3, Nov 1929)

Herrick, Robert
"What is dirt?" (pp. 258-262)

re: A Farewell To Arms.
Includes Scribners' reply: "Is it
dirt or is it art?" on insert.

Periodicals

CONTACT (Vol.1, No.2, May 1932)

Periodicals

BRENTANO'S BOOK CHAT (Vol.7, No.5, Sept-Oct
1928)

Cowley, Malcolm
"The Hemingway legend" (pp.25-29)

Periodicals

IL CONVEGNO (No.6 & 7, 30 Jun & 30 Jul 1925)

Hemingway, Ernest
"Il ritorno del soldato" (pp. 339
-347)

Periodicals

BULLETIN OF THE INTERNATIONAL OCEANOGRAPHIC
FOUNDATION (Vol.2, No.2 Jul 1956)

Reference to The Old Man and the Sea
in photograph caption p. 73.

Periodicals

THE CO-OPERATIVE COMMONWEALTH (Vol.3, No.3,
(1 Oct 1921)

Periodicals
CORONET (Feb 1937)

Periodicals
ESQUIRE (Autumn 1933)

Hemingway, Ernest
"Marlin off the Morro, a Cuban
letter" (p.8+)

Photographs

Periodicals
COSMOPOLITAN (Vol.123, No.4, Oct 1947)

Hemingway, Ernest
"The short happy life of Francis
Macomber" (pp. 203-212)

Periodicals
ESQUIRE (Dec 1933 - May 1934)

Volume 1 bound with "Ernest
Hemingway Esquire" tooled in gold
on cover

Periodicals
DAS TAGE BUCH (Vol.10, No.50 14 Dec 1929)

Polgar, Alfred
"Hemingway" p. 2180-2182.

Pencil notes on cover, p. 2181 and
p. 2182.

Periodicals
ESQUIRE (Feb 1934)

Hemingway, Ernest
"A Paris letter" (p.22+)

Color illustrations.

Periodicals
THE DOUBLE-DEALER (Vol.3, No.17, May 1922)

Hemingway, Ernest
"A divine gesture" (pp. 267-268)

Periodicals
ESQUIRE (Jun 1934 - Dec 1934)

Volume 2 bound with "Ernest
Hemingway Esquire" tooled in gold
on cover

Periodicals
THE DIAL (Vol.84, No.4, Apr 1928)

Rothman, N.L.
"Hemingway whistles in the dark"
(pp. 336-338)

Re: Men without women

Periodicals
ESQUIRE (Oct 1934)

Hemingway, Ernest
"Genio after Josie, a Havana
letter" (pp. 21-22)

Photographs

Periodicals

ESQUIRE (Dec 1935)

    Hemingway, Ernest
       "Million dollar fight, a New York
letter" (pp. 35+)

Periodicals

ESQUIRE (Aug 1936)

    Hemingway, Ernest
       "The snows of Kilimanjaro" (p.27+)

    Pencil note on cover.

Periodicals

ESQUIRE (Feb 1936)

    Hemingway, Ernest
       "The tradesman's return, a short
story" (p. 27+)

Periodicals

ESQUIRE (Dec 1938)

    Hemingway, Ernest
       "The butterfly and the tank" (p.
51+)

Periodicals

ESQUIRE (Apr 1936)

    Hemingway, Ernest
       "On the blue water" (p. 31+)

Periodicals

EUROPAISCHE REVUE (Nov 1929)

    Hemingway, Ernest
       "Drei tage sturm" (pp. 556-563)

Periodicals

ESQUIRE (May 1936)

    Hemingway, Ernest
       "There she breaches, or Moby Dick
off the Morro" (p. 35+)

Periodicals

EVERYMAN (Vol.2, No.46, 12 Dec 1929)

    Jordan, Philip
       "Ernest Hemingway, a personal
study" (p. 541)

Periodicals

ESQUIRE (Jun 1936)

    Hemingway, Ernest
       "The horns of the bull" (p. 31+)

Periodicals

EX LIBRIS (Vol.1, No.7, Jan 1924)

Periodicals

EXPERIMENT   (May 1929)

      Phare, Elsie Elizabeth
        "Ernest Hemingway"   (pp. 13-16)

Periodicals

HOUND AND HORN   (Oct - Dec 1932)

      Hemingway, Ernest
        (Letter to the editors) (p.135)

Periodicals

'47 THE MAGAZINE OF THE YEAR   (Jul 1947)

Periodicals

HOUND AND HORN   (Jan - Mar 1933)

      Kirstein, Lincoln
        "The canon of death"   (pp. 336-341)

      Review of: Death in the Afternoon

Periodicals

GACETA ILUSTRADA   (8 Aug 1959)

      Castillo Puche, José Luis
        "Ernesto volvió a cantar el
      'riau-riau'"   (pp. 18-29)

      Photographs, some color

Periodicals

ILUSTRACION FEMENINA   (Aug 1957)

      Anon.
        "Hemingway: escritor aventurero"
      (p. 10)

      Photographs.

Periodicals

HOUND AND HORN   (Fall 1929)

Periodicals

INTERNATIONAL LITERATURE   (Dec 1934)

Periodicals

HOUND AND HORN   (Winter 1931)

Periodicals

INTERNATIONAL LITERATURE   (May 1935)

      Kashkeen, J.
        "Ernest Hemingway: a tragedy of
      craftsmanship"   (pp. 72-90)

      Notes in ink p. [120] signed "J.K."

Periodicals

INTERNATIONAL LITERATURE (Sep 1935)

Cartoon of EH (p.117)

Periodicals

KEN (Prospectus, ca. Feb 1938)

Reference to EH as an editor.

Illustrated with drawing of EH.

Periodicals

KEN (Vol.1, No.1, 7 Apr 1938)

Hemingway, Ernest
"The time now, the place Spain"
(pp. 36-37)

Periodicals

KEN (Vol.1, No.2, 21 Apr 1938)

Hemingway, Ernest
"Dying, well or badly" (pp. 68-71)

Photographs.

2 copies

Periodicals

KEN (Vol.1, No.3, 5 May 1938)

Hemingway, Ernest
"The Cardinal picks a winner"
(pp. 38-39)

Photographs.

2 copies

Periodicals

KEN (Vol.1, No.4, 19 May 1938)

Hemingway, Ernest
"The old man at the bridge" (p. 36)

Periodicals

KEN (Vol.1, No.5, 2 Jun 1938)

Hemingway, Ernest
"United we fall upon Ken" (p. 38)

Periodicals

KEN (Vol.1, No.7, 30 Jun 1938)

Hemingway, Ernest
"Treachery in Aragon" (p.26)

Periodicals

KEN (Vol.2, No.1, 14 Jul 1938)

Hemingway, Ernest
"Call for greatness" (P. 23)

Periodicals

KEN (Vol.2, No.2, 28 Jul 1938)

Hemingway, Ernest
"My pal the gorilla gargantua"
(p. 26)

Periodicals

LIBERATOR (Oct 1920)

Periodicals

LIFE EN ESPANOL (14 Nov 1960)

Hemingway, Ernest
"El verano sangriento" Part II
(pp. 68-82)

Photographs.

Periodicals

LIFE (Nov 22 1929)

Anonymous
"A farewell to charms" (by Very
Ernest Deitrick) (pp. 11+)

Periodicals

LIFE EN ESPANOL (28 Nov 1960)

Hemingway, Ernest
"El verano sangriento" Part III
(pp. 66-81)

Photographs.

Periodicals

LIFE (1 Sep 1952)

Hemingway, Ernest
"The old man and the sea" (pp.
34-54)

Illustrations, some color.
2 copies

Periodicals

THE LITTLE REVIEW (Winter 1922)

Periodicals

LIFE (14 Jul 1961)

"Hemingway, driving force of a great
artist" (pp. 59-68)
Photographs.

MacLeish, Archibald
"His mirror was danger" (pp. 71-
73).
Photographs

Periodicals

THE LITTLE REVIEW (Autumn 1922)

Periodicals

LIFE EN ESPANOL (31 Oct 1960)

Hemingway, Ernest
"El verano sangriento" part I
(pp. 43+)

Color photographs.

Periodicals

THE LITTLE REVIEW (Spring 1923)

Hemingway, Ernest
"In our time" (pp. 3-5)
"They all made peace--what is
peace?" (pp. 20-21)

2 copies.

Periodicals

THE LITTLE REVIEW (Autumn, Winter 1923-1924)

Periodicals

LOOK (4 May 1954)

    Hemingway, Ernest
      "The Christmas gift" Part II
    (pp. 79-89).

    Photographs.

Periodicals

THE LITTLE REVIEW (Spring 1925)

Periodicals

MANIKIN (No.3)

Periodicals

THE LITTLE REVIEW (May 1929)

    Hemingway, Ernest
      (Letter) (p. 41)
      "Valentine" (p. 42)

    Photograph of EH (P. 42).
    2 copies.

Periodicals

MAN'S MAGAZINE (Sep 1959)

    Ditzel, Paul
      "Ernest Hemingway's private war
    with Adolf Hitler" (pp. 18-21+)

Periodicals

THE LIVING AGE (Vol. 354, No. 4463, Aug 1938)

Periodicals

MUNDO HISPANICO (Feb 1960)

    Puche, Jose Luis Castillo
      "Hemingway, los toros y los toreros"
    (p. 35).

Periodicals

LOOK (20 Apr 1954)

    Hemingway, Ernest
      "The Christmas gift" (pp. 29-37)

    Color photographs.

Periodicals

THE NATION (Vol.136, No.3524, 18 Jan 1933)

    Fadiman, Clifton
      "Ernest Hemingway: an American
    Byron" (pp. 63-64)

Periodicals

THE NATION   (Vol.147, No.24,   10 Dec 1938)

Wilson, Edmund
"Hemingway and the wars" (pp. 628-630)

Reviews of The Fifth Column and The Spanish War.

Periodicals

THE NEW STATESMAN   (Vol.34, No.866,   30 Nov 1929)

E.S.
Review of A Farewell To Arms (pp. 267-268)

Periodicals

LE NAVIRE D'ARGENT (Mar 1926)

Hemingway, Ernest
"L'Invincible" (pp. 161-194)

2 copies, one signed by EH

Periodicals

THE NEW YORKER   (20 Sep 1947)

Handwritten note inserted between pp. 6-7

Periodicals

NEW MASSES (Dec 1929)

Dos Passos, John
Review of A Farewell To Arms.
(p. 16)

Periodicals

LA NOUVELLE REVUE FRANCAISE (May 1927)

Periodicals

NEW MASSES (17 Sep 1935)

Hemingway, Ernest
"Who murdered the vets, a first hand report on the Florida hurricane"
(pp. 9-10)

Periodicals

LA NOUVELLE REVUE FRANCAISE (Jun 1927)

Periodicals

NEW REPUBLIC (18 May 1927)

Hemingway, Ernest
"Italy, 1927" (pp. 350-353)

EH handwritten notes on cover, typo correction in pencil p.353.

2 copies

Periodicals

LA NOUVELLE REVUE FRANCAISE (Jul 1927)

2 copies

Periodicals
LA NOUVELLE REVUE FRANCAISE (Aug 1927)

      Hemingway, Ernest
        "Cinquante mille dollars" (pp.
161-192)

Periodicals
NOW AND THEN (No.46 Winter 1933)

Periodicals
LA NOUVELLE REVUE FRANCAISE (Feb 1928)

      2 copies

Periodicals
NOW AND THEN (No.48, Summer 1934)

Periodicals
LA NOUVELLE REVUE FRANCAISE (Jun 1928)

      Hemingway, Ernest
        "Le village indien" (pp. 736-741)

Periodicals
NOW AND THEN (No.49, Winter 1934)

Periodicals
LA NOUVELLE REVUE FRANCAISE (May 1931)

Periodicals
OAK LEAVES (11 Oct 1919)

Periodicals
NOW AND THEN (No.22, Christmas 1926)

Periodicals
THE OAK PARKER (4 Oct 1919)

Periodicals
OMNIBUS (1931)

Hemingway, Ernest
"A farewell to arms" (pp. 73-74)

Exerpts.

Periodicals
DER QUERSCHNITT (Nov 1924)

Hemingway, Ernest
"The lady poets with foot notes"
(p. 317)

Periodicals
PARIS MATCH (25 Dec 1954)

"Hemingway, le chasseur de fauves, s'est
fait porter malade au rendez-vous du
roi" (pp. 58-61)

Photographs.

Periodicals
DER QUERSCHNITT (Feb 1926)

Hemingway, Ernest
"The age demanded" (p. 111)

Periodicals
PLAYBOY (1 Dec 1961)

Hemingway, Leicester
"My brother, Ernest Hemingway"
Part I (pp. 41-78)

Photographs.

Periodicals
DER QUERSCHNITT (Jul 1926)

Periodicals
POETRY (Vol.21, No.4, Jan 1923)

Hemingway, Ernest
"Wanderings" [5 poems, cut out
of magazine presumably by EH himself]

Periodicals
DER QUERSCHNITT (Aug 1926)

Periodicals
PRINCETON UNIVERSITY LIBRARY CHRONICLE (Vol.5,
No.2, Feb 1944)

Mizener, Arthur
"Edmund Wilson, a checklist" (pp.
62-78)

Reference to Wilson Introduction to
In Our Time (p. 67) and essay "Letter
to the Russians about Hemingway", New
Republic 11 Dec 1935 (p. 73)

Periodicals
DER QUERSCHNITT (Sep 1926)

Periodicals

DER QUERSCHNITT (Feb 1927)

Periodicals

THE ROYAL MILITARY COLLEGE MAGAZINE & RECORD
            (Christmas 1924)

            [Dorman-Smith, E.G.]
                "A bull fight at Pamplona" (pp. 19
            -29).

Periodicals

DER QUERSCHNITT (Mar 1927)

Periodicals

THE ROYAL MILITARY COLLEGE MAGAZINE & RECORD
            (Easter 1925)

            "Chink" [Dorman-Smith, E.G.]
                "Il encierro" (pp. 87-92)

            Photographs.
            Handwritten note by MH identifying
        author as Capt. Major Dorman-Smith now
        Brig. Gen. Smith-O'Gorman. (p. 92)

Periodicals

DER QUERSCHNITT (Feb 1928)

Periodicals

EL RUEDO (25 Aug 1960)

            "Hemingway crea--en el diario 'Pueblo'
                un gran concurso literario sobre
                temas taurinos" (p. [21])

Periodicals

DER QUERSCHNITT (Sep 1929)

Periodicals

ST. NICHOLAS (Feb 1890)

Periodicals

LA REVUE EUROPEENNE (Jan 1930)

        Hemingway, Ernest
            "Je vous salue Marie" (pp. 76-86)

Periodicals

THE SATURDAY REVIEW (Vol.6, No.12, 12 Oct 1929)

        Canby, Henry Seidel
            "Story of the brave" (p. 231-232)

        Review of A Farewell To Arms.

Periodicals

THE SATURDAY REVIEW (23 Aug 1958)

    Beatty, Jerome
      "Who owns the past? Hemingway
    vs. Esquire" (pp. 10-11+)

Periodicals

SCRIBNER'S MAGAZINE (Vol.81, No.6, Jun 1927)

    Lewis, Gordon
      Letter (p. 706d) [requesting
    more stories by EH]

Periodicals

SCRIBNER'S MAGAZINE (Vol.46, No.6, Dec 1909)

Periodicals

SCRIBNER'S MAGAZINE (Vol.85, No.5, May 1929)

    Hemingway, Ernest
      "A farewell to arms" Part I
    (pp. 493-504, 597-610)

    Photograph of EH p.492

Periodicals

SCRIBNER'S MAGAZINE (Vol.81, No.3, Mar 1927)

    Hemingway, Ernest
      "The killers" (pp. 227-233)

    2 copies

Periodicals

SCRIBNER'S MAGAZINE (Vol.85, No.6 Jun 1929)

    Hemingway, Ernest
      "A farewell to arms" PartII
    (pp. 649-660)

    2 copies

Periodicals

SCRIBNER'S MAGAZINE Vol.81, No.4, Apr 1927)

    Hemingway, Ernest
      "In another country" (pp. 355-
357) "A canary for one" (pp. 358-360)

Periodicals

SCRIBNER'S MAGAZINE (Vol.86, No.1, Jul 1929)

    Hemingway, Ernest
      "A farewell to arms" Part III
    (pp. 20-32)

    2 copies

Periodicals

SCRIBNER'S MAGAZINE (Vol.81, No.5, May 1927)

    Note regarding first published
    stories of EH (p. 578f)

Periodicals

SCRIBNER'S MAGAZINE (Vol.86, No.2, Aug 1929)

    Hemingway, Ernest
      "A farewell to arms" Part IV
    (pp. 169-181)

    2 copies

Periodicals

SCRIBNER'S MAGAZINE (Vol.86, No.4, Oct 1929)

Hemingway, Ernest
"A farewell to arms"   Part VI
(pp. 373-385)

Periodicals

SCRIBNER'S MAGAZINE (Vol.97, No.5, May 1935)

Hemingway, Ernest
"The green hills of Africa" (pp.
257-268) Part I

Periodicals

SCRIBNER'S MAGAZINE (Vol.88, No.2, Aug 1930)

Hemingway, Ernest
"The wine of Wyoming" (pp. 195-
204)

2 copies

Periodicals

SCRIBNER'S MAGAZINE (Vol.97, No.6, Jun 1935)

Hemingway, Ernest
"The green hills of Africa" (pp.
334-344) Part II

Periodicals

SCRIBNER'S MAGAZINE (Vol.93, No.3, Mar 1933)

Hemingway, Ernest
"A clean, well-lighted place"
(pp. 149-150)

2 copies

Periodicals

SCRIBNER'S MAGAZINE (Vol.98, No.4, Oct 1935)

Hemingway, Ernest
"The green hills of Africa" (pp.
200-206) Part VI

Periodicals

SCRIBNER'S MAGAZINE (Vol.93, No.4, Apr 1933)

Hemingway, Ernest
"Homage to Switzerland" (pp. 204+)

Article cut out of magazine

Periodicals

SCRIBNER'S MAGAZINE (Vol.98, No.5, Nov 1935)

Hemingway, Ernest
"The green hills of Africa" (pp.
262-273) Part VII

Periodicals

SCRIBNER'S MAGAZINE (Vol.93, No.5, May 1933)

Hemingway, Ernest
"Give us a prescription doctor"
(pp. 272-278)

Periodicals

SCRIBNER'S MAGAZINE (Vol.101, No.1, Jan 1937)

Hemingway, Ernest
"The killers" (pp. 83-86)

Periodicals

3 4 N (Sep 1923 - Jan 1924)

Periodicals

THIS QUARTER (Spring 1925)

Hemingway, Ernest
"Big two hearted river" (pp. 110-128)

Special dedication to EH on flyleaf

Periodicals

SPAIN TODAY (No.3, October 1937)

Periodicals

THIS QUARTER (Vol.2, No.2, 1925)

Walsh, Ernest
"Mr. Hemingway's prose" (pp. 319-321)

Review of In Our Time

Periodicals

THE SPUR (1 Dec 1929)

Periodicals

THIS QUARTER (Oct - Dec 1929)

Maurois, Andre
"Ernest Hemingway" (pp. 212-215)

Periodicals

TABULA (Vol.23, No.1, Nov 1916)

Hemingway, Ernest
"Sepi jingan" (pp. 8-9)

Periodicals

THIS QUARTER (Vol.3, No.1, Jul - Sep 1930)

Periodicals

TABULA (Apr 1930)

Hemingway, Carol
"The eleven o'clock mail plane"
(p. 17)

Periodicals

THIS QUARTER (Vol.4, No.2, Dec 1931)

Hemingway, Ernest
"The sea change" (pp. 247-251)

Periodicals

THE TRANSATLANTIC REVIEW (Vol.1, No.4, Apr 1924)

Hemingway, Ernest
Literary supplement III from work in progress (pp. 230-234)

Periodicals

THE TRANSATLANTIC REVIEW (Vol.1, No.5, May 1924)

Hemingway, Ernest
[Letter from the United States] (pp. 355-357)

Periodicals

THE TRANSATLANTIC REVIEW (Vol.2, No.1, Jul 1924)

Periodicals

THE TRANSATLANTIC REVIEW (Vol.2, No.3, Sep 1924)

Hemingway, Ernest
"Pamplona letter" (pp. 300-302)
"Conrad, optimist and moralist" (pp. 341-342)

Periodicals
TRANSITION (May 1927)

Periodicals

TRANSITION (Jun 1927)

Periodicals

TRANSITION (Jul 1927)

Periodicals

TRANSITION (Nov 1927)

Periodicals

TRANSITION (Dec 1927)

Periodicals
TRANSITION (Feb 1928)

Periodicals

THE VIRGINIA QUARTERLY REVIEW (Vol.10, No.1, Jan 1934)

Kerstein, Lincoln
"The cream of the crop" (pp. 145-148)

Review of Winner Take Nothing and others

Post/Telegraph

Receipts and envelopes, 1922 - 1953, for EH and Hadley. Also printed book of rates. 27 items

---

Photo Papers

Envelopes and receipts from photo development. Papers removed from photographs, including the original labels from the boxes of transparencies, 1931 - 1954 and undated. 24 items

---

Press Passes

Passes, identification cards, and letters of certification, 1922 - 1938. 11 items

---

Pilar Papers

Purchase papers, manifests, shipping papers, rules and regulations, inspection certificates, etc. 1934 - 1942 and undated. 41 items

---

Press Papers

Printed materials from the Society of Authors, Playwrights and Composers, the Authors' League, and the Association de la Presse Anglo-Americaine de Paris, 1924 - 1926. 4 items

---

Plane Tickets

Tickets, receipts, schedules and envelopes for EH, MH, Carlos Gutierrez, and Bill Davis, 1935 - 1959. 11 items

---

Publicity

Newspaper advertisements, flyers, posters, balleys of advertisements, journal advertising and brochures from Contact Press, The Three Mountains Press, Boni and Liveright, Scribner's, Jonathan Cape, and Scribner's Magazine announcing publication of works by EH. 45 items

---

Post Cards

Unused cards from Oak Park, Windemere, Italy, Spain, France, bullfighters, etc. 121 items

---

Publishing Notes

Notes by EH and MH on rights, mentions Jack London's Adventure Magazine. 2 items

Quotations

    From Baudelaire and Lord Byron. 2 items

Scrapbooks

    Newspaper Clipping Scrapbook. Two large scrapbooks containing clippings on EH. Arranged chronologically.

Scores

    Harvard/Yale football, Yankees/Cardinals 1942 World Series, game four (score 9 - 6, St. Louis), cards between "P," "H," and "E," and Correos. Scores kept by EH and other. 4 items

Scrapbooks

    Torrents of Spring/Sun Also Rises. Contains reviews on both Torrents of Spring and The Sun Also Rises, 1926 - 1927.

Scrapbooks

    Mother's Scrapbooks. Five books kept by Grace Hall Hemingway, containing photographs, clippings, souvenirs, and handwritten narrative, 1899 - 1917.

Scrapbooks

    Fifty Grand Scrapbook. Contains French reviews of Cinquante Mille Dollars, published in 1928.

Scrapbooks

    Grandparent's Scrapbook. Book kept by Hemingway's paternal grandparents from EH's birth through World War I. Contains photographs, clippings and letters.

Scrapbooks

    Magazine Scrapbook. Contains clippings of Hemingway's articles in Esquire, Ken, Colliers, The New Republic, and Double Dealer.

Scrapbooks

    Star Scrapbook. Contains articles, mostly by EH, from 1920 through 1924, from the Toronto Star and other papers.

Scrapbooks

    China Trip Scrapbook. Titled Whampoa Military Academy in Canton (translation). Includes photographs, some of which picture EH and Martha, 1941

Scrapbooks

Old Man Scrapbook. Contains reviews of
The Old Man and the Sea, compiled by
Scribner's.

Service/Store Receipts

General

Hardware, groceries, drugs, heat,
furniture, etc. 1924 - 1960 and undated.
59 items

Scrapbooks

Antelope/Zebra Scrapbooks. Contains
clippings and congratulatory telegrams
on the Hemingways' survival of the Africa
plane crashes, 1954.

Service/Store Receipts

Liquor

1925 - 1959 and undated. 7 items

Scrapbooks

Scrapbook 54. Contains clippings on
the Hemingways' Africa crashes and the
Nobel Prize from American, German, Cuban,
French, Spanish and Italian periodicals,
1954. W/the visiting card of De Simon
Adamo taped to inside front cover.

Service/Store Receipts

Sporting/Hunting/Fishing Goods

1928 - 1956 and undated. 14 items

Scrapbooks

Feast Scrapbook. Includes newspaper
reviews, articles and other material on
the publication of A Moveable Feast.

Sightseeing/Souvenirs

Admission tickets to Versailles and to
visit Cruiser Patria. 2 items

Service/Store Receipts

Clothing

Purchase and cleaning, 1921 - 1959.
10 items

Spanish Civil War   News clippings

The War in Spain: A Weekly Summary
pub -- United Editorial Ltd.; London

- #43 12 Nov 1938

- #58 25 Feb 1939

Spanish Civil War   News Clippings

    <u>Spanish News</u>

  #16   3 May 1938

  #18   24 May 1938

Spanish Civil War   Receipt   2/4/37

Receipt. Contribution receipt issued
by American Friends of Spanish Democracy
to Ernest Hemingway on 4 Feb 1937

Spanish Civil War   News Clippings

  <u>News of Spain</u>   pub -- Spanish Information
Bureau; New York, NY

  #   6 July 1938

  vol II   #6   9 Feb 1939

  vol II   #7   16 Feb 1939

Spanish Civil War   Report 4/29/38

Report. Information report from the
Ministerio de Defensa Nacional dated
29 Apr 1938. Stamped by Secretaria
del Ministerio de Defensa Nacional.
1p. w/envelope

Spanish Civil War   News Clippings

  Misc news clippings

Spanish Civil War   Report 17 Oct 1937

Report. EH typescript battle report
for Oct 17 [1937] on events in Aragon
and Asturias. 1p. w/envelope

Spanish Civil War   Notes

Miscellaneous notes by EH, typed by EH, and
typed by others, concerning ambulance shipments,
American wounded, on promoting film. Lists,
things to do. 9pp.

Spanish Civil War   Report   3 Nov 1938

"Requete du Gouvernment Espagnor aus Fins
d'Obtenir l'Assistance Technique de la
Societe des Nations dans l'Etude des Mesures
Propres a Assurer le Ravitaillement des
Refugies," by Sir Denys Bray and M. L.
Webster. UN Report C.416.M.261.1938.VII,
dated Geneva, 3 Nov 1938. 9pp.

Spanish Civil War   Quotations

  Typescript fragment of quotations of
  Joseph F. Thorning. Slight insect
  damage. page 3, 1p.

Spanish Civil War   Report

  Manuscript. Report About the Ambulance
  Factory written by Jefetura de Sanidad;
  Madrid. 6pp.

Sports

Tickets, programs, newspapers, etc.
1918 - 1934 and undated. 18 items

To do's

Various notes, reminders, shopping
lists written by both EH and MH, on
scraps of paper, envelopes, cardboard,
etc. Mostly undated. 41 items

Stationery

Dr. Hemingway's, Kenilworth Avenue in
Oak Park, 153 Lyndhurst Avenue, Toronto,
and San Francisco de Paula envelope.
4 items

Train Tickets

Tickets and receipts for purchases on
trains for EH, Hadley, Pauline, and
Archibald MacLeish, 1922 - 1931 and
undated. 22 items

Steamship Crossings

Tickets, correspondence, and menus, etc.
1919 - 1956 and undated. 19 items

Translations

Typescript of a French translation of
"The Killers." 17pp.

Storage

Receipt for New York Storage, 18 May 1962.
1 item

Travel Papers

Tickets, receipts, correspondence and
notes on travel for EH, Archibald MacLeish,
and Lee Samuels. Notes by EH and MH
including itineraries. 1923 - 1956 and
undated. 26 items

Theatre/Concerts

Programs and tickets, 1916 - 1928 and
undated. 14 items

Travel Brochures

Europe. 2 items

Travel Brochures

France. 2 items

Travel Brochures

USA, including the L-T Ranch. 3 items

Travel Brochures

Germany. The Lent School for Skiing.
1 items

Visiting Cards

Including cards of Ernest M. Hemingway
at The Toronto Star, Robert McAlmon, Sylvi-
Beach, Elliot Paul, George W. Brown, etc.
29 items

Travel Brochures

Italy. 4 items

War between Greece and Turkey, 1922

Report. Typescript report titled American
Relief Work concerning the operations of the
American Red Cross in Constantinople in 1922.
6pp.

Travel Brochures

Spain. 3 items

War between Greece and Turkey, 1922

Note. EH?

Travel Brochures

Switzerland, including Schruns. 8 items

Wedding to Hadley

EH notes on things to buy, expenditures,
travel arrangements, and guest list.
7pp.

Word Counts

    10 Oct 1959 - 28 May 1960 and one scrap undated. 8 pp.

World War I

    Medals and Awards.
        Croce al Merito di Guerra, signed 18 Dec 1918
        Medaglia d'Argente al Valor Militare, signed 15 Mar 1921, w/correspondence
        Croce al Merito di Guerra (medal only)
for William D. Horne

World War I

    American Red Cross. Discharge papers and certificates, 1918 - 1919. 3 items

---

World War I

    Milt Runkle's War Jokes and Kaiser's Last Will and Testament. 3pp.

World War I

    France's Army and Navy in Peace, 1923. Six-page brochure, publisher unknown.

World War I

    Misstatements and Facts Concerning Conditions in the Ruhr, published by the Franco-American Committee, Nov 1923.

World War I

    I Bollettini della Vittoria, published by the Italian Supreme Command, 1918. 38pp.

World War I

    Note (by EH?), on American Red Cross, Vicenza envelope

World War I

    Instruction Book. Instructions and Information for Red Cross Workers in France compiled by American Red Cross in France. 1 Apr 1918

World War I

    Patriotic and Popular Songs, published by War Recreation Board, USA. 40pp.

World War I

    Program. Dedication Service of the Roll
of Honor of those who served in W.W. I
at the 1st Congregational Church in
Oak Park, Ill. on 28 Dec 1919. Ernest
Hemingway's name include on Roll of Honor.
4pp.

World War II

    Spain. Typewritten index, in Spanish, to
information reports on Spain. Titled
"Characterizaciones." 59pp.

World War I

    Report.   Report of the Department of
Military Affairs   January to July
1918 [Italy - Rome]

World War II

    Spain. Typewritten index to reports on
Spain, in Spanish. Titled "Resumen de
Informacion Sobre Espana." Dated on last
page, 31 Oct 1942. 30pp.

World War I

    The War in Italy: Arms and Ammunition,
published by the Italian General
Headquarters, 1918. Soldiers Edition #18.
32pp.

World War II

    Spain. Continuation of the typewritten
index titled "Resumen de Informacion Sobre
Espana." 27pp.

World War I

    War Poems, by Will M. Cressy, 14pp.

World War II

    Spain. Typewritten report on Spain in 1939
titled "Informe sobre la Situacion de
Espana." 19pp.

World War I

    Western Union Telegram facsimile dated
4 Dec 1918, from Henry P. Davison, Chairman, Red Cross War Council to all Red
Cross members. 4pp.

World War II

    Spain. Report titled "The United States
and Cuban-Spanish Relations," dated
28 Oct 1942. 10pp., w/1p. cover memo
(from/to?) dated 26 Oct 1942.

World War II

Caribbean Submarine Watch. Submarine
sighting reports, EH notes, and <u>Axis
Submarine Manual</u>." TL unsigned, to ?
dated 9 Nov 1942, 2pp. 12 items

World War II

Reports on Defence of Rambouillet/
Investigation of Activities of EH.
Materials concerning the investigation,
including orders to report for questioning,
and testimony of EH and others.
2 Oct 1944 - 26 June 1952 and undated

World War II

EH Notes. Pencil notes on Easy Red,
Fox Green, Overlord, and ships. 7pp.

World War II

Journals -- 22nd Infantry Regiment.
Typewritten reports:
  Narrative Report for CT-22 Action during
Month of November, 1 Nov 1944, 26pp.
  Journal, 22nd Infantry, 16 Nov 1944 -
3 Dec 1944, 91pp.

World War II

  General
6/7/42   Press News--Dorothea L. Dix
7/28/44   Royal Air Force Message "Plane
            Fragments found in possession of War
            Correspondent
10/23/44   Press Release, Supreme Hq., AEF
12/24/44   Photographs
undated   "The Story of the 4th Infantry Divi-
            sion, and letter
undated   "The Story of the 35th Infantry
            Division"

World War II

Narrative Report of Battle Plan. Report
and maps of Stolberg, Roetgen, and
Lendersdorf, 10 Nov 1944.

World War II

Reports, etc. Untitled report on violation
of secrecy code; "Time Over Targets, the
Story of the 9th Bombardment Division," Lt.
Cressori's statement of battle action, to
Gen. Barton; "Summary of the Battle of
Hurtgen Forest, 9 Nov 1944; "The Ivy Leaf,"
22 Nov 1944; letter by Col. Lanham praising
Combat Team 22, 13 Dec 1944.

World War II

Periodic Reports. Declassified G-2
Periodic Reports on Stenningen, Zweifall,
Luxembourg, etc. 30 Nov 1944 - 4 Jan 1945.

World War II

Citations, Awards, Orders, Authorizations.
Travel orders, and other authorizations,
and letters and certificates: Bronze Star,
service with Third Army, European-African-
Middle Eastern Campaign Ribbon, Appreciation for servcies as War Correspondent.
27 July 1944 - 7 May 1947 and undated

World War II

Colonel Moore (Charges). Testimony
concerning the charges made by Lt. Col.
Scott against Col. Moore. 30 Apr 1945 -
1 May 1945

World War II

    22nd Infantry Association, 3rd Convention,
Washington, D.C. Report of the Convention,
5 Aug 1949 - 7 Aug 1949. pp. 5-16 only

World War II

    Anniversary of 1945 American-Russian
Link-Up at Elbe River. Newsclippings and
printed material from the American
Veterans of the Elbe River Link-up.
25 Apr 1945 - 28 Mar 1960